GAMES FOR BUSINESS
AND ECONOMICS

ROY GARDNER

Indiana University

WILEY

www.wiley.com/college/gardner

Acquisitions Editor   *Leslie Kraham*
Marketing Manager   *Charity Robey*
Associate Production Manager   *Kelly Tavares*
Production Editor   *Sarah Wolfman-Robichaud*
Managing Editor   *Lari Bishop*
Illustration Editor   *Kris Pauls*
Cover Design   *Shoshanna Turek*
Cover Image   *Christopher Baldwin/Stock Illustration Source*

This book was set in 10/12 Minion by Leyh Publishing LLC and printed and bound by Malloy, Inc. The cover was printed by Lehigh Press.

This book is printed on acid free paper. ∞

ISBN: 0-471-23071-5

Printed in the United States of America

10 9 8 7 6 5 4 3 2 1

To Carla, Sara, and James

Brief Contents

Contents

Chapter 6

■ NONCOOPERATIVE MARKET GAMES IN NORMAL FORM 127

Part Three
GAMES WITH IMPERFECT INFORMATION 237

Chapter 10

■ SIGNALING, SCREENING, AND SEQUENTIAL EQUILIBRIUM 238

Part Five
GAMES, MARKETING, AND POLITICS 373

Chapter 15
■ TWO-SIDED MARKETS AND MATCHING GAMES 374

Preface

This edition aims to update and improve the first. The need for updates is clear, as almost a decade has elapsed between editions. Numerous readers, listed below, pointed out the need for corrections in places. Among the changes, four stand out. First, I have taken a much more active learning approach. Although this is evident to some extent in the text, it will be most apparent in the *Instructor's Resource Manual* that accompanies the text. There, I offer one or more in-class experiments and demonstrations for each chapter. My students have found that participating in these experiments and demonstrations enhances their learning. Indeed, in some cases, the experience itself can be quite memorable. Second, I have reduced the amount of calculus used in the text. Calculus is now found mostly in the footnotes and in appendices, with some calculus intuition still in the text. This should make the text accessible to an even larger audience, without any sacrifice of essential content. You can do a great deal of useful mathematics, even without calculus.

Third, I have created an entirely new chapter, Chapter 2, on dealing with chance in games. This chapter includes a tour of the gaming and entertainment industry of the United States, a topic of interest to many students taking game theory. Finally, I have linked the material where possible to popular media, such as movies and the Internet. A movie like *A Beautiful Mind* leaves its mark in many ways.

I could hardly have done this edition without the help of many others. I thank my co-authors of long standing, Andrew Herr, Claudia Keser, Molly Morris, Elinor Ostrom, Roger Stover, Juergen von Hagen, Thierry Verdier, James A. Walker, and Christopher J. Waller, with whom working has been so fruitful and has had a positive influence on this edition. I thank the following for research support: Chair, Department of Economics, Dean, College of Arts and Sciences, Dean of Faculties, and Chancellor of the Bloomington campus, Indiana University; National Science Foundation (Grants #Sbr-9319835 and #SBR-9521918), as well as the NSF-funded initiative "Mathematics Across the Curriculum," in which I developed the active learning approach presented here. I thank the Center for European Integration Studies, University of Bonn, and in particular Co-Director Juergen von Hagen, for research and writing support, as well as considerable inspiration. I thank the Department of Economics and the Center for Russian and East European Studies, Stanford University, for inviting me to their campus. It was during a very fruitful stay at Stanford that I was able to finish the first draft of this edition, free from the usual distractions. I thank my students at Indiana University, the Institute for Advanced Studies, Vienna, Austria, and National University "Kyiv-Mohyla Academy," Kyiv, Ukraine, for their patience as I worked out the material for this edition. I thank Reinhard Selten, who has long been an inspiration and supportive of my work. I thank my friend and colleague, Robert Becker, who read the entire second draft of this edition, and who has made numerous improvements to the text. I thank Tom Merz, who read the entire first and second drafts of this edition, and who likewise made numerous improvements to the text. I thank Kyung Hwan Baik, Hae-Kwon Bao, Friedrich Breyer, James Gardner, Sara Gardner, Basil Golovetsky, Joseph Harrington, Manfred Koenig, Michael Kopel, Percy Ling, Ioanna Moldovan, Liliana Pasyeka, Ekaterina Peneva, Ulrich Schwalbe, Jim Stodder, Mark Walker, and Jinyang Zhao for numerous suggestions for improvement.

A number of colleagues have reviewed drafts of the manuscript, and their comments have resulted in a substantially improved book. I thank all of these reviewers for their helpful comments:

Robert Becker	Indiana University
Nick Feltovich	University of Houston
Andrew Herr	St. Vincent College
Tom Merz	Michigan Tech University
Lynne Pepall	Tufts University
Tim Salmon	Florida State University
Mike Shor	Vanderbilt University
Rafael Tenorio	DePaul University
Eduardo Zambrano	University of Notre Dame

I thank the entire team at John Wiley & Sons, Inc., for their tireless efforts on behalf of this edition, especially my Acquiring Editor Leslie Kraham, without whose support this edition would never have got off the ground. At Wiley I also thank Jessica Bartelt, Jenny Cardozo and Cindy Rhoads. At Leyh Publishing, which handled production, I thank Lari Bishop, Managing Editor, Kris Pauls, Production Coordinator, and Chris Thillen, Copy Editor, who whipped the final draft into publishable shape in record time.

Finally, I thank my family, and especially Sara, who had to put me up (and put up with me) while I was in Northern California, quite obsessed with writing this edition. I hope this edition is better than its predecessor, and apologize in advance to all if it is not.

Roy Gardner

About the Author

Roy Gardner was born in Peoria, Illinois and graduated summa cum laude from Bradley University. He served as an artillery officer in the U.S. Army-Vietnam, winning a Bronze Star. He earned his Ph.D. in economics from Cornell University in 1975. He has been at Indiana University since 1983, and holds the title of Chancellors' Professor of Economics. He is also Senior Fellow of the Center for European Integration Studies, Bonn, Germany.

Dr. Gardner specializes in the theory of games and economic behavior. He has applied game theory to such topics as class struggle, spoils systems, draft resistance, alliance formation, monetary union, and corruption. A major focus of his research has been on human dimensions of global environmental change, which has received over a dozen years of National Science Foundation support. Much of his research appears in this book.

Prior to coming to Indiana, Dr. Gardner was on the faculties of Iowa State and Northwestern. He participated in the first U.S.-France Exchange of Scientists (1979–80) to the Center for Mathematical Economic Planning (CEPREMAP) in Paris, and was an Alexander von Humboldt Fellow at the University of Bonn (1985–86). He has also been a research fellow at the Universities of Bielefeld, Mannheim, Amsterdam, the Institute for Advanced Studies (Vienna) and the National University of Ukraine (Kyiv). He has served on the National Research Council, Panel for Social and Behavioral Sciences (1989–92), is a member of eight professional societies, and serves as referee or consultant to thirty-six scientific journals, eight publishers, and four national science foundations.

PART ONE

Basic Game Theory

CHAPTER I

An Introduction to Games and Their Theory

1.1 WHAT IS A GAME?

In ordinary English, a **game** is any pastime or diversion. This definition covers a lot of terrain. Let's try to organize it somewhat. We can start by identifying different varieties of games. First, there are games played on a board, *board games*. These include Chess, Checkers, and Monopoly.[1] Chess and Checkers have exactly two players, whereas Monopoly can have anywhere from two to eight players. In Chess and Checkers, the outcome of the game is win, lose, or draw: either one player wins and the other loses, or both players draw. In Monopoly, the player with the most assets at the end of the game is the winner; all the rest are losers. Second, there are games played with cards, *card games*. These include Solitaire, Poker, and Blackjack. Solitaire is special, since it has only one player. Poker and Blackjack can have two to seven players—you study them in the next two chapters. Third, there are games played on a video screen against a computer, *video games*. These games are rather like Solitaire, in that they have only one human player. Computers can play many games; later in this chapter we see how and why. Finally, there are games played on a field or a court, *field games*. These include baseball, football, basketball, and hockey, the major professional sports in the United States. Field games are played by two aggregate players, the opposing teams, which are composed of individuals, the members of each team.

All these things are called games, so, according to Aristotle's theory of categories, they must have some feature in common that brings them all under the same name.[2] Let's look for what this feature, or set of features, might be. First, all games have *rules*. The rules specify what a player can and cannot do. A player who breaks the rules is penalized—again, according to the rules—and in extreme cases can be removed from the game altogether. Second, in every game *strategy matters*. There are good and bad strategies, and players can be and are criticized for choosing bad strategies. One of the tasks of game theory is to tell the difference between good and bad strategies. Third, there is an *outcome* to the game, for example, one player wins and the other loses. Fourth, this outcome depends on the strategies chosen by each of the players, a phenomenon we call **strategic interdependence.** Even

---

[1] Games have proper names, just as people do, so we capitalize them in this book.

[2] See Aristotle, *Categories and De Interpretatione* ed. J. L. Ackrill (Oxford: Oxford University Press, 1963).

a bad strategy can win if the opponent chooses a worse one. We combine these features to define a game as *any rule-governed situation with a well-defined outcome, characterized by strategic interdependence.* This describes the Aristotelian category to which games belong.

A lot of things that aren't called games in ordinary English satisfy this definition. Consider firms competing in the same business. There are rules governing their competition, including the law of contracts and property and government regulations, which specify what a firm can and cannot do. A firm that breaks the rules can be penalized, and in extreme cases, such as bankruptcy, can even be removed from the game. The outcome of firms' competition is typically something observable, such as the amount of money each firm makes or the amount of market share each firm has. These outcomes are often reported in a firm's financial statements. As we will see, a firm's strategies can include price, quantity, advertising, which markets it operates in, what kinds of contracts it offers its employees—a host of things. Finally—and this is the most important truth in this book—*the outcome for a given firm depends not just on what strategy it chooses, but also on what strategies its competitors choose.* A firm can have the greatest product line in the world and still get clobbered by the competition if its strategies are no good. When firms compete in a market, they operate in a rule-governed situation, with well-defined outcomes, characterized by strategic interdependence. We have a word for this: it's a *game,* in this case a **market game.** Firms competing in a market are just as much players in a game as are Poker players seated around a poker table. Indeed, the stakes in a business are almost always a lot higher. What began as a metaphor at the beginning of this century has become literally and categorically true.

Let's take an example that works on both sides of the literal and metaphorical aspect of *game:* a professional sports franchise, the Chicago Bulls.[3] The Bulls play professional basketball in the National Basketball Association (NBA), and in the 1990s they played it very well, winning six NBA championships. More recently, they have been among the worst teams in the league. The Bulls are also a corporation—owned by private investors, mostly from the Chicago area—that is in business to make money each year. The more games the Bulls win on the basketball court, the more money the owners of the Bulls make from ticket sales, broadcasting rights, and concessions. Although winning at basketball isn't the same thing as winning in business, the two are closely related in this case.

Another example, not at all sports related, is the cola industry. Cola was invented in Atlanta in 1886. The inventor later went on to found Coca-Cola Corporation. Other cola drinks entered the market soon thereafter. Since the 1920s, Coke and Pepsi, with the largest market shares and highest profits, have dominated the U.S. market and have battled head-to-head for cola business. Their competition, commonly known as the cola wars,[4] has included price wars, new product competition (Pepsi Twist is a recent entry), new packaging (the 2-liter plastic bottle), and advertising campaigns (Coke Is It! The Pepsi Generation). How much money Pepsi makes from its cola operations depends on what Coke does, and vice versa. This is strategic interdependence manifested in the market.

Business isn't the only arena in which we see games in the extended sense—they are at the very heart of economics, too. Think of domestic economic negotiations, such as those between the White House and Congress on domestic economic policy issues, for example, the budget, or between the White House and the Fed on monetary policy. Think of international

---

[3] All the examples in this book are drawn from real life. You will never encounter the word widget, to say nothing of the markets in which these mythological objects are bought and sold.

[4] The title is from J. C. Louis, The Cola Wars (New York: Everest House, 1980).

economic negotiations, such as those among the G-8 countries, involving international trade and finance.[5] **Economic negotiations** such as these have all the makings of a game. There are rules (domestic and international law) governing what each party to the negotiations can do. Strategy matters—if you are absent from the negotiations, you should not be surprised if your interests are not represented. There is a clearly defined outcome—the status quo if negotiations break down, some sort of agreement if negotiations are brought to a successful conclusion. Finally, the outcome of negotiations depends not only on what your side does, but on what the other side does, too. Various forms of bargaining, negotiation, and arbitration—all games with at least an element of cooperation—are studied in the last third of this book.

◼ 1.2 WHAT IS GAME THEORY, AND WHY?

Game theory is the science that studies games and takes games seriously enough to solve them. Game theory is a product of the twentieth century, the brainchild of one of the century's greatest minds, John von Neumann.[6] Von Neumann discovered one of the central regularities of games, the solution for 2-person, zero-sum games, which is covered in Chapter 3. He provided the framework that this book uses to study games in general. Together with Oskar Morgenstern, his fellow refugee from fascism, Von Neumann was the first to solve games in business and economics.[7]

We use game theory to solve games, to help players avoid mistakes and find the right strategy if there is only one. Sometimes the best we can do is narrow a player's choice down to a set of strategies. A solution of a game should tell each player what outcome to expect and how to achieve that outcome. This involves some mathematics; indeed, game theory began as pure mathematics. Von Neumann was first and foremost a mathematician, as was his star student, John Nash. Nash formulated a central idea in solution theory, Nash Equilibrium (NE), which we study from Chapter 3 onward. This is *the* John Nash portrayed in the movie *A Beautiful Mind*. Nash, along with two other game theorists, Reinhard Selten and John Harsanyi, won the Nobel Prize in economics in 1994 for their advances in game theory. You will learn about those advances as you go through this book.

Although some mathematics is unavoidable, we try to make that mathematics as user-friendly as possible, applying the adage that you should tell beginners the truth, but not the whole truth. If you are a beginner and you master this book, then you are ready to go on to more advanced material, which we suggest for further reading throughout the text. At the beginning, you are spared the theoretical niceties and the jargon you don't yet need or can't yet appreciate. Game theory is a subject that gets deep fast enough as it is. Think of it as a swimming pool in which even the shallow end can be over your head.

Although game theory began as applied mathematics, it has become a powerful mode of reasoning in business and economics, and is heavily used in other fields like formal political

---

[5] The G-8 countries are the world's seven largest economies (United States, Japan, Germany, France, United Kingdom, Italy, Canada) plus Russia; their representatives meet frequently to negotiate issues that involve economic relations among them.

[6] Besides creating game theory, von Neumann also provided the mathematical foundation for quantum mechanics, designed the implosion lens for the atomic bomb, and created the architecture of the computer. An excellent biography is Norman McRae, *John von Neumann* (New York: Pantheon Books, 1992.)

[7] The title of their magnum opus, John von Neumann and Oskar Morgenstern, *The Theory of Games and Economic Behavior* (Princeton, N.J.: Princeton University Press, 1944), shows how much their work was driven by the possibility of economic applications. Later on, after the creation of game theory, it became apparent that earlier economists, among them Cournot, Bertrand, Edgeworth, and Stackelberg, had also found solutions to games.

theory, evolutionary biology, psychology, and philosophy. The Nobel Prize–winning macro-economist Robert Lucas argues that the most important contributions to macroeconomics since Keynes have been the result of formulating macroeconomic problems as games and then solving those games.[8] It is easy to see why this is true. In the heyday of Keynesian economics, economists designed policies for the government to use assuming that the public's expectations, government policies of other countries, and the like would not be affected. This assumption is tantamount to assuming that the public and other governments are not play-ers in a game. We know better now. Expectations held by the public—which show up, for instance, in the investment and portfolio decisions taken in the private sector—make an enormous difference to the outcome of economic policy. When the energy sector was dereg-ulated in the early 1990s, that opened up all sorts of strategies for firms like Enron. Enron was playing a whole new game, and grew (at least on paper) into a $50-billion firm by playing that game in fairly unique fashion—before it imploded into bankruptcy at the end of 2001. When something is a game—and the entire economy surely is one—you have to treat it as a game if you are going to understand it at all well.

Another example, which arises both in business and in economics, is called *mechanism design*. Suppose you have a certain goal in mind—for example, collecting $2 trillion in gov-ernment revenue—and you want to achieve that goal as inexpensively as possible. You need to design a set of mechanisms—foremost among them, the tax system—to achieve the goal. The mechanisms so designed lead to games, since taxpayers have strategies that respond to various kinds of taxation. If you don't include taxpayer strategies in your mech-anism, you can be sure that it will fail miserably. Mass transit riders will change their rid-ing strategy to some extent when fares double, and a transit authority that ignores this will not set fares in a strategically sound way. Of course, taxes aren't the only source of govern-ment revenue. Until recently, the federal government gave away rights to the electromag-netic spectrum, even though those rights are extremely valuable. Since the mid 1990s, advised and influenced to a large extent by game theorists, the federal government has auc-tioned off those rights, in the process raising billions of dollars for the U.S. Treasury. We study various kinds of mechanism design problems in Chapters 11 and 12.

There are several purely selfish reasons for studying game theory, above and beyond the desire to know the truth that this science has to offer. These reasons might apply to your job or your career someday, even if you aren't going to be the next John Nash. First and foremost, game theory can improve your strategic decision making. It makes you more aware of when you are in a situation in which strategy matters, to say nothing of making you aware of strategic nuance on the part of your competitors or opponents. Second, it can improve your ability to run a business and to evaluate changes in policy. The phrases "com-petitive advantage," "everyday low pricing," and "winner's curse" will make a lot more sense to you after they have been strategically explicated (in Chapters 3, 4, and 12, respectively). Finally, game theory can help you become a better economist or a better manager. Game theory is the central paradigm of economics and finance. It contains or informs all the cur-rent buzzwords, such as market failure, credibility, incentive contracts, hostile takeovers, and coalition building, to name just a few. And—if you are into that sort of thing—game theory might even make you a better Blackjack player.

Like any theory that involves mathematics, there is no royal road to understanding game theory. You have to follow the arguments, understand the proofs, work the problems

---

[8] Lucas is one of the principal architects of the rational expectations revolution in macroeconomics. See his *Models of Business Cycles* (Oxford: Basil Blackwell, 1987).

(there are problems at the end of each chapter), study the examples, and think about it all in terms of your own life and your own work. If you do the work, then you will complete this book knowing how to set up and solve a whole arsenal of games—and even more important, knowing how to think about games in an intelligent way. You won't fall for the wrong answers in strategic situations, if you have analyzed them correctly.

The book is organized as follows. Part One covers the fundamentals, ideas and techniques that are used throughout game theory. Part Two looks at games within games (subgames), repeated games, and games that are out of equilibrium. Part Three is especially concerned with games of imperfect information, where mechanism design is the central objective. Part Four focuses on games in which cooperation pays off—negotiation, bargaining, and arbitration. Part Five deals with the interaction between games, markets, and politics and introduces the link with micro- and macroeconomics.

This is a lot of material to cover, so let's get started. Theory is something you do, not something you talk about doing. We begin with the simplest possible games, those with a single player and perfect information.

■ 1.3 ONE-PERSON DECISIONS WITH PERFECT INFORMATION

Situations with a single person involved are called **decisions,** to distinguish them from games, which need at least two players. At the same time, some of the same language and machinery that are useful in decisions are useful in games as well. In any science, it makes sense to start with really simple problems, real morale boosters. Solving these prepares you for tackling tougher problems later on. That's precisely why we start with 1-person decisions.

The information available to the players in a game makes a big difference in what they can or should do. A player has **perfect information** if he or she knows exactly what has happened every time a decision needs to be made. A game has perfect information if every player in it has perfect information. Chess is a game with perfect information. As long as both players can see the board, they can see exactly what has happened every time they have to make a move.[9] If some player does not have perfect information, then the game is one of **imperfect information.** Poker is a game with imperfect information. One player does not know—unless he or she is cheating—what cards have been dealt to another player. Games with imperfect information are very important, but they are more difficult to solve than games with perfect information. In this section we study games with perfect information; later, we tackle games with imperfect information.

As a paradigm for a 1-player decision with perfect information, consider a player about to enter the maze in Figure 1.1. Give this player a number—say, 1. Although a number isn't needed to identify a single player, numbers do become useful to identify the players once there are several of them. Action begins when player 1 enters the maze. Player 1's goal is to get to the pot of gold at the end of the maze without running into a wall first. The minute the player runs into a wall, the call is over. The pot of gold is worth M (for money) dollars, and if the player reaches it, the outcome is M. Player 1 gets paid the amount M, which is positive. If player 1 runs into a wall, the game ends and the outcome is 0. In this book, and for the vast majority of time in real life, a player prefers more money to less, and so prefers the outcome M to the outcome 0. These are the two possible outcomes when the player enters the maze shown in Figure 1.1.

---

[9] There is a version of Chess, called Kriegspiel, in which players do not see the board; Kriegspiel thus has imperfect information.

FIGURE 1.1 **THE MAZE**

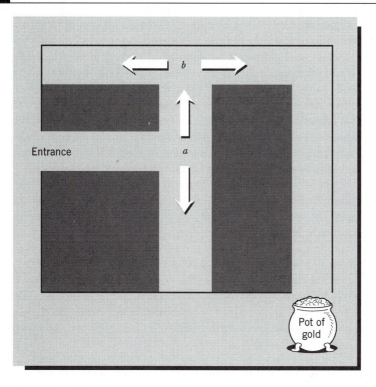

Now we are going to walk with player 1 through the maze. Player 1 reaches a *decision point*, marked *a*, soon after entering the maze. At this decision point, player 1 has two choices: go left or go right. If player 1 goes right, she runs into a wall and the game ends. If player 1 goes left, she encounters a second decision point, marked *b*. At this decision point, player 1 can go either left or right. If player 1 goes left, she runs into a wall and the game ends. If player 1 goes right, she eventually reaches the pot of gold.

Now let's see how decision looks at this maze. Decision theory has a precise way of describing any decision, a description called the **extensive form** of the decision. Figure 1.2 shows the extensive form of the maze in Figure 1.1. The decision is dubbed Pot of Gold. We will walk you through the extensive form of Pot of Gold, and then look at some definitions.

Decision theory is all about the decisions the player makes, so the description of Pot of Gold begins with the first decision point, *a*, shown as the circled *a* and 1 at the left of Figure 1.2. A circle means that some player must make a decision at that point. The number of the player whose decision it is—here, player 1—is included inside the circle. Coming out of this decision point are two straight lines. These straight lines represent the two choices player 1 can make at decision point *a:* left or right. The line labeled Right runs into a wall, causing the game to end. The end of the game is represented by an *endpoint*. An outcome is attached to each endpoint. Since running into a wall means getting $0, the outcome 0 is attached to this endpoint. If player 1 goes left, then she reaches another decision point, *b*. At this decision point, player 1 has two choices, left or right. These choices (also called moves) are again represented by lines coming out of decision point *b*, labeled Left and

Right. If player 1 goes left, she again runs into a wall (an endpoint) and the outcome is 0. If player 1 goes right, she exits from the maze and reaches the pot of gold, the outcome M.

The extensive form shown in Figure 1.2 contains all the information about Pot of Gold that is needed to solve it. Mathematically speaking, the extensive form is a *tree diagram*, so called because it looks like a tree if you are at the starting point, facing right. There are fancy names for the elements of the extensive form. Points in the tree are called *nodes*. Every game begins with an *initial node*. In Pot of Gold, this is the node a. A node with a circle around it and a player number inside is called an **information set.** An information set shows which player has to move and what the player knows when making the move. The lines coming out from a node are called *branches,* again in keeping with the tree metaphor. The outcomes attached to endpoints are called *payoffs.* Pot of Gold has perfect information: whenever a decision has to be made, that is, at nodes a and b, player 1 knows exactly where he or she is in the maze. Later we will see what imperfect information looks like in a tree diagram.

There is a way to solve Pot of Gold and games like it that always works: start from the pot of gold and work backward until the entrance is reached. Working from the end of a game back to the beginning in order to solve it is called **backward induction** and is the procedure used to solve every 1-person game with perfect information. Here's how backward induction is used to solve Pot of Gold (see Figure 1.3).

Start at the last decision point of the game, node b. At node b, player 1 reaches the pot of gold by going right. We denote this by an arrow on the branch labeled Right coming out of node b. Now it is up to player 1 to reach node b, since this puts the player in position to get the gold. The only way to reach node b is by going left at node a. We denote this by an

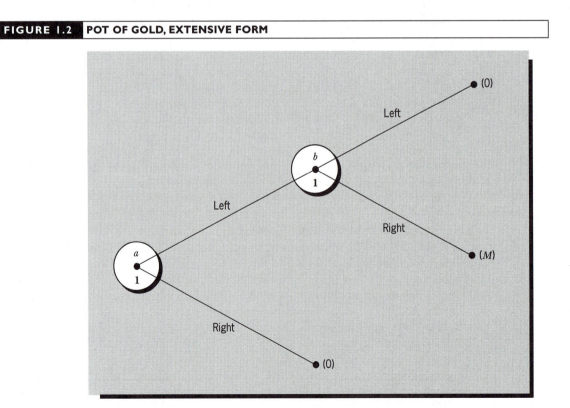

FIGURE 1.3   **POT OF GOLD, BACKWARD INDUCTION**

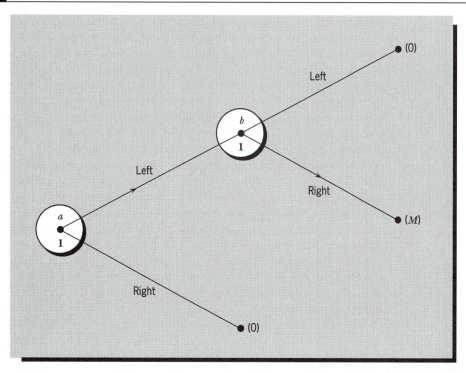

arrow on the branch labeled Left coming out of node *a*. We now have a complete path from the initial node *a* to the endpoint where the pot of gold is:

go left at *a*, go right at *b*

This plan of play solves Pot of Gold and gets the payoff *M*, the pot of gold. We have just solved your first game.

It is possible to get the payoff 0 in Pot of Gold. All it takes is a bad strategy. A **strategy** is a complete plan of play for a game. The good strategy in Pot of Gold leads to the pot of gold. There are three other strategies for Pot of Gold, all of which are bad because they run into a wall and get payoff 0. To construct a strategy, you first identify every decision that a player might make. Here, player 1 has to make a decision at node *a* and again at node *b*. At node *a*, player 1 has two choices; at node *b*, two choices. A strategy for Pot of Gold fills in the following blanks:

_____ at *a*, _____ at *b*

Since there are two possible ways to fill in the blank at *a* and two possible ways to fill in the blank at *b*, there are (2)(2) = 4 strategies for Pot of Gold. We have already identified the good strategy. Here are the three bad strategies:

right at *a*, right at *b*

left at *a*, left at *b*

right at *a*, left at *b*

Good play avoids these three strategies.

We have seen that the extensive form of Pot of Gold consists of nodes, branches, endpoints, and payoffs. Game theory has another way to describe Pot of Gold. This description, based only on strategies, is called the **normal form.** The normal form of a 1-player game lists each of the player's strategies and the payoff alongside each. Figure 1.4 shows Pot of Gold in normal form. It lists player 1's four strategies and the payoff, 0 or M, alongside each. The normal form codes all the information of the extensive form into a matrix, here a matrix with four rows and one column. In this code, it is easy to spot the solution to Pot of Gold: pick the strategy (left at a, right at b) that pays M. This is the best strategy, as it is the only one to pay a positive payoff. The three other strategies pay zero.

You ought to be wondering why there are two representations, normal form and extensive form, of the same game. Some purists think that we should study games only in extensive form. In particular, for games where the sequence of moves is crucial, the extensive form has a lot of appeal. Von Neumann and Morgenstern, the originators of the distinction, thought studying games in normal form led to more general insights. For games where all players move simultaneously, the normal form has a lot of appeal. This book takes a pragmatic approach: pick the form that is easier to write down and solve. This is usually the normal form. However, if the game is already written down in extensive form, you can solve it in that form without bothering with the normal form. In 1-player decisions of perfect information, the same solution is derived from both the extensive form and the normal form.[10]

FIGURE 1.4 **POT OF GOLD, NORMAL FORM**

Player 1	
Left at a, left at b	0
Left at a, right at b	M
Right at a, left at b	0
Right at a, right at b	0

---

[10] Chapter 7 shows to what extent this is true for more complicated games.

1.4 TWO-PERSON GAMES WITH PERFECT INFORMATION

The decision we studied in the last section had only one player. The rest of this chapter is devoted to games with two players. For now, we restrict our attention to 2-person games with perfect information, a simple example of which is shown in Figure 1.5, Two-Person Pot of Gold.

Player 1 moves first, and can go either left or right. If player 1 goes right, the game ends. At the endpoint is attached the payoff vector **u,** given by

$$\mathbf{u} = (u_1, u_2) = (0,0)$$

where u_i is the notation for the payoff to player 1. So each player gets 0 at this endpoint. If player 1 goes left, then it is player 2's turn to move. Player 2 can go either left or right. If player 2 goes left, then the game ends with the payoff vector

$$\mathbf{u} = (0,0)$$

If player 2 goes right, then the game ends as well. In this event, the players have found the pot of gold, whose value they divide evenly:

$$\mathbf{u} = M/2, M/2$$

Solving Pot of Gold with two players is no different from solving Pot of Gold with one player. We use backward induction, starting with player 2, the last player to move. Player 2, who prefers half the pot of gold to none, moves right. This brings us to player 1's move.

FIGURE 1.5 | **TWO-PERSON POT OF GOLD, EXTENSIVE FORM**

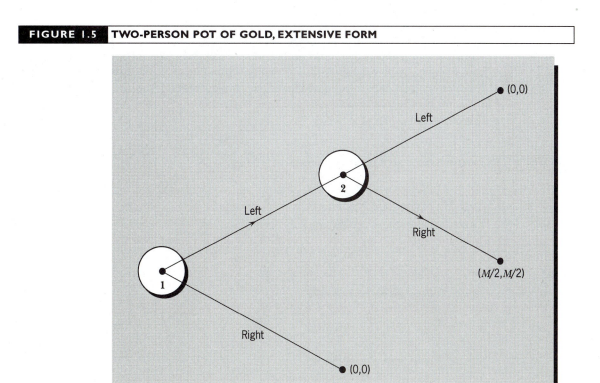

Player 1, who also prefers half the pot of gold to none, moves left. This solution is denoted by the arrows through Figure 1.5. We have just solved our first 2-person game.

Pot of Gold with two players is a parable—it tells a large story in a small space. Consider any business deal that has profit potential for both parties. The pot of gold valued M represents the deal. What the two sides have to do is find their way to the deal. The path by which 1 goes left, 2 goes right represents how the two sides find their way to the deal. This path is called the *solution path*. In 2-person Pot of Gold there is only one solution path, the path that gets to the pot of gold. All the other paths get zeros instead. Of course, most business deals are a lot more complicated than 2-person Pot of Gold; this complexity is addressed in later chapters.

Although the extensive form of 2-person Pot of Gold closely resembles the extensive form of the 1-person version (compare Figures 1.2 and 1.5), its normal form looks a lot different (compare Figures 1.4 and 1.6). To construct its normal form, we list the strategies for each player. Player 1 is the row player, and player 2 is the column player. Player 1 has a single information set, with two choices at that set, so player 1 has $(1)(2) = 2$ strategies. These are Left or Right, listed alongside the rows of the matrix. Similarly, player 2 has a single information set, with two choices at that set, so player 2 also has two strategies, Left or Right. These are listed above the columns of the matrix. We array these strategies in a 2 x 2 matrix (that is, a matrix with two rows and two columns). The rows correspond to player 1's two strategies; the columns, to player 2's two strategies. We move the payoff vectors from the endpoints of the extensive form into the appropriate cell of the normal form matrix. For instance, the pair of strategies

> 1 goes left, 2 goes right

leads to the payoff vector $(M/2, M/2)$, which appears in row 1 (player 1 goes left) and column 2 (player 2 goes right) in the matrix. In every payoff vector, player 1's payoff comes first, followed by player 2's payoff. Throughout game theory, 2 x 2 games prove useful as parables of larger questions, a good reason to avail ourselves of them as often as possible. Let's now turn to a class of very special 2-person games with perfect information—games like Chess.

FIGURE 1.6 TWO-PERSON POT OF GOLD, NORMAL FORM

	Player 2	
Player 1	Left	Right
Left	(0,0)	$\left(\frac{M}{2}, \frac{M}{2}\right)$
Right	(0,0)	(0,0)

■ 1.5 GAMES LIKE CHESS

A 2-person game with perfect information is a **game like Chess** if it satisfies the following requirements. First, the players have perfect information. Second, each player has at most a finite number of strategies. Third, the outcomes are limited to win, lose, or draw. Either player 1 wins and player 2 loses (w,l) or both players get a draw (d,d) or player 1 loses and player 2 wins (l,w).

Chess is a game like Chess. The fact that both players can see the board at all times means that it has perfect information. Chess is finite; it can't go on forever, because of a special stopping rule. If the same configuration appears on the board three times, the game is ruled a draw. The two players alternate turns, and the outcomes are limited to win, lose, or draw. So Chess qualifies. The first theorem ever proved about games says:

Theorem on Games like Chess.   In games like Chess, exactly one of the following is true: player 1 can guarantee a win, player 2 can guarantee a win, or each player can guarantee a draw.[11]

FIGURE 1.7   GAMES LIKE CHESS

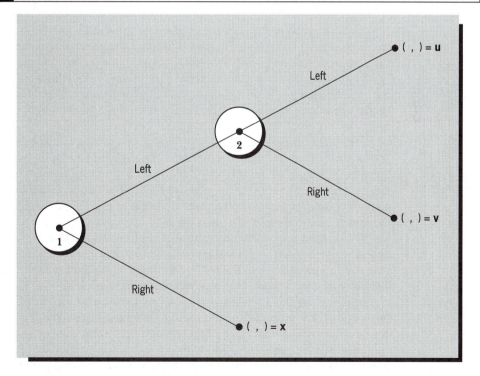

---

[11] This theorem was essentially stated and proved by the mathematician Zermelo in 1913. See U. Schwalbe and P. Walker, "Zermelo and the early history of game theory," *Games and Economics Behavior* 34 (2001): 123–137, for the latest research on Zermelo's theorem.

We will prove this theorem for the class of extensive form games like Chess shown in Figure 1.7, all of whose normal forms are 2 x 2. Player 1 moves first and can move either left or right. If player 1 moves right, the game ends with the payoff vector **x.** If player 1 moves left, then it is player 2's turn. Player 2 can move either left or right. If player 2 moves left, the payoff vector is **u;** if player 2 moves right, the payoff vector is **v.** The payoff vectors **u, v,** and **x** can take any of the following forms:

$$(w,l) \quad (d,d) \quad (l,w)$$

Since each possible payoff vector can take any of three forms, and there are three payoff vectors, $3^3 = 27$ possible games are represented in Figure 1.7. The following proof applies to each of these 27 games.

The proof works via backward induction. Start with player 2, at the end of the game. Player 2 maximizes payoff, given the payoff vectors **u** and **v.** There are three possible cases facing player 2.

- *Case 1.* Player 2 can reach a win in at least one of the payoff vectors **u** or **v.** Then player 2 so moves. In this case, if the play reaches player 2, he can guarantee a win.
- *Case 2.* Player 2 cannot reach a win with either move, but he can reach a draw from at least one of the payoff vectors **u** or **v.** Then player 2 so moves. In this case, if the play reaches player 2, he can guarantee a draw.
- *Case 3.* Player 2 faces a loss no matter what move he makes: $\mathbf{u} = \mathbf{v} = (w,l)$. In this case, player 1 can guarantee a win by moving left. The play reaches player 2, who is sure to lose.

Now we come back to the start of the game, and player 1's move. If case 2 holds, then the worst player 1 can do is get a draw. If the payoff vector $\mathbf{x} = (w,l)$, then player 1 moves right and guarantees a win. Otherwise, player 1 moves left and guarantees a draw. Finally, suppose that case 1 holds. If $\mathbf{x} = (l,w)$, then player 1 loses no matter what she chooses, left or right. In this case, player 2 guarantees a win. If $\mathbf{x} = (d,d)$, then player 1 guarantees a draw by moving right. Finally, if $\mathbf{x} = (w,l)$, player 1 guarantees a win. This completes the proof.

There are a lot of games like Chess. Tic-Tac-Toe is one popular example. In Tic-Tac-Toe, the two players play on a 3 x 3 matrix. Player 1 marks an "X" in one of the 9 cells of the matrix. Then player 2 marks an "O" in one of the 8 remaining open cells of the matrix. Play continues until one of the players has a row, column, or diagonal with all of her or his marks in it, in which case that player wins. If the players have filled the matrix and no player has won, the game is declared a draw.

The theorem says something general about games like Chess. For any specific game like Chess, if we understand it well enough, then we can determine which of the three possible conclusions holds. For Tic-Tac-Toe, we know the following: each player in Tic-Tac-Toe can guarantee a draw. You can check this with your classmates. Pair off, and play 5 rounds of Tic-Tac-Toe. In the early rounds, you may observe wins by player 1 or player 2. By the end of the fifth round, however, all you will observe are draws. Experienced Tic-Tac-Toe players know the strategies that prevent defeat for either player 1 or player 2.

Chess is a lot more complicated than Tic-Tac-Toe. In Tic-Tac-Toe, the player who moves first has 9 possible moves; the player who moves second, 8 possible moves. By contrast, in Chess, player 1 (white) has 20 possible opening moves, and player 2 (black) has 20 possible responses to each opening move by white. Already the extensive form of Chess is challenging the capabilities of conventional human graphics. Moreover, Tic-Tac-Toe ends in at most 9 moves, while in most Chess games it takes 40 moves before it is clear what the outcome will be. It is estimated that the extensive form of Chess would require something on the order of 10^{30} nodes to write down.

Chess is so complicated that it is still not known which of the three possible conclusions of the theorem is true. In Chess played at the world-class level, we observe all three of the possible conclusions of the theorem. However, we observe wins by player 1 more often than wins by player 2, and draws are more common than a win by either player. This suggests that there is some advantage to being player 1. To level the playing field in tournament conditions, such as the World Championship, there are an even number of matches (12), with the two finalists each playing as first mover an equal number of times (6). Whether player 1 can guarantee a win, or whether each player can guarantee a draw, remains an open question. Fame and fortune await the person—or machine—that ultimately decides this question.

◼ 1.6 MAN VS. MACHINE: KASPAROV LOSES TO DEEP BLUE

Part of what keeps Chess interesting is that we do not understand it well enough to know which of the three possible conclusions of the theorem is true.[12] If we knew that player 1 can guarantee a win, there would be little or no suspense left in any given match. Player 1 should be the favorite to win, and any other outcome is an upset. But this is precisely what we don't know.

Roughly a hundred million people play Chess, and even more follow the game, making it a business. Important matches, such as the World Championship, are now broadcast over the Internet to large audiences. The most-followed Chess match of all time took place in 1997, pitting the then World Champion, Garry Kasparov, against the highest-ranking Chess machine of all time, Deep Blue. Deep Blue was a creation of IBM, named after the corporation's color. Deep Blue was designed to do nothing else except play. Deep Blue operated by brute force, literally crunching Chess problems to death. Able to calculate the consequences of 200 million moves per second, thanks to its configuration of 32 processors in parallel, Deep Blue was ranked 60th in the world when this match was scheduled. That means Deep Blue was already better than all but 59 human players on the whole planet.

Games like Chess were the first games that machines could play. The only thing a machine needs to play a game like Chess is a program to determine its strategy. Once the machine has a complete plan of play, or a rule for computing the various pieces of a complete plan, it is ready to play. In a game like Chess, strategy is all that matters. Machines have been able to play Tic-Tac-Toe as well as humans for the past 30 years. Chess-playing programs on personal computers can often beat their owners. Still, it came as a shock to most humans when Deep Blue beat Kasparov in their 6-game match. This was the first time in history that a machine beat the World Champion at Chess. Although Kasparov came back to win a subsequent 6-game rematch, it is now established that, on any given day, a sufficiently powerful and well-designed machine can beat any human on the planet at Chess.

Games like Chess, or nearly so, are important not just as amusements. Chapter 7 shows that, with only a slight alteration of the payoffs in Figure 1.7, we get an important game played in business, involving possible entry into a market and attempts by established firms to deter that entry. Games like Chess show with crystalline clarity that strategy matters.

---

[12] Material in this section is drawn in part from the *Chicago Tribune,* "Deep Blue Association is a Windfall for IBM," 17 August 1997.

FIGURE 1.8 | **IS THERE MORE TO THE DECISION BY IBM TO RETIRE DEEP BLUE?**

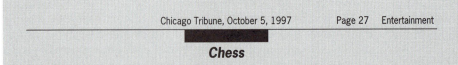

Chicago Tribune, October 5, 1997   Page 27   Entertainment

Chess

By Shelby Lyman

America has not had good luck with its chess superstars.

Bobby Fischer became world champion in 1972 and played no more. Gata Kamsky—a phenomenal prodigy and the United States' strongest player—abandoned chess last year to study medicine. And now the computer Deep Blue has been retired only months after a brilliant victory over Garry Kasparov.

According to IBM spokespersons, the scientists who created the machine are looking for new challenges. There is also a reluctance in some corporate quarters to risk defeat and a possible marketing setback in a rematch. But there may be more to the decision than is being publicly acknowledged.

At a press conference immediately following his defeat, the distraught world champion told a skeptical audience that there may have been human intervention during some of the computer's moves. He further undermined his relationship with IBM by criticizing its role in the organization of the event.

It is possible that these and other accusations and complaints have made IBM shy of another round with Kasparov. If so, the decision to have no match at all is understandable. The charismatic world champion is arguably the greatest player ever. A match with anyone else would be a much lesser event.

Deep Blue's "retirement" may only be temporary. But until IBM resumes the project—or another computer preempts Deep Blue's role—a wonderful adventure marrying science and chess is no longer ours.

Reprinted with permission.

Suppose you are player 1 in such a game, and it is known that player 1 can guarantee a win. Somehow you manage to lose instead. You have no excuses. You can't blame luck, since there are no chance moves. You can't blame missing information, since you have perfect information. The only reason you lost is that you chose a bad strategy. You snatched defeat from the jaws of victory. You have no one to blame but yourself when you play a bad strategy and get a bad outcome as a result.

■ 1.7 WEAK DOMINANCE OF STRATEGIES AND WEAK DOMINANCE SOLVABILITY

When a player goes about comparing two strategies, the comparison involved is usually not straightforward. Usually the player finds that in some situations, one strategy does better than the other, while in other situations, the reverse is the case. Suppose you are head football coach, your team has the ball, and you are comparing the two strategies Pass and Run. The payoff from each of these strategies, in terms of yards gained, depends on what strategy the defense chooses. If the defense sets up in a 9-man line, then Run pays very little, while Pass stands to gain many yards. Just the opposite is true if the defense sets up in a prevent formation, with 7 or 8 players defending against the pass. This is the usual situation in games.

However, when one strategy always does at least as well as another in every situation, and does better in at least one situation, then the comparison between them is straightforward. We say that the strategy that does at least as well as another in every situation, and does better in at least one situation, **weakly dominates** the other. You will see why we need the adverb *weakly* in the next section, where we study a stronger kind of domination. If a player has two strategies, and one weakly dominates the other, then she or he has every reason to choose the strategy that weakly dominates; and no good reason to choose the strategy that gets weakly dominated. The strategy that weakly dominates is a good strategy; the strategy that gets dominated is a bad strategy.

To see an example of this, recall the game in Figure 1.6; this is the normal form of 2-person Maze with perfect information. Consider player 1, comparing her two strategies Left and Right. Here is the comparison:

> If player 2 chooses Left, then player 1 gets 0 if she chooses Left and 0 if she chooses Right. Since $0 = 0$, the result is a tie in this case.
>
> If player 2 chooses Right, then player 1 gets $M/2$ if she chooses Left and 0 if she chooses Right. Since $M/2 > 0$, Left is better for player 1.

To sum up, Left pays player 1 at least as much as Right in every situation, and Left pays more than Right in one situation, so Left weakly dominates Right.

You can check that for player 2, the strategy Right weakly dominates the strategy Left. So each of the players in this game has a strategy that dominates her or his other strategy. The strategic choice in this game is really straightforward for each of the two players: choose the strategy that weakly dominates. When each player chooses his or her strategy that weakly dominates, player 1 chooses Left and player 2 chooses Right. The result is the payoff $M/2$ to each player in Figure 1.6.

When every player in a game has a strategy that dominates all his or her other strategies, we say the game is **weakly dominance solvable.** Solely by determining which strategy is weakly dominant, and choosing that strategy, we can solve such a game. Although games that are weakly dominance solvable are rare, when they do occur players who understand the game know exactly how to play them.

Often times, games in extreme situations tend to be dominance solvable. Here is an extreme case where this is so. A group of prisoners of war is about to be executed. This is not supposed to happen in war, according to the Geneva Convention of 1925; however, in the 2001 war in Afghanistan, the Geneva Convention was not always followed. Each of the prisoners has a pair of strategies, Do Nothing and Revolt. If a prisoner chooses the strategy Do Nothing, then he will be executed. If a prisoner chooses the strategy Revolt, and if enough other prisoners choose that same strategy, then at least some of the prisoners avoid execution. Thus, Revolt weakly dominates Do Nothing. And Revolt is exactly what happened at the prisoner of war camp outside Mazaar-e-Sharif, Afghanistan. Of some 600 prisoners of war, roughly 90 survived the revolt and fell into the hands of the Red Cross, which does observe the Geneva Convention.

Here is a second example, not involving life-and-death calculations but rather more economics. In a **second-price auction,** each player bids on the item being auctioned. The high bidder wins, but pays a price equal to the second-highest bid. In this kind of auction, bidding what the item is worth to you weakly dominates underbidding. If you bid what the item is worth and win the auction, then you pay a price lower than what the item is worth to you. In this case, you come out with a positive payoff; you come out ahead. If you underbid and still win the auction, then you pay a price lower than what the item is worth to you—a tie. Finally, if you underbid and lose the auction, you get a zero payoff (the status quo hasn't changed), when you might have won the auction by bidding what the item is worth to you. That's precisely where the weak domination comes in. Auctions are complicated, and second-price auctions are fairly rare; we defer further study of them to Chapter 12.

◼ 1.8 STRICT AND WEAK DOMINATION OF STRATEGIES AND STRICT DOMINANCE SOLVABILITY

In the last section, we considered the comparison of two strategies, one of which was at least as good as the other in every situation, and better than the other in at least one situation. If one strategy is better than another in every situation, we say it **strictly dominates.** If every player in a game has a strategy that strictly dominates all other strategies, then playing the strictly dominating strategy is best for the player. We call such a game **strictly dominance solvable.** Solely by determining which strategy is strictly dominant, and choosing that strategy, we can solve such a game. Games that are strictly dominance solvable are even rarer than those that are weakly dominance solvable.

Figure 1.9 shows a game that is strictly dominance solvable. This game represents a certain kind of Teamwork. If each player chooses the strategy Left, then teamwork succeeds, and the payoff is +1 to each player. If the players do not choose the same strategy, then teamwork breaks down, and the payoff is 0 to each. Finally, if each player chooses the strategy Right, then teamwork leads to infighting and lots of other negativity, and each player gets the payoff −1.

Notice that for player 1 in the game of Teamwork, the strategy Left always pays better than the strategy Right: there are no ties. Similarly, for player 2 in Teamwork, the strategy Left always pays better than the strategy Right: again, there are no ties. Each player choosing his or her strictly dominant strategy, Left, leads to the outcome +1 for each player. This is the strictly dominant solution of Teamwork.

FIGURE 1.9 GAME THAT IS STRICTLY DOMINANCE SOLVABLE

It is instructive to compare Figure 1.9, where the game is strictly dominance solvable, and Figure 1.6, where the game is weakly dominance solvable. In Figure 1.9, there are no ties; the dominance all goes one way, in favor of the teamwork strategy Left. In Figure 1.6, there are ties; the dominance kicks in only when player 1 uses the strategy Left and player 2 uses the strategy Right.

Here is a version of Teamwork that you may not want to play in class. Suppose the pay-off represents points toward your final grade. "Left" means "Attend Class"; "Right" means "Skip Class." If all students skip class, then the professor deducts one grade point from each—that's harsh. If some students skip class and some attend class, then each student who attends is awarded one grade point, but there is no deduction from any student who does not attend. Finally, if each student attends class, then each student is awarded one grade point. In such a class, attending class is a strictly dominant strategy and attendance in class, the strictly dominant solution.

■ 1.9 EXTENSIVE FORM, NORMAL FORM, AND COALITION FUNCTION FORM

Sometimes the line between a game like Chess and a game that is not like Chess can be very fine indeed. Consider the two extensive form games in Figure 1.10. The game in Figure 1.10a is like Chess, and player 1 can guarantee a draw by going left. The game in Figure 1.10b is not like Chess, since it has imperfect information. This imperfection shows up in the information set of player 2, which has 2 nodes. Player 2 doesn't know how player 1 has moved, and so does not know at which node play has arrived when it is his turn to move. However, if we look at the normal forms of these two games, we see that they are exactly the same! The normal form of both is shown in Figure 1.11. Each player has one information set, with two choices at that information set, so each player has two strategies. That makes the normal

FIGURE 1.10   GAMES NEARLY LIKE CHESS

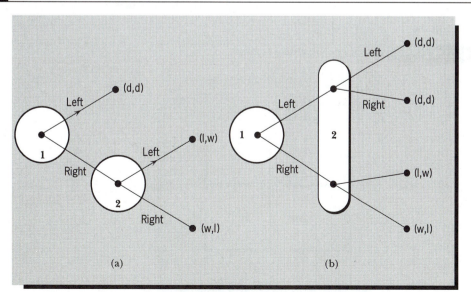

(a)   (b)

form a 2 x 2 matrix in each case. When both players go left, the outcome is a draw (d,d), and so on; so that the payoffs match up. Even though the game in Figure 1.10b is not like Chess, it is close enough that it has the same normal form as a game that is like Chess.

It often happens that games with different extensive forms have the same normal form, because the normal form suppresses some information that is available in the extensive form. For instance, you can see at once that the game in Figure 1.10a has perfect information, but this inference is no longer available in the normal form. Every extensive form has a unique normal form representation. However, for every game in normal form there are usually several possible games in extensive form that could give rise to it. Thus things that are true for games like Chess may also be true for games nearly like Chess.

In Figure 1.10a, just as in Figure 1.11, player 1 can guarantee a draw by moving left. In the extensive form, we find this out by backward induction. In normal form, we get this outcome by a rather different route. For player 2, choosing the strategy Left weakly dominates choosing the strategy Right. For player 1, neither strategy weakly dominates the other. So this game is not weakly dominance solvable, to say nothing of strictly dominance solvable. However, suppose player 1 takes this weak domination on the part of player 2 into account. Then player 1 does best by choosing the strategy Left and getting a draw. What player 1 has done is appeal to player 2's **rationality;** a rational player, here player 2, has no reason to use a weakly dominanted strategy. In such a case, we say a game outcome is **rationalizable,** when it is based on an appeal to rationality. If you can follow an argument like that just given, you are well on your way to thinking like a true game theorist!

In addition to the extensive and normal forms, there is a third form of games, especially useful for games with a largely cooperative character, called the **coalition function form.** This form requires the answers to only two questions: what can each player guarantee for himself or herself, and what can the two players acting together guarantee for themselves? For the win, lose, or draw game, such as that shown in Figure 1.11, the coalition function form simply says that player 1 can guarantee a draw, as can player 2. The players acting together cannot guarantee anything more. For 2-person Pot of Gold, the coalition function form says that player 1 can guarantee 0 (because player 2 goes left), player 2 can guarantee 0 (because player 1 goes left), but together they can guarantee M (because player

---

FIGURE 1.11   **GAMES IN NORMAL FORM**

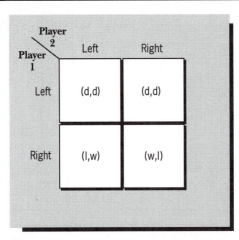

FIGURE 1.12   **TWO-PERSON POT OF GOLD, COALITION FUNCTION FORM**

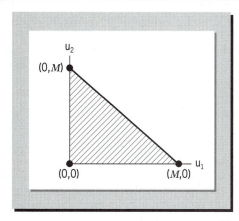

1 goes right and player 2 goes left). This coalition function form is depicted in Figure 1.12: the three points we have just identified are the vertices of a payoff triangle, and the striped area shows various ways of dividing less than M among the two players. The coalition function form is used primarily when studying how the gains of cooperation are divided up among those involved in a deal—a question focused on in Chapter 13 and beyond.

◼ SUMMARY

1. A game is any rule-governed strategic situation with a well-defined outcome, characterized by strategic interdependence among the players.

2. There is a great variety of games in the literal sense: board games, card games, video games, and field games. Business and economics exhibit games in the extended sense. The Chicago Bulls provide an example of both senses.

3. Game theory is the science that studies games and takes them seriously enough to solve them. Game theory began as applied mathematics, but is now central to the way we think about business and economics.

4. Games serve as models for market interactions and economic negotiations. For example, the cola wars between Coke and Pepsi are a market game; negotiations among the G-8 countries are a game in international economics.

5. The extensive form is the basic description of a game. An extensive form is a tree diagram, with nodes, branches, an initial node, information sets, and endpoints.

6. A 1-player decision with perfect information can be solved by backward induction, starting at the end and working back to the beginning.

7. A game has perfect information if every information set contains a single node.

8. Two-person games with perfect information can be solved by backward induction, just like 1-person decisions with perfect information.

9. For a game like Chess, exactly one of the following is true: player 1 can guarantee a win, player 2 can guarantee a win, or each player can guarantee a draw.

10. A strategy that pays at least as well as another in every situation, and that pays better than another in at least one situation, weakly dominates. A game where every player has a weakly dominant strategy is weakly dominance solvable.

11. A strategy that pays better than another in every situation strictly dominates. A game where every player has a strictly dominant strategy is strictly dominance solvable.

12. There are three representations of games: extensive form, normal form, and coalition function form. The normal form looks at the implications of strategies, while suppressing some of the detail contained in the extensive form. The coalition function form suppresses even more detail than the normal form and is used mainly for studying cooperation among players.

■ KEY TERMS

game	extensive form	second-price auction
strategic interdependence	information set	strictly dominant
market game	backward induction	strictly dominance solvable
economic negotiation	strategy	rationality
game theory	games like Chess	rationalizable
decisions	weakly dominant	coalition function form
perfect/imperfect information	weakly dominance solvable	

■ PROBLEMS

1. Give examples of strategic interaction in each of the following industries: entertainment, beer, automobiles, and financial services.

2. Draw the extensive form of the maze in Figure 1.13, and then solve it. Player 1 moves at a; player 2, at b.

FIGURE 1.13   THE MAZE II

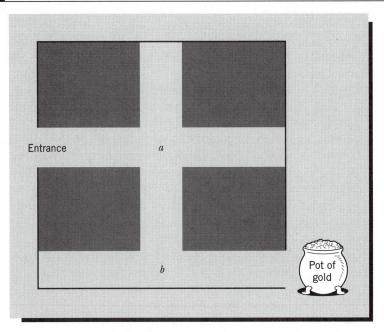

Entrance   a

b   Pot of gold

3. Transform the game in problem 2 into normal form. Next, find a weakly dominant strategy for each player. Finally, show that the game is weakly dominance solvable by finding its weak dominance solution.

4. Consider the schema of Figure 1.7. Find payoff vectors **u, v,** and **x** such that (a) player 1 can guarantee a win; (b) player 2 can guarantee a win; and (c) either player can guarantee a draw. (There are many right answers.)

5. Suppose you play Tic-Tac-Toe on a 2 × 2 board, as shown in Figure 1.14. The usual rules apply. Player 1, who goes first, puts an *X* in any one of the cells. Player 2, who goes second, puts an *O* in one of the remaining cells. The first player to fill a row, column, or diagonal with his or her marks wins. Show that this game is like Chess. Draw its extensive form. Which player can guarantee a win?

6. In section 1.5, we said experienced Tic-Tac-Toe players on a 3 x 3 board never lose. Show how the player moving second can always get a draw, by considering how to counter the three kinds of opening moves: (1) player 1 puts *X* in a corner; (2) player 1 puts *X* on the side, but not a corner; (3) player 1 puts *X* in the middle.

Violate any one of the conditions that make a game like Chess and the game may no longer satisfy the conclusion of the theorem for games like Chess. This is the theme of the next four questions.

7. The theorem on games like Chess breaks down if there are three or more players. See if you can find a counterexample. If you can't, here's a big hint: see Chapter 5, section 5.1.

8. The game Pick the Largest Number is a 2-player, win, lose, or draw game with perfect information. Player 1 picks any number. Player 2 hears player 1's number, then picks any number he wants. If player 1's number is bigger than player 2's, the game ends in a win for player 1. If player 1's number equals player 2's number, the game ends in a draw. If player 1's number is smaller than player 2's number, then player 1 gets to choose again. Show that Pick the Largest Number is not like Chess because it is not finite: There is no largest number. In particular, show that player 2 need never lose—and so the game never ends.

9. Now consider the game Pick the Largest Number, as in problem 8, only now the largest number a player is allowed to pick is 3. This game is finite. Show that it is like Chess. In particular, either player can force a draw. For extra credit, show that this game is weakly dominance solvable, and find its weak dominance solution.

FIGURE 1.14 **TIC-TAC-TOE ON A 2 x 2 BOARD, PLAYER 1 HAS JUST MOVED**

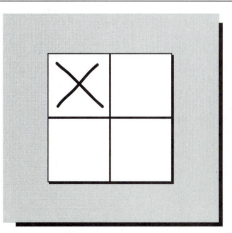

10. The game Escape and Evasion (shown in Figure 1.15) is a 2-person, win, lose, or draw finite game. Player 1, the escapee, has just escaped from jail, and can go either top or bottom. Player 2, the jailer, can also go either top or bottom, but does not know which way the escapee has gone. If the jailer goes the same way as the escapee, the jailer catches the escapee—a win for the jailer. If the jailer goes a different way from the escapee, the escapee gets away—a win for the escapee. Show that Escape and Evasion has imperfect information. Then show that neither player can guarantee a win. Since draws aren't allowed, you have a counterexample to the theorem on games like Chess.

11. According to the doctrine that "a dollar is a dollar," the same principles apply to the game Pot of Gold whether M is $1 or $1 million. Do you agree or disagree? Why?

FIGURE 1.15 **ESCAPE AND EVASION**

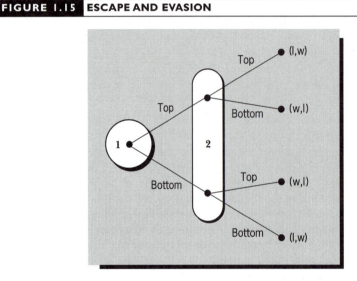

CHAPTER 2

Games of Chance

◼ 2.1 THE CHALLENGE CHANCE POSES TO PLAYERS OF A GAME

In the previous chapter, all games involved nothing but strategy—chance played no role. In this chapter, we look at what happens in a game when chance does play a role. In some games, for instance the state lottery and games played in casinos, chance plays a dominant role. This chapter explores the implications of the role chance plays for game theory.

The first thing we have to do is extend the notion of payoff to that of expected payoff. Since chance means more than one thing can happen, with probabilities attached to the various possible outcomes, it is a nontrivial task to process those possibilities and possible outcomes into a number that players can use to guide their play. Indeed, there are many ways to accomplish this task. The first of these is expected value, which you may already have encountered in a basic statistics class. Expected value implies that players are neutral toward risk in a sense that we will make precise.

To commence our study of chance, consider the following basic situation. Player 1 is faced with the following **risky situation:**

> Win $1 with probability 0.5.
> Lose $1 with probability 0.5.

We portray this risky situation in Figure 2.1. The figure begins with an information set belonging to a player numbered 0—player 0 will always represent Chance in a game. Player 0 is not a true strategic player—it does not receive payoffs and its strategy is not decided in the way that a true player's is. Chance picks either the outcome +1 (player 1 wins $1) or the outcome −1 (player 1 loses $1), each with probability 0.5. The probability of a possible outcome lies along the branch connecting that outcome to the initial node where Chance moves. Chance itself never gets a payoff, so only player 1's payoffs appear at the endpoints. Player 1 has a payoff, but no strategy whatsoever—he or she is simply at the mercy of chance in this risky situation.

Our goal is to replace the game represented in Figure 2.1 with a single number—a number that can be compared to monetary values that do not involve chance. Reaching

FIGURE 2.1 | **RISKY SITUATION**

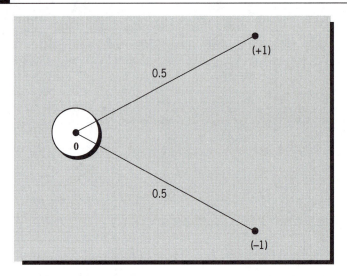

that goal means a player can put situations involving chance on a par with situations that do not involve chance.

To reach that goal, consider the following proposal, first put forward by the French mathematician Blaise Pascal in the seventeenth century.[1] Compute the **expected value,** which is simply a weighted average where the weights are the assigned probabilities and items being weighed are the possible outcomes. Player 1 can compare the expected value (which is a single number) of the risky situation to the value of a situation that does not involve chance, to see what the consequences are of being involved in the risky situation in Figure 2.1.

Doing just that, we get

$$\text{Expected Value} = (0.5)(+1) + (0.5)(-1) = 0.5 + (-0.5) = 0$$

The expected value to player 1 of playing the game in Figure 2.1 is zero; this game represents a break-even proposition for player 1.

A physical model of this situation is a coin toss, in particular, a **fair coin toss.** It is fair, because neither heads nor tails has a greater chance of occurring. Since heads and tails come up with the same probability, and one of them must come up, the probability of each is 0.5. If player 1 wins if the coin lands heads, and loses if the coin lands tails, then we have precisely the situation depicted in Figure 2.1.

Now consider the equation $0 = 0$. Let the 0 on the left represent the status quo, while the 0 on the right represents the expected value of the game of chance. What the equation tells us is that player 1 is indifferent between a sure 0, the status quo, and a risky 0, the expected value generated by the game in Figure 2.1. When a player is indifferent between a sure value and the same value arising as an expected value, we say the player is **risk neutral.** And when a game of chance has a zero expected value to a player, we call that a **fair game.**

---

[1] An excellent source for this connection is Richard A. Epstein, *The Theory of Gambling and Statistical Logic* (London: Academic Press, 1995).

2.2 TWO PLAYERS IN A FAIR GAME

Let's look at how two players might interact in a fair game. The physical situation is the same as that underlying Figure 2.1, only now there are two players involved. We will call them player 1, the Gambler, and player 2, the Casino. When the Gambler wins +1, she wins that dollar from the Casino; when the Gambler loses –1, she pays that dollar to the Casino. The game that results is depicted in Figure 2.2.

The expected value to the Gambler is as before, 0. The expected value to the Casino is

$$\text{Expected Value}_2 = (0.5)(-1) + (0.5)(+1) = 0,$$

also zero, where the subscript "2" denotes player 2, the Casino.

Notice in particular that the expression for the Expected Value to the Casino is precisely the expression of the Expected Value to the Gambler multiplied by a minus sign: the same probabilities attached to the negative of the payoffs. Thus, if a game is fair to one of two players, and their monetary payoffs add up to zero, then the game is fair to the other player.

2.3 TWO PLAYERS IN AN UNFAIR GAME OF CHANCE

Of course, games of chance need not be fair to either of the players. Consider the game of chance in Figure 2.3, which as we will show is unfair in the sense that it is biased against player 1. Although the payoffs attached to possible outcomes have not changed, the probabilities attached to them have changed. In particular, the possible outcome (–1,+1) happens with a slightly greater probability, 19/37, than the possible outcome (+1,–1), which occurs with only probability 18/37. Let's compute the expected values of this game of chance to each of the players. For the Gambler, we get

$$\text{Expected Value}_1 = (18/37)(+1) + (19/37)(-1) = -1/37$$
$$\text{or about } -.028.$$

FIGURE 2.2   **GAME OF CHANCE BETWEEN GAMBLER AND CASINO**

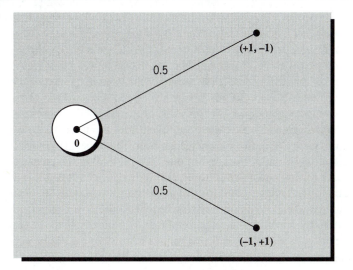

FIGURE 2.3 | **UNFAIR GAME OF CHANCE BETWEEN GAMBLER AND CASINO**

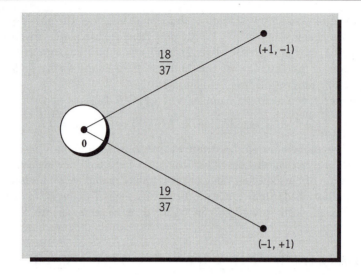

While for the Casino we get

$$\text{Expected Value}_2 = (18/37)(-1) + (19/37)(+1) = +1/37$$
$$\text{or about } +.028.$$

Notice that value in expected value terms is conserved:

$$\text{Expected Value}_1 + \text{Expected Value}_2 = -1/37 + (+1/37) = 0.$$

The game in Figure 2.3 neither creates nor destroys value; it merely conserves value, transferring (in expected value terms) some value from the Gambler to the Casino.

Here is a physical model for the game of chance in Figure 2.3. One popular game played in casinos is **Roulette.** In Roulette, a ball rolls by chance into slots on a wheel. In the kind of Roulette played in casinos in Europe, there are 37 slots in the wheel. Of these 37 slots, 18 are colored red, 18 are colored black, and 1 is colored white. A gambler may place a bet on one of the colors. Suppose the gambler puts 1 monetary unit on the color red. If the ball lands in a red slot, the gambler gets 2 monetary units back—the one he or she bet, plus an additional one paid by the casino. If the ball does not land in a red slot, the gambler gets no money back. This is exactly the situation portrayed in Figure 2.3. You can convince yourself that the same analysis applies if the gambler places a bet on the color black.

Notice that if it were not for the white-colored slot in the roulette wheel, European Roulette would be a fair game, as far as betting on the colors is concerned. The white-colored slot was invented by the casinos three centuries ago to create an advantage for themselves in this game. With that advantage, for every dollar bet on Roulette, the casino stands to win 2.8 cents—a small margin, but one that builds over the course of millions of bets. By the same token, a gambler betting on a color stands to lose 2.8 cents for every dollar bet—again a small margin, but one that again builds with repeated bets.

Casinos in the United States have taken this concept one step further by adding two white slots to the roulette wheel instead of one. The advantage to the casinos in the United States is thus even greater than the advantage enjoyed by the casinos in Europe. The casinos in America are a really big business, as we shall now see.

◼ 2.4 America's Love Affair with Gambling

Americans love to gamble.[2] At least 50 million Americans patronize the businesses in this sector every year. Indeed, some Americans love to gamble so much that they are clinical—some 5 million are diagnosed as compulsive gamblers, suffering from addiction. These are the kind of people who are prone to lose everything they have gambling—like the former owner of the Philadelphia Eagles, who lost $20 million, including control of the Eagles, during a particularly bad losing streak in Atlantic City, New Jersey.

It wasn't always this way. Go back two generations, and basically the only legal gambling was in the state of Nevada—and even there, it wasn't the big deal it is today. Las Vegas began to blossom casinos after World War II—but as late as 1959, the heaviest betting action still took place offshore, in Havana, Cuba. The communist takeover of the island changed all that. Now Las Vegas is the fastest-growing city in the United States—with a population well over 1 million, all built on the foundation of the country's largest concentration of land-based casinos.

Americans place about $600 billion in legal bets annually. We don't have data on illegally placed bets, but if we did they might add as much as 25 percent to this total. The betting public is the consumer; the industry that serves them calls itself the **"gaming and entertainment"** industry. The firms are offering the service of playing games of chance for money, while at the same time keeping the players of those games entertained.

The industry enjoys substantial profits. For every dollar bet, the gaming and entertainment industry earns about 8 cents of profit. So the $600 billion bet by Americans translates into about $50 billion in profits to the industry—a handsome rate of return on a somewhat unusual service. What it boils down to is that the betting public is handing its money over to the industry, while the industry keeps the customers entertained.

The gaming and entertainment industry consists of three parts, each with roughly a one-third share of total bets placed. These three segments are state lotteries, land-based casinos, and water-borne casinos.

Today most states—37 states plus the District of Columbia—have state lotteries, compared to 1960, when no states had a lottery. The state lotteries are notorious for having the industry's lowest payout rate to players—half of every dollar bet in the state lotteries stays with the states. Although people who play the state lottery are at least somewhat aware that they can expect to lose half of every dollar they bet, this does not deter them from playing.

Land-based casinos include the entire state of Nevada; Atlantic City, New Jersey; New Orleans, Louisiana; and almost every Indian reservation in the United States. A U.S. Supreme Court ruling in 1978 recognized the right of Indian tribes to set up casinos on tribal lands, free from interference from or regulation by the states in which those tribal lands are located. Some tribes, like the Pequod in New England, have earned lavish profits from their casino operations.

While only three states (as of this writing) allow land-based casinos, many states allow casinos that float on water. Indiana, for instance, has seven casino boats, floating either on Lake Michigan or on the Ohio River. These seven boats pay $500 million in taxes each year. Indiana levies the highest tax rate, 34 percent, on casino profits in the nation. So the seven riverboats in Indiana collectively make over $1.5 billion in profits each year.

Although the gaming and entertainment industry is making lots of money, it is a tough place to work. Most casino workers—like Blackjack dealers—start out at minimum wage

---

[2] Some material for this section is taken from *The Economist*, "Busted Flush," January 25, 1997, pp. 26–28.

and don't get much higher. These workers have to rely on tips to get their pay above the poverty line. A few workers rise from the ranks into management, where compensation is better. But even there, most of the casino's profits are going to the casino's owners.

2.5 WHY PLAY UNFAIR GAMES OF CHANCE?

Our study of the gaming and entertainment industry in the United States presents us with a paradox. If people use expected value to evaluate the games offered by this industry, then they shouldn't play. Figure 2.4 presents the basic situation facing a potential gambler. Player 1 is the Gambler, and player 2, the Casino, as before. Player 1 has two strategies, either to Enter the Casino or to Stay out of the Casino. If Player 1 enters the casino, she can expect to lose 8 cents to the casino on every dollar bet. If Player 1 stays out of the casino, then she—and the casino—breaks even. Applying backward induction to this game, Player 1 should stay out of the casino. Nevertheless, millions of people do enter casinos and play state lotteries every year.

This is where the "entertainment" in "gaming and entertainment" comes in. The casinos try to make things as entertaining as possible for the gamblers. They ply the players with cheap drinks and food. Before the laws changed, they plied the players with free drinks. They have big-name stars from Hollywood; singers, dancers, and magicians all put on shows. They sponsor boxing matches and other sports attractions. There's never a dull moment in a casino; the action is nonstop. For the millions of steady customers, it may be that the entertainment aspect takes their minds off the money they are losing.

Chance is tricky. Even though the odds favor the casino, on any given night a few lucky players will beat the odds and leave the casino with more money than they came with. If you get a $100 payout on your first pull of a slot machine—and make an immediate getaway—you walk out a winner, despite what expected value says. But the lucky few are outnumbered by the unlucky many—and when all is said and done, the casino comes out ahead.

FIGURE 2.4 | TO ENTER, OR NOT TO ENTER, A CASINO

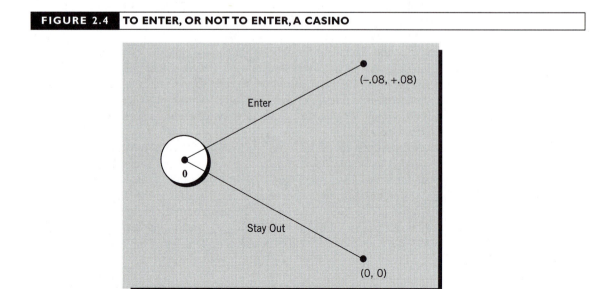

Still, the entertainment argument is hard to swallow. It's hard to believe that the entertainment offered by casinos and state lotteries is worth almost 10 times the entertainment offered by Hollywood movies each year, which sell roughly $6 billion a year in tickets. We now turn to an added explanation, besides that of entertainment.

■ 2.6 A DIFFERENT ATTITUDE TOWARD RISK: RISK SEEKING

Expected value says that a dollar lost and a dollar gained offset each other, as long as the probabilities attached to the loss and gain are equal. This is the hallmark of risk neutrality. But perhaps not all people are neutral to risk in this way. Let's see what happens when a dollar won and a dollar lost do not offset each other.

To model this possibility, consider the following psychology. Suppose that people attach to a gain or loss of money x, a number of points, $u(x)$. The function $u(x)$ that attaches points to gains or losses x is called the utility function. For a risk-neutral person, we have the equation

$$u(x) = x$$

In particular, $u(-1) = -1$, and $u(+1) = +1$. A dollar lost loses 1 point, but a dollar gained gains 1 point, so they offset one another when attached to the same probability.

For a **risk seeker,** if a dollar lost loses 1 point, then a dollar gained gains more than 1 point. A risk seeker who has a utility function with $u(-1) = -1$ and $u(1) = 1.5$ will be only too happy to play European or American Roulette or even the state lottery.

Figure 2.5 shows how this risk seeker views European Roulette. In the figure, the risk seeker is player 1, the Gambler, and we have replaced payoffs in money with payoffs in utility points. Player 2 is the Casino, still assumed to be risk neutral. Treating the points just as we treated dollars under expected value calculation, we have

$$\text{Expected Points}_1 = (18/37)(+1.5) + (19/37)(-1) = 8/37 > 0$$

This risk seeker thinks entering the casino to play European Roulette is a much better deal than staying out of the casino and avoiding risk. At the same time, the casino is glad to take the risk seeker's money, in expected value terms.

We can ask, how low would the probability of winning have to be before this risk seeker would refuse to play the game in Figure 2.5? Replace the known probability of winning, 18/37, in the preceding expression with the unknown probability of winning, p. We are looking for a solution to the equation

$$\text{Expected Points}_1 = (p)(+1.5) + (1-p)(-1) = 0$$

Solving for p, we get $p = 0.4$. This risk seeker would be just indifferent between winning a dollar with probability 0.4 and losing a dollar with probability 0.6—comparable to the odds offered by a typical state lottery. If 50 million Americans are actually risk seekers, and their risk seeking is described by the preceding calculation, then we can explain why they patronize casinos. That's where the risk is.

Risk seeking shows up in other contexts besides casinos. Take, for instance, opening a small business—like a family-style restaurant—in the United States. This is a risky proposition; roughly 80 percent of all such restaurants fail. Figure 2.6 portrays a typical situation. An investor has $10,000 of her own to sink into the small business—the rest of the money needed comes from a bank loan. Player 0, Chance, chooses from two possible outcomes. At the node

FIGURE 2.5 **A RISK-SEEKER SEEKS OUT RISK**

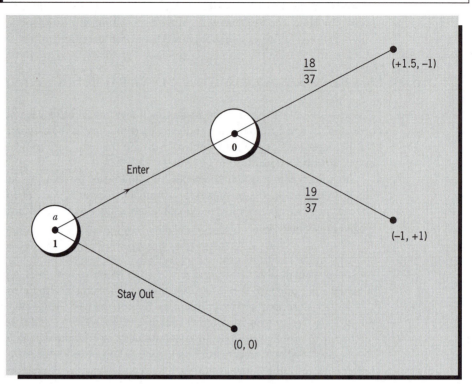

FIGURE 2.6 **SMALL BUSINESS, IMPERFECT INFORMATION**

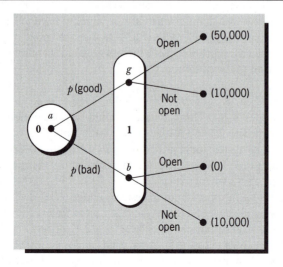

labeled g, the outcome is good for the investor, and the small business pays out $50,000 to the investor. At the node labeled b, the outcome is bad for the investor, and the small business pays back $0. The probability of reaching the bad outcome, the probability of failure of the small business, is 0.8. The probability of reaching the good outcome, small business success, is 0.2.

The investor, player 1, does not know which of these two possible outcomes will occur. The investor has two strategies, either Open the small business, in which case he or she is exposed to the risk of failure, or Not Open, in which case he or she hangs onto the $10,000 of starting value.

A risk-neutral player is indifferent between these two strategies, since

$$10{,}000 = \text{Payoff(Not Open)} = (0.8)(0) + (0.2)(50{,}000)$$
$$= \text{Expected Value(Open)}$$

To a risk-neutral player, an expected $10,000 is the same as a sure $10,000.

In any situation where a risk-neutral player is indifferent between a sure thing and a risky proposition, a risk-seeking player will definitely prefer the risky proposition. Here, a risk-seeking investor will prefer the strategy Open to the strategy Not Open.

Figure 2.7 illustrates this. The risk seeker in this situation transforms monetary pay-offs into points according to the utility function

$$u(x) = x^2/2$$

Notice that the risk seeker prefers Opening the small business to Not Opening it:

$$\text{Points from Not Open} = 5 \times 10^7 = u(50{,}000)$$
$$< \text{Expected Points from Open} = (0.8)u(0) + (0.2)u(50{,}000)$$
$$= (0.8)(0) + (0.2)(1.25 \times 10^9) = 2.5 \times 10^8$$

It's not even close: the risk seeker gets many more points by choosing the strategy that leads to risk, when the expected value of that risk is several orders of magnitude greater than the riskless alternative.

FIGURE 2.7 **SMALL BUSINESS, RISK-SEEKING PLAYER**

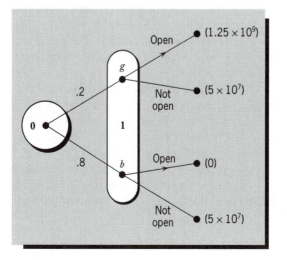

◼ 2.7 ANOTHER ATTITUDE TOWARD RISK: RISK AVERSION

Risk averters—people who like to avoid risk—are just the opposite of risk seekers, people who like to take risks. The attitude that risk averters have to risk, **risk aversion,** is the third possible attitude toward risk.

Let's see how risk averters respond to the fair coin toss depicted in Figure 2.1. That figure shows payoffs in dollars, but a risk averter, like a risk seeker, transforms those dollars into points before taking the expected value. In addition, for a risk averter, losing a dollar means more lost points than gaining a dollar means points gained. Suppose that for this risk averter, 0 dollars means 0 points, and winning one dollar means gaining one point. However, losing one dollar means losing more than one point. Suppose losing one dollar means losing two points. Summarizing, we have

$$u(+1) = +1, u(0) = 0, \text{ and } u(-1) = -2$$

For any risk averter, we would have

$$u(-1) < -1.$$

The toss of a fair coin does not appeal to a risk averter. In terms of expected points, it is a points loser:

$$\text{Expected utility(coin toss)} = (0.5)u(+1) + (0.5)u(-1)$$
$$= (0.5)(+1) + (0.5)(-2) = -0.5 < 0$$

The risk averter expects to lose one-half point by playing the fair game in Figure 2.1. By contrast, the risk averter experiences no change in points by sticking to the status quo.

Since risk averters do not play fair games, it follows that they do not play unfair games, either. It is bad enough to expect to lose points when the expected value of playing a game is zero; it is even worse to expect to lose points when the expected value of playing a game is negative. Someone who is averse to risk will avoid situations and places full of risk, like state lotteries, casinos, and opening small businesses.

Although risk averters do not patronize casinos, they do some other things that a risk seeker would never be caught dead doing. For instance, risk averters notably buy **insurance** to cover possible losses. Insurance reduces risk, and risk reduction appeals to risk averters. Risk averters are even willing to pay a premium, called a **risk premium,** above and beyond the expected value of loss for such insurance; those risk premiums are the basis for the profits earned by the insurance industry.

Risk-averse investors are willing to invest in those parts of the market where the odds are in their favor. Thus, they can be found in blue chip stocks, which over the past 100 years have outperformed all other financial investments. Still, stocks are risky. To deal with this risk, risk-averse investors **diversify** their portfolios, rather than putting all their eggs in one basket, as risk seekers routinely do. Given the 50 million Americans who seek out risk by playing state lotteries and gambling in casinos, that leaves 230 million Americans who do not so seek out risk. These are the risk-neutral and risk-averse segments of the population, who hold by far the majority attitude toward risk in the United States.

■ 2.8 INDIFFERENCE CURVES
FOR EXPECTED UTILITY THEORY

In this chapter, we have been studying how a player might reduce a situation involving chance down to a single number, either by computing the expected value of that situation, or more generally, by computing the **expected utility** of that situation. When a player does this, she or he is in essence ranking a special kind of object, probability distribution. A **probability distribution** is a set of possible outcomes, each associated with a corresponding probability. The probabilities are nonnegative, and add to 1. We can gain further insight into these rankings, as in any set of rankings, by studying the indifference curves they imply. Economists have gained some of their greatest insights from indifference curves analysis, ever since the world-famous economist V. Pareto invented indifference curves over a century ago. The diagrams that show indifference curves over probability distributions, called **Marshak-Machina diagrams** after their inventor (T. Marshak) and popularizer (M. Machina), provide an invaluable picture of what expected value and expected utility look like.

Suppose a risk-neutral player faces the following risky situation:

Win \$1 with probability p(+1).

Break even (win \$0) with probability p(0).

Lose \$1 with probability p(−1).

This risky situation includes the status quo as a possible outcome. The fair coin toss depicted in Figure 2.1 is a special case of the preceding risky situation, with the following specific values:

$$p(+1) = 0.5, p(0) = 0, \text{ and } p(-1) = 0.5$$

This risky situation is also a probability distribution: note that the probabilities add to 1 and are nonnegative.

Expected value, which a risk-neutral player uses to evaluate risky situations, allows a player to rank probability distributions, showing the probability distribution the player likes most, the probability distribution the player likes the least, and all the probability distributions in between.

Consider Figure 2.8, which does just that for a risk-neutral player. On the horizontal axis, we plot the probability of losing one dollar, $p(-1)$. On the vertical axis, we plot the probability of winning one dollar, $p(+1)$. Knowing these two probabilities uniquely determines the third value, since

$$p(0) = 1 - p(-1) - p(+1)$$

We already know how a risk-neutral player evaluates a fair coin toss: $p(+1) = p(-1) = 0.5$, $p(0) = 0$. He or she assigns an expected value of 0 to this probability distribution. This is the point labeled "A" in Figure 2.8, and it lies on the line marked $EU = 0$, for expected utility—here identical with expected value—equal to zero.

Let's now show that all the probability distributions that a risk-neutral player finds equal to the fair coin toss are lying on the straight line marked $EU = 0$ in the figure. In fact, this line is the 45-degree line joining the origin and the point marked A. If a probability

FIGURE 2.8 **INDIFFERENCE CURVES FOR RISK-NEUTRAL PLAYER**

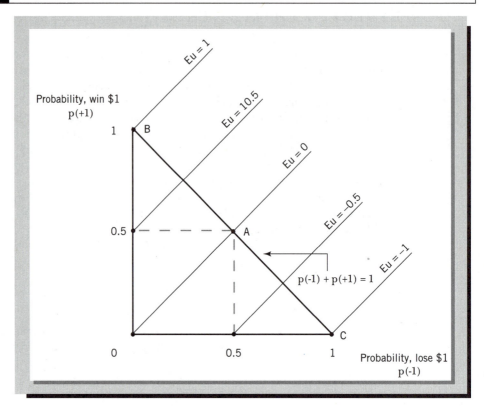

distribution over the outcomes of win one dollar, break even, or lose one dollar has an expected value of zero, that means

$$\text{Expected Value} = 0 = (+1)p(+1) + (0)p(0) + (-1)p(-1)$$

Simplifying, we have

$$0 = p(+1) - p(-1)$$

or

$$p(+1) = p(-1)$$

This is the 45-degree line through the origin, as promised. So the indifference curve for a risk-neutral player with expected value equal to zero is a straight line, connecting the origin, where

$$p(+1) = p(-1) = 0, \, p(0) = 1$$

with the probability distribution for a fair coin toss. That makes sense, since a risk-neutral player finds a sure dollar and an expected dollar worth the same.

Notice another thing about Figure 2.8: the three vertices of the triangle representing all possible probability distributions are the three sure things. The origin is the sure thing "break even," the intercept on the vertical axis is the sure-thing "win one dollar," and the intercept on the horizontal axis is the sure-thing "lose one dollar."

This identification allows us to find the most preferred and least preferred probability distributions for a risk-neutral player. First, the most preferred probability distribution is a sure one dollar: that has to beat an expected value of anything less than one dollar. The expected value attached to a sure one dollar is

$$\text{Expected Value} = (+1)p(+1) + (0)p(0) + (0)p(-1) = 1$$

or

$$p(+1) = 1$$

This probability distribution is labeled "B" in Figure 2.8—it is the only point on the highest indifference curve for a risk-neutral player. Similarly, you can check that the lowest ranking probability distribution for a risk-neutral player is a sure loss of one dollar. This is the probability distribution labeled "C" in Figure 2.8, and it has the expected utility (expected value) equal to −1.

We can now find the general equation for any indifference curve for this player, for expected value = u, where u is a number between −1 and +1. From the equation for expected value, we have

$$\text{Expected Value} = u = (+1)p(+1) + (0)p(0) + (-1)p(-1)$$

Solving this equation, we get

$$p(+1) = u + p(-1)$$

Notice that this equation checks for the points A (where $u = 0$), B (where $u = 1$), and C (where $u = -1$) that we have already determined. We plot two more indifference curves in the figure, those for $u = 0.5$ and $u = -0.5$.

From the equation, and from Figure 2.8, you can see that the indifference curves for a risk-neutral player are parallel straight lines. They all have slope = +1, which makes them parallel. They don't cross—that would be a contradiction—because each line has a different value of u. This is a very special pattern, actually. Indifference curves between a good outcome (winning one dollar) and a bad outcome (losing one dollar) should not cross and should have a positive slope, but that is all the structure that economic theory in general puts on them. Risk neutrality, in the guise of expected value, puts an enormous amount of extra structure on the indifference curves, making them not curves at all but straight lines, and parallel straight lines at that.

The two panels of Figure 2.9 show the indifference curves for a risk-seeking player (Figure 2.9, panel a) and a risk-averse player (Figure 2.9, panel b). They have the same pattern—parallel straight lines—but the slope differs from that of a risk-neutral player. Let's see why that is so.

1. Start with a risk seeker. From the equation for expected utility, we have

$$\text{Expected Utility} = u(+1)p(+1) + u(0)p(0) + u(-1)p(-1)$$

2. Take the risk seeker you studied earlier, with the point values

$$u(+1) = 1.5, u(0) = 0, u(-11) = -1$$

3. Substituting these values into the equation for expected utility, we get

$$\text{Expected Utility} = (1.5)p(+1) + (0)p(0) + (-1)p(-1)$$
$$= (1.5)p(+1) - p(-1)$$

FIGURE 2.9 | **INDIFFERENCE CURVES FOR RISK-SEEKING AND RISK-ABUSING PLAYERS**

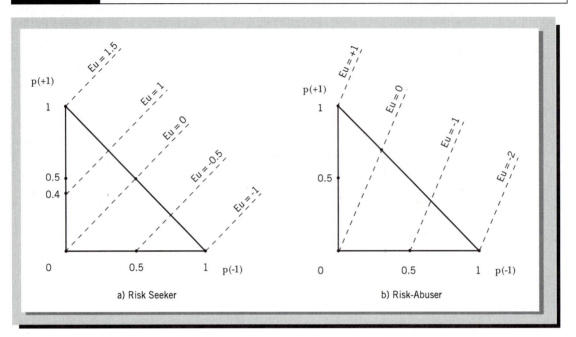

a) Risk Seeker

b) Risk-Abuser

4. Solving for $p(+1)$, we get

$$p(+1) = (\text{Expected Utility})/1.5 + p(-1)/1.5$$

where Expected Utility can be any number between +1.5, the highest-ranking probability distribution for a sure plus one dollar, and −1, the lowest ranking probability distribution for a sure minus one dollar. Figure 2.9a shows the indifference curves for this risk seeker, for the values of expected utility −1, −0.5, 0, +1, and +1.5. Notice in particular that the slope of each indifference curve is 1/1.5 or 2/3. The slope is less than one. This is how risk seeking manifests itself: compared to a risk-neutral agent, whose indifference curves have a slope equal to 1, a risk seeker's indifference curves have a slope less than 1.

Figure 2.9b show the indifference curves for a risk-averse player, in particular the player with the point values

$$u(+1) = 1, u(0) = 0, \text{ and } u(-1) = -2$$

You can see from the figure that the slope of an indifference curve for this player is greater than one. We can compute the exact value of the slope.

1. Start with the equation for expected utility:

$$\text{Expected Utility} = u(+1)p(+1) + u(0)p(0) + u(-1)p(-1)$$

2. Substitute the point values for this risk-averse player:

$$\text{Expected Utility} = (1)p(+1) + (0)p(0) + (-2)p(-1)$$
$$= (1)p(+1) - 2p(-1)$$

3. Solving for $p(+1)$, we get

$$p(+1) = \text{Expected Utility} + 2\,p(-1)$$

so the slope of an indifference curve is 2.

This is how risk aversion manifests itself: compared to a risk-neutral agent, whose indifference curves have a slope equal to 1, a risk averter's indifference curves have a slope greater than 1.

◼ 2.9 ALTERNATIVES TO EXPECTED UTILITY THEORY

In the last section, you saw what expected value and expected utility look like in a Marshak-Machina diagram. These hypotheses imply a very special shape of indifference curves, parallel straight lines. It should come as no surprise that people in experiments and in real life are not as consistent or as predictable as Figures 2.8 and 2.9 suggest. Indeed, the expected value and expected utility ways of comparing probability distributions remain controversial. People, when they are confronted with possible outcomes and probabilities, tend to behave in a fashion much less predictable than expected utility would predict. Here are three respects in which the evidence is against expected utility as a predictive theory:[3]

1. **Probability bias.** People systematically mistake the probabilities they face.
2. **Framing effects.** People behave differently depending on how the outcomes are posed.
3. **Nonlinearity.** Even people who avoid probability bias and framing effects incorporate probability into their judgments in nonlinear ways.

Many experiments have shown that, although people can handle the probability 0.5 without difficulty, they have trouble dealing with probabilities far away from 0.5. The average person tends to perceive (and act on those perceptions) as though probabilities near 0 are larger than they are, and as though probabilities near 1 are smaller than they are. This is probability bias.

Here is an extreme, almost pathological, case of probability bias. A person, confronted with any probability whatsoever, interprets that probability as the number 0.5. That is, faced with a probability distribution

Win one dollar with probability $p(+1)$.

Break even with probability $p(0)$.

Lose one dollar with probability $p(-1)$.

Whatever the values of $p(+1)$, $p(0)$, and $p(-1)$, this person processes the situation as though

$$p(+1) = p(0) = p(-1) = 0.5$$

Notice that such a person violates the Law of Probability—that the probabilities in a probability distribution add to 1. The implication is that every probability distribution in a Marshak-Machina diagram is ranked the same. So instead of parallel straight lines, this person subject to extreme probability bias has one giant indifference zone, covering the entire triangle—a very different pattern. Figure 2.10 portrays this situation, with a thick indifference curve covering the entire triangle of probability distributions in the Marshak-Machina diagram.

---

[3] See the survey by Colin Camerer, "Individual Decision Making," in *Handbook of Experimental Economics*, ed. John H. Kagel and Alvin E Roth (Princeton, N.J.: Princeton University Press, 1995).

FIGURE 2.10 | **PERSON SUFFERING FROM EXTREME PROBABILITY BIAS**

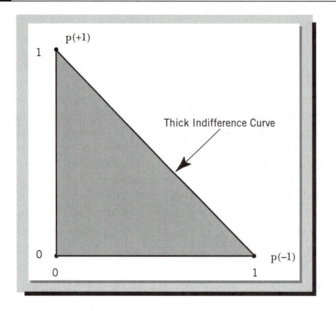

One place where probability bias is implicated is playing the state lottery. As you saw, a risk-neutral buyer can expect to lose part of every dollar bet when he or she plays the lottery. However, if a risk-neutral buyer acts on biased odds, then he or she could easily justify playing. Take an extreme case—the odds are 1 in 2 million that a ticket is a winner. The winning ticket takes home $1 million. Every ticket costs $1. Each ticket bought has an expected loss of $.50. However, a person who treats the probability (1/2000000) as though it were 0.5 thinks the lottery is a good deal—a 1-in-2 chance to win $1 million is worth a lot more than the $1 price of a ticket. Such a person will gladly buy a lottery ticket—and think he or she is getting a good deal!

Although the example just given seems extreme, it really isn't. Many people who play the state lottery, when asked why, will argue as follows. "I buy a lottery ticket because winning a million dollars will alter my lifestyle in a good way, but losing $1 will not affect my lifestyle." This expression essentially puts the same weight on winning $1 million as on paying the $1 price of the ticket.

A second problem that calls expected utility theory into question is framing effects—when a person's response to a question changes, depending upon how the question is asked. Experimental psychologists have uncovered these kinds of effects repeatedly in the laboratory. Consider the following comparison:

1. You start with $4. Would you rather keep the $4 or play the following lottery instead of keeping the $4?
   a. You win $1 with probability 0.6.
   b. You win $7 with probability 0.4.

2. You start with $10, which you don't get to keep. Would you rather lose $6 of it for sure or play the following lottery instead?
   a. You lose $3 with probability 0.4.
   b. You lose $9 with probability 0.6.

Take a close look at each member of the comparison—they are economically identical. To see this, note first that losing $6 for sure out of $10 is the same as keeping $4 for sure, so the sure things are economically identical. The risky situations are also identical, since in (2), we have the probability distribution over final outcomes

($10 − $3) = $7 with probability 0.4
($10 − $9) = $1 with probability 0.6

which is again identical to the probability distribution in (1).

Nevertheless, in a behavior experiment many people will keep the $4 in (1) but play the lottery in (2). According to expected utility theory, if a person keeps the $4 in (1), he or she should give up the $6 in (2). Behaving differently in (1) and (2) is due to a framing effect—(1) is framed in terms of gains, while (2) is framed in terms of losses—and many people behave differently depending on whether the frame is in terms of gains of losses. Expected utility theory cannot explain framing effects, although a rival theory, **prospect theory,** can.[4]

A third problem that calls expected utility into question is nonlinearity. Expected value and expected utility both assume that probabilities enter the calculation in a linear fashion. This shows up in the indifference curves being parallel straight lines. For many people, however, indifference curves are straight lines, but not parallel. This was first discovered in a famous experiment conducted in 1952 by the Nobel Prize–winning economist Maurice Allais, which discovery has been called **Allais' Paradox** ever since.[5] Allais was attending an international conference in Paris in 1952, where many of the world's top game theorists were assembled. He gave them a questionnaire consisting of two simple questions:

Question 1. Rank the following two probability distributions:

A: Win $500 million with probability 0.
Win $100 million with probability 1.
Win $0 with probability 0.

B: Win $500 million with probability .1.
Win $100 million with probability .89.
Win $0 with probability .01.

Question 2. Rank the following two probability distributions:

C: Win $500 million with probability 0.
Win $100 million with probability .11.
Win $0 with probability .89.

D: Win $500 million with probability .1.
Win $100 million with probability 0.
Win $0 with probability .9.

These four probability distributions are portrayed in Figure 2.11.

---

[4] See Daniel Kahneman and Amos Tversky, "Prospect Theory," *Econometrica* 47 (1979): 263–291. I also recommend Massimo Piattelli-Palmarini, *Inevitable Illusions: How Mistakes of Reason Rule Our Minds* (New York: Wiley, 1994), which delves into the psychology involved in Kahneman and Tversky's and other studies. Kahnemann won the Nobel Prize in economics in 2002 in large part for this work.

[5] If your French is good, you can find the original in M. Allais, "Le Comporetment de l'Homme Rationnel devant le Risque: Critique des Postulats et Axiomes de l'Ecole Amnericaine," *Econometrica* 21 (1953): 503–546.

FIGURE 2.11 **ALLAIS' PARADOX**

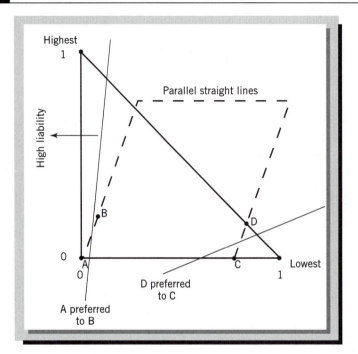

Most respondents in Allais' survey preferred A to B, citing the sure $100 million win, and D to C, citing the 10 percent chance of winning $500 million. However, this contradicts expected utility theory. Notice that A and B lie on a straight line, while C and D lie on another parallel straight line. So if a person prefers A to B and obeys expected utility theory, that person should prefer C to D.

Instead, the actual indifference curves for these respondents to Allais' survey are straight lines with different slopes, a pattern called **mixed fanning.**

All these departures from expected value and expected utility have lead researchers to look for better descriptive theories of how people behave when confronted with uncertainty. According to the latest evidence, four theories appear to be the main contenders for the title of best predictive theory.[6] These four theories are expected value, expected utility, prospect theory, and mixed fanning. People are complicated when it comes to probability and chance events, and no one theory will ever describe all the complexities of their behavior.

■ SUMMARY

1. In games involving chance, a player needs to be able to compare probability distributions to ordinary riskless alternatives.

2. We describe uncertainty by means of probability distributions. A probability distribution is a set of possible outcomes, with a probability attached to each outcome. We often depict decisions involving uncertainty in a tree diagram.

[6] See John Hey and Brian Orme, "Individual Choice under Uncertainty," *Econometrica* 63 (1995).

3. According to the expected value hypothesis, a player multiplies the monetary value attached to a possible outcome by the probability of that outcome, and then adds over all possible outcomes. The result is an expected value, which can then be compared to riskless alternatives.

4. A fair game has an expected value of zero to any player involved. Tossing a fair coin is an example of a fair game.

5. Games like the state lottery, or games like Roulette played in a casino, are unfair. The state and the casino have an advantage in expected value terms over gamblers who play these games.

6. A player who obeys expected value theory is risk neutral. For such a player, a sure dollar is the same as an expected dollar.

7. Expected utility theory extends expected value theory to account for different attitudes for risk, risk seeking, and risk aversion.

8. A risk seeker will gladly play a casino game for the risk involved, even though he or she expects to lose money. A risk averter will never enter a casino.

9. Indifference curves for expected value theory and expected utility are parallel straight lines, as shown by a Marshak-Machina diagram.

10. Expected utility theory is not consistent with probability bias, framing effects, or nonlinearity.

◨ KEY TERMS

risky situation	risk seeking	Marshak-Machina diagram
expected value	risk aversion	probability bias
fair coin toss	insurance	framing effects
risk neutral	risk premium	nonlinearities
fair game	diversify	prospect theory
Roulette	expected utility	Allais' Paradox
gaming and entertainment	probability distribution	mixed fanning

◨ PROBLEMS

1. Give three examples of games to which uncertainty attaches.

2. The state lottery sells 10 million tickets, one of which is a winner. The winning ticket pays the holder $5 million; all other lottery tickets are losers and pay $0. The price of each ticket is $1. Analyze the decision whether to buy a lottery ticket or not, using expected value theory. Assume risk neutrality.

3. In the state lottery in problem 2, explain why risk seekers might play the lottery. Also, assuming that all tickets are sold, compute the expected value to the state of running the lottery.

4. In American Roulette, there are two white slots on the roulette wheel instead of one. Compute the expected value to a gambler betting $1 on the color red, and to the casino, for American Roulette.

5. Recall the game in Figure 2.6, for opening a small business. Consider a risk-averse player with the utility function

$$u(x) = 2x^{0.5}$$

Compute the expected utility to this player of the strategy Open, and of the strategy Not Open. Which strategy does this risk-averse player prefer?

6. Recall the game in Figure 2.6, now with the following change in the rules. Instead of losing all of his money if he opens a business in the bad state, an investor is subsidized, and gets a payoff of $10,000—also in this state. Otherwise, payoffs are like those in Figure 2.6. Call

this game Subsidized Small Business. Show that for all three attitudes, the strategy chosen is Open. Then interpret your result in terms of the economic policy bias against subsidies.

7. Consider a risk seeker with utility function $u(x) = x^2$; a risk-neutral player with utility function $u(x) = x$; and a risk averter with utility function $u(x) = x^{0.5}$. Plot the utility function of each. Then show that the marginal utility of money for the risk (seeker/neutral/averter) is (increasing/constant/decreasing) as money increases.

8. Draw a Marshak-Machina diagram for a risk-neutral player playing the game Small Business in Figure 2.6. On the horizontal axis, put the probability of getting a payoff of $0. On the vertical axis, put the probability of getting a payoff of $50,000. Include indifference curves for the following expected values: $0, $5000, $10000, $20000, and $50000.

9. How do each of the following three concepts explain the fact that 50 million Americans patronize the gaming and entertainment industry each year: entertainment, risk seeking, and probability bias?

10. Prior to 1960, no state had a lottery and only Nevada allowed gambling. Describe the current situation with regard to gambling in the United States. What accounts for the change over the last four decades?

11. Describe three phenomena that cannot be explained by expected value and expected utility theory. Why do we use a theory when it cannot explain many observed phenomena?

12. The psychologist Richard Thaler and economist Matt Rabin have recently pointed out the following additional critique of risk aversion.[7] If a person is risk averse over moderate stakes, then that same person will be pathologically risk averse over large stakes. Here's an example you can work out for yourself. A risk averter has the utility function $u(x) = 1 - e^{-.01(x + 100)}$. Show first that this risk averter prefers the status quo $x = 0$ to the risky alternative

Lose $10 with probability 0.5.

Win $11 with probability 0.5.

That's risk aversion over moderate stakes. Then show that this same risk averter prefers the status quo to the risky alternative

Lose $100 with probability 0.5.

Win $1 trillion with probability 0.5.

That's pathological risk aversion.

■ APPENDIX. WINNING AT BLACKJACK

In the fall of 1961 a young mathematician, Edward O. Thorp, astounded the gambling world by enumerating a strategy to beat the dealer in the casino game Blackjack.[8] Previously, casinos had thought they had the advantage at every game they played, including Blackjack. Indeed, it is true that for every casino game except Blackjack, the casinos have a positive expected value. Thorp's shocking discovery was based on millions of computer simulations, backed up by extensive play in the casinos. To present the complete strategy, together with a summary of the argument behind it for the casino version of Blackjack, requires an entire book. The two

---

[7] The very readable article by these authors is R. Thaler and M. Rabin, "Anomalies: Risk Aversion'" *Journal of Economic Perspectives* 15 (2001): 219–232.

[8] This material is based on Edwin O. Thorp, *Beat the Dealer* (New York: Random House, 1961, 1966). For a recent update, see Ben Mezrich, *Bringing Down the House: The Inside Story of Six MIT Students Who Took Vegas for Millions* (New York: Free Press, 2002).

principles underlying it are fairly easy to understand, however. This appendix presents a simpler game, called Ten, which models Blackjack. Ten shares all the important strategic features of Blackjack, but can be solved without resorting to heavy-duty computing. Once you have mastered Ten, if you are still interested in beating the dealer at Blackjack, read Thorp's book.[9]

The rules of Ten are as follows:

1. **Players.** There are two players. Player 1 is you or me. Player 2 is the dealer, who represents the casino. From now on, we will call player 1 the player and player 2 the dealer.[10]

2. **The pack.** The pack consists of 11 cards, including four 10s and seven 5s. You can construct such a pack and play the game yourself.

3. **The deal.** Before play begins, the cards are shuffled by the dealer and cut by the player. Then two cards are removed by the dealer and shown to the player. These cards are said to have been burned. The dealer then deals one card face down to the player and one card face up to himself or herself.

4. **Betting.** The player bets before his or her card is dealt, but after the two cards have been burned. The minimum bet is $1; the maximum bet is $5. The minimum and maximum bet can be varied to suit the action.

5. **Value of the cards.** A 10 is worth 10 points; a 5, 5 points. If a player draws a second card, its value is added to that of the first to obtain the total value of the hand.

6. **Object of the player.** The player tries to obtain a total value that is greater than that of the dealer, but does not exceed 10—hence the name Ten.

7. **The draw.** The player looks at his or her card. If it is a 5, the player may elect either to draw a second card or to stand pat. If the player draws a second card and it is a 10, the total value of the hand is 15, which exceeds 10, and the player immediately loses to the dealer. This is called going bust. If the player draws a second card and it is a 5, the player has a total value of 10 and stands pat. Once the player has either drawn a card or stood pat, it is then the dealer's turn to draw. If the dealer has a 10, the dealer stands pat. If the dealer has a 5, he or she must draw. If the dealer draws a 10, the total is 15 and the dealer loses. If the dealer draws a 5, the total value is 10 and the dealer stands pat.

8. **The settlement.** If the player has not gone bust and the dealer has, then the player wins an amount equal to the bet. If neither the player nor the dealer has gone bust, the person with the higher total wins an amount equal to the bet of the player. If the player and the dealer both have the same total, not exceeding 10, no money changes hands.

This completes the set of rules for Ten. The biggest simplifications from Blackjack are the smaller deck (11 cards instead of 52) and the smaller number of different card values (2 different values instead of 11). It is not at all obvious from reading the rules of Ten that if the player bets $1 every hand, he or she can expect to lose on average 2 cents for every dollar bet. This is a losing experience consistent with that for average casino play. Now let's turn to the proof—not just for curiosity's sake, but because the proof will reveal a strategy for beating the dealer.

[9] Let the reader beware. Applying Thorp's system under casino conditions requires unflinching concentration and extraordinary devotion to detail for long periods of time. It is not meant for casual players.
[10] Actually, Ten can be played with a dealer and two other players, as shown in Chapter 5.

Let's begin our analysis with the burning of two cards, as shown in Figure 2.12. The original pack consists of four 10s and seven 5s, hereafter denoted (number of 10s, number of 5s) = (4,7). After burning two cards, there are three possible packs: (4,5), (3,6), and (2,7). The probabilities of each of these burns are given in the figure. The most likely burn is one card of each type, which happens a little more than 50 percent of the time (56/110), to be precise).

It is important to understand that the strategic situations represented by the different packs are different. The situation (4,5) is favorable to the player, whereas the situations (3,6) and (2,7) are favorable to the dealer. Note that the latter two situations are rich in 5s. In general (and this is true of casino Blackjack, too), the more 5s, the more likely a situation is to be unfavorable to the player.

Case 1. The pack is (4,5). The extensive form for this part of the game is shown in Figure 2.13. At this point, there are four possible deals: (player, dealer) = (10,10), (10,5), (5,10), or (5,5). The deal (10,10) is easy—an automatic tie, with payoffs (0,0). Now consider the deals (10,5) and (5,10). The dealer has to hit when the deal is (10,5), whereas the player wants to hit when the deal is (5,10). Since both face the same pack, at this point (3,4), they both face the same odds. So these two deals average out to a draw also. This situation is reflected by the payoff (0,0) reached with probability 52/72, the probability that at least one 10 has been dealt.

The only deal left to consider is (5,5). The player can either draw a card or stand pat. If the player draws a card, he or she gets a 10 with probability 4/7 and goes bust, payoff (−1,1). If the player draws a 5, a probability 3/7 event, then it is the dealer's turn. The dealer must draw a card. With probability 3/6, that card is a 10 and the dealer has gone bust—the player wins, payoff (1,−1). With probability 3/6, that card is a 5; and the dealer and the player tie at 10 apiece, payoff (0,0). The expected value to the player of drawing a card is the following:

1 with probability 3/14

0 with probability 3/14

−1 with probability 8/14, *EV* = −5/14

FIGURE 2.12 | **THE BURN IN TEN**

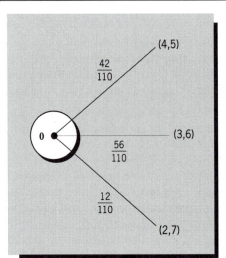

FIGURE 2.13   TEN AFTER THE PACK (4, 5)

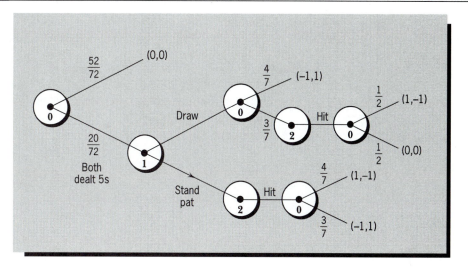

This is not promising. Now consider what happens if the player stands pat. The dealer must draw a card. With probability 4/7, that card is a 10 and the dealer has gone bust—the player wins, payoff (1,–1). With probability 3/7, that card is a 5 and the dealer wins, 10 to 5—payoff (–1,1). The expected value to the player of standing pat is

> 1 with probability 4/7
> –1 with probability 3/7, $EV = 1/7$

That's much better. The player stands on 5 when the dealer has a 5 and beats the dealer. The overall expected value to the player from the pack (4,5) is

> 0 with probability 52/72
> 1/7 with probability 20/72, $EV = 20/504$
> It's not big, but it's positive.

Case 2. The pack is (3,6). The game tree for this case is shown in Figure 2.14. As in case 1, play is even except when two 5s are dealt, a 30/72 probability event. In this case, if the player takes a card, he or she has the following expected value:

> 1 with probability 4/14
> 0 with probability 4/14
> –1 with probability, $EV = –1/7$

Not good. If the player stands pat and forces the dealer to take a card, the player's expected value is the following:

> 1 with probability 3/7
> –1 with probability 4/7, $EV = –1/7$

FIGURE 2.14 | **TEN AFTER THE PACK (3, 6)**

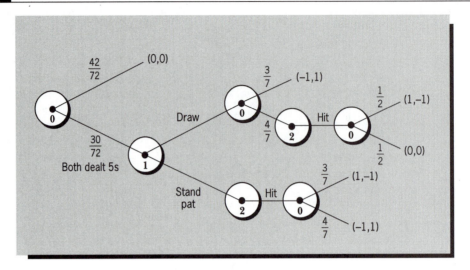

Not good either. This case is a loser for the player, with an overall expected value

0 with probability 42/72

−1/7 with probability 30/72, $EV = -30/504$

Case 3. The pack is (2,7). It is up to you to show that this case is also a loser for the player—you get a big hint in the form of Figure 2.15. You can show that the expected value to the player of play from a (2,7) pack is

0 with probability 30/72

−1/21 with probability 42/72, $EV = -14/504$

Again, not good.

We have exhausted the three cases and can now compute the expected value of betting the minimum, $1, each and every time, no matter what the pack is. We have

20/504 with probability 42/110 the pack (4,5)

−30/504 with probability 56/110 the pack (3,6)

−14/504 with probability 12/110 the pack (2,7)

so the expected value is

$$EV = -1008/55,440$$

The player can expect to lose about 2 cents of every dollar bet, as indicated.

You were promised a payoff for going to all this trouble, and here it is. We have just uncovered a valuable distinction for the player:

Principle of Ten 1. Some situations are favorable to the player, others are not. The player, as long as he or she can recognize the difference, can vary bets to exploit situations in his or her favor.

This leads to:

Principle of Ten 2. Bet the minimum in unfavorable situations; bet the maximum in favorable situations. These two principles imply the following strategy. Bet $5 when the burn leads to the situation (4,5); otherwise, bet the minimum, $1.

This strategy has the following expected value:

100/504 with probability 42/110 the pack (4,5) with $5 bet
–30/504 with probability 56/110 the pack (3,6) with $1 bet
–14/504 with probability 12/110 the pack (2,7) with $1 bet

$$EV = 2352/55,440$$

The player can expect to earn about 4 cents for every dollar bet using these two principles. These principles turn the player from a loser into a winner. *The player beats the dealer with this improved strategy.* And there is nothing the dealer can do about it—short of changing the rules or outright cheating.

Even though Blackjack is more complicated than Ten, the strategic principles just described for Ten apply to it with a vengeance. The biggest challenge in using a strategy like Thorp's is to identify the situations favorable to you under casino conditions. Naturally, the casinos take game theory seriously enough to have introduced various countermeasures to prevent the identification of favorable situations. These include increasing the number of decks (making it harder for the player to count), having the dealer count and reshuffle the deck whenever it is favorable to the player, and—as a last resort—banning players, like Thorp, who consistently win. [11]

FIGURE 2.15 TEN AFTER THE PACK (2, 7)

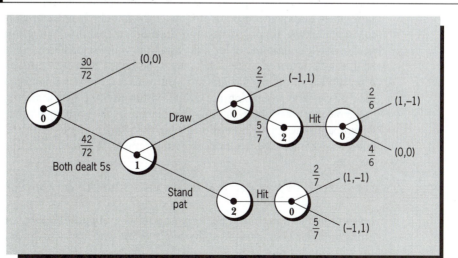

---

[11] Courts have upheld the constitutionality of this exclusion, which extends to Thorp himself (at least in Nevada).

CHAPTER 3

Nash Equilibrium for Two-Person Games

This chapter focuses on games with exactly two players, 2-person games. *Player* can be interpreted quite broadly. As indicated in Chapter 1, machines can be players. Chapter 9 shows that animals can be players, too. When game theory was invented, however, these possibilities were in the future, reason enough to stick with the traditional phrase 2-person games. Two-person games are the simplest, and therefore the most suitable for beginners. The more players in a game, the more complicated the game gets. The study of *n*-person games is deferred to Chapter 5.

Games where the players' interests are completely opposed are called *zero-sum* and *constant-sum* games. This chapter shows the relationship between these two types of games, and introduces a technique (the arrow diagram) to analyze them. The solution of a 2-person, zero-sum game is its Nash equilibrium outcome, so named after its discoverer, Nobel laureate John Nash. We shall have quite a lot to say about Nash equilibrium throughout this book. All Nash equilibria of a 2-person, zero-sum game have the same payoffs, as we shall show.

The chapter then presents the phenomenon of competitive advantage in market contexts, and shows why firms in competition with one another are driven by strategic forces to adopt new technologies. The same phenomenon arises, albeit in a different guise, in Poker. Games where the players' interests are not completely opposed are called *variable-sum* games. Such games arise in economics the minute there are gains from trade or from coalition building. Variable-sum games are more complicated than zero-sum games. In particular, they can have multiple Nash equilibria, with very different payoffs. Some of these Nash equilibria can be quite inefficient, as the game called the Prisoner's Dilemma shows. A practical application of the prisoner's dilemma is the tobacco industry, especially the banning of cigarette advertising on U.S. television in 1971. When advertising was banned, tobacco company profits went up—as explained by the Nash equilibrium of the Prisoner's Dilemma. In the appendix to this chapter, following in the footsteps of Nash himself, we prove an existence theorem for Nash equilibrium for 2-person, variable-sum games.

■ 3.1 ZERO-SUM GAMES AND CONSTANT-SUM GAMES

Let's start with a 2-person game. Suppose that for every possible outcome of the game, the utility of player 1, u_1, plus the utility of player 2, u_2, adds to zero. In an equation,

$$u_1 + u_2 = 0$$

One example is provided by a game like Chess, with win, lose, or draw outcomes. If the utility of a win to a player is +1, the utility of a draw is 0, and the utility of a loss is −1, the game is a **zero-sum game.** There are three possible outcomes:

Player 1 wins: payoff vector (+1,−1), sum = +1 + (−1) = 0

The players draw: payoff vector (0,0), sum = 0 + 0 = 0

Player 2 wins: payoff vector (−1,+1), sum = −1 + (+1) = 0

In every case, the sum of utilities is zero. This is the zero-sum condition. Poker is another example of a zero-sum game as long as the players are risk neutral and utility equals dollars. Both players put the same amount of money in the pot (the center of the table where all bets are placed). The winner takes all the money in the pot—the winner's gain is the loser's loss.

The former dean of the Sloan School at MIT, Lester Thurow, wrote an influential book, *The Zero-Sum Society,* describing in bleak terms how our economy would look if the entire economy were structured on the principle of "What I win equals what you lose." No value can be created in a zero-sum game: the players are forever at each other's throats. In such a society, economic change is nearly impossible; and when it is possible, it comes only at a very high cost.[1]

Zero-sum games are a special instance of constant-sum games. In a **constant-sum game,** whatever the outcome, the player's utilities add up to a constant k. If $k−$ happens to equal 0, then you have a zero-sum game. It often happens in business that $k = 1$. When firms are competing on the basis of market shares, then the market shares add up to 100 percent. Consider the game **Battle of the Networks,** the normal form of which is shown in Figure 3.1. Two television networks, which we will call 1 and 2, are battling for shares of total viewers. Viewer shares are important because the higher the viewer share, the more money the network can make from selling advertising time on that program. Each network can show either a sitcom or a sports event, and the networks make their programming decisions independently and

---

FIGURE 3.1 **BATTLE OF THE NETWORKS, NORMAL FORM**

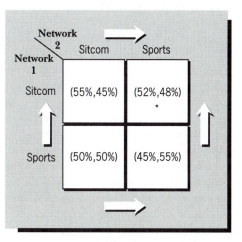

---

[1] For the complete argument, read Lester C. Thurow, *The Zero-Sum Society: Distribution and the Possibilities for Economic Change* (New York: Basic Books, 1980).

simultaneously. Game time and chronological time need not be the same, so playing simultaneously need not mean playing at the same chronological time. Network 1 might make its decision at 9:00 a.m. on a particular day, and network 2 might make its decision at 2:00 p.m. that same day. So long as network 2 makes its decision while it is unaware of what network 1 chose, then the game is characterized as simultaneous. Network 1 has a programming advantage in sitcoms. If both networks show sitcoms, then network 1 gets a 55 percent viewer share. Network 2 has a programming advantage in sports; if both networks show sports, then network 2 gets a 55 percent viewer share.

Nash equilibrium tells us how the two networks will play Battle of the Networks. In particular, a Nash equilibrium comprises actions that are best responses to each other. Network 1 has chosen its best strategy, given what network 2 has chosen. Similarly, network 2 has chosen its best strategy, given what network 1 has chosen. At a Nash equilibrium, each player has maximized his or her utility—a hallmark of rationality throughout economics.

One way to find a Nash equilibrium is by attaching arrows to the normal form of this game in Figure 3.1. The arrow on the left pointing up shows that network 1 prefers showing a sitcom and getting a viewer share of 55 percent to showing sports and getting a viewer share of 50 percent when network 2 is showing a sitcom. Similarly, the arrow at the bottom pointing to the right indicates that network 2 prefers showing sports and getting a viewer share of 55 percent to showing a sitcom and getting a viewer share of 50 percent when network 1 is showing a sitcom. There is a single situation in which arrows point in from both directions: network 1 is showing a sitcom and network 2 is showing sports, with network 1 getting 52 percent of the viewers. This situation is denoted by an asterisk (*).

A situation toward which arrows point from both directions is called a Nash equilibrium. At the Nash equilibrium of Battle of the Networks, neither network has an incentive to *unilaterally* adopt a different strategy from its Nash equilibrium strategy. If network 1 were to switch from its sitcom to a sports show, its viewer share would drop 7 percent, from 52 percent to 45 percent—not good for network 1. If network 2 were to switch from its sports show to a sitcom, its viewer share would drop 3 percent, from 48 percent to 45 percent—not good for network 2. Each network is getting the best ratings it can, given the competition it is up against. This is the sense of Nash equilibrium: each player is doing the best possible given the competition. The Nash equilibrium of Battle of the Networks is the pair of strategies (network 1 shows a sitcom; network 2 shows sports) that we expect to observe if this game is played for real.

We can say even more about this Nash equilibrium. For network 1, the strategy sitcom strictly dominates the strategy sports; for network 2, the strategy sports strictly dominate the strategy sitcom. So Battle of the Networks is strictly dominance solvable, and its strict dominance solution is the pair of strategies (network 1 shows a sitcom; network 2 shows sports)—also its Nash equilibrium. This is no accident: when a game is strictly dominance solvable, it has a unique Nash equilibrium that coincides with its strict dominance solution.

Just as economics is based on the study of market equilibrium, so game theory is predicated on the study of Nash equilibrium. Indeed, later (Chapter 6) you will learn that market equilibrium and Nash equilibrium are especially linked. For now, be sure you understand how the arrow diagram works. Such diagrams are used throughout the book to find Nash equilibria, so master this now before going any further.

There is an easy way to relate constant-sum and zero-sum 2-person games. Let u_1 and u_2 be the payoffs in a k-sum game. Now consider a new set of payoffs of the form

$$v_1 = u_1 - u_2$$
$$v_2 = u_2 - u_1$$

Clearly, $v_1 + v_2 = 0$, so we now have a zero-sum game. Substituting in the constant-sum condition

$$u_1 + u_2 = k$$

We have

$$v_1 = 2u_1 - k$$
$$v_2 = 2u_2 - k$$

These are positive, linear transformations of utility, and so they have no effect on decisions. What these transformations do is measure utility in terms of viewer share advantage. If v_1 is positive, network 1 has a larger viewer share than network 2, and v_1 measures how large network 1's advantage is.

Figure 3.2 shows Battle of the Networks as a zero-sum game. To see how the payoffs from Figure 3.2 follow from Figure 3.1, take the case where both networks show a sitcom. Network 1 gets a 55 percent viewer share in this case. Using the previous transformation with $k = 1$, we get

$$v_1 = 2(0.55) - 1 = 0.1$$

or 10 percent. This is the entry for network 1's utility in the cell (sitcom, sitcom). Network 1 has a 10 percent advantage in viewer share in this case. Similarly, for network 2,

$$v_2 = 2(0.45) - 1 = -0.1$$

or −10 percent. This is the entry for network 2's utility in the cell (sitcom, sitcom). Notice that these two entries do indeed add up to zero. You can work out all the other payoffs in Figure 3.2 in this way.

Notice that the arrow diagram of Figure 3.2 is exactly the same as the arrow diagram of Figure 3.1. This is no coincidence, but reflects the fact that strategic reasoning remains the same for any positive linear transformation of players' utilities. Whether these networks reason in terms of total viewer share, in which case the game is one sum, or in terms of viewer advantage, in which case the game is zero sum, the Nash equilibrium is the same. Network

---

FIGURE 3.2   BATTLE OF THE NETWORKS, ZERO-SUM VERSION

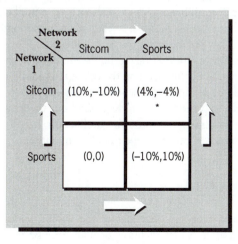

1 shows a sitcom; network 2, sports. The dollar reality behind these utilities is the same in either case. No matter how you look at them, higher ratings mean more advertising dollars.

3.2 WHY LOOK FOR NASH EQUILIBRIUM?

We have already seen what a Nash equilibrium looks like, in Figures 3.1 and 3.2—it has arrows pointing toward it from both directions. Those arrows point in the direction of maximum payoff for each player. Once players get to a Nash equilibrium—as the word *equilibrium* implies—each has an incentive to stay there.

Put another way, if players choose strategies that are not in Nash equilibrium, then at least one player will have an incentive to change his or her strategy. Consider the pair of strategies (sports, sports) in Figure 3.1. At this pair of strategies, player 1 is getting a market share of only 45 percent. Player 1 can get a higher market share by changing her strategy to sitcom. So we do not expect to see strategies played that are not a Nash equilibrium.

Notice also that the games in Figure 3.1 and 3.2 are strictly dominance solvable. For player 1, the strategy sitcom strictly dominates the strategy sports. For player 2, the strategy sports strictly dominate the strategy sitcom. So by playing strictly dominant strategies, and achieving the strict dominance solution, the players simultaneously achieve the Nash equilibrium. This is no accident: if a game is strictly dominance solvable, then it has a unique Nash equilibrium, and the strict dominance solution is its Nash equilibrium. Later in this chapter, we will show that if a game is weakly dominance solvable, its weak dominance solution is again a Nash equilibrium. So Nash equilibrium captures all the content of dominance solvability, if the latter is present.

But Nash equilibrium goes further, since it applies to the vast majority of games that aren't strictly or weakly dominance solvable.

Nash equilibrium also captures the logic behind the result for games like Chess. Consider the following normal form of the game like Chess shown in Figure 3.3. As you can see from panel a, this game like Chess ends in a draw. Player 2 chooses Left, seeking a win; player 1 chooses Right, to get a draw. In panel b, you see that the pair of strategies (right, left) is a Nash equilibrium, again leading to a draw. Also, this game is weakly dominance solvable. For player 1, the strategy Right strictly (and therefore weakly) dominates: for player 2, the strategy Left weakly dominates. The weak dominance solution, the pair of strategies (right, left), is a Nash equilibrium. There is also a Nash equilibrium, (right, right), leading to a draw, which is not consistent with backward induction and is not the weak dominance solution. We will have more to say about it in Chapter 7.

Basically, Nash equilibrium captures everything essential we have said so far about games. As economists, we ground our theories on the concept of equilibrium. If something is not an equilibrium, it will not persist, and it won't last long enough to matter to our economic calculations. Similarly, as game theorists, we ground our theories on the concept of Nash equilibrium. If a pair of strategies is not an equilibrium, it will not persist, and it won't last long enough to matter to our strategic calculations, either.

3.3 COMPETITIVE ADVANTAGE

In a technologically advanced economy like that of the United States, firms constantly encounter the following situation. A new technological advance becomes available. If one

FIGURE 3.3 | NASH EQUILIBRIUM OF A GAME LIKE CHESS

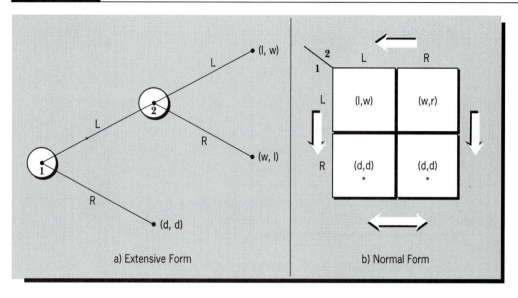

a) Extensive Form

b) Normal Form

firm adopts the new technology, it gains an advantage over its competitors, a **competitive advantage.** If all firms adopt the new technology, then the advantage vanishes. The game these firms are in is called Competitive Advantage. To take just one of many possible examples, consider the hospital industry. Magnetic resonance imaging (MRI) is a new technology that enhances conventional X-rays with the assistance of computers. It allows doctors to see body damage in ways that were not previously possible. Once MRI became available, any hospital that installed an MRI unit gained a competitive advantage over other hospitals in its area. It got more referrals and could offer a wider range of services.

Figure 3.4 shows Competitive Advantage in normal form. The payoff parameter *a* measures the size of the competitive advantage conferred by the new technology. Each firm has two strategies, either Stay put or Adopt the new technology. Firm 1 has an incentive to adopt the new technology. In the event that firm 2 stays put, then firm 1 gets the competitive advantage *a*—by adopting the new technology. This situation is represented by the arrow on the right, pointing up. In the event that firm 2 adopts the new technology, then firm 1 erases its competitive disadvantage *a* by adopting the new technology. This situation is represented by the arrow on the left, pointing up. The arrows on the top and bottom pointing to the left reflect similar incentives for firm 2. Indeed, you can see that the strategy New Technology strictly dominates the strategy Stay put for each firm.

The Nash equilibrium of Competitive Advantage, where arrows point in from both directions, occurs when each firm adopts the new technology. At the Nash equilibrium, which is also the strict dominance solution, the competitive advantage vanishes. No firm has a competitive advantage over the other, but no firm can afford to stay put, either. The firms in this game are driven to adopt any technology that comes along. The force behind this drive is the solution to Competitive Advantage. To return to the MRI example, it may not make much sense from a public policy standpoint for every hospital to have its own MRI unit. These units are expensive to buy and to operate—they can eat up millions of dollars. Also, one MRI unit can sometimes handle the traffic of several hospitals. At the

FIGURE 3.4 COMPETITIVE ADVANTAGE

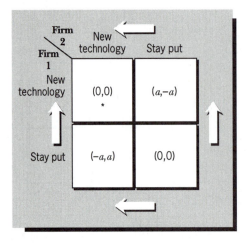

same time, an individual hospital would be at a competitive disadvantage if it didn't have its own MRI. As long as hospitals play Competitive Advantage, they are going to adopt every new technology that comes along.

In the Battle of the Networks and Competitive Advantage, strategy is all-important and luck plays no role. Let's now turn to a zero-sum game, Poker, where strategy is important and so is luck. Poker is all about being lucky *and* playing your cards right. We will study a simple version of Poker—so simple, in fact, that it has the same normal form that Competitive Advantage has.

3.4 ONE-CARD STUD POKER

This section looks at a version of Poker that, although very simple, exhibits many of the principles of good Poker play. Poker is a complicated game, the more so, the more cards a player holds. We will keep things simple by studying a version of Poker in which each player is dealt exactly one card, hence the name **1-card Stud Poker**.[2] We will also keep things simple by having only two players, although this game can easily be played by more than two players, as shown in Chapter 5.

Call the two players 1 and 2. The deck of cards consists of 50 percent aces and 50 percent kings. (You can create such a deck and play this game yourself). Prior to the deal, each player puts an amount of money a, called the *ante*, into the center of the table, called the *pot*. Each player is dealt one card face down, which neither the player nor the opponent sees.[3] At this point, a player can either bet an amount b (also placed in the pot) or pass. The players make this decision simultaneously.[4] Once the betting round has concluded, the

---

[2] In Draw Poker, as opposed to Stud Poker, players can discard some cards and replace them with new ones, a move called drawing cards. In Stud Poker, players have to play with the cards dealt them.

[3] This is another simplification, since in real-life Poker players have the option of seeing their own cards, but not those of their opponents. This assumption is relaxed in Chapter 4.

[4] In most Poker games, the players bet in sequence rather than simultaneously, which introduces an element of signaling into the game. Signaling is studied in Chapter 10.

game is over. If one player bet and the other passed, the player who bet takes the pot. If both players bet or both players passed, both turn over their card (the showdown). The player with the highest card wins the pot, with an ace beating a king. If both players in a showdown have equal cards, they split the pot.

Figure 3.5 shows 1-card Stud Poker in extensive form. One-card Stud Poker combines elements of sequential and simultaneous games. The sequential element is that Chance moves first, in the deal of the cards. The game begins with a chance move, the deal. A deal consists of a pair (card to player 1, card to player 2). For instance, the deal where player 1 gets an ace and player 2 gets a king is represented (A,K). There are four possible deals, each with probability 1/4. The simultaneous element is that players 1 and 2 each choose their strategies unaware of the other's choice. As shown in Figure 3.5, Player 1 is the next to move. Player 1 does not know which deal has occurred, and so her information set contains four nodes corresponding to the four possible deals. Player 1 either bets or passes. As shown in Figure 3.5,

FIGURE 3.5 ONE-CARD STUD POKER, EXTENSIVE FORM

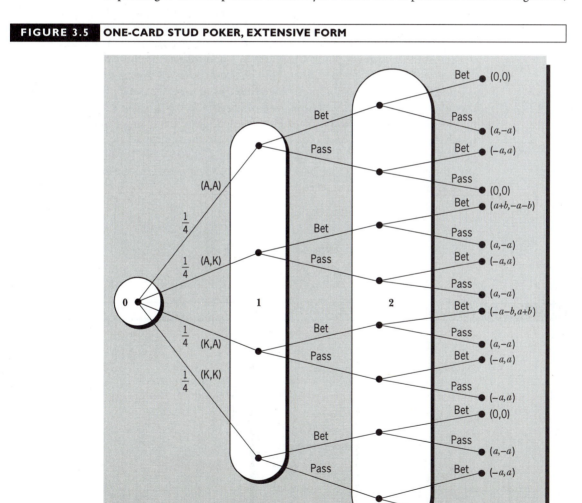

Player 2 is the last to move. Player 2 does not know which deal has occurred or what player 1 has done, and so his information set contains eight nodes, corresponding to the four possible deals times the two possible moves by player 1. Player 2 bets or passes. At this point the game ends. In Figure 3.5, we could also have shown player 2 as moving before player 1 and nothing in the analysis would change—this highlights the meaning of simultaneous moves.

There are 16 endpoints to 1-card Stud Poker in extensive form. These are shown in Figure 3.5, and we will walk through some of them. Suppose the deal is (A,A) and both players bet. The pot contains $2(a + b)$ dollars. At the showdown, the hands are equal, so the players split the pot. Each player breaks even—the outcome (0,0). The same outcome occurs when the deal is (K,K) and both players bet, when the deal is (A,A) and both players pass, and when the deal is (K,K) and both players pass. Next, suppose that player 1 bets and player 2 passes. Then, regardless of the cards, player 1 wins player 2's ante—the outcome $(a, -a)$. Player 2 may have the better card, or a card of equal value, but by folding he hands the ante over to player 1. There are 5 endpoints with the outcome $(a, -a)$. By reversing the strategies, with player 1 passing and player 2 betting, we get 5 endpoints of the form $(-a, a)$. Finally, suppose the deal is (A,K) and both players bet. The pot contains $2(a + b)$ dollars. At the showdown, player 1 beats player 2 and collects the entire pot. Player 1's gain, $a + b$, is what player 2 anted and bet. This is the outcome $(a + b, -a - b)$.

As is usually the case, it is pretty hard to see from the extensive form what each player should do. Fortunately, the extensive form of Figure 3.5 boils down to a much simpler normal form—Figure 3.6. Note first of all that each player has a single information set, at which there are two possible moves, bet or pass. Thus the strategy set for each player is (bet, pass). These are the rows and columns of Figure 3.6. Now we need to fill in the cells. Start with the pair of strategies (bet, bet). This pair of strategies leads to the following probability distribution over endpoints of the game:

(0,0) with probability 1/4; deal (A,A)

$(a + b, -a - b)$ with probability 1/4; deal (A,K)

$(-a - b, a + b)$ with probability 1/4; deal (K,A)

(0,0) with probability 1/4; deal (K,K)

FIGURE 3.6   ONE-CARD STUD POKER, NORMAL FORM

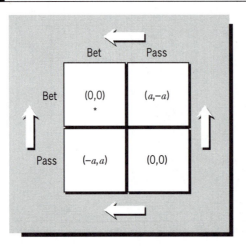

Taking expected values, we get for player 1

$$EV_1 = .25(0) + .25(a + b) + .25(-a - b) + .25(0) = 0$$

and similarly for player 2. This is the payoff vector (0,0) in the cell for (bet, bet) in Figure 3.6. Carrying out the same calculation for the strategies (pass, pass) yields the payoff vector for that cell. Finally, for the strategy vector (bet, pass), player 1 wins and player 2 loses regardless of the cards, the payoff vector $(a, -a)$.

Following the arrows, the Nash equilibrium of 1-card Stud Poker is for each player to bet. At this Nash equilibrium, both players break even.[5] A player who does not bet is beaten by a player who does bet. This result, players breaking even, reflects the fact that the deal is *fair*: each player has the same chance of getting a good hand. If the deal were unfair, then the solution to Poker would favor the player getting good cards more of the time (see end-of-chapter problem 6). Unfair deals are generated by cheating. With a fair deal, when both players adopt the same strategy, the cards even out and the payoff vector (0,0) results. Even though (pass, pass) is not a solution, if both players use this strategy, then they both break even. If you persistently lose at Poker and the deal is fair, you have only yourself to blame. You are not playing the best available strategy. If you were, you would at least break even. A loser fails to follow the strategic principles that could improve play. A loser who doesn't learn from his or her losses remains just that—a loser.

Now compare Figures 3.4 and 3.6. Except for the names of the games and the names of the strategies, they are exactly the same. 1-card Stud Poker and Competitive Advantage have the same strategic content. Just as adopting a new technology gives a business a competitive advantage, betting in Poker gives a Poker player a playing advantage over a player who passes. Nothing ventured, nothing gained—and in the case of Poker, nothing bet, the ante lost. At first it may seem rather remarkable that MRIs and Poker could have anything in common. However, this happens all the time in game theory, so you might as well get used to it. The same game can show up all over the economy, and even in the games we play at home.

We can say something even stronger about Competitive Advantage and 1-card Stud Poker, namely, that they are strictly dominance solvable. There is only one good way to play these games. As we have already pointed out, a strict dominance solution is a Nash equilibrium, and uniquely so. It is a serious and costly mistake in a game to play a strategy that is strictly dominated. No such strategy can be played as part of an equilibrium. An arrow would point away from such a strategy toward the strictly dominant strategy instead. In Competitive Advantage and 1-card Stud Poker, the parameter a measures just how costly a mistake it is to play the strictly dominated strategy.

■ 3.5 Nash Equilibria of Two-Person, Zero-Sum Games

Two-person, zero-sum games were the first to be solved, even before the concept of Nash equilibrium was discovered.[6] All such games we have encountered so far have either had a unique Nash equilibrium, or even if they had more than one Nash equilibrium, the multiple Nash

---

[5] This holds true for more general forms of Poker.

[6] This feat was accomplished by the father of game theory, John von Neumann, in an article in German entitled Zur Theorie der Gesellschaftsspiele (Toward a theory of social games), *Mathematische Annalen* 100 (1928): 295–320. This article is available in both English and German in von Neumann's *Collected Papers*.

equilibria led to the same outcome. This is no coincidence, as we are about to show. Even when a 2-person, zero-sum game has many Nash equilibria, they all must have the same payoffs.

Consider the game in Figure 3.7. Both players can move either left or right simultaneously. If player 2 moves left, he automatically loses regardless of what player 1 does; therefore, player 2 moves right. If player 1 moves left, the result is a draw; if player 1 moves right, likewise a draw. These two Nash equilibria (left, right) and (right, right) lead to the same payoffs—zero utility for each player.

Figure 3.8 gives an even more complicated example, a 2-person, zero-sum game with four Nash equilibria. Both players can move left, center, or right simultaneously. The only way player 2 can lose is by getting caught in the center when player 1 isn't in the center. The only way player 1 can lose is by getting caught in the center when player 2 isn't in the center. All other strategy combinations lead to a draw. Note the four equilibria: (left, left), (left, right), (right, left), and (right, right). All have the same payoffs, corresponding to a draw.

Here is a cultural interpretation of what the game in Figure 3.8 might represent—namely, a more complex version of competitive advantage. Suppose that the strategy Center represents a culture that does not have writing. Players 1 and 2 are cultures, and if they are at (center, center), neither has invented writing. Strategy Left represents writing from left to right, like we do in English. Strategy Right represents writing from right to left, as is done in Hebrew. If one culture has invented writing while another has not, this gives it a competitive advantage of 1. Thus, at the pair of strategies (center, left) culture 1 does not have writing, whereas culture 2 is writing left to right. At the four Nash equilibria of this game, both cultures have adopted the competitive advantage of writing. However, the question—whether a culture writes left to right or right to left—is left open by Nash equilibrium. Nash equilibrium says only that a culture will develop writing to stay even with rival cultures; Nash equilibrium does not specify which system of writing will be chosen. In practice, what players often do is settle on a **focal point,** one Nash equilibrium out of many that has some sort of special appeal to them. Returning to the cultural interpretation, many countries that succeeded the Roman Empire and no longer spoke Latin nevertheless used the Latin alphabet as their means of writing. You will see various kinds of focal points showing up throughout game theory.

FIGURE 3.7 **TWO-PERSON, ZERO-SUM GAME WITH TWO SOLUTIONS**

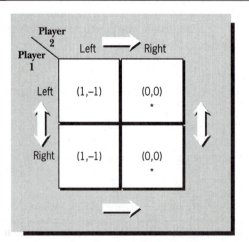

FIGURE 3.8   **TWO-PERSON, ZERO-SUM GAME WITH FOUR SOLUTIONS**

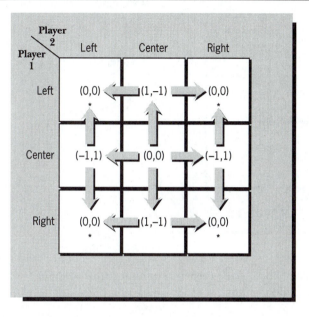

In games with more than two strategies per player, like the one in Figure 3.8, using the arrow diagram to see Nash equilibrium becomes rather cumbersome. In large-matrix games, you can also resort to brute force to find a Nash equilibrium (if one exists). Start with the payoff entry corresponding to the first row and first column. Check down the column to see if the payoff to player 1 is a maximum; check across the row to see if the payoff to player 2 is a maximum. If both checks pass, then you have found a Nash equilibrium. If at least one check does not pass, then you have not found a Nash equilibrium. Now repeat the process for every entry in the matrix. It's not too hard to write out the brute-force method as a computer algorithm; and there are software programs, such as Gambit, to do just that for you.

In both examples of multiple Nash equilibria, we see that payoffs to each player are the same at every equilibrium. This is no coincidence; rather, it is a mathematical necessity that every Nash equilibrium of a 2-person, zero-sum game have the same payoffs. We shall now prove that this must be the case.

Von Neumann's Theorem for 2-Person, Zero-Sum Games.   Every Nash equilibrium of a 2-person, zero-sum game has the same payoffs.

We will prove **von Neumann's theorem** for the case of 2 x 2 games, although it holds true for general m x n games as well. Consider the game in Figure 3.9. The proof is by contradiction. By hypothesis, the payoff vectors (a,a) and $(b, -b)$ are Nash equilibria, and a is not equal to b. These two different Nash equilibria cannot lie on the same row or column, which would be an immediate contradiction. We lose no generality by locating these two

---

FIGURE 3.9 **PROOF OF VON NEUMANN'S THEOREM**

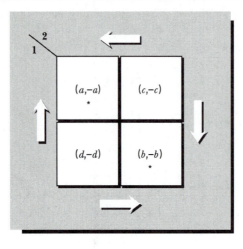

different Nash equilibria at the corners. From the arrow diagram, we have the following system of inequalities:

$$a > d$$
$$b > c$$
$$-a > -c$$
$$-b > -d$$

Solving this set of inequalities, we get

$$a > d > b > c > a$$

a contradiction. If we make any or all of the arrows two-headed, and thus replace an inequality with an equality, you still get a contradiction. Thus the two equilibria must have the same payoffs. This completes the proof.

Since all Nash equilibria of a 2-person, zero-sum game have the same payoffs, we can identify the solution payoffs with any of them. As you will soon see, this is not true for general variable-sum games. Once a game has variable-sum payoffs, it may have Nash equilibria with very different payoff values. In such a case, identifying any particular Nash equilibrium payoffs as the solution of a game is a challenge.

■ 3.6 A BEAUTIFUL MIND: THE STORY BEHIND NASH EQUILIBRIUM

Perhaps you have seen the Oscar-winning Hollywood movie *A Beautiful Mind*, starring Russell Crowe as the mathematician John Nash. Or you may have read Sylvia Nasar's book, *A Beautiful Mind: A Biography of John Forbes Nash, Jr., Winner of the Nobel Prize in Economics, 1994,* on which the movie is based. If you are familiar with either of these works, then you know there is a human-interest story behind the technical term "Nash equilibrium." Here is the short version of that story.

In 1928 the father of game theory, John von Neumann, writing in German, proved that all Nash equilibria of a 2-person zero-sum game have the same payoffs. He further proved that such games in normal form, whose matrix has a finite number of rows and columns, have at least one Nash equilibrium. Von Neumann called the payoffs at the Nash equilibrium of a game its "value," and used a complicated mathematical description, "minimax," to describe the strategies leading to the value. Von Neumann didn't use the language of Nash equilibrium, because it didn't yet exist. That language had to await the arrival of John Forbes Nash Jr. on Princeton's campus in 1947.

Von Neumann had already been at Princeton since 1938, at its world-renowned Institute for Advanced Studies, although he spent much of World War II and beyond working on weapons of mass destruction. Nash came to Princeton as a teenage Ph.D. candidate in mathematics. He became familiar with von Neumann's paper of 1928, and with his book on game theory, and began working on generalizing these results to games with two or more players, and not necessarily zero sum. The result was a paper, published in 1950, that made Nash world-famous himself, and gave rise to the term *Nash equilibrium,* a term Nash himself didn't use. In fact, the first-year graduate student was awarded his Ph.D. on the basis of this paper, even before it was published.

The amazing thing about all this was, von Neumann was arguably the greatest mathematician in the world, and here was a twenty-something student who had just proved theorems that von Neumann never dreamed of. Nash went on to prove other important results in game theory (we look at one of these, bargaining theory, in Chapter 13), but then abruptly stopped publishing on the subject in 1953. Later, Nash suffered an illness of many years' duration, during which he published nothing. Still, his achievement in game theory was so outstanding that he was awarded the Nobel Prize in economics in 1994, along with fellow game theorists Reinhard Selten of the University of Bonn, Germany, and John Harsanyi of Berkeley.

Without the concept of Nash equilibrium, game theory as we know it today would not exist. Progress in the subject, in particular getting beyond the point reached by von Neumann, required a "beautiful mind" if ever there was one.

■ 3.7 Two-Person Variable-Sum Games

Most of the games that are played in an economy are not constant sum. If the sum of players' utilities in a game varies at a single outcome, that game is a **variable-sum game.** Variable-sum games are more complex than constant-sum games, and the Nash equilibria for them are more complex than for zero-sum games. In particular, there can be many Nash equilibria, like in zero-sum games; but those Nash equilibria can have different payoffs, unlike in zero-sum games.

Here is an example, inspired by Hollywood, called **Let's Make a Deal.** Player 1, a movie star, and player 2, a director, are trying to put together a movie deal. They estimate that the movie is capable of making $30 million in profits. There is an offer on the table—to split the profits evenly. If both the movie star and the director say yes to the deal, it's a deal. If either player rejects the deal, the game is over and no movie gets made. The normal form for this game is shown in Figure 3.10.

As you can see from the arrow diagram, Let's Make a Deal has two Nash equilibria. One Nash equilibrium, (yes, yes), means there is a $30 million deal, from which both sides get $15 million. The second Nash equilibrium, (no, no), means there is no deal, and both sides get $0. If you are the movie star and you know the studio is going to reject the deal,

FIGURE 3.10 **LET'S MAKE A DEAL**

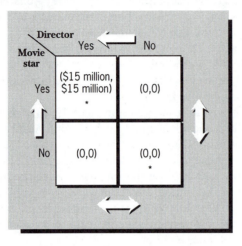

you lose nothing by rejecting it either. These two Nash equilibria have dramatically different payoffs, reflecting the variable-sum nature of the game.

Still, we can distinguish between these two Nash equilibria. First, we can distinguish between them on efficiency grounds—always favorite terrain for economic analysis. When payoffs are in money, it makes sense to add them. So compute the total payoff at a Nash equilibrium. Then compute the maximum total payoff possible in the game; you can do this by summing the payoffs in each of the cells of the matrix, then picking the cell with the largest sum of payoffs. Also compute the minimum total payoff possible in the game. Now take the difference between the Nash equilibrium payoff and the minimum payoff, and the difference between the maximum payoff and the minimum payoff. Finally, take the ratio of these two differences: that is the **efficiency** of the Nash equilibrium in question.

Let's compute the efficiency of the Nash equilibrium (yes, yes). Total payoffs at this Nash equilibrium are a goodly sum:

$$\$15 \text{ million} + \$15 \text{ million} = \$30 \text{ million}$$

Next, compute the maximum and minimum total payoff possible in the game in Figure 3.10. The total payoffs in the 4 cells of the matrix are $0, $0, $0, and $30 million, so the maximum total payoff is $30 million and the minimum total payoff is $0. This means the efficiency of the Nash equilibrium (yes, yes) is

$$\text{Efficiency} = (\$30 \text{ million} - \$0)/(\$30 \text{ million} - \$0) = 100\%$$

That's the best possible efficiency. An efficiency of 100 percent means that the Nash equilibrium (yes, yes) is a good equilibrium—an economy that achieves 100 percent efficiency is creating the most value possible.

Now contrast this efficiency to the efficiency of the Nash equilibrium (no, no). Total payoffs at this Nash equilibrium are nonexistent:

$$\$0 + \$0 = \$0$$

Since the maximum total payoff possible is $30 million, this implies an efficiency of

$$\text{Efficiency} = (\$0 - \$0)/(\$30 \text{ million} - \$0) = 0\%$$

That's a terrible efficiency; it implies total waste of value. So this is judged by economists, and perhaps others, to be a bad Nash equilibrium.

When we are faced with two Nash equilibria, one good and one bad, then we have an argument on efficiency grounds for favoring the good Nash equilibrium. Notice that this phenomenon does not arise in 2-person, zero-sum games. There, all Nash equilibria have total payoff equal to zero, and the maximum total payoff possible is zero—all this due to the zero-sum nature of the game. We don't even define efficiency in that case, because $(0 - 0)/(0 - 0)$ has no meaning in mathematics. This is another reason that zero-sum games are rare in a well-functioning economy. Such an economy creates value, and so allows for measurement of efficiency, neither of which is possible in a zero-sum situation, where at most value already created is being redistributed.

There is another way to distinguish between the two Nash equilibria of Let's Make a Deal, besides on efficiency grounds. Notice that the strategy Yes weakly dominates the strategy No, both for player 1 and for player 2. We already saw that the weak dominance solution is a Nash equilibrium—this illustration just reinforces that fact. So the Nash equilibrium (yes, yes) is the weak dominance solution of Let's Make a Deal, while the Nash equilibrium (no, no) is not. Instead, the latter is a Nash equilibrium in weakly dominated strategies.

So we have two reasons for arguing for the Nash equilibrium (yes, yes) and against the Nash equilibrium (no, no). The former is better on efficiency grounds, and it is the weak dominance solution. In this case, in game theory analysis, two strikes and you're out: the Nash equilibrium at (no, no) does not deserve further consideration. In Chapter 9, we will see yet a third strike against the Nash equilibrium at (no, no).

■ 3.8 TWO MORE TWO-PERSON, VARIABLE-SUM GAMES

There are many examples of 2-person, variable-sum games. Here are two especially instructive ones. Many games involve coordination among the players, in particular games that involve networks. You can't talk to another person on a cell phone unless there is a network that connects the two of you. You can't watch a television show unless you access the network that show is being televised on. These kinds of **network effects** can be modeled usefully as games.

A famous instance of a coordination game involving network effects is shown in Figure 3.11. This game, inspired by the market for videos and VCRs, is called **Video System Coordination.** In this game, there are two kinds of video systems, VHS and Beta. Both work equally well. A firm can adopt either VHS or Beta technology. However, once a firm adopts one of these technologies, it cannot successfully network with a firm using the other technology. A firm can successfully network only with a firm using the same technology as it is using. This is called a **coordination problem:** the problem is to get everybody to coordinate on a single strategy. Video System Coordination is shown in Figure 3.11. This coordination game has two Nash equilibria.[7] It doesn't really matter whether firms choose Beta or VHS, as long as they both choose the same system. At either of these Nash equilibria, the efficiency achieved is 100 percent, so from an efficiency standpoint, there is nothing to choose between

---

[7] The seminal work on coordination problems is Thomas C. Schelling, *The Strategy of Conflict* (New York, Oxford, 1960). See also Michael Chwe, *Rational Ritual: Culture, Coordination and Common Knowledge* (Princeton: Princeton, 2001). Chapter 4 exhibits a third Nash equilibrium, which you can't see from the arrow diagram here.

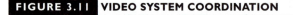

FIGURE 3.11 **VIDEO SYSTEM COORDINATION**

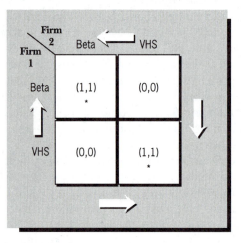

them. You can check that Video System Coordination is not dominance solvable, so that criterion does not apply. This is an ideal place for a focal point. Indeed, many analysts explain the ultimate market dominance by VHS over Beta as a focal point solution of the game.

All the 2-person variable-sum games you have seen so far have had a Nash equilibrium with an efficiency of 100 percent. This need not always be the case. The following counterexample is one of the most famous games of all time, the **Prisoner's Dilemma.**[8]

Consider the game in Figure 3.12. There are two players, called prisoner 1 and prisoner 2. These two have committed a serious crime together. Each prisoner has two strategies, to Cooperate or to Confess. If both prisoners cooperate, each gets a payoff R (for reward). The reward they get is keeping the loot from their crime. If exactly one prisoner confesses, thus implicating the other, then the confessing prisoner gets the payoff T (for temptation), while the other prisoner gets the payoff S (for sucker). T is the highest possible payoff in the game—making it very tempting, while S is the lowest possible payoff—which is why nobody wants to be played for a sucker. Finally, if both prisoners confess, then they are both convicted of a serious crime, and each of them gets the payoff P (for punishment). The rankings of the payoffs are T > R > P > S. These are the payoffs shown in Figure 3.12.

Notice that there is a unique Nash equilibrium for the Prisoner's Dilemma: (confess, confess). The strategic incentives are such that each prisoner confesses. However, the efficiency of this Nash equilibrium is not even close to 100 percent. It definitely has lower efficiency than the outcome (cooperate, cooperate), which pays each player more. To see a concrete example of this, consider the parameter values T = 2, R = 1, P = –1 and S = –2, shown in Figure 3.13. The total payoff at the Nash equilibrium is –2, while the maximum total payoff is +2 and the minimum total payoff is –2, so the efficiency of the Nash equilibrium is

$$\text{Efficiency} = [-2 - (-2)]/[2 - (-2)] = 0\%$$

This is an enormously wasteful efficiency. But it is hard to escape. To take an extreme scenario, suppose that the prisoners got to collude. Even then, absent an enforcement mechanism in place to deter cheating, collusion would not get them out of their

---

[8] This game is so famous it has an entire book devoted to it. See William Poundstone, *Prisoner's Dilemma: John von Neumann, Game Theory, and the Puzzle of the Bomb* (New York: Doubleday, 1992).

FIGURE 3.12   PRISONER'S DILEMMA

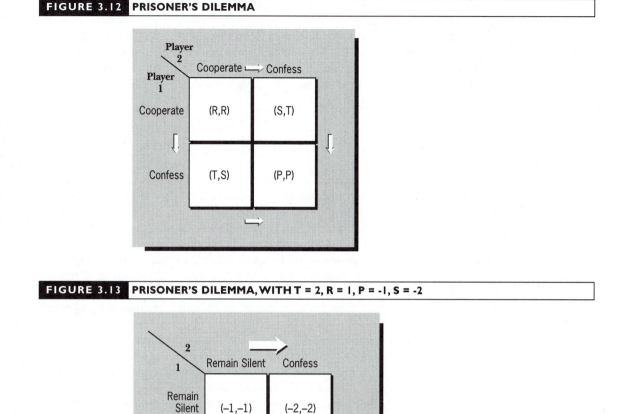

FIGURE 3.13   PRISONER'S DILEMMA, WITH T = 2, R = 1, P = -1, S = -2

dilemma. Each would still have an incentive to turn state's evidence on the other—the temptation payoff making it worth their while to "sing like a bird." Notice also that Prisoner's Dilemma is strictly dominance solvable: the strategy Confess strictly dominates the strategy Remain Silent for each player. Being strictly dominance solvable explains why the Nash equilibrium is unique, but it does not explain why the Nash equilibrium is so inefficient.

This potential inefficiency is one of the major distinctions between Nash equilibrium and market equilibrium. In a well-functioning market, we expect the outcome to be efficient or nearly so. However, in a game with a unique Nash equilibrium that is markedly inefficient, we do not expect the outcome to be efficient or nearly so. The expectation of equilibrium trumps the expectation of efficiency, where games are concerned.

A useful way to think of 2-person games like Let's Make a Deal, Video System Coordination, or the Prisoner's Dilemma is as parables. They reduce to the bare essentials the strategic aspects of a given situation, such as making a deal, getting a network to run, or dealing with a prosecutor. The way parables work is by showing us how to apply what we have learned in a bare-bones situation to the richer situations that we encounter in real life. Of course, a really good parable will also apply immediately to real life, as in the following surprise from the 1970s.

◼ 3.9 CIGARETTE ADVERTISING ON TELEVISION

In the years before 1964, all tobacco companies in the United States advertised heavily on television, **cigarette television advertising**.[9] You could see actors, celebrities, and ex-athletes lighting up all the time. In 1964 the surgeon general issued the first official warning that cigarette smoking might be hazardous to public health. At first, the cigarette companies were loath to carry the now-familiar warning label on their product. They feared, and rightly so, that carrying the warning would open them up to devastating liability lawsuits. After protracted negotiations, the industry and the U.S. government reached an agreement in 1970. According to the agreement, the companies would carry the warning label and would cease advertising on television in exchange for immunity from lawsuits based on federal law.[10]

The agreement went into effect on January 1, 1971. To see the effect of this agreement, we need to work out the strategic interaction in the industry before and after the agreement went into effect. Although four large tobacco companies were involved—American Brands, Reynolds, Philip Morris, and Liggett & Myers—and the same considerations operated for all firms in the industry, for simplicity let's consider the strategic interaction between only two of them. Then, for the sake of anonymity, let's refer to them as company 1 and company 2. Assume that when the companies adopt comparable strategies, they enjoy comparable market share and profits as well.

The strategies of each firm are to advertise on television or not. The entries of the payoff matrix are each company's profits in 1970 dollars. To convert these profits to current dollars, you should multiply by a factor of about 4. The 2-firm, variable-sum game that results is shown in Figure 3.14. You can see from the matrix that advertising on television is a powerful marketing tool. If company 1 advertises on television and company 2 doesn't, then company 1's profits go up 20 percent; the same is true when the roles are reversed. Each company has an incentive to advertise its cigarettes on television. Indeed, this is a strictly dominant strategy for each of the companies. What we see in the game in Figure 3.14 is a Prisoner's Dilemma, only this time with all positive payoffs. This game has a single Nash equilibrium: (advertise, advertise). And this was exactly what you saw on television—lots of tobacco companies advertising cigarettes.

Notice, however, what happens to earnings when both companies advertise on television at the same time. Earnings are only $27 million each, $23 million less than if the companies refrained from advertising on television. The reason for this result is that all

---

[9] Material in this section is drawn from Frederick M. Scherer, *Industrial Market Structure and Economic Performance*, 2d ed. (Boston: Houghton Mifflin, 1980), especially p. 389 and the references listed therein.

[10] The cigarette companies continue to be potentially liable under state law, since the states were not part of this agreement. All cigarette lawsuits now pending are being handled in state courts.

FIGURE 3.14 CIGARETTE TELEVISION ADVERTISING (ALL PAYOFFS IN MILLIONS OF DOLLARS)

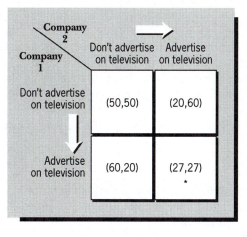

advertisements tend to cancel each other out, leaving industry sales about the same but costs much higher. The efficiency of this Nash equilibrium is the lowest possible:

$$\text{Efficiency} = (\$54 \text{ million} - \$54 \text{ million})/(\$100 \text{ million} - \$54 \text{ million}) = 0\%$$

In any Prisoner's Dilemma, the players are prisoners of their own strategies, unless something changes the game for them. In the case of the tobacco companies, that something was the U.S. government. By agreeing with the government to carry the warning label and stop advertising on television, the cigarette companies gave up the strategy of advertising on television. They were left with only the strategy: Don't Advertise on Television. Cigarette companies are heavy advertisers at all times. The big four companies spent $315 million on advertising their products in 1970, but only $252 million on advertising in 1971. This $63-million decrease came right out of the television advertising accounts. At the same time, it came as something of a surprise to the industry—and a welcome one at that—that profits rose by $91 million.

It often happens in variable-sum games that Nash equilibrium is not efficient. Note, however, that the solution is efficient in Let's Make a Deal and Video System Coordination. In the next section, we will study a class of games that includes Let's Make a Deal, and which always have an efficient Nash equilibrium. Since economists are always on the lookout for inefficiency, and ways to convert it to efficiency, so should you be on the lookout for inefficient Nash equilibria, and ways to improve their efficiency. An artful change in the rules of the game—such as in cigarette advertising on television—can often lead to large efficiency gains.

◼ 3.10 TWO-PERSON GAMES WITH MANY STRATEGIES

This chapter has presented normal form games with at most three rows and three columns. As you might suspect, there is nothing sacred about the number 3. A player could have billions of strategies—and we could still analyze the game. To do so requires some notation. This book never introduces more notation than is needed, and this particular piece is indispensable.

Let x_1 denote the strategy chosen by player 1 and x_2 denote the strategy chosen by player 2. Player 1's utility function, $u_1(x_1, x_2)$, depends on both strategies. Player 2's utility function, $u_2(x_1, x_2)$, also depends on both strategies. This is strategic interaction in a nutshell. Suppose that x_1 could take on 100 different values, and so could x_2. You need a 100 x 100 matrix to write down the game. Nobody wants to write down a matrix that big. It gets worse. Suppose that x_1 and x_2 could be any number between 0 and 1. There are uncountably many numbers to choose from—writing down that matrix would take longer than eternity. Nevertheless, we can still find the Nash equilibria of games with lots of strategies, even if we can't, or don't want to, write out their normal form as a matrix.

Here is an example to show how all this works. Individual effort by player j is denoted by x_j such that

$$0 \leq x_j \leq 1$$

As long as one team member is contributing positive effort, the more effort from the other team member, the more the team output. Specifically, player 1's payoff function, $u_1(x_1, x_2)$, is represented by the function

$$u_1(x_1, x_2) = (x_1)(x_2)$$

Since this is a team, player 2's payoff function is exactly the same as player 1's:

$$u_2(x_1, x_2) = (x_1)(x_2)$$

We call a game where each player has the same payoff function a **game of common interest.** Games of common interest always have an efficient Nash equilibrium.

In Figure 3.15, we show just the corner strategies of this game, where strategies take their extreme values of either 0 or 1 only. Notice that this game of Common Interest looks just like Let's Make a Deal, interpreting 1 as Yes, 0 as No, and the payoff to complete team

---

FIGURE 3.15   **GAME WITH MANY STRATEGIES: THE CORNERS**

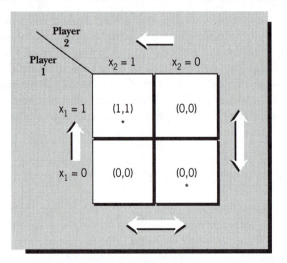

effort, 1+1, as \$30 million. We get a Nash equilibrium at (1,1) with efficiency of 100 percent, as promised; we get a bad Nash equilibrium at (0,0) with efficiency of 0 percent.

Now let's show that these are all the Nash equilibria, when we consider all the strategies between 0 and 1 for each player. Notice that for a fixed positive value of player 2's effort, $x_2 = c > 0$, player 1's payoff function is increasing in that player's strategy:

$$u_1(x_1, x_2) = (x_1)(x_2) = c\,x_1$$

Player 1 is not in equilibrium until her strategy reaches its highest value, 1.

Next, take a fixed positive value of player 1's effort, $x_1 = c > 0$. Player 2's payoff function is increasing in that player's strategy:

$$u_2(x_1, x_2) = (x_1)(x_2) = c\,x_2$$

Player 2 is not in equilibrium until his strategy reaches its highest value, 1. Together, these two findings show that there is no equilibrium for any pair of strategies (x_1, x_2), where the strategies are strictly between 0 and 1. So the Nash equilibria we see in Figure 3.15 are all the Nash equilibria of this game with infinitely many strategies. You can also show that this game of Common Interest is weakly dominance solvable, with maximum effort on the part of each player being the weakly dominant solution. The good Nash equilibrium is thus the weakly dominant solution as well.

■ SUMMARY

1. A game is zero-sum when the sum of the players' utilities is zero regardless of the outcome. Zero-sum games are a special case of constant-sum games. Every constant-sum game can be converted to a zero-sum game.

2. Two-person, zero-sum games can be solved using an arrow diagram. Arrows point toward an equilibrium. At an equilibrium, each player has maximized utility, given what the opposing player has done.

3. A firm can achieve a competitive advantage by adopting a new technology if its competitors stay put. In a game equilibrium, however, each firm adopts a new technology and no firm gains a competitive advantage.

4. One-card Stud Poker has the same normal form as Competitive Advantage, but strategy and luck are important in Poker.

5. Every equilibrium of a 2-person, zero-sum game has the same value.

6. When the sum of players' utilities in a game varies, the game is called variable sum. Variable-sum games are more complicated than zero-sum games, and they have different characteristics.

7. A variable-sum game can have Nash equilibria whose payoffs differ. Let's Make a Deal is an example of this.

8. A variable-sum game can have Nash equilibria that are inefficient. The Prisoner's Dilemma is an example of this.

9. Cigarette Television Advertising shows that the solution to a game may involve seriously eroded profits. Changing the rules of the game can lead to large profit increases in such a case.

10. We measure the efficiency of a Nash equilibrium by the ratio of observed minus minimum payoffs to maximum minus minimum payoffs. This efficiency measure varies between 0 percent and 100 percent. Nash equilibria rarely achieve 100 percent efficiency.

■ KEY TERMS

zero-sum game	focal point	Video System Coordination
constant-sum game	von Neumann's theorem	coordination problem
Battle of the Networks	variable-sum game	Prisoner's Dilemma
Nash equilibrium	Let's Make a Deal	Cigarette Television
competitive advantage	efficiency	Advertising
1-card Stud Poker	network effects	common interest

■ PROBLEMS

1. Suppose that in Battle of the Networks, if each network plays a sitcom, network 1 gets a market share of 66 percent. There are no other changes in the normal form. What is the solution of the game? Does this change make a difference? Why?

2. Convert the version of Battle of the Networks in problem 1 into a zero-sum game, then solve. Explain why the solution to the game in problems 1 and 2 are really the same.

3. Show that a win, lose, or draw game is not zero sum if each player has utility = 1 for a win, utility = 0.5 for a draw, and utility = –1 for a loss. What does this result imply about the generality of zero-sum games?

4. Give examples of competitive advantages in the following industries: personal computers, automobiles, pharmaceuticals.

5. In 1-card Stud Poker, suppose the ante is $2 and the bet is $1. Draw the normal form of the game and solve.

6. Unfair 1-card Stud Poker I. Suppose that player 1 always gets an ace, and player 2 always gets a king. Draw the normal form and solve. (This is called cheating on the part of player 1.) Does player 2 break even?

7. Solve Let's Make a Deal when there is only $35,000 to be split evenly. Draw the normal form and spell out all the steps of your reasoning.

8. Suppose that in Video System Coordination the payoff if both firms are on the VHS system is 2 instead of 1. How does this affect the solution? Why might firms prefer one equilibrium to another?

9. Suppose that the strategy set for each player is the unit interval, [0,1]. Payoff functions are as follows:

$$u_1(x_1, x_2) = x_1 + x_2 = u_2(x_1, x_2)$$

Show that this game is strictly dominance solvable. Find its strict dominance solution and its Nash equilibrium.

10. In a market economy where all goods are private and competition is perfect, an equilibrium is an optimum. However, in many 2-person games, Nash equilibria are not optimal. Why not?

■ APPENDIX. EXISTENCE OF NASH EQUILIBRIUM

Throughout this chapter, we have proceeded as if we can always expect to find a Nash equilibrium. Actually, that is something we can't take for granted: we need to prove it. One of the hallmarks of Nash's mathematical genius was to prove the existence of at least one Nash equilibrium for every matrix game with a finite number of rows and columns. We will sketch a proof along the lines of his here.

First, some setup is needed. Each player has the strategy space [0,1]. Player 1 picks strategy x_1 from this interval; player 2, strategy x_2. Player 1 has the utility function $u_1(x_1, x_2)$; player 2 has the utility function $u_2(x_1, x_2)$. These utility functions are continuous and smooth. Moreover, utility is strictly concave in a player's own strategy; this generalizes the notion of diminishing marginal utility from consumer theory.

Define player 1's best-response function $f_1(x_2)$ to be the value of x_1 that maximizes $u_1(x_1, x_2)$, for any fixed x_2. Moreover, assume that this best-response function is continuous. Similarly, define player 2's best-response function $f_2(x_1)$ as the value of x_2 that maximizes $u_2(x_1, x_2)$ for any fixed x_1. Again, assume that $f_2(x_1)$ is a continuous function of x_1.

Let $\mathbf{f} = [f_1(x_2), f_2(x_1)]$ be the vector function of these best-response functions. Since the component functions of $\mathbf{f}$ are continuous, $\mathbf{f}$ is continuous. The function $\mathbf{f}$ is called the best-response function for the entire game. Start out with a pair of strategies (x_1, x_2). Player 1 makes her best response to $x_2, f_1(x_2)$. At the same time, player 2 makes his best response to $x_1, f_2(x_1)$. The best-response function for the game records these responses. Play has gone from (x_1, x_2) to $[f_1(x_2), f_2(x_1)]$.

The easiest way to see how this works is in a game that is strictly dominance solvable. Suppose the strictly dominant solution of a game is (1,1). This means the best response functions are given by

$$f_1(x_2) = 1; f_2(x_1) = 1$$

Figure 3.16 plots these best responses and shows where they intersect—the vector (1,1).

A vector $\mathbf{x}^\star$ that satisfies both best-response conditions is a Nash equilibrium. Graphically, this means that the two best-response functions cross at $\mathbf{x}^\star$. For instance, in Figure 3.16, the

---

FIGURE 3.16 | **STRICTLY DOMINANCE SOLVABLE GAME, BEST-RESPONSE FUNCTIONS**

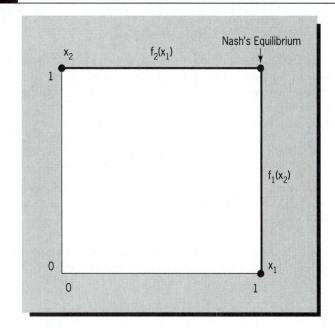

two best-response functions cross at $(1,1)$, which is the unique Nash equilibrium. That's no accident: when each player is making his or her best response to what the other player is doing, simultaneously, that's a Nash equilibrium. The intersection of best-response functions is the graphical equivalent of arrows pointing to a pair of strategies in a matrix.

Another way to relate a Nash equilibrium to best responses is the following. Indeed, this was the approach taken by Nash himself. Write down the system

$$x^*_1 = f_1(x^*_2)$$
$$\text{and}$$
$$x^*_2 = f_2(x^*_1)$$

Using vector notation, we can rewrite these equations more compactly as

$$(\mathbf{x}^*) = \mathbf{f}(\mathbf{x}^*) = [f_1(x^*_2), f_2(x^*_1)]$$

A point at which function $\mathbf{f}$ maps into itself is called a *fixed point*. A Nash equilibrium is a fixed point of the best-response mapping. At a Nash equilibrium, neither player has an incentive to make a response other than the one he or she is currently making. To guarantee that a game has a Nash equilibrium, we have to guarantee that the equation involving the best-response function for the game has a fixed point $\mathbf{x\emptyset}$. Fortunately, there is a mathematical answer to this question, contained in the following fixed-point theorem:

Fixed-Point Theorem.   If $\mathbf{f}$ is a continuous function from the unit square to the unit square, then f has a fixed point; namely, $\mathbf{x}$, where $x = \mathbf{f}(\mathbf{x})$.

Figure 3.17 illustrates the fixed-point property for a game whose strictly dominant solution is the vector $(1,1)$. The best-response mapping in this case is defined as

$$\mathbf{f}(x_1, x_2) = (1,1)$$

Notice that all points are mapped into $(1,1)$. In particular, the point $(1,1)$ is mapped into $(1,1)$. That makes $(1,1)$ a fixed point of the mapping—hence, a Nash equilibrium. Since the mapping $\mathbf{f}$ is continuous, it must have a fixed point according to the fixed-point theorem. Any such fixed point is a Nash equilibrium.

We can now collect our argument in the form of a theorem:

Existence of Equilibrium.   Suppose that for each player i, strategies are on the unit interval and best responses $f_i(.)$ are continuous functions. Then the game has a Nash equilibrium.

It is important to appreciate that the existence argument guarantees that there will be a Nash equilibrium when strategy sets are bounded intervals, and utility functions are well

FIGURE 3.17 STRICTLY DOMINANCE SOLVABLE GAME, BEST-RESPONSE MAPPING

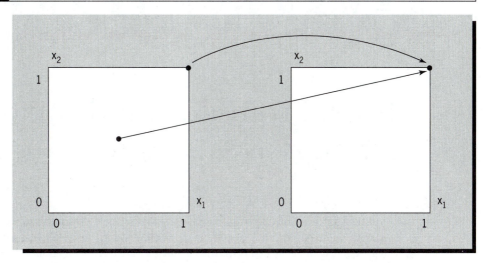

behaved (continuous and smooth, and concave in a player's own strategy). At the same time, the existence theorem is silent when strategy sets or utility functions are nasty. In those cases, a game might have a Nash equilibrium, or it might not. This topic is pursued relentlessly in advanced texts.

CHAPTER 4

Mixed Strategies and Mixed Strategy Nash Equilibrium

All the strategies considered so far have been completely deterministic: they have involved definite plans of play, with everything that a player has to do specified in advance. Any strategy that is completely deterministic is a **pure strategy.** A Nash equilibrium in which every player plays a pure strategy is called a **pure strategy Nash equilibrium.** All the games we have solved so far have had pure strategy Nash equilibria as solutions. Sometimes, however, a Nash equilibrium involves players' using strategies that are not completely deterministic. Any strategy that is not completely deterministic, but instead involves chance, is called a **mixed strategy.** When a player uses a mixed strategy, it is as if he or she is replaced by Chance, with the probabilities Chance uses set by the player. A Nash equilibrium in which at least one player plays a mixed strategy is called a **mixed strategy Nash equilibrium.** This chapter will show why a player might play a mixed strategy and so act randomly.

The first section defines mixed strategies and shows that the right way to play the game Matching Pennies is to employ a mixed strategy. Discussion then turns to how mixed strategies can be used in a game involving entry into a market niche, where there is room for only one firm. In the context of such market niche games, a contradiction between efficiency and fairness of Nash equilibria can be seen. Section 4.3 defines bluffing and shows how bluffing naturally arises in Liar's Poker. Coordination games are then introduced. These games always have mixed strategy Nash equilibria, but players would prefer not to play them. Next, we study Chicken, a game where players definitely want to avoid using the same strategy—just the opposite of Coordination. When firms playing Market Niche are asymmetrical, these Nash equilibria are asymmetrical, too. Then, this chapter reveals how sales involve mixed strategies. The strategy behind sales has a real-world analogue, Everyday Low Pricing. Sears' attempt in the late 1980s to charge everyday low prices proved to be a fiasco, which can best be appreciated from the cold glare of game theory. But that didn't stop Kmart from repeating the strategic error in 2001. The appendix examines in detail the mixed strategy bluffing that arises in a more complicated version of 1-card Stud Poker than the one you studied in Chapter 3.

■ 4.1 MIXED STRATEGIES

A pure strategy is a strategy that does not involve chance. All the strategies we have looked at so far have been pure. A player using a pure strategy is completely predictable—just like clockwork. A mixed strategy involves chance. A player uses a mixed strategy when he or she does not want to be completely predictable. This consideration comes up all the time in sports. In baseball, pitchers go to considerable effort to hide from the batter whether a pitch is going to be a fastball or off-speed. Batters would get many more hits if they knew the kind of pitch they were about to get, instead of having to guess. In football, both the defense and the offense call their play in a huddle, to keep the other side from hearing and knowing what play they have called. Again, each side wants to keep the other side guessing. In tennis, the server needs to mix up serves, going left and going right, to keep the other player guessing. The same consideration comes up in basketball, where the point guard wants to keep the defense guessing which direction he or she is taking the ball.

Mathematically, a mixed strategy is a **probability distribution** over pure strategies. Some pure strategies may not be used at all, but at least two pure strategies are used with some positive probability. A player playing a mixed strategy has in effect replaced himself or herself with a random device set and has set the probabilities governing that random device in an attempt to maximize expected utility.[1]

The simplest game in which mixed strategies are important is quite familiar: **Matching Pennies.** The normal form for Matching Pennies is shown in Figure 4.1. There are two players, and the game is zero sum. Each player has two pure strategies, Heads (H) and Tails (T). Each player bets a fixed amount, a penny. If both players choose heads or if both players choose tails—this is called a match—then player 1 wins player 2's bet. If there is no match, then player 2 wins player 1's bet.

Notice from the arrow diagram in Figure 4.1 that Matching Pennies has no Nash equilibrium in pure strategies. Take (H,H). Player 2 has an incentive to switch to tails, T, thereby turning a 1-cent loss into a 1-cent gain. The same thing happens at each of the four pure strategy combinations. One of the players wants to switch strategy. Thus, none of the pure

---

FIGURE 4.1   MATCHING PENNIES (ALL PAYOFFS IN CENTS)

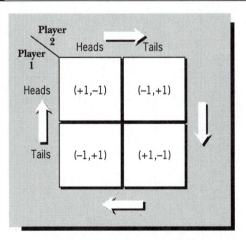

---

[1] This is not the only possible interpretation of mixed strategies. For an alternative interpretation of players' beliefs, see John Harsanyi, "Games with Randomly Disturbed Payoffs: A New Rationale for Mixed Strategy Equilibrium Points," *International Journal of Game Theory* 2 (1973): 1–23. For a study of how well tennis players replace themselves with randomness, see Mark Walker and John Wooders, "Minimax Play at Wimbledon," *American Economic Review* 91 (2001), 1521–1538.

strategy combinations is a rest point. Matching Pennies cannot be in equilibrium at any of its pure strategies combinations.

Nevertheless, Matching Pennies does have a Nash equilibrium—you just can't see it from the arrow diagram. To find this Nash equilibrium, we resort to mixed strategies. This should not come as a complete surprise. The way people usually play Matching Pennies is by tossing a coin. The act of tossing a coin is a random device for picking between heads and tails. As we shall soon see, the Nash equilibrium of Matching Pennies requires that each player toss a coin whose probability of coming up heads is exactly .5. The way people play this game in real life thus makes sense from the stand-point of game theory.

Here is another example, called **Market Niche,** where the importance of mixed strategies is not so apparent. There are two firms, 1 and 2, and a single market niche that either of them could occupy. If one firm occupies the market niche, it gets a return of 100. If both firms occupy the market niche, each loses 50. If a firm stays out of this market, it breaks even. The firms decide simultaneously whether to enter the market niche or not. Figure 4.2 shows the normal form of Market Niche.

You can see from the arrow diagram that Market Niche has two pure strategy equilibria: (enter, stay out) and (stay out, enter). These involve exactly one firm occupying the market niche. The firm entering the market niche enjoys a much greater payoff than the firm staying out of the market niche. Also notice that this game is symmetrical: both firms get the same payoff when they choose the same strategy. When the firms switch strategies, they switch payoffs. The two pure strategy equilibria, where the players use different strategies and get different payoffs, are asymmetrical: the firms get very different payoffs. Market Niche also has a symmetrical equilibrium, which you cannot see from the arrow diagram. This equilibrium is in mixed strategies and pays each player the same. We now turn to the task of describing mixed strategies and solving for a mixed strategy equilibrium. Then we will solve for the mixed strategy equilibria of Matching Pennies and Market Niche.

FIGURE 4.2 | **MARKET NICHE**

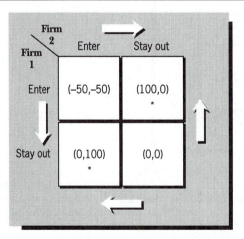

◼ 4.2 Computing Mixed Strategy Nash Equilibria in 2 x 2 Games

Let's begin our computations with Matching Pennies (recall Figure 4.1). We know that Matching Pennies does not have a pure strategy equilibrium, which forces us to look for a mixed strategy equilibrium. The key insight to a mixed strategy Nash equilibrium is the following: *Every pure strategy that is played as part of a mixed strategy Nash equilibrium has the same expected value.* If one strategy pays less than another, then you should play only the strategy that pays more to the exclusion of the strategy that pays less. This is just domination of one strategy by another, when probability is involved. The only strategies that are not excluded pay the same. We will apply this principle over and over again to find mixed strategy Nash equilibria.[2]

Before proceeding, we need a little more notation. Let $p_1(H)$ equal the probability that player 1 plays heads, and $p_1(T)$ equal the probability that player 1 plays tails. Similarly, let $p_2(H)$ be the probability that player 2 plays heads and $p_2(T)$ be the probability that player 2 plays tails. Now take player 1's payoffs. Suppose that player 1 uses the pure strategy Heads and player 2 uses some mixed strategy $p_2 = [p_2(H), p_2(T)]$. Since player 2 is using a mixed strategy, player 1 faces an expected value, $EV_1(H)$, from playing heads:

$$EV_1(H) = p_2(H)(+1) + p_2(T)(-1)$$

When player 2 picks heads, the result is a match and player 1 gains, +1; when player 2 picks tails, the result is a mismatch and player 1 loses, −1. Now suppose that player 1 is using the other pure strategy, Tails. Since player 2 is using a mixed strategy, player 1 faces an expected value, $EV_1(T)$, from playing tails:

$$EV_1(T) = p_2(H)(-1) + p_2(T)(+1)$$

When player 2 picks heads, the result is a mismatch and player 1 loses, −1; when player 2 picks tails, the result is a match and player 1 gains, +1.

All we have to do now is set the payoffs of player 1's two strategies equal to each other:

$$EV_1(H) = EV_1(T)$$

Substituting, we have

$$p_2(H)(+1) + p_2(T)(-1) = p_2(H)(-1) + p_2(T)(+1)$$

To this condition we add the requirement that player 2's mixed strategy be a probability distribution, the probabilities of whose events add up to 1:

$$p_2(H) + p_2(T) = 1$$

At this point we have two equations to solve in two unknowns, $p_2(H)$ and $p_2(T)$. A little algebra will show that the solution to these two equations is

$$p_2(H)^\star = p_2(T)^\star = .5$$

---

[2] The existence proof given in Chapter 2 for pure strategy equilibria can be adapted to guarantee the existence of mixed strategy equilibria as well. In particular, for a game with a finite number of pure strategies, the operation of mixing strategies supplies the needed continuity. See J. Nash, "Noncooperative Games," *Annuals of Mathematics* 54 (1951): 289–295, for details.

Use of * here indicates that these are mixed strategy equilibrium values for player 2. Player 1 chooses this equilibrium strategy, even though it is one of an infinite number of strategies that gives the same payoff, given that player 2 is also choosing his equilibrium strategy. That infinite number of strategies is created by the infinite number of probability distributions over Heads and Tails. Only one of these probability distributions satisfies the requirements for Nash equilibrium.

Notice that when the pure strategies Heads and Tails have the same expected value, then player 1 is indifferent as to which pure strategy she plays. If she were not indifferent, that would be bad news for player 2—it would imply that player 1 was enjoying a gain at player 2's expense. For instance, if player 1 preferred playing Heads to Tails, this would mean that player 2 was playing Heads too often. And we can say the same thing about player 2.

There is an odd thing about mixed strategies that you have to get used to. The value of a player's own pure strategy depends on the opponent's mixed strategy. The condition that the player's pure strategies pay the same implies something about the opponent's mixed strategy, and vice versa. At a mixed strategy equilibrium, the opponent has made the player indifferent about his or her pure strategies, just as the player has made the opponent indifferent about his or her pure strategies.

We are now in a position to compute player 1's expected value from either pure strategy in her mixed strategy:

$$EV_1(H) = (.5)(+1) + (.5)(-1) = 0 = EV_1(T)$$

Player 1 breaks even by using either of the pure strategies, as long as she uses them in a mixed strategy. At this point we also know what probabilities player 2 must use in a mixed strategy to keep player 1 honest. If player 2 chose heads more than tails, then player 1 could guarantee a winning percentage by always choosing heads. For instance, if player 2 used Heads 60 percent of the time, then player 1, by using Heads also, would match 60 percent of the time for a gain of 1 and would mismatch 40 percent of the time for a loss of 1, a net gain of 20 percent.

We can go through the same process for player 2. When we do so, we find that player 1 plays heads with probability $p_1(H)^* = .5 = p_1(T)^*$, the probability with which she plays tails. This situation leads to an expected value to player 2 from using either of the pure strategies of:

$$EV_2(H) = p_1(H)^*(-1) + p_1(T)^*(+1)$$
$$= (.5)(-1) + (.5)(+1)$$
$$= 0$$
$$= EV_2(T)$$

Notice that when the pure strategies Heads and Tails have the same expected value, then player 2 is indifferent as to which pure strategy he plays. If he were not indifferent, that would be bad news for player 1—it would imply that player 2 was enjoying a gain at player 1's expense—the same phenomenon we saw for player 1 earlier.

Even though Matching Pennies is not a symmetrical game, it has a symmetrical Nash equilibrium. At this symmetrical Nash equilibrium, each player plays heads with probability .5 and tails with probability .5. In the process, each player can expect to break even in dollar terms. This mixed strategy Nash equilibrium explains why people, when they play Matching Pennies (for whatever stakes), toss their coins. The coin toss is an effort to implement 50–50 odds of heads and tails that break even at the mixed strategy Nash equilibrium.

Since our linear equations had a unique solution, we are also assured that this mixed strategy Nash equilibrium is the only Nash equilibrium. The only way for people to play

Matching Pennies is to replace themselves with random devices with equal probabilities of Heads and Tails.

Suppose, like the pitches in baseball, the play calling in football, and the serve in tennis, the situation where the player wants to use a mixed strategy is repeated. Then an extra consideration comes in—patterns over time have to be avoided, even if they lead to the same observed frequency. Suppose in football that the mixed strategy dictates passing with probability 0.5. If the offense called a passing play on the first play from scrimmage, the third play from scrimmage, the fifth play from scrimmage, and so on over 80 plays, it would have called 40 passing plays, for an observed frequency of 40/80 = 0.5. However, this offense would be completely predictable: the defense would know exactly when a pass is coming. To avoid this, and to keep the defense guessing, the offense has to replace itself with a random device each and every play from scrimmage.

Let's now turn to Market Niche (recall Figure 4.2). As you can see from the arrow diagram, Market Niche has two pure strategy Nash equilibria, (enter, stay out) and (stay out, enter). At these pure strategy Nash equilibria, the firm that enters the market niche gets a much higher payoff than the firm that stays out of the market niche. Market Niche also has a mixed strategy Nash equilibrium. This mixed strategy Nash equilibrium is symmetrical: both firms adopt the same mixed strategy and get the same payoff.

To find this mixed strategy Nash equilibrium, we can employ the same argument used for Matching Pennies. Let p_1(enter) equal the probability that firm 1 enters the market niche and p_1(stay out) equal the probability that firm 1 stays out of the market niche. Similarly, let p_2(enter) equal the probability that firm 2 enters the market niche and p_2(stay out) equal the probability that firm 2 stays out of the market niche. Now compute firm 1's payoffs. Suppose that firm 1 chooses the pure strategy Enter, whereas firm 2 uses some mixed strategy $p_2 = [p_2(\text{enter}), p_2(\text{stay out})]$. Since firm 2 is using a mixed strategy, firm 1 faces an expected value, EV_1 (enter), from entering the market niche:

$$EV_1(\text{enter}) = p_2(\text{enter})(-50) + p_2(\text{stay out})(100)$$

This equation results because when firm 2 enters the market niche as well, both firms lose 50. When firm 2 stays out of the market niche, then firm 1 gets the market niche all to itself, a payoff of 100.

Now suppose that firm 1 uses its other pure strategy, Stay Out of the market niche. Regardless of what firm 2 does, this strategy pays 0. All we have to do now is set the payoffs of player 1's two pure strategies equal to each other:

$$EV_1(\text{enter}) = EV_1(\text{stay out}) = 0$$

Substituting, we have

$$p_2(\text{enter})(-50) + p_2(\text{stay out})(100) = 0$$

To this condition we add the requirement that player 2's mixed strategy be a probability distribution, the probabilities of whose events add up to 1:

$$p_2(\text{enter}) + p_2(\text{stay out}) = 1$$

At this point we have two equations to solve in two unknowns, p_2(enter) and p_2(stay out). A little algebra will show that the solution to these two equations is

$$p_2^*(\text{enter}) = 2/3; \ p_2^*(\text{stay out}) = 1/3$$

We are now in a position to compute firm 1's expected value from either pure strategy:

$$EV_1(\text{enter}) = 2/3(-50) + 1/3(100) = 0 = EV_1(\text{stay out})$$

Firm 1 breaks even when firm 2 uses the equilibrium mixed strategy, which puts a 2/3 probability on entering the market niche. You can show that the same probabilities apply to firm 1:

$$p_1{}^*(\text{enter}) = 2/3; \; p_1{}^*(\text{stay out}) = 1/3$$

with an expected value to either pure strategy of 0.

As you can see, the payoffs from this symmetrical mixed strategy Nash equilibrium, (0,0), are inefficient. One of these firms could make a lot of money by entering the market niche, if it was sure that the other firm would not enter that same niche. This assurance is precisely what is missing. It's a free country and a free market: each firm has exactly the same right to enter the market niche. The only way for *both* firms to exercise their right to enter the market niche is to play the inefficient, but symmetrical, mixed strategy Nash equilibrium.

You can think of Market Niche as a parable. In most industrial markets there is room for only a few firms; here, there is room for only one firm to operate profitably, and either firm is perfectly capable of filling that niche—a situation called a *perfectly contestable market*. Chance plays a major role in the identity of the firms that ultimately enter such markets. If too many firms enter, then there are losses all around, and in the long run some firms must exit. If we know the mixed strategy equilibrium, we can actually predict how often there will be too many entrants. Since the probability of entry by either firm is 1/3, the probability that both firms enter is $(1/3)^2 = 1/9$. A little over 11 percent of the time, two firms enter the market niche when there is room for only one firm. In the long run, one of these firms must leave the market. This is a process we observe all the time—as illustrated by the several hundred now-defunct U.S. automobile companies.

It is hard to keep firms from adopting the same strategy in Market Niche. Here we confront a clash of important principles—efficiency and fairness. Efficiency says to play a Nash equilibrium with the highest total payoffs; here, 100. Equity says to play a Nash equilibrium that pays each player the same, which in this case has total payoffs of 0—drastically lower. The two principles cannot be reconciled in a game like Market Niche. The clash between efficiency and equity pervades economics, so it comes as no surprise to find it reflected in game theory.[3]

There is a fancy name for efficiency as it applies to Nash equilibria:

Payoff Dominance.   If every player gets a higher payoff at one Nash equilibrium than at another, then the former Nash equilibrium payoff dominates the latter.

Payoff dominance is in many respects an attractive principle. Unfortunately, if we try to impose both payoff dominance and equity as conditions a Nash equilibrium should satisfy, we encounter a nasty contradiction. In general, no Nash equilibrium can satisfy both payoff dominance and equity at the same time. The game Market Niche provides a ready-made

---

[3] One rubric under which this clash appears is the liberal paradox. The original presentation is by A. K. Sen, *Social Choice and Welfare* (San Francisco: Norton, 1970), chap. 9. There is a vast literature on the subject.

counterexample: its one and only symmetrical Nash equilibrium is payoff dominated by either of its asymmetrical Nash equilibria. The conflict between efficiency and equity is not only pervasive; it is often intractable. Nevertheless, efficiency is desirable, so we should try whenever possible to advocate Nash equilibria that embody it. This issue is further elaborated in section 4.4.[4]

■ 4.3 MIXED STRATEGIES AND BLUFFING: LIAR'S POKER

Whenever a player uses a mixed strategy, he or she is trying to be unpredictable—just like the weather. "The probability of rain today is 30 percent" and "the probability that I will go to the hot fishing spot today is 30 percent" are statements on the same logical footing. Many times in a game with imperfect information, a player has information that might be valuable to an opponent and detrimental to the player were it to be revealed. In such cases the player has a strong incentive to keep this information secret. The trouble is, strategic behavior might give the information away. This situation gives rise to bluffing.[5]

Bluffing is any attempt to mislead or deceive. The purpose of the deception is to prevent the opponent from being able to infer what the player knows, what information he or she is privy to. Bluffing all the time just doesn't pay: a bluff is too often called, and the bluffer pays a heavy price. A player wants to bluff just enough to keep the opponent guessing—to keep the opponent from being able to read what the player knows by observing how he or she plays. Mixed strategies are the vehicle for bluffing, and a mixed strategy equilibrium tells just how much a player needs to bluff to protect the value of his or her information.

Here is a simple example of how protecting information can be valuable. The game is called **Liar's Poker,** because it resembles Poker and lying plays a large part in its solution.[6] There are two players, 1 and 2, and two cards in the pack, an ace and a king. An ace ranks higher than a king. Player 1 is dealt a card, face down, which she can look at but which player 2 never sees. All player 2 knows is that with probability .5 the card is an ace; with probability .5, a king. Now player 1 says something. Player 1 can say what the card is, or lie about it and say that she has a higher-ranking card. If the card is an ace, player 1 can't lie about having a better card and must say that it is an ace. If the card is a king, player 1 can say ace or king. Player 2 hears what player 1 says. If player 1 says ace, then player 2 can either call or fold. If player 2 calls and player 1's card is not an ace, then player 1 loses and pays $1 to player 2. If player 2 calls and player 1's card is an ace, then player 2 loses and pays $1 to player 1. If player 2 folds, then player 1 automatically wins $0.50 from player 2. Finally, if player 1 says king, then the game ends and both players break even.[7]

The extensive form of this game is shown in Figure 4.3a. Notice that player 1 has two strategies in this game, based on the one information set she has:

---

[4] For a careful argument of why rights-based notions such as equity might have priority over the notion of efficiency, see John Rawls, *A Theory of Justice* (Cambridge, Mass.: Harvard University Press, 1971).

[5] An entire chapter is devoted to this issue (Chapter 10). The idea of a strategy's revealing private information is central to modern theories of finance and financial economics.

[6] The form of Liar's Poker analyzed here is the simplest possible. To see what a real-life game of Liar's Poker looks like, read the first chapter of Michael Lewis's best-seller, *Liar's Poker* (New York: Norton, 1989).

[7] In real-life versions of Liar's Poker, the possible hands are ranked as in 5-card Stud Poker (straight flush beats four of a kind beats a full house, etc.), and player 1 loses whenever she is caught lying; that is, when she says the hand is better than it really is and is called. If player 1 claims to have the lowest possible hand (no pair), then she can't be lying about its strength and the outcome is a tie.

FIGURE 4.3 | **LIAR'S POKER: (a) EXTENSIVE FORM; (b) NORMAL FORM**

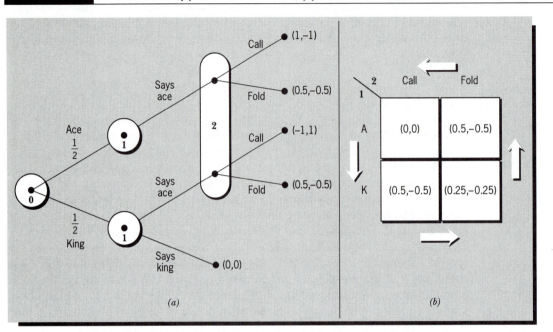

(a)   *(b)*

A: Say ace when the card is an ace, and say ace when the card is a king.

K: Say ace when the card is an ace, and say king when the card is a king.

Player 1's strategy A contains an element of bluffing when the player's card is a king. If player 2 believes player 1 when she says her card is an ace although it is a king, then player 1 wins $0.50 even though she has a bad hand. By contrast, player 1's strategy K is not bluffing; rather, it is entirely honest, without a trace of deception. Unfortunately for player 1, this strategy also doesn't make any money. Similarly, player 2 has two strategies in this game, Call and Fold, based on the one information set he has. We now show that Liar's Poker has a unique Nash equilibrium, which is in mixed strategies. In particular, the solution to Liar's Poker involves quite a bit of lying.

The best way to see all this is in the normal form, which is shown in Figure 4.3b. Here is the story behind the payoffs. Take (A, fold): player 1 always says the card is an ace, whether the card is in fact an ace or a king, and player 2 always folds. With probability .5, player 1 is dealt an ace. Player 1 says the card is an ace, and player 2 folds, so player 1 wins $0.50. With probability .5, player 1 is dealt a king, in which case player 1 again says the card is an ace, and player 2 again folds, so player 1 again wins $0.50. These are the payoffs in the cell (A, fold).

Now suppose that player 1 always says the card is an ace, but player 2 calls instead of folding. With probability .5, player 1 is dealt an ace. Player 1 says the card is an ace, and player 2 calls, so player 1 wins $1. With probability .5, player 1 is dealt a king, in which case player 1 again says the card is an ace. Player 2 calls, so player 1 loses $1. The expected value to player 1 is

$$EV_1 = (.5)(+1) + (.5)(-1) = 0$$

Both players expect to break even in the cell (A, call).

Next, suppose that player 1 says the card is an ace when she is dealt an ace, and says the card is a king when a king is dealt, and player 2 calls. With probability .5, player 1 is dealt an ace and says so. Player 2 calls, so player 1 wins $1. With probability .5, player 1 is dealt a king and says so. The payoff to player 1 in this case is $0. Player 1's expected value is

$$EV_1 = (.5)(1) + (.5)(0) = 0.5$$

The payoffs to the cell (K, call) are (0.5, –0.5).

Finally, suppose that player 1 says the card is an ace when an ace is dealt and the card is a king when a king is dealt, and player 2 folds. With probability .5, player 1 is dealt an ace and says so. Player 2 folds, so player 1 wins $0.50. With probability .5, player 1 is dealt a king and says so. The payoff to player 1 in this case is $0. Player 1's expected value is

$$EV_1 = (.5)(0.5) + (.5)(0) = 0.25$$

The payoffs to the cell (K, fold) are (0.25, –0.25). This completes the setup of the normal form.

As you can see from the arrow diagram of Figure 4.3b, Liar's Poker does not have a pure strategy Nash equilibrium. This means we have to look for a mixed strategy Nash equilibrium, at which neither player is completely predictable. Denote by $p_2(\text{call})$ the probability that player 2 calls; by $p_2(\text{fold})$, the probability that player 2 folds. Player 1's strategies A and K pay the same when

$$(0.5)p_2(\text{fold}) = (0.5)p_2(\text{call}) + (0.25)p_2(\text{fold})$$

From this we infer that

$$0.25p_2(\text{fold}) = 0.5p_2(\text{call})$$

that is, player 2 should fold twice as much as he calls. By the laws of probability, this means that

$$p_2{}^*(\text{fold}) = 2/3; \, p_2{}^*(\text{call}) = 1/3$$

We now turn to player 2. Denote by $p_1(A)$ the probability that player 1 says the card is an ace when it is an ace and says the card is an ace when it is a king. Denote by $p_1(K)$ the probability that player 1 says the card is an ace when it is an ace and says it is a king when it is a king. Player 2's strategies Call and Fold pay the same when

$$p_1(K)(-0.5) = p_1(A)(-0.5) + p_1(K)(-0.25)$$

From this we infer that

$$0.25p_1(K) = 0.5p_1(A)$$

that is, player 1 should use the strategy K twice as often as the strategy A. By the laws of probability, this means that

$$p_1{}^*(K) = 2/3; \, p_1{}^*(A) = 1/3$$

This pair of probability distributions is the Nash equilibrium of Liar's Poker.

Notice that this mixed strategy equilibrium involves quite a bit of bluffing on player 1's part. In fact, the probability is 1/6 that player 1 is lying. When player 1 gets an ace (probability .5), she says so. That's telling the truth. When player 1 gets a king (probability .5), two-thirds of the time she says so, but the rest of the time she lies. So the probability that player 1 is lying is (1/2)(1/3) = 1/6.

All that bluffing pays for player 1, who gets a positive expected value at the mixed strategy Nash equilibrium from this zero-sum game. Liar's Poker isn't fair. To see this result, substitute the mixed strategy equilibrium values $p_2\emptyset(\text{call})$ and $p_2\emptyset(\text{fold})$ into player 1's expected value from saying the card is an ace when it is a king. You get

$$EV_1{}^* = (1/3)(0) + (2/3)(0.5) = \$0.33$$

You would also get the same answer if you substituted into player 1's expected value from saying the card is a king when it is a king. No matter how you look at it, for every $1 bet, player 1 expects to make $0.33, for a handsome rate of return of 33 percent. Since Liar's Poker is zero sum, player 2 expects to lose that $0.33. Only a fool would willingly play the role of player 2 in Liar's Poker, over and over again. It's a much worse proposition than anything a casino offers. Indeed, the only fair way to play Liar's Poker in real life is via a rotation: each player gets the same chance of going first.[8]

◼ 4.4 Mixed Strategy Nash Equilibria of Coordination Games and Coordination Problems

You were warned that some of the games studied in Chapter 3 had Nash equilibria you could not see from an arrow diagram. Now that you know how to compute mixed strategy Nash equilibria, we can go back and find these invisible Nash equilibria. Let's begin with Video System Coordination (Figure 3.11). This game has two pure strategy Nash equilibria, both of which are symmetrical. There is nothing to suggest that there are any other Nash equilibria. One diagnostic, however, is the following. Neither Beta nor VHS dominates the other, and the two pure strategy equilibria are at opposite corners of the game matrix. When this happens, it is usually the case that the equations governing a mixed strategy solution have a solution.

Let $p_1(\text{Beta})$ be the probability that firm 1 chooses Beta, and $p_1(\text{VHS})$ be the probability that firm 1 chooses VHS. Similarly, let $p_2(\text{Beta})$ be the probability that firm 2 chooses Beta and $p_2(\text{VHS})$ be the probability that firm 2 chooses VHS. Now take firm 1's payoffs. Suppose that firm 1 chooses Beta and firm 2 uses some mixed strategy, $p_2E = [p_2(\text{Beta}), p_2(\text{VHS})]$. Since firm 2 is using a mixed strategy, firm 1 faces an expected value, $EV_1(\text{Beta})$, from choosing Beta:

$$EV_1(\text{Beta}) = p_2(\text{Beta})(+1) + p_2(\text{VHS})(0)$$

This equation is obtained because when firm 2 chooses Beta, the result is a match and firm 1 gains, +1, and when firm 2 chooses VHS, the result is a mismatch and firm 1 gets 0.

Now suppose that firm 1 is using its other pure strategy, VHS. Since firm 2 is using a mixed strategy, firm 1 faces an expected value, $EV_1(\text{VHS})$, from choosing VHS:

$$EV_1(\text{VHS}) = p_2(\text{Beta})(0) + p_2(\text{VHS})(1)$$

This equation is obtained because when firm 2 chooses Beta, the result is a mismatch and firm 1 gets 0, and when firm 2 chooses VHS, the result is a match and firm 1 gains, +1.

All we have to do now is set the payoffs of firm 1's two pure strategies equal to each other:

$$EV_1(\text{Beta}) = EV_1(\text{VHS})$$

---

[8] The players can use a 50–50 random device to determine who goes first. This is just like the public signal in a correlated equilibrium. Alternatively, they can use a deterministic rotation, with each player going first half of all rounds, with the total number of rounds even.

Substituting, we have

$$p_2(\text{Beta})(+1) + p_2(\text{VHS})(0) = p_2(\text{Beta})(0) + p_2(\text{VHS})(1)$$

To this condition we add the requirement that firm 2's mixed strategy be a probability distribution, the probabilities of whose events add up to 1:

$$p_2(\text{Beta}) + p_2(\text{VHS}) = 1$$

At this point we have two equations to solve in two unknowns, $p_2(\text{Beta})$ and $p_2(\text{VHS})$. A little algebra will show that the solution to these two equations is

$$p_2{}^*(\text{Beta}) = p_2{}^*(\text{VHS}) = 0.5$$

An appeal to symmetry shows that the same mixed strategy is an equilibrium for firm 1. At the mixed strategy Nash equilibrium for Video System Coordination, each firm has an expected value of 0.5. This low payoff arises because half the time, the two firms are not on the same system. Even though this payoff satisfies symmetry (it has the same payoff for both firms), it pales in comparison to either of the symmetrical pure strategy Nash equilibria, both of which pay twice as much. Here is an instance in which there is no conflict between efficiency and equity. We can have both as long as we throw out the low-paying mixed strategy Nash equilibrium

4.5 CORRELATED EQUILIBRIUM

We have seen that mixed strategy Nash equilibria tend to have low efficiency, and that that may set up a potential conflict between efficiency and equity. The clearest instance you have seen of this so far is Market Niche, where the pure strategy Nash equilibria have 100 percent efficiency but are very asymmetric, while the mixed strategy Nash equilibrium has 50 percent efficiency but pays both firms the same in expected value terms. In certain circumstances, there is a way out of this conflict, called **correlated equilibrium.**

At a correlated equilibrium, each player utilizes a public signal to determine his or her choice of strategy. This public signal is observed by all players, all of whom utilize it to determine strategy. After each possible signal, players play a Nash equilibrium on the game that follows the signal. That's what makes a correlated equilibrium an equilibrium. The public signal is what generates the correlation.

So we need two things for a correlated equilibrium:

1. A public signal, observable by all players prior to play
2. Nash equilibrium play on the game that follows

Here's an example of how correlated equilibrium can address the conflict between efficiency and equity. Recall Market Niche from Figure 4.2. Market Niche has three Nash equilibria—these will be the equilibrium play on the game that follows. For the public signal, suppose that before the two firms play Market Niche they observe the outcome of a coin toss. The coin can come up either Heads or Tails, each with probability 0.5. The two firms observe the outcome of the coin toss before they choose between Enter and Stay Out.

There are many ways the firms could use the outcome of the coin toss to determine their strategy choice in Market Niche. Here's one that will generate 100 percent efficiency and equity:

If the coin is Heads, then firm 1 enters and firm 2 stays out.

If the coin toss is Tails, then firm 1 stays out and firm 2 enters.

This is a correlated equilibrium. It's an equilibrium because neither firm has an incentive to move differently. If the coin toss is Heads and firm 1 stays out, then it gets a 0 payoff when it could have had a payoff of 100 by choosing Enter. So that deviation doesn't pay firm 1. Similarly, if the coin toss is Heads and firm 2 enters, it gets a payoff of −50 when it could have had a payoff of 0 instead. So that deviation doesn't pay firm 2. You can show the same is true for deviations if the coin toss is Tails.

Now let's show that this correlated equilibrium generates 100 percent efficiency in expected value terms. First, let's compute the expected value for firm 1:

$$EV_1 = p(H)(\text{payoff if Heads}) + p(T)(\text{payoff if Tails}) = (0.5)(100) + (0.5)(0) = 50$$

Similarly, the expected value for firm 2 is

$$EV_2 = p(H)(\text{payoff if Heads}) + p(T)(\text{payoff if Tails}) = (0.5)(0) + (0.5)(50) = 50$$

Adding to get the expected total payoff, we have $50 + 50 = 100$, a sum equal to the maximum total payoff. So that's an efficiency of 100 percent.

If you think this is all a trick, you're not mistaken—but correlated equilibrium is a useful trick, and it gets used in real life all the time. Here are just two examples, one from sports and one from the stock market. First, consider the coin toss before a football game begins. This signal is very informative: it tells everyone involved which team has the ball first, and which team defends which end of the field. Otherwise, there would be need for a device (a melee, perhaps) to determine who gets the ball and who defends what. Second, consider **program trading** on the stock market. A program trade is a computer program that determines which trades to make, and when. Program trading is triggered by certain publicly available signals, such as large movements up or down in the stock market. On a quiet day there is no program trading, since nothing initiates the programs. But on a trading day with a lot of up-and-down action, you can be sure that the program traders are active.

■ 4.6 ASYMMETRICAL MIXED STRATEGY NASH EQUILIBRIA

So far all our mixed strategy Nash equilibria have been symmetrical. Mixed strategy Nash equilibria can also be asymmetrical. Go back to the game Market Niche (Figure 4.2). When we make things ever so slightly asymmetrical, then we get an asymmetrical mixed strategy Nash equilibrium. Consider the following slightly asymmetrical version of Market Niche (see Figure 4.4). In this version, firm 1 gets a payoff of 150 if it gets the market niche to itself. Otherwise, the game is precisely the same as shown in Figure 4.2. The change reflects the competitive advantage firm 1 has over firm 2 in the event that it is the sole entrant. Firm 1 creates more value out of the market niche, when it is the sole occupant, than does firm 2. This competitive advantage could be due to lower costs, better marketing, or many other factors. **Asymmetrical Market Niche** has pure strategy equilibrium payoffs of (150,0) and (0,100). It also has an asymmetrical mixed strategy equilibrium, which we now compute.

Let $p_1(\text{enter})$ equal the probability that firm 1 enters the market niche; $p_1(\text{stay out})$ equal the probability that firm 1 stays out; $p_2(\text{enter})$ equal the probability that firm 2 enters the market niche; and $p_2(\text{stay out})$ equal the probability that firm 2 stays out. Now compute firm 1's payoffs. Suppose that firm 1 enters while firm 2 is using the mixed

FIGURE 4.4   **ASYMMETRICAL MARKET NICHE**

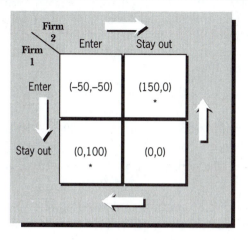

strategy $p_2 = [p_2(\text{enter}), p_2(\text{stay out})]$. Since firm 2 is using a mixed strategy, firm 1 faces an expected value, $EV_1(\text{enter})$, from entering the market niche:

$$EV_1(\text{enter}) = p_2(\text{enter})(-50) + p_2(\text{stay out})(150)$$

Next, suppose that firm 1 uses its other pure strategy, Stay Out. In this case, firm 1 is guaranteed the payoff 0 regardless of what firm 2 does. Setting these two expected values equal to each other, we get

$$p_2(\text{enter})(-50) + p_2(\text{stay out})(150) = 0$$

To this condition we add the requirement that firm 2's mixed strategy be a probability distribution, the probabilities of whose events add up to 1:

$$p_2(\text{enter}) + p_2(\text{stay out}) = 1$$

At this point we have two equations to solve in two unknowns, $p_2(\text{enter})$ and $p_2(\text{stay out})$. Again, a little algebra will show that the solution to these two equations is

$$p_2{}^*(\text{enter}) = 3/4; \, p_2{}^*(\text{stay out}) = 1/4$$

Compared to the symmetrical version of Market Niche, the less efficient firm enters the market niche with a somewhat higher probability (3/4 versus 2/3). As before, firm 1 breaks even at the mixed strategy equilibrium:

$$EV_1(\text{enter}) = 3/4(-50) + 1/4(150) = 0 = EV_2(\text{stay out})$$

Since firm 2's payoffs have not changed, player 1's mixture probabilities do not change:

$$p_1(\text{enter})^* = 2/3; \, p_1(\text{stay out})^* = 1/3$$

Firm 2 still expects to break even at the mixed strategy equilibrium:

$$EV_2(\text{enter}) = 2/3(-50) + 1/3(100) = 0 = EV_2(\text{stay out})$$

Because this version of Market Niche is asymmetrical, considerations of symmetry no longer apply. Since symmetry was the only thing the mixed strategy Nash equilibrium had going for it, it is very tempting to exclude that Nash equilibrium from further attention. Moreover, we can rank the three Nash equilibria in terms of efficiency. Since the maximum total possible payoff is 150 and the minimum total payoff is −100, we get the following efficiencies for the three Nash equilibria:

$$\text{Nash equilibrium(enter, stay out): efficiency} = [150 + 0 - (-100)]/[150 - (-100)]$$
$$= 100\%$$
$$\text{Nash equilibrium (stay out, enter): efficiency} = [0 + 100 - (-100)])/[150 - (-100)]$$
$$= 80\%$$
$$\text{Mixed strategy Nash equilibrium: efficiency} = [0 + 0 - (-100)])/[150 - (-100)]$$
$$= 40\%$$

In terms of efficiency, the Nash equilibrium that sends firm 1 into the market niche and keeps firm 2 out is first best; the Nash equilibrium that sends firm 2 into the market niche and keeps firm 1 out is second best; the Nash equilibrium that sends both firms to the market with probabilities 2/3 and 3/4 respectively, is a distant third best. Moreover, the pure strategy Nash equilibria pay at least zero to both firms. Thus, it (weakly) payoff dominates the mixed strategy Nash equilibrium, where both firms expect zero.[9]

■ 4.7 CHICKEN

One of the most famous 2-person games of all, in the same league with Prisoner's Dilemma, is **Chicken.** The name comes from the slang word for "coward." Perhaps the most visible instance of the game occurs near the end of the Hollywood film, *Rebel Without a Cause*, when James Dean and another actor drive their cars toward the edge of a cliff in Los Angeles. Each driver has two strategies: Drive Straight Ahead, or Swerve.

Each driver makes his choice (this version of the game was played with guys behind the wheel—although a girl does give the signal for the game to start) simultaneously and independently of the other driver. Typical payoffs are shown in Figure 4.5. If both drivers drive straight ahead, they hit their brakes just as they reach the edge of the cliff and are seriously injured—a large negative payoff. If both drivers swerve, that makes them chickens. They get a zero payoff, because even though their reputations are damaged, they're otherwise unharmed. Finally, if just one driver swerves, that makes him a chicken—again a negative payoff, but not as large as if he gone over the cliff. In this case, the driver who goes straight ahead is able to stop just before the edge of the cliff. He's the winner, and gets a positive payoff.

From the arrow diagram in Figure 4.5, you can see two pure strategy Nash equilibria:

(swerve, straight ahead)

and

(straight ahead, swerve)

At either of these pure strategy Nash equilibrium, one player gets to be the "chicken" while the other is the winner-hero. Those are very asymmetric outcomes; if you were going

---

[9] The tie in payoff to the firm that stays out prevents this dominance from being strict.

FIGURE 4.5 **CHICKEN**

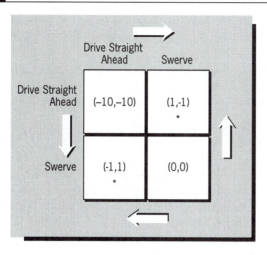

to play Chicken, would you really want to play the Nash equilibrium where you wound up being the chicken?

As with Market Niche, which has the same arrow diagram, there is a third Nash equilibrium in mixed strategies that pays each player the same. Here is a quick calculation for player 1, using the criterion that each pure strategy must pay the same:

$$EV_1(\text{drive straight ahead}) = p_x(\text{drive straight ahead})(-10) + p_2(\text{swerve})(+1)$$
$$= EV_1(\text{swerve}) = p_x(\text{drive straight ahead})(-1) + p_2(\text{swerve})(0)$$

After rearranging, this implies

$$9\, p_x(\text{drive straight ahead}) = p_2(\text{swerve})$$

and since these two probabilities must add to 1, we have

$$p_x(\text{drive straight ahead}) = 1/10,\ p_2(\text{swerve}) = 9/10$$

You can show that the same probabilities apply to driver 1 at the mixed strategy Nash equilibrium. Most of the time—nine times out of ten—a driver swerves. So the most common outcome, with probability $(9/10)^2 = 0.81$, both of the players come in as chickens. The rarest outcome, with probability $(1/10)^2 = 0.01$, has both players going over the cliff.

This equilibrium pays each player a slightly negative value. Substituting into the expression for expected value for player 1, we get

$$EV_1(\text{drive straight ahead}) = p_x(\text{drive straight ahead})(-10) + p_2(\text{swerve})(+1)$$
$$= (1/10)(-10) + (9/10)(1)$$
$$= -1 + (0.9) = -0.1$$

slightly below 0

Chicken is a famous game, not just from the movie, but again as a parable of **brinkmanship** in domestic or international affairs. Just like the cliff in the movie, countries may approach a metaphorical brink as they threaten each other with war ("drive straight ahead"), even though they really want to avoid war ("swerve"). According to the pure strategy equilibria of Chicken, one of the countries always backs down. That doesn't seem to be a very good description of fairly evenly matched countries, like India and Pakistan in their latest nuclear confrontation. Indeed, these two could be playing the mixed strategy Nash equilibrium, at which some conflicts are observed.

Although Chicken doesn't sound like a parable for a domestic economy, the same kind of strategic situation does arise when we talk about firms' competing with one another on price. Aggressive pricing is an awful lot like aggressive driving, as we show in Always Low Prices.

■ 4.8 ALWAYS LOW PRICES

In the spring of 1989, retailing giant Sears announced with great fanfare a new pricing policy, Everyday Low Prices.[10] Sears argued that it was running too many sales and that its sales were not generating enough volume. Therefore, it was going to charge low prices every day from then on. Unfortunately for Sears, the policy of everyday low prices did not reverse its troubled retailing fortunes. The policy may even have exacerbated the situation. Game theory will provide some clues as to why this is so.

When firms like Sears use price as a strategic variable, they try hard to keep price above marginal cost. Giant retailers like Wal-Mart, Kmart, Target, and Sears are household names—a definite sign of differentiation. These are also the biggest four firms in the industry. Still, there are competitive pressures driving price toward marginal cost. A simple model of **sales** that captures these features is presented here. For a much more general model, consult the Varian article, "A Model of Sales."

Two differentiated firms, called 1 and 2, are locked in price competition. Each firm has a choice between two different prices for a large appliance, a normal price, NP, and a sale price, SP, with NP higher than SP. Even the sale price is above cost. To keep things as simple as possible, unit cost is constant. For purposes of a concrete example, take the following numbers: NP = $600, SP = $500, unit cost = $450. This is the supply side of the model.

On the demand side of the model, there are two kinds of buyers. First, there are buyers who are in the market for the appliance no matter what the price is, as long as it does not exceed the normal price, NP. These buyers also don't shop around for the lowest price:; they simply take the first price they see. Such buyers are often called u-buyers (u for uninformed). Suppose there are 100 such u-buyers in the market, and they show up randomly at either firm, so each firm can expect to make 100/2 = 50 sales to u-buyers regardless of price. Second, there are buyers who are in the market for the appliance only if it is on sale, and then only if they find it at the sale price. These buyers shop around for the lowest price, and if they don't find that price, they don't buy. Such buyers are often called i-buyers (i for informed). Suppose there are 120 such i-buyers in the market. These are the buyers that a sale price might attract.

We now have enough data to construct a game matrix. First, suppose that both firms charge a normal price. In this case, each firm sells only to u-buyers (50 units) at a profit margin of $150/unit (NP − unit cost = $600 − $450) for a profit of $7,500. This is not an equilibrium. Suppose that firm 1 decides to run a sale. By cutting its price to the sale price of $500, it reduces its profit margin to $50/unit, but it increases its sales from 50 units (to the u-buyers, who don't even notice there is a sale going on) to 170 units (adding all 120 i-buyers). Firm

[10] This material is inspired in part by Hal Varian, "A Model of Sales," *American Economic Review* 70 (1980): 651–659. See also "Expensive Ad Circulars Help Precipitate Kmart President's Departure," *Wall Street Journal*, 18 January 2002, pp. B-1, B-6.

1's profits are now \$50/unit times 170 units = \$8,500. Firm 1 raises profits by lowering its price, so it is not a Nash equilibrium for all firms to charge a normal price.

What if both firms charge the sale price? That isn't a Nash equilibrium either. In this case, each firm sells to 50 u-buyers plus 60 i-buyers (the i-buyers get distributed randomly in the market, too). The profit margin for each firm is \$50 at the sale price, and so profits for each are \$50/unit times 110 units, or \$5,500. This is not an equilibrium. Take firm 2 this time, and suppose that it raises its price back up to the normal level. It triples its profit margin, from \$50 to \$150, and it still keeps its customer base of 50 u-buyers. The profit from this price increase is \$150/unit times 50 units, or \$7,500. So when all firms charge the sale price it is not an equilibrium either.

The normal form of the game Everyday Low Pricing is shown in Figure 4.6. As you can see from the arrow diagram, there are two pure strategy Nash equilibria. At each one of these, a single firm is charging the low price, and that firm is making more money. These are important for our story about retailing in America. On its way to being number 1, Wal-Mart made the crucial strategic decision to identify itself as the low-price seller in the industry—with slogans like "Always Low Prices." If a firm is able to reach the low-price strategy, it achieves a pure strategy Nash equilibrium that is very hard to dislodge. Research has shown that Wal-Mart does really charge lower prices. For instance, in a recent survey of 130 commonly purchased products conducted by UBS Warburg, a large market research firm, the average price at Target was 3.2 percent above Wal-Mart's, while the average price at Kmart was 3.8 percent above Wal-Mart's.

The game in Figure 4.6 is symmetric, so it must have a symmetric Nash equilibrium. Since the pure strategy equilibria as not symmetric, that symmetric Nash equilibrium must be in mixed strategies. In particular, at this mixed strategy equilibrium, the firms run sales with a given probability. Mixed strategies lead to a **pricing cycle,** with firms' prices constantly fluctuating between normal and sale prices as they employ their mixed strategies. At a mixed strategy, a firm charges the normal price some of the time and the sale price the rest of the time. Whatever firms do contains an element of surprise.

To nail this down, let's find this mixed strategy. Let $p(NP)$ be the probability of charging the normal price and $p(SP)$, the probability of charging the sale price.[11] At a mixed

---

FIGURE 4.6 | **EVERYDAY LOW PRICING**

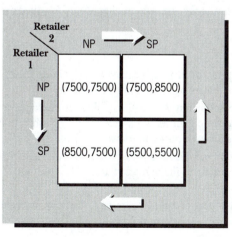

[11] The game looks the same to both firms, so we don't need to know the firms' identities in this calculation.

strategy equilibrium, the expected profit from charging the normal price, $EV(NP)$, and the expected profit from charging the sale price, $EV(SP)$, are equal. By charging the normal price, a firm locks in a profit of \$7,500. At a sale price, it expects a profit of

$$EV(SP) = \$8,500p(NP) + \$5,500p(SP)$$

At a mixed strategy equilibrium, the profits from normal pricing, \$7,500, have to equal the profits from sale pricing, $EV(SP)$. The probabilities that do this are the following:

$$p(NP)^* = 2/3; \, p(SP)^* = 1/3$$

At this mixed strategy equilibrium, each firm expects to earn \$7,500, just as if it were normal pricing.

If a firm runs sales one-third of the time, then it will defend its profits against its competitor. Its sales will be effective, because they will come as a surprise. Running sales at the right frequency will defend profits at the same level as at normal prices. Sale pricing is just like bluffing in Poker: good players do it, but they don't do it more often than necessary. Finding the mixed strategy equilibrium answers just how much surprise is needed.

It takes all firms' running sales to maintain the mixed strategy Nash equilibrium. In the period prior to Wal-Mart's dominance, this was the competitive environment in the industry. Retailer's rates of return were comparable, and they all ran sales. Once Wal-Mart established itself as the Always Low Price firm, then outcomes became quite asymmetric, with Wal-Mart as a clear #1 in market share and profits. Wal-Mart's competitors, like Sears, were in no position to improve their profits by also using a low-price strategy. That would just cut their profits further, as Sears found out the hard way in the early 1990s.

History repeats itself, sometimes eerily so. In 2001, Kmart launched its "Blue Light Always" strategy. This strategy cut prices permanently on 38,000 products, while drastically cutting back on circulars advertising weekly sale prices. On the cost side, Kmart's reasoning was clear enough: the circulars were eating up 10.4 percent of operating expenses, compared to 0.4 percent at Wal-Mart. Remember, Wal-Mart doesn't have to advertise weekly sale prices very much if it is the "Always Low Price" seller already. Although Kmart did cut its advertising costs with this move, Blue Light Always backfired on the profits front, as shoppers, accustomed to the advertising circulars, stayed away from Kmart stores in droves. In January 2002, the Kmart president who dreamed up Blue Light Always was sacked. A few days later, Kmart, beset by many troubles—including but not limited to strategic pricing blunders—filed for bankruptcy.

◼ SUMMARY

1. A pure strategy does not involve chance; a mixed strategy does. Players use a mixed strategy when they do not want their behavior to be predictable.

2. A mixed strategy Nash equilibrium is a Nash equilibrium where players use mixed strategies. The solution to Matching Pennies is a mixed strategy Nash equilibrium. One way to realize the equilibrium is for each player to toss a fair coin.

3. The game Market Niche is a parable for a perfectly contestable market, where there is room for only a limited number of firms in the market. It has both pure strategy and mixed strategy Nash equilibria.

4. Every pure strategy that is part of a mixed strategy must pay the same expected value. A mixed strategy must also obey the laws of probability. Finding a mixed strategy equilibrium

in a 2 x 2 game requires solving two systems of two linear equations in two unknowns, one such system for each player.

5. The conditions of efficiency and equity are incompatible, as the game Market Niche shows. This incompatibility reflects a similar conflict within economics at large. However, correlated equilibrium may offer a way out of the conflict.

6. Bluffing is any attempt to mislead or deceive. The purpose of bluffing is to protect the value of information that only you hold. Mixed strategies, as in Liar's Poker, offer an effective way to bluff.

7. Coordination games, such as Video System Coordination, have mixed strategy Nash equilibria that are inefficient compared to the pure strategy Nash equilibria of such games.

8. Asymmetrical Market Niche has asymmetrical pure strategy Nash equilibria and an asymmetrical mixed strategy Nash equilibrium. The most efficient of these Nash equilibria is the pure strategy equilibrium that has the most efficient firm enter the market niche; the least efficient of these Nash equilibria involves mixed strategies.

9. Chicken offers a model of brinkmanship. At its mixed strategy Nash equilibrium, conflict occurs, but only rarely.

10. Sales involve a mixed strategy. For sales to be profitable, some buyers have to be uninformed about prices.

◼ KEY TERMS

pure strategy	Matching Pennies	Asymmetrical Market Niche
pure strategy Nash equilibrium	Market Niche	Chicken
	payoff dominance	brinkmanship
mixed strategy	bluffing	sales
mixed strategy Nash equilibrium	Liar's Poker	pricing cycle
	correlated equilibrium	
probability distribution	program trading	

◼ PROBLEMS

1. Asymmetrical Matching Pennies. Suppose that player 1 wins +2 in the event of a match on heads, and player loses –2 in this same event. Otherwise the game is the same as in Figure 4.1. Find the mixed strategy equilibrium. How does the difference in payoffs affect the fairness of Matching Pennies?

2. Suppose that in Market Niche, only firm 1 is aware of the fact that a market niche has opened up. What equilibrium would you predict in this case? Should firm 2 enter the market niche if firm 1 is already there?

3. Suppose that in Liar's Poker, player 1 wins $0.60 if player 2 folds. The rest of the payoffs are the same. How does this affect the solution? Does player 1 lie more or less often with this rule change?

4. In a variant of Video System Coordination, suppose that it matters whether players coordinate on Beta or VHS in the sense that coordinating on Beta pays 2, while coordinating on VHS pays 1. Find the three Nash equilibria for this game (two pure, one mixed), and then solve, using payoff dominance and symmetry.

5. Make symmetrical Market Niche (Figure 4.2) asymmetrical in the following way. The market niche is worth 90 to firm 2. Nothing else about the game changes. Find the three Nash equilibria (two pure, one mixed) for this game.

6. Give three examples of bluffing in business, politics, or public relations. For each example, what happens to the bluffer if he or she is found out?

7. Here is a game that arises in resource economics. There are two fishing spots, one hot and one cold. The hot spot has 20 fish, whereas the cold spot has only 12 fish. There two fishers, 1 and 2. A fisher can go to either spot to fish, but only to a single spot. If two fishers go to the same spot, they divide the catch equally. Find three Nash equilibria for this game.

8. In fishing games such as that of problem 7, conflicts often break out over the fishing grounds. How might an asymmetrical equilibrium, such as that provided by the 200-mile fishing limit among nations, lead to a more efficient outcome? Also, could a correlated equilibrium work here as well?

9. Work out the mixed strategy equilibrium to Everyday Low Pricing when there are 90 u-buyers in the market instead of 100. What is the intuition behind your result?

10. In Everyday Low Pricing, suppose there are only 20 i-buyers in the market instead of 120. How does this affect the solution? Might there be times when firms would never want to run sales?

■ APPENDIX. BLUFFING IN ONE-CARD STUD POKER

Now that we have studied the basics of bluffing in Liar's Poker, we're ready to tackle a version of 1-card Stud Poker that has plenty of bluffing. To get bluffing as part of Nash equilibrium behavior, two complications are essential, beyond the 1-card Stud Poker you studied in the last chapter: more types of cards, and players see their cards.

First, the deck for 1-card Stud Poker now consists of three kinds of cards: aces (A), kings (K), and queens (Q), each appearing with frequency 1/3. The game begins with an ante of size a. Each player is dealt one card face down. The players see their own card, but not that of their opponent. Each player either bets an amount of size b or passes; this decision is taken simultaneously. From here on the rules are the same as before, with an ace beating a king beating a queen.

There are nine possible deals in this version of 1-card Stud Poker. In our notation for hands, (1's hand, 2's hand) = (A,K) when 1 is dealt an ace and 2 is dealt a king. Since the deal is fair and each card is equally likely, each of these nine deals is equally likely and has probability 1/9. Since a player sees his or her own card (three possibilities) and can either bet or pass after seeing that card (two possibilities), $2^3 = 8$ pure strategies are available to the player. They are as follows:

I: Bet an ace, bet a king, bet a queen.

II: Bet an ace, bet a king, pass a queen.

III: Bet an ace, pass a king, bet a queen.

IV: Bet an ace, pass a king, pass a queen.

V: Pass an ace, bet a king, bet a queen.

VI: Pass an ace, bet a king, pass a queen.

VII: Pass an ace, pass a king, bet a queen.

VIII: Pass an ace, pass a king, pass a queen.

The following discussion refers to these pure strategies by their roman numerals.

Strategy I bets everything—a very aggressive strategy, designed especially for defending one's ante. Strategies I, III, V, and VII all bet a queen. Since a queen can never win a showdown, all these strategies contain an element of bluffing. Strategy IV bets only when a player can't lose—a very conservative strategy, and the very opposite of bluffing. The minute you see a player using strategy IV bet, you know he or she has an ace. This strategy alerts a player's opponent to the fact that he or she is up against an ace. Strategy VIII is the ultimate in timidity—it never bets. Strategy VII is obviously perverse—it only bets a card that can't win (a queen). This strategy is just as informative as strategy IV—only it lets the opponent know that a player can't beat him or her.[12]

Not all these strategies deserve our attention. For instance, you can show that strategies V, VI, VII, and VIII, all of which share the feature that they pass an ace—a card that can't lose—are all bad. Every one of them is dominated by the strategy that bets the ace instead (I dominates V, II dominates VI, and so on). The only strategies that really deserve our attention are I, II, III, and IV, all of which share the feature that they bet an ace. Next, the game is symmetrical: both players have the same strategies and get on average the same quality of cards. Therefore, if we solve the game for player 1, say, then that solution also works for player 2. Next, again because of symmetry, if the same strategy is played against itself, I against I for instance, then the strategy breaks even. Finally, and again because of symmetry plus the fact that Poker is zero sum, the payoff for I versus II when player 1 uses strategy I is minus the payoff of II versus I when player 1 uses strategy II. All of this means we have to compute only six pairs of strategies (I vs. II, I vs. III, I vs. IV, II vs. III, II vs. IV, and III vs. IV). The results of this computation are shown in Figure 4.7.

FIGURE 4.7 ONE-CARD STUD POKER (PAYOFF MATRIX, PLAYER I)

Player 1 \ Player 2	I	II	III	IV
I	$(0,0)$	$\left(\dfrac{a-2b}{9},\dfrac{2b-a}{9}\right)$	$\left(\dfrac{2a}{9},\dfrac{-2a}{9}\right)$	$\left(\dfrac{4a-2b}{9},\dfrac{2b-4a}{9}\right)$
II	$\left(\dfrac{2b-a}{9},\dfrac{a-2b}{9}\right)$	$(0,0)$	$\left(\dfrac{b}{9},\dfrac{-b}{9}\right)$	$\left(\dfrac{a-b}{9},\dfrac{b-a}{9}\right)$
III	$\left(\dfrac{-2a}{9},\dfrac{2a}{9}\right)$	$\left(\dfrac{-b}{9},\dfrac{b}{9}\right)$	$(0,0)$	$\left(\dfrac{2a-b}{9},\dfrac{b-2a}{9}\right)$
IV	$\left(\dfrac{2b-4a}{9},\dfrac{4a-2b}{9}\right)$	$\left(\dfrac{b-a}{9},\dfrac{a-b}{9}\right)$	$\left(\dfrac{b-2a}{9},\dfrac{2a-b}{9}\right)$	$(0,0)$

[12] Of course, since the players are moving simultaneously, this information is not immediately available.

Notice that there are only two unequivocal cases in which one strategy beats another, regardless of the size of the ante and the size of the bet. These are I versus III, which pays $2a/9$, and II versus III, which pays $b/9$. Every other pairing could go either way, depending on the size of the ante relative to the bet. This situation has implications for the solution. Let's fix the ante ($a = \$1$) and vary the bet b. Suppose the bet is $2. Substituting into Figure 4.7 yields Figure 4.8. There is a pure strategy equilibrium at (IV,IV); indeed, this is the only Nash equilibrium. Thus the solution to 1-card Stud Poker (with queens) when the ante is $1 and the bet is $2 is to bet only an ace. The bet is too large relative to the ante to risk losing it on hands that can be beaten. Each player breaks even at this solution, which is to be expected from symmetry.

Now suppose that the bet is the same size as the ante, $1. The resulting payoff matrix is given in Figure 4.9. The unique pure strategy Nash equilibrium occurs at (II,II). Each player bets both an ace and a king, but passes a queen. Again, no bluffing is present, and both players break even. Somewhere between a bet size of $1 and $2, the solution of the game jumps from strategy II to strategy IV. It is in this zone, where the solution jumps, that mixed strategy Nash equilibria and bluffing are found.

Set the bet at $b = \$1.50$. Figure 4.10 shows the payoffs that result. Notice that neither II nor IV is a pure strategy Nash equilibrium. Indeed, there is no pure strategy equilibrium, so this size bet lies in the zone we just talked about. Now we have to look for a mixed strategy solution to Poker. You can check that the following probabilities are the mixed strategy equilibrium we are looking for:

$$p(\text{I})\emptyset = 1/7; \ p(\text{II})\emptyset = 2/7; \text{ and } p(\text{IV})\emptyset = 4/7$$

FIGURE 4.8 ONE-CARD STUD POKER (PAYOFF MATRIX, PLAYER 1, $a = \$1$, $b = \$2$)

		I	II	III	IV
	Player 2 ↘ Player 1				
I		$(0,0)$	$\left(\frac{-3}{9}, \frac{3}{9}\right)$	$\left(\frac{2}{9}, \frac{-2}{9}\right)$	$(0,0)$
II		$\left(\frac{3}{9}, \frac{-3}{9}\right)$	$(0,0)$	$\left(\frac{2}{9}, \frac{-2}{9}\right)$	$\left(\frac{-1}{9}, \frac{1}{9}\right)$
III		$\left(\frac{-2}{9}, \frac{2}{9}\right)$	$\left(\frac{-2}{9}, \frac{2}{9}\right)$	$(0,0)$	$(0,0)$
IV		$(0,0)$	$\left(\frac{1}{9}, \frac{-1}{9}\right)$	$(0,0)$	$(0,0)$ *

FIGURE 4.9 ONE-CARD STUD POKER, (PAYOFF MATRIX, PLAYER 1, $a = b = \$1$)

Player 1 \ Player 2	I	II	III	IV
I	$(0,0)$	$\left(\frac{-1}{9}, \frac{1}{9}\right)$	$\left(\frac{2}{9}, \frac{-2}{9}\right)$	$\left(\frac{2}{9}, \frac{-2}{9}\right)$
II	$\left(\frac{1}{9}, \frac{-1}{9}\right)$	$(0,0)$ *	$\left(\frac{1}{9}, \frac{-1}{9}\right)$	$(0,0)$
III	$\left(\frac{-2}{9}, \frac{2}{9}\right)$	$\left(\frac{-1}{9}, \frac{1}{9}\right)$	$(0,0)$	$\left(\frac{1}{9}, \frac{-1}{9}\right)$
IV	$\left(\frac{-2}{9}, \frac{2}{9}\right)$	$(0,0)$	$\left(\frac{-1}{9}, \frac{1}{9}\right)$	$(0,0)$

FIGURE 4.10 ONE-CARD STUD POKER (PAYOFF MATRIX, PLAYER 1, $a = \$1, b = \$1.50$)

Player 1 \ Player 2	I	II	III	IV
I	$(0,0)$	$\left(\frac{-2}{9}, \frac{2}{9}\right)$	$\left(\frac{2}{9}, \frac{-2}{9}\right)$	$\left(\frac{1}{9}, \frac{-1}{9}\right)$
II	$\left(\frac{2}{9}, \frac{-2}{9}\right)$	$(0,0)$	$\left(\frac{1.5}{9}, \frac{-1.5}{9}\right)$	$\left(\frac{-0.5}{9}, \frac{0.5}{9}\right)$
III	$\left(\frac{-2}{9}, \frac{2}{9}\right)$	$\left(\frac{-1.5}{9}, \frac{1.5}{9}\right)$	$(0,0)$	$\left(\frac{0.5}{9}, \frac{-0.5}{9}\right)$
IV	$\left(\frac{-1}{9}, \frac{1}{9}\right)$	$\left(\frac{0.5}{9}, \frac{-0.5}{9}\right)$	$\left(\frac{-0.5}{9}, \frac{0.5}{9}\right)$	$(0,0)$

There is a considerable amount of bluffing going on according to this mixed strategy. To see this, let's consider what this mixed strategy does on the basis of 21 deals. In 7 of 21 deals, a player is dealt an ace. Since strategies I, II, and IV all bet an ace, in these 7 deals the player always bets an ace. In another 7 of 21 deals, a player is dealt a king. Strategies I and II bet a king, which happens 3 of 7 times ($1/7 + 2/7$), whereas strategy IV passes a king, which happens 4 of 7 times. This strategy is already deceptive: sometimes this player bets a king, sometimes he or she doesn't. In yet another 7 of 21 times, a player is dealt a queen. Strategy I bets this queen, which happens 1 of 7 times, whereas II and III pass the queen, which happens 6 of 7 times. In 21 deals, the player using this strategy bluffs in the purest form (betting a card that cannot win, a queen) once, a bluffing rate of 1/21 (5 percent) on hands that cannot win. This level of bluffing is on the order of magnitude of what you observe in real-world Poker games involving good players. The whole point of this mixed strategy is to throw the opponent off, to prevent the opponent from drawing any information from the fact that a player bet—and it does this admirably. Play this strategy and no one will know what your cards are. This strategy also breaks even:

$$EV(\text{I}) = EV(\text{II}) = EV(\text{IV}) = 0$$

As usual in Poker, you go to an awful lot of work just so you won't lose money. In order to make money, you still have to find a sucker who doesn't play the right strategy. Then your strategy *will* make money.[13]

---

[13] For more material on 1-card Stud Poker, go to www.indiana.edu/~weur/_faculty/_gardner/poker.html.

C H A P T E R   5

n-Person Games in Normal Form

Every game that we have studied so far, such as Battle of the Networks, Let's Make a Deal, Video System Coordination, Cigarette Television Advertising, Competitive Advantage, and Market Niche, had exactly two players. All these games, however, can be played by more than two players. There is nothing sacred about the number 2. For instance, there are more than two television networks, more than two cigarette companies, and more than two principals usually involved in putting together a movie deal. Sometimes it makes a big difference whether there are exactly two players in a game or more than two. Since we want to apply game theory to the real world, we need to be able to write down and find good Nash equilibria of games that have more than two players. The goal of this chapter is to meet that need.

This chapter begins with two main results for 2-person games—the theorem for games like Chess and the solution theorem for 2-person, zero-sum games—and shows that these results no longer hold when there are three players, one of whom plays the role of a spoiler. Next, 3-person versions of Competitive Advantage and Market Niche are introduced to show what difference a third player makes, and the method for writing down and solving Video System Coordination and Let's Make a Deal with three players is explained. Cigarette Television Advertising with four players—the big four tobacco companies in 1971—is described. A famous episode in U.S. history, Stonewalling at Watergate, is a 3-person Prisoner's Dilemma that brought down the Nixon presidency.

For games with more than three players, the concept of symmetry provides a useful shortcut, both for modeling the game and for finding symmetric Nash equilibria. A symmetrical game looks the same to every player. The condition of payoff symmetry holds that the solution of a symmetrical game should pay each player the same amount. *N*-Person Stag Hunt offers some especially valuable lessons about free riding and the choice between pure and mixed strategy Nash equilibrium. The chapter then presents a phenomenon known as the tragedy of the commons, which occurs when a resource, such as rangeland, is used in common by a large number of players. The tragedy of the commons is a parable for negative aspects of global environmental change. It is also bad for power companies, as the game Geothermal Tragedy of the Commons shows. The tragedy of the commons can be recreated in the laboratory. Laboratory experiments in game theory are an exciting way to enhance understanding of strategic behavior, and they lead to some surprises, too.

◼ 5.1 FUNDAMENTAL DIFFERENCES WITH THREE PLAYERS: THE SPOILER

When there are three players in a game instead of two, fundamental differences arise. It is as if there were a continental divide between the cases $n = 2$, and $n = 3$ (the parameter n refers to the number of players from now on); sometimes a result gets across the divide and sometimes it doesn't. One result that definitely doesn't hold for $n = 3$ is the theorem for games like Chess (section 1.5). The easiest way to show that a result is not general is to provide a **counterexample,** an example that runs counter to the generalization.

Figure 5.1 shows an extensive form game called Spoiler, for reasons that will soon become apparent. Spoiler has perfect information; the players move in sequence; it is win, lose, or draw; and it is finite. Unlike the determinate games of Chapter 1, it has three players. Players 1 and 2 get payoffs but do not actually have any choices to make. A player who gets a payoff but does not have any choices to make is called a **strategic dummy.** In this game, only player 3 has any choices to make. Player 3 chooses either top or bottom. Payoff vectors **u** are of the form $\mathbf{u} = (u_1, u_2, u_3)$. Player 3 is indifferent about top and bottom—he or she loses no matter what—therefore, both get arrows. Then player 1 could win—player 3 chooses top and the payoff vector is (w,l,l)—or player 2 could win—player 3 chooses bottom and the payoff vector is (l,w,l). For this game, it is not the case that exactly one of the following is true: player 1 wins, player 2 wins, player 3 wins, or the result is a draw. Two of these are possible: player 1 wins, or player 2 wins. That's the counterexample.

You might wonder why player 3 would bother to play, given that this player loses no matter what. We haven't given player 3 an outside option to playing the game in Figure 5.1. But if we did give player 3 an outside option that was even worse than losing, then the counterexample would still stand. Indeed, we could make the counterexample of Figure 5.1 much more complicated, for instance by having lots of moves for players 1 and 2. As long

FIGURE 5.1 INDETERMINATE THREE-PERSON GAME

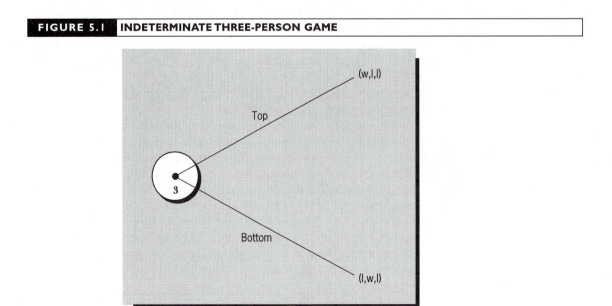

as at the end of the game the determination boils down to a move by player 3 and the payoffs attached to that move are (w,l,l) and (l,w,l), the game is indeterminate.

Another result that cannot be generalized to three players is the solution theorem for 2-person, zero-sum games (section 3.4). Once there are more than two players, a zero-sum game in normal form can have Nash equilibria that do not have the same payoffs. To follow the counterexample for this case, one more introductory remark is needed. As usual, player 1 controls the rows of the matrix and player 2 controls the columns of the matrix. Now, the additional player, player 3, controls the matrix. The counterexample given, now in normal form, shows that the solution theorem is not true for $n = 3$ (see Figure 5.2). Let the utility of winning be 1 and the utility of losing, $-1/2$. Since players 1 and 2 are strategic dummies, the matrix they play on is 1 x 1. Player 3 picks either the matrix on the left, corresponding to the move Top in Figure 5.1, or the matrix on the right, corresponding to the move Bottom in Figure 5.1. Player 3 is indifferent between these two choices, as shown by the two-headed arrow between the two matrices. Player 3 loses no matter what he or she does. We have two Nash equilibria with very different payoffs, $(1,-1/2,-1/2)$ and $(-1/2,1,-1/2)$. Player 3, while maximizing his or her own utility, can be simultaneously maximizing or minimizing player 1's utility—all because player 2 is also part of the picture.

There is an explanation for what is going on in these games, at least for politics or sports. In politics, a player is a called a **spoiler** if he or she cannot win but can determine who does win. For example, take the 1992 presidential election: 1 Bush Sr., 2 Clinton, 3 Perot. Perot can't win, at least not after dropping out of the race in June. If Perot stays out of the race, Bush Sr. gets just enough of the voters in the middle to win. If Perot gets back in the race, he pulls just enough votes away from Bush Sr. that Clinton wins. Perot plays the spoiler in this campaign, just as shown in Figures 5.1 and 5.2. In a two-way race, no one can play a spoiler; in a three-way race, there is room for a spoiler like Perot. Indeed, it appears that Perot wanted especially to see fellow Texan Bush Sr. lose in 1992, so Perot's utility function included more than just his own loss as an argument. It is possible that the same thing happened again in the 2000 presidential election, with Green Party candidate Nader playing the role of the spoiler.

You can have spoilers in team sports, too. Any individual game between two teams is win, lose, or draw. However, when an entire league of teams is fighting for a championship, then a team that is out of the running could play the spoiler. For all of you USA men's ice hockey fans, 1980 was a magic year—the last time the United States won the gold medal in the Olympics. You could win a bar bet with the statement, "I'll bet you think that when the USA beat the USSR 4 to 3, they won the gold medal." The problem with this statement is

FIGURE 5.2   MULTIPLE SOLUTIONS FOR 3-PERSON ZERO-SUM GAME

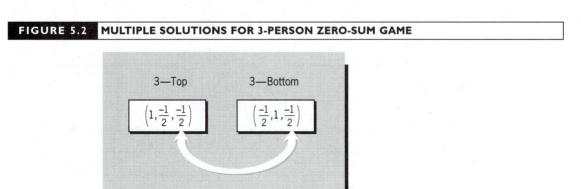

that the Olympics weren't over yet, and the United States still had to play Finland, a tough team. Finland was out of the medal race, but it could have played the spoiler. If Finland had beaten the United States, the USSR would have won the gold medal. As it turned out, the United States beat Finland 4 to 1. That's when the United States clinched its gold medal.

When spoilers don't occur, then the results for 2-player games work for 3-player games as well. The next section shows that this is true for Competitive Advantage and Market Niche.

■ 5.2 COMPETITIVE ADVANTAGE AND MARKET NICHE WITH THREE PLAYERS

Recall the game Competitive Advantage from Chapter 3. This game can actually be played by more than two firms. Let's consider what Competitive Advantage looks like with three firms, labeled 1, 2, and 3. As before, each firm has a choice between staying put or adopting the new technology. If no firm adopts the new technology, then there is no competitive advantage and the payoff vector is (0,0,0). If exactly one firm adopts the new technology, then that firm gets the competitive advantage a, while each firm at a competitive disadvantage loses $a/2$. Thus if only firm 1 adopts the new technology, then the payoff vector is $(a, -a/2, -a/2)$. You can think of this as firm 1 taking market share away from both firm 2 and firm 3. If exactly two firms adopt the new technology, then these two firms split the competitive advantage, and the firm at a disadvantage loses a. Thus, if firms 1 and 2 adopt the new technology, the payoff vector is $(a/2, a/2, -a)$. The firm that lags behind loses big. Finally, if all three firms adopt the new technology, there is again no competitive advantage and the payoff vector is (0,0,0). Figure 5.3 shows the normal form of Competitive Advantage with three players.

FIGURE 5.3 | **COMPETITIVE ADVANTAGE, THREE FIRMS**

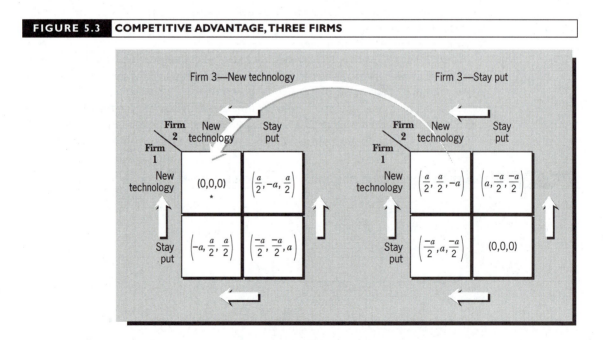

There is one new aspect of the arrow diagram you should be aware of. When firm 3 is choosing, it must compare identically located cells across the matrices—northwest with northwest, southwest with southwest, and so on. As you can see from the arrow diagram in Figure 5.3, the unique equilibrium occurs when each firm adopts the new technology. This is precisely what happens when there are only two firms. No firm can afford to be left behind in the race to adopt the new technology—this is just as true for *n* players as it is for two or three players. This is our first example of a result that extends from two players to more than two players. Indeed, this Nash equilibrium is the strict dominance solution for the 3-player game, just as it was for the 2-player game.

Let's turn to Market Niche with three firms—1, 2, and 3 (recall Figure 4.2). As before, each firm has to choose between entering the market niche or staying out, and there is room in the market niche for only a single firm. Any firm that stays out breaks even. If exactly one firm enters the market niche, it gains 100. If more than one firm enters the market niche, each firm that does so loses 50. The normal form of Market Niche with three players is shown in Figure 5.4.

As you can see from the arrow diagram, Market Niche has three pure strategy Nash equilibria: (stay out, stay out, enter), (enter, stay out, stay out), and (stay out, enter, stay out). At each of these pure strategy Nash equilibria, exactly one firm occupies the market niche and the other two firms stay out. Each of these pure strategy Nash equilibria has 100 percent efficiency. However, their payoff consequences are very different: each firm would like to be the one that enters the market niche. These outcomes are lopsided.

In addition to the three asymmetrical pure strategy Nash equilibria, there is a symmetrical mixed strategy Nash equilibrium. At this Nash equilibrium, each firm uses the same mixed strategy and gets the same payoff. To compute the mixed strategy that each firm

FIGURE 5.4   MARKET NICHE, THREE FIRMS

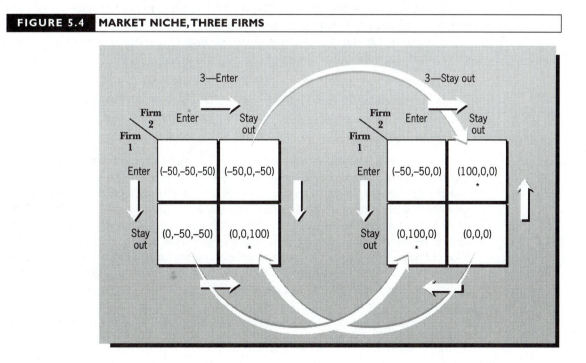

uses, let p(enter) be the probability that a firm enters the market niche and p(stay out) be the probability that a firm stays out of the market niche. Consider the choice facing firm 1. If firm 1 enters the market, it encounters the following probability distribution:

With probability p(enter)^2, two other firms are present.

With probability $2p$(enter) p(stay out), one other firm is present.

With probability p(stay out)^2, no other firm is present.[1]

Thus, the expected value to firm 1 of entering the market niche, EV_1(enter), given the mixed strategies played by its competitors, is

$$EV_1(\text{enter}) = (-50)[1 - p(\text{stay out})^2] + (100)p(\text{stay out})^2$$

because if one or both other firms are present, firm 1 loses 50. Firm 1's alternative is to stay out, and that pays a sure 0, hence an expected 0, EV_1(stay out) = 0. Setting these two expected values equal to each other, we get

$$0 = (-50)[1 - p(\text{stay out})^2] + (100)p(\text{stay out})^2$$

where $[1 - p(\text{stay out})^2]$ is the probability that at least one other firm is present. We now have one equation in one unknown, p(stay out). Solving this equation, we arrive at

$$p(\text{stay out})^* = .58$$

At the mixed strategy Nash equilibrium, the probability that an individual firm will stay out of the market is .58; the probability that it will enter the market, .42. At this symmetrical equilibrium, each firm expects to break even. Notice that the maximum sum of payoffs is 100, while the minimum sum of payoffs is −100. So the efficiency of this Nash equilibrium is $[0 - (-100)]/[100 - (-100)] = 50\%$, compared to the 100 percent efficiency earned by any of the pure strategy Nash equilibria.

From the standpoint of the market, the distribution of number of firms in the market niche, according to the mixed strategy equilibriums is as follows:

With probability p(enter)^{*3} = $(.42)^3$ = .08, three firms enter.

With probability $3p$(enter)^{*2} p(stay out)* = $3(.42)^2(.58)$ = .31, two firms enter.

With probability $3p$(enter)* p(stay out)^{*2} = $3 (.42)(.58)^2$ = .42, one firm enters.

With probability p(stay out)^{*3} = $(.58)^3$ = .19, no firm enters.

It is very likely (probability =.81 = .08 + .31 + .42) that the market will be served by at least one firm. It is also rather likely (probability = .39 = .08 + .31 that the market will be overserved, with 2 or 3 firms. This high probability of overserving the market is the price the firms will pay if they are all to get the same payoff—and that payoff is 0. Although in one respect—namely, the firms all break even—this outcome is like perfect competition, in another respect it is not. The only outcomes that guarantee that the market niche will be filled, the pure strategy equilibria, must be upheld by some form of limitation on free entry, perhaps by a correlated equilibrium. Only in that way does exactly one firm know that, at equilibrium, it is safe to enter the market niche.

---

[1] These probabilities are derived from the binomial probability distribution. You can also generate them from a tree diagram, with random devices in the role of players 2 and 3.

■ 5.3 Three-Player Versions of Video System Coordination, Let's Make a Deal, and Cigarette Television Advertising

This section reviews three more games in which spoilers play no role; consequently, the outcomes are fairly close to those of the 2-player versions. Consider first Video System Coordination, shown in Figure 5.5. As in the 2-player version, in the 3-player version every firm has to be on the same system in order for networking to take place. You can think of these players as three firms under the same corporate umbrella—unless they are on the same system, they can't make anything. Either system, Beta or VHS, does equally well. As you can see from the arrow diagram, there are two pure strategy Nash equilibria, one with all firms on the Beta system and another with all firms on the VHS system. The payoffs associated with these outcomes are the same, so we can't say that one is better than the other.

Just as in the 2-player version of Video System Coordination, in the 3-player game there is an additional Nash equilibrium in mixed strategies. At this mixed strategy Nash equilibrium, it is easy to show that each firm is on either system with equal probability:

$$p(\text{Beta})^\star = p(\text{VHS})^\star = .5$$

With probability $.5^3 = .125$, all firms are on the Beta system; with probability .125, on the VHS system. Thus, the chance that firms coordinate on some system is only 25 percent. This result implies a large failure-to-coordinate rate of 75 percent. Things only get worse as the number, *n*, of firms grows. You can show that the chances of coordinating in the *n*-player

FIGURE 5.5 **VIDEO SYSTEM COORDINATION, THREE FIRMS**

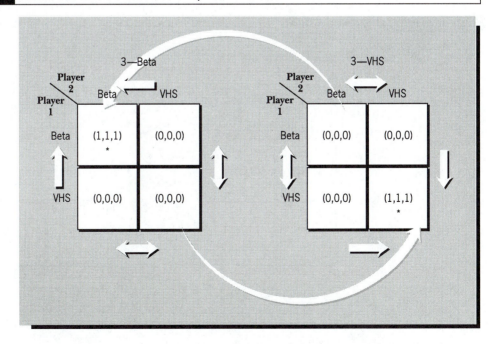

version of Video System Coordination at the mixed strategy equilibrium go to zero as *n* gets large. The moral of all this is that coordination is too important to be left to chance. Firms must somehow solve the game they are in for one of its pure strategy Nash equilibria or pay the consequences. One obvious way to solve the coordination problem is by a focal point. For instance, setting an **industry standard** provides a focal point. Although VHS did not start out as the industry standard, it did become one later.

Next let's look at Let's Make a Deal, now with three players. The three players are 1, the movie star; 2, the director; and 3, the producer. The producer is important because he or she usually arranges the financing for the movie. As before, there is $15 million at stake. If all three players say yes, they split the $15 million equally. If one of them says no, then it's no deal and each player gets $0. The normal form of this game is shown in Figure 5.6.

As you can see from the arrow diagram, Let's Make a Deal with three players has five pure strategy equilibria. One of these pays well—everybody says yes. All the rest pay poorly—nobody gets anything. Any strategy vector where at least two people say no is an equilibrium. This situation explains why there are so many bad equilibria. However, saying no is weakly dominated by saying yes. If everyone else says yes, then saying yes pays $5 million while saying no pays $0. In every other case, saying either yes or no pays $0. That's enough for weak dominance. Hence, by favoring the Nash equilibrium that is both the weak dominance solution and efficient, we solve Let's Make a Deal with the Yes vector: (yes, yes, yes).

As the final multiplayer game in this section, consider Cigarette Television Advertising. The cigarette companies are labeled companies 1, 2, 3, and 4 to protect their anonymity. When we looked at two cigarette companies in the case in Chapter 3, each company had a strictly dominant strategy to advertise on television. This situation holds true for four companies as well. The solution of the game is for each company to advertise on television. In

---

FIGURE 5.6 **LET'S MAKE A DEAL, THREE PLAYERS (PAYOFFS IN MILLIONS OF DOLLARS)**

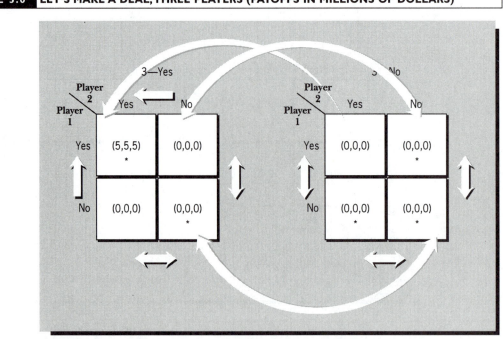

the 2-player version, when both companies advertised on television their profits were less than when both refrained from advertising on television. Again, this holds true with four cigarette companies. All four cigarette manufacturers made more money when the government banned television advertising.

The phenomenon where every player in an *n*-player game has a strictly dominant strategy that leads to an inefficient outcome has a special name: the **prisoner's dilemma.** You've seen the 2-player version of this game already. The *n*-player version pervades our lives as well, and we need to be alert to its danger. The following famous episode from twentieth-century U.S. history shows what happens when the incentives of the dilemma are present.

■ 5.4 STONEWALLING WATERGATE

On June 17, 1972, burglars broke into the headquarters of the Democratic National Committee at the Watergate Hotel in Washington, D.C.[2] Thus began a strategic odyssey that ended with Richard Nixon's resignation from the presidency 2 years later. This section considers one of many aspects of the Watergate affair, namely, the way those closest to the president dealt with the investigating authorities.

White House spokesmen publicly denounced the break-in as a third-rate burglary and continued to run the Committee to Reelect the President (CREEP) as if nothing had happened. Behind the scenes, however, plenty was happening. In White House tape recordings dated June 21, 1972, and subsequently released by the National Archives, we can hear the president discussing what to do about the break-in. Nowadays, this kind of activity is called damage control. According to the Associated Press report of the tape, Nixon said, in a mocking tone, "It's a horrible thing to bug. . . . Most people around the country think it's probably routine, everybody's trying to bug everybody else, it's politics. That's my view." Then he added, "I don't think you're going to see a great, great uproar in the country about the Republican Committee trying to bug the Democratic headquarters."[3]

The Nixon administration decided to control the damage by a combination of denial and cover-up. In the weeks that followed, three members of the Nixon team—in alphabetical order, John W. Dean III, counsel to the president; John D. Ehrlichman, assistant to the president for domestic affairs; and H. R. Haldeman, White House chief of staff—took full charge of the Watergate damage control plan. The primary objective of the plan was to reelect the president. If it could be proved that the White House was involved in the break-in, the president's overwhelming lead in the polls would be jeopardized. The secondary objective of the plan was to keep the cover-up itself covered up. Obstruction of justice and conspiracy were just two of the felony charges available to federal prosecutors in the event that the cover-up failed. The White House even coined a new word to describe this aspect of the plan: **stonewalling.** Just as Union troops ran into a stone wall whenever they attacked the Confederate general Thomas (Stonewall) Jackson, so federal investigators would run into a stone wall whenever they tried to attack the White House cloak of silence.

In the 1972 election, Nixon won a landslide victory against McGovern, carrying 49 of 50 states. CREEP had done its job, but the stonewalling had only just begun. The plan at this stage was given a code name: Operation Candor. The three players in the game were

[2] This material is inspired in part by Carl Bernstein and Robert Woodward, All the President's Men (New York: Simon & Schuster, 1974).

[3] See the Bloomington (Ind.) Herald-Telephone, 15 May 15 1993.

the three White House insiders entrusted with carrying out Operation Candor: Dean, Ehrlichman, and Haldeman. Boiled down to its simplest terms, each player had a pair of strategies. A player could stonewall or talk. Stonewalling meant refusing to cooperate with federal prosecutors, making reporters' lives as difficult as possible, and keeping up the pressure on all lower-ranked personnel involved. Given the speedy apprehension and conviction of the Watergate burglars, even this strategy invited some loss—and the prospect of loss grew, the closer the investigation got to the White House. Talking meant either talking to the federal prosecutors, talking to reporters, such as Woodward and Bernstein, or talking to the player's own lawyer. Talking would begin to rip apart the cloak of secrecy and would leave coconspirators to twist in the wind, as the White House tapes put it.

Again keeping things simple, there were four possible outcomes to the game. Once reporters and federal investigators got sufficiently close to White House involvement in the break-in—in March 1974, when indictments were handed down—the payoff to stonewalling looked pretty bad. Even if all three players toughed it out, there was still a good chance that they would get felony convictions and do some hard time. Call the utility of this outcome –3. The least undesirable outcome was to talk, especially if the player talked to federal authorities and copped his own plea. We won't distinguish here between talking to the federal authorities and other forms of talking. For instance, a player could accomplish much the same thing by talking to his own lawyers and instructing them to start negotiations with the federal prosecutor in the hope of leniency. In any event, if a player talked, the payoff was –2, rather better than –3. Also, if a player talked, he left his coconspirators to twist in the wind, a payoff of –5. Finally, if all players talked, the prosecutors had an open-and-shut case, but would ask for slightly less than maximum penalties. Call the utility of this outcome –4. The game that results is shown in Figure 5.7.

FIGURE 5.7 | **STONEWALLING WATERGATE (D = DEAN; E = EHRLICHMAN; H = HALDEMAN)**

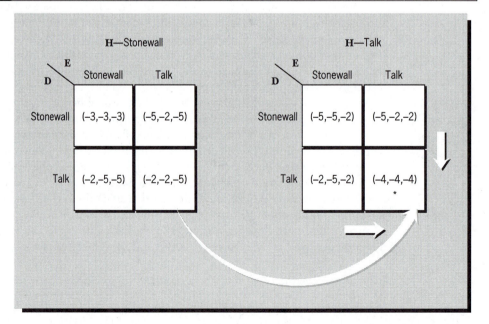

As you can see from the arrow diagram, there is a unique pure strategy Nash equilibrium. At this Nash equilibrium, Dean, Ehrlichman, and Haldeman all talk. This Nash equilibrium is also the strictly dominant solution. And that's exactly what happened. The temptation to give up on stonewalling and seek a better deal from the prosecutors was too much to resist. The outcome for each player is worse than if he had been the only one to quit stonewalling. Indeed—and this is what makes the Prisoner's Dilemma so fiendish—the outcome is worse than if they had all stuck to stonewalling in the first place. The payoff to stonewalling is (–3,–3,–3); hardly great, but better than the (–4,–4,–4) at equilibrium. The moral of the story is, as long as there is a more attractive option available than staying inside a conspiracy, someone is going to take it. There is a good strategic reason why cover-ups uncover themselves.

At the end of the story, all the players—Dean, Ehrlichman, and Haldeman—met the ultimate fate of players in Prisoners' Dilemma: they went to prison. Their boss, President Nixon, resigned soon afterward. All the players of this particular game have now passed away. But contemporary versions of the game continue to be played—almost every Wall Street scandal of 2002 has an *n*-person Prisoner's Dilemma being played as part of the scandal. See if you can work out the strategic details for one of these, for instance Imclone insider trading.

■ 5.5 Symmetry and Games with Many Players

Once a game has more than three players, or each player has more than eight strategies or so, writing down the entire game in extensive or normal form becomes rather impractical. We need a notation that allows us to study more involved games. Just as utility functions of many variables came to the rescue in Chapter 3, so they will come in handy here.

Suppose that there are *n* players, indexed by the letter $i = 1, 2, \ldots, n$. Each player *i* has a set of available strategies, $X(i)$. The strategy that player *i* actually chooses, x_i, must belong to the set of strategies $X(i)$. Finally, each player *i* has a utility function of the form $u_i(x)$, where $\mathbf{x} = (x_1, x_2, \ldots, x_n)$ is a vector of the strategies chosen by all the players individually. This compact notation covers every *n*-person game studied so far, including 2-person games.

To see how this notation works in an example, consider Video System Coordination with three firms. First we need to code the strategies. For each firm *i*, let $X(i) = \{0, 1\}$, where $x_i = 1$ means that firm *i* is on the Beta system, and $x_i = 0$ means that firm *i* is on the VHS system. Then we can write the utility function for firm *i* succinctly as

$$u_i(\mathbf{x}) = 1 \text{ if } \sum x_i = 3 \text{ or } 0$$
$$u_i(\mathbf{x}) = 0 \text{ otherwise}$$

where $\sum$ is the symbol for "sum." This functional notation contains all the information in Figure 5.5. See if you can write down Competitive Advantage, Market Niche, and Let's Make a Deal in this notation.

This notation enables us to write down games with many players, each with many strategies. All we need to do is specify the utility function of each player as a function of *n* variables, one variable for each player's strategy. We will soon put this notation to work in solving games.

First, however, we need a new concept, *symmetry*. Intuitively, a game is a **symmetrical game** when it looks the same to each player. "Looks the same" boils down to two major considerations. First, each player *i* has the same set of strategies $X(i)$; one player does not have more strategies than, or different strategies from, another. Second, every pair of players i and j have the same utility function in the sense that, given the strategies of all the other players, interchanging the strategies of players interchanges their payoffs:

$$u_i \,(x_i, x_j, \text{rest of strategies}) = u_j \,(x_j, x_i, \text{rest of strategies})$$

In particular, when two players choose the same strategy, they get the same payoff.

As an example of a symmetrical game, consider Let's Make a Deal. To check the first condition, note that the strategies Yes and No are available to each player. To check the second condition, note that when they all say yes, they get the same payoff ($5 million), and when they all say no, they get the same payoff ($0). Finally, to check the rest of the payoff **interchange condition,** taking $1 = i$ and $2 = j$ and letting Yes = 1 and No = 0,

$$u_1(1,0,0) = u_2(0,1,0) = 0$$
$$u_1(0,1,0) = u_2(1,0,0) = 0$$
$$u_1(1,0,1) = u_2(0,1,1) = 0$$
$$u_1(0,1,1) = u_2(1,0,1) = 0$$

You can check the interchange condition for every other pair of players; the result is exactly the same as the one shown here. The game Let's Make a Deal looks just the same to the movie star as to the director as to the producer.

Symmetrical games are important for two reasons. First, they provide good approximations to complicated games when the players are not very different, and they are easier to solve. Second, if a symmetrical game has a Nash equilibrium, then it has *at least one* symmetric Nash equilibrium in *either pure or mixed strategies.* Nash himself proved this in his 1950 paper.[4] This is important, because a symmetrical game looks the same to every player, so there is no reason to believe that one player has an advantage over another. All players have equal opportunity. The play of a symmetrical game ought to reflect this equality of opportunity, by the play of a **symmetrical Nash equilibrium.**[5]

To see the power of symmetry, consider 3-player Let's Make a Deal, which has five Nash equilibria. Two of these, the Yes vector and the No vector, are symmetrical. The three other Nash equilibria are asymmetrical: two players do different things. Even these three asymmetrical Nash equilibria satisfy **payoff symmetry,** however, since every player gets paid $0. This game already shows that a symmetrical game can have asymmetrical Nash equilibria.

Now compare the two symmetric Nash equilibria on efficiency grounds. The symmetric Nash equilibrium where every player says Yes has an efficiency of 100 percent, while the symmetric Nash equilibrium where every player says No has an efficiency of 0 percent. Symmetry, together with efficiency, rules out all Nash equilibrium except (yes, yes, yes). This is the right way to play Let's Make a Deal with three, or many more than three, players.[6]

The combination of efficiency and symmetry creates a powerful focal point for selecting one Nash equilibrium among many, as you will see repeatedly in your study of game theory.

Market Niche (with two or three players) provides an example of a symmetrical game whose asymmetrical pure strategy equilibria do not satisfy payoff symmetry. Recall Figures

---

[4] The proof is tricky and requires some abstract algebra, which you are spared! See J. Nash, "Noncooperative Games," Annals of Mathematics 54(1951): 289–295, for details.

[5] Recall, however, the conflict raised in the last chapter between efficiency and equity, which is reflected here as well.

[6] For an extensive argument for applying symmetry prior to payoff dominance, see John Harsanyi and Reinhard Selten, *A General Theory of Equilibrium Selection in Games* (Cambridge, Mass.: MIT Press, 1988).

4.2 and 5.4. Market Niche satisfies the interchange and diagonal conditions: the asymmetrical equilibria are (enter, stay out) and (stay out, enter), and the firm that enters gets a much higher payoff. The only symmetrical equilibrium of Market Niche is in mixed strategies.

■ 5.6 SOLVING SYMMETRICAL GAMES WITH MANY STRATEGIES

When the players in a symmetrical game have a lot of strategies, we can exploit a shortcut to find symmetric Nash equilibria. Remember, the game looks to the same to every player. If we find the utility maximizing strategy for one player, and then **exploit symmetry** by having every other player use that strategy, then we have found a symmetrical Nash equilibrium. Here is an example to see how this works, for a 3-player game of Common Interest—you studied the 2-player version in Chapter 3.

Each player has the strategy set $[0,1]$—any number between 0 and 1. Player 1 has the utility function

$$u_1(\boldsymbol{x}) = (x_1)(x_2)(x_3)$$

Since this is a game of common interest, players 2 and 3 have the same utility function. For general $n > 3$, this becomes

$$u_1(\boldsymbol{x}) = (x_1)(x_2)...(x_n)$$

We can see that these utility functions satisfy the payoff interchange condition, because each player's strategy enters utility functions in the same way, as a factor in the overall multiplication. Alternatively, we can say that a player's payoff depends only on his or her own strategy, and (in this case) on the product of all the other players' strategies.

Any time a player's utility function can be written in the form $u_i(x_i, \sum x_i)$ and the form of the function u is the same for all players, then the payoff interchange condition is satisfied. There is a reason for this. Each player's payoff depends only on his or her own action and on the aggregate action of all the players. In the aggregate, each player is the same as every other player. That is where the symmetry lies.

Now let's solve the game when there are three players. In Chapter 3, we solved the game by considering the corner strategies, and then showing that there are no Nash equilibrium inside the corners. We could do that again here; instead, let's exploit symmetry. To do that, we first maximize utility for one player, say, player 1. Then, we exploit symmetry—the fact that at a symmetrical equilibrium, each player does the same thing.

Maximizing player 1's utility means, for a given $(x_2)(x_3) > 0$, find the maximum of

$$u_1(\boldsymbol{x}) = (x_1)(x_2)(x_3)$$

with respect to player 1's strategy. Clearly, this maximum occurs at

$$x_1 = 1$$

Now, at a symmetrical Nash equilibrium all players will be doing the same thing that player 1 is doing:

$$x_1 = 1 = x_2 = x_3$$

We have found a symmetrical Nash equilibrium of Common Interest with three players:

$$\mathbf{x} = (1,1,1)$$

We can find the other symmetric Nash equilibrium of Common Interest by dropping the condition that the product of player 2's and 3's strategies be positive.

You can better appreciate the power of this technique by seeing how it solves this game with 100 players. Instead of letting $n = 100$ stop us, we simply perform these two steps, where the product of strategies is

$$(x_1)(x_2) \ldots (x_{100})$$

The notation says that you can fill in the dots easily. Holding all other players' strategies constant at a positive product, player 1 maximizes utility by setting

$$x_1 = 1$$

Now set every other player's strategy equal to player 1's:

$$x_1 = 1 = x_2 = x_2 = x_{100}$$

We have just found a symmetrical Nash equilibrium of Common Interest.

Games with many players can get pretty crowded. Think of perfect competition, where there are many, many firms, each with a tiny market share. There are so many firms that market price is driven down to cost, and none of the firms makes very much money. Of course, consumers make out like bandits. Something similar occurs when too many firms exploit the same resource in common, only in this case consumers aren't any better off, either. Everybody is a loser in the tragedy of the commons, as we show in section 5.9.

◨ 5.7 THE NASH DEMAND GAME

In this section, we showcase the power of the solution technique for symmetric games with a famous game invented by John Nash for just that purpose. This game is now called the Nash Demand game in his honor, and it's simple enough for you to play in class.

We will start with the 2-player version. There is an integer amount M of money on the table. If the two players can agree on how to divide the money, they get to keep some or all of it. If the two players cannot agree on how to divide the money, it disappears. So the strategic situation is a lot like Let's Make a Deal, only the division of the deal amount is now endogenous.

Each player has the set of strategies:

Ask for $0, ask for $1, . . ., ask for $M

So the game is symmetric in that respect. Now here are the payoff rules. Let x_i be the amount of money that player i demands. A player gets what he or she asks for, as long as total demand does not exceed M:

$$u_i(\boldsymbol{x}) = x_i \text{ if } x_2 + x_2 \leq M$$

Otherwise, a player gets nothing:

$$u_i(\boldsymbol{x}) = 0 \text{ if } x_2 + x_2 > M$$

Since the payoff functions are the same for every player, the game satisfies symmetry in this respect also.

Figure 5.8 shows the Nash Demand game for the case $M = 2$. You can see from the figure that there are four pure strategy Nash equilibria. (There aren't any mixed strategy Nash

FIGURE 5.8 **NASH DEMAND GAME**

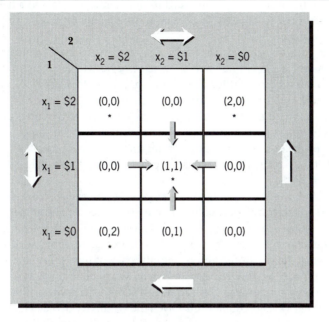

equilibria.) Of these, the three Nash equilibria along the diagonal where total demands equal $2 all have 100 percent efficiency. In addition, there is a Nash equilibrium where each player demands all the money. This Nash equilibrium has 0 percent efficiency; in the Nash Demand game, as in life, greed doesn't pay.

Two of these Nash equilibria are symmetric: $x = (1,1)$ and $(2,2)$. The vector of strategies $(1,1)$ is the good symmetric Nash equilibrium—the players divide the money equally. The vector of strategies $(2,2)$ is the bad symmetric Nash equilibrium—each player asks for everything and gets nothing. Using efficiency and symmetry, we endorse the play of the good symmetric Nash equilibrium.

One interesting feature of the Nash Demand game is that it can be played with any number n of players. The same pair of symmetric Nash equilibria, one good and one bad, will reappear, as long as M is evenly divisible by n. This is where the power of symmetry really comes in. With large n, there are many other bad equilibria. For instance, any vector of demands where every player asks for at least $[M/(n-1)]$ of the money on the table is a pure strategy Nash equilibrium paying every player 0.

Just because a Nash equilibrium has 0 percent efficiency, this is no guarantee we won't observe it on rare occasions. Consider the case of a movie star who refuses to play in a movie unless he or she gets all the profits. The movie doesn't get made if the producer and director are also demanding all the profits. In this case, there is a way out—each party to the deal asks for somewhat less than everything.

■ 5.8 STAG HUNT WITH TWO OR MORE PLAYERS

Sometimes, moving from two to three or more players creates qualitatively new Nash equilibria. We will now look at such a phenomenon, in the game called **Stag Hunt.** This game has a long history, in two senses. First, it was invented by the French political philosopher J. J. Rousseau in the mid-eighteenth century—two and a half centuries ago. And it describes the technology of human hunting going far back into the Stone Age— many millennia ago.

We start with the simplest version, with two players. The two players are hunters. A hunter can hunt for something small, in which case he catches something small for a pay-off of 1. Or a hunter can hunt for something big. If a hunter hunts for something big (like a stag, or deer) and he hunts alone, he comes back empty handed, for a payoff of 0. However, if a hunter hunts for something big and there are two hunters hunting for something big, then you've got a hunting party. The hunters do catch something big. Even after accounting for the extra effort (1 unit) of hunting for something big as opposed to hunting for something small, they still get a net payoff of 3 each (4 for the big animal minus 1 for extra effort).

Figure 5.9 shows Stag Hunt with two players. As you can see from the arrow diagram, there are two symmetric Nash equilibria in pure strategies. At one of these, (hunt big, hunt big), the players form a hunting party and achieve the efficient outcome. This is the efficient and equitable Nash equilibrium. At the other of these, (hunt small, hunt small), the players get much lower payoffs, 1 each. The efficiency of this Nash equilibrium is only $(2 - 1)/(6 - 1) = 1/5 = 20\%$. This is a very inefficient way to allocate human resources.

Since we have pure strategy Nash equilibria at opposite corners of the game matrix, we also have a mixed strategy equilibrium. Given the symmetry of Stag Hunt, let's assume this mixed strategy equilibrium is symmetric. Let p denote the probability of hunting big, and $1 - p$ the probability of hunting small. Also notice that the strategy Hunt Small pays 1 for certain. Then we have

$$1 = EV(\text{hunt small}) = EV(\text{hunt big}) = p(3) + (1 - p)(0) = 3p$$

Solving, $p = 1/3$ is the probability of hunting big at the mixed strategy equilibrium; $1 - p = 1 - (1/3) = 2/3$ is the probability of hunting small. This mixed strategy Nash equilibrium is just as inefficient as the pure strategy Nash equilibrium where every player hunts small.

FIGURE 5.9	**STAG HUNT**

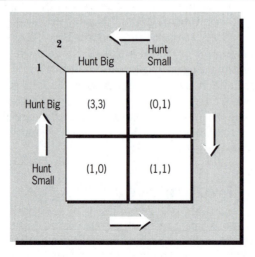

Now let's consider Stag Hunt with three players, where three large qualitative differences emerge. The hunting technology is still the same, so if two or more hunters hunt something big, they catch something big. Indeed, this something big is enough to feed everybody, even those who did not hunt for it. This creates the first qualitative difference, the possibility of **free riding.** A player free-rides if he gets something without having to work for it: here, one player can get some of the big catch without hunting for it. Instead, a free rider can hunt for something small and get an even larger payoff.

Assume that a successful hunt for something big means a payoff of 3 to those who actually do the hunting, but a payoff of 4 to a free rider, while hunting for something small pays 1. Figure 5.10 shows the 3-player Stag Hunt that results. From the arrow diagram, you can see that there are four pure strategy Nash equilibria. Three of these are efficient, but no longer pay the players the same. These are the Nash equilibria by which two players hunt for something big, while the third player free-rides, hunting for something small. The free rider gets a larger payoff. This brings us to the second qualitative difference: the efficient, symmetric Nash equilibrium is no longer present. The inefficient Nash equilibrium (hunt small, hunt small, hunt small) is still present, however. The bad equilibrium doesn't go away.

You can show that the symmetric mixed strategy Nash equilibrium is still present also. At this symmetric equilibrium, each player hunts big with the same probability, 6/7. We leave the details of this calculation to an end-of-chapter problem.

The third large qualitative difference that emerges is Nash equilibria at which some players use a mixed strategy, while other players use a pure strategy. These are a kind of hybrid Nash equilibrium. Stag Hunt with three players has several of these; we will work out the details of one of them. Suppose player 3 uses the pure strategy hunt for something big, while players 1 and 2 use mixed strategies. In particular, let p denote the probability

FIGURE 5.10 STAG HUNT, THREE PLAYERS

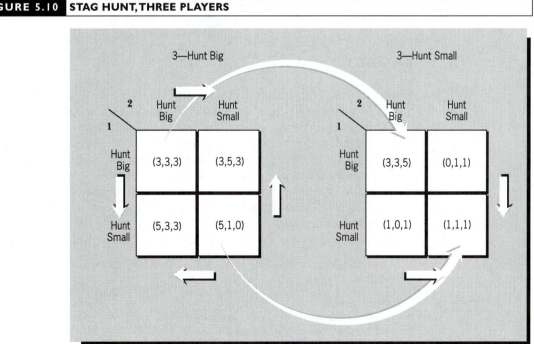

that player 1 (and independently, player 2) hunts for something big, and let $1 - p$ be the probability that player 1 hunts for something small. The expected value to player 1 of hunting for something big, EV_1(hunt big), is a sure value of 3, since at least one other player, 3, is hunting for something big so it is certain that a 2-player hunting party will form. The expected value of hunting for something small, EV_1(hunt small), is given by

$$EV_1(\text{hunt small}) = p(5) + (1 - p)(1)$$

where the first term on the right reflects the probability that players 2 (and 3) are hunting for something big while player 1 free-rides, and the second term on the right reflects the probability that only player 3 went hunting for something big. Equating the two expected values, we get

$$3 = EV_1(\text{hunt big}) = 5p + 1 - p = 4p + 1$$

Solving, $p = 1/2$. At this hybrid Nash equilibrium, players 1 and 2 hunt for something big with probability 1/2, while player 3 hunts for something big for sure. Notice that all three players get the same payoff, however—3. So this Nash equilibrium, which is neither mixed nor pure but some of both, achieves the symmetric outcome paying each player 3. Still, this equilibrium leaves something to be desired on efficiency grounds, with an efficiency of $(9 - 2)/(11 - 2) = 7/9 = 88\%$, rather less than 100 percent.

Besides its direct applicability to Stone Age hunters, Stag Hunt has more modern applications. Here is just one, where free riding is quite pronounced. Suppose that public goods—such as law and order, and national defense—are paid for by taxes, and that payment of taxes is voluntary. Since everyone gets the benefits from a public good, whether they pay for it or not, we have a situation strategically like that of Stag Hunt. The strategy Hunt Big is analogous to paying taxes voluntarily; the Group Hunt, to producing a public good with the taxes voluntarily paid; and Hunt Small to using one's resources for private gain. Call this version of Stag Hunt **Voluntary Taxes.** At any Nash equilibrium of Voluntary Taxes with more than two players, one observes some free riding.

■ 5.9 THE TRAGEDY OF THE COMMONS

The following scenario is played out the world over.[7] A group of individual producers or firms access a resource that no one of them owns. The resource is a **commons,** freely available to all. One example of a commons is an underground aquifer, such as the Ogallala aquifer, which extends under the Great Plains from the Dakotas to Texas. No one owns the aquifer, and anyone who wants to pump its water up to the surface, usually for agricultural production, can do so. When such underground water sources are hot, such as in geysers, they offer a valuable source of geothermal energy. Another example of a commons is a species of whale, such as the minke whale, swimming the high seas. No one owns the whales, and any nation that wants to hunt them is free to do so.[8] Yet another example of a commons is the atmosphere. Any firm can store its waste in the atmosphere at essentially no cost.[9]

[7] Material for this section has been drawn from Richard A. Ken, "Geothermal Tragedy of the Commons," *Science* 253 (1991): 134–135.

[8] The hunting of whales is currently subject to an international agreement. This agreement is a direct result of the tragedy of the commons.

[9] As in the case of the whales, the commons tragedy of the atmosphere, manifested as degraded air quality, had led to changes in the rules of the game, in particular the Montreal Protocol on hydrofluorocarbons and the Kyoto Protocol on global warming.

A **tragedy of the commons** occurs when too many players exploit the resource. This practice leads to a double-edged disaster. First, the resource is either degraded or destroyed. Second, rates of return of all the producers involved are lower than they could be. In its most virulent form, the tragedy plays out as destruction of the resource and a zero rate of return to the firms involved. We will see this in a simple game model as well as in real life.

Let i be an index of potential users of the commons—these could be individuals, firms, or even governments. Let x_i represent player i's strategy; let n be the total number of players, and let X be the number of players using the commons, $X \leq n$. The expression $x_{i\_} = 1$ means that i uses the commons; $x_i = 0$ means that i does not use the commons. If i does not use the commons, it gets an outside opportunity equal some constant, say 0.1. If i uses the commons, the payoff depends on how many other players use the commons as well. The production function for the entire commons, $F(X)$, measures how much is produced in total, depending on how many players are using the commons (X).

To keep things symmetrical, assume that all players that use the commons get an equal share of the commons production. If all n players are using the commons, then an individual player using the commons gets $F(n)/n$ as its payoff.[10] The payoff function for player i, $u_i(x)$, is given as follows:

$$u_i(x) = 0.1 \text{ if } x_i = 0$$
$$= F(X)/(X) \text{ if } x_i = 1$$

This utility function can be written more compactly as

$$u_i(x) = (0.1)(1 - x_i) + x_i[F(X)/X]$$

When i's strategy equals 0, he or she gets the term on the left, the outside opportunity 0.1; when their strategy equals 1, the term on the right, $F(X)/X$. Each player has the same set of strategies and the same form of utility function, differing only by subscript, so the game is symmetrical.

We will first solve the game with two players, $n = 2$. To fix ideas, let's take a specific commons production function, $F(X)$, namely,

$$F(X) = 1.2X - .1X^2$$

This production function is shown in Figure 5.11. Total use of the commons X is shown on the horizontal axis; output from the commons, on the vertical axis. This production function exhibits diminishing returns, with total output reaching its maximum value, 3.6, when total use of the resource $X = 6$. When a single player is using the commons, the payoff is fantastic:

$$F(1) / 1 = 1.1/1 = 1.1 > 0.1$$

That's 11 times the payoff from the outside opportunity. In particular, this computation provides a test for whether a single player would want to use the commons or not. If the payoff from using the commons is greater than the outside opportunity, then the player uses the commons; otherwise, the player exploits the outside opportunity instead.

---

[10] The tragedy of the commons does not depend on symmetry. It takes place in asymmetrical situations as well as in symmetrical ones.

FIGURE 5.11 | **COMMONS PRODUCTION FUNCTION**

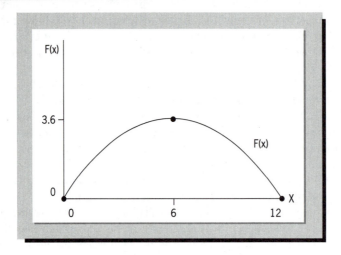

As the number of players using the commons increases, the returns drop off dramatically. This is the economic signal of the game Tragedy of the Commons. To see this, let's compare the Nash equilibria of two games, the first with five players, the second with 10. Notice that with only five players, each player has an incentive to use the commons:

$$F(5)/5 = [(1.2)(5) - (0.1)5^2]/5 = [6 - 2.5]/5 = 0.7 > 0.1$$

Even with five players, returns from the commons are 7 times those from the outside opportunity. In addition, the outcome is still in the economic zone of production, where total output is increasing and marginal product is positive. The efficiency of this Nash equilibrium is therefore high.

Now contrast this equilibrium outcome with that when the number of players doubles, to 10. By the time there are 10 players using the commons, returns are down to a very low level:

$$F(10)/10 = [(1.2)(10) - (0.1)10^2]/10 = [12 - 10]/10 = 0.2, > 0.1$$

Returns are now scarcely above those of the outside opportunity. Moreover, production is now deep into the uneconomical zone, where total output is falling, and marginal product is negative. The result is terribly inefficient. Figure 5.12 contrasts these two Nash equilibria. One Nash equilibrium, with fewer players, is in the economic zone, where the marginal product of an extra player in the commons is positive; the other, with more players, in the uneconomical zone, where the marginal product of an extra player in the commons is negative. It is irrational to put more productive resources into a production process when the marginal product is negative, but this is exactly what happens at the Tragedy of the Commons.

Remember, in a commons there is nothing to stop anyone from using the resource. As long as there are enough potential players, more players will continue to use the resource at Nash equilibrium. The limit of this process is reached only when individual returns from the resource are driven down to the return from the outside opportunity:

$$F(X)/X = 0.1$$

Substituting $F(X) = 1.2X - .1X^2$ into this expression and solving for X, we get $X = 11$. As soon as there are at least 11 players, then the commons is almost completely wasted. With

11 players using the commons and earning an individual return equal to that of the outside opportunity, it is as if the commons didn't even exist as a potentially economic resource. All its potential value has been wiped out by overuse. Figure 5.13 shows the average and marginal products from the commons, and compares the efficient solution, where the marginal product equals the outside opportunity value, with the Nash equilibrium with 11 players, where the average product equals the outside opportunity value.

FIGURE 5.12   TRAGEDY OF THE COMMONS

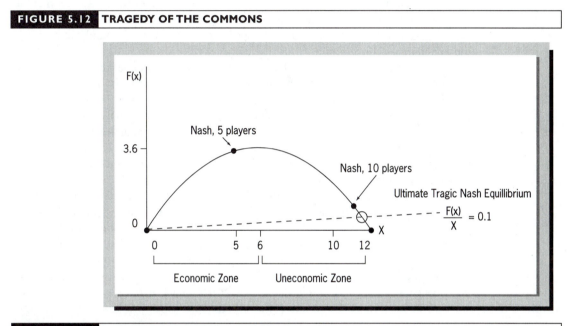

FIGURE 5.13   EFFICIENT COMMONS VS. TRAGEDY

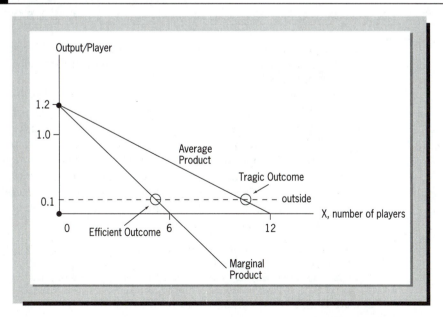

The inefficient Nash equilibria found in the Tragedy of the Commons reflect a larger economic truth. The **First Theorem of Welfare Economics** gives conditions under which a market equilibrium outcome is economically efficient. This theorem does not hold when there are **externalities.** Commons problems are one kind of externality, the externality imposed on existing users when a new user enters. Because of the externality, individual optimization leads to a bad outcome for the group as a whole.

Figures 5.12 and 5.13 provide only a snapshot of the inefficiency involved in overuse of a commons. Overuse in the short run can lead to degradation or even destruction of the commons in the long run. Overgraze rangeland long enough, and it won't be rangeland any more, but desert. Such examples of the Tragedy of the Commons abound; we now give another, more specific example.

Game theory predicts overuse of a commons with a large number of players. Let's see how the theory works in practice. The Geysers of northern California is the nation's largest geothermal energy field, producing more than 6 percent of California's energy and 75 percent of the nation's geothermal energy. When the field was first developed in 1960, rates of return were very high. Pacific Gas and Electric (PG&E), the principal developer, was earning a hefty rate of return. By California law, the field was a commons, open to all. Attracted by high rates of return and unrestricted entry, many companies entered the area. By 1990, there was more than 2000 megawatts of installed energy capacity at the surface.

Unfortunately, much of this capacity is currently idle, despite the power crisis in California. Even worse, the underground steam capacity is steadily falling. Quite simply, the geysers for which the field was named are drying up. Without sufficient water underground, they cannot produce steam to drive the turbines at the surface. The culprit in all of this is clear. As one developer put it, Put simply, there are too many straws in the teapot.

The future of the Geysers is bleak. Energy production continues to fall, even as we write this paragraph. This is not just a tragedy for fans of alternative energy sources or for the companies and their shareholders—it's a tragedy for the geysers, too.

■ 5.10 TRAGEDY OF THE COMMONS IN THE LABORATORY

The goal of any scientific theory is to explain and to predict.[11] In this respect, game theory is no different from any other theory. Most applications of game theory to real life are explanatory. Occasionally, there is enough information to make a sound prediction as well. One of the exciting developments in game theory in recent years has been the application of controlled laboratory experiments to games. Although *experimental games* are reported as early as Luce and Raiffa (1957), this activity has become a major industry in the last two decades.[12] This section reports on the results of games played in an experimental commons. Some results are not surprising—the tragedy of the commons appears in the laboratory just as it does in the field. Some results are surprising—a change in the game that should not affect the Nash equilibrium (the change only makes the players richer, potentially) does affect it. This is why we run experiments: not just to tell us what we already know but also to tell us what we don't suspect, but should.

[11] This material is based on E. Ostrom, R. Gardner, and J. Walker, *Rules, Games, and Common-Pool Resources* (Ann Arbor: University of Michigan Press, 1993).

[12] The earliest experiments are reported in R. Duncan Luce and Howard Raiffa, *Games and Decisions* (New York: Wiley & Sons, 1957). An excellent overview of what has been done with experimental games is given in John Kagel and Alvin E. Roth, eds., *Handbook of Experimental Economics* (Princeton, N.J.: Princeton University Press, 1994).

The experiments described here are run as follows. Volunteers are recruited from undergraduate classes at Indiana University. Recruits are told that they will be making decisions in an economic choice situation. They will be paid in person, in private, at the end of the experiment, based on the decisions they and others in the experiment have made. They are told that they will be paid $3 for showing up for the experiment and that they can make substantially more than that in the experiment proper. *The experimenter never lies to the subjects.* The experiment begins with subjects signing a federally mandated release form, in accordance with federal regulations on the treatment of human subjects in experiments. Subjects then go through a set of instructions to teach them the game they are about to play. Subjects have to pass a quiz on their understanding of the game before they go on to actual play. Finally, subjects play the game three times for practice before they begin to play for real money. Since the average subject makes about $15 for a 90-minute experimental session, in addition to the show-up bonus, there is no difficulty recruiting volunteer subjects.

Eight subjects played the following Commons game.[13] Each player i picks a number x_i between 0 and w. The parameter w is the number of tokens a player has—10 or 25, depending on the experimental design. A player can put as many tokens as he or she wants into the bank; for each token deposited, he or she is paid 5 cents. Tokens not put into the bank go into the commons, where the rate of return depends on how many tokens the player has invested in the commons, and on the total number of tokens invested in the commons. Player i's payoffs, in cents, is given by

$$u_i(\boldsymbol{x}) = 5(w - x_i) + x_i F(X)/X$$

where X is the number of tokens invested in the commons. Note the similarity with the payoff function in the Tragedy of the Commons game of section 5.9. The only differences are an outside opportunity worth $.05 per unit instead of $.10; $w = 10$ or 25 instead of 1; and X equal to the number of tokens in the commons instead of the number of players in the commons. We made these changes in order to separate the effect of more tokens per player, versus more players.

The production function in these experiments is given by

$$F(X) = 23X - 0.25X^2$$

where output is measured in U.S. cents. Substituting, we have the payoff function,

$$u_i(\boldsymbol{x}) = 5(w - x_i) + x_i(23 - 0.25X)$$

Note that this payoff function depends on player i's decision as well as on the aggregate decision, so the game is symmetrical.

This symmetrical experimental game has a unique symmetrical Nash equilibrium. At this symmetrical Nash equilibrium, each player invests 8 of his or her tokens in the commons. The subjects were given a table, showing them that the marginal cost to them of the eighth token invested, $.05, was equal to the marginal revenue generated by that same token invested, $.05, when total investment in the commons equaled 63 tokens already. Thus, subjects were looking at the Nash equilibrium in tabular form. Of course, the table contained much more information besides.

As designed, this experimental Nash equilibrium leads to a tragedy of the commons, since commons output reaches its maximum value at $X = 46$, substantially below the $X = 64$ of Nash equilibrium. Indeed, the efficiency of the symmetric Nash equilibrium (here, we

---

[13] Ten subjects were recruited for each experiment. If more than eight showed up, the surplus subjects were paid $5 for showing up and a place was reserved for them in the next experiment.

take the minimum total payoff to be zero, even though much lower values are possible) is only 40 percent this far into the uneconomical zone.

Figure 5.14 shows the average total payoff in each round of the experiment, divided by the maximum possible total payoff. This is a measure of efficiency, although different from the one we are using in this book, because it does not take into account the minimum possible payoff. The Commons game is played for money 20 straight times. When players have 10 tokens each, the outcome fluctuates around the symmetrical Nash equilibrium. The average efficiency over the 20 periods is 43 percent, quite close to the Nash equilibrium prediction. The fluctuations have yet to be explained, but the fact that the average behavior is close to Nash equilibrium is reassuring. That's the good news.

FIGURE 5.14 TRAGEDY OF THE COMMONS IN THE LABORATORY

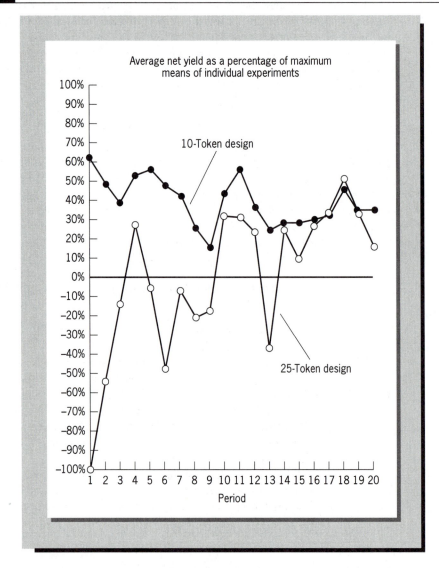

Average net yield as a percentage of maximum means of individual experiments

The bad news is what happens when subjects have 25 tokens to invest instead of 10. This is a wealth effect, making the subjects 150 percent richer as far as money in the bank is concerned. This wealth effect does not affect the rate of return from investment in the commons, so we should see no difference in commons behavior according to Nash equilibrium predictions. Subjects should simply put the extra 15 tokens in the bank and play the same as before.

As you can see from Figure 5.14, this is not what subjects with 25 tokens do. Instead, they invest way too many tokens in the commons in the early decision periods, driving returns negative. After about a dozen periods, subjects have finally got the negativity out of their systems, but even then they are still below the symmetrical Nash equilibrium efficiency of 40 percent. On average over all 20 periods, these subjects earn slightly negative earnings (−4 percent). They are doing *worse* than the tragedy of the commons, which predicts that earnings approach zero without going negative. This experimental result is also yet to be explained.

The tragedy of the commons is real, both in the field and in the laboratory. We as individuals and as firms ignore it at our own peril.

■ SUMMARY

1. When there are three players in a game instead of two, fundamental differences may arise. The theorem for games like Chess and von Neumann's theorem for 2-person, zero-sum games no longer hold, because in zero-sum games a third player can play the spoiler.

2. Spoilers are less frequent in markets than they are in politics and sports. Most of the time, when there is a third or fourth firm in a market, the impact on profits or market shares is not that dramatic.

3. When each player has a strictly dominant strategy, a game has a unique Nash equilibrium. The unique Nash equilibrium for Cigarette Television Advertising, taking into account all four firms, is for each cigarette company to advertise on television.

4. The phenomenon where every player has a strictly dominant strategy that leads to a very bad outcome for all players is called the prisoner's dilemma. The game Stonewalling Watergate exemplifies the prisoner's dilemma in real life, and all of its players went to prison.

5. Once a game has more than three players or each player has more than eight strategies, writing it down in its entirety becomes impractical. A more compact mathematical notation is used to study such games.

6. A game is symmetrical when it looks the same to each player. Each player has the same set of strategies, and utility functions satisfy the interchange property.

7. Every symmetrical game has a symmetrical Nash equilibrium. If a game has more than one symmetrical Nash equilibrium, we can rank the equilibria on efficiency grounds.

8. When each player's payoff depends only on that player's own action and on the aggregate action of all the players, and when all utility functions have the same form, a game is symmetrical.

9. Stag Hunt is a parable for human hunting in the Stone Age, as well as for private provision of public goods in a modern economy. The Nash equilibria of Stag Hunt with three or more players exhibit free riding, as do the Nash equilibria of the analogous game Voluntary Taxes.

10. A commons is a resource that is freely available to all. A tragedy of the commons occurs when too many players exploit the resource, leading to inefficiency in the short run and degradation or destruction of the commons in the long run.

11. The tragedy of the commons is observed in the drying up of the Geysers of California as well as in laboratory experiments.

■ KEY TERMS

counterexample	interchange condition	Voluntary Taxes
strategic dummy	symmetrical Nash equilib-	commons
spoiler	rium	tragedy of the commons
industry standard	payoff symmetry	First Theorem of Welfare
prisoner's dilemma	exploit symmetry	Economics
stonewalling	Stag Hunt	externalities
symmetrical game	free riding	

■ PROBLEMS

1. Suppose that there are now three networks in Battle of the Networks. The market shares of the existing two networks have fallen by 10 percent each to make room for the new network. Redraw the normal form and find the solution. Interpret your new result in terms of network programming strategy.

2. Do enough research on the 2000 U.S. Presidential election to find out how many votes Nader got in Florida, the swing state, and how many of these votes came at the expense of Gore. Then argue that Figure 5.1, suitably redrawn, applies to this election.

3. Suppose that in Stonewalling Watergate, only Dean and Ehrlichman get to make choices. Haldeman is under complete control of the president and must stonewall until the bitter end. Redraw the normal form and find the solution. (*Hint:* Haldeman is a strategic dummy in this version of the game.)

4. Find the mixed strategy equilibrium of Video System Coordination with three firms.

5. Write down the 3-player versions of Market Niche, Competitive Advantage, and Let's Make a Deal in the $u_i(x)$ notation. Show that each of these is symmetrical.

6. In 3-player Let's Make a Deal, there is $40 million on the table. Player 1 gets paid twice as much as either player 2 or player 3 in the event there is a deal. Find all the equilibria you can, then solve.

7. Show that Let's Make a Deal with two or three players does not have a mixed strategy equilibrium. (*Hint:* Suppose that it does, and show that the resulting equations have no solution.)

8. Find all the Nash equilibria of the Nash Demand game with three players and $M = 3$. Then find the symmetric Nash equilibrium with the highest efficiency. What is its efficiency?

9. Find the symmetric mixed strategy Nash equilibrium of Stag Hunt with three players.

10. In Tragedy of the Commons, the commons production function $F(X) = 1.6X - 0.2X^2$. The rate of return outside the commons remains 0.1. Find the symmetric Nash equilibrium when there are seven players. Is your solution tragic?

11. You are the Governor of California, a state facing a serious energy crisis. Formulate a geothermal policy that will effectively address your state's energy crisis. Remember, the main geothermal resource you have at your disposal is the Geysers.

C H A P T E R   6

Noncooperative Market Games in Normal Form

The previous chapters have reviewed games that arise in an economy: Competitive Advantage, Market Niche, Let's Make a Deal, Cigarette Television Advertising, and Tragedy of the Commons. However, the economic structure available when a game is played in a market has not yet been fully exploited. Now that you have experience studying games and finding Nash equilibria, you are ready to exploit the structure that a market gives to a game.

This chapter looks at **noncooperative market games in normal form.**[1] In such games, each buyer or seller in a market picks its strategy. For buyers, that strategy can be a willingness to buy something, expressed as a bid offer. For sellers, that strategy can be a willingness to sell something, expressed as an asking price. Each player gets a payoff—a payoff, in terms of gain or loss, after the market has processed all the strategic information submitted to it. Since each player is acting independently, the game is noncooperative. As such, there is no presumption that a Nash equilibrium outcome will be efficient.

We first study the simplest possible market, with one buyer and one seller. We show how this market can have both good Nash equilibria and bad Nash equilibria. The good Nash equilibria resemble perfectly competitive outcomes, although the behavior underlying those outcomes is hardly in accord with perfect competition. Then we extend our results from a simple market with one buyer and one seller to markets with many buyers and sellers. Here, we focus mainly on good Nash equilibria, although the bad Nash equilibria do not go away. We illustrate these results with a section on price formation on the New York Stock Exchange.

Next, we shift gears to study markets where only sellers are strategic, while buyers honestly report willingness to pay in the form of market demand. These models were the first games economists ever solved, a century before the birth of game theory. Quantity competition between two firms selling products that are perfect substitutes is presented first. Then the chapter describes what happens when the number of firms grows large. In this case, quantity competition approaches as a limit perfect competition, a result known as the Cournot limit theorem. Then price competition—also known as Bertrand competition—is studied, first between two firms and then among many firms, each selling perfect substitutes. Competing on price does not lead to the same equilibrium as does competing on

---

[1] Chapters 7 and 8 present market games in extensive form. Chapter 15 presents market games in coalition function form.

quantity. In particular, price competition can lead to a Nash equilibrium outcome consistent with perfectly competition with as few as two firms. This rather startling contrast between quantity and price competition has real-world implications, which we see in the 0 percent financing programs of the Big 3 automobile manufacturers in the United States at the end of 2001. Oligopoly can be a lot more competitive than those enamored of perfect competition give it credit for.

◼ 6.1 A MARKET WITH ONE BUYER AND ONE SELLER

We start with the simplest possible market game, one buyer and one seller. The buyer is in the market for a single unit of an item. This buyer is characterized by a single piece of information, his or her willingness to pay for that item, denoted $b\#$. The seller has one unit of that same item for sale. This seller is again characterized by a single piece of information, his or her willingness to sell that item, denoted $a\#$.

Let's look at the market interaction between this buyer and seller through the lens of classical microeconomics. The two panels of Figure 6.1 show the market fundamentals, with quantity Q on the horizontal axis and price P on the vertical axis. Figure 6.1a shows the individual (and market) demand for the buyer. Note that market demand is zero at any price above $b\#$, while market demand is one at any price below $b\#$. This reflects the buyer's willingness to buy. Figure 6.1b shows the individual (and market) supply for the seller. Note that market supply is zero at any price below $a\#$, while market supply is one at any price above $a\#$. This reflects the seller's willingness to sell. These market demand and supply graphs are constructed on the twin pillars of **price-taking behavior** and **honest revelation of potentially valuable information.** Both the buyer and seller are passive, nonstrategic agents who simply do what the market tells them: that's price-taking behavior. Furthermore, both the buyer and the seller tell the market exactly what the item is worth

FIGURE 6.1 **MARKET FUNDAMENTALS**

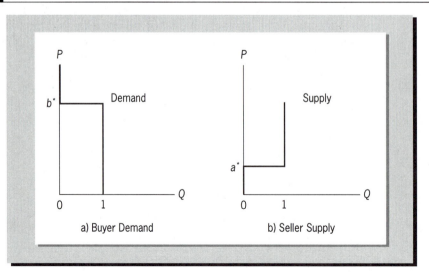

a) Buyer Demand   b) Seller Supply

to them: that's honest revelation of crucial information. As we will show in this chapter, these are decent assumptions for markets with many buyers or sellers, but they don't correspond to Nash equilibrium when there is one buyer and one seller.

Now put demand and supply together to get market equilibrium. Figure 6.2 does just that. As long as willingness to pay $b\#$ is greater than willingness to sell $a\#$, there is an **active market equilibrium** where a positive quantity of the good is traded, with a positive quantity $Q^* = 1$ and a positive price P^* anywhere between $a\#$ and $b\#$. This is the answer that classical market analysis gives to the simplest market, where price-taking behavior and honest revelation of crucial information reign supreme. We now turn to a game theoretic analysis of the same market situation, where both these pillars of classical microeconomics are the first things to go.

◨ 6.2 THE MARKET GAME BETWEEN ONE BUYER AND ONE SELLER

To define a market game between the buyer and the seller, we will first need to set up the rules for trading. The rules for the buyer are as follows. The buyer chooses a bid price b; this is the buyer's strategy. In principle, b could be any number not exceeding the buyer's ability to pay. For simplicity, we restrict b to be an integer, and assume that the buyer's ability to pay far exceeds the potential cost of this item, so we can safely ignore the buyer's budget constraint.

The rules for the seller are as follows. The seller chooses an asking price a; this is the seller's strategy. In principle, a could be any number. For simplicity, we restrict a to be an integer.

The market price P is a function of the ask a and bid b submitted by the seller and buyer respectively. We denote the market price function by $P(a,b)$. In particular, the market price is the average of the ask and bid:

$$P(a,b) = (a + b)/2$$

| FIGURE 6.2 | CLASSICAL MARKET EQUILIBRIUM |

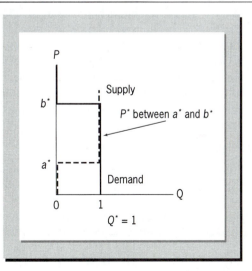

Of the many possible price rules, this one has the feature of treating both sides to the transaction the same. As we show in section 6.7, this is the rule used for over two centuries on the New York Stock Exchange. There are infinitely many other pricing rules, each favoring one side of the market or the other. Here are the two extremes:

$$P(a,b) = a$$

completely favors the buyer, since the buyer pays the lowest price in the range from a to b. By contrast,

$$P(a,b) = b$$

completely favors the seller, since the seller receives the highest price in the range from a to b.

The trading rules require that no one be forced to trade, relative to his or her ask or bid. For the buyer, this means that the buyer is not forced to buy. Since the buyer has told the market his or her willingness to pay is the bid b, the buyer buys only if the market price does not exceed his or her bid:

$$Q \text{ Demanded} = 1 \text{ only if } b \geq P(a,b)$$

Similarly, the seller is not forced to sell. Since the seller has told the market his or her willingness to sell is the ask a, the seller sells only if the market price is at least as great as his or her ask:

$$Q \text{ Supplied} = 1 \text{ only if } a \leq P(a,b)$$

Putting the two sides of the market together, there is a transaction with $Q = 1$ units bought and sold when

$$Q = 1 \text{ only when } a \leq P(a,b) \leq b$$

Otherwise, there is no deal and $Q = 0$.

These market trading rules are based on the rules actually used in **open outcry** markets, like the Chicago Board of Trade. Still, if you aren't familiar with them, they may all seem a bit abstract, so let's put them to work in a concrete example. Suppose the buyer's true willingness to pay is $4 ($b\# = 4$), and the buyer has the bids $4, $3, and $2 to choose from. At the same time, the seller's true willingness to sell is $2 ($a\# = 2$), and the seller has the asks $2, $3, and $4 to choose from.

The matrix in Figure 6.3 puts bids and asks together in the form of market outcomes, the price $P(a,b)$ based on bids and asks, and the quantity Q transacted, either 0 or 1. Let's walk through a couple of market outcomes to see how the trading rules work. Take the (ask, bid) pair ask = 4, bid = 2 in the upper left hand corner of the matrix. At this bid-ask pair, the price $P(a,b)$ is

$$P(a,b) = P(4,2) = (4 + 2)/2 = 3$$

The price 3 is higher than what the buyer is bidding, so there is no transaction:

$$Q \text{ Demanded} = 0, \text{ since } P(4,2) = 3 > 2 = b$$

The seller would be willing to sell at this price, since the ask is 2 and the price is 3, but willingness on one side of the market does not suffice to make a deal. It takes both sides of the market to make a deal.

FIGURE 6.3 OUTCOME MATRIX

Buyer\\Seller	b = 2	b = 3	b = 4
a = 4	P=3 Q=0	P=3.5 Q=0	P=4 Q=1
a = 3	P=2.5 Q=0	P=3 Q=1	P=3.5 Q=1
a = 2	P=2 Q=1	P=2.5 Q=1	P=3 Q=1

Now consider the (ask, bid) pair ask = 3, bid = 3, in the center of the matrix. At this ask-bid pair, the price $P(a,b)$ is

$$P(a,b) = P(3,3) = (3 + 3)/2 = 3$$

The price 3 is exactly what the buyer is bidding, so the buyer is willing to buy:

$$Q \text{ Demanded} = 1, \text{ since } P(3,3) = 3 = b$$

Similarly, the price 3 is exactly what the seller is asking, so the seller is willing to sell:

$$Q \text{ Supplied} = 1, \text{ since } P(3,3) = 3 = a$$

At this ask-bid pair, there is a transaction.

We are now one step away from a market game in normal form. Converting the market outcome matrix in Figure 6.3 into a game matrix requires converting market outcomes into payoffs.

For the seller, the payoff function $u_1(a,b)$ is given by

$$u_1(a,b) = P(a,b) - a\# \text{ if there is a deal;}$$
$$0 \text{ otherwise}$$

Regardless of what the seller asks, he or she gets rewarded based on true willingness to sell, $a\#$. The difference between market price and true willingness to sell is the **producer's surplus.** If there is no deal, then there is neither loss nor gain, so the payoff is zero. Of course, whether there is a deal or not depends on both the ask and the bid:

$$Q = 1 \text{ only when } a \leq P(a,b) \leq b$$

For the buyer, the payoff function $u_2(a,b)$ is given by

$$u_2(a,b) = b\# - P(a,b) \text{ if there is a deal;}$$
$$0 \text{ otherwise}$$

Regardless of what the buyer bids, he or she gets rewarded based on true willingness to buy, $b\#$. The difference between true willingness to buy and market price is the **consumer's surplus.** If there is no deal, then there is neither loss nor gain, so the payoff is zero.

Finally, we have a game. Using the payoff functions just derived to convert market outcomes into payoffs, we have the game matrix in Figure 6.4. Let's walk through a couple of the payoff cells, to make sure you understand where they come from. First, consider the payoffs corresponding to ask = 4, bid = 2, in the upper left-hand corner of Figure 6.4. These payoffs are (0,0). Since there is no deal, neither the buyer nor the seller gains (or loses) anything—the meaning of zero, staying at the status quo. Next, consider the payoffs corresponding to ask = 3, bid = 3, in the center of Figure 6.4. These payoffs are (1,1). Since there is a deal, both the buyer and the seller gain something—in this case, both their gains are equal to one.

■ 6.3 Nash Equilibrium versus Perfectly Competitive Equilibrium

We are now in position to find the Nash equilibria of the market game between one buyer and one seller, and compare those to the predictions of perfect competition. Figure 6.4 provides the arrows necessary to identify all the Nash equilibria of the market game—4, in total. We can categorize the Nash equilibria into good and bad. The good Nash equilibria have an efficiency of 100 percent; the bad Nash equilibrium has an efficiency of 0 percent.

FIGURE 6.4 MARKET GAME MATRIX

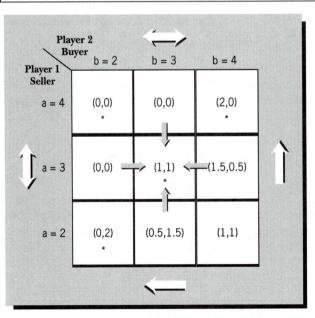

Here are the good Nash equilibria:

- (ask, bid) = (2,2). At this Nash equilibrium, the seller asks exactly what the item is worth to him or her, and the buyer bids well below what the item is worth to him or her. As a result, the buyer gets all the gain from trade: payoff to the buyer = 2. This Nash equilibrium achieves 100 percent efficiency, but with very one-sided payoffs. This Nash equilibrium is consistent with the market equilibrium where $P^* = 2$ in Figure 6.2.

- (ask, bid) = (4,4). At this Nash equilibrium, the buyer bids exactly what the item is worth to him or her, and the seller asks well above what the item is worth to him or her. As a result, the seller gets all the gain from trade: payoff to the seller = 2. This Nash equilibrium achieves 100 percent efficiency, but with very one-sided payoffs. This Nash equilibrium is consistent with the market equilibrium where $P^* = 4$ in Figure 6.2.

- (ask, bid) = (3,3). At this Nash equilibrium, the buyer bids one less unit than what the item is worth to him or her (slight underbidding), while the seller asks one unit above what the item is worth to him or her. As a result, the buyer and seller divide the gains from trade equally, one unit each. This Nash equilibrium achieves 100 percent efficiency, with equal payoffs. This Nash equilibrium is consistent with the market equilibrium where $P^* = 3$ in Figure 6.2.

Here is the bad Nash equilibrium:

- (ask, bid) = (4,2). This is the greedy Nash equilibrium, at which each side of the market chooses a strategy that essentially asks for all the gains from trade. Since a pair of such strategies leads to no deal, greed doesn't pay: payoff = 0 to each side. This Nash equilibrium achieves 0 percent efficiency, and corresponds to no market equilibrium in Figure 6.2.

It should not surprise you that there is a bad Nash equilibrium in this market game. Compare the payoffs in Figure 6.4 with those in Figure 5.8, for the Nash Demand game. From purely a payoff standpoint, you are looking at similar symmetric game matrixes, and the same arrow diagram. This market game is symmetric, so it has at least one symmetric Nash equilibrium—here there are two, a good one and a bad one.

Now notice the following two features of the good Nash equilibria that correspond to market equilibria. At none of these equilibria are both players revealing honest potentially valuable information to the market. Indeed, at the good Nash equilibrium with equal payoffs, both players are choosing a strategy other than true value. The buyer is putting in a lowball bid, and the seller is putting in a padded ask. When you think about it, this is a very reasonable way to act. If a new car dealer were to ask you, How much are you willing to pay for this car? and you answered truthfully, you can guess what the seller would say next: You can have it for that! Good strategic play means not revealing honest potentially valuable information.

Second, these players are not taking price as given. The seller is not taking price as given, but is trying to drive the price up. The reason for the seller to ask more than true value, a#, is that a higher ask raises the price—as long as the price stays in the zone where the buyer is willing to buy. The price

$$P(a,b) = (a + b)/2$$

is increasing in a. Likewise, the buyer is not taking price as given, but trying to drive the price down. The reason for the buyer to bid less than true value, b#, is that a lower bid lowers the price—again, as long as the price stays in the zone where the seller is willing to sell. Putting these two forces together yields the good Nash equilibrium with equal payoffs.

There is one more thing to notice about all the good Nash equilibria in Figure 6.4. At every one of these equilibria, the bid and ask are equal. This makes sense; it means there is no more room for the price to move. If the bid and ask were different, creating a **spread,** then either side to the transaction could still move the price in its favor—they wouldn't be in equilibrium.

There is yet another argument for the good Nash equilibrium with equal payoffs. Notice that the strategy $a = 3$ weakly dominates the strategy $a = 2$ for the seller; likewise, the strategy $b = 3$ weakly dominates the strategy $b = 4$ for the buyer. Notice what this means: honesty is not the best policy. In fact, honesty is a dominated policy. Bidding slightly less, or asking slightly more, is a better policy. Eliminate the weakly dominated strategies that involve honest revelation of underlying value. We are left with the reduced 2 x 2 game in Figure 6.5, and its iterated dominance solution is ask = 3, bid = 3. The process by which we have reached a single pair of strategies is called **iterated elimination of weakly dominated strategies,** and the pair of strategies that survives iterated elimination of dominated strategies is the iterated dominance solution. Ultimately, greed looks like a bad strategy from the viewpoint of domination—regardless of what the characters in the movie *Wall Street* say.

There are three important things to note about iterated elimination of dominated strategies. First, elimination of weakly dominated strategies can fail to reveal all the Nash equilibria that exist. Going from Figure 6.4 to Figure 6.5, two Nash equilibria disappear. Second, the Nash equilibria that one ends up with depend on how one proceeds—this is called **path dependence.** To see this, consider the following alternative path. First eliminate the weakly dominated strategy, $a = 2$, and only this strategy. You get the matrix in Figure 6.6. Next, eliminate the weakly dominated strategy, $b = 2$, leading to the game matrix in Figure 6.7. If you stop here, you are looking at two pure strategy Nash equilibria. One of these, $(a,b) = (3,3)$, we reached by the first iterated elimination path; the second of these, $(a,b) = 4,4$, we did not. Third, elimination of weakly dominated strategies

---

FIGURE 6.5 **MARKET GAME: ITERATED DOMINANCE SOLUTION**

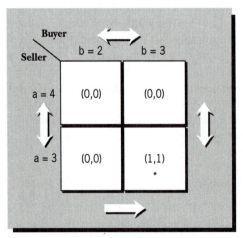

can lead to Nash equilibria in the reduced game that are not Nash equilibria in the original game.

The preceding argument also shows why we were able to ignore bids by the buyer higher than $4 and asks by the seller lower than $2 when we set up the market game. These strategies would also be dominated. So we actually used elimination of weakly dominated strategies even when we set up the game. Similarly, we were able to ignore bids by the buyer lower than $2 (the minimum the seller is willing to accept) and asks by the seller higher than $4 (the maximum the buyer is willing to pay)—these strategies are again dominated.

One moral to draw from this very simple market game is that institutions such as markets are capable of yielding very efficient outcomes. But such efficiency depends crucially on the strategies used by the players. Bad strategies can lead to bad outcomes—even with good institutions. And honesty is not always the best policy.

FIGURE 6.6 MARKET GAME: ITERATED ELIMINATION OF WEAKLY DOMINATED STRATEGIES (ALTERNATIVE PATH: STEP 1)

	b = 2	b = 3	b = 4
a = 4	(0,0)	(0,0)	(2,0)
a = 3	(0,0)	(1,1)	(1.5,0.5)

FIGURE 6.7 MARKET GAME: ITERATED ELIMINATION OF WEAKLY DOMINATED STRATEGIES (ALTERNATIVE PATH: STEP 2)

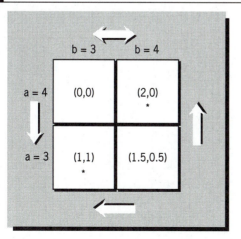

	b = 3	b = 4
a = 4	(0,0)	(2,0) *
a = 3	(1,1) *	(1.5,0.5)

■ 6.4. MARKET GAMES WITH MANY BUYERS AND SELLERS

In the previous section, we looked at the market game between a single buyer and a single seller. Such markets are rare; most of the time a market has many sellers and many buyers. In this section, we consider how the market described earlier works with more than two players.

The simplest next step is to consider two buyers and two sellers. We identify the buyers by their true willingness to pay, $6 and $4 respectively. We identify the sellers by their true willingness to sell, $1 and $2 respectively.

First, suppose that buyers and sellers honestly report their potentially valuable information to the market. This results in the Demand and Supply arrays in Figure 6.8. Demand is arrayed from highest willingness to pay (at $6) on down; Supply is arrayed from lowest willingness to accept (at $1) on up. These demand and supply arrays obey the Law of Demand and Law of Supply, respectively.

As you can see from Figure 6.8, market equilibrium under price-taking behavior occurs at $Q^* = 2$, with any price P^* between $2 and $4. We call the pair that sets the bounds on equilibrium price (here, the buyer willing to pay $4 and the seller willing to accept $2) the **marginal pair.** The marginal pair determines the limits on market price.

We now consider the 4-person market game based on the true willingness to pay of the two buyers and the true willingness to sell of the two sellers. Each buyer has as possible strategies a bid b; each seller has as possible strategies an ask a. Implicit in everything we have done (and will do in this chapter) is **complete information;** each player in the 4-person market game knows all the information in Figure 6.8. It is as if there was a "blue book" for every market participant's willingness to buy and sell, that any market participant could look up. We consider the implications of relaxing that assumption in Chapter 12 on auctions.

First we need some trading rules. Suppose that there is an **auctioneer** who provides the service of price formation to the market. Each buyer submits a bid to the auctioneer, who

FIGURE 6.8   DEMAND AND SUPPLY: MARKET GAME WITH FOUR PLAYERS

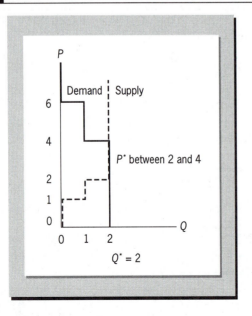

arrays them from highest to lowest, as in Figure 6.6. Simultaneously, each seller submits an ask to the auctioneer, who arrays them from lowest to highest, as in Figure 6.8. The auctioneer then executes all pairs of transactions for which there is a willing buyer and willing seller, starting with the highest bid and lowest ask pair, until no more transactions can be executed.

To see how this trading rule works, suppose the two buyers submit the bids $6 (this is honest revelation) and $3; the two sellers submit the asks $1 (this is honest revelation) and $3. The auctioneer then arrays these bids and asks, some of which are strategic, as market demand and supply. Figure 6.9 shows the market that results. The auctioneer first executes the transaction between the buyer bidding $6 and the seller asking $1; this pair is certainly willing to trade. The auctioneer then executes the transaction between the buyer bidding $3 and the seller asking $3; this is the marginal pair. At this point, the auctioneer is finished executing transactions, since there are no more potential traders available on either side of the market.

The auctioneer isn't quite done, however; he or she still needs to determine the price at which transactions occur. Here, the auctioneer uses the price formula of the previous section, with the bid and ask of the marginal pair. For the market in Figure 6.9, that implies

$$P(a,b) = P(3,3) = (3 + 3)/2 = 3$$

$3 is the price at which the auctioneer executes all transactions.

At the price = $3, every buyer and seller gains. Here are those gains:

The buyer with $b\# = \$6$ gets the payoff $b\# - P = \$6 - \$3 = \$3$.
The buyer with $b\# = \$4$ gets the payoff $b\# - P = \$4 - \$3 = \$1$.
The seller with $a\# = \$1$ gets the payoff $P - a\# = \$3 - \$1 = \$2$.
The seller with $a\# = \$4$ gets the payoff $P - a\# = \$3 - \$2 = \$1$.

FIGURE 6.9 STRATEGIC BID-ASK ARRAYS

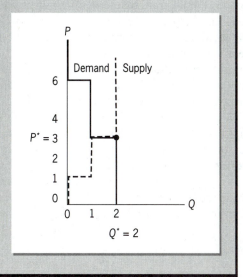

Now we argue that this vector of bids and asks is a Nash equilibrium. Here we argue that no player in the market game can increase his or her payoff by unilaterally changing behavior—that's the test for Nash equilibrium. First consider the buyer with true willingness to pay of $6, who is bidding that true willingness, and getting the largest payoff of any player in the game. The only way this player could increase that payoff is by lowering the price. That would imply putting in a bid lower than $3. That would lower the price all right—and shut this buyer right out of the market. At a price below $3, there is only one willing seller, and that seller would be matched with the now high bidder at $3. So any attempt by the highest bidder to lower the price below $3 would wipe out that buyer's payoff.

Similarly, consider the seller with true willingness to pay of $1, who is asking that true willingness, and getting the second largest payoff of any player in the game. The only way this player could increase the payoff is by raising the price. That would imply submitting an ask higher than $3. That would raise the price all right—and shut this seller right out of the market. At a price above $3, there is only one willing buyer, and that buyer would be matched with the now low bidder at $3. So any attempt by the lowest ask to raise the price above $3 would wipe out that seller's payoff.

These two players pass the test for Nash equilibrium. That leaves the marginal pair, at ask = bid = $3. These two players are in effect playing the game shown in Figure 6.4—the fact that there are other players in the game does not affect the price formation by and payoffs to these two players. So they pass the Nash equilibrium test also.

Notice the Nash equilibrium just described is a good Nash equilibrium—it achieves a total payoff of 7, which is the maximum total surplus, consumer surplus plus producer surplus, available. You can see the total surplus as the area between demand and supply in Figure 6.8. Since the maximum total payoffs possible are 7 and the minimum total payoff is zero (no trades), the total payoff at this Nash equilibrium is $3 + 1 + 2 + 1 = 7$, and achieves an efficiency of 100 percent.

The preceding market game has many good Nash equilibria, depending on how the total payoff of 7 is distributed among four players; see if you can find one. This market game also has bad Nash equilibria, which lead to inefficient outcomes. Here is a bad Nash equilibrium, which exhibits maximum greed on the part of every player. At this Nash equilibrium, both buyers bid $1 and both sellers ask $6. At these asks and bids, no units are transacted, so efficiency = 0%. Moreover, no individual player can profitably make a transaction happen, by unilaterally changing his or her ask or bid.

We see that the main features of the simplest market game extend to market games with more than one buyer and one seller. There are good and bad Nash equilibria. The good Nash equilibria involve some strategic behavior, while the bad Nash equilibria require greedy behavior. We gain an extra insight by observing the following. Suppose at a good Nash equilibrium, # of buyers = # of sellers = n, and let n be large. Then for $n - 1$ buyers and $n - 1$ sellers, the ones who aren't the marginal pair, asking or bidding true value is a Nash equilibrium strategy. So for large n, the fraction of buyers (sellers) for whom honest behavior is $[(n - 1)/n]$; as n gets large, this fraction approaches 1. So the classical assumptions have a strategic foundation after all: with a large number n of buyers (sellers), price-taking behavior and revelation of valuable information are consistent with Nash equilibrium.

◼ 6.5 PRICE FORMATION ON THE NEW YORK STOCK EXCHANGE

Let's consider a real-life example of price formation, the way stock prices are determined on the New York Stock Exchange (NYSE). The NYSE was founded in 1792 by all-around founding father Alexander Hamilton (he also sold the first U.S. bonds and created the U.S. dollar). The NYSE has always had specialists on the floor of the exchange, who form prices of individual stocks from bid-ask arrays.

Individuals and institutions who want to buy or sell shares relay their buying and selling orders to the floor of the exchange, usually via a member firm. Unlike the market games of this chapter, those orders can be for more than one share of stock. Orders take two forms, **limit** and **at the market.** A limit order is just like the strategies you have seen in this chapter: a buyer gives the market a price at (or below) which they are willing to buy one (or more) shares, and that order immediately goes into the demand-side market array. A market order is different from the strategies you have seen in this chapter: a buyer asks to buy a set number of shares at whatever price is currently available. The buyer does not know what price he or she will actually pay; that depends on the exact time when the buyer's order reaches the trading floor. The specialist is supposed to execute a market order as soon as possible, by finding willing sellers immediately.

Traditionally, limit buy and sell orders were in terms of fractions of a dollar divisible by two. This fits nicely into the pricing rule you have studied, since the average of any pair of prices divisible by two is itself divisible by two. Until the year 2001, bids and asks were expressed in terms of 1/16 of a dollar, and market prices were expressed in terms of 1/32 of a dollar. [Prior to the 1960s, coarser units were the norm.] So in the specialist's array, if the lowest bid for a stock was 5 1/4 and the highest ask was 5 3/8, the transactions price would be the average of these, 5 5/16. The market rules forbade transactions involving wider spreads than 1/8 of a dollar, the spread in this example. The NASDAQ ran into a great deal of legal trouble and bad publicity, over allegations that spreads there were wider than at the NYSE. Wide spreads allow the specialist to favor one side of a transaction over another, especially when market orders are involved.

In the year 2001, following the lead of the NASDAQ, the NYSE went to decimal pricing. Now all bids and asks can be in increments of $.01, as are the transaction prices. Essentially, with bid-ask spreads as fine as a penny, it is no longer necessary to split the difference of a penny. However, it is not yet clear whether this rule change in price formation has reduced price formation spreads down to a penny—this question needs further research.

◼ 6.6 QUANTITY COMPETITION BETWEEN TWO FIRMS

We now turn to markets with a large number of buyers, so price-taking behavior makes sense for them, but with a small number of sellers, who have sizeable market shares and thus can influence the market price. In some markets like this, firms compete in terms of quantity. Each breakfast cereal company, for example, tries to get as much shelf space in the grocery store as possible. In other markets, firms compete in terms of price. The number of seats offered by the airlines is roughly constant, but they are continually offering all kinds of deals on fares. The first market games we consider involve markets where firms compete in terms of quantity. This type of game was the first studied by a French economist, Augustin Cournot, a century and a half ago. His model of competition is now called Cournot competition, and the equilibrium of his market game, Cournot equilibrium, is named in his honor.[2] We will study Cournot competition as a noncooperative game in normal form, showing that the Nash equilibrium of this game leads to a market outcome where price is above marginal cost and is therefore inefficient.

In **Cournot competition,** each firm i brings a quantity x_i to market. For the moment, we keep things simple by having only two firms in the market. Each firm has constant returns to scale, hence constant average variable costs, denoted by c. The products of the two firms, numbered 1 and 2, are perfect substitutes, and so must sell at the same market price. Market price, P, is determined by market demand:

$$P = 130 - Q \text{ if } Q \text{ does not exceed } 130$$

$$0 \text{ otherwise}$$

where Q denotes total market quantity. We assume that each firm i wants to maximize profits. Let $\mathbf{x} = (x_1, x_2)$ be the vector of each firm's quantity delivered to the market. Firm's 1's profits, written $u_1(\mathbf{x})$, are determined by firm 1's revenue minus cost:

$$u_1(\mathbf{x}) = \text{revenue} - \text{cost}$$
$$= Px_1 - cx_1$$
$$= (P - c)x_1$$

The term $P - c$ represents the profit margin on each unit firm 1 sells. Firm 2's profits have the same look:

$$u_2(\mathbf{x}) = (P - c)x_2$$

The strategic interaction between the two firms comes about because the market price, P, is determined by how much *both* firms produce and sell.

For purposes of this example, set $c = \$10$ for both firms. Let's first work out the case where each firm has three strategies: produce and sell 30, 40, or 60 units. The normal form game that results is shown in Figure 6.10. The entries of the matrix can be computed as follows. Take $x_1 = x_2 = 30$. Sixty units are shipped to market. The price at which these 60 units sell is:

$$P = 130 - Q = 130 - 60 = \$70$$

Since average cost = \$10, the profit margin is $P - c = \$70 - \$10 = \$60$/unit. Finally, since each firm i is selling 30 units, it earns a profit

$$u_i(\mathbf{x}) = (P - c)\, x_i = (\$60/\text{unit}) \ (30 \text{ units}) = \$1{,}800$$

These are the entries corresponding to the quantities ($x_1 = 30$, $x_2 = 30$). You can work out the other entries of the matrix in a similar fashion.

Restricted to only these three strategies, the market game has a single equilibrium: each firm produces 40 units. Arrows point in to this outcome from both directions,

---

[2] Cournot's remarkable work appeared in the last chapter of his book, *Researches into the Mathematical Principles of the Theory of Wealth* (New York: Macmillan, 1897; originally published in 1838). Cournot's solution thus predates von Neumann's famous paper by 90 years.

FIGURE 6.10 **COURNOT MARKET GAME, TWO PLAYERS**

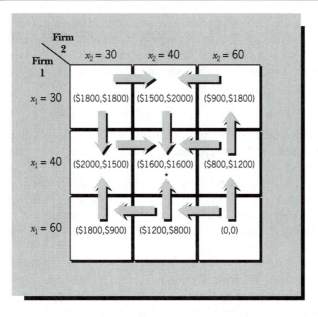

whereas arrows point away from every other outcome in at least one direction. This is the **Cournot equilibrium: $x^* = (40,40)$**. At this equilibrium, the market price is \$130 – \$80 = \$50, which is substantially above marginal cost, \$10. The firms involved are making considerable profits, with a profit margin of \$40 on each of the 40 units they sell, for total profits of \$1,600, above and beyond the normal profits built into the cost function.

Notice that the efficiency of the Cournot equilibrium—we could also call this the Nash equilibrium of the market game where firms use quantity as their strategy and buyers are nonstrategic—is less than 100 percent.

In particular, the maximum total payoffs in Figure 6.8 occur at the quantities 30 each, where total payoffs are \$1,800 + \$1,800 = \$3,600. So the efficiency of Cournot equilibrium is 3200/3600 = 89%, somewhat less than 100 percent.

Now suppose that the firms are not restricted to the strategies 30, 40 and 60, but quantity can be any number between 30 and 60. We will check that the quantity 40 for each firm remains the Cournot equilibrium even when these other strategies are allowed. To see why, consider what happens to firm 1's profit if it reduces quantity from 40 to 39, while firm 2 continues to produce and sell 40 units. In this case, the price rises 1 unit from \$50 to \$51, so firm 1's profit margin rises one unit from \$40 to \$41. Multiplying firm 1's profit margin of \$41 by its quantity of 39 units, we get a total profit of (41)(39) = \$1,599—one dollar less than the profit at a quantity of 40 units. You can check that the same one-dollar reduction in profit occurs if the firm increases output to 41 units, driving price down to \$49. Indeed, the further firm 1 gets from a quantity of 40 units, the lower its profit becomes, until profit is all the way down to \$0 at the quantities of either 0 or 80, 40 units away from the Cournot equilibrium quantity of 40.

The one thing we haven't shown you is where we got the Cournot equilibrium quantities of 40 each. That requires further argument, which is in the appendix to this chapter.

◼ 6.7 THE COURNOT LIMIT THEOREM

We can now compare Cournot equilibrium with other kinds of market outcomes. In *perfect competitive equilibrium,* market price equals marginal cost. If this market were perfectly competitive, the price would be $10, since marginal cost is $10. In *monopoly equilibrium,* market profits are as large as possible. A monopoly[3] in this market would maximize total market profits, *u,* where *u* is given by

$$u = u_1 + u_2 = (P - c)Q = (120 - Q)Q$$

We show in the appendix that the maximum profits occur at $Q = 60$. A monopoly will produce and sell 60 units, with a corresponding price of $70, a profit margin of $60, and total profits of ($60)(60) = $3,600.

The monopoly equilibrium, Cournot equilibrium, and perfectly competitive equilibrium are shown in Figure 6.11. Monopoly is associated with the highest price, lowest quantity, and highest profits. Perfect competition is associated with the lowest price, highest quantity, and lowest profits ($0). Cournot equilibrium lies in between on all three dimensions.

Thus, *Cournot competition between two firms leads to an outcome between monopoly and perfect competition.* The same thing is true for more than two firms. Notice that if we start with just two firms, each of them will be making positive profits, with price above the long-run average total cost. Since these two firms enjoy constant returns to scale, there are no natural barriers to entry by other firms in search of above-normal returns. So we would expect more firms to enter the market. Indeed, the more firms that enter the market, the closer the situation comes to perfect competition. In the limit as the number of firms in Cournot competition becomes large, the market outcome is identical to perfect competition. We show this, using some calculus, in the appendix to this chapter.

In Chapter 5, when we took the limit as the number of energy firms using the commons grew large, we called the outcome tragic: the resource was wasted, and there was no offsetting gain for anyone else involved. No one stands to gain from the destruction of a

FIGURE 6.11 | **COURNOT MARKET GAME: MARKET OUTCOMES COMPARED**

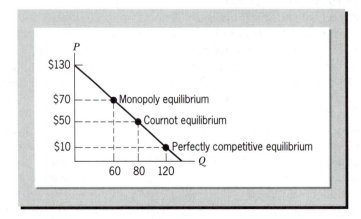

[3] One way to create such a monopoly is to have all the firms in the market form one gigantic merger. The Federal Trade Commission, which has the responsibility for keeping markets competitive, typically disallows such mergers.

commons. The situation here is different. In a market, there are buyers involved as well as sellers. Rather than being a tragedy, from the standpoint of the buyers, prices near marginal cost are a really good deal. When we consider both buyers' and sellers' gains from trade in a market, we will see that the limit of Cournot equilibrium as the number of firms grows large is a good thing.

We can use market surplus analysis to show why the Cournot outcome with many firms is no tragedy. Every market generates a **total surplus**, equal to the sum of consumer's and producer's surplus, reflecting the total gain to both sides of the market. The consumer's surplus is the area between the demand curve and the market price; the producer's surplus is the area between market price and marginal cost. Figure 6.12 shows the consumer's surplus, producer's surplus and total surplus in the Cournot limit. For $n = 1$ (Figure 6.12a), the producer's surplus is the area $60 \times 60 = 3600$; the consumer's surplus is the area $60 \times 60/2 = 1800$; and the total surplus is $3600 + 1800 = 5400$. For $n = 2$ (Figure 6.12b), the producer's surplus is $40 \times 80 = 3200$; the consumer's surplus, $80 \times 80/2 = 3200$; and the total surplus is $3200 + 3200 = 6400$. Sellers lose as their numbers grow, but buyers gain, and the gains of the buyers more than make up for the reduced gains of the sellers. For very large n (Figure 6.12c), producer's surplus = 0; consumer's surplus = $120 \times 120/2 = 7200$. The total surplus is $0 + 7200 = 7200$. As expected, perfect competition maximizes the total surplus; unfortunately for the sellers (and their shareholders), all that gain goes to the buyers. In contrast, monopoly maximizes gain to the seller, but to do this it has to minimize total surplus.

Notice that, when comparing monopoly with perfect competition, in principle, the winner under competition, the buyers, could compensate the loser, the monopolist, $3,600 and still have $3,600 > $1,800. This is the sense in which perfect competition is a good thing: the switch from monopoly to perfect competition need not have any losers. Without such compensation, the switch to competition is bad for the seller.

◨ 6.8 PRICE COMPETITION BETWEEN TWO FIRMS

The next market games we will consider involve markets where firms compete in terms of price. This market game was first studied a century ago by a French critic of Cournot,

FIGURE 6.12 **CONSUMER AND PRODUCER SURPLUS UNDER VARIOUS STRATEGIC SITUATIONS**

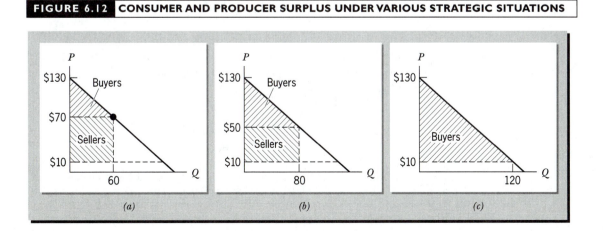

J. Bertrand. Bertrand's model of competition is now called **Bertrand competition,** and the equilibrium of his market game, **Bertrand equilibrium,** is named in his honor. This section presents Bertrand competition as a noncooperative game in normal form, and shows that the equilibrium of this market game, Bertrand equilibrium, is different from Cournot equilibrium.[4]

Intuitively, using the experience of monopoly as a guide, you might think that it doesn't matter whether firms use price or quantity as a strategic variable. It certainly doesn't matter for a monopoly. But then a monopoly doesn't have competitors. In both Cournot and Bertrand competition, competitors are present, and the way their presence is felt depends on how the market aggregates their behavior. In a market where quantity is the strategic variable, market price depends on market quantity, which is *the sum of the firm's quantities.* In a market where price is the strategic variable, it is *the minimum of all the firms' prices* that determines market price. Informed buyers will not pay more than they have to, and they don't have to pay more than the lowest price being offered. This in a nutshell is why Bertrand competition and Cournot competition differ.

To elaborate on this difference, start with the same market demand used before, only inverting price and quantity:

$$Q = 130 - P$$

Firm 1's profits are revenue minus cost, here

$$u_1(\mathbf{p}) = (p_1 - c)\, x_1(\mathbf{p})$$

where $\mathbf{p} = (p_1, p_2)$ is the vector of firms' prices, and $x_1(\mathbf{p})$ is the demand facing firm 1. Firm 2's profits are given analogously:

$$u_2(\mathbf{p}) = (p_2 - c)\, x_2(\mathbf{p})$$

We retain the cost structure of section 6.7, with unit cost $c = \$10$; the firms are selling products that are perfect substitutes.

A problem we immediately encounter is how to define firm 1's quantity demanded, $x_1(\mathbf{p})$. The quantity firm 1 sells depends both on its price and on the price of its competitor, firm 2. There are three cases to consider. First, firm 1 is asking the lowest price, $p_1 < p_2$. In this case, firm 1 gets the entire market, since consumers maximize their utility by buying at the lowest available price. We have $x_1(\mathbf{p}) = 130 - p_1$. Second, firm 2 is asking the lowest price, $p_2 < p_1$. In this case, firm 2 gets the entire market and firm 1 sells nothing. Firm 1 has been *undersold* by firm 2. We have $x_1(\mathbf{p}) = 0$. Third, suppose that both firms ask the same price,

$$p_1 = p_2$$

In this case they somehow share the market. For the sake of symmetry, let's assume that the firms share the market equally.[5] We summarize this discussion succinctly by the following demand curve for firm 1:

$$\begin{aligned}
x_1(\mathbf{p}) &= 130 - p_1 \text{ when } p_1 < p_2 \\
&= (130 - p_1)/2 \text{ when } p_1 = p_2 \\
&= 0 \text{ when } p_1 > p_2
\end{aligned}$$

---

[4] The reference is J. Bertrand, Review of "Théorie mathématique de la richesse sociale," by A. Cournot, *Journal des Savants* 68(1883): 499–508. This was the first published review of Cournot's book, 45 years after it was written. The pace of science in the nineteenth century was a lot more relaxed than it is today.

[5] The Bertrand equilibrium has the same form, regardless of the exact market sharing rule used.

This is the demand curve for firm 1 in Bertrand competition, and it is shown in Figure 6.13. The strategic interaction in this form of competition shows up solely through the demand curve. The demand curve for firm 2 is similar:

$$x_2(\mathbf{p}) = 130 - p_2 \text{ when } p_2 < p_1$$
$$= (130 - p_1)/2 \text{ when } p_1 = p_2$$
$$= 0 \text{ when } p_2 > p_1$$

Notice that demand is discontinuous at the point where prices are equal, as shown in Figure 16.3.

We now go about finding a Bertrand equilibrium. We first consider a matrix version as we did for Cournot equilibrium, with prices corresponding to the quantities in Figure 6.10. Each firm can charge one of three possible prices, $70, $50, and $10. The matrix game to which this leads is shown in Figure 6.14.

We will walk through two of the profit entries. If both firms charge price = $70, then both sell $(130 - 70)/2 = 30$ units. The profit margin is $70 - $10 = $60/unit, so profits are $60(30) = $1,800, as shown by the outcome for $p_1 = p_2 = $70.

By contrast, if at least one firm charges a rock-bottom price equal to cost, then nobody in the market will make any money. This accounts for all the zeros along the bottom and the right side of the matrix.

There are two Bertrand equilibria. The first is right in the middle of the matrix, just as the Cournot equilibrium was, at price $p_1{}^* = p_2{}^* = $50. The other is at the rock-bottom price $p_1{}^* = p_2{}^* = $10. This second equilibrium is in weakly dominated strategies, however—notice that the strategy Price = $50 weakly dominates the strategy Price = $10, for both row and column player. The most attractive Nash equilibrium in Figure 6.14 is the equilibrium $\mathbf{p}^* = (\$50, \$50)$.

Unfortunately for the firms involved, if they aren't restricted to just three prices and can charge any price they want, only the zero-profit equilibrium, price = $10, is left to them. Let each firm's set of strategies be the price interval [0,130]. A firm charging a price above $130 has *priced itself out of the market* and guarantees that it will sell nothing. A price

FIGURE 6.13 BERTRAND DEMAND, FIRM 1

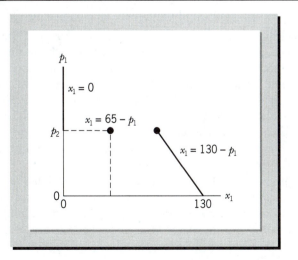

FIGURE 6.14 BERTRAND MARKET GAME, TWO PLAYERS

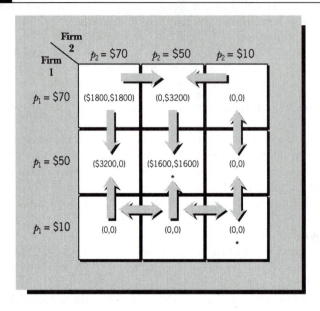

just below \$130 may actually sell something, and so has a chance of actually making a profit. A firm charging \$0 *is giving its product away*. Again, this is no way to make money. We don't expect to see firms charging extreme prices, such as \$130 or \$0, in equilibrium, and we won't.

Since the two firms have the same costs and sell perfect substitutes, they are economically symmetrical. Since they have the same strategy sets and same-shaped profit functions, the market game they are in is symmetrical. To solve the game, we look for a symmetrical equilibrium, where $p_1 = p_2$. There are two different cases to consider:

Case 1: $p_1 = p_2 > 10$. Let p denote the price common to both firms. The payoff to firm 1 is the following:

$$u_1 = (p - 10)(130 - p)/2$$

This is not an equilibrium for firm 1. If firm 1 raises its price above p, it loses all sales, so this is not the right way to go. If firm 1 lowers its price ever so slightly, then it doubles its sales, while reducing its profit margin by only a tiny amount. For all practical purposes, it doubles its profits. For example, let the common price $p = \$50$, which was an equilibrium in Figure 6.14. Then profits at a price of \$50 are $(50 - 10)(40) = \$1,600$, whereas profits at a price of \$49.99 are $(49.99 - 10)(130 - 49.99) = \$3,200$ to the nearest dollar. The same argument shows that this is also not an equilibrium for firm 2. Any price above cost gets undercut.

Case 2: $p_1 = p_2 = 10$. Prices are now down to unit cost, so both firms break even. If a firm cuts the price any further, it cuts its own throat—and goes into the red. Moreover, if a firm raises its price above \$10, it gets no sales, and so continues to break even. This is the only symmetrical equilibrium left to the firms. *The Bertrand solution in this case is precisely the perfectly competitive outcome, price marginal cost.* Although it takes a lot more than two firms in Cournot competition to get perfect competition, in Bertrand competition with perfect substitutes and lots of prices possible, two firms constitute just enough competition to yield perfect competition. This result is the conclusion of the Bertrand limit theorem, that the limit of Bertrand competition is perfectly competitive equilibrium, already with $n = 2$.

Although two firms in Cournot competition would be a tight oligopoly with outcomes not too far from monopoly, two firms in Bertrand competition essentially cut each other's throats. Price competition, even among a few firms, tends to be much more intense, and much more corrosive of profits, than quantity competition. For this reason, such competition is often called **ruinous competition.** If carried to extremes, it can ruin profits.

■ 6.9 ZERO-PERCENT FINANCING IN THE U.S. AUTOMOBILE MARKET[6]

You have just seen that Cournot and Bertrand equilibrium in the same market lead to very different outcomes. You should be asking yourself, does this theoretical difference matter in the real world? Actually, it does. In an oligopoly, where a few firms dominate the market, if competition is Cournot-style, involving quantities, then price tends to be higher than if competition is Bertrand-style, involving price.

For most of the past century, the U.S. automobile industry has been a tight oligopoly, with a few domestic firms (currently two—General Motors and Ford—DaimlerChrysler is a German firm) dominating the market. In the last 30 years, imports have also gained a substantial market share, now constituting 30 percent of the market.

The market leader since the 1920s, General Motors, has seen its market share slide in recent years, with market share lost to both domestic competitors and foreign imports. In response to this loss of market share, from 50 percent in 1980 to 30 percent today, General Motors decided to implement what is essentially a price-cutting strategy, just as in Bertrand competition. Most new car buyers finance their new car purchase—these are big-ticket items, with an average price in excess of $20,000. Most new car buyers don't have that kind of cash at their disposal. Reducing the interest rate on financing for a new car is tantamount to offering these new car buyers a price cut.

When General Motors announced its 0 percent financing strategy, this was good news for buyers. Instead of paying 7 percent or higher interest on new car debt, these buyers were getting that credit for free. So it was no surprise when the Law of Demand kicked in, and new car buyers in droves rushed to buy General Motors products.

To see the impact on General Motors profits, it is important to remember that General Motors makes more money financing a new car sale (through its financing subsidiary, GMAC), than it does producing the new car. Giving away the financing also meant giving away the lion's share of the profits.

Bertrand competition says that price cuts (above cost) will be followed by competitors. This is exactly what happened in the U.S. auto industry. Ford and DaimlerChrysler quickly followed the General Motors 0 percent financing offer with comparable 0 percent financing offers of their own.

Fall of 2001 was a banner quarter for new car buyers, as has been the fall of 2002, which again saw 0 percent financing deals. Unbelievably low interest rates speak volumes to new car buyers, and record new car sales are the result. As far as oligopoly profits are concerned,

---

[6] This material is drawn in part from Gregory L. White, *Wall Street Journal,* "GM's 0% Finance Plan is Good for Economy, Risky for the Company," 30 October 2001.

however, the news is completely Bertrandian. Profit margins have fallen to razor-thin levels, and none of the firms' involved profits have gone up. As for General Motors, it may have gained slightly in market share, but its bottom line is nothing to make shareholders happy.

■ SUMMARY

1. The simplest market game involves one buyer and one seller. The price in such a market is formed by the actions of the buyer and seller.

2. Perfect competition assumes that all market participants are price-takers, and they honestly reveal potentially valuable information.

3. The market game between one buyer and one seller has many Nash equilibria. Some of these Nash equilibria are efficient, but others are not. None of the Nash equilibria has all market participants taking price as given, or honestly revealing potentially valuable information.

4. The results of the simplest market game between one buyer and one seller extend to markets with many buyers and sellers. There exist good and bad Nash equilibria for such markets.

5. The price formation service on a stock exchange, like that in New York, is provided by specialists, who play the role of auctioneers.

6. In Cournot competition, firms use quantity shipped to market as their strategic variable. The Nash equilibrium of a Cournot market game is often called a Cournot equilibrium, in honor of the economist who first studied such competition.

7. In a Cournot equilibrium, when firms' products are perfect substitutes, price lies below monopoly levels but above marginal cost. Neither monopoly nor perfect competition is a Cournot equilibrium.

8. As the number of firms selling perfect substitutes in Cournot competition grows large, the Cournot equilibrium price approaches marginal cost. This phenomenon is called the Cournot limit theorem.

9. In Bertrand competition, firms use price called out in the market as their strategic variable. The equilibrium of a Bertrand market game is called a Bertrand equilibrium.

10. In a Bertrand equilibrium, when firms' products are perfect substitutes and firms' costs are the same, price equals marginal cost.

■ KEY TERMS

noncooperative market games in normal form	spread	Cournot competition
price-taking behavior	iterated elimination of weakly dominated strategies	Cournot equilibrium
honest revelation of potentially valuable information	path dependence	Cournot limit theorem
active market equilibrium	marginal pair	Total surplus
open outcry	complete information	Bertrand competition
producer's surplus	auctioneer	Bertrand equilibrium
consumer's surplus	limit order	ruinous competition
	market order	

■ PROBLEMS

1. There is a single buyer, with $b\# = \$10$; a single seller, with $a\# = \$6$. Plot the market demand and supply for this simple market. What does perfect competition predict?

2. Assume the same market fundamentals as in problem 1. Now bids and asks are even numbers. Find all the Nash equilibria you can for the market game. Which of these Nash equilibria are efficient? Which are in dominated strategies?

3. Conduct a competitive market analysis of the simple market when b# = $6 and a# = $10. Then analyze this as a market game in normal form. To what Nash equilibria do such market fundamentals lead?

4. Find another good Nash equilibrium for the large market in section 6.5.

5. Verify that the bad Nash equilibrium in section 6.6 is indeed an equilibrium.

6. There are three buyers with true willingness to buy #b = $7, $5, and $1 respectively. There are three sellers with true willingness to sell a# = $2, $5, and $9. Find the outcomes of perfect competition; then find a good Nash equilibrium of the market game, where asks and bids are whole numbers.

7. Market demand is given by P = 140 – Q. There are two firms, each with unit costs = $20. Firms can choose any quantity. Find the Cournot equilibrium and compare it to the monopoly outcome and to the perfectly competitive outcome. Why aren't the latter equilibria of the market game?

8. What is the outcome of the oligopoly in problem 7 as the number of firms grows large? Why will the number of firms grow large? Is this outcome a tragedy?

9. Suppose that two firms both have average variable cost $50. Market demand is given by Q = 100 – P. Find the Bertrand equilibrium. Would your answer change if there were three firms?

10. Explain why 0 percent financing is good for consumers, but bad for the profits of firms involved. Use consumer and producer surplus in your answer. Is 0 percent financing a Cournot equilibrium?

11. We showed in section 6.8 that with continuous pricing, the Bertrand equilibrium has zero profits. This depends crucially on the feature that the products involved were perfect substitutes. If their products are differentiated instead, then Bertrand equilibrium can lead to positive profits. Here's a 2-firm example. Firm 1 has the demand function

$$x_1(\mathbf{p}) = 180 - p_1 - (p_1 - \text{average price})$$

where the average is taken over the price of the two firms. Firm 2's demand function is the same, only with its price replacing firm 1's price. Each firm has average (and marginal) cost = $20 per unit. Suppose the firms use the three prices {$94, $84, $74} as strategies. Draw the 3 x 3 matrix game and find its Bertrand equilibrium. What are profits at this equilibrium?

■ APPENDIX. DERIVING THE COURNOT EQUILIBRIUM, THE MONOPOLY SOLUTION, AND THE COURNOT LIMIT THEOREM

In this section, we first derive the Cournot equilibrium and monopoly solution for section 6.7. First, consider firm 1 in Cournot competition. It has the payoff function:

$$u_i = (P - c)x_i$$

Let P^* and Q^* denote the market price and quantity at Cournot equilibrium. Given firm 2's quantity at that equilibrium, firm 1's quantity x_i^* maximizes 1's profit. Any deviation h

from that quantity, $x_i^* + h$, cannot lead to great profits. Note that h can be either positive or negative.

Substituting the maximum profit condition into 1's payoff function,

$$u_i(\mathbf{x}^*) = (P^* - c)x_i^* \geq (P^* - h - c)(x_i^* + h) = u_i(x_1^* + h, x_2^*)$$

where the asterisk (*) denotes the Cournot equilibrium.

Simplifying the preceding inequality, we get

$$0 \geq (P^* - h - c)h - h\,(xi^* + h)$$

Rewriting this once more

$$h^2 \geq (a - 2x_i^* - x_2^* - c)h$$

where a is the vertical intercept of the market demand line.

Now divide both sides by h. For h positive, we have that

$$h \geq (a - 2x_i^* - x_2^* - c)$$

while for h negative, we have that

$$(a - 2x_i^* - x_2^* - c)\,?\,h$$

Now take the limit as h goes to 0, and we get the equation

$$(*)\ 0 = (a - 2x_i^* - x_2^* - c)$$

Applying symmetry, so that the Cournot equilibrium quantities of the two firms are equal, we have

$$0 = (a - 3x_i^* - c)$$

Finally, substituting in the values $a = 130$ and $c = 10$, we get

$$0 = (120 - 3x_i^*)$$

Solving, we get the Cournot equilibrium quantities

$$40 = x_i^* = x_2^*$$

as promised.

Now apply a similar argument to the monopoly problem, maximize market profits, which are given by

$$\text{Market profits} = (P - c)Q = (120 - Q)Q$$

Let Q^* be the monopoly solution, and consider a small deviation h from Q^*. Following the above steps, you will reach the equation

$$0 = 120 - 2Q^*$$

leading to the monopoly solution, $Q^* = 60$.

Finally, we derive the Cournot limit theorem for the specific market where market price P and quantity Q obey

$$P = 130 - Q$$

Each firm has constant average (and marginal) cost = 10.

And total quantity Q is the sum of individual firm's quantities sold:

$$Q = x_1 + x_2 + \ldots x_n$$

There are $n > 2$ firms, and we want to show that as the number of firms n grows large, the symmetric Cournot equilibrium approaches the perfectly competitive outcome given in Figure 6.11.

Since we are going to exploit symmetry, it suffices to focus on a single firm, say firm 1. Firm 1's profits are given by

$$u_i = (P - c)x_i$$

Substituting the market demand curve and average cost, we get

$$u_i = (120 - Q)x_i$$

Appealing to the condition (*) which we derived for 2-firm Cournot equilibrium, only replacing "x_2" with "$x_2 + \ldots x_n$" we have

$$0 = 120 - (x_1 + x_2 + \ldots x_n) - x_1$$

Now exploit symmetry, so that all firm quantities equal firm 1's:

Substituting, we have

$$0 = 120 - (nx_1) - x_1 = 120 - (n + 1)x_1$$

Solving, we get

$$x_1{}^* = 120/(n + 1)$$

In the limit as n goes to infinity, $x_1 = 0$:

$$\text{Lim } x_1{}^* = 120/(n + 1) = 0$$

Firm 1 has a $1/n$ market share, so total market quantity $Q = nx_1 = [n/(n + 1)120$.

In the limit as n goes to infinity, $Q = 120$:

$$\text{Lim } Q = [n/(n + 1)120 = 120 \text{ lim } [n/(n + 1)] = 120$$

This is the market quantity corresponding to perfect competition, as promised.

PART TWO

Games with Sequential Structure

CHAPTER 7

Credibility and Subgame Perfect Equilibrium

Threats and promises are a major part of everyday life and a major part of economic activity. When to believe someone's threat or promise and when not to is a key part of decision making. As long as we stick to games in normal form, the question whether a strategy containing a threat or a promise is credible or not doesn't come up. Threats and promises are tied to the future, while all strategic choices in normal form games are made simultaneously in the present. However, in games in extensive form, the issue of credibility comes up in a big way. Making a threat or making a promise becomes a move in the game, and it may have an impact on players who have to move later in the game. For this reason, all the games studied in this chapter are in extensive form.

The chapter begins by introducing the crucial notion of a **subgame**. A subgame is a part of an entire game that, when detached from its parent game, can stand alone as a game. Normal form games cannot have subgames, but extensive form games can. Then the related concept of *subgame perfection*, which is how credibility is expressed in game theory, is discussed. A strategy is subgame perfect when it plays a Nash equilibrium on every subgame. Reinhard Selten won the Nobel Prize in 1994, in part for his work on subgame perfection—even the term is his. This chapter shows how subgame perfection relates to dominated strategies, and why subgame perfection enshrines a notion of credibility. When every strategy in a Nash equilibrium is subgame perfect, that Nash equilibrium itself is subgame perfect. Next, subgame perfection is applied to two episodes a century apart in U.S. history, both of which raise interesting credibility issues. The first of these deals with conscription during the American Civil War (1861–65); the second involves the Cuban missile crisis (1962).

Discussion then returns to noncooperative market games, only now in extensive form. We consider asymmetric price formation, where a monopoly on one side of the market creates a big asymmetry. We consider how much power a monopoly has over buyers, depending on market rules, and how strategic buyers are in the bidding behavior. Finally, we study *Stackelberg competition,* where one firm gets to move before its rivals. Stackelberg competition affects Cournot and Bertrand equilibria in different ways. In Cournot competition, the firm that moves first has the advantage; in Bertrand competition, the firm that moves second has the advantage. As a final example of credibility, the strategic detail of the often-heard marketing claim, "This offer is good for a limited time only," is presented. As you will see, it takes powerful precommitment devices to make this claim credible. The appendix looks at some experiments involving ultimatums, which by their very nature contain credibility issues.

■ 7.1 SUBGAMES AND THEIR EQUILIBRIA

Roughly speaking, a subgame is any part of a game that can itself be played as a game. We can make this quite precise. A subgame is a collection of nodes and branches that satisfies three properties: (1) it begins at a single node; (2) it contains every successor node to this node—a successor to node x is all the nodes that can be reached by following some sequence of branches beginning at x; and (3) if it contains any part of an information set, then it must contain all the nodes in that information set. Consider the game in Figure 7.1a. It has a subgame, shown by the nodes and branches surrounded by a dashed square. Notice that it satisfies the three formal requirements: (1) it begins at a single node, player 2's decision point: (2) it contains the two successor nodes to this node, which are the two endpoints; (3) it contains all of player 2's information set. We will have more to say about this subgame shortly. Next, consider the game in Figure 7.1b. This game does not have a subgame. Player 2 has imperfect information and does not know whether player 1 has gone left or right. When it is player 2's turn to move, there is no way to start a game there.

The difference between these two games comes down to one of timing and information. In the game in Figure 7.1a, each player has perfect information. Player 1 moves first,

---

<table>
<tr><td>**FIGURE 7.1**</td><td>**TELEX VERSUS IBM, EXTENSIVE FORM: ([a] SUBGAME, PERFECT INFORMATION; [b] NO SUBGAME, IMPERFECT INFORMATION)**</td></tr>
</table>

(a)   *(b)*

and when he has to move, player 2 knows what player 1 has done. *Every game with perfect information has subgames.* A complicated game with perfect information has many subgames. In the game in Figure 7.1b, both players move simultaneously. Player 2 does not see what player 1 has done. This makes the game one of imperfect information. This game does not have a subgame. *No game in which the players move simultaneously once and for all has subgames other than itself.* In particular, this statement applies to games in normal form. The difference between the two games in Figure 7.1 is sufficiently subtle that they have the same normal form (see Figure 7.2).

The game in Figure 7.1a is called Telex versus IBM.[1] These two computer firms, one a giant (IBM), the other an upstart (Telex), were battling for market share and profits in the late 1960s. Telex was making inroads into IBM's market share by creating almost perfect substitutes for IBM's hardware. Telex products, such as computer printers and memories, were plug compatible, which meant they could be plugged right into an IBM machine and work fine. Call player 1 Telex, and player 2, IBM. Telex moves first. Telex can either enter IBM's market or stay out. If Telex stays out, it earns a normal profit somewhere else in the economy ($u_1 = 1$) and IBM makes monopoly profits in its market ($u_2 = 5$). If Telex enters IBM's market, then IBM has to move. IBM can accommodate Telex by letting it into the market without a fight. Or IBM can smash Telex, slashing prices to the bone so that both companies are making no profit. The term *smash* for this strategy comes from an internal IBM memorandum of the period, entitled Operation Smash, which outlined precisely this response to Telex's entry attempt.[2] If IBM accommodates Telex's entry, then they each get the payoff 2. If IBM smashes Telex, then they each get the payoff 0. After either of these moves by IBM, the subgame ends and the overall game ends.

FIGURE 7.2 **TELEX VERSUS IBM, NORMAL FORM**

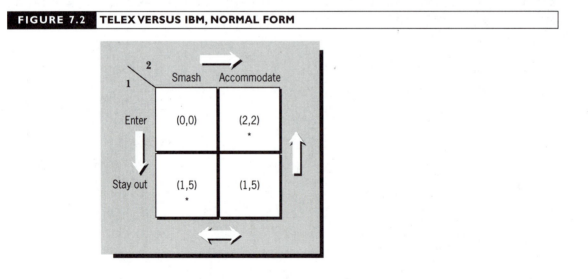

[1] This game was invented by Reinhard Selten, "The Chain Store Paradox," *Theory and Decision* 9 (1977): 127–159. Another name for it is Entry.

[2] This memorandum became a key piece of evidence in the court case involving Telex and IBM. See Gerald W. Brock, *The U.S. Computer Industry* (Cambridge, Mass.: Ballinger, 1975), especially pages 114–124, for further details. It should be noted that strategies that smash a business competitor are sometimes illegal in the United States.

As you can see from the arrow diagram of Figure 7.2, Telex versus IBM has two pure strategy Nash equilibria. Figure 7.3 shows the same Nash equilibria via labels on the game tree: (stay out, smash) is an equilibrium; so is (enter, accommodate). The former equilibrium presents a **credibility problem.** A credibility problem is present if, at the moment when a threat must actually be carried out, a player does not maximize utility by carrying out the threat. Smash is a threat designed to discourage Telex from entering. It is as if IBM said to Telex, "If you enter my market, I will smash you." Suppose Telex stands up to the threat by entering IBM's market. Now it's time for IBM to make good its threat to smash Telex. The trouble with carrying out the threat is that it minimizes IBM's payoff ($u_2 = 0$) instead of maximizing that payoff ($u_2 = 2$). There is a further problem with the strategy Smash: it is weakly dominated by the strategy Accommodate. Arrows point in toward Accommodate along both rows of the payoff matrix. As we shall soon see, this is no coincidence. Where there is a credibility problem, strategic domination is usually a problem, too.

No credibility problem attends the strategy Accommodate. It maximizes utility on the subgame that begins with player 2's decision. Indeed, it represents the unique equilibrium on that subgame (Figure 7.4). The equilibrium (enter, accommodate), which does not have a credibility problem, turns out to be the solution of Telex versus IBM with perfect information. A Nash equilibrium is **subgame perfect** if every player plays a Nash equilibrium on every subgame. In IBM vs. Telex, the subgame perfect equilibrium is (enter, accommodate). Subgame perfection contains the solution to the credibility problem. The other Nash equilibrium, (stay out, smash), is not subgame perfect and contains a credibility problem.[3]

Here is a second example, called Centipede, which contains a promise that is not credible.[4] In Centipede, there are two players. Player 1 moves first, and player 2 moves second. After at most two moves, the game ends. The game begins with $1 sitting on the table. Player 1 can either take the dollar or wait. If player 1 takes the dollar, the game is over, and

| FIGURE 7.3 | **TELEX VERSUS IBM, EXTENSIVE FORM EQUILIBRIA: (a) NONCREDIBLE EQUILIBRIUM; (b) CREDIBLE EQUILIBRIUM** |

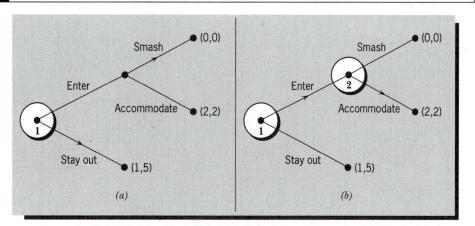

[3] Things get a lot more complicated if the game can be played multiple times and reputation matters to the outcome, as we show in later chapters.

[4] This game was introduced by Robert Rosenthal, "Games of Perfect Information, Predatory Pricing, and the Chain Store Paradox," *Journal of Economic Theory* 25 (1982): 92–100.

FIGURE 7.4 | **TELEX VERSUS IBM, SUBGAME EQUILIBRIUM**

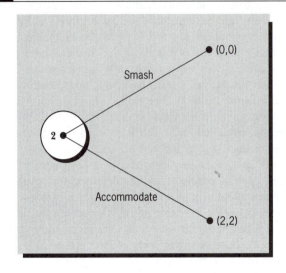

she gets to keep the dollar. If player 1 waits, the dollar on the table quadruples to $4. Now it is player 2's turn. Player 2 can either take the entire $4 on the table or split the $4 evenly with player 1. Figure 7.5a shows Centipede in extensive form.

Player 2's strategy to split the money with player 1 implicitly contains the following promise addressed to player 1: If you wait, then I will split the $4 with you. The trouble is, this promise has a credibility problem. Suppose player 1 does wait. Now it is player 2's turn to make good on the promise to player 1 to split the money on the table. If player 2 makes good on the promise, player 2 minimizes his utility ($u_2 = 2$) instead of

FIGURE 7.5 | **CENTIPEDE: (a) EXTENSIVE FORM; (b) NORMAL FORM**

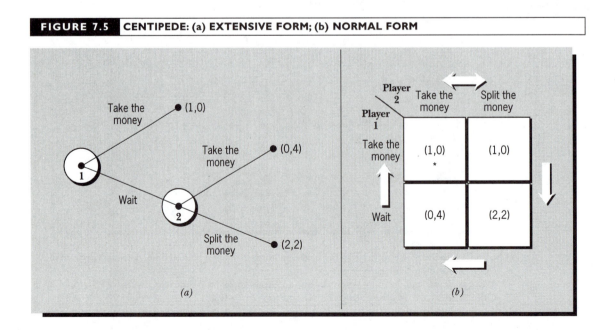

maximizing it ($u_2 = 4$). Player 2 has every reason in the world to break the promise and take all the money instead.

The credibility problem posed by the promise to split the money is apparent; the only equilibrium on the subgame beginning with player 2's move is for player 2 to take all the money. There is an even bigger problem with player 2's promise to split the money: it is not part of *any* Nash equilibrium. You can see this in Figure 7.5b, which shows Centipede in normal form. The only Nash equilibrium for Centipede is (take the money, take the money). Each player takes the money if the opportunity ever presents itself. Indeed, the strategy Take the Money strictly dominates the strategy Split the Money for player 2. Again, this strategic domination is due to the credibility problem adhering to the strategy Split the Money.

A credibility problem attends any strategy containing a threat or promise, the carrying out of which is costly to the player making it. Players who make such threats or promises and then do not carry them out are said to lose their credibility, a phenomenon familiar in economics and more so in politics. Here are three recent examples from American politics. During the presidential campaign of 1988, candidate Bush Sr. famously promised, "Read my lips—no new taxes." When President Bush Sr. later signed the tax increase bill of 1990, the consequences for his credibility were immediate; they were a major factor in his not being reelected. In a state example, Governor Pete Wilson of California, campaigning for reelection in 1994, promised the voters he would not run for president if he were reelected. When still Governor Wilson did run for president in 1996, his credibility vanished and his fellow Republican contenders made quick work of him, even before the Democrats got the chance. And it's not just Republican politicians who make promises. In the aftermath of the presidential election of 2000, Connecticut's Senator Joe Lieberman promised not to run for president in 2004 if former Vice President Al Gore were to run again. In 2002, Lieberman is gearing up for a presidential bid, as is Gore. You can be sure that Lieberman's credibility will take a big hit if he runs against Gore. The moral here is that you should not make a promise unless you are prepared to keep it.

The same holds true for threats. For a threat to be successful in getting an opponent to yield to your demands, it must inflict mutual harm if carried out. This then raises an issue of establishing credibility; otherwise, the threat won't work. You can see the process of establishing credibility live in the Sean Connery movie *The Rock*. It's loaded with strategic moves and issues of credibility.[5] A threat won't work if your opponent knows you aren't prepared to carry it out.

There is one intrinsic asymmetry between threats and promises that games don't always capture, but that is a part of our moral norms. We have a moral norm saying, "You should keep your promises," but we don't have a moral norm saying, "You should carry out your threats." In this sense, breaking a promise is worse than not carrying out a threat— regardless of credibility. Even this moral norm has its limits, though. A person who never breaks a promise can just as easily be a monster as a hero. Take the story of Jephthah from the Bible (Judges 11:29–31). Jephthah commands the Israelites in battle against the Moabites. He promises God that if he prevails in battle, he will sacrifice the first living thing he sees in the wake of victory. Jephthah does prevail in battle, and the first living thing he sees in the wake of victory is his daughter. Jephthah keeps his promise, promptly turning his live daughter into a dead sacrifice. In so doing, Jephthah commits a terrible crime. It is not good to make a promise whose consequences might be dire, especially if you are someone who keeps promises at all costs.

---

[5] A word of caution: it's also loaded with violence and strong language.

■ 7.2 MAINTAINING CREDIBILITY VIA SUBGAME PERFECTION

The advice game theory gives on the credibility problem is simple: never make a threat or promise unless you are prepared to carry it out. To make your threat or promise credible to others, it must pay you to make good on your threat or promise if the time comes to do so. In a game in extensive form, that means playing a subgame perfect equilibrium. In economics, we often assert the following:

The solution of a game in extensive form is subgame perfect.

Notice that this assertion has force only in games in extensive form, where typically

Subgame Perfect Equilibria is a subset of Nash Equilibria.

It says nothing about games in normal form, all of which lack subgames, and for which we have the following equation:

Subgame Perfect Equilibria = Nash Equilibria

All strategies and Nash equilibria that fail the test of subgame perfection are called *imperfect.* The imperfection of a strategy consists in the fact that at some point in the game, it has a credibility problem.

The condition just given would be no good if a game in extensive form had no subgame perfect equilibrium. This is another example of an existence problem. Fortunately, if a game is finite, it has equilibria, and we can construct a subgame perfect equilibrium for it by **backward induction,** the same reasoning we used to determine the outcome of games like Chess in Chapter 1. To construct a subgame perfect equilibrium, start at the final subgame of the game. When the game is finite, it has one or more final subgames. Find a subgame equilibrium for each of those subgames. Now work back through the game tree from each final subgame to the next subgame that strictly contains it. Find a subgame equilibrium for this larger subgame. Now work back through the game tree once more from this subgame, and so on until you reach the start of the game. Following the equilibrium path you have just taken through the game tree yields a subgame perfect equilibrium. We have constructed an equilibrium on every subgame.

We are now in a position to solve, via backward induction, the games we looked at in the last section. Consider first the perfect information version of Telex versus IBM (see Figure 7.3b). The final subgame (the only subgame) has a single equilibrium, with IBM choosing Accommodate. Working back to the next subgame, we reach the start of the game. Telex has the choice between staying out and getting $u_1 = 1$ or entering and getting $u_2 = 2$. The subgame perfect equilibrium path has Telex entering and IBM accommodating. This is the only subgame perfect equilibrium of Telex versus IBM with perfect information, and hence the solution to Telex versus IBM.

When we turn to the imperfect information and normal form versions of Telex versus IBM, we get the same solution, but for a different reason. Subgame perfection has no bite here, since the games are in normal form. In both these games, however, IBM's strategy Accommodate dominates Smash. Hence, by applying dominance solvability, we get the solution (enter, accommodate)—the same as before.

Next consider Centipede, which has a unique Nash equilibrium (see Figure 7.5). On the final subgame, player 2 takes all the money. At the start, player 1 takes all the money, rather than waiting for player 2 to take it. This is the subgame perfect equilibrium path, indeed, the only equilibrium path.

7.3 CREDIBLE THREATS AND PROMISES

So far we have looked at threats and promises with a credibility problem. There are plenty of threats and promises that you had better believe. Depending on the **type of opponent** you are playing against, a strategy that has a credibility problem might instead be credible. We turn to some of these now. Consider the game in Figure 7.6, Telex versus Mean IBM. The only difference between this perfect information version of Telex versus IBM and the version we solved previously is that the payoff to IBM when it smashes Telex is $u_2 = 4$. Mean IBM is so called because it gets more utility from driving rivals out of business than from making profits. Mean IBM has a perfectly credible threat to smash—smash is the only Nash equilibrium on this player's final subgame. The only Nash equilibrium, hence the solution, for Telex versus Mean IBM is (don't enter, smash). A firm would be foolhardy to enter a market against such a rival—the rival wants the other firm to enter, it so enjoys smashing others.

An example of a game with a credible promise is Centipede with a Nice Opponent (Figure 7.7). The only difference between this version of Centipede and the version we

FIGURE 7.6 TELEX VERSUS MEAN IBM

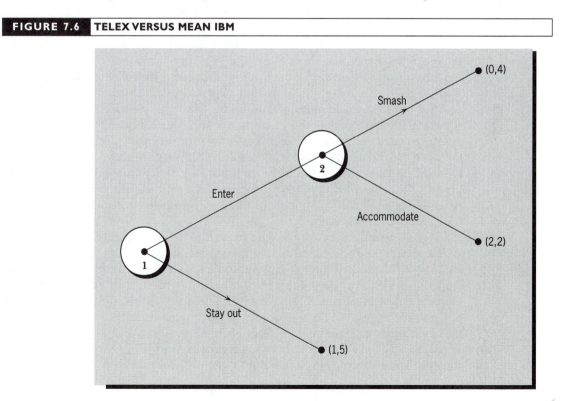

FIGURE 7.7 | **CENTIPEDE WITH A NICE OPPONENT ([a] EXTENSIVE FORM; [b] NORMAL FORM)**

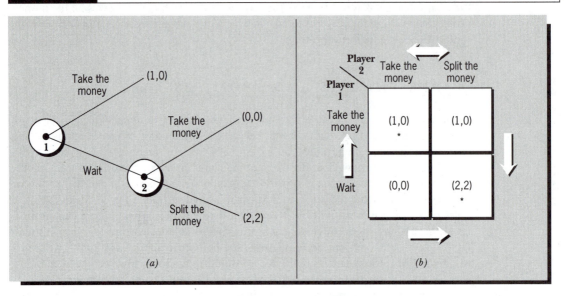

reviewed earlier is in the payoff to player 2 when he takes all the money. Player 2 gets called "nice" because he would much rather divide the money evenly ($u_2 = 2$) than take it all ($u_2 = 0$). We could explain this by appealing to player 2's sense of fairness or equity. Games can model emotions, such as meanness, kindness, or fairness, but they have to stray from monetary payoffs to do so. Now player 2's promise to split the money evenly is perfectly credible. Indeed, player 1's strategy Take the Money, which before was the only sensible one, now is dominated by the strategy Wait. Curiously enough, Centipede with a Nice Opponent has a second, imperfect equilibrium, (take the money, take the money); see Figure 7.7b. At this equilibrium, player 2 noncredibly threatens to take all the money, and player 1, believing this threat, takes the money first. In the extensive form version of Centipede with a Nice Opponent, this noncredible equilibrium is ruled out by subgame perfection. In the normal form version of the game, this equilibrium is ruled out by dominance considerations. For player 2, the strategy Split the Money dominates the strategy Take the money. Thus, in either form, the solution to Centipede with a Nice Opponent is (wait, split the money), and the players split the $4 evenly.

If you compare the outcome of Telex versus IBM to that of Telex versus Mean IBM, it is clear that it would pay IBM to pretend to be mean, even if it wasn't, if information was less than perfect. Again, if you compare the outcome of Centipede to Centipede with a Nice Opponent, it would pay player 2 to pretend to be nice, even if he wasn't, if information was less than perfect. In the case of Telex versus IBM, IBM would be bluffing Telex; in the case of Centipede, player 2 would be misleading player 1 to make it easier to betray her. These kinds of behavior, called Machiavellian after the notorious political philosopher of Renaissance Italy who first advocated them, are rife in games of imperfect information.[6] If you don't know who you are playing against, you really have to be on your guard against

---

[6] See Niccolo Machiavelli, *The Prince*, trans. Peter Bondanella and Mark Musa (Oxford, U.K.: Oxford University Press, 1984).

deception. Chapter 10 returns to this important topic. For now, we look at two episodes in U.S. history instead—important episodes, full of strategic content and credibility issues. The first of these comes from the American Civil War.

■ 7.4 RELUCTANT VOLUNTEERS: CONSCRIPTION IN THE AMERICAN CIVIL WAR, 1862–65

The American Civil War was the bloodiest war America ever fought.[7] Over 3 million soldiers and civilians fought in this war, serving either the United States of America (USA) or the Confederate States of America (CSA). Some 700,000 of these died. USA President Lincoln originally called for 75,000 soldiers to serve for 90 days; CSA President Davis called for 50,000 soldiers to serve for 1 year. Once it became clear to both sides that the war would be protracted, replacement of the initial regular forces and state militias became of great concern. Both sides needed more soldiers. Both the USA and the CSA constitutions granted to their respective congresses the power to raise armies. This constitutional privilege was the basis for legislation on both sides to institute national conscription—the first such in U.S. history. The CSA Congress enacted its Conscription Act in 1862, just before the 1-year enlistments expired. The USA Congress enacted its Conscription Act in 1863, just prior to the pivotal victories at Vicksburg and Gettysburg.

The possibility of conscription put those eligible for service into a strategic quandary: should I volunteer or should I wait for the draft, which might or might not catch up with me? Since enlistment dates, ages, and other call-up criteria were sequential in nature, one person might have to make this decision earlier or later than another. The version of the game Conscription described here was played by literally millions of men. According to the census of 1860, at least 5 million men were eligible to serve on one side or the other. The age limits of 15 to 50 years were quite broad, and there were almost no exemptions. In the USA, you could be exempted if you were the sole supporter of your parents or if you had at least four (!) brothers already serving. In the CSA, you could be exempted if your being drafted would reduce the ratio of white men to African American slaves on a plantation below 1:25. That was pretty much it for exemptions.

In the version of Conscription presented here, there are only two men—although the same basic principle applies to the game played by millions. Again for simplicity, we consider the situation facing two men eligible for induction into the army of the USA. Similar incentives applied to men eligible for induction into the army of the CSA. The army needs one of these two for armed service. Player 1 has to move first. He can either volunteer, in which case the game ends, or he can wait for the draft. If player 1 volunteers, he gets the payoff $b - c$, and player 2 gets the payoff 0. The payoff parameter b represents the bonus for volunteering, which was substantial, about one year's wage for an average industrial worker.[8] The payoff parameter c represents the cost of serving, which is composed of two components: the expected loss of life and limb and the certain loss of civilian earnings. The payoff value 0 represents the civilian reference point. If player 1 waits for the draft, then player 2 faces the choice whether to volunteer or wait for the draft. If player 2 volunteers,

---

[7] Material has been drawn from Roy Gardner, "Resisting the Draft: A Perfect Equilibrium Approach," in *Game Equilibrium Models* vol. 4, *Social and Political Interaction,* ed. Reinhard Selten (New York: Springer-Verlag, 1991), 141–154.
[8] The bonus was $300 in 1863 dollars, roughly equal to the average annual wage for an industrial worker in the North.

the game ends; he gets the bonus for volunteering and serves in the army. If player 2 also waits for the draft, then the government conducts an equal-chance lottery to fill its draft quota. The catch is that a draftee serves, but does not get the bonus for volunteering. The only way to get the bonus, *b*, is to actually and truly volunteer. The extensive form of Conscription is shown in Figure 7.8a.

The subgame perfect equilibrium of Conscription depends very heavily on the size of the payoff parameters *b* (the bonus for volunteering) and *c* (the cost of serving). The values *b* = $300 and *c* = $400 (in 1863 dollars) are fairly realistic for this war. Let's find the subgame perfect equilibrium for these values (see Figure 6.8b). At the final chance subgame, reached if each player waits, the payoff vector is $(-c/2, -c/2) = (-200, -200)$. At the final subgame where he has a move, player 2 can volunteer, in which case he gets –$100, or wait for the draft. If he waits for the draft, he has a 50% probability of losing $400, and a 50% probability of remaining civilian. Since this is an expected loss of –$200, this player maximizes utility by volunteering for the draft. Any player who takes a sure loss rather than risking an even greater loss is called a **reluctant volunteer.** Player 2 in this case is a reluc-

---

FIGURE 7.8 | **CONSCRIPTION: (a) EXTENSIVE FORM; (b) B = $300, C = $400**

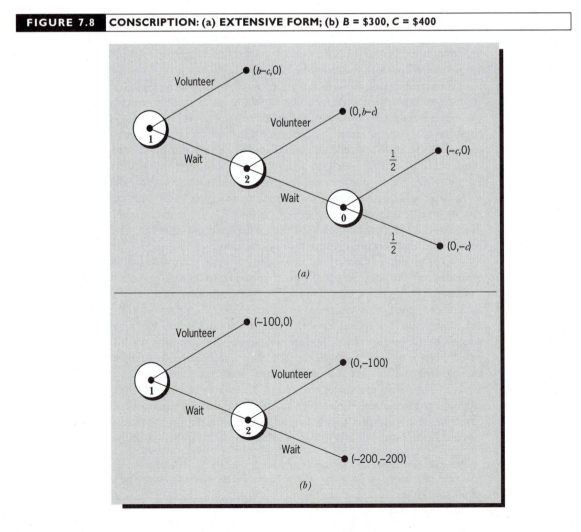

tant volunteer. He would rather volunteer and cut his losses than take a larger expected loss in the draft. We now work backward to player 1 at the start of the game. If player 1 volunteers, he gets –$100; whereas if he waits, player 2 will do the volunteering for him, and he gets $0. Player 1 can safely afford to wait. This is the subgame perfect equilibrium, (wait, volunteer). The player who moves last reluctantly volunteers.

The imperfect equilibrium here is just the opposite. Player 2, noncredibly, threatens to wait for the draft. Player 1, believing this threat, volunteers. At the imperfect equilibrium, it is the player who goes first who reluctantly volunteers. So both equilibria lead to the same behavioral conclusion: the draft quota is filled by reluctant volunteers.

What does all this have to do with America's bloody Civil War?[9] Just this. Of the 2.1 million soldiers who served in the Union army, only 50,000 were draftees. An astonishing 96% of all those who served were volunteers. Given the well-known costs of serving—over a quarter of these soldiers died—this number is truly remarkable. The volunteer rate for the Confederate army, at about half the size of the Union army, was similar. This terrible war was fought by vast volunteer armies, many of whose members were reluctant volunteers.

■ 7.5 Mutually Assured Destruction

Extensive form games with only two moves, one for each player, are by far the easiest to solve. All the games we have considered to this point could be represented by 2 x 2 matrices in normal form, since one of the moves by the first player terminated the game. This section examines a complicated game and finds increasingly complicated credibility issues as a result.

The game we consider is called **Mutually Assured Destruction** (MAD). MAD is played by two superpowers, country 1 and country 2. It will help to think back to the days when there were two superpowers, the United States and the Soviet Union. An international incident has just occurred, precipitated by country 2. Country 1 can either ignore the incident, in which case the status quo is maintained and the game ends, or country 1 can escalate the situation with an ultimatum to country 2. In the event that country 1 escalates the conflict, country 2 can either back down from the confrontation, at a small loss of utility, or country 2 can escalate further. If country 2 escalates further, both countries are in a nuclear confrontation subgame. In this nuclear confrontation subgame, each country moves simultaneously. Each country gets one last chance to back down. Each country may also go nuclear, imposing large losses on both countries by an all-out attack, with the code name Doomsday. The loss parameter L associated with Doomsday is a large negative number.[10] In either of these two events, the game ends.[11] Figure 7.9a shows the extensive form of MAD.

MAD is a model of a nuclear weapons doctrine that was popular during the Cold War. Each superpower kept massive stockpiles of nuclear weapons, deliverable on short notice by bombers, submarines, and missiles. In the event of serious escalation, a superpower had the wherewithal to impose massive assured destruction on its adversary. There was always controversy over whether the threat to use such weapons of mass destruction

---

[9] More soldiers died in three days at Gettysburg than in the heaviest year of fighting in Vietnam.

[10] Saint Anselm would call it a number larger than which none can be imagined. The classic treatment of brinkmanship is due to Thomas C. Schelling, *The Strategy of Conflict* (New York: Oxford, 1960).

[11] According to some authorities, in the event of Doomsday, the world ends, too. See R. P. Turco et al., "Nuclear Winter: Global Consequences of Multiple Nuclear Explosions," *Science* 222 (December 23, 1983): 1283–1300.

FIGURE 7.9	MAD, EXTENSIVE FORM: (a) ENTIRE GAME; (b) PATH TO FINAL BACKING DOWN; (c) PATH TO DOOMSDAY

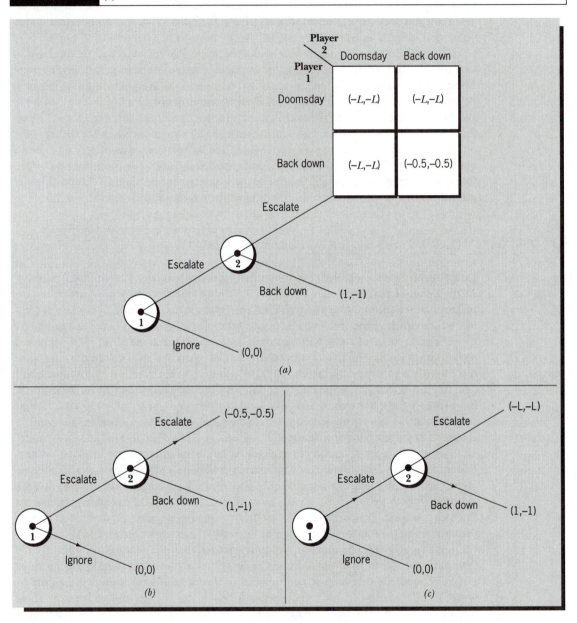

was credible. Let's see why, by computing the subgame perfect equilibria—of which there are two—for MAD.

The multiple subgame perfect equilibria arise from the fact that the final subgame has two equilibria: (back down, back down) and (Doomsday, Doomsday). Either of these could be the subgame equilibrium that starts the backward induction path. For instance, suppose that the equilibrium played on the subgame is (back down, back down). Then the backward induction begins by replacing this subgame with the payoffs of this equilibrium (–0.5, –0.5). Given that the final subgame is going to end in both countries backing down, country 2 prefers to escalate to reach this desirable conclusion, rather than to back down by itself beforehand. A payoff of –0.5 is preferred to a payoff of –1. Since country 2 is escalating, country 1 prefers to ignore the provocation. This backward induction reasoning is reflected in the subgame perfect equilibrium path of Figure 7.9b, the path to final backing down. The equilibrium we have just found supports the payoffs (0,0). The strategies used by each country are as follows:

> country 1: Ignore, then back down.
> country 2: Escalate, then back down.

This is not the only subgame perfect equilibrium. Suppose that the equilibrium chosen in the final simultaneity subgame is (Doomsday, Doomsday). Then the backward induction begins by replacing this subgame with the payoffs of this equilibrium (–L –L). Given that the final subgame is going to end in very large negative payoffs for both countries, country 2 prefers to back down early rather than to go nuclear. Since country 2 is backing down, country 1 prefers to escalate. This backward induction reasoning is reflected in the subgame perfect equilibrium path of Figure 6.9c, the path to Doomsday. This second subgame perfect equilibrium supports the payoffs (1, –1). The strategies used by each country are as follows:

> country 1: Escalate, then Doomsday.
> country 2: Back down, then Doomsday.

MAD was played at least once, during the Cuban missile crisis of 1962. At that time, the USA and USSR each had over a thousand nuclear weapons, capable of striking the other country via bomber or missile. There is a great movie about this—*Thirteen Days*, starring Kevin Costner; the movie is named for the duration of the crisis, which lasted exactly 13 days. The crisis was precipitated by the U.S. discovery of Soviet nuclear missiles on the island of Cuba. Instead of ignoring the incident, the United States escalated the crisis by quarantining Cuba, in an act just short of declaring war. At the brink, rather than going to all-out nuclear war, the USSR backed down, agreeing to remove its missiles from Cuba.[12] This is precisely the behavior that the inventors of the doctrine of mutually assured destruction had in mind. Each superpower had a credible threat to use its nuclear forces. Given that these threats were credible, a country that provoked a confrontation would not take the final escalatory step toward the nuclear showdown. Instead, that country would have to back down at the brink, thus losing the confrontation.

These are not the only Nash equilibria of MAD. To make the other equilibria easier to see, Figure 7.10 shows the normal form of MAD. The normal form is 4 x 4, since each country has two choices to make at each of two information sets. As you look at these strategies, you immediately see a problem. If country 1 ignores the provocation at the start, then country 1 should never have a chance to back down later. So the complete plan of play (ignore, then back down) appears to be self-contradictory. Appearances are deceiving, however. The reason we require *complete* plans of play is to be ready for all contingencies, including the contingency that not everything goes according to plan. Of course, this raises

---

[12] In a face-saving gesture for the USSR, the United States agreed to remove U.S. missiles that had been in Turkey for several years.

FIGURE 7.10	MAD, NORMAL FORM (*b* = BACK DOWN; = *D* DOOMSDAY; *e* = ESCALATE; *i* = IGNORE; * = EQUILIBRIUM; CIRCLED * = SUBGAME PERFECT EQUILIBRIUM)

Country 2 → Country 1 ↓	e,D	e,b	b,D	b,b
e,D	$(-L,-L)$	$(-L,-L)$	$(1,-1)$ ⊛	$(1,-1)$ *
e,b	$(-L,-L)$	$(-0.5,-0.5)$	$(1,-1)$	$(1,-1)$
i,D	$(0,0)$ *	$(0,0)$ *	$(0,0)$	$(0,0)$
i,b	$(0,0)$ *	$(0,0)$ ⊛	$(0,0)$	$(0,0)$

the further question, why doesn't everything go according to plan? And if it doesn't, why isn't that included in the description of the game? These are tough questions, and in recent years they have increasingly vexed game theorists.[13]

As you can see from Figure 7.10, MAD has four pure strategy equilibria in addition to its two subgame perfect equilibria. Three of these—

[(ignore, Doomsday), (escalate, Doomsday)]

[(ignore, Doomsday), (escalate, back down)]

[(ignore, back down), (escalate, Doomsday)]

have payoffs equivalent to those of the subgame perfect equilibrium where country 1 backs down. Their imperfection shows up later, in the parts of the game that should not be reached if everything goes according to plan. Their imperfection would be major, should country 1 escalate by mistake. This mistake would trigger Doomsday by country 2—just as in the movie *Dr. Strangelove*. The other pure strategy equilibrium—

[escalate, Doomsday), (back down, back down)]

---

[13] Chapter 9 studies a model in which mistakes happen by chance, with a small probability. If a mistake happens in the middle of a game that calls into question the very rationality of the other player, things quickly get really complicated. See Philip Reny, "Rationality in Extensive Form Games," *Journal of Economic Perspectives* 6 (1992): 103–118.

has payoffs equivalent to those of the subgame perfect equilibrium where country 1 escalates and country 2 backs down. This equilibrium again could have a Strangelovian ending. Suppose that country 2 escalates by mistake after country 1 has escalated. Then, according to the rest of the plan, country 1 goes Doomsday. This kind of nuclear nightmare, based on the possibility of mistakes, is the dark side of the MAD doctrine. A mistake by either side in this game could have disastrous consequences.

MAD has, in addition to the six pure strategy Nash equilibria, an infinite number of mixed strategy Nash equilibria. We will construct one of these now; the rest are left for the "Problems" section. Suppose that country 2 uses the strategy (escalate, then Doomsday). Then country 1 can play the strategy (ignore, then back down) with probability .5 and the strategy (ignore, then Doomsday) with probability .5. This situation is tantamount to ignoring the provocation every time at the first move and then mixing over the strategies Doomsday and back down at the second move. Both pure strategies in this mixture pay zero. However, since these mixed strategies put positive probability on a move with a credibility problem—Doomsday—they, too, are imperfect and so are not candidates for a solution.

The two subgame perfect equilibria meet the requirements for a solution for MAD. They represent equally credible doctrines of how to behave in the event of an international incident. The first equilibrium endorses brinkmanship; that is, both countries go to the very brink of destruction before both back down simultaneously. The second doctrine makes the escalatory ladder very short (a single escalation step) and has the perpetrator of the incident back down quickly. However, this quick resolution to the conflict relies on the mutual threat of destruction—credible in this case. If something should go wrong, in particular if player 2 should fail to back down as planned, then mutually assured destruction would be triggered. It might seem unsatisfactory for a game to have two solutions as different as these two. However, we might wonder whether one of these solutions should be excluded on other grounds.[14]

■ 7.6 MARKET GAMES WITH SUBGAMES: TAKE-IT-OR-LEAVE-IT MONOPOLY

We now turn to market games that have subgames. The first such game we consider is the simplest market with one buyer and one seller, which you saw in the last chapter. This time there are two major changes. One of the players, the seller, moves first. Call the seller player 1. Also, the seller is going to name the price. In terms of bid-ask behavior, this implies the price formation rule

$$P(a,b) = a$$

The ask is the price, but there is a deal only if the ask is less than or equal to the bid. The price depends only on what the seller asks. Indeed, in the version we consider now, the buyer doesn't even make a bid. The buyer, player 2, simply says Yes or No to the seller's ask. We call this a **take-it-or-leave-it market.** The buyer is literally at the mercy of the seller—and monopoly sellers aren't known for being merciful.

---

[14] For a theory of how to select a unique equilibrium for a game such as that in Figure 7.10, see John Harsanyi and Reinhard Selten, *A General Theory of Equilibrium Selection in Games* (Cambridge, Mass.: MIT Press, 1988).

Suppose, as in Chapter 6, section 6.2, the buyer's true value $b\# = \$4$, while the seller's true value $a\# = \$2$. The seller can pick any ask a divisible evenly by \$.50; that ask a becomes the price. The buyer hears what the seller asks, and then responds with a Yes or a No. If the buyer says Yes, it's a deal and each participant earns his or her surplus from the transaction. Remember, any choice of strategy that leads to a negative payoff is dominated in a market game. If the buyer says No, there is no deal and each participant gets 0.

Figure 7.11 shows the extensive form of this Take-It-or-Leave-It market game. To keep the extensive form simple, we show only the asks \$3.50 and \$4; you can show that any lower ask than \$3.50 and any higher ask than \$4 is weakly dominated by one of these two asks. So we have already eliminated some weakly dominated strategies in getting to Figure 7.11. This market game has two subgame perfect equilibria, depending on how the buyer reacts to the asking price of \$4. Notice that the buyer maximizes utility by saying Yes to the asking price \$3.50. A gain of half a dollar is better than no gain. The reason there are two subgame perfect

FIGURE 7.11 **TAKE-IT-OR-LEAVE-IT MARKET**

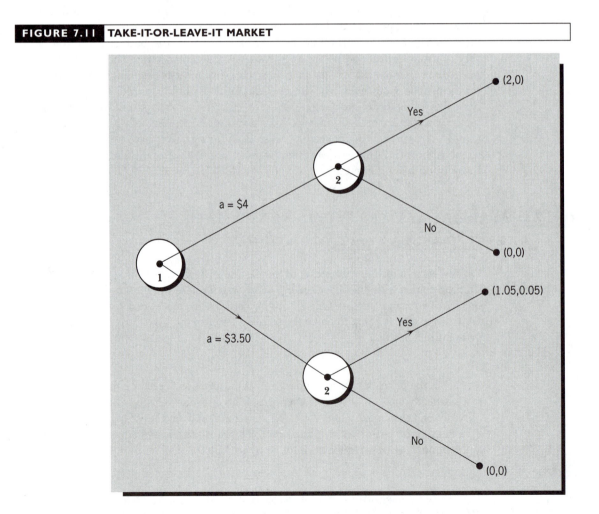

equilibria is that the buyer is indifferent between saying Yes and getting a deal with $0 and saying No and getting no deal, also worth $0:

Subgame perfect equilibrium I.   The buyer says Yes to the asking price of $4. This means the seller gains $2. Since $2 > $1.50, the seller prefers to ask $4 than to ask $3.50. At this subgame perfect equilibrium, the strategies are

> Seller, ask $4
>
> Buyer, say Yes to $4, say Yes to $3.50
>
> and the payoffs are (2,0).

Subgame perfect equilibrium II.   The buyer says No to the asking price of $4. This means the seller gains $0. Since $0 < $1.50, the seller prefers to ask $3.50 than to ask $4. At this subgame perfect equilibrium, the strategies are

> Seller, ask $3.50
>
> Buyer, say No to $4, say Yes to $3.50
>
> and the payoffs are (1.5, 0.5).

Subgame perfect equilibrium II shows again why greed doesn't always pay. If buyers are going to reject extremely greedy offers, then sellers who make such offers will be punished by making no deals.

Actually, there is quite a bit of experimental evidence to suggest that buyers will say No to proposals that offer them little or nothing, as we show in the appendix. Indeed, even offers that split the gain 3 to 1 in favor of the monopoly stand a good chance of being rejected.

Nevertheless, the market game setup just described is the precise formulation of classical monopoly theory. The monopoly states a price, and buyers either take it or leave it. We can extend this model to the case of many buyers and many units for sale; here, considerations of marginal revenue and marginal cost become paramount.

To see one easy example, suppose there are now two buyers, with willingness to pay $b\#$ equal $8 and $4, respectively. The seller can now produce two units, each a marginal cost $a\# = $2. To focus attention on just one subgame perfect equilibrium, we rule out all asking prices that leave one buyer indifferent. In this case, the seller's strategic choice boils down to the following:

> Ask = $7.50. This high price soaks the buyer most willing to pay, and leaves the lower-value buyer out. Profit to the monopoly = $5.50.
>
> Ask = $3.50. This lower price lets both buyers into the market.
>
> Profit to the monopoly = Revenue − Cost = $7 − $4 = $3, a lower number

The reason for this is that when the seller lowers the price from $7.50 to $3.50, revenue falls from $7.50 to $7, so marginal revenue is negative, equal to minus half a dollar. Meanwhile, marginal cost is $2, so marginal profit is −$2.50. This is the profit differential between the high and low asking price.

7.7 How Powerful Is Monopoly?

The rules for a take-it-or-leave-it market really favor a monopoly. When price formation is somewhat fairer, then monopoly profits will not be nearly as great as suggested by classical economic theory or the subgame perfect equilibria of the previous section.

In this section, we consider the price formation rule

$$P(a,b) = a$$

In conjunction with the rule for making a deal, the bid must be at least as great as the price; otherwise, no deal. The way this market game works is that the monopoly and the buyer submit an ask and a bid simultaneously. The ask is the price; but there is a deal only if the ask does not exceed the bid.

Suppose all asks and bids are divisible by $0.50 and lie between $2 and $4. Figure 7.12 shows the market game that results. There is a lot happening in this 5 x 5 game:

10 outcomes lead to no deal; these are the payoffs (0,0). These occur when $a > b$.

15 outcomes lead to a deal; these are the payoffs that add up to 2.

FIGURE 7.12 SIMULTANEOUS MOVE MONOPOLY MARKET

Seller Asks \ Buyer Bids	b = $2	b = 2.50	b = 3	b = 3.50	b = 4
a = $4	(0,0) *	(0,0)	(0,0)	(0,0)	(2,0) *
a = 3.50	(0,0)	(0,0)	(0,0)	(1.5,0.5) *	(1.5,0.5)
a = 3	(0,0)	(0,0)	(1,1) *	(1,1)	(1,1)
a = 2.50	(0,0)	(0.5,1.5) *	(0.5,1.5)	(0.5,1.5)	(0.5,1.5)
a = 2	(0,2) *	(0,2)	(0,2)	(0,2)	(0,2)

5 outcomes are pure strategy Nash equilibria with efficiency = 100%. These lie on the diagonal where $a = b$.

1 outcome is the pure strategy Nash equilibrium with efficiency = 0%. This is the greedy equilibrium, where the seller asks \$4 and the buyer bids \$2, each trying to steal the item.

Except for the asymmetry in pricing, the pattern of Nash equilibria and payoffs is rather like that of an ordinary market game, as in Figure 5.5: efficient Nash equilibria along the diagonal, and a bad Nash equilibrium in the upper left-hand corner. In a strategic situation this complex, the seller and the buyer have a difficult equilibrium selection problem. Even though the game is not symmetric—the pricing rule still favors the seller exclusively—in a real-life setting the players might still use symmetry considerations (equal payoff, being in the center of the matrix) to settle on a deal and achieve efficiency. In such a scenario, monopoly is far from all-powerful.

◼ 7.8 CREDIBLE QUANTITY COMPETITION: COURNOT-STACKELBERG EQUILIBRIUM

We now consider market games where only the sellers are strategic, and buyer behavior is reflected by market demand. The first such games we will consider have quantity competition, hence, Cournot competition. In the original Cournot model, all firms move simultaneously, so there are no subgames. In the model we are about to study, one firm sends its quantity to market first. This sort of competition is named Stackelberg competition, after the economist who first studied it.[15] Putting the Cournot quantity element and the Stackelberg sequence element together results in Cournot-Stackelberg competition. This is the competition presented in this section.

Consider the market game in section 6.7. Market price, P, satisfies

$$P = 130 - Q$$

where Q is market quantity, the sum of firm 1's and firm 2's quantities. Each firm has a constant average and marginal cost = \$10. Firm 1 ships its quantity, x_1, to market first. Firm 2 sees how much firm 1 shipped and then ships its quantity, x_2, to market. The sum of quantities shipped equals quantity Q, which then determines price. The firms' profits are the market price times the quantity they shipped, minus their costs. We will now see that *the unique subgame perfect equilibrium of Cournot-Stackelberg competition* is the pair of strategies

Firm 1 ships 60 units.

Firm 2 ships $60 - 0.5\,x_1$ units.

In particular, firm 2 ships $60 - 0.5(60) = 30$ units. So firm 1 has twice the market share and twice the profits of firm 2. In **Cournot-Stackelberg competition,** the firm that moves first has a first mover advantage.

---

[15] See Heinrich Freiherr von Stackelberg, *The Theory of the Market Economy* (London: William Hodges, 1952; originally published in German in 1934).

We start at the final subgame. Firm 2 has just observed firm 1's shipment, x_1. Firm 2 thus faces the following demand curve:

$$P = (130 - x_1) - x_2$$

where the intercept $(130 - x_1)$ reflects the fact that firm 2 only gets a residual demand, what is left after firm 1's goods are sold. Firm 2 now maximizes profits,

$$\max u_2(\mathbf{x}) = x_2(130 - x_1 - x_2 - 10) = x_2(120 - x_1 - x_2)$$

with respect to its own quantity, x_2. We actually solved this maximization problem in the appendix to Chapter 6, only for firm 1 instead of firm 2. Recalling that solution,

$$0 = a - x_1 - 2x_2 - c$$

and making the necessary substitutions, we get

$$0 = 120 - x_1 - 2x_2$$

Solving this equation, we get firm 2's profit maximizing output, as a function of what it observes firm 1 to have produced:

$$x_2 = g(x_1) = 60 - x_1/2$$

Notice that firm 2's strategy is a function of firm 1's shipments. For every possible shipment by firm 1 from 0 to 130, firm 2 has a profit-maximizing response. Figure 7.13 shows this function. Let's consider three points on it. When firm 1's quantity is 0, firm 2 has the market to itself and it monopolizes it, with a quantity of 60. If firm 1's quantity is 40, firm 2 has a best response of 40 also—this is just the Cournot equilibrium of section 6.7. Finally, if firm 1's quantity is 120, it has flooded the market, driving price down to cost. In this situation, firm 2 does best by staying out of the market, with a quantity of 0.

FIGURE 7.13 **COURNOT-STACKELBERG COMPETITION: FIRM 2'S BEST RESPONSE**

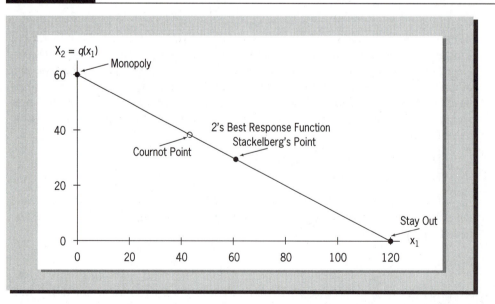

Since firm 2 has maximized profits on its subgame, it has played its part of the subgame perfect equilibrium. We can now use backward induction to return to the start of the game and to firm 1's decision of how much to ship, x_1. Firm 1 faces the original demand, but also takes into account the profit-maximizing reaction by firm 2 contained in the function $g(x_1)$. Thus, firm 1 wants to maximize its profits, which are given by

$$u_1(\mathbf{x}) = [130 - x_1 - g(x_1) - 10]x_1$$

Firm 1 has induced firm 2's sales backward, using profit maximization as a guide. Essentially, what firm 1 does is to choose the point on Figure 7.132 that is most favorable to itself. Therein lies firm 1's first-mover advantage. Let's do a quick calculation of four suggestive possibilities for firm 1's quantity: 40 (the Cournot quantity), 50, 60, and 70. Substituting these values into firm 1's profit function

$$u_1(\mathbf{x}) = [120 - x_1 - 60 + x_1/2]x_1$$

we get

$$u_1(40) = 1600, \ u_1(50) = 1750, \ u_1(60) = 1800, \ u_1(70) = 1750$$

Firm 1's highest profit along firm 2's reaction line occurs at a quantity of 60 units. We prove this, using calculus, in the appendix.

Here is how the subgame perfect equilibrium path is played. Firm 1 ships 60 units. Firm 2, seeing these 60 units shipped, ships $60 - 60/2 = 30$ units. The total shipments are $Q = 60 + 30 = 90$, and the market equilibrium price P is the same for both firms (recall section 6.7). Since the firms' products are identical, Cournot competition where the firms ship to market simultaneously leads to a symmetrical situation ($x_1 = x_2 = 40$) and a market price of $50. Each firm has a one-half market share. However, when firm 1 gets to ship first and firm 2 responds by maximizing profits, then firm 1 gets a two-thirds market share as opposed to a one-third share for firm 2. Firm 1 enjoys a **first-mover advantage** in Cournot-Stackelberg competition. Also, more units are shipped to market ($60 + 30 = 90$) and buyers enjoy a lower price ($130 - $90 = $40).

If we relax the assumption that $c = $10 and allow for other values of c, we find that the firm that moves first will retain its first-mover advantage and its market share as long as average variable costs are the same for both firms. It takes a substantial cost advantage for the firm that moves second to offset the advantage of the firm that moves first.

The solution we have just computed is the unique subgame perfect equilibrium to the Cournot-Stackelberg market game, but it is not the only Nash equilibrium. There are infinitely many other Nash equilibria, but all of them have a credibility problem. For some of these, the credibility problem is extreme.

Here is just one example. If you follow this example, you should be able to come up with as many others as you want. We will construct a Nash equilibrium that supports the Cournot outcome, where each firm sells 40 units. The idea is to create an incredible threat on the part of firm 2, which, despite its lack of credibility, firm 1 believes. The trick that makes this easy is to have firm 2 do something really stupid—like flood the market with its product—if firm 1 ships anything other than 40 units. Here is an incredible, market-flooding strategy for firm 2:

$$x_2 = 40 \text{ if } x_1 = 40$$
$$x_2 = 120 \text{ otherwise}$$

This strategy guarantees a price no greater than marginal cost unless firm 1 ships the quantity $x_1 = 40$. Note the credibility problem that pervades this strategy. If firm 1 shipped 42 units, firm 2 would make a lot of money by shipping 21 units. The resulting market price of $130 - 63 = 67$/unit would lead to a profit margin of $67 - 10 = 57$/unit, and so firm 2 would make $21(\$57) = \$1,197$. However, since firm 1 did not ship 40 units, firm 2's strategy says it must ship 120 units instead. This floods the market, and these units have to be given away. Firm 2 loses a lot of money, $(120 \text{ units})(-\$10) = -\$1,200$. This is a pretty high price to pay to keep a promise that isn't worth keeping in the first place. Try explaining this strategy to the stockholders at the next annual meeting.

Threats like that embodied in firm 2's function, which involve dire consequences (like market flooding) in the event that things don't go according to a player's plan, are called *dire threats* and the strategies that embody them, *dire strategies*. Dire strategies, which are triggered by deviation from what a player is aiming for, are also called *trigger strategies*. These are especially important in repeated games, presented in Chapter 8. If you know you are playing a market game against somebody rational, or somebody who has to answer to stockholders (which is roughly the same thing), you don't have to take dire threats seriously unless they are credible. And you can check for credibility by asking yourself whether carrying out this threat will pay your opponent when it comes time for the threat to be carried out.

◼ 7.9 CREDIBLE PRICE COMPETITION: BERTRAND-STACKELBERG EQUILIBRIUM

In Bertrand competition, price is the strategic variable. The Stackelberg element adds sequence to the moves. So in **Bertrand-Stackelberg competition,** firms use price as their strategic variable and one of the firms, say firm 1, goes first. In the event of perfect substitutes, it is easy to see what the subgame perfect equilibrium of such competition is.

To keep things concrete, let's stick to the model of the last section. Demand is given by

$$P = 130 - Q$$

The two firms produce and sell perfect substitutes. Unit costs are constant at $10. All buyers are informed, so the lowest-priced firm gets all the customers. If prices tie, then the each firm gets half the customers.

To find a subgame perfect equilibrium, we start with the final subgames, where firm 2 is reacting to the price firm 1 has announced, p_1. Unless firm 2 matches or undercuts this price, it makes no sales and therefore makes no money. If firm 2 undercuts this price ever so slightly—say, by the minimum monetary unit—then it gets the entire market to itself, which is always better than splitting the market. Finally, firm 2 would like to monopolize the market if possible. This is a fairly realistic goal, since firm 2 has to beat only one price, p_1, and that price is already posted. Thus, if firm 1 charges a price above $70, the monopoly price, then firm 2 would want to go down to $70. Let $0.01 be the minimum monetary unit. Then firm 2's profit-maximizing response to firm 1's price is

$$p_2 = \$70, \text{ if } p_1 \text{ is greater than } \$70$$
$$p_2 = p_1 - \$0.01, \text{ if } p_1 \text{ is between } \$70 \text{ and } \$10.02$$
$$p_2 = p_1, \text{ if } p_1 = \$10.01$$
$$p_2 = \$10 \text{ otherwise}$$

Notice that once again firm 2's strategy is a function, $p_2 = g(p_1)$. Unlike the case of Cournot-Stackelberg competition, this function is not a straight line, but rather three straight-line segments spliced together.

Facing this pattern of profit-maximizing responses, firm 1 is in a real quandary. Any price it charges that is above $10.02 will get underbid. The best it can do is call out a price of $10.01. It makes almost no money at this price—the profit margin is only a penny. Firm 2 will match this price, and both firms will make a pittance. Figure 7.14 focuses on the crucial part of the game tree.

FIGURE 7.14 **BERTRAND-STACKELBERG COMPETITION**

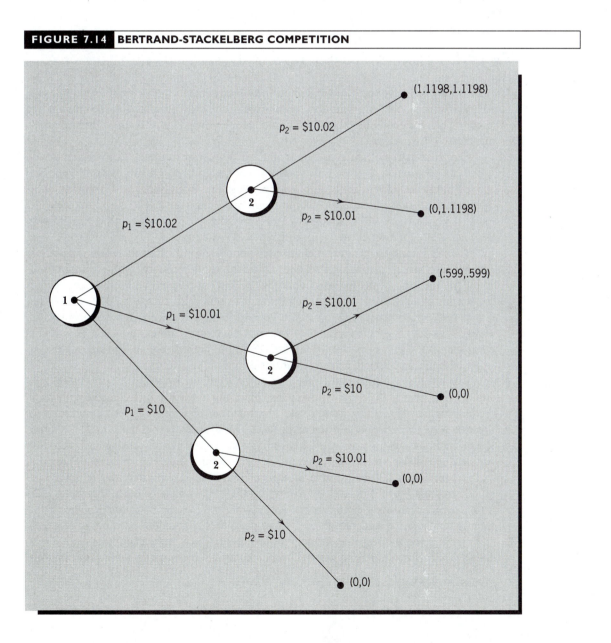

You can show that this solution can be generalized to the case in which firms have constant average costs c other than $10. You can also adapt this solution to cover cost asymmetries. These generalizations are left as end-of-chapter problems.

Besides the profit-maximizing function given here, which does not have a credibility problem, there are plenty of response functions that do. These are typically of the form, I won't undercut you if you charge the price I want. The trouble is, such a promise is inherently not credible. The firm that moves last can undercut you any time it wants, if you move first. Having to make your bid first is a serious disadvantage. And this disadvantage to moving first is just the opposite of getting to ship first in Cournot competition—this is a **first-mover disadvantage,** or **second-mover advantage.**

◼ 7.10 THIS OFFER IS GOOD FOR A LIMITED TIME ONLY

How many times have you heard this phrase on advertisements on television?[16] Should you believe it? The Nobel Prize–winning economist Ronald Coase gives us plenty of reason for doubt. When the good offered is durable, and has a long shelf life, then the offer has a serious credibility problem.

Here is an extreme case. A seller has 10 Civil War commemorative chess sets in stock, which can be stored at no cost for two periods. The seller can charge two prices in a period, either $100 or $20. There are 10 fully informed and interested buyers in the market, each of whom wants at most one Civil War commemorative chess set. Five of the buyers are willing to pay as much as $100 for a set, whereas the other five buyers are only willing to pay as much as $20 for a set. Buyers are indifferent as to whether they buy now or later.

The seller wants to make as much money as possible from selling these sets and prefers getting the money sooner rather than later. To get this result means charging a price of $100 in the first period, selling five sets, pocketing the $500 in revenue, and leaving the rest of the sets in the warehouse. This is much better than selling all the sets for $20 each in the first period, which nets only $200. If you watch television, you can imagine such a seller saying, This offer is good for a limited time only. That limited time is period 1. The seller's complete plan of play is to post a price of $100/set. In the first period, five sets sell at this price; in the second period, no sets sell at this price.

Suppose that the seller chose this plan, and now we are in period 2. Five sets are still sitting in the warehouse, and five buyers are still willing to pay $20 apiece for them. It is not credible for the seller at this point to say, "I refuse to sell these sets." The seller wants to sell these five sets for $20, pocketing an extra $100. The strategy to hold the price at $100 has lost its credibility. Those who would have bought in the first period, sensing the credibility problem, should wait until the second period, and so enjoy their 80% price reduction.

Extreme cases call for extreme measures. Here is an extreme measure to solve this seller's credibility problem: *Destroy five of the Civil War commemorative chess sets!* This action definitely limits the offer to one period and prevents the first-period buyers from waiting for the price reduction in the second period. This situation illustrates in an especially graphic way the principle of **costly commitment,** which pervades economic life. Every time a business incurs a fixed cost, it incurs a costly commitment to some future action,

---

[16] This material is inspired in part by Ronald Coase, "Durability and Monopoly," *Journal of Law and Economics* 15 (1972): 143–149.

which it may or may not take. A fixed cost represents the cost of a forgone opportunity, here the opportunity to sell Civil War commemorative chess sets in the second period.

Of course, there may be less costly solutions to the credibility problem as well. Suppose the seller establishes a **most-favored customer** program. When you buy a chess set, you automatically are enrolled in the program. As a most-favored customer, you enjoy the following guarantee: if this chess set is ever sold for a lower price to someone else, the seller will refund you the price difference. As long as the seller has the funds to back up the guarantee, then the most-favored customer program solves the credibility problem too. In the second period, with five chess sets left to sell, the seller makes $100 by selling them at $20 each, but loses $400 in refunds to the first-period buyers, for a payoff of –$300; not an attractive option.

Companies that sell things that last, **durable goods,** have to worry about the credibility of their offers. A number of durable goods industries have evolved rather ingenious techniques to make their claims credible. In textbook publishing, for example, the answer is called the second edition. The first edition of a textbook is good for roughly 3 years, and this is the time limit during which the book is offered for sale. The second edition, if there is one, is waiting in the wings. So even if there are some copies of the first edition left in the warehouse when the 3 years are up, you won't see them in any bookstore. What you will see is the second edition instead. The model year in automobiles operates on the same principle, only with a shorter revision span. You should look for such patterns in other industries.

The next time you hear the words "This offer is good for a limited time only," ask yourself whether there is a good reason to believe them before you run out to buy whatever is being offered. And if you are working for a company trying to sell its merchandise with these words, ask yourself whether your company has incurred any costly commitment that might give them weight.

■ SUMMARY

1. A subgame is any part of a game that can be played by itself. Every game with perfect information has subgames.

2. A credibility problem is present if, at the moment when a threat (or promise) must actually be carried out, a player does not maximize utility by carrying it out. Players who make such threats or promises and then do not carry them out lose their credibility.

3. A strategy that is subgame perfect will always be credible. All strategies and equilibria that fail the test of subgame perfection are called imperfect; they have credibility problems.

4. The solution of a game in extensive form is subgame perfect. Subgame perfect equilibria are found by backward induction, solving a game starting with its final subgames.

5. Whether a threat or promise made by an opponent is credible or not depends on what type of payoffs that opponent has. If a threat or promise is not credible, a player will not have an incentive to carry it out when the time comes.

6. The doctrine of mutually assured destruction holds that nuclear deterrence is credible. This doctrine relies heavily on a particular subgame perfect equilibrium.

7. A monopoly in a take-it-or-leave-it market can exploit most, if not all, the gain from trade from the buyer at subgame perfect equilibrium.

8. Cournot competition in a market game where one firm goes first is called Cournot-Stackelberg competition. The Cournot-Stackelberg equilibrium of such competition is its subgame perfect equilibrium. The first mover in such competition has an advantage.

9. Bertrand competition in a market game where one firm goes first is called Bertrand-Stackelberg competition. The Bertrand-Stackelberg equilibrium of such competition is its subgame perfect equilibrium. The second mover in such competition has an advantage.

10. Credibility concerns help explain why publishers and durable goods manufacturers have instituted the second edition and the model year.

■ KEY TERMS

subgame	take-it-or-leave-it market	costly commitment
credibility problem	Cournot-Stackelberg	most-favored customer
subgame perfect equilibrium	competition	durable goods
backward induction	first-mover advantage	
type of opponent	Bertrand-Stackelberg	
reluctant volunteer	competition	
Mutually Assured	first-mover disadvantage	
Destruction (MAD)	second-mover advantage	

■ PROBLEMS

1. In the perfect information version of Telex versus IBM, suppose that IBM goes first. How does this affect the solution? Is there still a credibility problem with the strategy Smash?

2. Suppose that Centipede has three moves. If player 2 waits at his move, then the money on the table quadruples again, and player 1 either takes it all or splits it. Draw the extensive form and solve. How would you play this game if you were player 1 and you thought player 2 was a nice opponent?

3. Solve the Conscription game when the bonus b = $500 and the cost of serving c = $400. How does this solution differ from that when b = $300? Interpret your answer in terms of an all-volunteer army.

4. MAD has a lot of mixed strategy equilibria; you saw one in the text. Find two more. Why aren't these mixed strategy equilibria credible?

5. Suppose in MAD that at the endgame, if both players back down, the payoffs are −1.5 each. How does this affect the solution? Why is the solution so sensitive to the endgame payoffs?

6. The seller in a take-it-or-leave-it market with two buyers sets the price. The buyers have true willingness to pay $b\#$ of $8 and $6 respectively. Price is an even multiple of $.50, and $a\#$ is $2 for each unit. Find the subgame perfect equilibrium that leaves no buyer indifferent between buying and not buying. Relate your answer to the classical theory of monopoly.

7. In Cournot-Stackelberg competition, each firm faces the market demand $P = (90 − Q$ Each firm has unit cost $30 for each unit it ships to market. Firm 1 moves first. Find the Cournot-Stackelberg equilibrium. Show that firm 1 has a big first-mover advantage, evidenced by its profits. (*Hint:* Firm 2's best response function is a straight line, with a vertical intercept of 60, the monopoly solution.)

8. Find an imperfect equilibrium for the Cournot-Stackelberg model of section 6.6 with $x\emptyset_1$ 30. (*Hint:* Try to mimic the dire strategy given in the text.)

9. In Bertrand-Stackelberg competition, firm 1 moves first and sets its price. Firm 2 sees that price, and then sets its price. The pricing interval is $1. Market demand and cost are the same as in problem 7. Find the Bertrand-Stackelberg equilibrium. How does it compare to the Cournot-Stackelberg equilibrium? How does it compare to Bertrand equilibrium?

10. Give three examples of industries or individual firms that have found a way to make This Offer is Good for a Limited Time Only a credible strategy. Are there are industries for which this strategy is automatically credible?

■ APPENDIX 1. TAKE IT OR LEAVE IT, IN THE LABORATORY

We alluded in section 7.6 to the fact that human subjects are likely to reject small amounts of money in laboratory settings. An internationally renowned team of researchers ran a version of Take It or Leave It in the laboratory to see to what extent human subjects actually play subgame perfect equilibrium in such a situation.[17] To defend against the criticism that the results might somehow be country specific, the experiments were run in four very different countries: the United States, Slovenia, Israel, and Japan. In the U.S. version of the experiment, there was $10 on the table. Payoffs were calibrated by country to the same level of purchasing power and were made in the local currency. The minimum monetary unit was 5 cents.

In this situation a lot of pure strategies are available to the players. Player 1 is the player who goes first, and proposes a division of this $10 to the other player. For player 1, the set of pure strategies is {$0, $0.05, . . .,$10}; that is, offer any amount between $0 and $10 that is divisible by 5 cents. There are 201 such strategies. For each of player 1's 201 pure strategies, player 2 says either Yes or No to player 1's offer, for a total of 2^{201} pure strategies. This is an immense number of strategies; we could never write down the normal form.

Nevertheless, the subgame perfect equilibria are simple enough. There are just two:

Subgame Perfect Equilibrium I: Player 1, offer $0; player 2, say Yes to any offer.

Subgame Perfect Equilibrium II: Player 1, offer $.05; Player 2, say Yes to any offer except $0.

However, nothing like that happened in the laboratories of these four countries. Only about 1% of all offers observed were consistent with subgame perfection, and those offers were *always* rejected. Most observed offers were in the range of $4 to $5. For the United States and Slovenia, the most common offer was $5; for Japan and Israel, $4. Moreover, the observed frequency of acceptance for any offer was never 100%. In the United States, for example, an offer of $3 or less by player 1 was rejected almost 75% of the time. Even an offer of $5 was rejected 10% of the time. You have to wonder what the people who rejected $5 were thinking. At any rate, human subjects just don't play a subgame perfect equilibrium of Take It or Leave It. Game theory, in the form of subgame perfection, can't explain what is going on here.

Nevertheless, there appears to be a certain amount of rationality contained in this behavior. Suppose that player 1 knew the function relating the probability of acceptance to the size of the offer and maximized expected value with respect to the offer accordingly. Then, for each of the four countries, player 1's maximum expected value occurs at the mode of the actually observed offers for that country. What was observed in these experiments makes a certain amount of sense when we think of it as out-of-equilibrium behavior. We will return to the themes of bounded rationality and out-of-equilibrium behavior in Chapter 9.

---

[17] See Alvin E. Roth, Vesna Prasnikar, Masahiro Okuno-Fujiwara, and Shmuel Zamir, "Bargaining and Market Behavior in Jerusalem, Ljubljana, Pittsburgh, and Tokyo: An Experimental Study," *American Economic Review* 81 (1991): 1068–1095.

These results show that there are serious limits to subgame perfection as a predictive theory, at least in situations involving ultimatums. Many other psychological considerations come into play in such situations besides simply a player's own payoffs, in particular notions of fairness. A very clever theory has recently been proposed to explain the deviations from subgame perfection in these experiments, based on a quantifiable version of player's notions of fairness. See Ernst Fehr and Klaus M. Schmidt, "A Theory of Fairness, Competition and Cooperation," *Quarterly Journal of Economics* 114 (1999): 817–868.

■ APPENDIX 2. CALCULUS DERIVATION OF A BEST RESPONSE

In our analysis of Cournot-Stackelberg competition, we needed to find the maximum of the function

$$u_1(\mathbf{x}) = [120 - x_1 - 60 + x_1/2]x_1$$

which is a quadratic function of one variable. Simplifying, we have

$$u_1(\mathbf{x}) = [60 - 0.5x_1]x_1 = 60x_1 - 0.5x_1^2$$

Taking the first derivative of this function with respect to x_1, and setting the result equal to zero, we get

$$0 = 60 - x_1$$

Solving, we get $x_1 = 60$, the answer we gave in section 7.8. Note that this is a true maximum, since the second derivative of the function is everywhere negative.

CHAPTER 8

Repeated Games

Many, if not most, of the strategic interactions in our daily lives take place more than once. There is an enormous difference between a single date with someone, and dating that same person more than once. In many markets—durable goods, insurance, financial services, and meals and entertainment, to name just a few—repeat buyers are essential to profitability. This chapter examines repeated games, games where the same players meet to play a game more than once. Repeating a zero-sum game does not create anything new, strategically. For variable-sum games, however, repetition creates exciting new possibilities for new outcomes, some of which are far more attractive than the outcome of the game played once. Repeated games capture an important part of what enduring relationships are all about.

The chapter begins with strategies and payoffs for repeated games. One reason that repeated games possess such attractive possibilities is that they have so many more strategies than do games played once. Finite repetition of a Cournot market game is not enough for an industry to maximize profits, a fact well known to the members of OPEC. However, finite repetition of a variable-sum game with multiple equilibria creates many new payoff opportunities. A theorem about finitely repeated games, called the folk theorem for finitely repeated games, is introduced. The folk theorem describes subgame perfect equilibria of a repeated game and shows how even finite repetition can approach an efficient outcome. Discussion next turns to infinitely repeated games, which are fundamentally different from finitely repeated games. Infinitely repeated games are especially relevant to corporate interactions, where the corporation is viewed as having an infinite life ahead of it. An analogous folk theorem for infinitely repeated games is used to describe subgame perfect equilibria of infinitely repeated Cournot and Bertrand market games. The pricing pattern prevalent in the ready-to-eat cereals industry, called price leadership, illustrates some of the issues in industrial economics that surround these equilibria.

■ 8.1 STRATEGIES AND PAYOFFS FOR GAMES PLAYED TWICE

Consider a generic 2 x 2 game in normal form—two players with two strategies each—the only difference being that this game is going to be played twice. Figure 8.1 depicts the situation schematically. There are four possible outcomes of the first play of the game. Each of these becomes a **possible history** leading up to the second play of the game. Each line from a cell of the initial matrix to the second matrix in Figure 8.1 represents a possible history. The game that is played each time is called the **one-shot game,** and the game that consists of all plays of the one-shot game is called the **repeated game.** In Figure 8.1, each of the five matrices is an instance of the one-shot game, whereas the entire figure represents the repeated game.

We can now define what a strategy, a complete plan of play, looks like for the game in Figure 8.1. Call the two strategies of the one-shot game Left (L) and Right (R). A strategy specifies what a player does at the first repetition, either L or R. Next, a strategy specifies

FIGURE 8.1 | **A 2 X 2 GAME PLAYED TWICE**

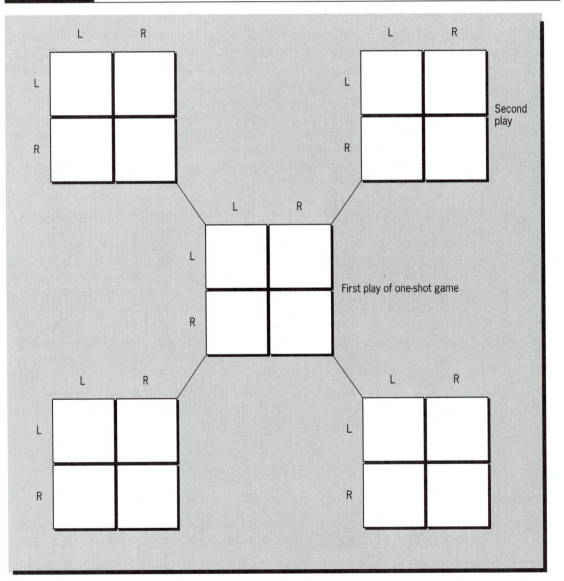

what a player does at the second repetition, following each logically possible history leading to it. Since there are four possible histories and two choices for each possible history, there are 16 possible choices at this stage. Multiplying, we have $(2)(16) = 32$ strategies for the entire repeated game. These strategies are listed in Figure 8.2.

Some of these strategies are important enough to get special names. Strategy 1 plays left at the first play and plays left at the second play, regardless of what happened on the first play. Such a strategy is an **unconditional strategy.** Strategy 32 is likewise unconditional, playing right instead of left. Strategy 16 is called a **rotation strategy.** It plays left at the first play, then plays right at the second play, regardless of what happened on the first play. in the second repetition after any possible history. Strategy 17 is the reverse rotation. Strategy 6 is called a **trigger strategy.** This strategy plays left on the first play and plays left in the second play if and only if the opponent played left in the previous history. If instead the opponent plays right on the first play, this triggers the play of right at the second play. Trigger strategies are useful when you want your opponent to play only one pure strategy in the one-shot game. Strategy 27 is the trigger strategy for right. It plays right on the first play and plays right on the second play if and only if the opponent played right in the previous history.

FIGURE 8.2	STRATEGIES FOR PLAYING A 2 X 2 GAME TWICE

		Outcome on the First Play Was:			
Strategy No.	First Play	(L,L)	(L,R)	(R,L)	(R,R)
1	L	L	L	L	L
2	L	L	L	L	R
3	L	L	L	R	L
4	L	L	L	R	R
5	L	L	R	L	L
6	L	L	R	L	R
7	L	L	R	R	L
8	L	L	R	R	R
9	L	R	L	L	L
10	L	R	L	L	R
11	L	R	L	R	L
12	L	R	L	R	R
13	L	R	R	L	L
14	L	R	R	L	R
15	L	R	R	R	L
16	L	R	R	R	R
17	R	L	L	L	L
18	R	L	L	L	R
19	R	L	L	R	L
20	R	L	L	R	R
21	R	L	R	L	L
22	R	L	R	L	R
23	R	L	R	R	L
24	R	L	R	R	R
25	R	R	L	L	L
26	R	R	L	L	R
27	R	R	L	R	L
28	R	R	L	R	R
29	R	R	R	L	L
30	R	R	R	L	R
31	R	R	R	R	L
32	R	R	R	R	R

To write down the normal form for a 2 x 2 game played twice, we would have to write down a 32 x 32 matrix. The matrices only get bigger with further repetition. There must be a better way to analyze repeated games, and there is—the extensive form. Repetition creates subgames. The 2 x 2 repeated game played twice has four final subgames. By exploiting the subgame structure inherent in repeated games, we can solve them without having to spend our lives writing down enormous matrices.

Payoffs for repeated games are reasonably straightforward. All we have to do is somehow add up the payoffs at each round. The most general way to do this is in terms of present value, the phenomenon according to which a dollar today is worth more than a dollar tomorrow. Let R be the **discount factor,** a number between 0 and 1. $R = 0$ means the future has no value; $R = 1$ means the future is just as important as the present. A payoff of \$1 T periods from now is worth \$$1R^T$ now. Let $u_1(t)$ be player 1's payoff in the one-shot played in period t. Then the present value for player 1 of a game played twice, u_1, is

$$u_1 = u_1(0) + Ru_1(1)$$

when the game starts now, at time $t = 0$. We define the present value for player 2 of a game played twice, u_2, similarly.

Here are two interpretations of the discount factor. One interpretation of R is as a discount factor purely for time. If r is the discount rate (often identified with the market interest rate), then the discount factor, R, satisfies

$$R = 1/(1 + r)$$

An interest rate of 10 percent per period ($r = 0.1$) implies a discount factor of $1/1.1$, or $10/11$. At this discount factor, a dollar 10 periods from now is worth only $(10/11)^{10} = \$0.38$ today. A second interpretation of R is probabilistic. Under this interpretation, R is the **continuation probability,** the probability that the game will be played again. Suppose a player is uncertain whether a game will be continued or not. Then it makes sense to weight an uncertain future less than a certain present. A bird in the hand is better than one in the bush—you may not find the one in the bush. Under either interpretation, we get exactly the same expression for u_1.

For all the finitely repeated games we study, we will set $R = 1$. Either the time between repetitions is very short, or the one-shot game is certain to be repeated. Also, we will normalize payoffs, so that payoffs from the repeated game have the same magnitude as the payoffs of the one-shot game. This is accomplished by dividing the payoff stream by the number of times the one-shot game is played, T. Thus, for a game played twice, we express the utility of player i in the one-shot game played twice, u_i, as

$$u_i = (1/2)[u_i(0) + u_i(1)]$$

Armed with payoffs and strategies, we are now ready to tackle some **finitely repeated games.** We turn to 2-person, zero-sum games first.

■ 8.2 Two-Person, Zero-Sum Games Played More than Once

Solving a 2-person, zero-sum game played more than once is a cinch. Value isn't created when a zero-sum game is repeated. If the game is one in which both players break even when it is played once, then they continue to break even by playing their break-even strategy however many times the game is played. If the game is one in which player 1 can guarantee a positive payoff at player 2's expense, then player 1 can guarantee that positive payoff each and every time the game is played by using her winning strategy. Here are two examples.

Suppose that two firms are playing Competitive Advantage (section 3.3) twice. The first time they play Competitive Advantage, the innovation is an MRI unit. The second time they play Competitive Advantage, the innovation is a positron emission tomography (PET) unit. Firm 1 has a strictly dominant strategy in the one-shot game, adopt the new technology. Firm 1 selects the repeated game strategy that always plays its strictly dominant strategy:

> First play: Firm 1 adopts the new technology.
> Second play: Whatever happened at the first play, firm 1 adopts the new technology.

This is also a strictly dominant strategy for firm 2 to play. An equilibrium path of a repeated game is what is observed each and every period when the players play a certain equilibrium. Along the subgame perfect equilibrium path of Competitive Advantage played twice, we observe that each firm adopts the new technology and gets a payoff of 0 each period. Just as in the Nash equilibrium of the one-shot game, where $u_1 = u_2 = 0$, we get in the repeated game

$$u_1 = (0 + 0)/2 = 0$$

and likewise for firm 2. If it is a strictly dominant strategy to adopt the new technology next year, and it is a dominant strategy to adopt the new technology this year, then it is a strictly dominant strategy to adopt the new technology both years.

Next, suppose that two television networks play Battle of the Networks (section 3.1) twice. Since the networks run their programs every week, they actually play this game a lot more than twice—more like 52 times a year. Every week, network 1 enjoys a 4 percent viewer share advantage over network 2 if it plays its Nash equilibrium strategy, Show a Sitcom. Network 1 will, of course, stick with a winner, using the strategy

> First play: Show a sitcom.
> Second play: What happened at the first play, show a sitcom.

Firm 2 uses a similar strategy, only with sitcom replaced by sports. The average viewer share advantage over 2 (or more) weeks is 4 percent, in favor of network 1. The subgame perfect equilibrium path of repeated Battle of the Networks is for network 1 to show a sitcom each period and for network 2 to show a sports show each period. This equilibrium is a subgame perfect, since it programs an equilibrium on each of the four possible subgames that arise in the second play.

As you can see, nothing new happens when a 2-person, zero-sum game is repeated. You just get the same behavior and the same outcome over and over again. There really is nothing to correspond to a relationship in a 2-person, zero-sum game, no matter how often it is played. Things have the potential to be a lot more interesting when the game that is being repeated is variable sum. Even in that case, however, a lot depends on how many Nash equilibria the one-shot game has.

◼ 8.3 VARIABLE-SUM GAMES WITH A SINGLE NASH EQUILIBRIUM, PLAYED TWICE

Repeating a variable-sum game can give rise to a valuable relationship between the players. The major qualification to this concerns credibility. Since repeated games have a rich subgame structure, subgame perfection plays an especially prominent role in their solution. Whether repetition will create extra game value depends on how many Nash equilibria the one-shot game has. If the one-shot game has a single Nash equilibrium, then repetition is no more interesting than in a zero-sum game. The solution of a repeated game whose one-shot game has a unique Nash equilibrium is that equilibrium played on every subgame.

We will prove this result for Prisoner's Dilemma played twice (see Figure 8.3). Prisoner's Dilemma played once has a unique Nash equilibrium, where each player confesses. We can show, via backward induction, that the unique subgame perfect equilibrium of Prisoner's Dilemma played twice is for each player to confess on each subgame. As always with backward induction, we start with the final subgames. On each of the four final subgames, there is a unique equilibrium. Since a subgame perfect equilibrium must play a Nash equilibrium on every subgame, and (confess, confess) is that subgame equilibrium, each player confesses on each subgame. This brings us back to the first play of the game, with the subgame equilibrium payoffs (2,2) added to each player's payoff. At the first play, there is again a unique Nash equilibrium, with each player confessing (see Figure 8.4). The total payoff for the two plays of the game is 4 for each player, which gives an average payoff of 4/2 = 2 per period. The complete plan of play for each player is the following unconditional strategy:

> Confess in the first period, and in every subsequent period, regardless of what has happened prior to that period.

Credibility prevents the prisoners from reaching a better outcome than the one-shot equilibrium. A prisoner's promise not to confess in the second round, which is what it would take to get higher payoffs, just doesn't stand up to the scrutiny of credibility.

The result we have just shown for a 2 x 2 game with a unique equilibrium played twice is true for any game played finitely many times:

◼ ◼ ◼

Selten's theorem. If a game with a unique Nash equilibrium is played finitely many times, its unique subgame perfect equilibrium is that Nash equilibrium played each and every time.[1]

This result was first noted by Nobel laureate Reinhard Selten. Selten's theorem does not mean that there aren't other Nash equilibria for such repeated games. There always are other Nash equilibria, but they all have credibility problems. Take Prisoner's Dilemma played twice. Here is an equilibrium with a credibility problem:

First play: Confess.

Second play: Confess if at least one player confessed at the first play; otherwise, do not confess.

[1] Reinhard Selten, "A Simple Model of Imperfect Competition, Where 4 Are Few and 6 Are Many," *International Journal of Game Theory* 2 (1973): 141–201. Selten was the first to prove this theorem in English.

FIGURE 8.3 PRISONER'S DILEMMA PLAYED TWICE

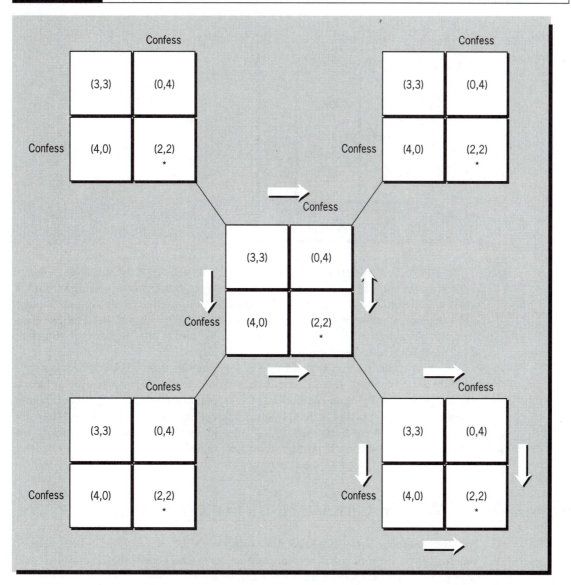

This strategy, when played by each player, has the same equilibrium path and pay-offs as the subgame perfect equilibrium does. Its imperfection arises only on the subgame reached by the first-period play (do not confess, do not confess). Since, according to the complete plan of each player, (confess, confess) is to be played in the first period, the first-period play (do not confess, do not confess) that activates the imperfection does not occur. If things did not go according to plan, and both players unintentionally did not confess at the first play, each would face a serious credibility problem at the second play. Their strategy would tell them not to confess, but they could get a higher pay-off by confessing.

FIGURE 8.4 **PRISONER'S DILEMMA (FIRST PLAY, AFTER BACKWARD INDUCTION)**

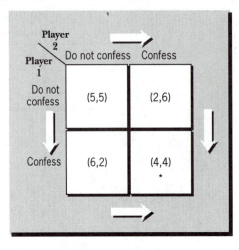

In a Prisoner's Dilemma game that is played a finite number of times (and players know when the end will occur), the dominant strategy of each player is to confess from the outset and continue to do so through the last play. Intuitively this can be seen through backward induction. Once it's determined that both players will confess on the last play, then each player will confess on the second-to-last play and so on, eventually arriving back at the first play, where cheating will occur by both players.

The same principle that applies to finitely repeated Prisoner's Dilemma applies with equal force to finitely repeated Cournot or Bertrand market games when these have a unique Cournot or Bertrand equilibrium. The one-shot market game Nash equilibrium, played each and every period, is the subgame perfect equilibrium path of the repeated market game (see problem 1 for details). The world market for oil, and especially the Organization of Petroleum Exporting Countries (OPEC) within that market, provides a good example of a repeated Cournot market game. To this market we now turn.

8.4 OPEC WON'T CURB OIL UNTIL OTHERS DO

The Organization of Petroleum Exporting Countries, **OPEC,** was founded in 1960.[2] Led by Venezuela in the beginning, the oil-exporting countries who joined OPEC had as their goal raising world oil prices substantially above marginal cost. As long as the United States was an oil exporter, that is, until 1967, OPEC had no opportunity to realize this goal.

OPEC's magic moment came in 1973, in the wake of the Yom Kippur War. OPEC raised the price of a barrel of oil from $2 to $10, and the price increase stuck. This situation was helped by OPEC's embargo of oil to the United States—an embargo violated only by the then shah of Iran. OPEC repeated this success in 1979, driving prices up to a new record level, $30/barrel.

Like any cartel, OPEC was faced with the problem of maintaining the cartel price. Since price was substantially above marginal cost, each country had an incentive to produce

---

[2] This section draws on material from Thaddeus Herrick and Bhushan Bahree, "OPEC Won't Curb Oil Until Others Do," *Wall Street Journal,* 15 November 2001.

and sell more oil and thereby to make more money. This is just another reflection of the fact that a price near monopoly is not a one-shot game equilibrium.

OPEC decided to address the price maintenance problem by instituting a set of quotas, one for each of the member countries. Saudi Arabia, the world's largest oil exporter, got the largest quota; smaller producers got smaller quotas. Bitter enemies, Iraq and Iran, got exactly the same quota. The total amount of the quotas led to a market quantity that would support the OPEC target price (see Figure 8.5). The OPEC target price, denoted $P+$, corresponds to the total quotas supplied to buyers. The observed market price, denoted P^*, corresponds to the one-shot Cournot equilibrium.

The members of OPEC were aware of the unfortunate consequences to cartel profits of deviations by member countries. Nevertheless, each member continually exceeded its quota. Saudi Arabia, with a daily quota of 5 million barrels, was known at times to produce twice that (for instance, during the Gulf War).

One way, it would seem, for OPEC to escape this fate would be to exploit the efficiency-enhancing properties of repeated game equilibria. Unfortunately, for the cartel, two facts conspire to prevent this from occurring. One is that member countries are rapidly running out of oil. Both Venezuela and Indonesia expect to run out entirely by the middle of the twenty-first century. This makes the game finite for them in a hurry. Even if the countries act as if they are going to last forever, their oil is not. Second, given the structure of world demand for imported oil, there is a unique one-shot equilibrium involving the members of OPEC. Thus, Selten's theorem comes into play with a vengeance. The only subgame perfect, repeated game equilibrium is for all the members to cheat on their quotas each and every period—precisely what they do.

Even worse for OPEC, nonmember countries made major oil strikes in the past decades: the United Kingdom, Norway, and the Netherlands in the North Sea; Mexico, in the Gulf of Mexico; Russia, in Siberia, and the United States, on the north slope of Alaska. All these strikes made available vast new supplies of oil to the world market. OPEC has seen the world market price in real terms steadily erode, until it returned to near 1973 levels.

FIGURE 8.5 OPEC QUOTAS

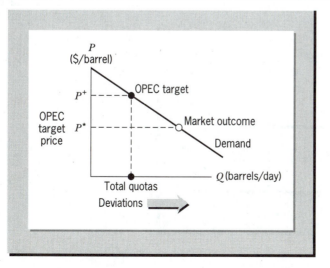

Despite recurring pleas at OPEC oil ministers' meetings for discipline in the ranks, the countries have continued to exceed their quotas. In the fall of 2001, in an effort to bolster prices, OPEC members proposed a cut in actual production of 1.5 million barrels a day (about 8 percent of their output), as long as non-OPEC producers—mainly Russia—also agreed to cut their production by 0.5 million barrels a day (again, about 8 percent of their output). Given a demand elasticity with respect to price of about –0.5, these overall output decreases of 8 percent would drive up price 16 percent, to the benefit of all oil producers.

Although Russia has agreed in public to such a cut, it remains to be seen if oil sent to the world market will indeed drop by 8 percent, with the attendant price increase. It should be borne in mind that Russia could produce an extra 2 million barrels/day and counteract all the efforts of OPEC members to raise the price—and make more money, to boot.

■ 8.5 VARIABLE-SUM GAMES WITH MULTIPLE NASH EQUILIBRIA, PLAYED FINITELY MANY TIMES

As we have just seen, playing Prisoner's Dilemma or a Cournot market game a finite number of times doesn't do the players any more good, on average, than playing the game once. When a one-shot game has multiple equilibria, then repeated play opens up a lot of interesting new payoff possibilities. What's more, these new payoff possibilities are subgame perfect, so they pass the test of credibility.

To fix ideas, let's look at a new one-shot game, called Market Niches (note the plural). There are two players, firms 1 and 2, and two market niches, A and B. The one-shot game is shown in Figure 8.6. If both firms occupy market niche A, they get a payoff of 3 each. However, if either firm leaves market niche A for market niche B, it gets a higher payoff (4). Finally, there is room at market niche B for only one firm, so if both firms go there, both get payoff 0. As you can see from the arrow diagram of Figure 8.6, Market Niches is exactly like Chicken.

As you can see, the one-shot version of Market Niches has two very different pure strategy Nash equilibria, (A,B) and (B,A), with payoff vectors (4,1) and (1,4). In addition

FIGURE 8.6   MARKET NICHES: THE ONE-SHOT GAME

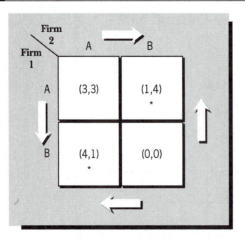

to these pure strategy Nash equilibria, there is a mixed strategy Nash equilibrium. At this equilibrium, firm 1 goes to market niche A with probability 1/2 and to market niche B with the same probability. Firm 2 plays the same mixed strategy. Each firm has the expected value of 2 at this mixed strategy equilibrium. These one-shot game payoffs are recorded in the utility possibility diagram of Figure 8.7.

Each firm would rather have market niche B to itself. If Market Niches is played twice, then a rotation is possible. In particular, each firm can have the market niche B to itself once. Here is the subgame perfect equilibrium that sends firm 1 to market niche B in the first round, and then sends firm 2 to market niche B in the second round. Firm 1's complete plan is the following:

First play: Go to B.

Second play: After every possible history, go to A.

Firm 2's complete plan is the following:

First play: Go to A.

Second play: After every possible history, go to B.

These strategies are subgame perfect because they play a Nash equilibrium on every subgame. The equilibrium path corresponding to these strategies is (B,A) first, followed by (A,B). This rotation yields the average payoffs in the repeated game of (2.5, 2.5). By reversing roles, we can program the rotation in the reverse order, with firm 2 going to market niche B in round 1. That, too, is subgame perfect, and again yields the repeated game payoffs (2.5, 2.5). This average utility of this rotation payoff is also shown in Figure 8.7.

We do not lose any feasible payoff vectors when the one-shot game is repeated. For instance, the payoff vector (4,1) corresponds to a subgame perfect equilibrium of Market Niches played twice. All we need is to play the same one-shot game equilibrium twice in a

FIGURE 8.7 **MARKET NICHES PLAYED TWO AND THREE TIMES (PAYOFF POSSIBILITIES)**

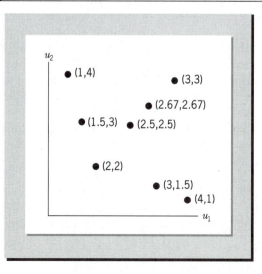

row. Firm 1's complete plan at the subgame perfect equilibrium that sends it to market niche B both periods is

First play: Go to B.

Second play: Whatever happened on the first play, go to B.

Firm 2's complete plan at this equilibrium is

First play: Go to A.

Second play: Whatever happened on the first play, go to A.

Notice that these strategies are unconditional. At this subgame perfect equilibrium we observe the sequence of outcomes and repeated game payoffs:

(B,A), (B,A); paying (4,1)

Using unconditional strategies that reverse the roles of two players, we get the subgame perfect equilibrium path

(A,B), (A,B); paying (1,4)

Let MIX denote the mixed strategy Nash equilibrium in the one-shot game. Here are seven more subgame perfect equilibrium paths:

MIX, MIX; paying (2,2)

MIX, (A,B); paying (1.5, 3)

MIX, (B,A); paying (3, 1.5)

(A,B), MIX; paying (1.5, 3)

(B,A), MIX; paying (3, 1.5)

(A,B), (B,A); paying (2.5, 2.5)

(B,A), (A,B); paying (2.5, 2.5)

Along all these paths, we play one Nash equilibrium of the one-shot game at the first play and at the second play. The payoff possibilities that result are shown in Figure 8.7. Playing Market Niches greatly increases the number of utility possibilities achieved by the subgame perfect equilibrium.

If we play Market Niches three times, we get a fundamentally new possibility in addition to all possible combinations of one-shot Nash equilibria. The new subgame perfect equilibrium that arises when Market Niches is played three times is very attractive. Here is the equilibrium path. Both firms go to market niche A in period 1. In periods 2 and 3 they rotate on the market niches. What was not a Nash equilibrium in the one-shot game, both firms going to market niche A, becomes part of a subgame perfect equilibrium in the repeated game. The average payoff vector

$$u_1 = u_2 = (3 + 1 + 4)/3 = 2.67$$

that each firm gets from this path dominates any other symmetrical equilibrium of Market Niches played three times. To support the equilibrium path (A,A) followed by (A,B) and then (B,A), the firms play the following strategies. For firm 1, the strategy is

First play: Go to A.

Second play: Go to A if the first play is (A,A) or (B,B)

and on the third play go to B unconditionally;

go to B if the first play is (A,B)

and on the third play go to B unconditionally;

go to A if the first play is (B,A)

and on the third play go to A unconditionally.

For firm 2, the strategy is

First play: Go to A.

Second play: Go to B if the first play is (A,A) or (B,B)

and on the third play go to A unconditionally;

go to A if the first play is (A,B)

and on the third play go to A unconditionally;

go to B if the first play is (B,A)

and on the third play go to B unconditionally.

Let's see how these strategies work. The equilibrium path is (A,A), followed by (A,B) and (B,A). Along the equilibrium path, firm 1 gets the average payoff

$$u_1 = (3 + 1 + 4)/3 = 2.67$$

which firm 2 also gets:

$$u_2 = (3 + 4 + 1)/3 = 2.67$$

Why doesn't one of the firms, say, firm 1, occupy niche B on the first play and thereby get a payoff 4 instead of 3? Notice what happens if firm 1 occupies niche B on the first play. Since firm 2 is sticking to its complete plan in this thought experiment, the first play is (B,A). If (B,A) is what happened, then on the second play firm 1 goes to A and firm 2 goes to B. This is a second play payoff vector (1,4), which is repeated on the third play. If firm 1 deviates from the strategy paying 2.67 by occupying market niche B at the first play, it gets the payoff

$$u_1 = (4 + 1 + 1)/3 = 2 < 2.67$$

It does not pay firm 1 to deviate, so this is indeed an equilibrium for firm 1. Similarly, you can show that a deviation by firm 2 on the first play also does not pay. Moreover, since all subsequent play involves one-shot game Nash equilibria, we have shown that this pair of strategies is a subgame perfect equilibrium. Every threat in the event that one of the firms deviates from the equilibrium path involves a one-shot game Nash equilibrium, making it credible. The payoff vector (2.67, 2.67) can therefore be included in Figure 8.7.

The generalization of the preceding strategies to a large number of plays T is as follows: Play (A,A) as much as possible. Then near the end of the game, switch to the rotation between (A,B) and (B,A). Support this play with the threat to play the worst one-shot equilibrium for a firm that deviates. We call this kind of strategy a trigger strategy, because a deviation from equilibrium triggers a credible punishment for the deviator—playing the worst possible one-shot equilibrium for that player until the game ends.

Suppose these firms play Market Niche 101 times. Using trigger strategies like those just presented, we send each firm to market niche A for the first 99 plays, then rotate the final two plays. Using an argument similar to that given earlier, we can show that this is a subgame perfect equilibrium path. Moreover, we can get very close to the average payoffs (3,3):

$$[99(3,3) + (4,1) + (1,4)]/101 = (2.99, 2.99)$$

This is no accident, but rather a general result. Let w_i be the worst equilibrium payoff to player i in the one-shot game and let **w** be the vector of such payoffs. Say that a payoff has **individual rationality** if a player can guarantee that payoff to himself or herself regardless of what the opponents do. We are now ready to state the folk theorem for games that are played a large, but finite, number of times:[3]

Folk Theorem for Finitely Repeated Two-Person Games. Suppose that a finitely repeated game has a one-shot equilibrium payoff vector that payoff dominates **w.** Then all individually rational and feasible payoffs are supported in the limit as average payoffs of subgame perfect equilibria.

This result is called the **folk theorem** because it was part of the folklore—what everybody in game theory knew and took for granted—years before anyone bothered to write down a proof and publish it.[4]

Figure 8.8 applies the folk theorem to Market Niches. Each firm can guarantee itself at least a payoff of 1 by playing A, so we get the reference vector for individual rationality, **IR:**

$$\mathbf{IR} = (1,1)$$

FIGURE 8.8 | **FOLK THEOREM: MARKET NICHES PLAYED FINITELY MANY TIMES**

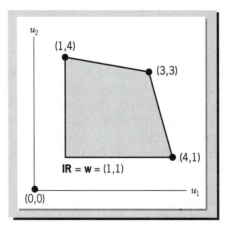

[3] This theorem is stated and proved for the 2-player game by J. Benoit and V. Krishna, "Finitely Repeated Games," *Econometrica* 53 (1985): 905–922. A similar result is true for more than two players, but requires more conditions in the hypothesis.
[4] This explanation of the origin of the term *folk theorem* is due to Robert Aumann.

The worst one-shot equilibrium payoff to player 1 is achieved by the equilibrium (A,B) and equals 1; the worst one-shot equilibrium payoff to player 2 is achieved by equilibrium (B,A) and equals 1. Thus we have

$$\mathbf{w} = (1,1) = \mathbf{IR}$$

The mixed strategy equilibrium paying (2,2) payoff dominates **w**. Feasible payoffs include the matrix entries (1,4), (4,1), and (3,3). Also feasible are payoffs on the lines connecting these three points, as well as payoffs below those lines. Combining individual rationality and feasibility, we get the quadrilateral depicted in Figure 8.8. For example, with enough plays, we can get arbitrarily close to the vector (3,3) using subgame perfect equilibria.

Repetition creates new subgame equilibrium possibilities, and some of these new subgame perfect equilibria are very attractive. At the same time, repetition creates new problems. Consider the two firms competing in Market Niches. Thanks to the folk theorem, they face a plethora of equilibria. One of these is best for firm 1: play (B,A) every time. Another of these is best for firm 2: play (B,A) every time. The strategic problem facing the firms—namely, which firm gets market niche B—is merely pushed up to a higher level by repetition. Instead of fighting over which firm gets market niche B in a one-shot equilibrium, now the firms fight over which equilibrium to play in the repeated game. Game theory can exhibit the possible solutions in a case like this, but game theory alone cannot supply the answer.

■ 8.6 Infinitely Repeated Games: Strategies and Payoffs

We are about to study infinitely repeated games, and there's no avoiding the inevitable question—why? We are all going to die someday, and definitely a lot sooner than an infinitely repeated game will ever end, so what's the use of such games? Here are three reasons for this madness. First, even though you're going to die, with any kind of luck your company is going to survive you. Since a corporation is not a person, there is no reason a corporation cannot live—and therefore play—forever. Some of the best examples of infinitely repeated games involve corporations. Second, even if you know you are going to die, it's unlikely that you will act as if death is around the corner. A lot of people act as if they are going to live forever. And that is all it takes for an infinitely repeated game: two or more players who act as if they will play the game forever. In this case, "as if" is as good as "is." Finally, even though the folk theorem for finitely repeated games shows how repetition creates good subgame equilibria for one-shot games with several Nash equilibria, it doesn't do anything for one-shot games with a single equilibrium. For instance, it doesn't create new, credible equilibrium payoff possibilities for the Prisoner's Dilemma. Only infinitely repeated games can do that.

A strategy for an infinitely repeated game must specify infinitely many choices for each play following each possible history. Such strategies could be infinitely complex. The strategies for infinitely repeated games we study here will be among the simplest possible.

Suppose two players are playing the Prisoner's Dilemma (recall Figure 8.3) forever. The simplest kind of strategy to play Prisoner's Dilemma forever, containing two program steps:

First play: Play Do Not Confess.

Subsequent play: At any time t, and after any possible history, play Do Not Confess.

This is the unconditional strategy to do the same thing—Do Not Confess—infinitely often. The analogous unconditional strategy, to Confess, is equally simple.

Trigger strategies are especially important for infinitely repeated games with a unique, inefficient one-shot Nash equilibrium. The players in Prisoner's Dilemma would like to escape the dilemma, and the combination of infinity and the right trigger strategies is just the thing to do that.

To see how that works, we first need to be able to evaluate payoffs for an infinitely repeated game. A dollar a hundred years from now is not worth the same as a dollar right now—and a dollar infinitely delayed is worth a whole lot less. To handle the problem posed by time, future payoffs are discounted relative to the present. For mathematical reasons, the discount rate is set at $R < 1$; otherwise, infinitely long streams of payoffs would not converge. We have to evaluate expressions of the form

$$u_I = (1 - R) \sum R^T u_1(t)$$

where t goes from zero (now) to infinity (the distant future). You will see in a minute why we multiply in front of the sum by the term $(1 - R)$; this keeps the payoffs for the infinitely repeated game on the exact same scale as those of the one-shot game.

Infinite sums can be a challenge to calculate, but as long as the terms in an infinite sum are constant, an exact answer can be found. This property is useful for finding subgame perfect equilibria for infinitely repeated games; it also allows us to approximate series whose terms vary. Suppose that player 1 gets the payoff 2 every time she plays a game, forever. Then, in the formula given, $u_1(t) = 2$ for all t. This player wants to find the value of the infinite series

$$u_1 = (1 - R)(2)(1 + R + R^2 + R^3 + \ldots)$$

For discount factors R between 0 and 1, $0 < R < 1$, the infinite series sums to

$$(1 + R + R^2 + R^3 + \ldots) = 1/(1 - R)$$

so we get the payoff in the infinitely repeated game

$$u_1 = (1 - R)(2)(1/(1 - R)) = 2$$

which is precisely the one-shot equilibrium payoff of Prisoner's Dilemma in Figure 8.3.

Figure 8.9 shows all the possible payoffs to Prisoner's Dilemma played infinitely many times when payoffs are normalized in this way. Notice that the payoffs form a triangle with vertices (4,0), (0,4) and (3,3)—all payoff vectors of the one-shot Prisoner's Dilemma. The final one-shot game payoff vector, (2,2), lies on the line connecting (4,0) and (0,4). Any payoff that can be written as a weighted combination of the vertices, with weights adding to one, can be achieved by infinite repetition of the game. Thus, we can get the payoff vector $(7/3, 7/3)$ as

$$(7/3, 7/3) = (1/3) (4, 0) + (1/3) (0, 4) + (1/3)(3, 3)$$

where 1/3 is the frequency with which each of those vertices is played. Armed with payoffs and strategies, we are now ready to tackle this infinitely repeated game.

FIGURE 8.9 | TRIGGER STRATEGIES FOR INFINITELY REPEATED PRISONER'S DILEMMA

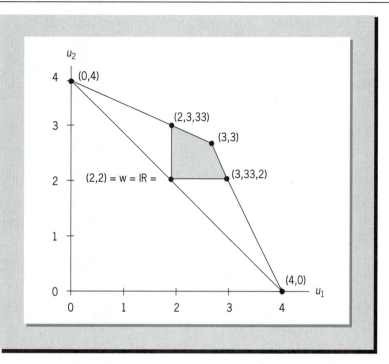

8.7 THE EFFICIENT OUTCOME OF PRISONER'S DILEMMA VIA SUBGAME PERFECTION

We saw that in Prisoner's Dilemma played finitely many times, subgame perfection led to a unique outcome, the inefficient Nash equilibrium of the one-shot game:

(confess, confess)

Now we want to show how infinite repetition allows the prisoners an escape. The idea behind the strategy that does this is just like in Market Niches played many times: play the efficient one-shot outcome, even though it is not a one-shot Nash equilibrium. Punish any deviation from this behavior with eternal play of the one-shot Nash equilibrium. As long as eternity means enough to the players—in our language, as long as R is close enough to 1—this **grim trigger strategy** (grim because it involved eternal punishment of any deviation) will be a subgame perfect equilibrium.

Here is the strategy we want each player to consider. Since the game is symmetric, it makes sense to have each consider the same strategy:

First play: Play Do Not Confess.

Subsequent play: If at any time t Confess has been played, then play Confess from $t + 1$ forever; otherwise play Do Not Confess.

Let's show first that this is a Nash equilibrium; no player can gain from deviating from the proposed equilibrium path (Do Not Confess, Do Not Confess), $t = 0$, 1, 2, . . . To see this, suppose that player 1 deviates right off the bat, in period $t = 0$. This is the most promising time to deviate, since this is the one and only payoff that will not be discounted. Waiting to deviate later will mean lower payoffs due to discounting. If player 1 deviates at time $t = 0$, she gets the payoff 4. Then, from $t = 1$ to eternity, this player is stuck playing the one-shot Nash equilibrium as a punishment, getting the payoff 2, discounted. Adding up these payoffs, we get

$$u_1 = (1 - R)[4 + 2R + 2R^2 + \ldots]$$

Adding and subtracting 2 to the last term on the right

$$u_1 = (1 - R)[4 - 2 + 2 + 2R + 2R^2 + \ldots]$$

Simplifying,

$$u_1 = (1 - R)[2 + (2)/(1 - R)] = 2 - 2R + 2 = 4 - 2R$$

The same payoff would face player 2 if he were to do the deviating.

Now compare the payoff from Confessing right off the bat to always playing Do Not Confess. That pays 3 every time:

$$u_1 = (1 - R)(3)(1 + R + R^2 + R^3 + \ldots) = 3$$

Let's solve the inequality

$$3 > 4 - 2R$$

This is the condition that guarantees that playing the efficient one-shot outcome forever is a Nash equilibrium. Solving, we have

$$2R > 1, \text{ or } R > 0.5$$

Here's another way to express what we just found. A player will confess so long as the marginal benefit from confessing exceeds the marginal cost of confessing. The marginal benefit of confessing is $4 - 2R$; the marginal cost of confessing is 3. Thus, confessing pays if and only if

$$4 - 2R > 3$$

By having $R > 0.5$, the preceding inequality is not satisfied, and confessing doesn't pay.

If this game is played every day, and if a dollar tomorrow is worth at least $.50 today, then it pays not to confess. Indeed, for anyone who puts money in the bank at an interest rate of 3 percent, a dollar one year from now is worth $.97 today—way above $.50.

Next, we show that the strategies just given are subgame perfect. Notice that they specify the play of a Nash equilibrium in the event of any deviation—that's credible. So we've got subgame perfection, too.

We have just exhibited an efficient subgame perfect equilibrium solution to the Prisoner's Dilemma. What we have shown is not specific to Prisoner's Dilemma but works for any one-shot game with a unique Nash equilibrium that is inefficient. This is the content of another folk theorem, this one for infinitely repeated games like Prisoner's Dilemma. As in the folk theorem for finitely repeated games, w_i refers to the worst one-shot equilibrium payoff to each player.

Folk Theorem for Infinitely Repeated Games. Suppose that an infinitely repeated game has a payoff vector that exceeds w_i for each player i. Then all feasible payoffs that payoff dominate **w** are supported as payoffs of subgame perfect equilibria using trigger strategies, as long as discount factors are sufficiently close to 1. In particular, efficient payoff vectors are supported as subgame perfect equilibrium outcomes when discount factors are sufficiently close to 1.

Figure 8.9 illustrates this theorem for Prisoner's Dilemma. Every point in the quadrilateral bounded by (2,2), (2, 3.33), (3,3) and (3.33, 2) can be supported as a subgame perfect equilibrium outcome, as long as the discount factors are at least 0.5.

Infinity and wise choice of strategies lets players out of the Prisoner's Dilemma. Notice, however, that the bad equilibrium does not go away. Playing (confess, confess) forever remains a subgame perfect equilibrium outcome. The players face a difficult equilibrium selection problem here, with infinitely many equilibria to choose from.

■ 8.8 ROBERT AXELROD'S TOURNAMENT

It should be noted that there is a much simpler strategy that leads to the payoffs (3,3) in infinitely repeated Prisoner's Dilemma.[5] This strategy, which is intuitively very appealing and appears a great deal in real life, is called **Tit-for-Tat.** Tit-for-Tat calls for the following play:

> First play: Do Not Confess. Play at time t: Do Not Confess if your opponent played Do Not Confess at time I − 1; Confess at time t if your opponent played Confess at time $t − 1$.
>
> Play at time $t + 1$: Do Not Confess.

Tit-for-Tat starts out playing the efficient one-shot outcome by not confessing. As long as the other player does not confess, play stays there. If the other player does confess—falling prey to temptation as it were, the player using Tit-for-Tat confesses at the next play, before returning to Do Not Confess.

Now consider what happens if two Tit-for-Tat strategies play against each other. They both start out not confessing, and keep on not confessing forever. So these strategies are **observationally equivalent** to the grim trigger strategies that we used in the last section to get the efficient, equal-paying outcome.

The political scientist Robert Axelrod has studied Tit-for-Tat behavior in a variety of settings, perhaps most tellingly on the Western Front of World War I. Think of "do not confess" as "do not use poison gas," and "confess" as "use poison gas." Think of the armies on the Western Front as being locked in a repeated Prisoner's Dilemma. Then for long stretches of time, the opposing armies (French and British vs. German) did not use poison gas against each other. Life on the front lines was no so bad during such "quiet" times. However, the minute one side used poison gas (usually ordered by Headquarters far to the rear), then so did the other.

---

[5] There is an excellent book devoted to this topic: Robert Axelrod, *The Evolution of Cooperation* (New York: Basic Books, 1985).

In a famous experiment, Axelrod invited game theorists around the world to submit strategies to play Prisoner's Dilemma 200 times, the idea being that 200 was close enough to infinity to get results like those of the folk theorem for infinitely repeated games. Over 50 strategies were submitted, including Tit-for-Tat, trigger strategies, and the strategy Confess. Strategies were paired against each other in a preliminary round of play, and a strategy was ranked depending on how well it did on average in all its pairings. The top-ranked strategies in the preliminary second advanced to the finals.

When the tournament was over, to the surprise of many participants and observers, the top-ranked strategy was Tit-for-Tat, submitted by Axelrod himself.

■ 8.9 INFINITELY REPEATED MARKET GAMES

Cournot and Bertrand competition between two firms, playing infinitely often, has the right structure for the preceding folk theorem to apply. Let's see how that works, turning first to Cournot competition.

Each period, two firms, 1 and 2, bring quantities of their products, which are perfect substitutes for each other, to market. Each period, the market demand they face is

$$P = 130 - Q$$

where P is market price and Q is market quantity. Each firm produces its product at a constant average (and marginal) cost $c = \$10$. If these firms play this game once, the Cournot equilibrium is $x_1^* = x_2^* = 40$ (recall section 6.7). The market price is 50, the profit margin for each firm is 40, and each firm makes $\$1,600$ in profits. This information is recorded as the point C (for one-shot Cournot) in the profit possibility diagram of Figure 8.10.

The one-shot monopoly solution is, of course, much more profitable. Monopoly would restrict output to 60 units, set the price at 70, enjoy a profit margin of 60, and

---

FIGURE 8.10   **FOLK THEOREM: INFINITELY REPEATED COURNOT MARKET GAME**

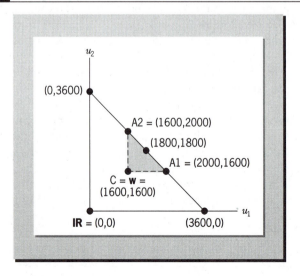

make \$3,600 in profits. This possible profit is recorded as the line $u_1 + u_2 = 3600$ in Figure 8.10. If firms 1 and 2 could somehow play a better equilibrium in the infinitely repeated game, they could enjoy profits this high. When these two firms play this market game infinitely often, there is a subgame perfect equilibrium that lets them do just that: monopolize.

Of course, playing the one-shot Cournot equilibrium is a subgame perfect equilibrium of the infinitely repeated game, but that won't earn these firms monopoly profits. The following strategy played by each will:

First play: Ship 30 units.

Subsequent play: Ship 30 units after any history where both firms have shipped 30 units; otherwise, ship 40 units forever.

Every trigger strategy has a "carrot-and-stick" nature. The first part of this strategy is the carrot—it programs monopoly profits forever. A firm plays its part by shipping just enough to maintain monopoly profits. The second part of this strategy is the stick. Suppose that a firm does something it is not supposed to. Then all firms switch to playing the one-shot Cournot equilibrium from then on. This means lower profits for the firm that spoiled the monopoly, as well as for every other firm. This is a stick that hurts. A deviation from the monopoly pattern of behavior triggers punishment in the form of the stick. What is worse, this punishment is eternal—it never ends.

One feature of trigger strategies does cause concern. If a player deviates *by mistake* from the monopoly solution for a single period (out of infinitely many plays), this triggers eternal punishment. Usually, we don't think the consequences of a lone mistake are that staggering. In such a case, one can always appeal to the Tit-for-Tat strategy, which is observationally equivalent if players don't ever make mistakes, but limits the damage a mistake might cause to at most 2 plays out of equilibrium.

In Figure 8.10, we show the payoff triangle that follows from the folk theorem for this infinitely repeated game. This triangle has as vertices the one-shot Cournot equilibrium payoffs, (1600, 1600) and the most asymmetric monopoly payoffs (2000, 1600) and (1600, 2000) compatible with any asymmetric trigger strategy. Our trigger strategy splits the market evenly, with each firm selling 30 units each period forever, whence the payoffs (1800, 1800).

Now let's check that for sufficiently patient firms, this trigger strategy that monopolizes the market is a Nash equilibrium. As before, the best time to deviate is right now. You can check from Figure 7.13 that the best response to a quantity of 30 is a quantity of 45. So suppose firm 1 ships 45 units today instead of 30. The market price falls from \$60 to \$45, and firm 1's profit margin falls from \$50 to \$35. However, firm 1's short-term profits go up from \$1,600 to ($45)(45) = \$2,025. Right now, firm 1 earns a lot more money. But then the fun is over—it is Cournot play for eternity, at \$1,600 per period.

Following the inequality argument of the previous section, firm 1 gets

$$u_1 = (1 - R)[2025 + 1600R + 1600R^2 + \ldots]$$

Add and subtract 1600 on the right-hand side, and perform the algebra as before, and you get

$$u_1 = 2025 - 425R$$

This is the payoff from deviating. Comparing this to the payoff 1800 forever, we have the inequality to solve:

$$2025 - 425R < 1800$$

Solving, we get

$$9/17 < R$$

Any discount factor over 9/17, or 53 percent, is enough to make firm 1 stick to the monopoly and not try to cheat.

Again, we can express this in the language of marginal benefit and marginal cost. The marginal benefit to a player from deviating is $2025 - 425R$, while the marginal cost to a player from deviating is 1800—the opportunity cost of forgoing the proposed Nash equilibrium. Marginal cost exceeds marginal benefit when the discount factor is high enough; here, "high enough" means greater than 9/17.

This subgame perfect equilibrium for the infinitely repeated Cournot market game has exciting new payoff possibilities—in particular monopoly profits at the levels of $1,800 for each firm. By sharing the market differently, one firm could get as much as $2,000 in profit from a subgame perfect equilibrium involving monopolization, as Figure 8.10 shows. And this would be monopolization achieved by completely independent play, a Nash equilibrium, and so seemingly immune from antitrust regulation.

We can perform the same kind of analysis for Bertrand competition in a market game played infinitely many times. The major difference between Cournot and Bertrand competition shows up in the location of the one-shot game Nash equilibrium in the profit possibilities diagram (see Figure 8.11). In Bertrand competition with perfect substitutes, the one-shot Nash equilibrium with infinitely divisible prices are the payoffs (0,0). In this case, the folk theorem gives an even bigger set of equilibria to fight over, the triangle with vertices (3600, 0), (0, 3600), and (0,0). Here is how to program the infinitely repeated profits (1800, 1800):

First play: Set price $70.

Subsequent play: Set price = $70 as long as price = $70 has always been set; otherwise, set price marginal cost $10 forever.

FIGURE 8.11 **PAYOFF POSSIBILITIES: INFINITELY REPEATED BERTRAND MARKET GAME**

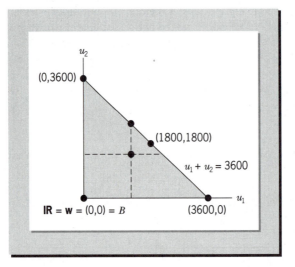

You can show that this is an equilibrium for any discount factor greater than .5. This particular equilibrium is intuitively quite plausible under the probability of continuation interpretation if you are risk neutral. If the odds are greater than 50–50 that you will play this same game tomorrow, then having half the market today and half the market tomorrow are better than having all the market today and nothing forever after.

Corporations interacting on a daily basis for over a century approximate an infinitely repeated game. Any time the economic fundamentals change—demand shifts or costs change—the profit possibilities and the set of infinitely repeated game equilibria change, too. The problem of coordinating among infinitely many equilibria becomes overwhelming in such a case. We now look at how one industry, the ready-to-eat breakfast cereal industry, adapted to the challenge posed by the many subgame perfect equilibria of infinitely repeated games.

◼ 8.10 PRICE LEADERSHIP IN THE READY-TO-EAT CEREALS INDUSTRY

Ready-to-eat cereal was invented by health-food advocates in the United States in the 1890s.[6] Two of the inventors, Kellogg and Post, gave their names to the companies they founded. Two other companies, General Mills and Ralston-Purina, have also had important market shares in this industry. These four companies have been rivals throughout the twentieth century. Large corporations with strong earnings and bright futures, the big four in the ready-to-eat cereals industry have had every reason to think that they would interact in this market into the indefinite future. Thus they could act as if they were playing an infinitely repeated market game, one of whose equilibria is monopoly pricing.

There is one real-life constraint to the folk theorem for infinitely repeated games that hasn't been mentioned. Since 1890, U.S. federal statute (the Sherman Act and subsequent legislation) has forbidden monopolizing, the attempt to monopolize, or the conspiracy to monopolize a market. This antitrust legislation is enforced by two separate agencies of the executive branch, the Department of Justice and the Federal Trade Commission. Typically, the U.S. government does not prove that firms have monopolized a market—the evidentiary requirements for a conviction are too great. Instead, the government proves that firms have conspired to monopolize a market. To do this, it traces smoke-filled rooms and paper trails indicating that companies have intentionally gotten together to fix prices at monopoly levels. The behavior underlying the folk theorem, which involves not even a whiff of conspiracy, hardly fills the bill for an antitrust violation. Nevertheless, companies with long horizons walk a fine line between antitrust legality and illegality.

Suppose that the major firms in an industry have reached the solution of an infinitely repeated game that supports monopoly profits. Their work has only begun. Every time an economic fundamental, such as cost or consumer preferences, changes, the set of subgame

---

[6] This material draws on Frederick M. Scherer, "The Breakfast Cereal Industry," in *The Structure of American Industry*, 6th ed., ed. W. Adams (New York: Macmillan, 1982), and John Sutton, *Sunk Costs and Market Structure: Price Competition, Advertising, and the Evolution of Concentration* (Cambridge, Mass.: MIT Press, 1991), especially chapter 10. For readers already familiar with the story, problem 11 in this chapter makes the same main point. The NCAA is another cartel that operates with something approximating trigger strategies. See Brain L. Goff, Robert D. Tollison and Arthur A. Fleisher, *The National Collegiate Athletic Association: A Study in Cartell Behavior* (Chicago: University of Chicago Press, 1992).

perfect equilibria to the infinitely repeated game change, too. The firms need some mechanism to move from the old equilibrium they were playing to a new one. Failing such a mechanism, they could wind up back at the one-shot equilibrium, with lower profits all around. The solution to this problem that evolved in the ready-to-eat cereals industry, as well as in a number of other industries, is called **price leadership.** Under price leadership, one firm, the price leader, takes charge of the industry pricing policy. Every time a change in prices is called for by a change in economic fundamentals, the price leader makes that change. The members of the industry depend on the price leader to make the correct price changes, so that industry profits are as high as they can possibly be.

For most of the twentieth century, the price leader in the ready-to-eat cereals industry was Kellogg's, which also happens to be number one in market share, consistently with more than 40 percent of all dollar sales. Considering the background inflation in the United States, especially since World War II, most of the price changes have involved price increases. In the period from 1950 to 1972, 99 percent of all price changes were price increases—and this figure controls for package size. A large fraction of all price increases, 80 percent in the period 1965–70, were led by Kellogg's. Other firms in the industry usually followed this lead promptly; occasionally they did not. Even when other firms did not follow, Kellogg's did not rescind its price increases. Instead, it advertised more intensively and waited for the rest of the industry to catch up to the price increase.

Price leadership helped the ready-to-eat cereals industry enjoy very high profit margins on their products and well-above-average rates of return on their assets. The Federal Trade Commission, ever alert to signs of conspiracy, brought suit against the firms in this industry. While admitting that it had no evidence of an outright conspiracy, the commission argued that, by their pattern of behavior, the cereals manufacturers were in effect a **shared monopoly,** and thus subject to antitrust remedies. The commission's notion of shared monopoly, if correct, confirms the view that the firms in this industry, following the price leadership of Kellogg's, have indeed found and maintained the profit-maximizing solution to their repeated game.

This case dragged on for several years in court, with all kinds of legal maneuvering over who would be the judge. The case also became heavily politicized. During the 1980 presidential campaign, candidate Reagan wrote to Kellogg's, expressing concern for their legal plight. At the same time, organized labor, fearing the loss of thousands of jobs in Battle Creek, Michigan, and the surrounding area, leaned hard on President Carter to give Kellogg's a break. It became apparent to the commission that, even if it proved that a shared monopoly existed, it would still not prevail in court. The newly appointed judge in the case dismissed all charges against the ready-to-eat cereal companies in 1981. Kellogg's and its price followers continue to earn impressive rates of return to this day.

◼ SUMMARY

1. A strategic interaction that takes place more than once is called a repeated game. Repeated games are more complicated than the one-shot game of which they are composed.

2. Repetition creates subgames. Subgame perfection is a powerful tool for solving a repeated game.

3. A repeated zero-sum game is still zero sum. Its payoff possibilities are not enriched by repetition.

4. According to Selten's theorem, if a one-shot game with a unique Nash equilibrium is played finitely many times, its unique subgame perfect equilibrium is that Nash equilibrium played each and every time.

5. Variable-sum games with multiple equilibria played finitely many times have large sets of subgame perfect equilibrium outcomes. Payoffs in the repeated game are measured as the average per play of the game.

6. According to the folk theorem for finitely repeated games, if a one-shot game with multiple equilibria is played enough times, an efficient outcome can be approximated by subgame perfect equilibrium play.

7. The members of OPEC appear to be playing a finitely repeated game in the world oil market.

8. Two or more players who act as if they will play a game forever constitute an infinitely repeated game. Payoffs in an infinitely repeated game are discounted either by time or by uncertainty.

9. Infinite repetition allows players to escape the inefficient Nash equilibrium of the Prisoner's Dilemma, provided they are patient enough. Two repeated game strategies that achieve this are grim trigger strategies and Tit-for-Tat.

10. The folk theorem for infinitely repeated games shows that infinitely repeated market games have large sets of subgame perfect equilibrium outcomes, including monopoly outcomes.

11. The ready-to-eat breakfast cereal industry in the United States has been characterized by price leadership, a device that appears to help the firms involved coordinate on efficient repeated game equilibria.

■ KEY WORDS

one-shot game
possible history
repeated game
unconditional strategy
rotation strategy
trigger strategy/grim trigger
   strategy

discount factor
continuation probability
finitely/infinitely repeated
   game
Selten's theorem
OPEC
individual rationality

folk theorem
Tit-for-Tat
observationally equivalent
price leadership
shared monopoly

■ PROBLEMS

1. Show that the 2-person Cournot market game (Chapter 6), played twice, has a unique subgame perfect equilibrium. Also show that the 2-person Prisoner's Dilemma (Figure 8.3), played three times, has a unique subgame perfect equilibrium.

2. Find the average payoffs of subgame perfect equilibrium for Market Niche (Figure 5.2) played twice.

3. Find another strategy that achieves the average payoffs (2.5, 2.5) for Market Niches played twice. How would a discount factor $R < 1$ affect how firms feel about rotations over the two market niches?

4. Find the average utility possibilities of subgame perfect equilibria for Market Niches played four times if the firms use only pure strategies. How close can you get to (3,3) by playing the one-shot game four times?

5. Compare the strategic situation facing Russia with that facing the members of OPEC. Why might Russia agree to OPEC's proposal? Use the discount factor R in your answer.

6. Show that in the infinitely repeated Prisoner's Dilemma of Figure 8.3, it does not pay player 1 to deviate from the efficient subgame perfect equilibrium at time $t = 0$.

7. Here is your chance to run your own tournament à la Axelrod. Prisoner's Dilemma is to be played three times. Four strategies are entered in the tournament: two Tit-for-Tat, and two Confess. In the preliminary round, each strategy is paired against the other three. How do the four strategies rank? If the top two strategies advance to the finals and play each other, which strategy wins the tournament?

8. Show that in the infinitely repeated Cournot market game of section 8.8, it does not pay a firm to restrict output, if the firms are playing the one-shot Cournot equilibrium forever.

9. Find a subgame perfect equilibrium that supports monopoly payoffs, $(1900, 1700)$, for the Cournot market game of section 8.8. Find the condition needed for this on the discount factor of each firm.

10. Solve for the profit possibilities in problem 8 if the firms are in Bertrand competition, and unit cost is \$30 instead of \$10. If firm 1 is the price leader, what price should it pick?

11. You are called as an expert witness by a corporate defendant in a case such as *United States v. Kellogg's et al.* Your job is to convince a jury that your client has done nothing wrong by acting as a price follower. Why would the corporation want your testimony on the witness stand? What would your testimony focus on?

CHAPTER 9

Evolutionary Stability and Bounded Rationality

We have taken for granted that the players of the games we have been studying were human—*Homo sapiens,* the smart hominid—with the exception of Deep Blue, the Chess-playing computer from chapter 1. In addition, we have assumed that these hominids were capable of tremendous feats of reasoning, such as are needed to play efficient subgame perfect equilibria of infinitely repeated games. We have also relied on the players' being capable of rather exquisite inferences, such as those needed in Mutually Assured Destruction or in Market Niches played finitely many times. With such players, it is a foregone conclusion that they find a Nash equilibrium to a game at once and play that equilibrium from then on. In the real world, however, even the best players are not this good. They don't always find a Nash equilibrium to a game right away; rather, they spend a lot of time learning to play the game. Also, they sometimes make mistakes. Players who have to learn how to play a game and who sometimes make mistakes are boundedly rational. This chapter studies the implications of **bounded rationality** for game theory.

We've already seen some examples, most notably the results from ultimatum experiments, where players appear to be out of equilibrium. Although we hardly expect a disequilibrium to persist, it is useful to know how players might get to an equilibrium. This chapter begins by introducing a dynamic system, called the **replicator dynamics,** to describe how play evolves when it is out of equilibrium. We did not pull this system out of a hat; rather, it is fundamental to the way biologists study the evolution of animal behavior—and since we're animals too, it applies to us.[1] The big difference between human players and other animal players in games is that humans are really smart and can learn really fast. But when humans are having a slow learning day—this seems to happen a lot in behavior laboratories when games are involved—then the replicator dynamics is not a bad model for humans, too.

The replicator dynamics is first applied to symmetrical 2 x 2 games in normal form. Boundedly rational players obeying the replicator dynamics eventually find a Nash equilibrium, called an evolutionarily stable strategy, if one exists. Thus, even dimwits can play games. This result leads to the example Frogs Call for Mates. The mating strategies of modern frogs—

---

[1] A good introduction to the mathematics and its applications is found in Josef Hofbauer and Karl Sigmund, *The Theory of Evolution and Dynamical Systems* (Cambridge, UK: Cambridge University Press, 1988).

definitely boundedly rational players—have something to tell us about our own strategic behavior. The discussion then turns to asymmetrical 2 x 2 games in normal form. After extending the replicator dynamics to handle asymmetry, this chapter shows that slow learners can still figure out Telex vs. IBM. Some modifications of the replicator dynamics for games with a finite number of players who are capable of fast learning are then considered. The chapter concludes by studying the evolution of the video game—a very fast evolution that is far from over. The appendix presents an example of the evolution of strategic behavior in a behavior laboratory.

9.1 HOW BOUNDEDLY RATIONAL PLAYERS PLAY GAMES

Have you ever missed a question on an exam, or failed to understand something the first time you heard it? Did it take you more than an instant to learn how to play your first game? Then you are boundedly rational—just like me. Any limit to computing power or understanding, especially of the sort employed in game theory, imposes a bound on rationality. Boundedly rational players have to learn how to play a game, using some form of trial and error. This section builds a model of trial-and-error play called replicator dynamics and shows how that play eventually leads to the solution of Let's Make a Deal (see Figure 9.1).

Suppose there is a large population of players. At each point in time, one player is randomly paired with another to play Let's Make a Deal. Let x be the percentage of all players who choose yes and $1 - x$ be the percentage of all players who choose no. These are the *player types*. In a random matching, the probability of being matched with a Yes type is x and the probability of being matched with a No type is $1 - x$. On the basis of this random matching, we can compute expected payoffs for each of the two player types, Yes and No. We will use the notation $u(\text{yes})$ and $u(\text{no})$ to denote the expected payoffs of the corresponding player types. We have

$$u(\text{yes}) = (x)1 + (1 - x)0 = x$$
$$u(\text{no}) = (x)0 + (1 - x)0 = 0$$

FIGURE 9.1	LET'S MAKE A DEAL (STAKE = $2)

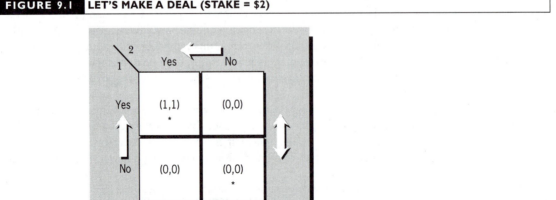

Clearly, Yes player types get paid at least as much as No player types, regardless of how many of them are present in the population. This reflects the fact that the strategy Yes weakly dominates the strategy No.

The replicator dynamics says that if a player type earns an above-average payoff, then its percentage in the population increases; if a player type earns a below-average payoff, then its percentage in the population decreases. Finally, if a player type earns an average payoff, then its percentage in the population stays the same. The player types getting a below-average payoff will want to copy the player types getting an above-average return. Since they are slow learners, not all the below-average player types will switch all at once, but eventually all player types still present in the population will earn the average payoff. Any player type earning an average payoff in the population keeps its percentage of the population constant. These considerations apply in a straightforward way to business. No manager wants to be below average or to get below-average results. The job of a manager whose results are consistently below average is in real jeopardy. Being above average pays better. Replicator dynamics expresses precisely this logic mathematically.

Let's see what the replicator dynamics have to say about Let's Make a Deal. The average payoff in the population is

$$\text{average } u = (x)u(\text{yes}) + (1 - x)u(\text{no}) = (x)(x) + (1 - x)0 = x^2$$

For $0 < x < 1$, we have

$$u(\text{yes}) = x > x^2 > 0 = u(\text{no})$$

Yes types are above average in payoffs, and their proportion increases; No types are below average, and their proportion in the population decreases. This process does not end until the limit $x = 1$ is reached: a population of all Yes types. The strategy Yes, played by the entire population, is evolutionarily stable. In other words, Yes will persist if played by everyone.

Notice that evolution has led to a Nash equilibrium of the game. This is no accident. Remember, at a Nash equilibrium no player has an incentive to change his or her strategy. In a symmetric game like Let's Make a Deal, every player playing the same strategy gets the same payoff. Thus, the condition for Nash equilibrium links up with the condition for the proportion of players in a population remaining constant. Equilibrium applies both to the Nash equilibrium of the game and the equilibrium of the evolutionary dynamics.

Figure 9.2, called a *phase diagram*, illustrates the argument we just made. The arrows on the line

$$x + (1 - x) = 1$$

point in the direction evolution takes. When $x > 0$, the strategy Yes is increasing in the population, so x increases—just as replicator dynamics suggests. The proportion of players saying yes continues to increase in the population until it reaches $x = 1$. In the phase diagram, this direction to the dynamics is denoted by the arrows pointing to the right. We have just created a representation of the learning process. Players in this population are learning to play the strategy Yes. Eventually, all the players in the system learn to play the strategy Yes. At that point, represented by the value $x = 1$, learning ceases.

Even though learning has ceased, these boundedly rational players can and will still make **mistakes.** Next we see that the same learning process that brought them to the point $x = 1$ in the first place will keep them there, despite their mistakes. Suppose that, with probability e, a player makes a mistake and switches from yes to no. Mistakes don't occur all that

---

FIGURE 9.2 | **LET'S MAKE A DEAL, PHASE DIAGRAM**

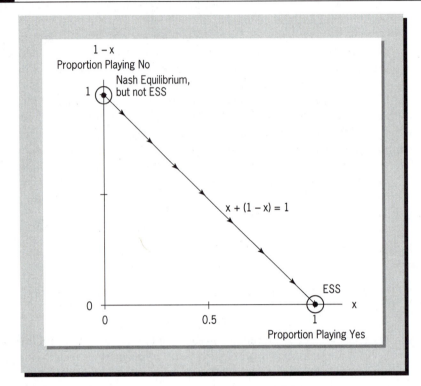

often, however, so e is a number near zero. Then $1 - e$, the proportion of the population that still chooses yes, is a number close to 1. In the population with mistaken players, the strategy Yes pays

$$u(\text{yes}) = (1 - e)(1) + e(0) = 1 - e$$

and the mistaken strategy No pays

$$u(\text{no}) = (1 - e)(0) + e(0) = 0$$

Since $u(\text{yes}) = 1 - e > 0 > u(\text{no})$, the mistaken players are below average and will correct their mistakes.

A Nash equilibrium is an **evolutionarily stable strategy,** or **ESS** for short, when two things happen: the replicator dynamics points toward this equilibrium, and low-probability mistakes do not destroy it.[2] The population $x\emptyset = 1$, all of whom choose yes, is an ESS for Let's Make a Deal.

Let's Make a Deal has another Nash equilibrium, in which all players say no, represented by the population $x = 0$. *This Nash equilibrium is not an ESS.* The replicator dynamics points away from this equilibrium. To see why, suppose that everyone in the population

---

[2] The exact definition of ESS and related concepts becomes more complicated in more complicated games. See P. Bomze, "Noncooperative 2-person Games in Biology," *International Journal of Game Theory* 15 (1991): 31–58 for details.

chooses No, when a small percentage e of players mistakenly switch to Yes. The players who have switched expect the payoff

$$u(\text{yes}) = (e)1 + (1 - e)0 = e$$

while the rest of the players, all saying No, get

$$u(\text{no}) = i(0) + (1 - e)0 = 0$$

Even when they are rare, the Yes types do better than the No types. The learning process kicks in, as more and more players switch from no to yes. Hence, the Nash equilibrium at $x = 0$ is not an ESS.[3]

We have just seen that boundedly rational players can find the weak dominance solution to Let's Make a Deal, even if they can't figure it out immediately. The next section shows to what extent this happy conclusion can be generalized.

■ 9.2 EVOLUTION AND EFFICIENCY

The replicator dynamics that solved Let's Make a Deal applies to any symmetrical game with two players and two strategies each. Every such game is a special case of the game in Figure 9.3; we consider some more examples of ESS in this section. Our result from Let's Make a Deal is quite optimistic: evolution in a world of boundedly rational players led to the best of all possible worlds, where total utility is maximized. In the nineteenth century, during the heyday of uncritical Darwinism, the doctrine of social Darwinism arose, alleging that evolution *always* leads to the best of all possible worlds. We now know better. Evolution can lead to outcomes that may be quite efficient

FIGURE 9.3 SYMMETRICAL 2x2 GAMES

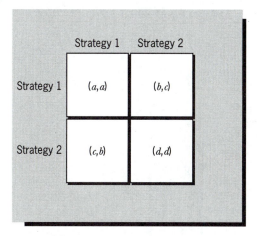

	Strategy 1	Strategy 2
Strategy 1	(a, a)	(b, c)
Strategy 2	(c, b)	(d, d)

[3] A special game theory concept applies just to the mistake part of ESS, and not to the learning part: perfect equilibrium. This concept is due to Reinhard Selten, "Reexamination of the Perfectness Concept for Equilibrium Points in Extensive Games," *International Journal of Game Theory* 4 (1975): 25–55. An ESS is always perfect, but not the converse.

Consider the game Coordination in Figure 9.4. This is a special case of Figure 9.3 with $a = 50$, $b = 49$, $c = d = 0$ in Figure 9.3. It has pure strategy Nash equilibria at (strategy 1, strategy 1) and (strategy 2, strategy 2), as well as a mixed strategy equilibrium. Let's first show that both pure Nash strategy equilibria are ESS. Then we will show the mixed strategy equilibrium is not an ESS. To find the ESS, first compute the payoff to strategy 1, $u(1)$, in a population where proportion x of the players play strategy 1:

$$u(1) = x(50) + (1 - x)(49) = 49 + x$$

Similarly, one has the payoff to strategy 2:

$$u(2) = x(0) + (1 - x)(60) = 60(1 - x)$$

Finally, the population average payoff is

$$\text{Average} = xu(1) + (1 - x)u(2) = 49x + x^2 + 60(1 - x)^2$$

First consider the case where x is close to 1; nearly everyone is playing strategy 1. Then we have

$$u(1) = 49 + x > 49x + x^2 + 60\ (1 - x)^2 > 60(1 - x) = u(2)$$

So strategy 1 is an ESS.

Next consider the case where x is close to 0: nearly everyone is playing strategy 2. Then we have

$$u(1) = 49 + x < 49x + x^2 + 60(1 - x)^2 < 60(1 - x) = u(2)$$

so strategy 2 is an ESS.

There is also a mixed strategy Nash equilibrium, with population proportions $x = 11/61$, $1 - x = 50/61$. We get this mixed strategy Nash equilibrium precisely when the two pure strategies in the population pay the same:

$$u(1) = u(2)$$

Substituting for $u(1)$ and $u(2)$, we get the equation

$$u(1) = 49 + x = 60(1 - x) = u(2)$$

FIGURE 9.4   **COORDINATION**

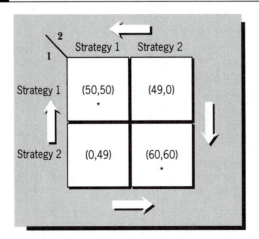

Rearranging, we have

$$11 = 61x, \text{ or } x = 11/61 \text{ as we claimed.}$$

This Nash equilibrium is not an ESS. You can see this in the phase diagram of Figure 9.5. What the mixed strategy Nash equilibrium does is divide the interval [0,1] into two zones. To the left of $x = 11/61$, the phase diagram points toward the ESS at $x^* = 0$. So if slightly fewer than 11/61 of the population plays strategy 1, either by mistake or by mutation or some other cause, strategy 2 pays better than strategy 2 and evolution heads toward $x^* = 1$. Likewise, if slightly more than 11/61 of the population plays strategy 1, then strategy 1 pays better than strategy 2 and evolution heads toward the ESS at $x^* = 1$. The arrows in the phase diagram of Figure 9.5 portray these two directions of evolution.

The two ESSs of the game are $x^* = 0$ (all players choose strategy 2) and $x^* = 1$ (all players choose strategy 1). Notice that the pure strategy equilibrium at (strategy 2, strategy 2) payoff dominates that at (strategy 1, strategy 1). In the event that learning converges to the equilibrium at $x^* = 1$, it leads to a less-than-best of all possible worlds. *Where learning winds up depends crucially in this case on where it starts.* For this reason the theory is not complete, since it doesn't predict where it starts. If the initial proportion of type 1 players in the population is less than 11/61 ($x < 11/61$), then the population heads toward the ESS where every player chooses strategy 2. Otherwise, the population heads toward the inefficient ESS. In particular, if any point on the unit interval is equally likely as a starting point for the learning process, then most of the time (50/61 = 82%), the population will evolve to the inefficient ESS.

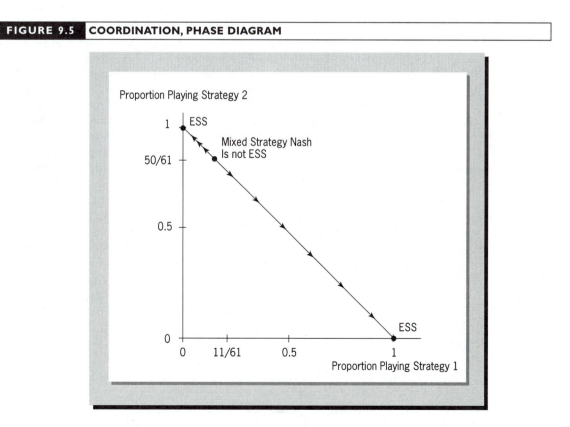

This bottom line is bad news for evolution. Unfortunately for this doctrine, replicator dynamics need not lead to an efficient outcome. If it did, we wouldn't be stuck with the keyboard we have—a rather complicated story we tell 2 paragraphs below. Nor would we divide the day into 24 hours, with each hour struck twice. These are just two examples of large-scale social coordination outcomes that harbor inefficiencies. Unfortunately, inefficient coordination outcomes are rather to be expected according to the replicator dynamics.

The punch line of this discussion is hardly comforting for old-style social Darwinists and their modern descendants. And the implications are not simply limited to social philosophy; they are very much real life. Here are two examples, one blatant, the other more subtle, where evolution has led to a world that is definitely not the best possible.

Here in the United States, we take it for granted that the day is 24 hours long, and each hour is struck twice each day. We keep the two "1 o'clocks" apart by the a.m/p.m. distinction. That goes back to the Romans, who invented a.m. (*ante meridiem,* "before noon") and p.m. (*post meridiem,* "after noon") to keep their times straight. For Romans, whose timekeeping was very low tech—sundials and the like—this may have been efficient. However, in modern times of 24/7 activity, it is much more efficient to divide the 24-hour day into 24 separate units. So the two "1 o'clocks" are 0100 (1 a.m.) and 1300 (1 p.m.). This innovation seems to have first been made by modern armies, since confusing two times can be a fatal error in warfare. By now, a good part of the world has gone to the 24-hour clock. Here in the United States, the armed forces are on 24-hour time, but the rest of us still have to keep our a.m.'s and p.m.'s straight, because Romans of two thousand years ago had to. Count your blessings: at least we did give up Roman numerals for doing mathematics.

Did you ever wonder where the keyboard on your computer came from? The Stanford economist Paul A. David found the answer.[4] Back in 1874, the inventor of the first typewriter, C. L. Sholes, faced a big problem. The keys on his machine kept jamming. To avoid such mechanical jams, he arranged the keys on the keyboard very oddly—an arrangement now called QWERTY after the first six letters on the top alphabet line. In particular, the most common letters, starting with "e," were moved to the fringes of the keyboard to prevent jams. This was noted almost immediately by rival inventors, who developed a different keyboard, called the "Ideal," based on a different technology (the forerunner of the typeball on electric typewriters). The Ideal puts the letters "dhiatensor" on the middle letter line. You can type 70 percent of all the words in English by staying on that middle letter line: that's efficient! Unfortunately, once the number of typists and typing teachers who knew QWERTY had reached a critical mass, replicator dynamics took over. By 1905, all typewriters on the market in the United States had QWERTY keyboards. A similar evolution took place with keyboards in other languages using the Latin alphabet (those Romans again!)—they're all QWERTY-based too. Once electric typewriters with modern typeballs replaced mechanical typewriters, the mechanical reason for the QWERTY keyboard ceased to exist. The same is true with even more force now that computers have replaced electric typewriters. However, the QWERTY keyboard had become **locked in**—it was and is the keyboard every user and every teacher of keyboarding knows, and it's the keyboard every learner is taught. To escape from this evolutionary outcome, we have to break with evolutionary processes, and introduce change some other way—just like with a.m and p.m.

---

[4] See Paul A. David, "Clio and the Economics of QWERTY," *American Economic Review* 75 (May 1985): 332–337. For a rather different take on this example, see Daniel F. Spulber, *Famous Fables of Economics: Myths of Market Failures* (New York: Blackwell, 2001).

9.3 EVOLUTION AND CONFLICT

Humans have evolved some remarkable weapons of mass destruction, for example, but it is not clear that we are better off because we now have such weapons. We may only have created the means of our own mass destruction. This gloomy thought has occurred to biologists in the following terms.[5] Most animals of the same species are rather heavily armed, but they rarely use their armaments on each other. To take just one example, think of poisonous snakes. These snakes fight all the time with each other over territory, mating opportunities, prey, and the like. They could easily kill each other with one bite in a fight, but they almost never do. Instead of biting each other, they wrestle. They save their poison for use on members of other species.

The game called Hawk vs. Dove explains why serious conflicts are rare, among animals as well as among boundedly rational humans. The normal form of Hawk vs. Dove is shown in Figure 9.6; this is a special case of Figure 9.3 with $a = (V - C)/2$, $b = V$, $c = 0$, and $d = V/2$. The language originates from the Vietnam War era, when hawks wanted to escalate the fighting in Vietnam to the limits of conventional warfare (or even go nuclear), while doves wanted to deescalate the fighting to a cease-fire. There is a military value, V, at stake, and this value is being contested by two countries. There are two country types. Hawk is an aggressive type. When two hawks meet, there is sure to be heavy fighting. The expected value of a fight is

$$1/2(V) + 1/2(-C)$$

With probability 1/2, a combatant wins the fight and therefore V; with probability 1/2, a combatant loses the fight and incurs cost C.[6] In keeping with the assumption that the fighting is serious, we have

$$V < C.$$

FIGURE 9.6 HAWK VS. DOVE

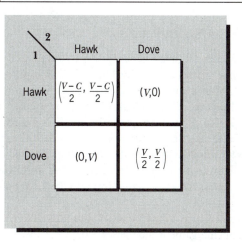

[5] See the classic article by John Maynard Smith and George Price, "The Logic of Animal Conflicts," *Nature* 246 (1973): 15–18.
[6] You can think of V as already containing the cost of capturing it in war. The cost C is therefore the marginal cost of losing.

in which case the Hawk vs. Dove that results is a game of Chicken. If we assume instead that

$$V > C$$

then the Hawk vs. Dove that results is a Prisoner's Dilemma.

Dove is a nonaggressive player type. When a hawk meets a dove, the dove leaves the battlefield and the hawk takes the resource without a fight. Finally, when two doves meet, there is no fight. Instead, they share the value equally, getting half each. The doves reach a resolution by diplomatic means, without resorting to their weapons—just like the wrestling matches of poisonous snakes.

Consider the parameter values $V = 2$ and $C = 12$. Let x be the percentage of hawks in the population. Let hawk payoff be u_1 and dove payoff be u_2. The payoff to the strategy Hawk is

$$u(\text{Hawk}) = x(2 - 12)/2 + (1 - x)(2) = -5x + 2 - 2x = 2 - 7x$$

The payoff to the strategy Dove is

$$u(\text{Dove}) = x(0) + (1 - x)(2)/2 = 1 - x$$

The dynamics in Hawk vs. Dove are just the reverse of those in Coordination. When x is near zero, we have

$$u(\text{Dove}) = 1 - x < 2 - 7x = u(\text{Hawk})$$

So the population at $x = 0$, all playing Dove, is not an ESS. When x is near 1, the inequalities are reversed:

$$u(\text{Dove}) = 1 - x > 0 > 2 - 7x = (\text{Hawk})$$

So the population at $x = 1$, all playing Hawk, is not an ESS. The ESS is the mixed strategy equilibrium in between these two pure strategies, where

$$u(\text{Hawk}) = 2 - 7x = 1 - x = u(\text{Dove})$$

Rearranging, we get

$$1 = 6x, \text{ so } x = 1/6, 1 - x = 5/6$$

This mixed strategy Nash equilibrium is the ESS.

Figure 9.7 shows the dynamics leading to this ESS. The ESS requires a proportion 1/6 of hawks and 5/6 of doves. When two countries are matched in a potential conflict, the probability is only $(1/6)^2 = 1/36$ that a serious fight will actually occur. Almost all the time, $(1/6)(5/6) + (5/6)(1/6) + (5/6)(5/6) = 35/36$, potential conflicts are resolved by peaceful means—either by retreat of one of the two sides, or by a diplomatically arranged partition. You can show (end-of-chapter problem) that, as the cost of fighting goes up (as in an arms race), the probability of a fight becomes extremely small. The world can support only a small percentage of warlike states, and these states don't do any better at the ESS than the peace-loving states do.

The three phase diagrams (Figures 9.2, 9.5, and 9.7) exhaust all the ESS possibilities for a 2 x 2 symmetrical game. Such a game has either one or two ESSs, and when it has two ESSs the outcome of the game depends crucially on the starting point.

There is one other possibility, namely, that no ESS exists. Suppose that $a = b = c = d$. Every strategy combination is a Nash equilibrium, but none of these is stable. Move the population from x to $x + e$, and the population will stay at $x + e$. This example is extreme,

FIGURE 9.7 **HAWK VS. DOVE, PHASE DIAGRAM**

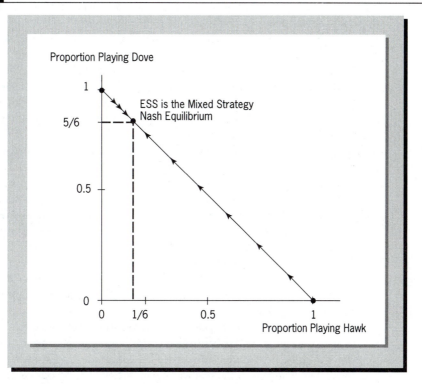

but many interesting possibilities arise in more complicated games—including the emergence of chaos when no ESS exists. The subject gets very mathematical very fast. In the meantime, however, let's come back down to Earth and take a look at some very boundedly rational beings, frogs.

9.4 FROGS CALL FOR MATES

Humans are not the only boundedly rational players on Earth.[7] Indeed, we are the least boundedly rational players. All other animals have much greater bounds on their rationality—and most of them are simply mindless. Nevertheless, animals manage to play many of the same games that people play, but the mechanism by which they play them is very different. Animals don't solve games by finding Nash equilibria—that's what you're supposed to be doing. Rather, animals solve games by the process of natural selection. We will review just enough biology to see how this works.[8]

The *genome* of any creature contains all its genetic information—its DNA content. This information is arrayed along the chromosomes. A particular spot on a chromosome, called a

---

[7] The material for this study is based on Roy Gardner, Molly Morris, and Craig Nelson, "Conditional Evolutionary Stable Strategies," *Animal Behavior* 35 (1987): 141–155.

[8] The following two paragraphs represent an enormous simplification of the relevant biology—rather like trying to compress all the information in this book in two paragraphs.

locus, governs some aspect of a creature's form and behavior. In frogs, for instance, calling behavior is governed by their genetic code. Females do not call at all—the same genetic information that determines sex also shuts down the calling system. The code stored at a locus is called the *genotype,* and the possible factors that may be present in the code are called *alleles.* The information stored at the genetic level is expressed at the level of form and behavior. This is called the *phenotype* of the creature. In our context, the phenotype is the strategy chosen.

Now consider the game in Figure 9.8. Each male frog has two strategies, Call and Don't Call. The simplest genetic code for this behavior consists of a pair of alleles, *A* and *B,* at a single locus.[9] With sexual reproduction, there are three possible genotypes: *AA, AB,* and *BB.* The genotypes *AA* and *AB* produce the phenotype Call; the genotype *BB* produces the phenotype Don't Call. We have to worry about payoffs as well as strategies. Instead of payoffs in dollars, frogs get payoffs in units of *fitness,* which can be measured by number of offspring. Fitness is just like utility—the more the better. The higher an animal's payoff, the more likely it is to transmit its genes to the next generation. The process by which genetic code is transmitted from one generation to the next is called natural selection. In *natural selection,* if a behavior has above-average fitness, then it increases as a percentage of the population as time goes on. This should sound familiar—it is exactly the same replicator dynamics we have used already. The limit of the process of natural selection, if such a limit exists, is an evolutionary equilibrium, where every surviving animal in a species has the same fitness. At the same time, this evolutionary equilibrium is a game equilibrium, where every strategy being played maximizes payoff.

There are many ways to test game theory, to see how well it predicts. We can run experiments in a laboratory, under controlled conditions, and see what happens. We can run experiments in the field, under less-controlled conditions, and see what happens. We can also watch what happens in the real world, completely beyond our control, and ask why it happened. Studying frogs combines elements of the last two kinds of science: making something happen that is not completely under our control, and watching something happen that is completely out of our control.

FIGURE 9.8 | **FROGS CALL FOR MATES**

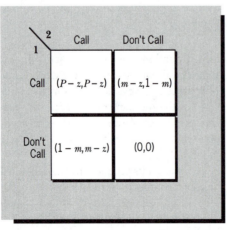

[9] Actually, the genetic code for frogs is much more complicated than this. However, the additional complexity does not affect the conclusions.

Some 300 million years ago, the ancestors of frogs did not have ears and did not make sounds. After a long period of evolution, all frogs have ears and the males can make sounds—they can call. The females do not have vocal chords, and so they remain silent. Females do have excellent hearing, though: they can hear a male calling from a kilometer away. Enemies of frogs, especially snakes, also tune into the calls of males—the better to find and eat them. Male frogs are thus caught in this terrible dilemma. If they call, they may attract a predator and get eaten; if they don't call, they may never attract a female.

The species this section discusses in detail is *Hyla cinera,* the tree frog native to Indiana. The males of this species spend most of their time in trees, coming down to the ground to feed and to mate. The females are dispersed, and congregate with the males only during mating season, when females hear the calls of males and approach them. The game played by males, which are roughly the same size, is a 2-player symmetrical game. It is a 2-player game because in the overwhelming number of cases in the field (more than 95 percent), exactly two males are found in the same 4-meter radius of territory. The game is symmetrical because, as far as we can tell, females cannot tell the difference between one male frog and another.

An interesting experiment in this regard was conducted by Steve Perrill of Butler University. He placed two males in an arena with a 4-meter radius in a field at night. He then released a gravid female[10] on the edge of the arena. There were two treatments. In one treatment, both males were calling or both males were silent. In this treatment, the probability of the female mating with a given male was about 50 percent. At this short distance at night, the female was groping in the dark and basically mated with the first male she encountered.[11] In the second treatment, one male was calling and the other male was silent. In this treatment, the probability of the female mating with the male who called was 60 percent.

We can now set out some parameters to describe the game played by the male frogs. Let z be the cost of calling. This cost includes the danger of becoming prey as well as the danger of running out of energy. Calling takes a lot of energy, especially on a cold night. Both becoming prey and running out of energy are equally fatal. Let m be the probability that a male who calls in a pair of males, the other of whom is not calling, gets a mate. For the Perrill data, we have

$$m = .6$$

Next, we normalize the attraction of females such that 1 male call = 1 female attracted, 0 male calls = 0 females attracted. Finally, frog calls display diminishing returns in the sense that two males calling attract P females each, with $0 < P < 1$. There is some interference between the frog calls, just as there is interference between competing advertisements for essentially the same product.

We can now write down the matrix for the game played by a pair of male frogs (see Figure 9.8). Each frog has two strategies, Call and Don't Call. If both frogs call, each attracts P females and pays cost z. If only one frog calls, he attracts 1 female with probability m and 0 females with probability $1 - m$; in either event, he pays cost z. The frog that doesn't call attracts 1 female with probability $1 - m$ and 0 females with probability m; in either event, he pays cost 0. Finally, if both are silent, 0 females are attracted and no cost is paid. These are the payoffs shown in Figure 9.8.

---

[10] That is, a female carrying unfertilized eggs.

[11] Think if you can see any analogies between this scene and the typical bar scene among humans.

There are three possible ESSs for this game, depending on the values of the payoff parameters (m,z,P). First, when $m < z$, it doesn't pay even a single male to call. Since $P < 1$, it also follows that $(P - z) < (1 - m)$. Thus we get an ESS at Don't Call for each male—the area marked Don't Call in Figure 9.9. Don't Call strictly dominates Call, and natural selection of behavior obeys strict dominance. In terms of the Perrill data, an example of this zone is $m = .6 < z = 1$, the point labeled "A" in Figure 9.9. A frog that calls is sure to be eaten.

Next, suppose that the cost of calling falls, so that $z < m$, but not too much, so that $(P - z) < (1 - m)$. Then we get a mixed strategy equilibrium, with some males calling and some males not calling. This is the zone marked Mix in Figure 9.8. In terms of the Perrill data, an example of this zone is $P = m = .6 > .4 = z$, the point labeled "B" in Figure 9.9. The two pure strategies must pay the same, so

$$u(\text{Call}) = x(P - z) + (1 - x)(m - z) = x(1 - m) + (1 - x)(0) = u(\text{Don't Call})$$

Substituting our parameter values, we get

$$x(.6 - .4) + (1 - x)(.6 - .4) = x(1 - .6)$$

Simplifying and rearranging, we get

$$.2 = .4x, \text{ or } x = 0.5$$

At this mixed strategy ESS, half of the male frogs are calling and the other half are not.

Finally, suppose that the cost of calling drops even further, so that $(P - z) > (1 - m)$. The strategy Call is a strictly dominant strategy in this event, and so Call is an ESS. This eventuality is shown by the zone Call in Figure 9.8. In terms of the Perrill data, an example of this zone is $P = .6 = m > 0 = z$, the point labeled "C" in Figure 9.9. If a frog that calls is never eaten, then it makes sense to call.

FIGURE 9.9 **FROGS CALL FOR MATES, REGIME DIAGRAM**

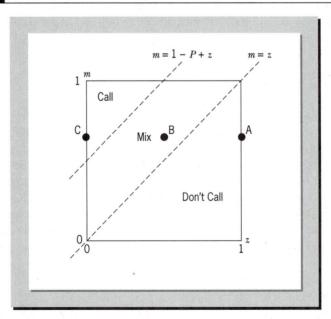

Economic reasoning comes through loud and clear here: the cheaper it is to call, the more the frogs call. Not only can frogs play games, they can also obey the laws of economics, in this case the law of supply. When it costs too much to supply a call, they don't supply it.[12]

Of these three possible ESSs, the one most likely under typical Indiana summer conditions is Mix. About 80 percent of the males on a typical night are calling, and 20 percent are not—but both are getting the same payoff in expected value terms. On a really cold night, none of the frogs call (really high z in terms of energy cost), whereas on the warmest night of the year, they all call (really low z in terms of energy cost). We can call these strategies **conditional,** since they depend on the atmospheric condition (temperature). ESSs that involve conditional strategies give animal behavior much more flexibility than we humans once assumed. Conditional ESS is the best way to organize all this frog data in a single explanation. Three hundred million years of amphibian evolution has led to some very strategic frogs.

■ 9.5 ESS FOR 2 X 2 ASYMMETRICAL GAMES

The ESS of a symmetrical game is itself symmetrical, a **symmetrical ESS.** In such games, all the boundedly rational players are essentially alike. However, boundedly rational players can also play asymmetrical games. In an asymmetrical game, the players are different and recognize the difference. The ESS of an asymmetrical game is called an **asymmetrical ESS,** and players at such an ESS may use different strategies. In such a case, you should think of ESS as standing for evolutionarily stable strategies, one for each player. We will study in detail how boundedly rational players play Telex vs. IBM (recall chapter 7), given in normal form in Figure 9.10.[13] The player in the role of Telex controls the rows of the matrix; the player in the role of IBM controls the columns. There are two Telex types: those who enter, called Entrants, and those who stay out, called Hesitators. There are also two IBM types: those who smash, called Smashers, and those who accommodate, called Accommodators. As you can see from Figure 9.10, this game has two Nash equilibria: (stay out, smash) and (enter, accommodate). Only (enter, accommodate) is evolutionarily stable. The credibility problem that (stay out, smash) has in extensive form shows up as evolutionary instability. This makes a lot of sense. If you do something that is not credible, generations a long time from now will not believe it any more than the current generation does.

The asymmetry that shows up in Telex vs. IBM is quite natural. All the ingredients necessary for a game like this are present whenever an upstart firm enters the turf of a large, established firm. Comparable asymmetries arise as cost advantages, first-mover advantages (Cournot competition), second-mover advantages (Bertrand competition), and information advantages—the subject of Part Three of this book. Whatever the source of the asymmetry, it is clearly present in the minds of the players.

In an asymmetrical game, we apply replicator dynamics to each role separately. In Telex vs. IBM, this means applying replicator dynamics to the Telex player types (Entrant and Hesitator) and to the IBM player types (Smasher and Accommodator) separately. We

---

[12] Animals have been studied intensively in the laboratory to see if their behavior accords with the law of economics. See, for example, John Kagel, Raymond Battalio, Howard Rachlin, Leonard Green, Robert Bassman, and W. Klemm, "Experimental Studies of Consumer Behavior Using Laboratory Animals," *Economic Inquiry* 13 (1975): 22–38.

[13] This game is analyzed here in normal form. It could also be analyzed in extensive form, yielding similar results. See R. Selten, "Evolutionary Stability in Extensive Two-Person Games," *Mathematical Social Sciences* 5 (1983): 269–363.

FIGURE 9.10 **TELEX VS. IBM, NORMAL FORM**

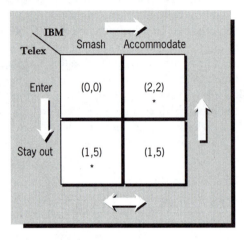

need two dimensions to represent these dynamics. Let x be the percentage of Entrants, and $1 - x$ the percentage of Hesitators. Similarly, let y be the percentage of Smashers, and $1 - y$ the percentage of Accommodators.

We now compute for each role the expected payoff of each player type in that role. On the Telex side of the game, we have for Entrants

$$u(\text{enter}) = (y)0 + 1(1 - y)\,2 = 2(1 - y)$$

since the probability of being matched with a Smasher is y, and the probability of being matched with an Accommodator is $1 - y$. Again, for Hesitators, we have

$$u(\text{stay out}) = (y)1 + (1 - y)1 = 1$$

Staying out of the market yields a sure-thing payoff. On the IBM side of the game, we have for Smashers

$$u(\text{smash}) = (x)0 + (1 - x)5 = 5 - 5x$$

since they are matched with an Entrant with probability x (in which event they get 0) and with a Hesitator with probability $1 - x$ (in which case they get 5). By the same token, Accommodators can expect the payoffs

$$u(\text{accommodate}) = (x)2 + (1 - x)5 = 5 - 3x$$

Notice that $u(\text{accommodate}) = (5 - 3x) > (5 - 5x) = u(\text{smash})$ unless $x = 0$, in which case they are equal. This result shows right away that Accommodate weakly dominates Smash (which we saw in a different context in chapter 7), although not strictly so.

Evolution takes place simultaneously on both Telex and IBM sides of the game. On the Telex side, we have

$$u(\text{enter}) = 2(1 - y) \text{ and } u(\text{stay out}) = 1$$

The average Telex player gets

$$\text{average Telex} = xu(\text{enter}) + (1 - x)\,u(\text{stay out}) = x[2(1 - y)] + (1 - x)1$$

Notice that the percentage of Entrants increases if

$$2(1 - y) > 1, \text{ or } y > 1/2$$

What this inequality means is that if the fraction of Smashers in the IBM population is less than 1/2, it pays to enter. Figure 9.11 depicts the phase diagram for Telex vs. IBM. The arrow below the line $y = 1/2$ pointing to the right shows that in this zone, x is increasing. The arrow above the line $y = 1/2$ pointing to the left shows that in this zone, x is decreasing.

Replicator dynamics is also at work on the IBM side. Here we have

$$u(\text{smash}) = x(0) + 5(1 - x)$$
$$u(\text{accommodate}) = x(2) + 5(1 - x)$$

Notice that $u(\text{smash})$ is always less than $u(\text{accommodate})$ when x is not zero. So the proportion of IBM types y playing smash is always decreasing long as there are any Entrants. This is reflected by the arrows pointing down in the phase diagram of Figure 9.11.

Telex vs. IBM has two Nash equilibria. One of these, (enter, accommodate), is played by a population with $x\emptyset = 1$ and $y\emptyset = 0$. All Telex player types are Entrants, and all IBM player types are Accommodators. This Nash equilibrium is an ESS. Arrows point toward it from both directions. If an IBM player type were to make a mistake and smash, that player type would get a below-average return and be driven out of the population. Likewise, if a Telex player type made a mistake and stayed out, that player type would get a below-average return and be driven out of the Telex population.

FIGURE 9.11 | **TELEX VS. IBM, PHASE DIAGRAM**

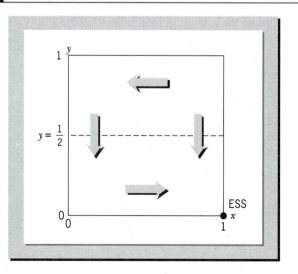

The other Nash equilibrium, (stay out, smash), is played by a population with $x = 0$ and $y = 1$. All Telex types are Hesitators, and all IBM player types are Smashers. This Nash equilibrium is not an ESS. Replicator dynamics favors any IBM type who accommodates. Suppose a mistake is made some Telex-type players, and x increases from 0 to e, where e is a small positive number. Then on the IBM side we have

$$u(\text{smash}) = 5[1 - (1 - e)] = 5e < u(\text{accommodate}) = (e)2 + 5[1 - (1 - e)] = 2e + 5e = 7e$$

and replicator dynamics is off and running, leaving the Smashers in the dust. The equilibrium with the credibility problem when played by rational players still has a problem when played by boundedly rational players—it's unstable.

For asymmetrical games, there is a very simple test for whether a Nash equilibrium can possibly be an ESS. A Nash equilibrium is a **strict Nash equilibrium** if each player has a unique best response to the other player's strategy. In an arrow diagram for the matrix game, this means that all arrows point in to an equilibrium, but no arrow points out (no two-headed arrows). Here is the test, called **Selten's test** after its discoverer:

ESS for Asymmetrical Games.   If (x^*, y^*) is an ESS, then (x^*, y^*) is a strict Nash equilibrium.[14]

This test is very effective when applied to Telex vs. IBM. The equilibrium (stay out, smash) is not strict, since Accommodate is also a best response to stay out. Accordingly, (stay out, smash) played by the population $(x, y) = (0, 1)$ cannot be an ESS. For 2 x 2 asymmetrical games, the converse is also true:

ESS for 2 x 2 Asymmetrical Games.   If (x^*, y^*) is a strict equilibrium, then (x^*, y^*) is an ESS.

Taken together, these two results give us an effective shortcut to finding all the ESS of a 2 x 2 asymmetrical game. We look for strict equilibria, and that's all. Since mixed strategy equilibria have multiple best responses (every strategy in the mixture pays the same), they can't possibly be strict, and so they can't be ESSs of asymmetrical games.

As in the case of symmetrical games, where there may not be an ESS, in asymmetrical games there may also fail to be an ESS. Matching Pennies (Figure 3.1) offers the simplest example. This is an asymmetrical 2-person game. Its only equilibrium is in mixed strategies. Since mixed strategies cannot be strict, Matching Pennies has no ESS. Indeed, it is often difficult for boundedly rational players to learn a mixed strategy. The information-processing requirements exceed all but the highest rational capabilities.

---

[14] This result was first proved by R. Selten, "A Note on Evolutionarily Stable Strategies in Asymmetrical Animal Conflicts," *Journal of Theoretical Biology* 84 (1980): 93–101. A short mathematical proof is given in Jose Hofbauer and Karl Sigmund, *The Theory of Evolution and Dynamical Systems* (Cambridge, UK: Cambridge University Press, 1987), chap. 17.

◼ 9.6 FAST LEARNING WITH A FINITE NUMBER OF PLAYERS

This chapter has proceeded under two assumptions: the learning studied has been quite slow; and only some of the players adopt a higher-paying strategy at any given time. If we allow players to adopt a higher-paying strategy immediately, and we allow for a finite number of players, then we can achieve sharper results for symmetrical 2 x 2 games.

This section again studies the game Coordination of Figure 9.4. Now, however, instead of a large number of players, there are only five players. Moreover, instead of being governed by replicator dynamics, the out-of-equilibrium behavior is described by **best-response dynamics.** In best-response dynamics, each player picks the strategy this period that maximizes payoff, assuming the rest of the population behaved the same as last period. Best-response dynamics allow for very fast learning. We leave the technical details to the appendix.

Before we state the main theorem about best-response dynamics that applies to 2 x 2 games, we need an additional concept, **risk dominance.**[15] First, define the *deviation loss* to player *i* of not playing a certain Nash equilibrium by how much that player loses by switching to another strategy, and then define the *deviation loss product* of a Nash equilibrium to be the product of the deviation losses for each player. One Nash equilibrium has risk dominance over another if its deviation loss product is larger.

To see how risk dominance applies to Coordination, let's walk through the steps of the calculation. The deviation loss to a player from switching from strategy 1 to strategy 2 is $50 - 0 = 50$. The deviation loss product for this equilibrium is $50^2 = 2500$. The deviation loss to a player from switching from strategy 2 to strategy 1 is $60 - 49 = 11$. The deviation loss product for this equilibrium is $11^2 = 121$. The equilibrium (strategy 1, strategy 1) risk dominates the equilibrium (strategy 2, strategy 2), since

$$2500 > 121$$

Armed with the concept of risk dominance, we can now express our main result:

◼ ◼ ◼

Theorem on Best-Response Dynamics. In 2 x 2 coordination games with best-response dynamics, learning almost always converges to the risk-dominant equilibrium.[16]

This means, in the Coordination game of Figure 9.4, the best-response dynamics converges to the inefficient Nash equilibrium (strategy 1, strategy 1), rather than the efficient Nash equilibrium (strategy 2, strategy 2).

---

[15] This notion is introduced in J. Harsanyi and R. Selten, *A General Theory of Equilibrium Selection in Games* (Cambridge, Mass.: MIT Press, 1988), chap. 3.

[16] A large number of papers have demonstrated this result. Two good examples are M. Kandori, G. J. Mailath, and R. Rob, "Learning, Mutation, and Long Run Equilibrium in Games," *Econometrica* 61 (1993): 29–56; and H. Peyton Young, "The Evolution of Conventions," *Econometrica* 61 (1993): 57–89.

The preceding prediction on inefficiency is very strong, and cries out to be run in the laboratory. It has.[17]

Consider the games shown in Figure 9.12. The game in Figure 9.12a has a unique pure strategy Nash equilibrium that is also strictly dominant, namely (s_2,s_2). Replicator and best-response dynamics both predict its play:

Prediction 1. In the game in Figure 9.12a, play will evolve to the Nash equilibrium (s_2,s_2).

The game in Figure 9.12b has two pure strategy Nash equilibria, namely, (s_1,s_1) and (s_2,s_2). This game also has a mixed strategy Nash equilibrium involving a probability distribution over strategies s_1 and s_2, with each player playing s_1 with probability .67. The phase diagram for this game would resemble that for Coordination (see Figure 9.4), where the mixed strategy Nash equilibrium is not an ESS but the two pure strategy Nash equilibria are.

Prediction 2. In the game in Figure 9.12b, play will evolve to either the ESS at s_1 or the ESS at s_2, depending on where play begins. If the percentage of the population playing s_1 is sufficiently great (at least .67) at the outset, then the system will evolve to the ESS where all players choose s_1.

A team of four researchers from the University of Iowa and Carleton University (in Ontario, Canada) conducted a series of experiments to study out-of-equilibrium behavior by boundedly rational players. The sample consisted of volunteers drawn from the ranks of upper division undergraduates and M.B.A. students at the University of Iowa. Subjects earned between $5 and $20 for participation in an experiment, depending on the strategies they and their opponents chose.

Subjects reviewed a set of instructions prior to play, after which the instructions were read out loud to them, all for the sake of making their choices as mistake free as possible. Each

FIGURE 9.12 **EXPERIMENTAL GAMES IN NORMAL FORM: (a) ONE ESS; (b) TWO ESSs**

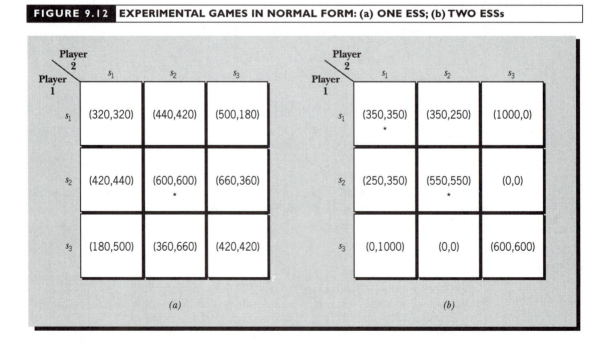

(a)

(b)

[17] See Russell W. Cooper, Douglas V. DeJong, Robert Forsythe, and Thomas W. Ross, "Selection Criteria in Coordination Games: Some Experimental Results," *American Economic Review* 80 (1990): 218–233.

subject then played the game in Figure 9.12a for 10 periods, each period against a different opponent. This game, which is really easy to solve, served as a warm-up for the subjects. Each subject then played the game in Figure 9.12b for 21 periods, each time against a different opponent. This game was meant to be a bigger challenge for the subjects, and so it was.

The main results of the experiment involving the games in Figure 9.12 are as follows. First, the data support for prediction 1 is outstanding. Of 820 subject choices for the game in Figure 9.12a, 770 (94 percent) chose s_2. The vast majority went to this strategy almost immediately and stayed there. This phenomenon not only provides strong evidence for fast learning but also yields an estimate of the error rate of 6 percent, which is well within the range of error rates (5–10 percent) observed in a wide variety of human behavior experiments. Second, the data support for prediction 2 is also strong, although not as strong as that for prediction 1. The authors observed that the first 10 periods of play of this game basically involved learning. During this learning phase, play approached the ESS at s_1. The authors reported detailed data for the last 11 periods. During these 11 periods, of 110 subject choices, 83 (75 percent) chose s_1. During the last 5 periods, behavior came even closer to the ESS, with 42 of 50 subjects (84 percent) choosing s_1. By the end of a 2-hour laboratory session, with the play of an easy game followed by that of a more difficult game, behavior had largely converged to Nash equilibria that are evolutionarily stable twice.

Although the results of this experiment are supportive of evolutionary theory, they also support the inefficiency that evolution may lead to. The Nash equilibrium at s_1 is inefficient relative to that at s_2, yet a large majority of human subjects choose to play s_1. The evolution of behavior, whether it is slow according to the laws of natural selection or fast according to the laws of cultural selection, may not lead to efficiency. If efficiency is the goal, then you can't depend solely on evolution to achieve that.

Best-response dynamics speeds up learning and gives human players a shortcut to a Nash equilibrium. The same adjustment, according to replicator dynamics, might take aeons, if it occurred at all. Part of the reason that our species has taken over the Earth from all other living things is our seemingly unlimited facility at exploiting this shortcut. Best-response dynamics is certainly important in rapidly evolving markets, such as that for video games, to which we now turn.

◼ 9.7 THE EVOLUTION OF VIDEO GAMES

In a perfectly coordinated world, any computer program could run on any computer.[18] Unfortunately, this is not the world we live in. Ever since John von Neumann laid down the architectural principles for computers in 1945, computers have had difficulty coordinating with each other. In the industry we are about to consider, **video games,** the inability to coordinate has evolved as a standard part of the industry. Let's see how this happened.[19]

The first computer games were created in the early 1960s. You could play these games only if you had a computer. Nolan Bushnell, a computer engineer, created the first video game, Pong, in 1972. To play Pong, all you needed was a television monitor and the program that ran the game, housed in a microprocessor-based circuit board. Pong was a big hit, first in arcades and later (1974) in a home version, and launched Bushnell's newly created Atari Corporation. About 100,000 copies of Pong were produced in 1974, but only about 10,000

---

[18] Material has been drawn from David Sheff, *Game Over* (New York: Random House, 1993).

[19] This conclusion continues to hold true if players make mistakes with a small probability.

of these were made by Atari. Video games were simple to copy, and pirate versions flooded the market. Also flooding the market were entrants, well over a dozen by 1978.

One of those entrants was Nintendo, a large Japanese card and toy company. In 1975, Nintendo cut a deal with Magnavox, one of Atari's principal rivals, to market Pong-like video games in Japan. Nintendo introduced its own games for the first time 2 years later, beginning with Color TV Game 6. Color, better sound and graphics, and more interesting and challenging games soon became Nintendo hallmarks. Nintendo introduced its first big hit, Donkey Kong, in the United States in 1980. Sales quickly reached the $100 million mark. In a heated bidding contest, Coleco beat out Atari and Mattel for exclusive rights to the home video version of Donkey Kong in 1982. Coleco ultimately sold over 6 million Donkey Kong cartridges. Despite its increased complexity, Donkey Kong also lost sales to counterfeit games—at least $100 million in sales, according to company figures. Nintendo pursued 35 counterfeiting cases in court, usually prevailing.

The year 1983 was a landmark year for the industry in the United States, especially if you consider cemeteries landmarks. Sales of video games fell dramatically, with Atari and Mattel nearly going under and Coleco barely hanging on. Nintendo, whose sales were still largely confined to Japan, where it had a dominant market share, saw the slump of the U.S. video game industry as a historic opportunity. Nintendo prepared to enter the U.S. market on its own in a big way. First, however, it had to make two strategic decisions. The first decision was how to introduce the rest of the games in its portfolio. Nintendo engineers developed a system, the Advanced Video System (or AVS, later known as the Nintendo Entertainment System, or NES) on which all the games could run. Second, Nintendo created an ingenious security system, called the *lockout system.* This system was basically nothing more than an electronic lock and key. The game-playing cartridge had to have a key to unlock the lock in the AVS player. The lockout system effectively put an end to counterfeiting. Its code wasn't broken for almost a decade, and then only by surreptitious access into the U.S. Patent Office, where it was on file.[20]

Nintendo brought its system to the U.S. market in 1984. Using the theme "The evolution of a species is now complete," Nintendo's marketing campaign featured pictures of Pong, color tennis, and a veiled video screen. Behind that screen, the buyer would uncover Donkey Kong, Super Mario Brothers, The Legend of Zelda—a panoply of great games. After a slow start, NES sales reached 7 million in 1988, with some 33 million game cartridges sold to go along with the system. The U.S. market recovered from the bottom of 1983, with sales reaching the $5 billion level in 1992. In this U.S. market, Nintendo was the dominant firm.

Nintendo's lockout system had a very profitable, if unintended, aspect. Software producers could not create games to run on NES unless they had the key. They could get the key only by dealing with Nintendo. As a virtual monopoly, Nintendo could, and did, extract extremely favorable terms from software producers, who soon numbered more than 100. The same was true of toy retailers. Even giant chains, such as Toys "R" Us, owed more than 20 percent of their profits to Nintendo sales. A further profitable feature was that the lockout system tended to lock players into the system. Once a player had acquired the system and a library of games, he or she (about 90 percent of all sales were to adolescent males) was much more likely to build a Nintendo library than to invest in another system.

One of Nintendo's biggest decisions came in 1990 and involved the 16-bit system that the company had developed, Super NES. Super NES could do everything better than NES.

---

[20] Atari finally obtained a copy of the code by illegal means from the U.S. Bureau of Standards, where it had been registered for safekeeping.

The only catch—and it was a big one—was that Super NES was not compatible with the NES. You couldn't run Super Mario Brothers 4 on NES, and you couldn't run Super Mario Brothers 3 on Super NES. With a price tag of $200 (the average annual expenditure on toys for a family of four) on Super NES, Nintendo was sure to encounter considerable buyer resistance. Nintendo was locked into its own success.

Despite all the negatives, Nintendo launched Super NES in the United States in 1991. In the decade that followed, evolution went far beyond the 16-bit system, reaching 256-bit systems. Sony's Playstation and Nintendo's GameCube continue to battle it out for market share, with an entrant, Microsoft, challenging both with its Xbox.

From a historical perspective, the speed with which video games are evolving is truly astounding. It took millions of years for natural selection to evolve the calling behavior of tree frogs. It took 30 years to go from Pong to Playstation. And the evolution is far from over.

■ SUMMARY

1. Boundedly rational players make mistakes and learn slowly. When boundedly rational players play a game, they are usually out of equilibrium.

2. Replicator dynamics describes the out-of-equilibrium behavior of boundedly rational players; it says that above-average play increases in the population. A Nash equilibrium that is stable in the replicator dynamics is called an evolutionarily stable strategy (ESS).

3. An ESS is a Nash equilibrium to which replicator dynamics leads and that cannot be destroyed by small percentages of players making mistakes.

4. Let's Make a Deal has a unique ESS, which agrees with the dominance solution.

5. Evolution may lead to inefficient ESS, as Coordination shows, and contrary to what social Darwinists claim.

6. Territorial contests are modeled by Hawk vs. Dove. If contests are costly, then the ESS permits almost no serious fights.

7. Boundedly rational players play two main types of games: symmetrical and asymmetrical. The properties of ESS for these two types of games are very different. In particular, the ESS of a symmetrical game must be in symmetrical strategies, and the ESS of an asymmetrical game cannot be in mixed strategies.

8. We observe inefficient ESS also in our economy and culture. Evolution explains why we are stuck with the keyboard of the 1870s, developed for manual typewriters, when we now have personal computers.

9. The ESS of a symmetrical game may be in mixed strategies, as in Hawk vs. Dove. The ESS of an asymmetrical game must be in pure strategies. All ESSs of an asymmetrical game are strict equilibria, with a unique best response.

10. In 2 x 2 coordination games, best-response dynamics selects the ESS that is risk dominant. Best-response dynamics is particularly applicable to markets where the product is rapidly evolving and where firms adopt short-term profit-maximizing strategies.

■ KEY TERMS

bounded rationality	locked in	Selten's test
replicator dynamics	conditional	best-response dynamics
mistakes	symmetrical/asymmetrical	risk dominance
evolutionarily stable strategy	ESS	video games
(ESS)	strict Nash equilibrium	

▪ PROBLEMS

1. State the basic principle of replicator dynamics. Do you think the compensation of managers is based on this principle? Do you think it should be?

2. Find an ESS for Prisoner's Dilemma in Figure 8.3. Is the ESS you found unique?

3. Interpret your answer in problem 2, in light of the claim that Tit-for-Tat is an ESS in Prisoner's Dilemma played twice.

4. Find two ESSs for Coordination (Figure 9.4), when the payoffs to (strategy 1, strategy 1) are (40,40) instead of (50,50). Why isn't the mixed strategy Nash equilibrium of this game an ESS? Why is an inefficient Nash equilibrium evolutionarily stable?

5. Find the ESS for Hawk vs. Dove (Figure 9.5) when $V = 2$ and $C = 100$. What is the probability of a fight occurring? What does this tell you about the probability of serious fights as cost gets large?

6. Set $m = .6$ and $P = .8$ in Frogs Call for Mates. Now find values of the cost of calling, z, such that each of the following happens: (a) Don't Call is an ESS; (b) Mix is an ESS; and (c) Call is an ESS. Relate your answer to standard economic theory, in particular the law of supply.

7. Suppose that there are two kinds of frogs in Frogs Call for Mates. Large frogs have a larger cost of calling (z_1) than do small frogs (z_2). Redraw the game matrix of Figure 9.8. What kinds of ESS are possible in this asymmetric game?

8. Assuming that $V_i < C_i$ for both i, construct a matrix game for Asymmetrical Hawk vs. Dove like that for Telex vs. IBM (Figure 9.10). Then find the two ESSs of this game. Why are there only two ESSs?

9. Two boundedly rational video companies are playing the asymmetrical game in Figure 9.13. Company XX has to decide whether to have an open system or a lockout system. Company XY has to decide whether to create its own system or copy that of company XX. Find an ESS for this game. Interpret the Nintendo story on the basis of this ESS.

10. Find the risk-dominant Nash equilibrium of the Coordination game in problem 3. Why is the risk-dominant Nash equilibrium so important in the best-response dynamics?

11. A Cournot equilibrium is an ESS. Tell why this should be true in the Cournot game of Figure 6.10. The player types are the quantities that could be shipped by the manager of a firm.

FIGURE 9.13 VIDEO MARKET GAME, TWO FIRMS

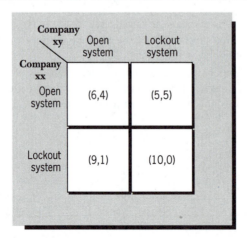

Company XX \ Company XY	Open system	Lockout system
Open system	(6,4)	(5,5)
Lockout system	(9,1)	(10,0)

■ APPENDIX. FAST LEARNING, USING THE BEST-RESPONSE DYNAMICS

Suppose that the players are arrayed on a circle, as in Figure 9.14a, and each player plays Coordination (Figure 9.4) with the neighbors to the left and to the right each period.[21] Thus player 1 plays each period with players 2 and 5; player 2, with players 1 and 3; and so on. The players against whom player i plays each period are his or her *neighbors*. A *state of the game* tells what each player did in the previous period (Figure 9.14b). There are $2^5 = 32$ possible states of this game. In this period, each player i picks a strategy to maximize utility, given the play of the neighbors in the previous period. Let $x_i(t)$ denote the number of player i's neighbors who played strategy 1 in period t; $2 - x_i(t)$, the number of player i's neighbors who played strategy 2 in period t. Then, in period $t + 1$, player i picks a strategy to maximize utility, based on the state of the game in period t. Player i picks strategy 1 if

$$x_i(t)50 + [2 - x_i(t)]49 > x_i(t)0 + [2 - x_i(t)]60$$

Rearranging, we have

$$x_i(t) > 22/61$$

Since $x_i(t)$ can take on only the values 0, 1, or 2, we have a simple rule for player i to follow:

Play strategy 1 this period if at least one neighbor played strategy 1 last period.

Finally, by symmetry, what is true of player i is true for any other player.

We will see that for all but one of the 32 possible states of the system, best-response dynamics leads to the ESS (strategy 1, strategy 1). To do this, we need to construct dynamics analogous to replicator dynamics. If every player in the game played strategy 2 at time t, then no player in the population has a neighbor who played strategy 1 at time t, so no player in the population plays strategy 1 in this period. Suppose that one player played strategy 1

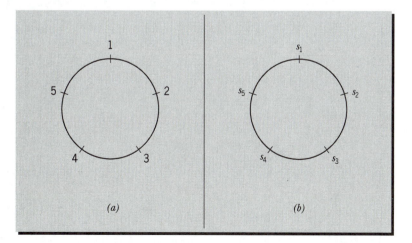

FIGURE 9.14 | **PLAYER NETWORK: (a) FIVE PLAYERS; (b) STATE OF THE GAME**

(a)

(b)

[21] A general model of this sort has been studied by S. K. Berninghaus and U. Schwalbe, "Evolution, Interaction, and Nash Equilibrium," *Journal of Economic Behavior and Organization* 37 (1998): 231–248.

at time *t*. Then two players this period have neighbors who played strategy 1 last period, and those two players will play strategy 1 this period, as shown in Figure 9.15a. Once at least one player plays strategy 1 in period *t*, the number of players playing strategy *i* in period *t* + 1 is greater than that in period *t*. This is what drives the players toward strategy 1.

In Figures 9.15b and c, we see what happens when two players played strategy 1 in period *t*. We have to distinguish between two cases, depending on how many players have a neighbor who played strategy 1. If the two players who played strategy 1 are themselves neighbors (Figure 9.15b), then four players have a neighbor who played strategy 1 in period *t*, and these four players will play strategy 1 in period *t* + 1, a big increase. If the two players who played strategy 1 are not neighbors (Figure 9.15c), then three players have a neighbor who played strategy 1 in period *t*, and these three players will play strategy 1 in period

---

FIGURE 9.15 **COORDINATION, TRANSITIONS**

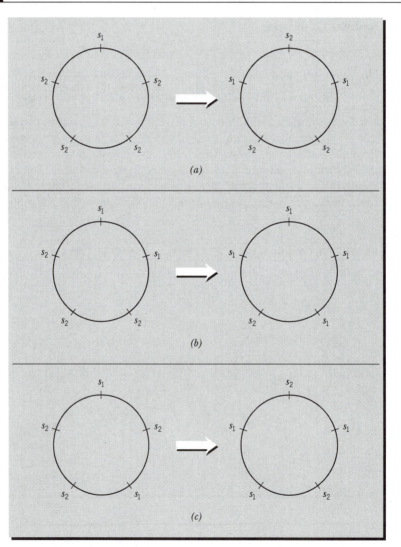

$t + 1$, again an increase. Once three players are playing strategy 1 in period t, four or five of them have neighbors who played strategy 1, depending on how they are arrayed. That means either four or five players play strategy 1 in period $t + 1$, again an increase. Either the system has converged to its dynamic equilibrium, or it has come very close. Finally, when four players are playing strategy 1 in period t, every player must have a neighbor who played that strategy, and all players play strategy 1 in period $t + 1$.

This result verifies the claim made earlier: once strategy 1 appears, it quickly takes over. A player adopts strategy 1 just as soon as one of his or her neighbors does. In this way, strategy 1 comes to predominate in a process that never takes more than the number of players. The dynamics described here has two fixed points, corresponding to the cases where all players play strategy 2 and all players play strategy 1. Each of these was an ESS when the game was analyzed using replicator dynamics. In best-response dynamics, however, the equilibrium where all players play strategy 2 is no longer dynamically stable. Once at least one player plays strategy 1—even if by mistake—strategy 1 takes over. It is the only dynamically stable equilibrium in best-response dynamics. Strategy 1, which had the largest probability of being the outcome under replicator dynamics (50/61), is even more likely (31/32) to be the outcome under best-response dynamics. This result also verifies the theorem, since strategy 1 risk dominates strategy 2. In addition, if we consider games with a larger number of players, then we can drive the likelihood that the best-response dynamics leads to the risk-dominant equilibrium arbitrarily close to 1.

P A R T   T H R E E

Games with Imperfect Information

C H A P T E R   1 0

Signaling, Screening, and Sequential Equilibrium

This chapter begins a new unit about games with imperfect information. Imperfect information has played a role in some of the games we have already studied. For instance, in Liar's Poker (see chapter 4, section 4.3), player 1's gain was due entirely to the fact that player 1 knew what her card was and player 2 did not. A situation in which one player knows something that another player does not know is called an *information asymmetry*. Information asymmetries are pervasive in markets and in life. This and the following two chapters explore the implications of imperfect information and informational asymmetries for strategy. Indeed, the work in this part was just recognized with the Nobel Prize in economics for 2001. Three Americans—George Akerlof (UCLA), Michael Spence (Stanford), and Joseph Stiglitz (Columbia) shared the prize for their work on market games with imperfect information. You see some of the contributions of each in this and coming chapters.

This chapter considers signaling and screening games. In a **signaling game,** one player knows more than another, and the player who knows more has to move first. For instance, the signaling game could be between you and a used-car dealer. The dealer knows a lot more about used cars than you do. The dealer also has to decide whether to put a given used car on the lot—and if so, what price tag to put on it—before you show up. Your decision is whether to buy a given used car or not. Signaling games go back to ancient times; the ancient Romans coined a phrase to apply to such games—*caveat emptor,* let the buyer beware. Another signaling game, played for significantly higher stakes, arises when a privately held corporation goes public, offering its stock for sale to the public. The corporation knows a lot more about what it is worth than even the best-informed outside investor. Thus, signaling games are well suited to the study of *inside information.*

By contrast, in a **screening game,** the uninformed player goes first. For instance, the screening game could be between you and an insurance company. You know a lot more about your driving habits than the insurance company does. That makes you the informed player. So when the insurance company offers its menu of car insurance contracts to the driving public, it is moving first with imperfect information about any individual member of the public. If the insurance company has insufficient information about the driving public, it may suffer heavy losses and be forced out of business. Thus, screening games are well suited to the study of *market failure.*

This chapter shows how to solve such games, beginning with a basic signaling game, where the informed player has two moves, one of which ends the game, and the uninformed player has two moves, either of which ends the game. The four kinds of market equilibria that can emerge from such a game are described. To describe these market equilibria, a new refinement of Nash equilibrium is presented, sequential equilibrium. Every sequential equilibrium is subgame perfect and Nash, but not vice versa.

Markets have a hard time functioning properly in the presence of asymmetrical information. A particularly notorious example is called the market for lemons—a lemon is something of poor quality sold at too high a price. The study of the market for lemons helped George Akerlof to the Nobel Prize in 2001.

Another example is the job market for recent college graduates. Prospective employers don't necessarily know how talented these graduates are, although the graduates have sent them a signal by having a college diploma. The study of job market signaling helped Michael Spence to the Nobel Prize in 2001.

Next, we study screening games, where again sequential equilibrium is a crucial game theory concept. These games again lead to a wide variety of market equilibria, including some that require the play of mixed strategies. The study of screening games helped Joseph Stiglitz win the Nobel Prize in 2001.

Sometimes, games involve elements of both signaling and screening. This is especially so in big Wall Street deals like mergers, acquisitions, leveraged buyouts, and management buyouts. We look at one such deal, the leveraged buyout of Nabisco, in detail.

Next, we study the effects of repetition on signaling games and screening games. In these games it is important for the uninformed player to learn what kind of player he or she is dealing with before entering into a long-term relationship, and repetition—especially the collection of information that repetition provides—makes that possible. The statistical technique called Bayesian updating is used to make strategically sound decisions in such games. If Bayesian updating is new to you, the appendix gives more information on how it works. Finally, we look at a classical case of a repeated screening game: the game played between a Hollywood studio and a talented producer.

◼ 10.1 TWO-PLAYER SIGNALING GAMES

This section examines a game of imperfect information between two players: one of them has the information (the **informed player**) and the other doesn't have the information (the **uninformed player**). This game is called Caveat Emptor—"Let the Buyer Beware"—after the ancient Roman saying that it embodies. The modern terms for this situation are **asymmetric information** (what the informed player knows and the uninformed player doesn't) and **adverse selection** (some of what is offered for sale may be bad for the buyer).

Player 1, the seller, is informed and moves first. Player 2, the buyer, is uninformed and moves second. The game starts with a random move, the outcome of which is known only to the seller (see Figure 10.1). The item that the seller is selling is either good or bad—that generates the adverse selection. The seller knows whether the item is good or bad—that generates the asymmetric information. All the buyer knows is that there is some probability $p(\text{good})$ that the item for sale is good, and some probability $p(\text{bad})$ that the item for sale is bad. After being informed about the quality of the good, the seller can either offer it for

FIGURE 10.1 **CAVEAT EMPTOR, EXTENSIVE FORM**

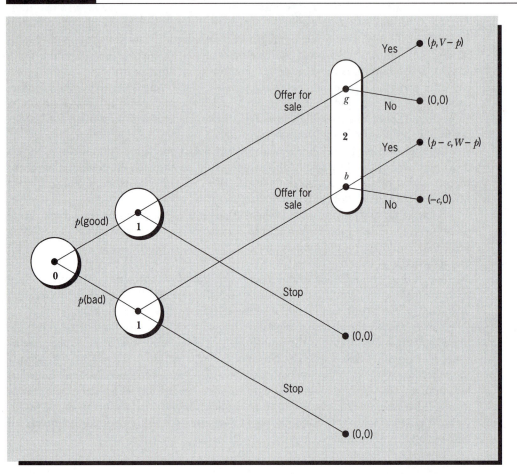

sale or withhold it from the market. If the seller withholds it from market, the game ends with the status quo payoffs of 0 each. If the seller offers the item for sale and it is good, it can be sold as is. If the seller offers the item for sale and it is bad, then it first needs to be cleaned up at cost c. After cleanup, a bad item looks just like a good item, and the buyer can't tell the difference. In any event, the buyer does not see this cleanup operation. Moreover, the price for the item, p, is the same whether it is good or bad. Price can't give away the information, either.[1]

If the item is offered for sale, it is the buyer's turn to move. The buyer has two nodes in the information set: node g, corresponding to a good item being offered for sale, and node b, corresponding to a bad item being offered for sale. The buyer does not know which node the play has reached—both of them are in the information set. The buyer can say either yes or no to the item offered for sale. If the buyer says no, there is no deal. The buyer

---

[1] Later in this chapter, the phenomenon whereby price does signal quality is studied. We should note that a fourth Nobel Prize winner is at work here. John Harsanyi introduced the first games with asymmetric information in 1967.

gets payoff 0, as does the good-type seller, but the bad-type seller gets the payoff –c. This seller cleaned up a bad item, only to see it go unsold. If the buyer says yes, there is a deal. The item sells for price p, which is the payoff to the good-type seller, and $p - c$ is the payoff to the bad-type seller. A good item is worth V to the buyer, from which the price paid, p, is subtracted, yielding the payoff $V - p$. A bad item is worth W to the buyer, from which the price paid, p, is subtracted, yielding the payoff $W - p$. The buyer gains from buying a good type, but loses from buying a bad type:

$$V > p > W$$

The buyer gets burned when he or she buys a bad item. This, in a nutshell, is why the buyer must beware.

Here are three instances of Caveat Emptor. In the first instance, the seller is a used-car dealer and the buyer is about to visit the lot. The seller either puts a car out on the lot or not. The price, p, is posted in the windshield of the car. The cost, c, of making a used car look good is the cost of a paint job. The buyer either buys or not. The buyer gets burned if the car is a lemon. In the second instance, the seller is a job applicant, who is either qualified or not. However, by going through coaching that costs c, the job applicant can put on a good enough front to get through a job interview unscathed. The buyer is an employer. The employer gets burned if he or she hires an unqualified job applicant. In the third instance, the seller is a company selling shares of stock. Let's call this company Enron. The company insiders know what the company's prospects are, but employees acquiring shares for their 401(k) plans do not. By going to extra legal and accounting expense, c, the company can paint as rosy a picture as it wants; in this case the accountant is called Arthur Andersen and charges Enron $55 million per year for its services. Buyers of the stock lose if the company is bad. In this event, Enron went bankrupt, taking thousands of employee 401(k) plans with it, while company insiders, starting with then-CEO Ken Lay, pocketed over $100 million in stock sales, stock options, and bonuses.

Even though Caveat Emptor is a very simple signaling game, a lot can still happen. Depending on the economic fundamentals represented by the parameters p(good), p(bad), p, V, W, and c, Caveat Emptor has four different possible game equilibria:

- **Complete market failure.** All sellers, even the good-type sellers, fearing rejection by the buyers, withhold their goods from the market. The market ceases to function, even though gains from trade are available. An equilibrium where all informed players do the same thing is called a pooling equilibrium. Complete market failure is an especially sinister pooling equilibrium.

- **Complete market success.** Only sellers with good items offer them for sale. Sellers with bad items withhold them from the market. Since all items offered for sale are good, buyers buy everything offered for sale. In this case, the market works perfectly. An equilibrium where the different types of informed players do different things is a **separating equilibrium.** In a separating equilibrium, behavior reveals type. The very act of offering the item for sale signals to the buyer that it is a good type. This signaling is the key to complete market success.

- **Partial market success.** All sellers offer their items for sale, good or bad. All buyers buy whatever is offered for sale. This is only a partial success: the market functions, but there are a lot of bad deals, which reduce market efficiency. This is another example of a pooling equilibrium. Unlike complete market failure, however, this pooling equilibrium does generate some gains from trade.

■ **Near market failure.** Some, but not all, bad-type sellers offer their items for sale. Buyers buy what is offered for sale with a certain probability, but reject what is offered with some probability also. Thus, both buyers and bad-type sellers adopt a mixed strategy response to the imperfect information. In this market, total gains from trade are smaller than in complete market success or partial market success.

Each of these possibilities is a signaling game equilibrium for some payoff parameter values and some initial probabilities. Before exploring these equilibria further, we need a new equilibrium concept, which is indispensable for studying signaling games: sequential equilibrium.

■ 10.2 SEQUENTIAL EQUILIBRIUM: PURE STRATEGIES

Caveat Emptor is the simplest possible signaling game there is. Still, it contains plenty of complexity. In particular, because of its imperfect information, this game has no subgames, which means subgame perfection can't be used as a solution device. This problem is endemic whenever information is imperfect; the imperfection gets in the way of subgame structure. Still, credibility has to be important in signaling. If you send a signal, and you want the person receiving it to believe it, then you had better be credible.

The need for an equilibrium concept that addresses credibility and applies more widely than subgame perfection is the inspiration for **sequential equilibrium.** A sequential equilibrium satisfies subgame perfection on subgames. On information sets like that of player 2 in Figure 10.1, which do not initiate subgames, sequential equilibrium requires that a player maximize expected utility—especially since the player may not know which node of the information set has been reached. To maximize expected utility presupposes a probability distribution over the nodes of the information set. A probability distribution over the nodes of player 2's information set {b,g} is a *belief.* Whenever possible, a belief should be based on hard evidence—the initial probabilities of the game, plus strategies of the other players. A sequential equilibrium for Caveat Emptor is a pair of strategies, one for each player, and a belief for player 2, which together satisfy backward induction on all information sets.[2]

Here is how to check whether an equilibrium is sequential, using an argument akin to backward induction on the signaling game. Suppose the probability of a bad item is very small, so the buyer knows that he or she is almost certain of buying a good item. Also suppose that the cleanup cost, c, is small relative to p. We can now show that the following is a sequential equilibrium:

> 1's strategy: Offer the item for sale if it is good, and offer the item for sale if it is bad.
>
> 2' strategy: Buy whatever is offered for sale.
>
> 2's belief: p(node g|offer) = p(good); p(node b|offer) = p(bad)

---

[2] Strictly speaking, the definition just given is for perfect Bayes equilibrium. A sequential equilibrium puts a further condition, called consistency, on beliefs. However, for all the games studied in this book, these two concepts are identical, and so only the term *sequential equilibrium* is used. See D. M. Kreps and R. Wilson, "Sequential Equilibrium," *Econometrica* 50 (1982): 863–894, for the original discussion. The authors prove an existence theorem for sequential equilibrium.

The notation "p(node g|offer)" stands for the conditional probability that node g has been reached, given that an offer has been made; similarly, the notation "p(node b|offer) = p(bad)" stands for the conditional probability that node b has been reached, given that an offer has been made. The appendix to this chapter tells you more about conditional probability, which is an essential mathematical tool for modeling and analyzing games with imperfect information.

According to the proposed plan of play, both types of sellers offer the item for sale, and the buyer says yes to all offers. First, note that the probability distribution over the nodes of the buyer's information set follows from the initial chance move and the strategy of the seller (see Figure 10.2). The node g of the buyer's information set is reached along the following path: chance picks good, and the seller offers the good item for sale. The probability that an item is good, given that it has been offered for sale, is given by the conditional probability

$$p(\text{good}|\text{offer}) = p(\text{good})p(\text{offer}|\text{good})/p(\text{offer})$$

where the probability of an offer, p(offer), is itself given by the conditional probability

$$p(\text{offer}) = p(\text{good})p(\text{offer}|\text{good}) + p(\text{bad})p(\text{offer}|\text{bad})$$

FIGURE 10.2 **PARTIAL MARKET SUCCESS: REACHING PLAYER 2'S INFORMATION SET**

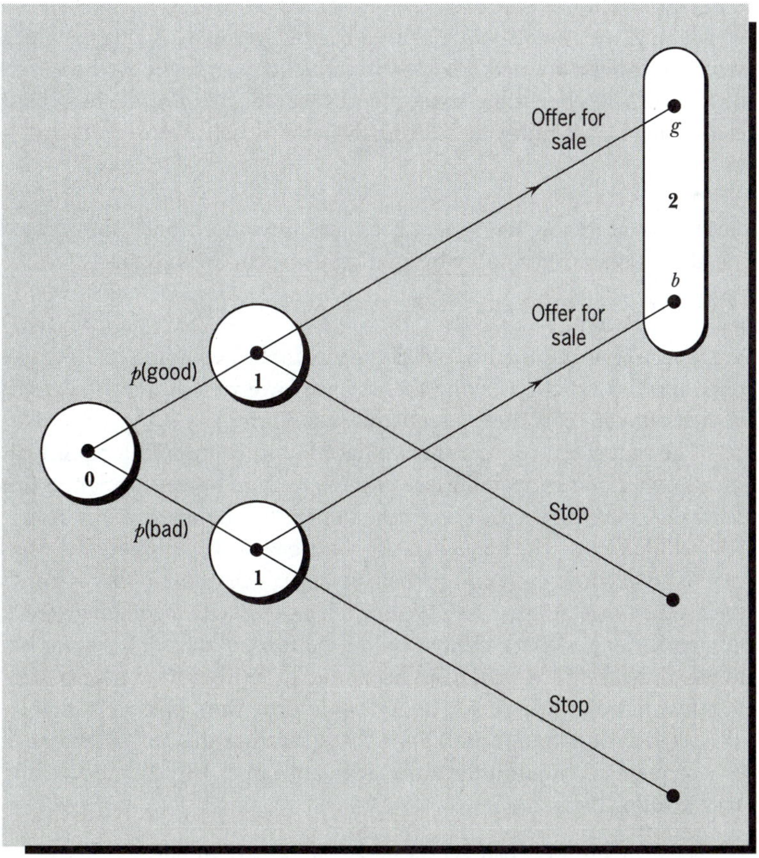

We have $p(\text{offer}|\text{good}) = 1$ and $p(\text{offer}|\text{bad}) = 1$, so that

$$p(\text{good}|\text{offer}) = p(\text{good})$$

The equation involving conditional probability is called **Bayes's rule** after its discoverer. What Bayes's rule does is take the information a player has at the beginning of the game and update it into information that a player can use during the game, or even later. Similarly, the probability that an item is bad, given that it has been offered for sale, is given by the conditional probability

$$p(\text{bad}|\text{offer}) = p(\text{bad})p(\text{offer}|\text{bad})/p(\text{offer}) = p(\text{bad})$$

Given an offer, the probability that player 2 is at node g of the information set is

$$p(\text{node } g|\text{offer}) = p(\text{good}|\text{offer})/[p(\text{good}|\text{offer}) + p(\text{bad}|\text{offer})]$$
$$= p(\text{good})/[p(\text{good}) + p(\text{bad})] = p(\text{good})$$

Likewise, the probability of being at node b of the information set, given an offer, is $p(\text{bad})$.

Now that we have a probability distribution over the nodes of player 2's information set, we can start a backward induction argument. If player 2 buys, he or she can expect the utility $Eu_2(\text{buy})$:

$$Eu_2(\text{buy}) = p(\text{node } g|\text{offer})(V - p) + p(\text{node } b|\text{offer})(W - p)$$
$$= p(\text{good})(V - p) + p(\text{bad})(W - p)$$

which for $p(\text{bad})$ small enough has to be positive. So the buyer maximizes utility by saving yes to any offer. Now, using backward induction, we can replace the information set of the buyer with its observable consequences (see Figure 10.3). The seller with a good item clearly maximizes utility by offering the item for sale, since

$$p > 0$$

At this point, this is an ordinary backward induction conclusion. Likewise, the seller with a bad item maximizes utility by offering that item for sale, since

$$p - c > 0$$

We have now backward induced all the way to the beginning of the game. Since we encountered no contradictions along the way, we have verified that the strategies and belief we started out with constitute a sequential equilibrium.

The sequential equilibrium we have found is a **pooling equilibrium,** partial market success. At a pooling equilibrium, a buyer gets no new information from seeing what the seller does. The buyer has exactly the same information once his or her information set is reached that he or she had when the game began. The probability $p(\text{bad})$ of buying a bad item is small enough to ensure that the buyer's expected utility is positive. If anyone were to do otherwise, utility would go down. If a seller with a good item were to withdraw from the market, their seller's utility would drop from p to zero. If a seller with a bad item were to withdraw from the market, utility would drop from $p - c$ to zero. Finally, if a buyer were to refuse to buy, the expected utility would drop from positive to zero.

We have just found conditions that guarantee that partial market success is achieved by a sequential equilibrium of the signaling game. The conditions in which this happens are the following:

$p > c$ (this gives bad-type sellers an incentive to sell)

FIGURE 10.3 | PARTIAL MARKET SUCCESS: BACKWARD INDUCTION, PLAYER 1'S MOVE

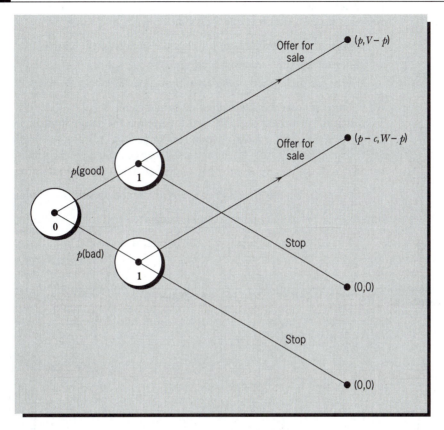

$p(\text{good})(V - p) + p(\text{bad})(W - p) > 0$ (this gives buyers an incentive to buy in a buyer-beware world)

Under the right conditions, we can get a market to function under this informational handicap, although far from perfectly.

Here is a real-life example of partial market success. The Ford Pinto, made by Ford Motor Company, was known to have a lot of problems, chief among them a gas tank that has a tendency to explode in an accident. However, despite all these problems, Ford continued to sell tens of thousands of Pintos each year to willing buyers. The reason people bought Pintos is that only a few Pintos manifested the problems, so that the probability of buying a bad Pinto was quite low. At the same time the Pinto was priced attractively, so $V - p$ was large when buying a good Pinto. The overall expected payoff then for a willing buyer was positive. Notice that this argument depends on risk neutrality; risk-averse drivers would be much less likely to buy such a vehicle.

One slight change to a parameter value gives an entirely different sequential equilibrium—indeed, the best of all possible outcomes. Suppose that the cost of fixing up a bad item to make it presentable is prohibitive:

$$c > p$$

Even if you go to the trouble of fixing up the item and selling it, you still lose money. This is not an attractive proposition, considering that a seller can always withdraw from the market at no cost. Consider the following strategies and belief:

1's strategy: Offer the item if it is good; stop if the item is bad.

2's strategy: Buy whatever is offered.

2's belief: prob(node g|offer) = 1; prob(node b|offer) = 0

We will now see that this is a sequential equilibrium.

First, note that the probability distribution over the nodes of the buyer's information set follows from the initial chance move and the strategy of the buyer (see Figure 10.4). The probability that an item is good, given that it has been offered, is the probability that chance picks a good item times the probability that a buyer offers the item for sale, given that it is good:

$$p(\text{good}|\text{offer}) = p(\text{good})p(\text{offer}|\text{good})/p(\text{offer}) = p(\text{good})$$

Similarly, the probability that an item is bad, given that it has been offered, is

$$p(\text{bad}|\text{offer}) = p(\text{bad})p(\text{offer}|\text{bad})/p(\text{offer}) = p(\text{bad})$$

FIGURE 10.4 **COMPLETE MARKET SUCCESS: REACHING PLAYER 2'S INFORMATION SET**

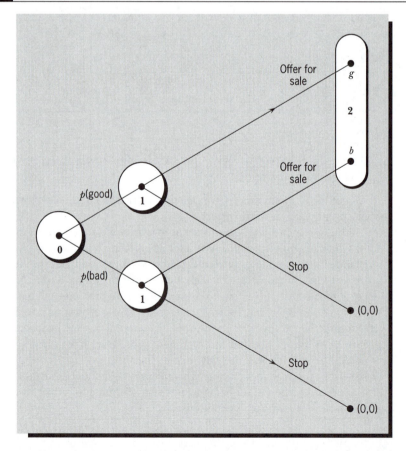

Given that an offer has been made, the probability that play has reached the node g is

$$p(\text{node } g|\text{offer}) = p(\text{good}|\text{offer})/[p(\text{good}|\text{offer}) + p(\text{bad}|\text{offer})]$$
$$= p(\text{good})/[p(\text{good}) + 0] = 1$$

Likewise, the probability that play has reached the node b, given an offer, is 0.

Now that we have a probability distribution over the nodes of player 2's information set, we can start a backward induction argument. If player 2 buys, he can expect the following utility:

$$Eu_2 = p(\text{node } g|\text{offer})(V - p) + p(\text{node } b|\text{offer})(W - p)$$
$$= (1)(V - p) + 0(W - p) > 0$$

so player 2 maximizes utility by buying. Now, using backward induction, we can replace the information set of the buyer with its observable consequences (see Figure 10.5). The seller with a good item clearly maximizes utility by offering the item for sale, since

$$p > 0$$

At this point, this is an ordinary backward induction conclusion. Likewise, the seller with a bad item maximizes utility by not offering that item for sale, since

$$p - c < 0$$

FIGURE 10.5 COMPLETE MARKET SUCCESS: BACKWARD INDUCTION, PLAYER 1'S MOVE

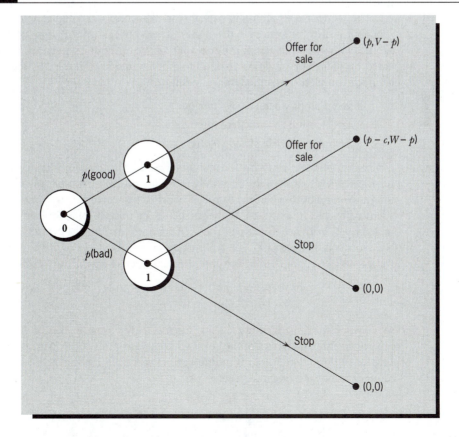

We have now backward induced all the way to the beginning of the game. Since we encountered no contradictions along the way, we have verified that the strategies and belief we started out with constitute a sequential equilibrium.

We have just found conditions that guarantee that complete market success is achieved by a sequential equilibrium of the signaling game. What we need is the following:

$p < c$ (this gives bad-type sellers an incentive not to sell)

This equation indicates that under the right conditions, we can get a market to function perfectly—to maximize gains from trade—even under this informational handicap. Complete market success is the first instance we have seen of an informative game equilibrium. The reason this sequential equilibrium is informative is that buyers, once they see an item offered for sale, know that it is good.

Here's a real-life example of complete market success. According to new rules passed by the Securities and Exchange Commission (SEC) and the U.S. Congress in the summer of 2002, CEOs and CFOs of large publicly traded corporations must publicly swear to the accuracy of their firms' financial statements. If firms so sworn later on are caught having deceived the public, à la Enron, then the CEOs and CFOs can be charged with felonies, punishable by up to 10 years in prison. This makes clean-up cost c extremely high relative to p. In addition, the accounting profession already has the example of bankrupt Arthur Andersen as a reminder of the risks inherent in providing clean-up services to clients. This rule change makes complete market success, in so far as such firms' stocks are concerned, much more likely.

The sequential equilibria in partial market success and complete market success used probability distributions over the nodes of the buyer's information set based on given probabilities and strategies. It can happen that the belief in a sequential equilibrium is not based on data. This situation underlies complete market failure. The sequential equilibrium for complete market failure is the following:

Player 1 stops whatever the item is.

Player 2 says no to any item offered.

$p(\text{node } g|\text{offer}) = 0$; $p(\text{node } b|\text{offer}) = 1$

Notice that the buyer's information set is never reached by this pair of strategies, since the seller never offers the item for sale. Thus the probability distribution over the nodes of the buyer's information is not based on any data. The belief at this sequential equilibrium is the most pessimistic possible. It says that if the seller should, by mistake, offer an item for sale, that item must be bad. With beliefs this pessimistic, it is no wonder that the market breaks down.

Now that we have a probability distribution over the nodes of player 2's information set, we can start a backward induction argument. If player 2 buys, he expects the following utility:

$$Eu_2 = p(\text{node } g|\text{offer})(V - p) + p(\text{node } b|\text{offer})(W - p)$$
$$= (0)(V - p) + 1(W - p) < 0$$

so player 2 maximizes utility by not buying. Now, using backward induction, we can replace the information set of the buyer with its observable consequences (see Figure 10.6). The seller with a good item is indifferent between offering the item for sale (where it is refused) or not offering it for sale:

$$0 = 0$$

FIGURE 10.6 **COMPLETE MARKET FAILURE: BACKWARD INDUCTION, PLAYER 1'S MOVE**

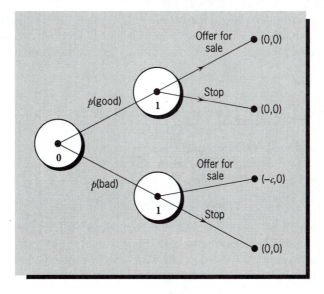

The seller with a bad item prefers not to offer it for sale:

$$-c < 0$$

We have now backward induced all the way to the beginning of the game. Since we encountered no contradictions along the way, we have verified that the strategies and belief we started out with constitute a sequential equilibrium.

At this sequential equilibrium, the market fails completely—nothing bought, nothing gained. We get an especially unfortunate type of pooling behavior on the part of sellers, as both withhold their products from the market. No gains from trade are realized, even though there is potential for such gains. Finally, this sequential equilibrium exists for all possible parameter constellations—a consequence of the fact that the belief crucial to it is not based on any data.[3]

Examples of Complete Market Failure are rare, but real in their implications. In macroeconomics, we refer to so-called **sunspot equilibria** where expectations not based on fundamentals can drive an outcome. A stock market mania is an example of a sunspot equilibrium. To see the connection, let's extend the concept of Complete Market Failure to include any market that fails to inform agents correctly about underlying value, either due to absence of transactions (as in the example just given) or because transactions take place at a highly inflated value. During the NASDAQ climb from 1000 points in 1995 to over 5000 points in March of 2000, the typical stock price rose by 400 percent. During that time, the economy (and corporate profits, to which a share of stock entitles the owner) grew by about 10 percent. As shown convincingly by economist Robert Shiller in his book, *Irrational Exuberance*, these stock prices were inflated beyond anything ever seen in U.S. history, and had to come back down. And come back down they have, to a level of 1300

---

[3] This sequential equilibrium ought to strike you as somehow bizarre. The strategy for player 1 (stop if good, stop if bad) is weakly dominated by the strategy (offer for sale if good, stop if bad).

points as of writing this (2002). The NASDAQ completely failed to inform investors about underlying value at the height of the mania.

We have just seen how partial market success, complete market success, and complete market failure can arise as pure strategy sequential equilibria of Caveat Emptor. The next section shows how near market failure can arise as a mixed strategy sequential equilibrium of Caveat Emptor.

■ 10.3 SEQUENTIAL EQUILIBRIUM: MIXED STRATEGIES

To show how near market failure can arise as a sequential equilibrium, two conditions have to be met. First, $p > c$, so that bad-type sellers have an incentive to offer their items for sale. Second, if buyers buy everything offered for sale, they lose:

$$Eu_2 = p(\text{good})(V - p) + p(\text{bad})(W - p) < 0$$

In this situation, buyers would refuse to buy. Then sellers with bad items would lose out. Mixed strategies provide the only way out of this situation.

The following example will help make clear what is going on. Suppose that this is a used-car market, and good and bad used cars are equally likely:

$$p(\text{good}) = p(\text{bad}) = .5$$

A good used car is worth \$3,000 to a buyer, whereas a bad used car is worthless to the buyer. The sticker price on all used cars is \$2,000:

$$\$3,000 = V > p = \$2,000 > 0 = W$$

It costs \$1,000 to clean up a bad used car. Notice that

$$c/p = 1000/2000 = 0.5$$

and that

$$p(\text{good})(V - p) + p(\text{bad})(W - p) = .5(1000) + .5(-2000) < 0$$

so we satisfy the regime inequalities. The version of Caveat Emptor that results is shown in Figure 10.7.

The following is a sequential equilibrium for Caveat Emptor with these payoff parameters:

1's strategy: Offer for sale if the used car is good; offer for sale with probability .5 if the used car is bad.

2's strategy: Buy the used car offered with probability .5.

$$p(\text{node } g|\text{offer}) = 2/3$$
$$p(\text{node } b|\text{offer}) = 1/3$$

Note first that the probability distribution over the nodes of player 2's information set follows from the strategies and probabilities. With probability .5, an item is good and is offered for sale, so node g is reached with probability .5. With probability .5, an item is bad,

FIGURE 10.7 **CAVEAT EMPTOR, NEAR MARKET FAILURE**

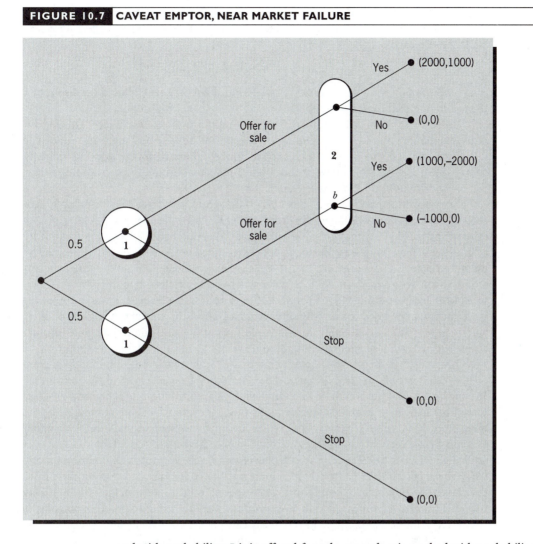

and with probability .5 it is offered for sale, so node g is reached with probability .25. The resulting conditional probability distribution is this belief.

Now we check that the buyer is indifferent about buying or not buying. With these probabilities, the expected value of buying is

$$Eu_2(\text{buy}|\text{offer}) = p(\text{node }g|\text{offer})(1000) + p(\text{node }b|\text{offer})(-2000) = 2/3(1000) + 1/3(-2000) = 0$$

the same payoff as for not buying. So the buyer passes the test for a mixed strategy equilibrium.

Next consider the seller with a good used car. If buyers buy with probability .5, then this seller expects

$$Eu_1(\text{offer}|\text{good}) = .5(2000) + .5(0) = 1000 > 0$$

The seller with a good used car maximizes utility by offering the car for sale. Finally, consider the seller with a bad used car. If this seller cleans up the used car and offers it for sale, he or she expects

$$Eu_1(\text{offer}|\text{bad}) = .5(1000) + .5(-1000) = 0$$

the same as not offering the used car for sale. Thus the seller of a bad used car also passes the test for a mixed strategy equilibrium.

We have just verified the sequential equilibrium for near market failure. This market is not functioning very well at all. Bad-type sellers and all buyers break even, and good-type sellers sell only half the time. Only complete market failure performs worse in terms of gains from trade than this mixed strategy sequential equilibrium. Imperfect information can really drive market performance down.

Do real-world markets ever work this badly? Think of player 1 as bringing a loan request to a lender, player 2. Lots of loan applicants are bad, in that they will fail to pay back interest and principal. Although some bad "apples" don't bother to apply for a loan, plenty of others do. Then there are good loan applicants—good because they will pay back interest and principal. The market for loans works when good loan applicants apply for loans and the loans are granted: such a loan made will benefit both lender and lendee. A lender, faced with both good and bad loan applicants, has a hard time telling them apart. A lender who can't separate good loan applicants from bad, winds up turning down lots of good loan requests. This phenomenon is called **credit rationing,** and you've just gone through main steps of the classic model of Stiglitz and Weiss.[4]

To sum up our discussion of Caveat Emptor, let's look at its complete solution in Figure 10.8, which is called a **regime diagram.** The crucial supply-side feature of the market, the cleanup post, c, is plotted on the x-axis. On the y-axis is plotted the crucial demand-side feature of the market—the expected value to the buyer if everything is offered and he or she buys: $p(\text{good})(V - p) + p(\text{bad})(W - p)$. There are three zones, or regimes, in the diagram. When $p < c$, we get complete market success. Only good types are offered for sale, and they are bought. This is the regime in which play is completely informative: you know exactly what type of good a seller has to sell the minute it is offered for sale (good) or withheld from the market (bad). When $p > c$ and the buyer's expected value is positive, then we get partial market success. Everything, good or bad, is offered for sale and bought. This outcome is completely uninformative: the good and the bad are pooled together. Finally, when $c < p$ and the expected value of buying everything is negative, we get near market failure. Both buyers and bad-type sellers adopt mixed strategies in order to survive this buyer-beware world.

Now that we have completely solved the basic signaling game, we are ready to take on the market for lemons. Lemons markets tell us the extent to which prices can signal quality when information is imperfect.

■ 10.4 THE MARKET FOR LEMONS

The price of a good or service is often thought to convey information about its quality. In Caveat Emptor, everything is sold at the same price, and so price could not possibly convey

[4] The classic paper is J. E. Stiglitz and A. W. Weiss, "Credit Rationing in Markets with Imperfect Information," *American Economic Review* 71 (1981): 393–410. Also worth reading is Stiglitz's Nobel award speech, "Information and the Change in the Paradigm in Economics," *American Economic Review* 92 (2002) 460–501.

FIGURE 10.8 CAVEAT EMPTOR, REGIME DIAGRAM

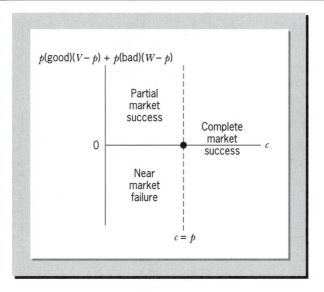

information.[5] Let's now relax this assumption and look for conditions under which price does reveal information about quality at a sequential equilibrium.

The game used to model this problem, called Lemons, is shown in Figure 10.9. There is a random move that determines the quality of the item in question (good or bad). Player 1, the seller, knows the quality and offers the items for sale, either at a high price, p, or at a low price, q. Player 2, the buyer, does not know the quality but does observe the price offered, high or low. The buyer says yes or no to the seller's offer. A good item (V) is worth more than a bad item (W) to the buyer. Even at a high price, buying the good item is better than buying the bad item at the low price; buying the bad item at a high price results in a loss:

$$V - q > V - p > W - q > 0 > W - p$$

Finally, the seller of a bad item must pay a cleanup cost, c, so that the item looks good. Otherwise, the seller can offer it for sale as is.

Lemons have the potential for price to signal quality. What is required is for the seller of a good item to charge a high price and for the seller of a bad item to charge a low price. Then price signals quality to the buyer: the buyer is getting exactly what he or she is paying for. The condition needed here is the same as that needed for Caveat Emptor: $c > p$. If it costs more to fix up a bad item and make it look good than it will return in sales, even at a high price, then it doesn't pay to clean it up at all. You can check (end-of-chapter problem) that the following is a sequential equilibrium when $c > p$:

1's strategy: Charge a high price with a good item; charge a low price with a bad item.

2's strategy: Buy any item offered for sale.

[5] This material has been inspired by Nobel laureate George Akerlof's classic article, "The Market for Lemons: Quality Uncertainty and the Market Mechanism," *Quarterly Journal of Economics* 89 (1970): 488–500. Also worth reading is Akerlof's Nobel award speech, "Behavioral Macroeconomics and Macroeconomic Behavior," *American Economic Review* 92 (2002): 411–433. You will see that economists have dreams, too.

FIGURE 10.9 LEMONS

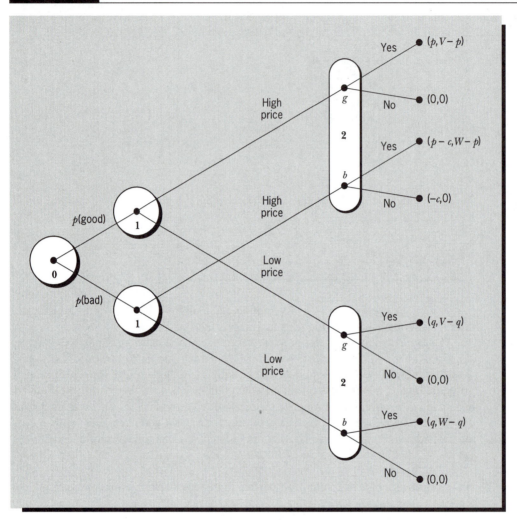

2's belief: p(node g|high price) = 1; p(node b|low price) = 1

In this case, thanks to the separating sequential equilibrium, Lemons has a complete market success solution.

Unfortunately, under other conditions, Lemons can have a complete market failure solution. Take the extreme case, where $c = 0$. A bad item can mimic a good item for free. A good item cannot be identified by putting a high price on it: a high price can be put on a bad item just as well. This situation dooms a separating sequential equilibrium and its attendant market success. Suppose that all good items are priced at p and all bad items at q. Buyers buy every item offered. This is not an equilibrium. A seller of a bad item can put a high price on it and sell it at a bigger gain: $p > q$. What one seller of a bad item can do, so can another. Price no longer signals quality. Even worse, suppose that the buyer's expected value if sellers pool at either high prices or low prices is negative:

$$Eu_2(\text{buy|high price}) = p(\text{good})(V - p) + p(\text{bad})(W - p) < 0$$

and

$$Eu_2(\text{buy|low price}) = p(\text{good})(V - q) + p(\text{bad})(W - q) < 0$$

In the very worst sequential equilibrium, the market breaks down completely:

1's strategy: Charge a high (or a low) price, good item or bad.

2's strategy: Do not buy at either price.

2's belief: $p(\text{node } g|\text{low price}) = p(\text{good})$; $p(\text{node } g|\text{high price}) = p(\text{good})$

The last belief, $p(\text{node } g|\text{high price}) = p(\text{good})$, is not pessimistic at all. The buyer believes that the probability of the sellers of either type asking a high price is the same as their frequency in the population. And at those odds, it doesn't pay to buy. Here is a reasonable sequential equilibrium for which no sales take place, and the market ceases to function. This is dubbed, after Akerlof, the **lemons principle:** the bad drives everything out of the market. The lemons principle is adverse selection with a vengeance.

In some markets that are especially information sensitive, the lemons principle is a major social problem. Take the market for initial public offerings (IPOs) of stock in firms. During the stock market boom of 1996–99, IPOs were extremely popular with investors, with some first-day closing prices several multiples of the initial asking price. However, the historic data on IPOs shows that the value of 90 percent of all IPOs are below the initial asking price, six months after the initial offer. Investors during the boom, ignoring the probability of a bad IPO, paid the price during the market correction of 2000–01, as most IPOs came back down to Earth, well below the initial offering price. This correction of asset values led to a complete drying up of the market for IPOs during the second half of 2001— a classic lemons market outcome. There were just too many lemons in the IPO market, and the only way for rational investors—some of whom had acquired their rationality the hard way, by losing lots of money—to play that market was to avoid it altogether for a while. Even IPOs with strong fundamentals could not be launched.

Other markets where economists have documented a lemons problem include used trucks, used business aircraft, wholesale used cars, and thoroughbreds.[6] This list shows just how pervasive a problem adverse selection is.

◼ 10.5 Costly Commitment as a Signaling Device

A powerful device for signaling purposes is to commit oneself to a considerable cost at the beginning of a game. For example, a man wants to marry a woman and gives her an

---

[6] For pickup trucks, see Eric W. Bond, "A Direct Test of the Lemons Model: The Market for Pickup Trucks," *American Economic Review* 72 (1982): 836–840; for business aircraft, Thomas W. Gillegan, "Adverse Selection and Trade in Used Durable Goods: Evidence from the Market for Business Aircraft," University of Southern California, working paper, 2002 <www-rcf.usc.edu/~gilligan.PVFJ>; for used cars, David Genesove, "Adverse Selection in the Wholesale Used Car Market," *Journal of Political Economy* 101 (1993): 644–665; and for thoroughbreds, Brian Chezum and Bradley S. Wimmer, "Adverse Selection in the Market for Thoroughbred Yearlings," *Review of Economics and Statistics* 79 (1997): 521–526.

engagement ring. This is a costly commitment. If he should later decide to dump her, it's going to cost him the ring—which she is entitled to keep, or better still, liquidate, and enjoy the money. As another example, a couple wants to buy a house. They put down $5,000 earnest money, which they forfeit if they do not go through with the transaction. This is a costly commitment—they will walk away from this deal only at great expense to themselves. The best kind of signal is a credible signal, and costly commitment is the best kind of credibility money can buy. This is called the principle of **costly commitment.**

Here is a game that illustrates how the principle of costly commitment works in a situation that would otherwise fall prey to the lemons principle. This game is called **Money-Back Guarantee** (Figure 10.10). Money-Back Guarantee is just like Lemons with $c = 0$, so every seller would charge the high price. There is one difference to payoffs, though. Along with charging a high price, there is a standard money-back guarantee in this market. If a buyer does not get high quality (V) when he or she pays a high price (p), the seller will pay the buyer the sum ($V - W$) to difference. This is a very costly commitment if you are selling bad stuff. The guarantee assures the buyer of the payoff $V - p$ no matter what is bought. If the buyer buys from a good source, that's fine. If the buyer buys from a bad source, the bad-type seller forks over an additional ($V - W$) to the unlucky buyer. . The money-back guarantee creates a sure-thing situation for the buyer.

If the money-back guarantee is costly enough; in particular, if

$$p + W - V < 0$$

then there is a sequential equilibrium leading to complete market success:

> 1's strategy: Charge a high price with a good item; charge a low price with a bad item.
>
> 2's strategy: Say yes to a high price; say no to a low price.
>
> 2's beliefs: p(node g\high price) = 1; p(node g|low price) = 0

A seller with a good item has a dominant strategy to charge a high price, and the buyer has a dominant strategy to say yes to a high price. Once these two strategies are in place, the rest of the sequential equilibrium follows immediately. The discovery on the part of mass retailers in the United States during the twentieth century of the money-back guarantee revolutionized the entire retailing industry. Sellers of good items have nothing to fear from sellers of bad items: the money-back guarantee protects them (and buyers) from lemons.

Here is an outline of another example of costly commitment. You should be able to fill in the details. In Telex vs. IBM, it makes a big difference to Telex whether IBM is mean or not. Suppose that the game begins with a random move that assigns a type to IBM. Although IBM does not get to set its price until the end of the game, it can send a costly signal after learning its type. In particular, IBM can create a large amount of capacity, incurring a large fixed cost—capacity it will need only in the event that it wants to smash Telex. Depending on the details of the game, you can construct sequential equilibria whereby mean IBM creates large capacity, whereas nice IBM does not. You can also construct sequential equilibria whereby both types of IBM create large capacity. In the latter case, nice IBM is bluffing, and gets away with it.

The principle of costly commitment also applies to international relations. During Operation Desert Storm, the United Nations put 500,000 men and women into Arabia to signal to Iraq that United Nations resolve should be believed. This commitment cost $50 billion. For reasons known only to Baghdad, this signal was not believed.

FIGURE 10.10 MONEY-BACK GUARANTEE

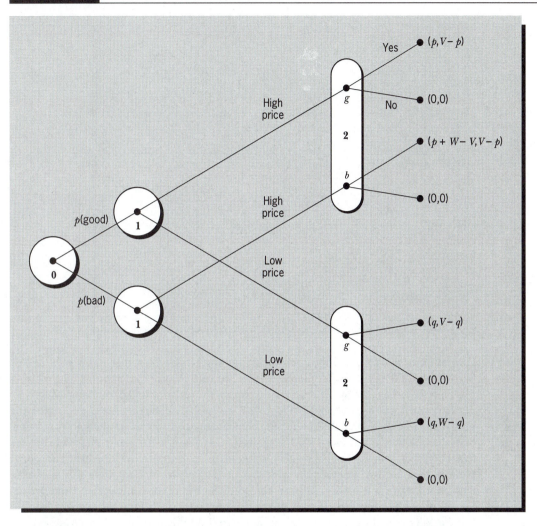

◼ 10.6 SCREENING GAMES

So far, we have looked at signaling games, where the informed player goes first. Now let's switch to screening games, where the uninformed player goes first. One of the prime markets where screening takes place is insurance. When an insurance company offers an insurance contract to a potential buyer, it doesn't know everything about that potential buyer. The buyer may be a good risk, in which case the insurance company will make money if it insures the buyer; the buyer may be a bad risk, in which case the insurance company will lose money if it insures the buyer. This setup applies to all kinds of insurance: life, health, automobile, and fire, to name just four kinds.

Figure 10.11 shows the screening game that arises in insurance. The insurance company, player 1, moves first. The insurance company has two strategies, Offer a Contract or

FIGURE 10.11 SCREENING GAME

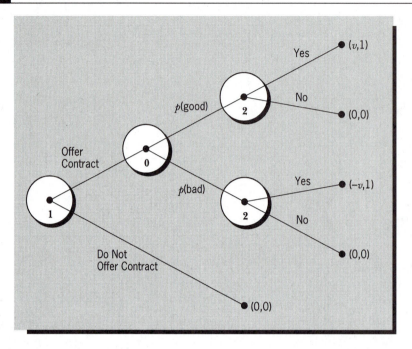

Do Not Offer a Contract. In the latter event, the game ends with status quo payoffs of 0 to both players. If the insurance company offers a contract, then a random move takes place—this represents the fact that the insurance company moves prior to the revelation of important information. With probability $p(good)$, the potential buyer is a good risk; with probability $p(bad)$, a bad risk. Player 2, the potential buyer, is informed, and knows whether he is a good risk or a bad risk. Using this information, Player 2 has two strategies, to say Yes to the contract or to say No. If a good risk says Yes to the contract, then the insurance company makes a profit V and the good risk also gains a positive amount, here 1. In this case, insurance creates a win-win situation for both the insurance company and the person being insured. If a bad risk says Yes to the contract, then the insurance company loses V, but the bad risk still gains a positive amount, here 1. In this case, insurance creates a lose-win situation: the company loses, but the person being insured wins.

This screening game is simple enough that we can use backward induction to solve it. First, note that both types of buyer say Yes to the insurance contract, since $1 > 0$ for each. This means that if a contract is offered, it is accepted by both risk types. The insurance company expects the value

$$EV_1 = p(\text{good})V + p(\text{bad})(-V) = V[p(\text{good}) - p(\text{bad})]$$

from offering the contract. If the preceding expected value is positive, which occurs when

$$p(\text{good}) > p(\text{bad})$$

then the insurance company prefers to offer the contract. If the expected value is negative, which occurs when

$$p(\text{good}) < p(\text{bad})$$

then the insurance company prefers not to offer the contract. In the former case, we see a pooling equilibrium with partial market success: all companies Offer a Contract, and all buyers say Yes. In the latter case, we see complete market failure: no company Offers a Contract, and all buyers say No. So the screening game shares some, but not all, of the same outcomes as the signaling game we studied earlier.

To get complete market success, if it is attainable at all, in a screening game, we need a lot more complexity. We will sketch what it takes here, but suppress all the mathematical details. First, the insurance company, player 1, needs to have more than a single, standard contract to offer. Indeed, what the insurance company needs is a menu of contracts. Suppose the insurance company has two contracts, I and II, and four pure strategies:

> Offer both contract I and contract II.
>
> Offer contract I only.
>
> Offer contract II only.
>
> Offer neither contract.

This replaces the first move in Figure 10.11 with 4 branches instead of 2. Next, make the two contracts very different. Contract I has a low premium and a large deductible: this contract is designed to appeal to the good-risk player 2, who almost never has an accident anyway. Contract II has a high premium but a small deductible: this contract is designed to appeal to the bad-risk player 2, who is quite likely to have an accident. Even a "fender-bender" nowadays will cause several thousand dollars of damage to a late-model car, way beyond a $500 deductible. If all the payoff details work out just right, then the following is a subgame perfect equilibrium:

> Player 1: Offer both contracts.
>
> Player 2, if good risk: Say Yes to contract I, no to contract II.
>
> Player 2, if bad risk: Say No to contract I, yes to contract II.

As with signaling games, however, such a separating equilibrium may fail to exist, depending on the payoff parameter values and the underlying type probabilities. This was just one of the insights that helped Joseph Stiglitz win the Nobel Prize in 2001.

◼ 10.7 BARBARIANS AT THE GATE: SIGNALING AND SCREENING IN THE SAME EVENT

RJR Nabisco, one of the 20 largest companies in the United States, was formed by the merger of Reynolds Tobacco (RJR, a company we saw in chapters 3 and 5) and the National Biscuit Company (Nabisco, maker of Oreos and other food products).[7] In the fall of 1988, RJR Nabisco stock was trading in the low $50s. CEO Ross Johnson, thinking the stock undervalued, formed a plan to take the company private in a financial maneuver called a **leveraged buyout** (LBO). In an LBO, someone—here the management—borrows a lot of money, enough to buy up all the shares of the company. The buyer then breaks up the company and sells off the pieces. If all goes well, the management makes a ton of money in the process.

---

[7] This material was inspired by B. Burrough and J. Heylar, *Barbarians at the Gate: The Fall of RJR Nabisco* (New York: Harper & Row, 1991). Also see Randall Smith, "Biggest Buyout Ever Finishes as Flop for KKR and Dozens of Large Investors," *Wall Street Journal*, 6 March 1995.

Anyone, not just the top management, can try to pull off an LBO. However, the top management has information an outsider does not. This creates an adverse selection problem for an outsider. As Burrough and Heylar put it, "In one way, an LBO is a lot like buying a used car. A target company's annual report and public filings can be compared to a classified ad. Like an advertisement, they contain useful information, although a savvy buyer knows that the numbers can convey anything a clever accountant needs them to."[8] The analogue to a used-car buyer inspecting the car—"kicking the tires"—in an LBO is called **due diligence.** During due diligence, a potential buyer in an LBO gets access to company insiders, questions them, and examines their financial records. This process, which usually lasts only a few days, generates a very noisy signal, especially when lawyers for the management group are present for most of the interviews, as they were in this case.

The RJR Nabisco management group commissioned a top-secret report on the value of the firm. Entitled "Corporate Strategy Update," and dated September 29, 1988, the report estimated the value of RJR Nabisco stock at between $82/share and $111/share. That's another noisy signal, but it is available only to CEO Johnson and his management team. With 230 million shares outstanding, this signals a value of the firm between $18.9 billion and $25.5 billion. Based on this signal, in mid-October Johnson offered to take the company private at $75/share—a $17 billion offer. A deal at this price would make CEO Johnson a billionaire almost overnight, if the noisy signal proved accurate.

In addition to the Johnson group, three other groups were interested in a buyout of RJR Nabisco: Kohlberg Kravis Roberts (KKR), Forstmann Little, and First Boston. Two of these, KKR and Forstmann Little, performed due diligence, based on which they came in with much higher bids: Forstmann Little at $85/share and KKR at $90/share. This was all the NYSE needed for investors to start believing an LBO was really going to happen, and the stock market price headed north to $90.

Now it was time for some screening by the board of directors of RJR Nabisco, which was legally empowered to make any decision as to who the LBO buyer would be. First, the board set an end-of-November deadline for bids. The board then turned the situation into a screening game, where the active bidders had to move first—without knowing how the board would decide its bids. Hoping to be the high bidder, the Johnson group raised its bid to $100/share just before the deadline. This bid was supposed to be held in secret by the board; however, there was enough information available for the outside bidders to realize the bidding was reaching very high levels. When, thanks to a leak, Forstmann Little learned the high bid really was $100, it dropped out of the bidding. At the same time, KKR raised its bid to $94/share. With less than 48 hours left to go before the deadline, First Boston jumped into the bidding at $105/share. Since First Boston had never performed due diligence, it was truly bidding in the dark.

The bidding was over, and the RJR Nabisco board of directors was perplexed. It had three very high bids, all of which were hard to compare. Cash was a tiny component of each, with most of the billions of dollars bid expressed in terms of junk bonds, warrants, and convertible preferred stock. So the board pulled a strategic surprise: it asked each of the final three bidders, "Give us your best offer in 24 hours or less." That move drove the Johnson group to bid $112/share—outside the bounds of its own secret signal of the value of the firm—while KKR upped its bid to $109/share. First Boston didn't budge.

The board of directors chose the KKR bid. At $109/share, KKR was paying (and borrowing) over $25 billion to buy RJR Nabisco, whose shareholders had basically doubled

---

[8] Burrough and Heylar, *Barbarians at the Gate,* 301.

their money in a few weeks' time. This remains to this day the biggest LBO of all time. Unfortunately for KKR, it was too big—the price they paid for RJR Nabisco was too high. When KKR finished selling off its RJR Nabisco holdings 7 years later, the *Wall Street Journal* called the biggest LBO of all time "a resounding flop" for KKR.

◨ 10.8 REPEATED SIGNALING AND TRACK RECORDS

Repeat buying is an important feature in many retail relationships, particularly for durable goods, such as automobiles and appliances. In a one-shot game where the type of the item sold can be clearly verified after purchase, the buyer will soon know whether to break off a retail relationship or not. If the item bought turns out to be a lemon, this indicates that the seller deals in bad items and should be avoided in the future. If the item bought turns out to be good, this indicates that the seller deals in good items and can be patronized in the future. With clear outcomes based on clear signals, then, the judgment whether to continue or terminate a business relationship is immediate. This is not the case, however, with noisy signals. A **noisy signal** contains information about the nature of the underlying type of business, but it also contains statistical noise, which confounds the attempt to determine underlying type.

To make matters concrete, suppose that you are in charge of a law firm and have just hired a young lawyer named Kane. Lawyer Kane has yet to try a case, but you know from experience that two kinds of lawyers get through your screening process. A star performer wins 90 percent of cases. In terms of probabilities, the probability that a star will win a case, $p(\text{win}|\text{star})$, is .9. An ordinary performer wins 50 percent of cases. The probability that an ordinary performer will win a case, $p(\text{win}|\text{ordinary})$, is only .5. You never hire lawyers worse than this. A star performer stochastically dominates an ordinary performer, and you would like to sign nothing but stars to long-term contracts.[9] Based only on what you know before lawyer Kane tries a single case, you think it equally likely that this person is a star performer or an ordinary performer. In terms of probabilities, this means:

$$p(\text{star}) = p(\text{ordinary}) = .5$$

You are faced with a decision. Ultimately, you have to decide whether to make this person a partner in the firm or let Kane go. And you have to make this decision under conditions of imperfect information.

To make this a full-fledged decision problem, we need to attach payoffs to decisions. Suppose that making a lawyer a partner in the firm means that the lawyer will be trying cases forever, and that your discount factor is .95 (corresponding to a 5 percent interest rate). Normalize utility so that $u(\text{win}) = 1$, and $u(\text{loss}) = 0$. Then, if you make a star performer a partner, you expect the value

$$EV = \sum (.95)t\,[.9(1) + .1(0)] = .9/(1 - .95) = 18$$

using the formula for infinitely repeated games from chapter 8. If, on the other hand, you make an ordinary performer a partner, you expect the value

$$EV = \sum (.95)t\,[.5(1) + .5(0)] = .5/(1 - .95) = 10$$

---

[9] This game assumes that the performance of a lawyer is determined solely by type, and not by effort. The next chapter looks at how to provide incentives for more effort through contractual clauses.

The lifetime consequence of making an ordinary performer a partner is a loss of almost 45 percent (8/18, to be exact), compared to making a star a partner.

You could make your decision on the basis of no data whatsoever—you could make someone a partner who has never tried a single case. That would be irresponsible, and no one with a sound mind would do that. What you do is give the new hire a **probationary period** instead. During the probationary period, the new hire builds a track record. The decision whether to make the person a partner or not depends on this track record.

During a probationary period, and afterward throughout a career, a person is judged on his or her track record. How many successes has the person had? What has the employee done for the company? This principle is called the **track-record principle.** A sequential equilibrium judges people by their track records. The better the track record, the more likely a person is to be judged as a good type and hence to enter a long-term relationship.

The biggest decision from a game theory standpoint is how long the probationary period should be—how much time new employees should have to prove themselves. For simplicity, we consider the shortest possible probationary period, one period long. The game One-Period Probation is shown in Figure 10.12. A random move at the beginning determines lawyer Kane's type; either type is equally likely. Lawyer Kane knows what the type is, but has no way to reveal this to you. (Why not? See end-of-chapter problem 8.) A second random move determines the outcome of lawyer Kane's first trial. This trial constitutes Kane's probationary period. You, as player 1, observe the outcome of the trial, win or lose. Your decision is whether to make Kane a partner or let Kane go. Kane automatically accepts all offers. If you let Kane go, then you have a vacancy for one period (utility = 0), and then get the expected value of what the market has to offer, $EV = [.5(18 - 1) + .5(10 - 1)] = 13$. We subtract 1 in this calculation, because that's the opportunity cost of a win at trial, and if you don't have a lawyer hired, you won't win.

You are going to make a decision based on what you see. Let's consider the four possible decisions, since here your strategy is the kind of decision you use:

I. *Yes no matter what.* This unconditional strategy has $EV = .5(18) + .5(10) = 14$.

II. *Yes if a win, No if a loss.*

Evaluating this conditional strategy requires Bayes's rule again. What you want to know is the probability that you've hired a star, given that the case was won, $p(\text{star}|\text{win})$. From Bayes's rule, we have

$$p(\text{star}|\text{win}) = p(\text{star})p(\text{win}|\text{star})/p(\text{win})$$

where

$$p(\text{win}) = p(\text{star})p(\text{win}|\text{star}) + p(\text{ordinary})p(\text{win}|\text{ordinary})$$

Substituting into this formula $p(\text{win}|\text{star}) = .9$; $p(\text{win}|\text{ordinary}) = .5$; and $p(\text{star}) = p(\text{ordinary}) = .5$;

$$p(\text{star}|\text{win}) = .45/.70 = 9/14, \text{ or } 64\%$$

If you see a win, you upgrade the probability that Kane is a star from 50 percent to 64 percent. Kane's stock just went up in your eyes, as well it should. Bayesian updating is the mathematical foundation of the track-record principle. On the other hand, the probability that you've hired an ordinary performer, who just happened to get lucky, $p(\text{ordinary}|\text{win})$, is given by

$$p(\text{ordinary}|\text{win}) = 1 - p(\text{star}|\text{win}) = 1 - 9/14 = 5/14 = 36\%$$

FIGURE 10.12 **ONE-PERIOD PROBATION**

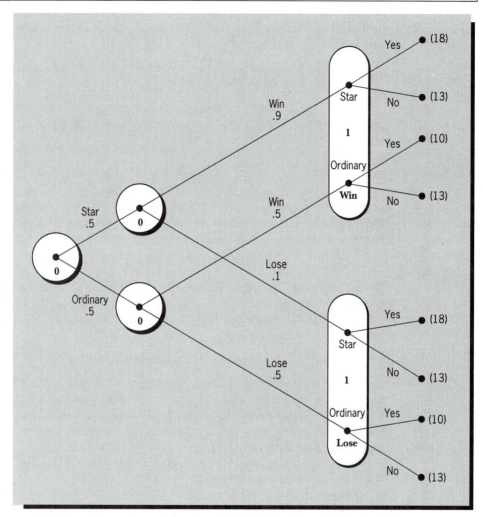

The probability that Kane is ordinary goes down when you observe a win, because stars produce wins much more often than ordinary performers do. This completes the calculations for what you do when you observe a win.

We next consider what you do when you observe a loss. Once again, we compute the probability that you are looking at a star who just got unlucky, $p(\text{star}|\text{loss})$. From Bayes's rule, we have

$$p(\text{star}|\text{loss}) = p(\text{star})p(\text{loss}|\text{star})/p(\text{loss})$$

where

$$p(\text{loss}) = p(\text{star})p(\text{loss}|\text{star}) + p(\text{ordinary})p(\text{loss}|\text{ordinary})$$

Substituting into Bayes's rule the information $p(\text{loss}|\text{star}) = .1$; $p(\text{loss}|\text{ordinary}) = .5$; and $p(\text{star}) = p(\text{ordinary}) = .5$;

$$p(\text{star}|\text{loss}) = .5(.1)/(.05 + .25) = 1/6, \text{ or } 17\%$$

The odds that your loss was produced by a star are rather small—only 1 chance in 6. By the same token, the odds that your loss was produced by an ordinary performer, $p(\text{ordinary}|\text{loss})$, are

$$p(\text{ordinary}|\text{loss}) = 1 - p(\text{star}|\text{loss}) = 1 - 1/6 = 5/6, \text{ or } 83\%$$

The odds are that the loss came from an ordinary performer.

Armed with all these probabilities, we can now compute the expected value of the strategy Yes if a win, No if a loss. A win occurs with probability .7. This follows from

$$p(\text{win}) = p(\text{win}|\text{star})p(\text{star}) + p(\text{win}|\text{ordinary})p(\text{ordinary})$$
$$= (.9)(.5) + (.5)(.5) = .7$$

When a win occurs, the decision is yes. In the event of a win, the probability is 9/14 that Kane is a star and therefore worth 18; the probability is 5/14 that Kane is ordinary and therefore worth 10. A loss occurs with probability .3. When a loss occurs, the decision is no. Here the payoff is 13. Adding this all up, we get

$$EV = .7[(9/14)(18) + 5/14(10)] + .3(13) = 14.5$$

Notice that Bayesian updating allows you to make a better decision than simply saying yes no matter what happens.

III. *No if a win, Yes if a loss.* This strategy sounds as bad as it is. Using the same probabilities as for strategy II, we get

$$EV = .7(13) + .3[(1/6)18 + (5/6)10 = 12.5$$

The strategy where you fire somebody the minute that person wins for you gets really low marks. You probably wouldn't want to spend much time working for such an outfit, anyway.

IV. *No, no matter what.* This unconditional strategy pays 13. If you fire everybody after the probation period, then you are always in the market for replacements and you can expect the replacement value.

We have clear rankings of the strategies: II beats I beats IV beats III. The best strategy if you are going to have one period of probation is to make Kane a partner with a win and let Kane go with a loss. This is the track-record principle at work.

There is an obvious problem with probationary periods this short. The odds of making a mistake are still pretty high. There are two kinds of mistake you can make, even when you use the best strategy. One mistake is to make an ordinary performer a partner. If you use strategy II, you will make this mistake with probability $(.7)(5/14)$. That is, 25 percent of the time you will make someone a partner just because he or she got lucky in court once. In the long run one-quarter of all your partners are going to be ordinary—hardly a star-studded law firm. Another mistake is to let a star performer go. If you use strategy II, you will make this mistake $(.3)(1/6)$ of the time. That is, 5 percent of the time you will let someone go whom you should have kept because that person got really unlucky in court once.

In a world of imperfect information and noisy signals, mistakes are inevitable. The way to cut down on mistakes is to have a **repeated signaling** over a longer probationary period. Relying on the law of large numbers—the same mathematical regularity that makes gaming and entertainment profits of $50 billion a year—will cut down on the number of mistakes. Using a strategy like II—a strategy that sticks with winners and gets rid of losers—will not only pay the best per period but also cut down on mistakes in the long run.

If your university has a football team, then you see this strategy at work with regard to head coaches. Star coaches, like the late Bear Bryant (Alabama) and Joe Paterno (Penn State), win most of their games over a period of decades. But even star coaches lose some games. A university doesn't fire a football coach for losing a single game, but almost any university will fire a football coach after five straight losing seasons.

So far we have looked at situations in which one side to a transaction has had all the information it needed, even if the other side did not. It often happens that even the informed trader has received only a noisy signal, not a perfectly clear one. In such a case, the informed trader has better information than the uninformed trader, even though the information is not perfect. This topic is pursued in the next two chapters, but we already have enough experience with imperfect information to follow the action in one of the biggest flops Hollywood ever made, called Hit and Run.

■ 10.9 HIT AND RUN: TRACK RECORDS IN HOLLYWOOD

Sometimes books aren't made into movies, and you wonder why not. Nancy Griffin and Kim Masters's book, *Hit and Run: How Jon Peters and Peter Gruber Took Sony for a Ride in Hollywood,* is such a case.[10] It contains enough "sex, drugs, and rock 'n' roll" to make a likely hit movie. Until the movie comes out though, it's still an instructive story about the power of track records in Hollywood.

We saw in the previous chapter the success Sony has had with its Sega video games division. In this section, we look at a less glorious page from Sony's recent past. In the early 1990s Sony was flush with cash and looking for investments with strong complementarities to its stereo, record, and video game products. The movie studio Columbia was for sale at a bargain price—its owner, Credit Lyonnais, the second largest bank in France, was going broke and needed to raise cash fast. Thus, Sony found itself with a Hollywood studio, albeit one with a single-digit market share, in a town where it had never operated before: Hollywood.

At the very same time that Sony acquired Columbia, two of the hottest directors in Hollywood were Jon Peters and Peter Gruber, who together had teamed up on such hits as *Flashdance* and *Yentl.* The track-record principle works with a vengeance in Hollywood, home of the saying "What have you done for me lately?" A director team with a string of recent hits is a hot commodity. In a heated bidding war, Sony signed the Peters-Gruber creative duo to a lucrative, multipicture contract.

In the game between Sony and Peters-Gruber, Sony was definitely the uninformed player, moving first. That makes the first piece of a screening game. The second piece is the two types of directors/creative types in Hollywood: one good for the movie studio, the other bad. We'll call the good type Productive; the bad type, Unproductive. Sony's Columbia studio in particular had no way of knowing whether its newly signed creative

---

[10] This material was inspired by Nancy Griffin and Kim Masters, *Hit and Run: How Jon Peters and Peter Gruber Took Sony for a Ride in Hollywood* (New York: Simon & Schuster, 1996).

duo would be productive, continuing their streak of recent hits, or turn to drugs and produce very little if any value.

As Sony's luck would have it, the type Chance drew for Sony was Unproductive, not Productive. During the time Peters-Gruber were under contract, Columbia made 23 pictures (admittedly, not all by Peters-Gruber), not a single one of which made money. This 23-movie losing streak cost Sony/Columbia a cool $3 billion. Considerable evidence suggests that at least one of the Peters-Gruber duo was heavily into drugs, and this was a cause of the disastrous turn in productivity. Whatever the case, Sony ultimately pulled the plug both on Peters-Gruber and on Columbia pictures, terminating the contract of the former and selling the latter.

Playing the role of uninformed player moving first in a screening game, where the downside is very large, can be very costly—especially if one plays that game unstrategically. And playing any market game in a town where hundreds of millions of dollars can be won or lost on a single movie is risky—riskier than playing any casino game.

◼ SUMMARY

1. In a signaling game of imperfect information, one player has a crucial piece of information that the other player does not have. The player with this crucial piece of information is called informed; the player without this crucial piece of information, uninformed.

2. When the informed player moves first, that play may convey information to the uninformed player. This possibility is called signaling.

3. When the uninformed player moves first, the game involves screening. The equilibria of both signaling and screening games may be very inefficient.

4. There are four possible outcomes of the market signaling game Caveat Emptor. Complete market success is separating; complete market failure and partial market success are both pooling; and near market failure is a mixture of separating and pooling.

5. A sequential equilibrium extends the concept of subgame perfection to signaling games. It requires that players make decisions that maximize expected utility on all their information sets. Probability distributions over the nodes of information sets are based on the data and on the strategies of the other players.

6. When complete market success is the solution of a market signaling game, the market equilibrium informs all traders. When partial market success is the solution, the market equilibrium provides no new information. When mixed market success is the solution, the equilibrium provides some information.

7. The lemons principle says that bad quality drives everything out of the market. This can happen as a sequential equilibrium of Lemons.

8. The principle of costly commitment says that a signal gains in credibility when it costs the sender to make the signal. The money-back guarantee is an example of a costly commitment that alleviates the lemons problem.

9. In repeated signaling games, a track record provides information about a player's type. The longer the probationary period, the better the information. Sequential equilibrium uses Bayesian updating of information to implement the best decision strategy. There is a trade-off between the length of the probationary period and the probability of mistaken judgment.

10. Sony's loss of $3 billion in Hollywood suggests the cost of playing a screening game badly.

■ KEY TERMS

signaling game	near market failure	leveraged buyout (LBO)
screening game	sequential equilibrium	due diligence
informed/uninformed player	Bayes's rule	money-back guarantee
asymmetric information	pooling equilibrium	repeated signaling
adverse selection	sunspot equilibrium	noisy signal
complete market failure	credit rationing	probationary period
complete market success	regime diagram	track-record principle
separating equilibrium	lemons principle	
partial market success	costly commitment	

■ PROBLEMS

1. An art dealer has offered you a disputed Rembrandt. Art experts are evenly divided over whether this is an authentic Rembrandt (in which case it is worth $20 million) or the work of a student of Rembrandt's (in which case it is worth $1 million). Set this up as a signaling game and solve it. The price you are being asked is $5 million, and you are risk neutral. It costs $100,000 to get an art critic to authenticate the painting.

2. You are considering a leveraged buyout of Corporation X. The stock of X is worth either $1/share or $5/share. The management of the company knows what it is worth, and is asking $2/share for the 10 thousand shares outstanding. All you know is that the probability that the company is worth $5/share is 50 percent. Should you buy the company at this price? It costs the management $50,000 to cook the books if it has to make the company look better than it really is.

3. Suppose in Caveat Emptor (Figure 10.1) that $p(\text{good}) = p(\text{bad}) = .5$. Give numerical examples of each of the following: complete market success; partial market success; and near market failure.

4. Suppose that in Caveat Emptor, the buyer goes first and has to say yes or no. That makes this a screening game, since the buyer is uninformed. Then it is up to the firm whether it wants to sell to the buyer or not. The seller of a bad type still has to incur the cleanup cost, c, or there is no deal. Draw the extensive form, and then find the sequential equilibrium. Show that there are three regimes.

5. Give three examples of costly commitments that effectively signal company type in business or daily life.

6. Show, using the numerical values $V = \$5,000$, $W = \$1,000$, $p = \$3,000$, $q = \$500$, and a positive c of your choice, what the sequential equilibrium of Lemons (Figure 10.9) is. Is there a lemons problem associated with this equilibrium?

7. In One-Period Probation, find the rankings of the four strategies if the discount factor is .8. What conclusion do you draw from your result?

8. You often hear the advice, "Why not just ask the person?" when you are trying to determine whether someone is a star performer or an ordinary performer. What is wrong, strategically, with asking a person this question and forgetting all about probationary periods? (*Hint:* What does it cost to say the words, "I'm going to be a star"?)

9. In most criminal court cases, a defendant has the opportunity to post bail. If the defendant does not show up for court, then he or she forfeits the bail bond, and in addition is charged

with a new felony, jumping bail. Explain this institution in terms of the principle of costly commitment.

10. You are in charge of a major Hollywood movie studio. What strategy or strategies might you employ to avoid the fate of Sony Hit and Run? Relate the strategy you favor to a sequential equilibrium of the corresponding screening game.

◼ APPENDIX. CONDITIONAL PROBABILITY AND BAYES'S RULE

Conditional probability is a key concept for expressing and analyzing information. This appendix gives you some practice in handling conditional probability.

We will use the standard 52-card deck, with 26 black cards and 26 red cards, to motivate the concept. Let A and B denote two events involving cards; for instance

A is the event "red card is drawn."

B is the event "black card is drawn."

Now suppose you know that the event B has happened. What does this tell you about the probability that A has happened? The answer to that is conditional probability, the conditional probability of A given B, which we write as

$$p(A|B)$$

For the two events just given, it is easy to see that

$$p(A|B) = 0$$

That is, if you know a black card has been drawn, then you know a red card has not been drawn—the latter could not have possibly happened—and the probability of something impossible is 0. That makes the conditional probability of having a red card, given that a black card has been drawn, 0.

Here is a nonzero example:

A is the event "club is drawn."

B Is the event "black card is drawn."

For these two events, we claim

$$p(A|B) = 0.5.$$

To see this, recall that there are 26 black cards. You know one of them has been drawn. Of these 26 black cards, 13 are clubs and 13 are spades. So the probability that one of the 26 black cards is a club is 13/26, or 0.5.

There is a general formula, called Bayes's rule, that defines conditional probability. Bayes's rule is expressed by the formula

$$p(A|B) = p(A \text{ and } B)/p(B)$$

We can think of Bayes's rule as a general way of calculating conditional probability. Let's apply Bayes's rule to check the two conditional probabilities we just found.

In the first case, the probability of A and B is the probability of the event "red card is drawn and black card is drawn." Since only one card is drawn, that's a 0-probability event. Substituting in Bayes's rule, we have

$$p(A|B) = p(A \text{ and } B)/p(B) = 0/(0.5) = 0$$

In the second case, the probability of A and B is the probability of the event "club is drawn and black card is drawn." That's the same event as "club is drawn," since a club is a black card, and the probability of drawing a club is 13/52, or 0.25. Substituting into Bayes's rule, we get

$$p(A|B) = p(A \text{ and } B)/p(B) = (0.25)/(0.5) = 0.5$$

both of which check with our previous results.

As further practice, let's leave the realm of cards behind and look at a problem involving medicine, where conditional probability can be a life-or-death matter. Consider an infant, to which one of the two events applies:

A = baby has blood disorder.

A' = baby does not have blood disorder.

We know that, in the population of all babies, 1 in 200 has the blood disorder. So 199 in 200 do not have the blood disorder. That implies the probabilities

$p(A) = 1/200 = .005$

$p(A') = 199/200 = .995$

A blood test has been developed, and like all medical tests, it doesn't yield absolutely certain results. The test generates two possible events:

B = the test is positive.

B' = the test is negative.

In addition, we know how effective the test is, thanks to the conditional probabilities generated during research leading to the test's being approved for human use. If the baby has the blood disorder, then the probability that a baby tests positive is .96. This is the conditional probability

$$p(B|A) = .96$$

That also means if the baby has the blood disorder, the probability that the test is negative is $1 - .96 = .04$. In this case, the test does not detect the disorder. That gives the conditional probability

$$p(B'|A) = .04$$

Finally, we know how effective the test is if the baby does not have the blood disorder. If a baby does not have the blood disorder, then the probability that a baby tests negative is .99. This is the conditional probability

$$p(B'|A') = .99$$

This also means that if a baby does not have the blood disorder, then the probability that a baby tests positive is $1 - .99 = .01$. This is the rate of "false positives." Write this as the conditional probability

$$p(B|A') = .01$$

Now suppose the baby tests positive. How likely is it that the baby has the blood disorder? This is the same as asking, What is the conditional probability that the baby has the blood disorder, given that the test is positive? Using the preceding notation, we are looking for

$$p(A|B) = p(A \text{ and } B)/p(B)$$

the right hand side term following from Bayes's rule. The probability of the event "A and B"—the baby has the blood disorder and tests positive—we don't yet know. Proceed by reversing the roles of A and B in Bayes's rule, which leads to

$$p(B|A) = p(A \text{ and } B)/p(A)$$

This we can solve to get $p(A \text{ and } B)$. Substituting our know values of $p(B|A)$ and $p(A)$, we have

$$.96 = p(A \text{ and } B)/(.005)$$

Solving,

$$p(A \text{ and } B) = .0048$$

So in 48 out of 10,000 cases, a baby has the blood disorder and tests positive.

Next, we need to find the probability of the event B. There are two ways that B occurs: a baby with the disorder tests positive, or a baby without the disorder tests positive. That is

$$p(B) = p(B|A)p(A) + p(B|A')p(A')$$

Substituting our known values for the right-hand side terms,

$$p(B) = (.96)(.005) + (.04)(.995) = .0048 + .0398 = .0446$$

Finally, substituting this result into our expression for $p(A|B)$, we get

$$p(A|B) = (.0048)/(.0446) = .1076$$

which is the desired result. If the baby tests positive, the probability is slightly more than 10 percent that it has the blood disorder.

If you can work an example like this, then you can deal with any of the conditional probabilities in Chapter 10.

CHAPTER 11

Games between a Principal and an Agent

Every day in a mature market economy, situations like the following arise. A person needs something done. Whether that person is capable of doing it or not, the cost is prohibitive. So, the person hires someone else to do this something. If information is reasonably complete, then the person hired can perform the task or service at a lower cost than can the person doing the hiring. This situation could be as simple as a person's going to the doctor or as complicated as a firm's stockholders' putting their stamp of approval on the management of the firm. This chapter studies such games, called games between a principal and an agent.

In legal language, a **principal** is any person or firm that hires another person or firm to perform services. An **agent** is any person or firm hired to perform services for a principal. This chapter looks first at situations where a principal has perfect information—the principal can monitor what the agent does at no cost. In this case, the principal can get exactly what he or she paid for at subgame perfect equilibrium. If the principal has imperfect information, then the principal has to offer the material incentives to the agent to get more work out of him or her. Otherwise, the agent might slack off—a problem called **moral hazard.** Moral hazard is always an issue when you pay someone to do something for you. **Incentive-based contracts** are a way to deal with moral hazard, and this chapter explores in detail how such contracts work.

When the principal does not have perfect information, then the game between the principal and agent becomes a screening game. In this case, both adverse selection and moral hazard come into play. As we saw in the last chapter, screening games can have ominous consequences for the principal, such as an uninformed player moving first. You play a game like this every time you walk into a financial institution to make a deposit; this chapter models that game with Depositor vs. S&L. As a depositor entrusting money to a financial institution, such as a savings and loan (S&L), you are a principal and the S&L is your agent. If the agent goes bankrupt, it's your money that is gone.

Next, the effect on incentive-based contracts of different attitudes toward risk is reviewed. Once we leave an all-risk-neutral world, significant inefficiencies can arise because of **agency costs**—this on top of adverse selection and moral hazard. The problem of heterogeneous agents is then addressed. The principal need not know at the outset of a relationship whether the agent is good or not. To solve this problem, certain kinds of repeated games—for instance, those involving a probationary period—can be played.

Fairly simple compensation schedules, resembling those observed in real life, can be generated that address the problems of long-term agency. Finally, corporate compensation is studied. Compensating corporate executives with incentives such as stock options, rather than with straight salaries, is very much in the interest of the stockholders.

11.1 PRINCIPAL VS. AGENT: PERFECT INFORMATION

This section looks at the game played by a principal and an agent, called for reasons that will soon become clear, Principal vs. Agent. We begin with the perfect information version, which provides a benchmark for what happens in the more realistic case when information is imperfect. Let player 1 be the principal and player 2, the agent. The principal moves first (see Figure 11.1) and has two choices. The principal can either offer a contract or not offer a contract. If the principal offers a contract, it must specify what wages will be paid if a **high effort** is observed and if a **low effort** is observed. If no contract is offered, then the game ends. If the principal offers a contract, then the agent has to decide whether to accept it or not. If the agent rejects the contract, then the game ends. If the agent accepts the contract, then the agent has to decide whether to put in a high effort or a low effort. If the agent puts in a high effort, the agent is paid the wage specified in the contract for high effort. If the agent puts in a low effort, the agent is paid the wage specified in the contract for low effort. In either case, the principal can verify what kind of effort the agent has put in and thus pay the agent accordingly.

Player 2, the agent, has the utility function

$$u_2(w, e) = w - e$$

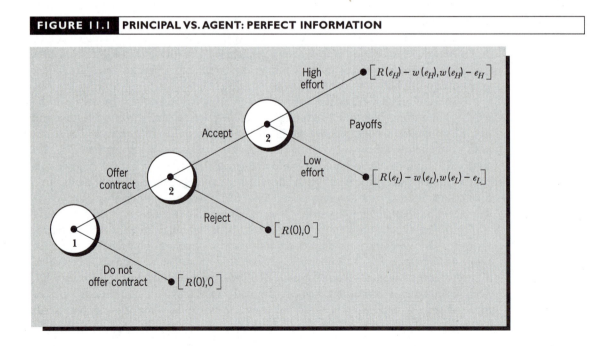

where w is the wage that player 2 receives, and $-e$ is the disutility that player 2 gets from putting in effort. The higher the effort the agent puts in, the lower that agent's utility; the higher the wage, the higher the agent's utility. In an incentive-based contract, where effort is observable, the wage is a function of effort:

$$w = w(e)$$

There are two things to note about this setup. First, since the principal can observe effort, the contract makes the wage paid conditional on effort. Second, since the agent's utility is linear in money, the agent is risk neutral. These assumptions are substantive and will be relaxed later.

Player 1, the principal, has the utility function

$$u_1 = R(e) - w$$

where $R(e)$ is the revenue the principal gets from the business, depending on how much effort the agent puts in, with the agent's wage w deducted as a cost. Since the principal's utility is linear in money, the principal is also risk neutral.

We can now spell out the payoffs for Principal vs. Agent in Figure 11.1. First, suppose that no contract is offered or that a contract is offered and rejected. Then the agent puts in no effort, makes no money from the principal, and has utility $u_2 = 0$. We can think of this utility level, 0, as a baseline from which the agent measures the attractiveness of all contract offers. The principal gets no help from the agent and incurs no cost, so the utility to the principal is the revenue corresponding to having no agent,

$$u_1 = R(0) - w(0) = R(0)$$

It makes sense that $w(0) = 0$; if you don't work, you don't get paid.

Next, suppose that a contract is offered and accepted. If the agent puts in a high effort $(e = e_H)$, then the agent is paid on the basis of high effort, $w(e_H)$. Taking into account the disutility of labor, the agent comes out with the utility

$$u_2 = w(e_H) - e_H$$

The principal in this case enjoys the revenue corresponding to high effort from the agent and pays the high-effort wage:

$$u_1 = R(e_H) - w(e_H)$$

Finally, if the agent puts in a low effort $(e = e_L)$, then the agent is paid on the basis of low effort, $w(e_L)$. Taking into account the disutility of labor, the agent comes out with utility

$$u_2 = w(e_L) - e_L$$

The principal in this case gets the revenue corresponding to low effort from the agent and pays the low-effort wage:

$$u_1 = R(e_L) - w(e_L)$$

These are the payoffs shown in Figure 11.1.

We will solve Principal vs. Agent in the next section. First, however, let's define what the best of all possible worlds involving a principal and an agent would look like. Since both players are risk neutral, it makes sense to add payoffs to get a measure of social welfare. Adding utilities, we get

$$u_1 + u_2 = [R(e) - w(e)] + [w(e) - e] = R(e) - e$$

where effort, e, can take the value high (e_H) or low (e_L) if an agent is involved, or 0 if no agent is involved. The best outcome possible would be one that maximized revenue net of effort. The wage paid corresponding to optimal effort would then be a social device for dividing the gains accruing to the principal-agent relationship. In the event that the maximum sum of utilities occurred at zero effort, then no gains would be available to society from an agency relationship, and no agent should be hired. Since one of the chief defenses of agency contracts and the legal system that enforces them is that such contracts enhance efficiency, it will be interesting to see to what extent solutions to Principal vs. Agent reflect efficiency.

■ 11.2 PRINCIPAL VS. AGENT: SUBGAME PERFECT EQUILIBRIUM

We will now solve the perfect information version of Principal vs. Agent for its subgame perfect equilibrium. For the time being, we take the wages $w(e_H)$ and $w(e_L)$ as given. You can think of these wages as standard provisions in a contract. Later in this section, we will make the wage choice strategic also, and give that choice to the principal. At the final subgame of Principal vs. Agent, the agent has to decide between putting forth a high effort or a low effort. Clearly, this decision depends on how much the agent is paid at each effort level and how much the effort costs. The agent will put in a high effort when

$$w(e_H) - e_H \geq w(e_L) - e_L$$

This inequality, called an **incentive compatibility constraint**, says that the wage net of the cost of effort for high effort is at least as great as that for low effort. Rewriting this inequality as

$$w(e_H) \geq w(e_L) + (e_H - e_L)$$

and since $e_H > e_L$ we get

$$w(e_H) > w(e_L)$$

If the agent chooses to put forth a lot of effort, he or she has to be paid more than if he or she puts in a low effort. If someone wants you to work harder, they have to pay you more—that's being compatible with incentives. An incentive compatibility constraint makes precise what the incentives must be to get an agent to put forth a predetermined effort. Of course, the principal might want only a low effort. The incentive compatibility constraint in that case is

$$w(e_L) - e_L > w(e_H) - e_H$$

Just as it takes a high wage to induce a high effort, a low wage may induce a low effort. One solution to this inequality is always

$$w(e_L) = w(e_H)$$

since we then have, from the incentive compatibility constraint,

$$-e_L > -e_H$$

You can always be sure that an agent will put in a low effort if every effort level is rewarded the same. In such a situation, the agent maximizes utility by minimizing effort. This situation is probably what occurs in dead-end, minimum-wage jobs.

Working our way back, the agent has another decision to make: whether to reject or accept the contract offered. Figure 11.2 focuses on this decision. In Figure 11.2a, the agent has chosen to put forth a high effort in response to the incentives provided by the principal. Now the agent must compare the result of putting forth a high effort to rejecting the contract altogether. The agent accepts the contract (and puts forth a high effort) when

$$w(e_H) - e_H \geq 0$$

where 0 is the utility of the outside option. This inequality is an example of a **participation constraint.** A participation constraint makes precise what the incentives must be to get an agent to participate in a certain contract with the principal. The agent rejects the contract when

$$w(e_H) - e_H < 0$$

When the high wages associated with high effort are still not high enough to compensate the agent, the agent will not sign on the dotted line.

FIGURE 11.2   **PRINCIPAL VS. AGENT, AGENT'S PARTICIPATION DECISION: (a) HIGH EFFORT, FINAL SUBGAME; (b) LOW EFFORT, FINAL SUBGAME**

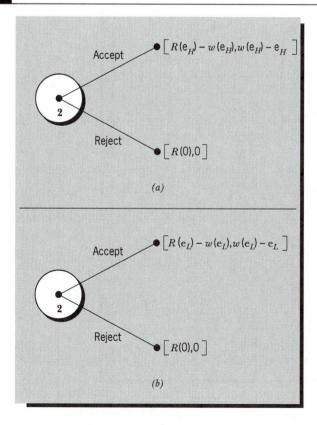

$$\left[R(e_H) - w(e_H), w(e_H) - e_H \right]$$

Accept

2

Reject

$$\left[R(0), 0 \right]$$

(a)

$$\left[R(e_L) - w(e_L), w(e_L) - e_L \right]$$

Accept

2

Reject

$$\left[R(0), 0 \right]$$

(b)

Figure 11.2b shows the case where the agent has chosen to put forth a low effort in response to the incentives provided by the principal. Again, the agent compares this payoff to that from rejecting the contract outright. The agent accepts the contract when

$$w(e_L) - e_L \geq 0$$

This inequality also exemplifies a participation constraint. The low-effort wage is still high enough to get the agent to sign on. The agent rejects the contract when

$$w(e_L) - e_L < 0$$

At this low a wage, the agent is not interested in working for the principal.

We have now worked our way back to the beginning of Principal vs. Agent, where it is the principal's turn to move. The principal faces the situation shown in Figure 11.3. If the agent's best move is to reject any contract, then it does not matter whether the principal offers a contract or not. In this case there will be no relationship, either because the principal does not offer a contract or because the agent rejects any contract the principal offers. Only two cases are left to consider, corresponding to high or low effort on the part of the agent. Figure 11.3a shows the case where the agent accepts the contract and puts forth a

FIGURE 11.3 **PRINCIPAL VS. AGENT, PRINCIPAL'S OFFER DECISION, AGENT ACCEPTS: (a) HIGH EFFORT; (b) LOW EFFORT**

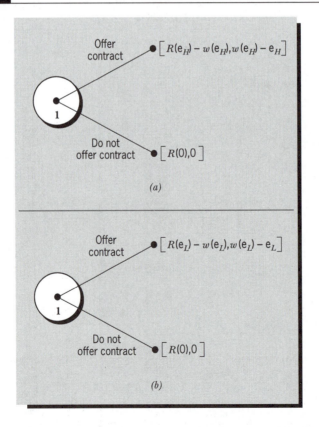

(a)

(b)

high effort. The principal has to decide between offering a contract or not. The principal offers the contract when

$$R(e_H) - w(e_H) \geq R(0)$$

When the profits from hiring a high-effort agent are greater than those of doing the job himself or herself, the principal offers a contract with incentives for high effort. The principal offers no such contract when the inequality is reversed:

$$R(e_H) - w(e_H) < R(0)$$

The principal faces a similar decision when the agent accepts the contract and puts forth a low effort, as shown in Figure 11.3b.

Now that we have worked our way through Principal vs. Agent, let's see how such a game plays out in practice. Suppose that the revenue function for the principal is quadratic in effort:

$$R(e) = 10e - e^2$$

Low effort $e = e_L = 1$; high effort $e = e_L = 2$. The wage for low effort is $w(e_L) = 2$; the wage for high effort, $w(e_H) = 4$. Substituting into the game tree of Figure 11.1, we get the game tree in Figure 11.4. At this high a wage, the agent has an incentive to put forth a high effort, since

$$w(e_H) - e_H = 4 - 2 = 2 > 2 - 1 = w(e_L) - e_L$$

Moreover, the agent has an incentive to accept the contract, since

$$w(e_H) - e_H = 4 - 2 = 2 > 0$$

Finally, the principal has an incentive to offer the contract, since

$$R(e_H) - w(e_H) = 10(2) - 2^2 - 4 = 12 > 0 = R(0)$$

This subgame perfect equilibrium is shown by the arrows in Figure 11.4.

Notice that the outcome is efficient. The sum of utilities, 14, that is achieved at the subgame equilibrium is the largest possible. To a large extent, this is a happy consequence of the wages that were fixed in the way they were. Otherwise, inefficiencies might arise. For instance, if the high-effort wage were fixed at the same level as the low-effort wage, $w(e_H) = 2$, then the agent would put in a low effort and the principal would still offer a contract (see Figure 11.5). Now, however, the subgame perfect equilibrium implies a total payoff of 8 units, even though a payoff of 14 is still possible, via $u = (14,0)$.

Fixed prices cause lots of mischief in economics, and we have just seen an example. As the Second Fundamental Theorem of Welfare Economics implies, efficiency has implications for prices—here, wages. Efficiency prescribes what sorts of wages are compatible with it. If wages are fixed without regard to incentives, then subgame perfect equilibrium need not lead to efficiency.

Let's now relax the assumption that the wages are fixed in advance and allow the principal to set the wages stated in the contract he or she offers. We can show that, with perfect information, the principal can always arrange to accomplish two things simultaneously: maximize profits and achieve efficiency. This again follows from the Second Fundamental Theorem of Welfare Economics. We get an **invisible-hand outcome,** that is, an efficient outcome that was part of no individual's intention.

FIGURE 11.4 | **PRINCIPAL VS. AGENT:** $R(e) = 10e - e^2$; $e_L = 1$; $e_H = 2$; $w(e_L) = 2$; $w(e_H) = 4$

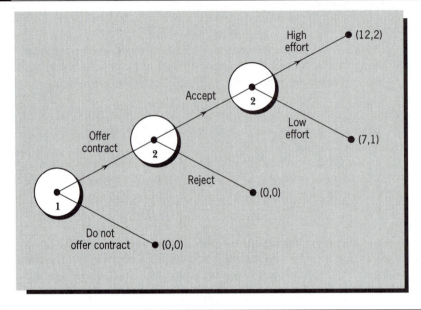

FIGURE 11.5 | **PRINCIPAL VS. AGENT:** $R(e) = 10e - e^2$; $e_L = 1$; $e_H = 2$; $w(e_L) = 2 = w(e_H)$

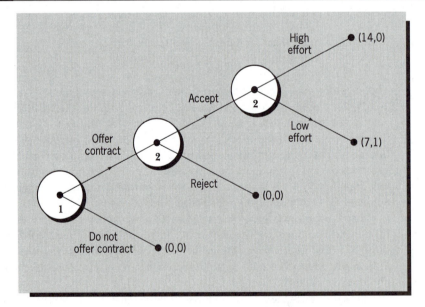

To see that when the principal sets the wages, the subgame perfect equilibrium is efficient, we will consider three possibilities in turn. Throughout, we assume that efficiency
leads to a total payoff that is positive; if so, the wages divide a positive net revenue (revenue
minus effort) between the principal and the agent. First suppose, as in the example just
given, high effort by the agent leads to efficiency. The principal needs to propose a contract

that the agent accepts (the participation constraint) and that provides incentives for the agent to put forth a high effort (the incentive compatibility constraint). The wages

$$w(e_H) > w(e_L) + e_H - e_L$$

satisfy the incentive compatibility constraint, and if the principal sets the low-effort wage equal to low effort, $w(e_L) = e_L$, we have

$$w(e_H) > e_H$$

Since net revenue is positive, we have

$$R(e_H) > w(e_H) > e_H$$

so the principal offers the contract. This also puts an upper bound on the high-effort wage. So we have shown that wages exist to support a subgame perfect equilibrium.

Second, suppose that low effort by the agent is the social optimum. Let the principal propose the wages

$$w(e_H) = w(e_L) > e_L$$

This induces low effort by the agent (incentive compatibility constraint), and the agent accepts the contract (participation constraint). Since net revenue is positive, we have

$$R(e_L) > w(e_L) > e_L$$

so the principal offers the contract. The efficient subgame perfect equilibrium (principal offers contract; agent accepts; agent puts forth a low effort) results.

Third, if zero effort is the social optimum, the principal need only propose the wages

$$w(e_H) = w(e_L) = 0$$

saying that the agent works for free. The agent will gladly say no to this—again the right answer for efficiency.

■ 11.3 PRINCIPAL VS. AGENT: IMPERFECT INFORMATION

In Principal vs. Agent with perfect information, the subgame perfect equilibrium drives the solution. If the principal has the power to set the terms of the contract, then the outcome that results is efficient.[1] In this section, we see to what extent this remains true when information is imperfect. Two degrees of imperfection are considered. In both, the principal's revenue is a random function of the agent's effort. When the principal can still observe the agent's effort, this randomness in revenue is not a big problem. Subgame perfect equilibrium can still achieve an efficient outcome. When the principal can no longer observe the agent's effort, this randomness in revenue poses a much larger problem—a challenge to efficiency that cannot be entirely overcome. In the latter case, the principal-agent game is a screening game, in which we expect subgame perfect or sequential equilibria to have efficiency problems. The asymmetric information present creates both adverse selection (the principal doesn't know what he or she is getting) and moral hazard (the agent's goals may clash with those of the principal).

---

[1] The same would be true if the agent had the power to set the terms of the contract (see end-of-chapter problem 3).

To model randomness in revenue, we need a little extra notation. Suppose, as before, that there are two revenue levels, high revenue, $R(H)$, and low revenue, $R(L)$, with

$$R(H) > R(L)$$

Revenue still depends on effort, but in a random fashion. When the agent puts forth a high effort, then high revenue is very likely. The probability of high revenue when the agent puts forth a high effort is a conditional probability, written $p[R(H)|e_H]$, that is a number close to 1. If your lawyer devotes a lot of effort to your case, you are likely to come out better than if your lawyer devotes little effort to your case. Still, even with high effort, revenue may still turn out to be low. This is the conditional probability $p[R(L)|e_H]$.

When the agent puts forth a low effort, then low revenue is likely. The probability of low revenue when the agent puts forth a low effort is again a conditional probability, written $p[R(L)|e_L]$. If your lawyer devotes little effort to your case, it will usually show up in the outcome in court. Still, it could happen that revenue is high even though effort is low: this is the conditional probability $p[R(H)|e_L]$. In the real world, we expect that conditional probability to be small.

In this respect, a principal-agent relationship has a bit of the casino in it. As principal, you could be really unlucky. Your agent puts forth a high effort, but there is little to show for it. Second, you could be really lucky. Your agent puts forth only a little effort, but you hit the jackpot. Neither of these events is going to happen very much of the time—nobody's luck is always bad or always good—but they happen enough of the time to make things interesting.

Now, as long as the principal can see what effort the agent puts forth, randomness in revenue may be a problem only for the principal. The agent continues to be paid according to effort rendered. If, in addition, the principal is risk neutral, then randomness in revenue may not be a problem for the principal, either. Here's an example to support this contention. Revenue can either be high, $R(H) = 20$, or low, $R(L) = 10$. A high effort produces high revenue 90 percent of the time, $p(20|e_H) = .9$; a high effort produces low revenue only 10 percent of the time, $p(10|e_H) = .1$.

A low effort is a different matter. A low effort produces low revenue 90 percent of the time, $p(10|e_L) = .9$; a low effort produces high revenue only 10 percent of the time, $p(10|e_L) = .1$. If no agent is present, the principal gets revenue = 0. All this is shown in Figure 11.6.

The final subgames are now random moves, but the principal can tell these two subgames apart. The principal knows when the probability distribution over his or her own revenue is based on high effort and when that probability distribution is based on low effort. The principal is able to **monitor** the agent. The principal keeps an eye on the agent, just as a professor monitoring an exam keeps an eye on the students. If the agent has chosen high effort, the principal can expect the revenue

$$ER_1(e_H) = .9[20 - w(e_H)] + .1[10 - w(e_H)] = 19 - w(e_H)$$

when he or she observes high effort by the agent. In this event, the agent gets the sure-thing payoff

$$w(e_H) - e_H$$

When the agent puts forth low effort, the principal can expect the revenue

$$ER(e_L) = .1[20 - w(e_L)] + .9[10 - w(e_L)] = 11 - w(e_L)$$

FIGURE 11.6   **PRINCIPAL VS. AGENT: IMPERFECT INFORMATION, MONITORING**

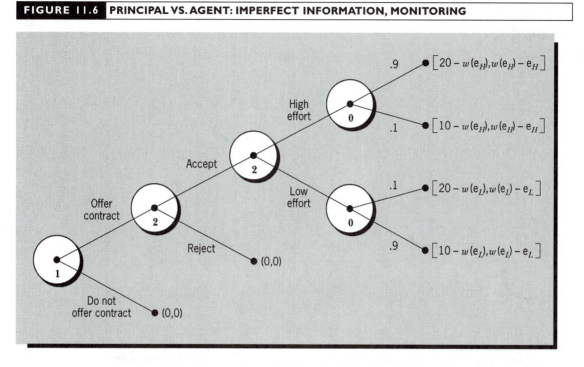

when he or she observes low effort by the agent. In this event, the agent gets the sure-thing payoff

$$w(e_L) - e_L$$

Notice that once we have replaced the final random-move endgames with their expected value to the principal and sure-thing value to the agent, we have essentially the same situation as in Principal vs. Agent with perfect information. To see this result, suppose further that high effort $e_H = 8$, low effort $e_L = 2$, the high-effort wage $w(8) = 9$, and the low-effort wage $w(2) = 2$. The game that results is shown in Figure 11.7. You can get to Figure 11.7 from Figure 11.6 by substituting the high and low revenue, effort and wage values from Figure 11.6. The conditional probabilities appear along the branches from the random events following high effort and low effort, respectively.

Replacing final subgames with their expected utilities, we see that high effort pays the principal the expected utility Eu_1

$$Eu_1(8) = ER(8) - w(8) = 19 - 9 = 10$$

and pays the agent the expected utility Eu_2

$$u_2(8) = w(8) - 8 = 9 - 8 = 1 > 0$$

leading to a total payoff of $10 + 1 = 11$.

Similarly, low effort leads to the payoffs

$$Eu_1(2) = ER(2) - w(2) = 11 - 2 = 9$$
$$Eu_2(2) = w(2) - 2 = 2 - 2 = 0$$

FIGURE 11.7	PRINCIPAL VS. AGENT, IMPERFECT INFORMATION, MONITORING: $e_H = 8$; $e_L = 2$; $w(e_H) = 9$; $w(e_L) = 2$

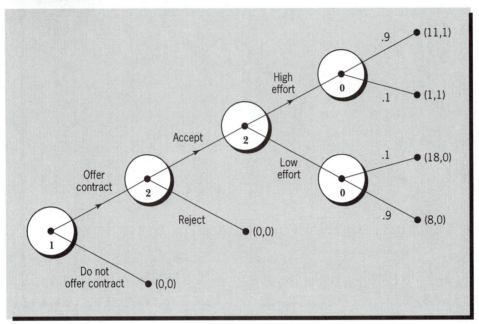

leading to a total payoff of $9 + 0 = 0$.

At the subgame perfect equilibrium, the principal offers this contract and the agent accepts and puts forth a high effort. The result is efficient, with maximum total payoff of 11. The additional uncertainty does not materially affect the equilibrium outcome. As far as the game is concerned, this is entirely the same outcome as if the principal knew $R(8) = 19$ and $R(2) = 11$ with certainty.

Things get stickier when the principal is even less informed and cannot monitor effort: he or she is now in a full-fledged screening game. The principal can no longer observe effort. When high or low revenue occurs, the principal knows only what the probabilities are of the agent's having put in a high effort or a low effort, but not what the agent actually did. In such a case, where the principal cannot monitor the agent's effort, the agent could have been lucky (low effort, high revenue) or unlucky (high effort, low revenue). Thus the principal can no longer pay the agent according to effort. The principal can pay the agent based only on the revenue that actually occurs. When an agent is lucky, the agent is overpaid relative to effort; when the agent is unlucky, he or she is underpaid relative to effort.

The wage paid the agent when revenue is high is written $w[R(H)]$; the wage paid the agent when revenue is low, $w[R(L)]$. Figure 11.8 shows the game of Figure 11.6 when the principal cannot monitor the agent's effort. This difference is evident in the final information set of the game, which is still a random move, but now the principal does not know which node of this information set has been reached. The two wages are $w(20)$ and $w(10)$, depending on revenue, which is observable; and not depending on effort, which is not. The

FIGURE 11.8 PRINCIPAL VS. AGENT: IMPERFECT INFORMATION, NO MONITORING

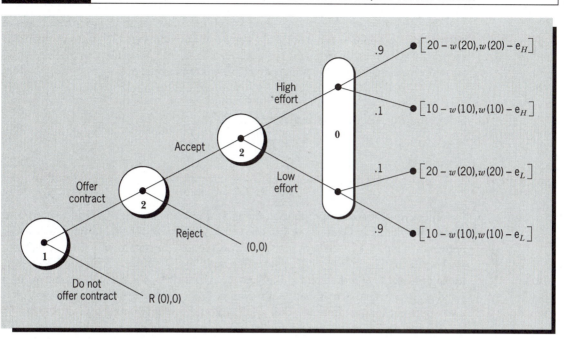

inability to monitor really complicates the principal's decision. This complication shows up at the agent's final decision, as expressed by the incentive compatibility constraint.

Suppose that the principal wants to provide an incentive for high effort—this makes sense, since high effort paid the principal the most when the principal could monitor. When the agent puts forth a high effort, he or she expects to produce high revenue and get the high-revenue wage 90 percent of the time. The rest of the time, the agent gets the low-revenue wage for high effort. The agent's expected value for high effort is

$$Eu_2(e_H) = .9w(20) + .1w(10) - e_H$$

When the agent puts forth a low effort, then he or she expects to produce low revenue and get the low-revenue wage 90 percent of the time. The rest of the time, the agent gets the high-revenue wage for low effort. The agent's expected value for low effort is

$$Eu_2(e_L) = .1w(20) + .9w(10) - e_L$$

To induce high effort, the principal needs to make sure that high effort pays at least as much as low effort:

$$Eu_2(e_H) \geq Eu_2(e_L)$$

Substituting the values $e_H = 8$ and $e_L = 2$ and solving the inequality, we get

$$.8w(20) \geq .8w(10) + 8 - 2 = .8w(10) + 6$$

or

$$w(20) \geq w(10) + 7.5$$

The agent is paid more for producing more revenue—whether he or she worked hard or not.

Now we can work our way back toward a solution. Given that the agent has chosen to put forth a high effort, the principal wants to make sure that the contract offered is accepted. This means satisfying the participation constraint. The agent accepts the contract when the expected value from a high effort exceeds the outside option:

$$Eu_2(e_H) > 0$$

Substituting the value $e_H = 8$ and solving the inequality, we get

$$.9w(20) + .1w(10) - 8 > 0$$

or

$$w(20) > 8.9 - .11w(10)$$

The inequalities corresponding to the incentive compatibility and participation constraints are plotted in Figure 11.9. The wages that satisfy both constraints have to lie above both lines in Figure 11.9. To keep matters simple, suppose the minimum monetary unit is 1, so all wages must be in integers. The point $(0,9)$ satisfies all these conditions and is less costly to the principal than is the point $(1,9)$. Thus the principal would offer the contract $w(20) = 9$ and $w(10) = 0$. The agent is paid \$9 if revenue is \$20 and is paid nothing otherwise. This is a very different contract from what the agent was offered when monitoring was possible.

We can now check to make sure that the principal wants to offer this contract, and then compute its payoff implications. If the principal offers the contract $w(20) = 9$ and $w(10) = 0$, and the agent accepts and puts forth a high effort, then the principal can expect

$$Eu_1 = .9(20 - 9) + .1(10 - 0) = 10.9 > 0$$

FIGURE 11.9	**PRINCIPAL VS. AGENT: NO MONITORING, INCENTIVE COMPATIBILITY, AND PARTICIPATION CONSTRAINTS**

An agent who puts forth a high effort can expect the payoff

$$Eu_2(e_H) = .9(9) - .1(0) - 8 = 0.1 > 0$$

Since the principal sets the price, the terms of the contract are especially favorable to the principal, who receives most of the gains from this relationship. Notice also that the total profit from the relationship, $10.9 + 0.1 = 11$, is exactly the same as when the principal could monitor the agent. We will see later that this is something of a fluke, since it depends on both parties being risk neutral. Now, however, let's look at a principal-agent game that is played every time a depositor goes to the bank or savings and loan and that was especially prominent during the S&L crisis of the 1980s.

■ 11.4 DEPOSITOR VS. S&L

The American humorist Will Rogers once said, "When I put money in the bank I'm more concerned about the return of the principal than I am concerned about the return on the principal."[2] He said this during the Great Depression, when one-quarter of all banks in the country failed. The 1980s were another bad time for banks in the United States, especially those in the **Savings and Loan (S&L)** sector.

Every time you walk into a financial institution to deposit your money, you are playing a form of Principal vs. Agent. You are the principal. You want the financial institution to take good care of your money, investing it wisely and paying back your principal plus interest when it is due. The financial institution is your agent. You cannot see behind the scenes and know what the institution is doing with your money, but you might want to. A version of Principal vs. Agent shows why.

This game is called Depositor vs. S&L. Player 1, the depositor, has $100,000 to invest, and moves first. The depositor can either deposit the money in the S&L or buy a 1-year U.S. government bond (G-bond). The G-bond is an absolutely sure thing—the U.S. government has never defaulted on its debt—and will repay the principal plus 3 percent interest, for a total of $103,000. If the depositor buys a G-bond, the game ends. If the depositor puts the money in an S&L, the game continues. The S&L is player 2. Since the S&L accepts all deposits, we do not have to model the accept/reject decision and there is no participation constraint. *The S&L always participates.* The S&L promises the depositor a rate of interest of 10 percent on an uninsured certificate of deposit (CD); however, this promise is not ironclad. If the S&L loses all the money, it does not have to repay it—it simply goes bankrupt instead. In order to make any money, the S&L has to find an investment that pays more than 10 percent interest.

Assume, for simplicity, that there is a single type of investment opportunity available to the S&L, a junk bond.[3] A $100,000 junk bond is either good, and pays back principal plus 12 percent interest, or it is junk—worthless, with a payback of $0. If the S&L puts forth a high research effort, it can guarantee that the probability of a junk bond's being junk is only 1 percent. However, it costs money to conduct the required junk bond market research, as measured by e_H. If the S&L puts in a low research effort, it can guarantee that the probability of a junk bond's being junk is 10 percent. It costs less to perform this

---

[2] Material for this section was inspired by Kathleen Day, *S&L Hell* (New York: Norton, 1993).
[3] The official name for this sort of security is high-yield bond. Junk bonds were invented by Michael Milken, and they played a major role in financing LBOs, as you saw in chapter 10 (section 10.7).

research, as measured by e_L. We now have the payoffs corresponding to the chance move at the end of Depositor vs. S&L, which determines whether a junk bond is good or junk. Suppose that the S&L has put in a high effort. Then with probability .99, the junk bond is good. The depositor gets his or her money back with interest, $110,000. The S&L gets the junk bond back with interest, $112,000. After paying off the depositor and deducting research costs, the S&L is left with $2,000 − e_H. With probability .01, the junk bond is junk. The depositor gets burned, losing all the money, and the S&L gets stuck with the research costs, $-e_H$. The same payoffs appear in the low-effort node—only the probabilities along the branches are different. This game is shown in Figure 11.10.

You can see what sort of jeopardy the depositor is in. Whether the S&L puts in a high effort or not depends on the following inequality:

$$.99(2000) - e_H \geq .9(2000) - e_L$$

or

$$180 \geq e_H - e_L$$

The cost of a high research effort cannot exceed by more than $180 the cost of a low research effort. Otherwise the S&L will put in a low effort, and the depositor will be burned 10 times as often. If research costs are low, as in $e_L = \$100$ and $e_H = \$200$, then the S&L puts forth a high effort and the depositor comes out ahead. The depositor expects a repayment of principal plus interest of $(.99)(110,000) = \$108,900$. Since the depositor is risk neutral, this result is better than the sure $103,000 from the G-bond. However, just a few dollars difference in research costs (say, $e_H = \$300$), and the outcome is completely different. The S&L puts in a low effort, and the depositor expects $(.9)(110,000) = \$99,000$, considerably less than the G-bond payoff.

The worst thing about all this is that the depositor may not even be aware that he or she is playing a game with the S&L. Consider the unfortunate depositors who bought

FIGURE 11.10 DEPOSITOR VS. S&L

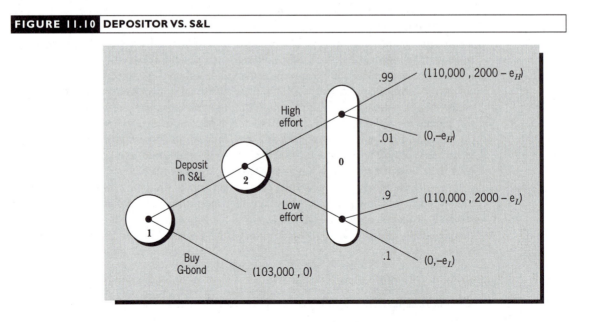

$100,000 uninsured CDs from Lincoln Federal, the infamous S&L run by Charles Keating. These depositors were told that uninsured CDs were the same as insured CDs, and not to worry. In fact, uninsured CDs were very different—there was no deposit insurance for them. When Lincoln Federal S&L went bankrupt, these depositors saw all their money in uninsured CDs go up in smoke. They had no idea what game they were playing—until their money was gone. The screening game outcome treated them very poorly.

■ 11.5 PRINCIPAL VS. AGENT WITH TWO TYPES OF AGENTS

In the situations we've reviewed so far, even if a principal could not monitor an agent, the principal did at least know what kind of agent he or she was dealing with. This is a bold assumption. It is tantamount to saying that all lawyers or all doctors are equally good, which isn't always so. In this section this assumption is relaxed, so that there are two **agent types.** High effort on the part of a good lawyer means something different from high effort on the part of a mediocre lawyer. This complication creates a full-fledged screening game, which this section addresses.

Figure 11.11 shows the sort of game that comes up with two types of agents. An initial random move determines whether the agent is good or mediocre. The agent sees the outcome of this move, but the principal does not. The principal then offers a contract or not. The same contract is offered to both types of agents, since the principal cannot tell the difference between them. Each type of agent can either accept or reject the contract. If either type of agent rejects the contract, then the game ends with the status quo payoffs (0,0). If an agent accepts the contract, then that agent can put in a high effort or a low effort. Let's assume that a good agent has the same characteristics as those of the agent in Figure 11.8: 90 percent of the time high effort leads to high revenue (20), and 10 percent of the time high effort leads to low revenue (10); 90 percent of the time low effort leads to low revenue, and 10 percent of the time low effort leads to high revenue. With a mediocre agent, high effort leads to high revenue only 60 percent of the time, whereas low effort leads to low revenue for sure. There is a big statistical difference between good agents and mediocre agents, and a good agent is always a better deal than a mediocre agent given the same contract. Since the principal cannot monitor effort, either, all of these endpoint possibilities come out of Chance's final information set.

If the game is going to be played just once, the principal is not terribly interested in finding out whether the agent is good or mediocre. The principal just wants to make as much money as possible from hiring an agent. Nevertheless, the response to a contract offer may reveal an agent's type. For example, when high effort $e_H = 8$ and low effort $e_L = 2$, offering the contract $[w(10), w(20)] = (0,9)$ to a good agent induces high effort—the subgame from Figure 11.8 that we already solved. Offering this same contract to a mediocre agent, we get for high effort

$$Eu_2(e_H) = .6(9) + .4(0) - 8 = -2.6$$

And high effort gets rejected. For low effort by a mediocre agent, we get

$$Eu_2(e_L) = 0 - 2 = -2$$

Since $-2.6 < -2$, low effort is better than high effort for a mediocre agent. However, no effort is best of all. The mediocre agent rejects the contract altogether, since he or she can always get 0. Thus offering the contract where high revenue of 20 pays 9, while low revenue

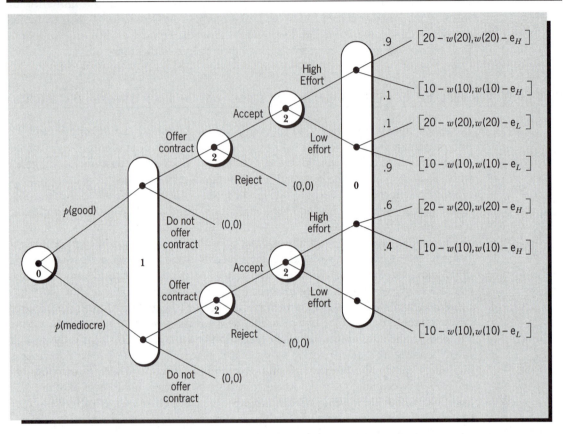

of 10 pays nothing, will actually serve two purposes. It induces a good agent to put forth a high effort, and it induces a mediocre agent to reveal type when he or she rejects the contract, as a mediocre agent will. This is a separating subgame perfect equilibrium.

Of course, in a one-shot game, getting the mediocre agent to reject the contract is not always the most desirable thing to do. If good agents are rare; that is, the probability of a good agent, $p(good)$, is small, then the principal may want to offer a contract that both types will accept and that will induce high effort by a mediocre agent and low effort by a good agent. In this case, it doesn't pay to cater to the incentives of a good agent. The principal is likely to be dealing with a mediocre agent, so it makes sense to cater to the incentives of a mediocre agent instead. You get to work out the details of this situation in end-of-chapter problem 9. In this event, the principal wants a pooling equilibrium instead.

If the principal-agent game is going to be played many times, there is a premium put on dealing with a good agent rather than with a mediocre agent. In such a case it is worthwhile for the principal to explore contracts that mediocre agents would reject and good agents would accept. If the difference between a mediocre agent and a good agent is slight, such a contract may not exist mathematically, and the principal can use the probation period technique described in chapter 10. The eventual establishment of a track record can determine, at least statistically, whether an agent in a repeated relationship is good or mediocre.

■ 11.6 PRINCIPALS COMPETING FOR AGENTS

So far in this chapter, the principal moved first, either taking the terms of the contract as given or setting those terms most favorably for him or herself.[4] The outcome that results is efficient, and is the most favorable possible from the viewpoint of the principal. When more than one principal is competing for the services of the same agent, then the distributive consequences of the principal-agent game that results are very different.

This is precisely what happens in the competition for the services of stars in athletics and entertainment. As Robert Frank and Philip Cook describe in their book, *The Winner-Take-All Society*, such competition can be very intense. A top-ranked provider of an entertainment service has extraordinary value in contemporary American society. As such, and despite the agency problems involved, principals will drive the bidding for such an agent to extraordinary levels. The outcome may be reminiscent of Barbarians at the Gates in the last chapter, with the principal that wins the bidding ultimately paying dearly for the services of the agent.

Here is an example from baseball. Alex Rodriguez, a shortstop for the Texas Rangers (formerly with Seattle Mariners), is perhaps the best player at his position in the history of baseball. Shortstop is the most challenging position in the field, and traditionally shortstops were mainly expected to be good fielders, providing defense on the left side of the field. Any offense they provided was a welcome extra. Rodriguez not only fields his position as well as anyone playing, but he provides offense at a level equal to the best Hall of Fame hitters at any position of all time. Here is just one statistic. In the history of baseball, prior to 2002, two hitters, Ralph Kiner and Duke Snider (both Hall of Famers), hit 40 or more home runs 5 years in a row. In 2002, Alex Rodriguez hit 40 or more home runs for the fifth straight year. Another comparison: the last (and only) shortstop to hit 40 or more home runs 2 years in a row—Ernie Banks—is also in the Hall of Fame.

So when Mr. Rodriguez became a free agent at the end of the 1999 season, the bidding for his services was fierce. The Seattle Mariners, his team at that time, would have loved to keep him, but they weren't willing to sign a 10-year contract at compensation averaging over $20 million/year. The Chicago Cubs, New York Mets, and Texas Rangers were all reported to be bidding that high. Ultimately, Mr. Rodriguez signed a 10-year, $252 million contract with the Texas Rangers. This made him by far the highest-paid baseball player of all time. The Rangers' owner—and new principal to Mr. Rodriguez' agency—hailed the acquisition of his new shortstop's services as the beginning of a new era of victory at Texas Stadium, home of the Rangers.

The first 2 years of the 10-year contract have seen Alex Rodriguez continue to field his position well and set records on offense. Unfortunately for the Rangers, they have been mired in last place in their division. Meanwhile Mr. Rodriguez' former team, the Mariners, tied a record for most victories in a single season (116), a record that had stood for 95 years. One great player—even the greatest at his position of all time—does not make a winning team.

---

[4] Material for this section has been drawn in part from Robert H. Frank and Philip J. Cook, *The Winner-Take-All Society* (New York: Free Press, 1995).

The downside of this kind of bidding war by principals over a single agent is clear. Unless the winning principal is able to get a contract with incentives for high effort, that principal may get stuck with an agent who puts forth low effort instead. And the extremely high levels the bidding reaches may leave little or no room for further incentives for high effort.

We see similar intense competition for the services of top-ranked agents in the markets for movie stars, opera stars, rock stars, and even professors. But the highest levels of compensation of all are reserved for corporate executive officers (CEOs)—they're agents too. We now turn to the issue of compensating the highest-paid people in the economy, CEOs.

■ 11.7 COMPENSATING CORPORATE EXECUTIVES

The owners of a corporation are the owners of the corporation's stock.[5] Taken as a whole, the stockholders are the principals in any game involving the corporation. All those working for the corporation are agents. In particular, the chief executive officer (CEO) and the other chief executives of a corporation act as agents of the stockholders. Designing compensation schemes for executives so that they have incentives to serve the stockholders' interests is a tricky and controversial issue. Given the high levels of executive compensation prevalent in the United States, overpaying executives relative to their effort poses a serious problem for corporate performance. A CEO drawing a big salary and at the same time running the corporation into the ground is every stockholder's worst nightmare—just ask the millions of people who held Enron stock when that company went bankrupt.

Information on executive compensation is available to stockholders from publicly held corporations and is contained in annual proxy statements. Kevin Murphy collected 18 years' worth of data (1964–81) from 73 firms that were on the 1981 Fortune 500 list. Executives were chairs, CEOs, presidents, and vice presidents. To be included in the study, an executive had to appear on the proxy statement during the first 6 years of the study (1964–70) and had to remain there for at least 5 years. These sample criteria were met by 461 executives, representing 4500 executive-years of experience. This is a large sample by almost any standard.

There are two major categories of executive compensation: salary and fringe benefits, which are not tied to firm performance; and **incentive payments,** which are tied to firm performance. Incentive payments include bonuses, deferred compensation (usually in the form of restricted shares of common stock), and stock options. All these forms of incentives have a strong tendency to rise in value when a corporation performs well. Bonuses are usually tied to annual profits. In a year when a corporation makes a lot of money, executives' bonuses are worth a lot. In addition, when a corporation makes a lot of money the price of its stock tends to go up, which directly raises the value of deferred compensation and indirectly raises the value of an option to buy the stock. **Total compensation** is the sum of salary and fringe benefits and incentives. The total compensation for an average executive in this sample in the year 1981 was $450,000,[6] divided roughly as follows:

Salary and fringe benefits: $260,000
Incentives: $190,000

---

[5] Material for this study was drawn from Kevin J. Murphy, "Corporate Performance and Managerial Remuneration: An Empirical Analysis," *Journal of Accounting and Economics* 7 (1985): 11–42.

[6] All figures reported are in constant-value 1983 dollars. To convert these figures to current dollars, multiply by 1.7.

More than 42 percent of total executive compensation was in the form of incentives.

Incentives are intended to increase in value when a corporation performs well. A good corporate performance is evidence that the executives are putting forth a high effort, which is showing up on the bottom line. (Of course, they could just be lucky, but the odds are against this.) The fact that nearly half of all compensation comes in the form of incentives makes corporate performance of considerable importance to the executives; the fact that they become owners (via deferred compensation and stock options) gives them a stake in the principal's side of the game as well as in the agent's side.

Whether the intention behind the incentives can actually be found in the data is a different issue. Although the data clearly indicate that total compensation rises with the size of the corporation, little hard evidence had been found previous to this study of a statistically significant link between corporate performance and total compensation. This study measured corporate performance by stockholders' annual rates of return, which is the sum of dividends and appreciation. All rates of return were adjusted for inflation and stock splits. The study found that when stockholders' rates of return went up (improved corporate performance), so did the total compensation of executives. For instance, for CEOs, a 20 percent increase in stockholders' rates of return led to a 3 percent increase in total compensation. If incentives constitute 42 percent of total compensation, this result indicates that incentive compensation rose more than 7 percent in response to a 20 percent increase in stockholders' rates of return. Effects of a similar magnitude were found for the other three categories of corporate officers.

Compensation in the form of incentives is an important part of the total compensation of corporate executives; these executives stand to gain a lot when the corporation performs well. It is nearly impossible for stockholders to monitor corporate executives, much less design schemes to weed out the good from the mediocre. Stockholders have a lot at stake in keeping agency costs down. Compensation in the form of bonuses, deferred compensation, and stock options appears to point corporate executives in the right direction, making their payoff go up with that of the stockholders.

■ SUMMARY

1. A principal is any person or firm that hires another person or firm to perform services. An agent is any person or firm so hired. Principal vs. Agent is the game played between the two.

2. In Principal vs. Agent, the principal offers or does not offer a contract to the agent. The agent either accepts or rejects the contract (the participation decision). If the agent accepts the contract, the agent can either put forth a high effort or a low effort (the incentive compatibility decision).

3. When there is perfect information and both the principal and the agent are risk neutral, the subgame perfect equilibrium of Principal vs. Agent is efficient. This outcome is an example of the invisible hand at work.

4. When information is imperfect but the principal can monitor the agent, the solution of Principal vs. Agent is a social optimum. This result holds true even if the principal cannot monitor the agent, as long as both are risk neutral.

5. When a depositor puts money into a financial institution, he or she is playing a form of Principal vs. Agent with the depositor as the principal. Such games played with some S&Ls as agents in the 1980s led to considerable losses by depositors.

6. When the agent is risk averse, agency costs rise, because the principal must implicitly insure the agent against unlucky outcomes. The subgame perfect equilibrium in this case does not guarantee efficiency.

7. When there is more than one type of agent and the principal cannot detect types, the principal is an uninformed agent in a screening game. The principal is constrained to offer the same contract to all types of agents, thus incurring an additional agency cost.

8. In a repeated-game setting, the principal has an added incentive to learn the agent's type before committing to a long-term relationship. When the two types of agents are sufficiently different, this determination can sometimes be made with a contract that one type accepts and the other type refuses.

9. A major form of Principal vs. Agent is played in a mature market economy between the stockholders of a corporation (the principal) and its top executives (the agents).

10. A little less than half the total compensation of top corporate executives derives from incentive payments, which include deferred compensation, bonuses, and stock options. At least one study has found a positive and significant relationship between corporate performance and incentives.

■ KEY TERMS

principal	high effort/low effort	monitoring
agent	incentive compatibility	savings and loan (S&L)
moral hazard	constraint	agent types
incentive-based contracts	participation constraint	incentive payments
agency costs	invisible-hand outcome	total compensation

■ PROBLEMS

1. Give three examples of principal-agent games that you, or a company you have worked for, have played. For each example, estimate how serious the agency problem was or might have been.

2. The principal has the revenue function $R(e) = 20e - e^2$, where e is effort by the agent. The agent has the utility function $u_2 = w - 2e$. Effort can be either high ($e_H = 4$) or low ($e_L = 0.5$). The wages are fixed in advance at $w(e_H) = 10$ and $w(e_L) = 4$. The principal can observe effort. Write down the principal-agent game in extensive form, and find its subgame perfect equilibrium. Compute the efficiency of this equilibrium.

3. Use the data from problem 2, except that now the principal gets to set the wages. Find the subgame perfect equilibrium, assuming that all wages must be multiples of 0.5. Is the subgame perfect equilibrium different from that in problem 2? Is it efficient?

4. Solve the game in problem 2 when the agent gets to set the wages. Is the outcome different from that in problem 3? Explain. Then relate your answer to the price formation process we usually encounter with doctors and lawyers.

5. A principal is considering hiring a lawyer to represent him or her in a lawsuit. The principal gets $250,000 if the suit is won and $0 otherwise. If the agent works hard (100 hours), there is a 50 percent chance that the principal will win the suit. If the agent does not work hard (10 hours), there is a 15 percent chance that the principal will win the suit. Without a lawyer, the principal is sure to lose the suit. The principal can monitor the agent, and both parties are risk neutral. The agent's utility function is $m - 50e$, where m is money in dollars and e is effort in hours. The agent's fee for this case is $100 per hour, and the outside opportunity is worth $500. Write down the game in extensive form, and find its subgame perfect equilibrium.

6. The data are the same as in problem 5, except that the principal cannot monitor the agent. The principal offers the agent a contingency contract. Instead of billing by the hour, the agent is paid on a contingency basis, getting one-third of whatever is won. Write down the game in extensive form and solve it. How does your solution compare to that in problem 5? What principle, if any, is operating here?

7. In Depositor vs. S&L, suppose that the S&L can invest $100,000 in a junk bond with the following rates of return: with high effort, the probability is .98 that the rate of return is 15 percent and .02 that the money vanishes; with low effort, the probability is .92 that the rate of return is 15 percent and .08 that the money vanishes. The rate of return on government bonds is 4 percent. Draw the extensive form and solve. Where should the depositor put the money? (*Hint:* Use Figure 11.10 as a guide.)

8. Asymmetric information in the principal-agent problem creates both adverse selection (principal goes first in a screening game) and moral hazard (agent's effort is unobserved). How might repetition of the game reduce both these problems. (*Hint:* Appeal to the track-record principle.)

9. In Figure 11.11, suppose that the probability of getting a mediocre agent is 95 percent. Show that a contract that induces high effort from the good agent is not the best possible for the principal.

10. The CEO of a large corporation, citing the need to hold the line on costs, has proposed getting rid of all existing incentive programs, citing them as too expensive. This proposal is on the ballot at the annual stockholder's meeting. As a stockholder, how would you vote on it? What would you need to know to cast your ballot wisely?

■ APPENDIX. RISK AVERSION IN THE PRINCIPAL-AGENT PROBLEM

Throughout the chapter, principal and agent alike were risk neutral, with the happy consequence that the subgame perfect equilibria of the games between them have been efficient, even when the principal could not monitor the agent's behavior. Once the players in Principal vs. Agent are not risk neutral, the efficiency of the interactions between principal and agent is no longer assured. In particular, when monitoring is no longer possible, a risk-averse agent will cost more to employ and the resulting subgame perfect equilibrium need not be efficient.

Recall the problem presented in section 11.3, with both players risk neutral (see Figure 11.8). An efficient outcome was achieved when the agent put forth a high effort. Now suppose that the agent is very risk averse, with the utility function

$$u_2(w,e) = \log(w - e + 1)$$

where log(.) denotes the natural logarithm of a number. Notice that the agent's indifference curves in (money, effort) space do not change. This is simply a monotonic transformation of utility, which does not change any deterministic decision. However, since this is a non-linear transformation of payoffs, it does affect decisions under uncertainty. The principal remains risk neutral. The efficient outcome, which produces the greatest value, is still equal to 11, and is still generated by a high effort from the agent. Now, however, it will cost the principal more to provide the incentives necessary for high effort. The wage contract that the principal offered previously, $w(20) = 8$ and $w(10) = 0$, is no longer acceptable to this risk-averse agent. The zero wage in the event that low revenue is observed would mean the agent would get the utility log(0)—that is, minus infinity—even if he or she put in zero effort! No agent would work for that kind of compensation—not when 0 utility is guaranteed just by saying no.

Let's work out the details of what it will take in this case for the principal to get the agent on board for a high effort. The game is shown in Figure 11.12. When the agent puts forth a high effort, he or she expects to produce high revenue and get the high-revenue wage 90 percent of the time. The rest of the time the agent gets the low-revenue wage for high effort. The agent's expected utility for high effort is

$$Eu_2(e_H) = .9 \log[w(20) - e_H + 1] + .1 \log[w(10) - e_H + 1]$$

Since the agent is now risk averse, all the wage payments net of effort get transformed accordingly. When the agent puts forth a low effort, he or she expects to produce low revenue and get the low-revenue wage 90 percent of the time. The rest of the time the agent gets the high-revenue wage for low effort. The agent's expected utility for low effort is

$$Eu_2(e_L) = .1 \log[w(20) - e_L + 1] + .9 \log[w(10) - e_L + 1]$$

To induce high effort, the principal needs to make sure that high effort pays more than low effort:

$$Eu_2(e_H) \geq Eu_2(e_L)$$

Substituting the values $e_H = 8$ and $e_L = 2$ and rearranging terms, we get

$$.9 \log[w(20) - 7] - .1 \log[w(20) - 1]$$
$$\geq .9 \log[w(10) - 1] - .1 \log[w(10) - 7]$$

FIGURE 11.12 | **PRINCIPAL VS. AGENT: IMPERFECT INFORMATION, NO MONITORING, RISK-AVERSE AGENT**

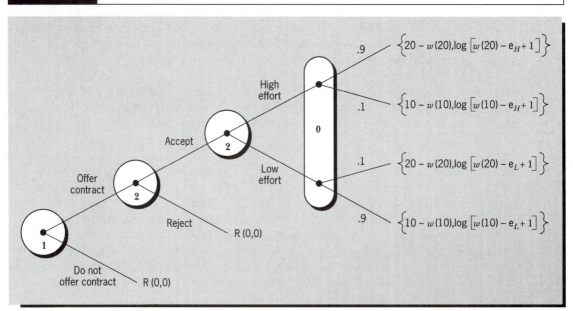

This nonlinear inequality represents the incentive compatibility constraint.

Next, consider the participation constraint. Given that the agent has chosen to put forth a high effort, the principal wants to make sure that the contract offered is accepted—the participation constraint. The agent accepts the contract when the payoff from a high effort exceeds the outside option:

$$Eu_2(e_H) \geq 0$$

Substituting the value $e_H = 8$ into the participation constraint and solving the inequality, we get

$$.9 \log[w(20) - 7] + .1 \log[w(10) - 7] \geq 0$$

Fortunately, we don't need an exact solution of these two constraints as long as all wages are in integers. From the participation constraint it is clear that the low-effort wage $w(10)$ is going to have to exceed 7, so let's set $w(10) = 8$. We know that $w(20)$ will have to be greater than $w(10)$ to provide the incentive needed for high effort, so $w(20)$ is at least 9. Plugging $w(10) = 8$ and $w(20) \geq 9$ into the participation constraint, we get

$$.9 \log[w(20) - 7] + .1 \log[w(10) - 7] \geq .9 \log[9 - 7] + .1 \log[8 - 7]$$
$$= .9 \log[2] + .1 \log[1] = .624 \geq 0$$

so we have satisfied the participation constraint. Notice that the low-revenue wage has already gone way up, to $w(10) = 8$ from $w(10) = 0$, compared to the case of a risk-neutral agent.

We're halfway to a solution. Now substitute $w(10) = 8$ into the incentive compatibility constraint, to get

$$.9 \log[w(20) - 7] - .1 \log[w(20) - 1]$$
$$\geq .9 \log[w(10) - 1] - .1 \log[w(10) - 7] = .9 \log[7] - .1 \log[1] = 1.751$$

We know that $w(20)$ has to be at least 9 to satisfy the participation constraint. Starting with $w(20) = 9$ and substituting into the incentive compatibility constraint, we get

$$.9 \log[9 - 7] - .1 \log[9 - 1] = .9 \log[2] - .1 \log[8] = .415 < 1.751$$

so $w(20) = 9$ is too low to satisfy the incentive compatibility constraint. Keep adding 1 and checking the constraint, until it is finally satisfied. You will find that that occurs at $w(20) = 17$. Substituting this into the incentive compatibility constraint, we get

$$.9 \log[17 - 7] - .1 \log[17 - 1] = .9 \log[10] - .1 \log 16] = 1.795 > 1.751$$

barely satisfying the constraint.

The wages $w(20) = 17$ and $w(10) = 8$ provide the necessary incentives for the agent to accept the contract and put forth high effort. These wages are much higher than the principal had to pay to a risk-neutral agent—those were $w(20) = 9$ and $w(10) = 0$. This means the principal's costs have risen and profit has fallen. Computing the expected payoff to the principal based on the higher wages, we find

$$Eu_1(e_H) = .9[R(H) - w(20)] + .1[R(L) - w(10)] = .9[20 - 17] + .1[10 - 8] = 2.9$$

which is a far cry from the expected profit of 10.9 that the principal enjoyed when the agent was risk neutral.

The intuition behind this result is the following. In any risky situation, efficiency dictates that the risk be borne by the party most willing to bear risk. In this case, that party is the risk-neutral principal. By bearing the risk, the principal is implicitly insuring the agent against bad outcomes. The low-revenue wage has to be at least 8 to keep the agent's utility from getting nuked. Providing this insurance is costly to the principal and thus drives the cost of the agent up.

The contract the principal would have to offer to get high effort from the agent would result in an expected profit of 2.9. However, the principal isn't required to get high effort if it is very costly. The principal can switch to a low-effort contract, which is always cheaper. All that is required for low effort is for the principal to offer the same low wage regardless of outcome. The contract $w(20) = w(10) = 2$ will automatically satisfy the incentive compatibility constraint—the agent wouldn't dream of putting forth high effort at those low wages. It will also satisfy the agent's participation constraint:

$$Eu_2(e_L) = .9 \log(2 - 2 + 1) + .1 \log(2 - 2 + 1) = 0 \geq 0$$

The agent accepts this contract and puts forth low effort. Moreover, the principal will now make more money, since

$$Eu_1(e_L) = .9[10 - 2] + .1[20 - 2] = 11 - 2 = 9$$

which is much higher than the 2.9 the principal earns from offering the contract with incentives for high effort. Thus, the principal offers the contract with incentives for low effort instead. The outcome that results is inefficient, and the combination of adverse selection, moral hazard, and risk aversion is to blame. This combination is more than any invisible hand can handle.

Following this same argument, you can show that it always costs a risk-neutral principal more to hire a risk-averse agent than a risk-neutral agent. Principals therefore have every incentive to deal with risk-neutral agents because they cost less, and risk-averse agents will be at a disadvantage in the market because they come with a higher price tag. You should not expect to find a great deal of risk aversion in professions such as medicine and law, whose practitioners are agents difficult to monitor.

CHAPTER 12

Auctions

Auctions are the most pervasive instance of Bertrand competition in our economy. Every day, firms bid to sell their services to the public and private sectors, and consumers bid to buy goods, services, and financial assets. Increasingly, much of this activity takes place on the Internet. This chapter studies auctions as normal form games. The text consistently refers to auctions to buy; the theory for auctions to buy is easily adapted to auctions to sell, and the adapters are supplied as needed.

The chapter begins with auctions with complete information, where each bidder knows what the item on the auction block is worth to each of the other bidders. These are the easiest auctions to understand, and they highlight principles that apply to all auctions. Two basic kinds of auctions are distinguished: first-price auctions, where honesty is not the best policy, and second-price auctions, where honesty is the best policy. Next, the assumption of complete information is relaxed, so that each bidder knows only what the item on the auction block is worth to him or her. Such auctions are called individual private-value auctions. The less information a bidder has, the more complicated strategic bidding gets. The best strategy for individual private-value first-price auctions is to bid less than what the item is worth to you, but not too much less. We also look at the behavior of human subjects in controlled laboratory auctions, to see how closely Nash equilibrium theory fits their behavior.

With this background, the chapter then turns to the cleanup of the biggest financial disaster in U.S. history—failed thrifts on the auction block. The Resolution Trust Corporation conducted a multibillion-dollar individual private-value auction to liquidate the assets of savings and loan associations that went bankrupt in the 1980s—an auction so large it had macroeconomic implications.

Next, the chapter addresses the most complicated auctions, where a bidder does not even know what the item on the block is worth to him or her, because no one can know the item's value. Such auctions are called common-value auctions. Bidding for offshore oil provides an important example of this type of auction. The result of bidding for oil anywhere is inherently uncertain, and especially so for offshore oil. Oil companies bid millions of dollars for drilling rights, with no way of knowing exactly what lies under the floor of the continental shelf. Some oil companies have lost substantial sums of money in these auctions. Strategic bidding could have avoided, or at least curtailed, some of these losses.

■ 12.1 SEALED-BID AUCTIONS WITH COMPLETE INFORMATION

Consider an auction to buy with two bidders, numbered 1 and 2. The item on the auction block is worth z_1 to bidder 1 and z_2 to bidder 2. These individual values are positive. Both bidders know both these values—an unrealistic assumption that will be relaxed shortly. Each bidder i makes a bid b_i, which for now is a positive integer or 0. Bidders make their bids simultaneously and put them in sealed envelopes—a **sealed-bid auction.** This constitutes the mechanics of bidding.

Let $\mathbf{b} = (b_1, b_2)$ be a vector of bids. In any auction, the winning bidder has bid the highest. Let $b(\max)$ equal the largest bid in the bid vector $\mathbf{b}$. We assume that ties are broken by an even-chance lottery among the tied bidders. The question is, what price does the winning bidder pay? Let's consider two possibilities. First, the winning bidder could pay a price P equal to the winning bid: $P = b(\max)$. This type of auction is a **first-price auction** and is the most common auction. Second, the winning bidder could pay a price P equal to the second-highest bid. This type of auction, called a **second-price auction,** is fairly rare, but it has some interesting features. In particular, it provides a strong incentive for a bidder to bid what the item is worth.

We will now set up a first-price auction as a game. Assume that bidders are risk neutral. Bidder i's utility function, $u_i(b_1, b_2)$, can be written

$$u_i(b_1, b_2) = z_i - b_i \text{ if } b_i = b(\max)$$
$$0 \text{ otherwise}$$

If you bid less than the object on the auction block is worth to you and you win the auction, you pocket the difference. This is buyer's surplus in its purest form. If you bid more than the object is worth to you and you win the auction, you lose money. Suppose that the item is worth $1,000 to you, you bid $2,000, and your bid wins. You have just lost ($1,000 − $2,000) = −$1,000. That's no way to come out ahead. Bidding $b_i > z_i$ is called **overbidding.** Overbidding may win you auctions, but it always costs you money when you win. By contrast, if you bid zero, you cannot lose. It is a common mistake in auctions, and potentially a very expensive mistake, to overbid. This observation is summarized by the following principle of bidding:

Bidding Principle 1. Never overbid. As a strategy, overbidding is weakly dominated by bidding zero.

To see that bidding zero weakly dominates overbidding, consider the following two cases. You overbid and you win the auction, but you lose money—in this case bidding zero would have saved you a lot of money. Or, you overbid and you lose the auction—in this case bidding zero would have led to the same result. Since bidding zero never pays less than overbidding and sometimes pays more, it weakly dominates overbidding as a strategy.

Given that you shouldn't overbid, maybe you should bid true value. Suppose that $z_1 > z_2$. If players bid their true value in a first-price auction, the resulting bid vector $\mathbf{b} = (z_1, z_2)$

is not a Nash equilibrium. To show that **b** is not a Nash equilibrium, consider player 1. Suppose that instead of bidding true value, this player bids a number z between z_1 and z_2. The utility to player 1 at the vector of honest bids, **b**, is

$$u_1(\mathbf{b}) = 0$$

since $z_1 - b(\max) = z_1 - z_1 = 0$. The utility to player 1 at the vector (z, z_2) is

$$u_1(z, z_2) = z_1 - z > 0$$

and player 1 still wins the auction. Player 1 does better by underbidding. This example shows that bidding true value is not a Nash equilibrium strategy in a first-price auction. The same would hold true for player 2, if player 2 had the high valuation. Bidding below true value is called **bid shaving,** a term inspired by language from the construction industry. This discussion leads to our second bidding principle:

Bidding Principle 2. If you know you are the high bidder in a first-price auction, you should always shave your bid.

The question is, how much should you shave your bid if you place the top value on the item being auctioned? To find the answer, we will proceed inductively. Consider the game in Figure 12.1, where $z_1 = \$2$, $z_2 = \$1$, and all bids must be multiples of $1. Given that players do not overbid, we need to consider only a 3 x 2 game, where players are at or below their true values using allowable bids. This game has three Nash equilibria: $\mathbf{b} = (1,1)$, $(1,0)$,

---

FIGURE 12.1 **FIRST-PRICE AUCTION, $1 BIDDING INTERVAL**

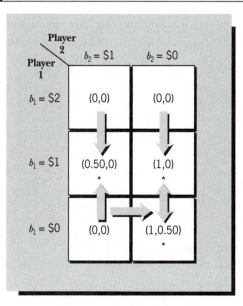

and (0,0). All these Nash equilibria involve underbidding by the high-value player. Notice that player 1 has a weakly dominant strategy at $b_1 = \$1$, the closest allowable bid below true value. If the high-value player uses his or her weakly dominant strategy, then the low-value player comes out of the auction the same as he or she went in, even.

To see the implications for efficiency of each of these Nash equilibria among the bidders, we need to include the seller in the discussion. Suppose the seller has put the item up for auction and is willing to accept any price, even zero. If this isn't the case—if the seller sets a price below which he or she will not accept—then the seller has set a positive **reserve price.** So the payoff to the seller, $u_{\text{seller}}(\mathbf{b})$, is

$$u_{\text{seller}}(\mathbf{b}) = b(\text{max})$$

So to compute the total payoff to bidders and the seller at the three Nash equilibria, we add the terms in the payoff vector $[u_1(\mathbf{b}), u_2(\mathbf{b}), u_{\text{seller}}(\mathbf{b})]$. The maximum total payoff is 2, which occurs whenever the high-value bidder wins the item for certain. This occurs, for instance, at bids (2,1)—which is not a Nash equilibrium—and at bids (1,0), which is. The minimum total payoff is 1, which occurs whenever the low-value bidder wins the item for certain. This occurs at bids (0,1), which is not a Nash equilibrium. Computing the efficiency of the Nash equilibria, we get:

$\mathbf{b} = (1,1)$, $P = 1$, payoff vector $= (0.5, 0, 1)$, efficiency $= (1.5 - 1)/(2 - 1) = 50\%$
$\mathbf{b} = (1,0)$, $P = 1$, payoff vector $= (1, 0, 1)$, efficiency $= (2 - 1)/(2 - 1) = 100\%$
$\mathbf{b} = (0,0)$, $P = 1$, payoff vector $= (1, 0.5, 0)$, efficiency $= (1.5 - 1)/(2 - 1) = 50\%$

Notice that only one of these Nash equilibria is efficient—that is, the equilibrium where player 1, the player who values the item the most, wins the item for sure. That is the test for an **efficient auction**—an auction is efficient only when the highest-value bidder wins. Although the Nash equilibrium at (0,0) is not efficient, there is something very interesting going on there. The bidders, by both bidding zero, have essentially stolen the item. At a winning bid of zero, the gain to the seller is zero. It is as if the bidders had conspired to drive down the price to the lowest possible level—even though they were bidding simultaneously and independently of one another.

Now let's see what happens as the bidding interval, the minimum difference between bids, gets smaller. Consider Figure 12.2, where the bidding interval has shrunk to $0.50. Player 1 contemplates bidding $1 or the two adjacent strategies, $1.50 and $0.50. Player 2 contemplates bidding $1, $0.50, and $0. Again, there are three Nash equilibria, at $\mathbf{b} = (1.5, 1)$, $(1,1)$, and $(1, 0.5)$. At Nash equilibrium, the high-value player always underbids. Now, the low-value player gets payoff 0 at every Nash equilibrium. Also, there are two efficient Nash equilibrium (and auctions), at $(1.5, 1)$ and $(1, 0.5)$. Finally, the Nash equilibrium where the seller gets zero has vanished.

Now we take the limit. Let $z_1 > z_2$, let the bidding increment be e, a small positive number. Player 1 bids player 2's underlying value, or either just above or below it: $b_1 = \{z_2 + e, z_2, z_2 - e\}$. Player 2 bids his underlying value, or just below it: $b_2 = \{z_2, z_2 - e\}$. Figure 12.3 shows the game between the two bidders in the neighborhood of the bid vector $\mathbf{b} = (z_2, z_2)$, where we saw Nash equilibrium when the bid interval was $1 (Figure 12.1) and the bid interval was $0.50 (Figure 12.2). In Figure 12.3, there are two pure strategy Nash equilibria, at $\mathbf{b} = (z_2 + e, z_2)$ and at $(z_2, z_2 - e)$. Both these pure strategy Nash equilibria, and the auctions associated with them, are efficient. The high-value bidder wins the item for certain.

FIGURE 12.2 FIRST-PRICE AUCTION, $0.50 BIDDING INTERVAL

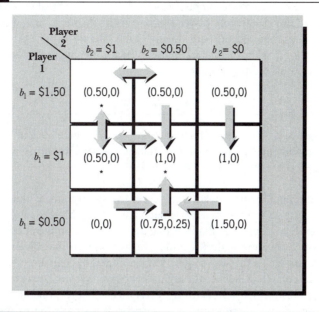

FIGURE 12.3 FIRST-PRICE AUCTION, BIDDING INTERVAL

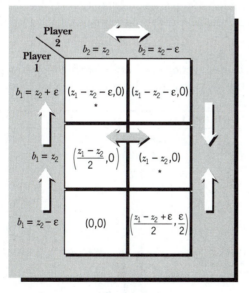

There is also a mixed strategy Nash equilibrium, with player 2 mixing on bidding true value and below true value. This equilibrium satisfies:

$$z_1 - z_2 - e = p_2(z_2)(z_1 - z_2)/2 + p_2(z_2 - e)(z_1 - z_2)$$

where $p_2(z_2)$ is the probability that player 2 bids true value z_2, and $p_2(z_2 - e)$ is the probability that player 2 bids just below true value. As e approaches zero, all these Nash equilibria get arbitrarily close to one another. Player 1 is bidding as close as possible to player 2's true value, and player 2 bids true value or just below it. Player 2, who breaks even at all these Nash equilibria, is bidding so as to keep player 1 from stealing the item with even lower bids. The limiting solution, as bids become perfectly divisible, is for the high-value bidder to win the auction and pay a price approximately equal to the second-highest valuation. This discussion leads to our third bidding principle:

Bidding Principle 3. If you have the high valuation in a first-price auction, you should bid as close to the second-highest valuation as the bidding interval allows.

This auction equilibrium makes sense from the standpoint of the theory of perfect competition. Figure 12.4 shows market demand and supply. Market supply is drawn under the assumption that supply is inelastic at one unit (the unit on the auction block), with a reserve price of 0. Demand is drawn under the assumption that bidders bid true value. Bidding true value yields the step-shaped market demand. Demand equals supply at any price P on the interval (z_1, z_2). Since the high-value player has no incentive to bid true value, the market equilibrium that results from a first-price auction is one unit traded at a price just above z_2. This result should come as no surprise. It is simply the analogue of the result in chapter 6: Bertrand competition between two competitors (here, buyers; there, sellers) with complete information suffices for perfect competition.

It is easy to generalize this result to n bidders. Simply rank the valuations from high to low:

$$z_1 > z_2 > \ldots z_n$$

Then you can show that all strategic action involves the two high-value bidders, and the rest of the players just watch (for instance, by bidding true value or bidding zero). This is

---

FIGURE 12.4 **FIRST-PRICE AUCTION AS A MARKET**

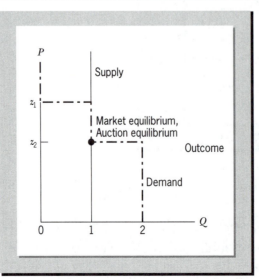

exactly how a market would work, too. All the buyers who put a value on the item less than z_2 are priced out of the market.

It is not quite as easy to generalize from a sealed-bid to an **English auction,** where bidders call out their bids and the last person bidding when the bidding stops wins the auction. However, once you abstract from the complexities of the extensive form, the action in an English auction once again boils down to the two highest-valuation bidders. Between them, once the bidding reaches the second-highest valuation, the auction has but one round of bidding to go. The auctioneer raises the bidding by the bidding increment, and only the high-value bidder is left, at which point an English auction ends. Thus, the result for an English auction is the same as the Nash equilibrium $\mathbf{b} = (z_2 + e, z_2)$ for a sealed-bid auction with the same small bidding interval. From the viewpoint of the seller, these two auctions are **revenue equivalent,** in that they generate the same revenue. Equilibrium quantity $Q = 1$ times equilibrium price $P = z_2 + e$ equals equilibrium revenue $z_2 + e$ to the seller, the same in both auctions. From the viewpoint of the economy, these two auctions are efficient: the unit traded goes to its highest value use. For a fascinating survey of revenue equivalence, go to Paul Klemperer's web site, http://www.nuff.ox.ac.uk/users/klemperer/papers.html.

12.2 SECOND-PRICE AUCTIONS

In first-price auctions, the highest bidder wins and pays a price equal to the winning bid. There is another kind of auction, rare in practice but with interesting incentives, called a second-price auction. In a second-price auction, the highest bidder wins and pays a price equal to the second-highest bid.[1] This situation might make little or no sense if you are a seller, until you realize that the high bidder in a first-price auction is going to be bidding as close as possible to the second-highest value anyway. At this point, second-price auctions start to make sense.

To see how a second-price auction works, look at Figure 12.5, which has the same individual valuations ($2 and $1) and bidding interval ($1) as Figure 12.1. Just as in Figure 12.1, there are three Nash equilibria, but they are different: $\mathbf{b}^* = (2,1)$, $(2,0)$, and $(1,0)$. At all these Nash equilibria, the player with the high value wins the auction, so all of these are efficient. This is the first difference between first-price and second-price auctions. At Nash equilibrium, a second-price auction is always efficient. This is its single biggest source of appeal for economics.

Next, notice that the Nash equilibrium at $(2,1)$ has both players bidding true value. This is the incentive-compatibility of second-price auctions. We can say something even stronger. For player 1, bidding true value, $2, strongly dominates bidding $0 and weakly dominates bidding $1. For player 2, bidding true value, $1, weakly dominates bidding $0. So each player has a weakly dominant strategy, and the game is weakly dominance solvable. Bidding true value is the weakly dominant solution of a second-price auction. This incentive property, that the institution gives each player an incentive to reveal important information, is again appealing.

---

[1] You can also define third-, fourth-, fifth-, and nth-price auctions by putting the corresponding adjective in place of *second.* Although such auctions have no appeal from the standpoint of the seller of a single item, they make a lot more sense when you are auctioning off a lot of items all at once.

FIGURE 12.5 **SECOND-PRICE AUCTION, $1 BIDDING INTERVAL**

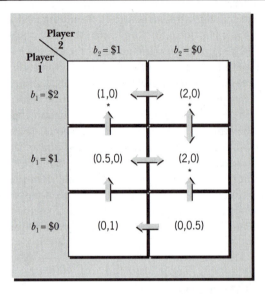

The result we have just seen holds for any number of strategies, not just two or three. In a second-price auction, bidding true value is a weakly dominant strategy. This insight is enshrined as a principle for second-price auctions:

Bidding Principle 4. In a second-price auction, always bid true value.

This principle also holds true regardless of the number of bidders. As in a first-price auction, the auction will come down to the top two valuations, at which point the results we just obtained provide the solution. Moreover, this principle does not depend on knowing your rival's valuation. It is just as true if you don't know your opponent's true value. Even in that case, paying the second-highest price means you can't lose when you bid true value. And you still can't do better by underbidding—you can only do worse.

Perfectly competitive markets work efficiently. For a market to be perfectly competitive, however, it needs perfect information. In particular, in order for the market demand curve to be correct, the individual buyers have to reveal their true demand curves. In an auction market, each buyer has to reveal his or her underlying true value in the market. The only auction in which all buyers have an incentive to reveal their underlying true value is a second-price auction. In any other auction, the market will operate based on biased information, and the efficiency of market outcomes will thereby be jeopardized.

In the last section, we mentioned the revenue equivalence of first-price auctions and English auctions. There is also a revenue equivalence involving second-price auctions. Consider an auction where the auctioneer starts the price very high—just the opposite of an English auction, where the auctioneer starts the price out low. None of the bidders says a thing. The auctioneer starts lowering the price at regular intervals (there is a clock ticking) by the bidding increment. The first bidder to signal willingness to buy gets the item, at a price equal to his or her stated willingness. Such an auction is called a **Dutch auction,** because it was invented in the Netherlands and is still used there to auction off flowers in the central flower market of Amsterdam. Suppose there are two bidders, with true willingness to pay of $2 and $1, and with each second of a clock, the price falls by one cent. The buyer willing to pay $2 can safely wait until the price ticks down to $1.01 before indicating willingness to buy. Thus (to the nearest cent), the price paid at a Dutch auction is the same as the price paid at a second-price auction: the revenue to the seller is equivalent. This is the second major revenue equivalence: a second-price auction and a Dutch auction are revenue equivalent, assuming complete information about valuations.

12.3 INDIVIDUAL PRIVATE-VALUE AUCTIONS

From now on we will consider only first-price auctions, which are by far the most common (second-price and Dutch auctions are a rarity, despite their attractive economic properties). However, we will drop the assumption that each bidder knows everyone's valuation. In an **individual private-value auction,** you know only your own valuation of the item on the auction block. You have some information about where the valuations of your bidding rivals come from, but you don't know what those valuations are. In particular, you know the probability distribution from which the valuations of your bidding rivals are drawn—and that is all. Such a situation is called **complete information.**[2] The information situation is symmetrical, in the sense that your rivals know the probability distribution from which your valuation is drawn. If all valuations are drawn from the same joint probability distribution, then we have an informational situation that is fully symmetric—just as when all the players in a card game know the distribution of cards in the deck before they are dealt.

From an informational standpoint, an individual private-value auction is just like Poker. You see your own hand and know its value, but this knowledge is your private information because no one else sees your hand. All you know about the other hands (values) is what probability distribution they came from—but you don't actually see the other hands before you have to bid.

The problem, as always in a first-price auction, is to determine how much to shave your bid. If you are bidder 1, you base your bid, b_1, on your individual private value, z_1. When you bid, you don't know whether you will win or not, so your utility is now an expected utility. For now we will assume risk neutrality, so that expected utility is expected value. Let $p_1(\text{win})$ denote the probability that player 1 wins the auction; $p_1(\text{lose})$, the probability that player 1 loses the auction. We can write expected value EV_1 as

$$EV_1 = p_1(\text{win})(z_1 - b_1) + p_1(\text{lose})(0)$$

If player 1 wins the auction, player 1 gets the individual value less the winning bid; if player 1 loses the auction, player 1 gets zero. This boils down to

$$EV_1 = p_1(\text{win})(z_1 - b_1)$$

As soon as we figure out the probability of winning, we can figure out the right way to bid.

---

[2] If bidders do not know the distribution from which valuations are drawn, the situation is one of incomplete information, and is vastly more complicated.

The probability of winning is going to depend on how high your bid is, which in turn depends on the probability distribution your rival's valuation is drawn from. We will consider the following **information situation**, again rather like poker. The auction starts out with signals Chance gives simultaneously to each player. These signals tell each player what his or her private value is, and are shown in Figure 12.6. Player 1 gets either a high or low signal with probability 1/2 each, and sees that signal: player 2 gets either a high or low signal with probability 1/2 each, and again sees that signal. What a player wants to bid depends on his or her individual value, z_1. The bidders' task is to find an entire **bidding function,** $b_1(z_1)$, that tells them what to bid given whatever valuation z_1 each of them has been given by chance.[3]

Finding an entire function is always a complicated proposition. Here, a big hint will help. Let's assume (which turns out to be true) that the higher an individual value is, the higher the player bids. In mathematical language, the bidding function is *monotonic*. Here are two linear, monotonic bidding functions that we will study. The bidding function $b_1(z_1) = z_1$ always bids true value. This is exactly the kind of bidding behavior that perfect competition postulates. We will show that the expected value of this bidding function is zero—the same as the bidding function $b_1(z_1) = 0$, which never wins. A player ought to be able to do better than zero in expected-value terms, and we will find a Nash equilibrium to do just that. The other bidding function we consider is $b_1(z_1) = z_1/2$. This bidding function underbids by 50 percent, so winning an auction with this bidding function leads to a positive payoff.

FIGURE 12.6 | **INFORMATION SITUATION**

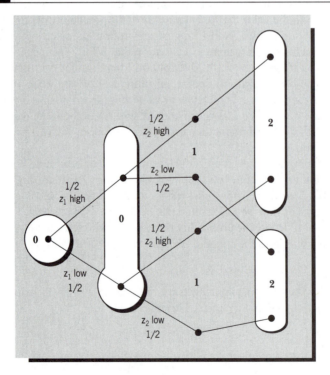

[3] These assumptions on information guarantee that the auction game is symmetric. Asymmetric auction games, based on informational asymmetries, are much more complicated; we won't study them at this level.

Now let's consider how these two strategies interact in a normal form game. In normal form, each player picks a strategy. Suppose first that both choose the strategy that bids true value. Then there are four different possible signal vectors, as shown in Figure 12.7; each of these signal vectors occurs with probability 1/4. Along the main diagonal of the matrix of signals, both bidders receive the same signal. Along the other diagonal, one buyer gets a higher signal than the other. If both bidders are bidding true value, then we can compute the probability that player 1 wins the auction, based solely on information in the signal matrix.

This is done in Figure 12.8. When both bidders receive the same signal, they bid that signal and the auction is a tie; in this case each player wins the auction with probability 1/2. If one player has a higher signal, then he or she bids that signal and has the higher bid, thus winning the auction. This is the logic underlying the probabilities you see in the figure.

Armed with the probability of a win, and a pair of bidding functions, we can compute the expected value to each bidding function over the various possible signal vectors, the probability distribution you see in Figure 12.7. Since the game is symmetric—each player

---

FIGURE 12.7 **MATRIX OF SIGNALS**

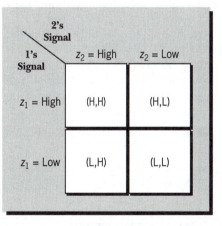

	2's Signal	
1's Signal	z_2 = High	z_2 = Low
z_1 = High	(H,H)	(H,L)
z_1 = Low	(L,H)	(L,L)

FIGURE 12.8 **MATRIX OF WIN PROBABILITIES**

	2's Signal	
1's Signal	z_2 = H	z_2 = L
z_1 = H	p_1 (win) = 1/2 p_2 (win) = 1/2	p_1 (win) = 1 p_2 (win) = 0
z_1 = L	p_1 (win) = 0 p_2 (win) = 1	p_1 (win) = 1/2 p_2 (win) = 1/2

has the same pair of strategies and the same information—we can exploit symmetry to fill in the entire normal form, shown in Figure 12.9.

Suppose player 1 is bidding true value. Here are the four possible signal vectors that might arise, together with their probabilities, and the probability that player 1 wins the auction, against another player also bidding true value:

Signal is (H,H), with probability 1/4; player 1 wins with probability 1/2.
Signal is (H,L), with probability 1/4; player 1 wins with probability 1.
Signal is (L,H), with probability 1/4; player 1 wins with probability 0.
Signal is (L,L), with probability 1/4; player 1 wins with probability 1/2.

Finally, to attach a number to winning the auction, suppose that $H = 2$ and $L = 1$ (any pair of values with $H > L$ will make the same point). Here is the expected value to player 1:

$$EV_1 = (1/4)[(1/2)0 + (1/2)0] \quad \text{Both receive the signal } H \text{ and bid } H, \text{ so } P = H.$$
$$+ (1/4)[(1)0] \quad \text{The signal vector is } (H,L); \text{ 1's bid } H \text{ wins, so } P = H.$$
$$+ (1/4)[0] \quad \text{The signal vector is } (L,H); \text{ 1's bid } L \text{ loses.}$$
$$+ (1/4)[(1/2)0 + (1/2)0] \quad \text{Both receive the signal } L \text{ and bid } L, \text{ so } P = L.$$
$$= (1/4)0 = 0$$

As you can see, bidder 1 expects a value of 0 by bidding true value. By symmetry, the same holds for bidder 2. These are the payoffs shown in the upper left-hand corner of Figure 12.9.

Now suppose that bidder 1 bids half of true value, while the other bidder continues to bid true value. Let's work out the payoff implications of this pair of strategies for the two bidders. There are four possibilities to consider, each with probability 1/4:

1. The signal is $\mathbf{z} = (2,2)$, the bids are $\mathbf{b} = (1,2)$, $P = 2$, and bidder 2 wins the auction; payoffs = $(0,0)$.
2. The signal is $\mathbf{z} = (2,1)$, the bids are $\mathbf{b} = (1,1)$, $P = 1$, and each bidder wins the auction with probability 1/2; payoff = $(1/2, 0)$.

FIGURE 12.9 INDIVIDUAL PRIVATE-VALUE AUCTION, NORMAL FORM

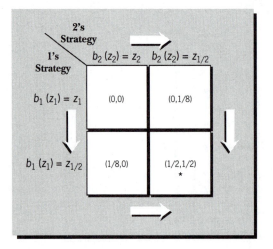

3. The signal is $z = (1,2)$, the bids are $b = (1/2, 2)$, $P = 2$, and bidder 2 wins the auction; payoffs $= (0,0)$.

4. The signal is $z = (1,1)$, the bids are $b = (1/2, 1)$ $P = 1$, and bidder 2 wins the auction; payoffs $= (0,0)$.

Adding up the consequences for each bidder, weighted by the appropriate probability, we get

$$EV_1 = (1/4)(0) + (1/4)(1/2) + (1/4)(0) + (1/4)(0) = 1/8$$
$$EV_2 = (1/4)0 + (1/4)0 + (1/4)0 + (1/4)0 = 0$$

These are the payoffs you see in the lower left-hand corner of Figure 12.9. By symmetry, these payoffs in the reverse order appear in the upper right-hand corner of Figure 12.9.

Finally, consider what happens when both bidders bid half the true value. Again, we consider the four possibilities:

1. Signal $z = (2,2)$, bids $b = (1,1)$, $P = 1$, each bidder wins the auction with probability 1/2; payoffs $= (1/2, 1/2)$.

2. Signal $z = (2,1)$; bids $b = (1, 1/2)$, $P = 1$, bidder 1 wins the auction; payoffs $= (1, 0)$.

3. Signal $z = (1,2)$; bids $b = (1/2, 1)$, $P = 1$, bidder 2 wins the auction; payoffs $= (0, 1)$.

3. Signal $z = (1,1)$; bids $b = (1/2, 1/2)$, $P = 1/2$, each bidder wins the auction with probability 1/2; payoffs $= (1/4, 1/4)$.

Adding up the consequences for bidder 1, weighted by the appropriate probability,

$$EV_1 = (1/4)(1/2) + (1/4)(1) + (1/4)(0) + (1/4)(1/2) = 1/2$$

By symmetry, bidder 2 gets the same payoff. These are the payoffs you see in the lower right-hand corner of Figure 12.9.

After doing all this work, you can see the unique Nash equilibrium to the individual private-value auction: each bidder bids half of true value. At this symmetric and efficient Nash equilibrium—each bidder expects to gain \$.50 based on the information situation and the strategy—bid half of what the item is worth to you, an outcome much better than breaking even. And since a high-value bidder always wins the auction at this symmetric Nash equilibrium, the auction is efficient too.

The preceding derivation has been pretty abstract. Let's put it into terms of the most popular auction site on the Internet, eBay, at www.ebay.com. eBay conducts auctions around the clock with bidders from all over the world. With revenue in the latest year of \$500 million, based on commissions charged to sales, that translates into some \$5 billion worth of goods sold at eBay auction in a year. This is a big auction business. As the macroeconomist Robert Hall suggests in his new book, *Digital Dealing: How e-markets are Transforming the Economy* (New York: Norton, 2002), this is hardly the only such example.

Suppose you and another bidder have registered and are ready to bid on an item. The signal you get starts with everything eBay tells you about the item. How a person processes that information depends on his wants, needs, and expectations, so not everyone gets the same signal of underlying value. At eBay there's a function called "reserve price auction," where you put in the highest price you are willing to bid (this is your reserve price), and they take care of the rest for you. If your reserve price wins, you win the auction. The highest price you are willing to bid, given what you know about the item, is precisely your bid function value based on that information. Since eBay doesn't tell any other bidder what you have told them, if every bidder uses the "reserve price auction" function, then this is tantamount to an auction in normal form. And that auction will go very fast, as fast as it takes eBay to compare the reserve prices. As long as you have taken care to bid half of what the item is really worth to you, you can expect to come out ahead—just as in Figure 12.9.

We have spent a lot of time on the game theory of auctions. Now is a good time to look at how one of the biggest auctions of all time played out: the auction to clean up the S&L crisis.

■ 12.4 AUCTIONING OFF FAILED THRIFTS

Congress passed the Financial Institutions Reform, Recovery, and Enforcement Act of 1989 to clean up the savings and loan (S&L) industry, which was by then in the throes of financial crisis.[4] A major provision of that law was the establishment of the **Resolution Trust Corporation (RTC),** a federal agency whose job it was to resolve (in most cases, that meant auction off) failed S&Ls that had been seized by federal regulators during the 1980s. The RTC conducted first-price, sealed-bid auctions of failed thrifts to accomplish its mission.

Of course, in some cases there wasn't much left of a failed thrift for the RTC to auction off. For instance, at Charles Keating's notorious Lincoln Savings and Loan, over 90 percent of all loans were in default.[5] Most of these loans were later declared uncollectible. Resolving this single S&L cost the U.S. Treasury (and therefore the taxpayers) about $2.5 billion. Since the basic criterion for S&L failure was for its deposit liabilities to greatly exceed its loan assets, large default rates on loans were typical of the failed thrifts on the RTC auction block. This situation led to one of the unique features of RTC auctions: negative bids were allowed. Indeed, if the winning bid was negative in an RTC auction, then the winning bidder got the failed thrift and in addition was paid by the RTC to accept the failed thrift. For instance, suppose that the winning bid was –$500,000. Then the RTC paid the winning bidder $500,000 to take over the failed thrift. This wasn't just a theoretical possibility; in a handful of cases it actually happened. In one especially prominent case (Silverado S&L in Denver), Neil Bush, brother of the current president, was one of the payees.

Prior to the auction of a failed thrift, the RTC held a bidders' conference. Every bidder who met the requirements (basically, a minimum amount of capital and no felony convictions) to bid was entitled—and encouraged—to attend this conference. At the bidders' conference, the RTC informed the bidders of the exact condition of the failed thrift—its assets and liabilities as of that moment. In addition to attending the bidders' conference, the bidders could take advantage of the due diligence procedure to determine exactly what the failed thrift was worth to them. Since many winning bids came from financial intermediaries located in the same region, locational and marketing considerations were built into a bidder's appraisal of the failed thrift. Finally, the rules provided for a winning bidder to withdraw a bid, for instance if the bidder had made a computational error in arriving at the bid. Since computational error could be interpreted extremely broadly, this provision practically guaranteed that a winning bidder did not overbid. These three features—the bidders' conference, due diligence, and the provision for withdrawal—made RTC auctions individual private-value auctions.

---

[4] Some of this material was drawn from Roger Stover and Roy Gardner, "The Role of Information in RTC Auctions of Failed Thrifts," *Journal of Financial Intermediation Services* 4 (1999): 141–152. For a very readable introduction to the entire S&L story, see Kathleen Day, *S&L Hell*.

[5] Keating was sentenced to a 10-year prison term for bank fraud.

In the period August 1989 to March 1992, for which data are available, the RTC handled 640 separate resolutions.[6] Resolutions fell into three categories. In purchase and assumption transactions, the most frequent resolutions (395), deposits, certain other liabilities, and a portion of assets were sold to the winning bidder. The buyer was purchasing assets and assuming liabilities, hence the name for these transactions. Of special importance to buyers were core deposits. The RTC defined core deposits as all nonbrokered deposits under $80,000. The incentive for any buyer of these deposits was the ability to lend them to make money the old-fashioned, financial intermediary way, by charging more interest on loans than is paid on deposits.[7] In insured deposit transfers, the next most frequent resolutions (157), the buyer served as paying agent for the RTC and established accounts for the failed S&L's depositors. In insured deposit payouts, the least frequent resolutions (88), the RTC directly paid depositors their insured amount and retained all assets.

Since the RTC computed core deposits down to the last dollar for the benefit of prospective bidders, the main task for bidders was performing due diligence of the assets. Determining whether loans were performing or not, or can reasonably be expected to perform in the future, becomes a due diligence nightmare—besides clogging up the cleanup. The RTC, facing a large backlog of auctions, changed the rules in April 1991 so that earnings assets were stripped out and handled separately. From that time on, bidders were able to treat all remaining assets as junk unworthy of due diligence attention.

You can show that strategic bidding in an individual private-value auction depends on the number of bidders. The more bidders, the higher the bid you should make based on your individual value, in order to have a chance of winning. In a statistical analysis of RTC auction data, there is a strong positive correlation between the winning bid and the number of bidders. This analysis is based on 201 winning bids in purchase and assumption transactions, for which the entire failed thrift was on the auction block.[8] This result makes sense, since the number of those attending the bidders' conference is a good signal of how many bidders there will actually be. The strongest explanatory variable by far for the winning bid is core deposits. This makes sense, too, since core deposits are the best possible signal of what the S&L is worth to a winning bidder. Both these empirical regularities are in accord with the theory of individual private-value auctions.[9,10]

The stated goal of RTC was to obtain the highest total premium to the RTC. By giving bidders access to the best possible information, and by holding bidders' conferences that

[6] Data on all these auctions were obtained from the Freedom of Information Office of the RTC and supplemented with discussions with RTC officials and bidders at RTC auctions.

[7] The conditions nonbrokered and under $80,000 guaranteed that such deposits would continue to be insured by an agency of the federal government, even after the demise of the Federal Savings and Loan Insurance Corporation (FSLIC) in 1989. Prior to its demise, the FSLIC had insured such deposits; after its demise, such deposits were insured by the Federal Deposit Insurance Corporation (FDIC).

[8] The excluded purchase and assumption transactions all have the feature that the RTC was auctioning off the failed thrift in pieces, a typical piece being a branch office.

[9] The regression equation for the bidding function based on this sample of bids is the following:

$$\text{bid} = -89980 + 8397\,core + 977n - 320\,repo + 5841\,put$$

where core represents core deposits, n is the number of bidders, repo is the ratio of repossessed assets to total assets (another measure of financial condition), and put represents the rule change of April 1991. All t-values exceed 3.6, and the adjusted R^2 is 0.24.

[10] For readers interested in pursuing this subject further, the best place to start is the excellent survey by Robert Wilson, "Strategic Analysis of Auctions," in *Handbook of Game Theory*, vol. 1, ed. R. J. Aumann and S. Hart (New York: Elsevier, 1992), 227–279.

made the bidders aware of the competition prior to bidding, it appears to have done just that. In the 5 years of its existence, the RTC collected over $35 billion in winning bids, ending its resolution assignment (and so happily going out of business) one year ahead of schedule. Compared to estimates of the cost of cleaning up the S&L crisis that ranged upward of $150 billion, the RTC helped save U.S. taxpayers $100 billion, give or take a little. As U.S. Senator Everett Dirksen (R–IL) once said, "A billion here, a billion there, and pretty soon you've got some real money."

◼ 12.5 COMMON-VALUE AUCTIONS

This section looks at the first-price auction with the least information, and therefore with the most complex bidding—**common-value auctions.** In a common-value auction, a bidder does not know what the item on the auction block is worth to him or her or to anybody else. All the bidder receives is a noisy signal about the value of that item. Each bidder knows that her own noisy signal, as well as that of every other bidder, is drawn from the same probability distribution. The bidder also knows what probability distribution this is. Still, this is not a whole lot of information to go on.

We'll use the same information situation that we did in the section on individual private-value auctions, with one crucial difference. Each bidder gets a signal on which to base his or her bid, but that signal is no longer equal to true underlying value. Suppose bidder 1 wants to base her or his bid, b_1, on the signal z_1. If there are two bidders, then the underlying true value V of the item is given by

$$V = (z_1 + z_2)/2$$

This true underlying value V is the same for all bidders, hence the name "common value" for this auction. Bidder 1 knows that the true underlying value of the item V is related to her or his signal, but that's all. The same is true for bidder 2. The information situation is therefore symmetric.

Otherwise, the rules for bidding are the same as in section 12.3. With risk-neutral bidders, let $p_1(\text{win})$ denote the probability that player 1 wins the auction; $p_1(\text{lose})$, the probability that player 1 loses the auction. We can write expected value EV_1 as

$$EV_1 = p_1(\text{win})(V - b_1) + p_1(\text{lose})(0)$$

If player 1 wins the auction, player 1 gets the common value less the winning bid; if player 1 loses the auction, player 1 gets zero. This boils down to

$$EV_1 = p_1(\text{win})(V - b_1)$$

As soon as we figure out the probability of winning, we can figure out the right way to bid.

The probability of winning is going to depend on how high your bid is, which in turn depends on the probability distribution that signals are drawn from. Consider the information situation given in Figure 12.10. Each bidder gets a High or Low signal (probability one-half each) of the underlying common value. This generates four possible signal vectors **z,** each of which has probability 1/4. The common value is the average of the individual signals. For instance, when one bidder gets a high signal and the other gets a low signal, the true common value is

$$V = (H + L)/2$$

FIGURE 12.10 MATRIX OF SIGNAL VALUES, COMMON-VALUE AUCTION

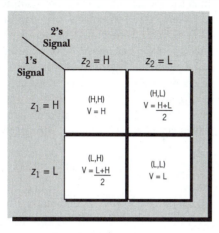

Since each bidder sees only her own signal, neither knows what the item at auction is truly worth. Although they aren't bidding in the dark—their signal does convey some information—they aren't exactly bidding in the light either.

As before, a bidding function, $b_1(z_1)$, specifies what player 1 bids, depending on the signal that player 1 has received. Unlike before, bidding signal value against a rival bidding signal value leads to an expected loss, a phenomenon in common-value auctions known as the **winner's curse.** Let's see why, by walking through the four possibilities in Figure 12.10.

- Signal $\mathbf{z} = (H,H)$, bid $\mathbf{b} = (H,H)$, $P = H$, $V = H$, and each player wins with probability 1/2; payoffs = (0,0).
- Signal $\mathbf{z} = (H,L)$, bid $\mathbf{b} = (H,L)$, $P = H$, $V = (H + L)/2$, and player 1 wins the auction; payoffs = $(-(L - H)/2, 0)$.
- Signal $\mathbf{z} = (L,H)$, bid $\mathbf{b} = (L,H)$, $P = H$, $V = (L + H)/2$, and player 2 wins the auction; payoffs = $(0, -(L - H)/2)$.
- Signal $\mathbf{z} = (L,L)$, bid $\mathbf{b} = (L,L)$, $P = L$, $V = L$, and each player wins with probability 1/2; payoffs = (0,0).

In three cases, a winning bidder gets 0 payoff; in one case, when the winning bidder gets the high signal and her or his rival gets the low signal, the winning bidder gets a negative payoff. With each signal vector having probability 1/4, this implies a negative expected value.

To see how this works with actual numbers, suppose that $H = 2$ and $L = 1$. Here is the expected value to player 1:

$$EV_1 = (1/4)(0) + (1/4)(-1/2) + (1/4)(0) + (1/4)(0) = -1/8 < 0$$

Unlike what happens in an individual private-value auction, bidding one's signal in a common-value auction leads to an expected loss. A bidder must bid well under signal value just to break even.

For the information situation we are considering, here is a very **safe bidding strategy:**

$$b(H) = (H + L)/2; b(L) = L$$

What this bidding strategy does is guarantee that a bidder never overbids. If the bidder receives a high signal of value, the bidder bids the lowest amount that the common value

V could possibly be, conditional on that bidder's information. If the bidder receives a low signal of value, the bidder again bids the lowest amount that the common value V could possibly be. Such a bidder will never overbid, and so expects to at least break even.

Figure 12.11 shows the normal form game between two bidders, with the two bidding strategies of Bid Signal Value and Bid the Safe Strategy. As before, the auction is symmetric, which we exploit in arriving at the payoffs in Figure 12.11. We have already shown that the payoffs to bidding signal value against itself are $-1/8$ each; these are the payoffs in the upper left-hand corner of the game matrix.

Now consider the implications of safe bidding against bidding signal value. Suppose bidder 1 bids safely, while bidder 2 bids signal value. As before, letting $H = 2$ and $L = 1$, the auction plays out as follows:

- Signal $\mathbf{z} = (2,2)$, bid $\mathbf{b} = (1.5,2)$, $P = 2$, $V = 2$, and player 2 wins the auction; payoffs $= (0,0)$.
- Signal $\mathbf{z} = (2,1)$, bid $\mathbf{b} = (1.5,1)$, $P = 1.5$, $V = 1.5$, and player 1 wins the auction; payoffs $= (0,0)$.
- Signal $\mathbf{z} = (1,2)$, bid $\mathbf{b} = (1,2)$, $P = 2$, $V = 1.5$, and player 2 wins the auction; payoffs $= (0, -1/2)$.
- Signal $\mathbf{z} = (1,1)$, bid $\mathbf{b} = (1,1)$, $P = 1$, $V = 1$, and each player wins with probability $1/2$; payoffs $= (0,0)$.

Bidder 1 expects the payoff

$$EV_1 = (1/4)(0 + 0 + 0 + 0) = 0$$

As you can see, bidder 1 expects a value of 0 by bidding safely. So the safe strategy does live up to its name. At the same time, bidder 2 still expects the value $-1/8$, the same expected loss as before. These are the payoffs shown in the lower left-hand corner of Figure 12.11. Reversing these payoffs, which symmetry allows, gives us the payoffs in the upper right-hand corner of Figure 12.11.

FIGURE 12.11 COMMON-VALUE AUCTION, NORMAL FORM

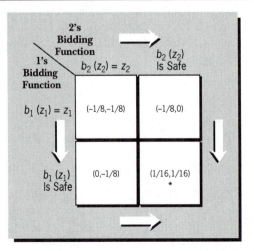

Finally, consider the implications of two bidders bidding safely against each other. The common-value auction plays out as follows:

- Signal $\mathbf{z} = (2,2)$, bid $\mathbf{b} = (1.5, 1.5)$, $P = 1.5, V = 2$, and each player wins with probability 1/2; payoffs = (1/4, 1/4).
- Signal $\mathbf{z} = (2,1)$, bid $\mathbf{b} = (1.5, 1)$, $P = 1.5$, $V = 1.5$, and player 1 wins the auction; payoffs = (0,0).
- Signal $\mathbf{z} = (1,2)$, bid $\mathbf{b} = (1, 1.5)$, $P = 1.5$, $V = 1.5$, and player 2 wins the auction; payoffs = (0, 0).
- Signal $\mathbf{z} = (1,1)$, bid $\mathbf{b} = (1,1)$, $P = 1$, $V = 1$, and each player wins with probability 1/2; payoffs = (0,0).

Now bidder 1 expects a positive payoff:

$$EV_1 = (1/4)(1/4) + (1/4)(0) + (1/4)(0) + (1/4)(0) = 1/16 > 0$$

By symmetry, bidder 2 expects the same positive payoff, 1/16. These are the payoffs in the lower right-hand corner of Figure 12.11.

Now we can see what the Nash equilibrium of the common-value auction is: each player bids safely. Moreover, this is also the strictly dominant solution of the auction game, since bidding safely strictly dominates bidding signal value. Bidding safely pays in a common-value auction, while bidding signal value leads to an expected loss.

This is perhaps the most abstract section in the entire book. Let's see that this abstraction does apply to the real world, in particular the world of oil exploration.

12.6 BIDDING FOR OFFSHORE OIL

The U.S. government has been leasing rights to drill for offshore oil since 1954. The government uses first-price, sealed-bid auctions to award the **offshore oil leases**.[11] Almost 20 percent of all oil produced in the United States comes from offshore wells, so the outcome of these auctions is important to the entire economy. The government typically provides no information beyond a legal description of the location of the area being leased, called a tract. Prior to these auctions, the oil companies are responsible for gathering whatever information they can about the oil-bearing potential of the tracts being offered. A typical tract covers about 5000 acres of ocean floor. Since the same geologic and seismological science and technology are available to all the oil companies, this information setup closely matches that of a common-value auction. This situation raises the possibility that oil companies might fall prey to the winner's curse in bidding for offshore oil.

Recently, three economists did an exhaustive study of these auctions for the period 1954–69. During this period, the government auctioned off 1200 tracts. All the major oil companies bid, as well as a large number of independent wildcatters. The total number of bids submitted on all tracts was 4050, meaning that a typical auction had three bidders. Winning an auction to drill for oil does not oblige the winning company to actually drill for oil. Of the 1200 tracts leased, the winner drilled on 872 of them, about 73 percent. In the other 27 percent of cases, the oil company, on further review, decided that the tract was

[11] Material for this study was drawn from Kenneth Hendricks, Robert H. Porter, and Bryan Boudreau, "Information, Returns, and Bidding Behavior in OCS Auctions: 1954–1969," *Journal of Industrial Economics* 35(1987): 517–542.

not promising enough to be worth exploring. This is a sure sign of a noisy signal. If the signal had been clear, then every winning bidder would have drilled for oil.

Everybody knows that the oil business is risky. Already, 27 percent of all tracts have shown up as losers. And just because a company drills for oil, that doesn't mean it's going to find any. Of the 872 wells that were actually drilled, 472 struck oil. So the conditional probability of striking oil, given that a company has decided to drill, is 54 percent—a little better than 50–50. This probability is even stronger evidence of a noisy signal about tract value. To sum up, of 1200 winning bids, 472 struck oil, or 39 percent. Winning the bidding for an offshore oil lease is no guarantee of finding oil.

It doesn't matter if a company strikes oil only 39 percent of the time it wins the auction, as long as its winning bid isn't too high. The industry as a whole came out very well in these 1200 auctions. The average winning bid was $2.26 million/tract, and industry profits for net of bids and exploration costs were about $2 million/tract. Overall, bids were low enough to absorb all the dry holes and all the above-average signals and still make money. There were some notable exceptions, however. Texaco, Phillips, and Sunoco all lost substantial amounts of money; Texaco was the biggest loser of all.

Now, you might be tempted to chalk this up to bad luck—the oil industry is certainly an environment replete with risk. Texaco won the bidding on 44 tracts; it drilled 38 of them, and it struck oil on 13 of them. Texaco's hit rate (13/38 = 34%) was below the industry average, whereas its drilling rate (38/44 = 86%) was above average. However, overall gross profits (that is, profits before deducting the winning bid) were positive for the 38 tracts that Texaco drilled. This situation provides some evidence that Texaco was overbidding.

To look further into the question whether Texaco was a winner cursed or not, the study used 20–20 hindsight. The economists asked, if Texaco had won every auction it bid on, what would it have made per tract? The answer was a whopping –$1.18 million/tract. Texaco could complain about its bad luck if it wanted to—but Texaco was really lucky. Had the company won all 128 tracts it bid on, it would have lost $151 million.

The U.S. government continues to auction off drilling rights for offshore oil. Stockholders of ChevronTexaco, the merger that includes Texaco, will be pleased to hear that Texaco's bidding performance has improved compared to 1954–69. There is a lot of money at stake in these auctions, and cursed is the winning bidder who has bid too much.

■ 12.7 AUCTIONS IN THE LABORATORY

No subject has received more attention in economics behavior laboratories than auctions. Kagel's admirable survey contains more than 115 references, and it is by no means exhaustive.[12] This section reviews two notable experiments from the survey, one an individual private-value auction and the other a common-value auction.

Experimental procedures for auctions are fairly standard. Subjects are volunteers recruited from the student population of the experimenter's university. Subjects are paid $3 to $5 for showing up. Subjects first read and sign a form, showing that they give their informed consent to participate in the experiment; this form is required by federal regulations on the use of human subjects in experiments. Subjects then work through a set of instructions concerning

---

[12] John H. Kagel, "Auctions: A Survey of Experimental Research," in *Handbook of Experimental Economics,* ed. John H. Kagel and Alvin E. Roth (New York: North Holland, 1994).

the auction they will be in. The instructions are couched in language as neutral as possible. Usually the subjects have to pass a quiz or practical exercise before they begin to play for real money. If there is a strong possibility that the subjects will lose money (not allowed by federal regulations), then they are given an initial capital stake. The idea is that the initial capital will keep them from going broke while they learn how to bid correctly.

The first auction we look at here is an individual private-value auction.[13] In this auction, subjects were told how many people they were bidding against, what their own individual value for the item was, and the uniform probability distribution from which individual values (their own and their rivals') would be drawn. Subjects then proceeded through a sequence of between 10 and 30 auctions.

A typical subject's behavior is shown in Figure 12.12. This subject was in a 3-person auction for 20 periods. In each period, the subject was given a new individual private-value and opportunity to bid. Individual private-value z is shown on the x-axis; the agent's bid, b, on the y-axis. The three straight lines shown are as follows: bidding true value, bidding two-thirds of true value, and the line that best fits the data. In a 3-person auction like this, a risk-neutral bidder has to raise his or her bid from 50 percent to 67 percent of true value in order to win the auction enough of the time to satisfy Nash equilibrium. Bidding true value guarantees that the subject breaks even. The straight line that best fit the data was as follows:

$$b(z) = 0.05 + 0.67z$$

Almost all observed bids lie between the break-even line and the Nash equilibrium bidding function for risk-neutral players, so the bidders are making money in the auction. These regularities appear in the data of several hundred subjects. Why the data do not fit the Nash equilibrium bidding function can be interpreted in many ways, such as asymmetric bidding

FIGURE 12.12 BIDDING FUNCTION OF A TYPICAL SUBJECT

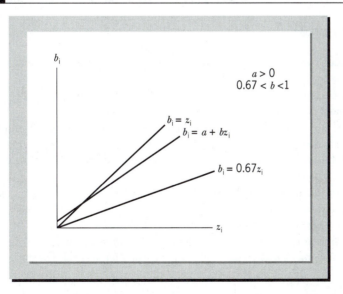

[13] James C. Cox, Vernon L. Smith, and James M. Walker, "Theory and Individual Behavior of First-Price Auctions," *Journal of Risk and Uncertainty* 1 (1988): 61–99. Vernon Smith won the Nobel Prize in Economics for 2002 in part for his work on auctions.

functions and differing attitudes toward risk. Indeed, interpreting these data has generated a good deal of controversy.

The next auction we look at is a common-value auction.[14] The subjects in this experiment were mostly M.B.A. students at the University of Houston. This experiment studied both first-price and second-price auctions. The major finding in both types of auctions was that subjects overbid. Inexperienced subjects were especially prone to overbidding. In first-price auctions, subjects bid on average more than $2.50 above the safe bidding strategy. As a consequence, more than 40 percent of the subjects went bankrupt: they ran out of money and had to be dismissed from the experiment before it was over. In second-price auctions, the overbidding was less severe. Still, in auctions where bidding underlying value weakly dominates all other strategies and is completely safe, subjects bid on average $1 more than underlying value.

This experiment provided very clear evidence of the winner's curse. With experience, about 70 percent of the subjects who didn't go bankrupt eventually did learn to avoid the winner's curse. These subjects bid at or even below the safe bidding strategy level. But even the subjects who survived barely broke even overall. Experience kept a dear school, as Benjamin Franklin would say.

These results raise a question. Considering that oil companies and others in real-world common-value auctions seem to do pretty well on average, why are laboratory rates of return so poor? In an effort to answer this question, the experimenters ran further trials with special subjects—bidding executives from Texas oil companies. Interestingly enough, the bidding behavior of the professionals in this experiment was statistically no different from that of the M.B.A. students. The experimenters did raise the stakes substantially to keep the executives interested. One possible explanation of this result is that there are features of real-world common-value auctions—known only to insiders—that lend a strong component of individual private value to these auctions. Such features could give bidders a benchmark from which to gauge overbidding—a benchmark more useful than just the signal of underlying value revealed in a pure common-value information situation.

■ SUMMARY

1. Auctions are the most pervasive instance of Bertrand competition in our economy. Auctions can be to buy or to sell a good, a service, or an asset.

2. Any auction in which the bidders simultaneously submit their bids is called a sealed-bid auction. Such auctions are modeled as normal form games.

3. There are three types of information conditions in an auction. Complete information means each bidder knows the valuation of every bidder. Individual private value means each bidder knows only his own valuation. Common value means each bidder has only a noisy signal of underlying valuation.

4. In any auction for a single item, the highest bidder wins. In a first-price auction, the winning bidder pays a price equal to the winning bid. In a second-price auction, the winning bidder pays a price equal to the second-highest bid.

5. In a first-price auction, regardless of the information condition, the bidder with the highest valuation or highest signal of valuation should underbid. The precise way in which to

[14] John H. Kagel, Ronald M. Harstad, and Dan Levin, "Information Impact and Allocation Rules in Auctions with Affiliated Private Values: A Laboratory Study," *Econometrica* 55(1987): 1275–1304.

underbid depends on the information condition. First-price auctions and English auctions produce equivalent revenue to the seller, at Nash equilibrium.

6. In a second-price auction where the bidder knows her own valuation, bidding that valuation is a dominant strategy. Second-price auctions and Dutch auctions produce equivalent revenue to the seller, at Nash equilibrium.

7. Symmetric auctions have symmetric Nash equilibria. At the symmetric Nash equilibrium of individual private-value and common-value auctions with two bidders, both bidders expect a positive payoff.

8. The Resolution Trust Corporation conducted a series of individual private-value auctions to clean up the savings and loan crisis in the United States in the early 1990s.

9. The winner's curse refers to a winning bidder in a common-value auction who had bid too close to the signal of underlying value. Such a bidder can expect to lose money. Bidding the signal of value in such an auction leads to a negative expected payoff.

10. The U.S. government has been conducting common-value auctions for rights to drill off-shore since 1954. The oil industry has profited from these auctions, with the notable exception of companies that overbid.

■ KEY TERMS

sealed-bid auction	English auction	bidding function
first-price auction	revenue equivalent	Resolution Trust
second-price auction	Dutch auction	Corporation (RTC)
overbidding	individual private-value	common-value auction
bid shaving	auction	winner's curse
reserve price	complete information	safe bidding strategy
efficient auction	information situation	offshore oil leases

■ PROBLEMS

1. Suppose there is complete information that valuations are $z_1 = \$5$ and $z_2 = \$4$. All bids must be multiples of $2. Draw the normal form for the first-price auction and solve.

2. Using the data in problem 1, solve the second-price auction.

3. In a first-price auction to sell, the low bidder wins and receives a price equal to the low bid. In an auction to sell, z_i represents the cost of providing the good or service, if sold. The utility function for a bidder i, u_i, is

$$u_i(\mathbf{b}) = b_i - z_i \text{ if } b_i = \min(\mathbf{b})$$

and 0 otherwise. Show that the three principles of bidding in first-price auctions apply to auctions to sell when you replace overbid with underbid.

4. Suppose that for the individual private-value auction in section 12.3, $H = 20$ and $L = 4$ instead of the signal values given there. Write down the normal form auction game that results, and find its Nash equilibrium. How does the solution change, if at all?

5. Consider the individual private-value auction in section 12.3. A bidder is considering bidding only 25 percent of individual private value. Compute the payoff consequences of this strategy against a bidder bidding true value, and against a bidder bidding half of true value. Is it a good idea to bid 25 percent of true value?

6. Consider the individual private-value auction in section 12.3. Now suppose that the high-value signal is three times as likely to be observed as the low-value signal. Write down the normal form auction game that results, and find its Nash equilibrium. Does this change in the information situation lead to a big change in strategy and payoffs?

7. You are contemplating bidding on a failed thrift. What information would you want before submitting your bid? Would this information be enough to form an individual private value?

8. The common value in a common-value auction is being determined by a coin toss. One coin toss provides a signal to bidder 1; a second coin toss provides a signal to bidder 2. Heads = 7; tails = 3. Underlying value is the average of the two tosses. Construct a table similar to that of Figure 12.10. Then write down the common-value auction in normal form, as in Figure 12.11. What is the Nash equilibrium of the auction?

9. In section 12.5, we considered only two strategies, Bid Signal Value and Bid the Safe Strategy. Consider the following lowball strategy: Always Bid L, Regardless of One's Signal. Include this strategy in the normal form of Figure 12.11 (now 3 x 3). What are the Nash equilibrium predictions now?

10. You are a large stockholder in Underwater Oil Company, which specializes in drilling for oil offshore. Underwater's earnings have been consistently negative, despite very strong earnings industry-wide. In its annual reports, the management attributes its earnings to bad luck. You have the microphone for 2 minutes at the annual stockholders' meeting. What do you say?

PART FOUR

Games Involving Bargaining

C H A P T E R   1 3

Two-Person Bargains

This chapter begins a new unit, games with substantial gains from and opportunities for cooperation. The simplest such games involve two players, and the coalition-function form, first mentioned in chapter 1, is often a useful way of describing them. The coalition-function form can be considered a shortcut to a solution—especially when the same answer can be derived from normal or extensive form versions of the game.

The real-world context in which gains to cooperation are present is bargaining. All games in this chapter are interpreted as bargaining games. We begin by recalling the Nash Demand game from chapter 5, which is the basic bargaining model on which all others are based. Two classic solutions to bargaining games are introduced, called the Nash bargaining solution and the Kalai-Smorodinsky bargaining solution after their discoverers. The properties of these solutions, and in particular how they handle various attitudes toward risk, are examined. Then we look at a recent example of bargaining, the deal struck between NextWave and the U.S. government, for which there was more than $10 billion on the table. Next the chapter turns to sequential bargaining, with its sequence of offers and counteroffers and the classic solution of Stahl and Rubinstein. Of particular importance are bargaining problems with imperfect information, in which offers, rejections of offers, and counteroffers may reveal private information. We then look at a special form of bargaining, called arbitration. Both sequential and imperfect information aspects surrounded trade talks between the world's two largest national economies, the United States and Japan. Finally, we consider some evidence on bargaining from experimental economics.

13.1 BARGAINING GAMES

In Chapter 5 we looked at a normal form game called the Nash Demand game. This section we take another look at this game and the general class of games to which it belongs, called bargaining games. Suppose there is a sum of money M on the table. There are two sides with an interest in the money, called player 1 and player 2. The players could be individuals, for example, the buyer and the seller of a house, bargaining over the terms of sale; one could be an individual and the other a corporation, such as a baseball player and the ball club, bargaining over contract terms; both sides could be corporations, such as GE and Honeywell bargaining over a merger; sides could even be countries or groups of countries, for example, the United States and the European Union (EU) bargaining over trade issues. The description of the bargaining game between the two sides is the same, regardless of the exact nature of those sides.

In a Nash Demand game, there is an amount of money M on the table. If the two sides agree on how to divide the money, each side gets what it asked for. If the two sides disagree, then the money disappears. The last time you saw this game, it was in normal form. Now we are going to model it as a bargaining game.

A **bargaining game** consists of two features: a **disagreement point** and **utility possibilities.** For the time being we will assume that both players are risk neutral, so that utility possibilities are equivalent to payoff possibilities. Disagreement occurs when both sides are unable to say yes to a proposal to divide the money at stake. We denote the disagreement point by the vector $\mathbf{d} = (d_1, d_2)$. This shows what the players get paid in the event they disagree. For now, we will assume that disagreement means that all the money on the table vanishes, so that $\mathbf{d} = (0,0)$. For instance, in the case of a house buyer and seller, disagreement means that there is no trade and hence no gains from trade available to these two parties. Similarly, in the case of the basketball player and the team, if they can't agree on a contract, the player doesn't play for the team. Again, neither side gains from the relationship. The same holds for larger entities, such as nations—if they can't reach an agreement on a deal, there is no deal and no gain to either side that might have been realized from the deal.

Payoff possibilities are represented by the set of all payoff vectors $\mathbf{u}$ that satisfy the budget constraint for risk-neutral players:

$$M \geq u_1 + u_2$$

Notice that the payoff possibilities, together with the disagreement point, put upper and lower bounds on what a player can get paid. First, a player cannot get less than zero out of a bargain: a player can say no to anything negative, that's the force of disagreement. By the same token, a player cannot get paid more than M. A payoff to player 1 larger than M means a negative payoff to player 2, who will automatically disagree to that. Efficiency in a bargaining situation means that players jointly get all the money on the table:

$$M = u_1 + u_2$$

where the payoff to each player is nonnegative. Remember, a player can always guarantee a payoff of zero by disagreeing, so that puts a lower bound on his or her payoff in this efficient division. An efficient division means the players do not leave any money on the table.

The disagreement point $\mathbf{d}$ and the utility possibility set together constitute the **coalition-function form** of the bargaining game. The coalition-function form presents information solely on payoffs, without going into any of the strategic detail underlying those payoffs. The coalition-function form of the bargaining game between risk-neutral players is shown in Figure 13.1.

We saw that the Nash Demand game in normal form has many Nash equilibria, some efficient, some not; some symmetric, some not. Suppose—in this we are following Nash himself—we require the solution to the Nash Demand game in coalition-function form to be efficient and symmetric. Efficiency says the solution pays out all the money. Symmetry says the solution pays each player equally, if the utility possibility set and disagreement point are symmetric. Both of these properties hold in the bargaining problem in Figure 13.1. The disagreement point is symmetric because each player gets the same payoff, 0, if negotiations

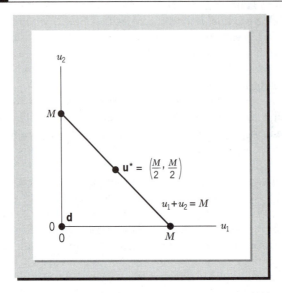

FIGURE 13.1 BARGAINING GAME, COALITION-FUNCTION FORM

break down. The utility possibility set is symmetric because for each payoff vector (x,y) in it, the payoff vector (y,x) is also in it—this is the payoff interchange condition from chapter 5. The **Nash bargaining solution** to the game in Figure 13.1 satisfies the pair of equations:

$$M = u_1 + u_2 \text{ (efficiency)}$$
$$u_1 = u_2 \text{ (symmetry)}$$

Solving these two equations, we get

$$u_1 = u_2 = M/2$$

The Nash bargaining solution to the symmetrical bargaining problem among risk neutrals is to split the money on the table evenly. Reaching an agreement by splitting the difference between the two parties is a time-honored and widely accepted principle of bargaining—a focal point, really—and we have just shown why, from a strategic standpoint.

The principles of efficiency and symmetry used to find the Nash bargaining solution are common to nearly all the bargaining solutions we study in this chapter. Let's highlight them once more. The first principle, bargaining symmetry, merely restates symmetry:

Bargaining symmetry. The solution of a symmetrical bargaining game is symmetrical.

For a symmetrical bargaining game like that shown in Figure 13.1, any feasible point on the line $u_1 = u_2$ satisfies symmetry. The second principle incorporates efficiency:

Bargaining efficiency. The solution of a bargaining game is efficient.

Bargaining efficiency means that the solution must lie on the efficient bargaining line. The symmetry line and the efficiency line cross at exactly one point—the equal division point—and this is the solution of the bargaining game, obtained via the shortcut of the coalition form.

These two principles suffice to solve all symmetrical bargaining games, but many interesting bargaining games are not symmetrical. How asymmetries arise and two competing concepts of how asymmetrical bargaining games should be solved are the subjects of the next section.

13.2 ASYMMETRIES AND THE NASH BARGAINING SOLUTION

There are four sources of asymmetry in a bargaining game. The players may be paid in different currencies, some alternatives may be irrelevant, the players may have different outside options, and the players may have different attitudes toward risk. This section looks at the first three sources of asymmetry, while the appendix considers the fourth.

The first possible asymmetry is that the players are paid in different currencies. For instance, suppose player 1 is paid in dollars, and player 2 in euros (€). Suppose that the exchange rate is €1.1 = $1. Thus both players' utilities have to be converted to a common currency in order to make them comparable. If there is $10,000 on the table, then efficiency in dollar terms is

$$10{,}000 = u_1 + u_2/1.1$$

where we have divided player 2's payoff in euros by 1.1 to convert those euros into dollars.

The disagreement point is still at $(0, 0)$, since $0 = 0$. Figure 13.2 shows the coalition function that results from the medium-of-payment asymmetry. If we apply symmetry to this asymmetrical game, we get $u_1 = u_2 = 5238$, to the nearest dollar. The odd thing here is that player 1 is getting paid $5,238, whereas player 2 is getting paid 5,238 euros, which is about $4,762, so the outcome is not really symmetrical at all.

Most people believe you should get paid the same economic value, whether you are paid in one currency or another. The following principle makes sure that players get paid the same, no matter what the currency:

Bargaining linear invariance. Suppose that $\mathbf{u}^* = (u_1^*, u_2^*)$ is the solution to the bargaining game with efficient division line $M = u_1 + u_2$. Then the solution to the bargaining game with efficient division line $M = u_1/k_1 + u_2/k_2$ is $(k_1 u_1^*, k_2 u_2^*)$.

What linear invariance does is convert the payoff to player 2 into dollars by multiplying by the exchange rate ($k_2 = 1.1$), thus keeping the dollar payoffs to the two players the same. The solution that satisfies linear invariance is shown by the vector

$$\mathbf{u}^* = (5000, 5500) \text{ in Figure 13.2.}$$

When both exchange rates are different from 1, both players are being paid in a third currency. This would happen when the money on the table is in British pounds, player 1 is paid in dollars, and player 2 is paid in euros. The bargaining solutions studied in this chapter satisfy linear invariance.

FIGURE 13.2 MEDIUM-OF-PAYMENT ASYMMETRY

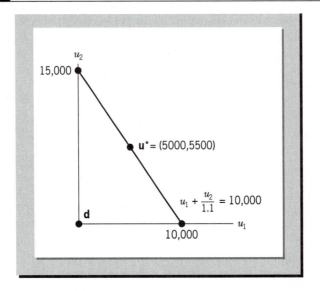

We can make the intuition behind linear invariance more precise by appealing to risk dominance (recall chapter 9). The risk-dominant Nash equilibrium maximizes the product of players' utilities, given that the alternative is a zero payoff. The maximum of the function

$$W = u_1 u_2$$

on the line $u_1 + u_2 = 10,000$ can be seen as the tangency solution between the efficient payoff line and the highest indifference curve generated by the function W. This is shown in Figure 13.3a, which is just like Figure 13.1. The maximum of this same function on the line $u_1 + u_2/1.1 = 10,000$ is shown in Figure 13.3b, which reproduces Figure 13.2. Notice that we satisfy linear invariance between the bargaining solutions in the two panels of Figure 13.3. This is no coincidence. Maximizing the product of players' utilities on a line will always satisfy linear invariance.

The first to notice this, and the inventor of the first bargaining solution, was Nobel Prize winner John Nash. We now call this the Nash bargaining solution in his honor.[1] When the disagreement point is (0,0), the Nash bargaining solution maximizes the product of players' utilities. We have seen that the Nash bargaining solution satisfies symmetry, efficiency, and linear invariance. We will now show one more crucial condition that it satisfies.

The second asymmetry we consider involves restrictions on what a player can get in a bargain. Such restrictions arise in bankruptcy. Suppose that players 1 and 2 have claims against the assets of a bankrupt company. By law, neither player can ask for more from the bankrupt company than that player is owed by the company. If the two players are owed different amounts, there is an asymmetry. Suppose that the bankrupt company owes $40,000 to player 1 and $50,000 to player 2. Suppose further that the bankrupt firm has

[1] See John F. Nash, "The Bargaining Problem," *Econometrica* 18 (1950): 155–162.

FIGURE 13.3 NASH BARGAINING SOLUTION AS TANGENCY SOLUTION

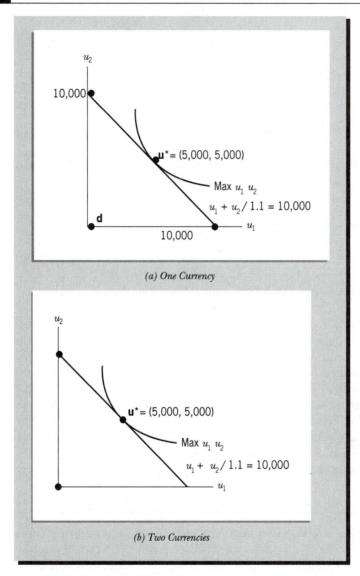

(a) One Currency

(b) Two Currencies

$80,000 in assets that can be paid out to the creditors if they can reach an agreement. Otherwise, the creditors are paid nothing. The efficient agreement line is

$$80,000 = u_1 + u_2$$

where u_1 cannot exceed $40,000, and u_2 cannot exceed $50,000. The coalition-function form is shown in Figure 13.4. Notice that the game is not symmetrical, and the vertices at (0, 80,000), and (80,000, 0) are unavailable. As you can see in Figure 13.4, the Nash bargaining solution ignores this asymmetry. It divides the $80,000 equally between the two

FIGURE 13.4 **BARGAINING GAME, BANKRUPTCY**

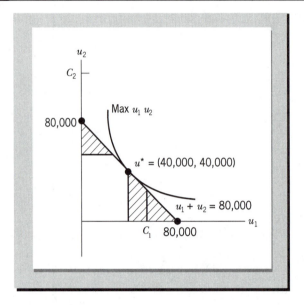

creditors, even though player 2 is owed $10,000 more than player 1. Other bargaining solutions are more sensitive to this asymmetry, as we show in the next section.

The third asymmetry we will study results from differences in the outside option. This asymmetry shows up as a nonzero disagreement point. Suppose there is $50,000 at stake in negotiations between player 1 and player 2. In the event that negotiations break down between the two, player 1 has a firm offer worth $15,000 from a third party, whereas player 2 gets $0. The disagreement point is then $\mathbf{d} = (15,000, 0)$ instead of $(0,0)$. Everyone agrees that this asymmetry is really important. The money on the table represents gains, and not money that players already have in their pockets from another source. We need another form of linear invariance to take this circumstance into account:

♟ ♟ ♟

Invariance with Respect to the Disagreement Point. Suppose that $\mathbf{u}^*$ is the solution to the bargaining problem with M at stake and disagreement point $(0,0)$. Then $\mathbf{u}^* + \mathbf{d}$ is the solution to the bargaining problem with disagreement point $\mathbf{d}$ and $M + d_1 + d_2$ at stake.

To see how this works, consider the bargaining problem between risk neutrals with $35,000 at stake. At the Nash bargaining solution $\mathbf{u}^*$, the players divide this money equally, $\mathbf{u}^* = (17,500, 17,500)$. Now suppose there is $50,000 at stake, but player 1 has an outside option worth $15,000. Then player 1 gets half the $35,000 plus the outside option ($15,000), for a grand total of $32,500. In equation format,

$$\mathbf{u}^* + \mathbf{d} = (17,500, 17,500) + (15,000, 0) = (32,500, 17,500)$$

The upshot is that the player with the better outside option comes out of the bargaining better. This is a very intuitive result. You know you have the upper hand when you can walk away from a deal and walk into another one nearly as good, when your bargaining partner has nothing to fall back on.

The Nash bargaining solution satisfies invariance with respect to the disagreement point by maximizing

$$W = (u_1 - d_1)(u_2 - d_2)$$

when the disagreement point is not equal to zero. In the bargaining game of Figure 13.5, the maximum of

$$W = (u_1 - d_1)(u_2 - d_2) = (u_1 - 15{,}000)(u_2 - 0)$$

on the line $50{,}000 = u_1 + u_2$ occurs at $u_1 = 32{,}500$, $u_2 = 17{,}500$. Intuitively, you think of this as the players first taking their outside options out of the money on the table, and then bargaining over what is left on the table. If they reach the agreement posited by the Nash bargaining solution, they divide what is left on the table after outside options have been cashed in evenly.

■ 13.3 BANKRUPTCY I: INDEPENDENCE OF IRRELEVANT ALTERNATIVES AND THE NASH BARGAINING SOLUTION

In the last section the Nash bargaining solution gave a puzzling answer to a **bankruptcy game.** With $80,000 of assets to divide between two risk-neutral creditors, one of whom was owed $40,000 and the other of whom was owed $50,000, the Nash bargaining solution gave each creditor $40,000. This section looks at the bankruptcy game in more detail to see why the Nash solution gives so much money to the smaller claimant. To accomplish this, we need some more notation.

Let A denote the assets of the bankrupt firm. We won't even bother to identify this firm—once in bankruptcy, it plays no role in the game. There are two claimants to the assets

FIGURE 13.5 BARGAINING GAME, d NOT 0

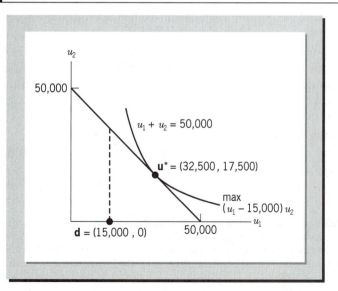

of the bankrupt firm, claimant 1 and claimant 2.[2] Claimant i has a claim C_i on the bankrupt firm. Each claim represents a legal liability on the part of the bankrupt firm. We first assume that both claimants are of equal seniority. In a bankruptcy game, claims exceed assets:

$$A < C_1 + C_2$$

This inequality of assets and liabilities is what creates the problem for the creditors; there is not enough left to pay them all off. We further assume that both claimants have the same outside option, 0, in the event that negotiations break down and no assets of the bankrupt firm are claimed. Finally, both claimants are risk neutral. With these assumptions, the only possible asymmetry lies with the claims. When $C_1 = C_2$, the game is symmetrical: equal seniority claims of equal value to the assets. The efficient division of assets line is

$$A = u_1 + u_2$$

and the disagreement point $\mathbf{d} = (0,0)$.

In the case of a symmetrical bankruptcy game, the Nash bargaining solution divides the assets equally:

$$A/2 = u_1{}^* = u_2{}^*$$

Notice that once the claims are equal, they play no further role. When the claims are unequal, then the bankruptcy game is asymmetrical. In this case the claims play a bigger, but still limited, role. It turns out to be handy to rank the claims in order of their size. Suppose the player with the lower number has the smaller claim:

$$C_1 < C_2$$

There are two cases to consider, depending on how much is left of assets relative to claims. These two cases are shown in Figure 13.6. To see why there are two cases, notice what happens when the assets are less than the smaller claim. In such a case, the Nash bargaining solution treats both claimants as if they were the same, because neither of them can feasibly get all their money back. The Nash bargaining solution continues to divide the money equally as long as assets are not too much bigger than the smaller claim.

- Case 1: $A/2 < C_1$. This case is shown in Figure 13.6a. The maximum product of utility occurs at the equal asset division.
- Case 2: $A/2 > C_1$. This case is shown in Figure 13.6b. The maximum product of utility occurs at the corner where $u_2{}^* = A - C_1$, and $u_1{}^* = C_1$. In this case, the smaller claimant is fully compensated, whereas the larger claimant gets what is left after paying off the smaller claimant. The larger claimant gets paid more than the smaller claimant.

This solution may strike you as odd. It is clearly not the way we usually settle bankruptcy cases among equally senior claimants. Indeed, it is as if the Nash bargaining solution is creating seniority where none exists. The smaller claim is treated as though it is senior once assets are double that claim. Prior to that point, both claims are treated the same.[3]

---

[2] The problem can be generalized to any number of claimants. Large bankruptcy cases, such as those involving bad debt of foreign countries, may have hundreds of claimants, chief among them U.S. banks. See chapter 14.

[3] In a strict seniority system, senior debt is fully paid off before a cent is paid to junior debt. If claimant 2 were truly senior in this case, then the seniority solution would also have two cases: $u_2 = A$ when $A > C_2$, and $u_2 = C_2$ when $A > C_2$.

FIGURE 13.6 | **BANKRUPTCY, NASH BARGAINING SOLUTION: (a) CASE 1; (b) CASE 2**

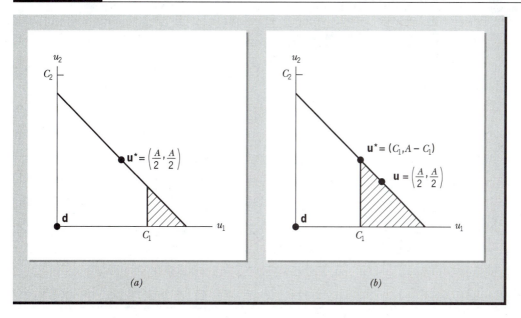

There is a special property, peculiar to the Nash bargaining solution, that is responsible for the way it solves bankruptcy games. This property is called the **independence of irrelevant alternatives,** and it works as follows. Suppose you know the solution $\mathbf{u}^*$ to a bargaining game. Then you get rid of some of the possibilities available in that bargaining game, but not $\mathbf{u}^*$. Then according to the independence of irrelevant alternatives, $\mathbf{u}^*$ is the solution of the game with fewer possibilities. The missing alternatives are simply irrelevant, as long as the original bargaining solution is still available.

Figure 13.7 shows how this works. Figure 13.7a is a standard bargaining game over an amount of money A. Efficiency and symmetry imply an even split of A. Now add player 2's claims to the game (see Figure 13.7b). Since claimant 2 cannot ask for more than he or she is owed, the claim C_2 eliminates alternatives. However, since none of these alternatives was the solution, they are irrelevant and can be disposed of without further ado. Next, add player 1's claim to player 2's claim (see Figure 13.7c). Since claimant 1 cannot ask for more than he or she is owed, the claim C_1 eliminates alternatives. Again, none of these alternatives was the solution. They, too, are irrelevant and can be disposed of without further ado. The same Nash bargaining solution, $\mathbf{u}^*$, solves all three cases in Figure 13.7.

Now we can explain why there are two cases in the Nash bargaining solution to the bankruptcy problem. In the argument for case 1, the picture is just like that in Figure 13.7c—the claims are small enough that only irrelevant alternatives are eliminated. If we go through this same argument for case 2, then the smaller claimant's claim eliminates a relevant alternative, the old solution. Once the payoff that divides the assets equally is unavailable, the Nash bargaining solution gives all the money it can to the smaller claimant.

Nash proved that the Nash bargaining solution is the only bargaining solution that satisfies symmetry, efficiency, linear invariance, and independence of irrelevant alternatives. Every bargaining solution worthy of serious attention satisfies the first three of these conditions. The independence condition is used to address relevant asymmetries, and controversy

---

| **FIGURE 13.7** | **INDEPENDENCE OF IRRELEVANT ALTERNATIVES: (a) GENERIC GAME; (b) WITH PLAYER 2'S CLAIM; (c) WITH PLAYER 2'S CLAIM AND PLAYER 1'S CLAIM** |

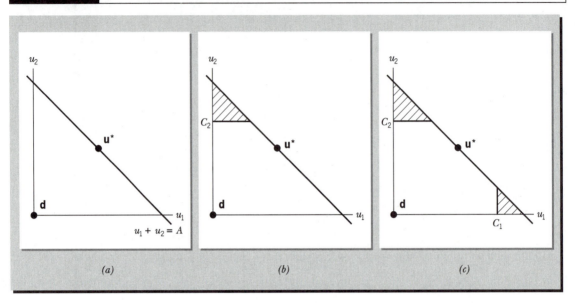

(a)   (b)   (c)

is bound to arise over which asymmetries are relevant and which are not. Still, it seems that what one is owed is always relevant to what one gets back in a bankruptcy proceeding.

■ 13.4 BANKRUPTCY II: MONOTONICITY AND THE KALAI-SMORODINSKY SOLUTION

Given the controversial way in which the Nash bargaining solution handles bankruptcy games, there has been considerable interest in proposing other solutions to bargaining games in general and to bankruptcy games in particular. The main idea behind such attempts has been to replace the independence of irrelevant alternatives with some other condition. Perhaps the most successful of these proposals is that of Kalai and Smorodinsky.[4] They proposed the following property for bargaining solutions, called **monotonicity.** Suppose that the utility possibilities shift out in player 1's direction. Then player 1's bargaining solution payoff does not go down. The same holds true for player 2, if there is a shift outward in player 2's direction. The spirit behind monotonicity is the old saying, "A high tide raises all the boats."

In general, the Nash bargaining solution does not satisfy monotonicity. Figure 13.8 provides a simple counterexample. Start with the bargaining game in Figure 13.8a, whose Nash bargaining solution $\mathbf{u}^* = (0.6, 0.6)$. Now shift utility possibilities out, as in Figure 13.8b, by

---

[4] See Ehud Kalai and Meir Smorodinsky, "Other Solutions to Nash's Bargaining Problem," *Econometrica* 43 (1975): 513–518. An early version of this bargaining solution is Howard Raiffa, "Arbitration Schemes for Generalized Two-Person Games," in *Contributions to the Theory of Games II*, ed. H. W. Kuhn and A. W. Tucker (Princeton, N.J.: Princeton University Press, 1953), 361–387.

FIGURE 13.8 | **NASH BARGAINING SOLUTION VIOLATES MONOTONICITY**

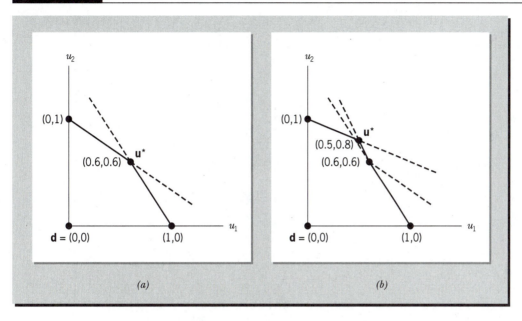

(a)   (b)

adding a new possibility, $(0.5, 0.8)$, to the efficient set. This new possibility becomes the new Nash bargaining solution $\mathbf{u}^*$ in Figure 13.8b. Player 1's payoff has gone down, even though player 2's has gone up. This violates monotonicity for player 1.

You might wonder if it is possible for a bargaining solution to satisfy monotonicity in every possible case. After all, this is a very strong condition. Kalai and Smorodinsky have shown that there is a unique bargaining solution satisfying efficiency, symmetry, linear invariance, and monotonicity.

The **Kalai-Smorodinsky bargaining solution** is easy to describe and to compute. Consider all the utilities available to the players that are at least as good as disagreement. Let U_1 be the highest such utility available to player 1 from bargaining; U_2, the highest such utility available to player 2. Write $\mathbf{U} = (U_1, U_2)$ for the vector of these maximum utilities. Now draw the line between the disagreement point $\mathbf{d}$ and the point $\mathbf{U}$. The Kalai-Smorodinsky solution is where this line crosses the efficient payoffs.

To see how the Kalai-Smorodinsky bargaining solution works, consider again the game given in Figure 13.8, now reproduced in Figure 13.9. We have the disagreement point $\mathbf{d} = (0,0)$, and the point of maximum payoffs $\mathbf{U} = (1,1)$. In Figure 13.9a, the Kalai-Smorodinsky solution agrees with the Nash solution, $\mathbf{u}^* = (0.6, 0.6)$, as it must, since both solutions satisfy symmetry and efficiency. In Figure 13.9b, the Kalai-Smorodinsky solution sticks to the (still efficient) solution $\mathbf{u}^* = (0.6, 0.6)$, despite the outward shift in utility possibilities. This solution will not make one player better off unless it can make both players better off. That is what enables the Kalai-Smorodinsky bargaining solution to satisfy monotonicity.

To take another example, consider the bankruptcy game with $C_1 = \$40,000$, $C_2 = \$50,000$, and $A = \$80,000$. We have $\mathbf{d} = (0,0)$ and $\mathbf{U} = (40,000, 50,000)$. The line between them is given by the equation

$$u_2 = 1.25u_1$$

FIGURE 13.9 KALAI-SMORODINSKY BARGAINING SOLUTION SATISFIES MONOTONICITY

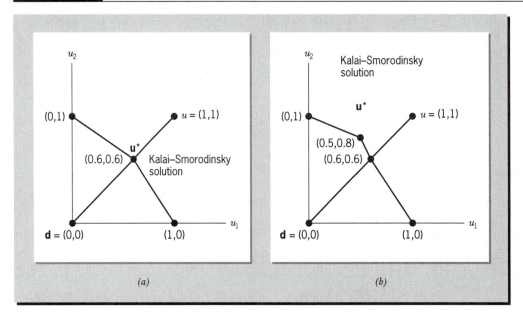

(a)   (b)

and the efficient payoff line is given by the equation

$$u_1 + u_2 = 80,000$$

These two lines cross at the point $\mathbf{u}^* = (35,556, 44,444)$, which is the Kalai-Smorodinsky bargaining solution. Compared to the Nash solution of (40,000, 40,000), the Kalai-Smorodinsky solution does not pay off claimant 1 in full. According to the Kalai-Smorodinsky bargaining solution, no claimant is paid off in full unless all claimants are paid off in full.

Often, the way in which bargainers represent the bargaining game they face has a major impact on the agreement they reach, if any. This factor is at work in a recent instance of 2-player bargaining, the deal between NextWave and the U.S. government.

13.5 NEXTWAVE AND THE FCC MAKE A DEAL

From the invention of radio until 1994, the U.S. government allocated frequencies on the electromagnetic spectrum to qualified broadcasters without charge, even though such frequencies, especially as they applied to television stations, could be quite valuable.[5] Instead of using market price as an allocation device, the regulatory arm of the government, the Federal Communications Commission (FCC), allocated frequencies on a variety of administrative criteria, such as "service to the public." Later, in the 1980s, the FCC used lotteries

---

[5] Material is drawn from John McMillan, "Selling Spectrum Rights," *Journal of Economic Perspectives* 8 (1994): 145–162; and from Yochi J. Dreazen, "NextWave's Wireless-License Accord Appears Washed Up," *Wall Street Journal*, 19 December 2001.

to allocate frequencies, sometimes getting up to 400,000 applicants for a single license to transmit on a frequency. In one widely publicized (but hardly unique) case, the lottery winner, who was an individual participating in the lottery solely in the hopes of reselling the license, did just that—for a cool $41 million, instantly.

This policy underwent a sea change in 1994. With heavy pressure on available frequencies from wireless telephone companies, and the undeniable evidence that the frequencies were scarce and valuable economic goods, the FCC decided to auction off rights to the electromagnetic spectrum instead of giving them away. The ensuing auction raised almost $1 billion for the U.S. Treasury, as well as creating a lot of jobs for game theorists specializing on auctions, who served as high-paid consultants to companies bidding for the spectrum

Given this initial success, the FCC conducted more such auctions of spectrum rights. In 1996, the FCC held one auction for large firms, with AT&T , McCaw (now part of AOL Time-Warner), Atlantic Bell (now Verizon), and SBC buying up most of the licenses. The FCC conducted a separate auction (the so-called C-block) for small firms. The C-block auction was intended to allocate licenses to small businesses.

NextWave, a small company, won a large chunk of the spectrum with its winning bid of $5 billion in the 1996 C-block auction. Indeed, the FCC gave very generous financing terms to any winner in the C-block auction. Those terms allowed small firms to bid like crazy in the hopes of then making a big splash on the IPO market to pay for them. Thus, the winners were generally the ones willing to take the biggest risks. Since the FCC did no screening for its financing, it got exactly what our adverse selection model in Chapter 10 predicts—a lot of credit risks who later defaulted.

NextWave was one of those defaults. Even with generous financing, its IPO never got off the ground, and before long it ran out of money. Under ordinary auction rules—like those on eBay—NextWave would have to withdraw its bid. But in this case, NextWave was the equivalent of that lottery winner—it had possession of a "winning ticket" worth a lot to the large firms which were excluded from the C- block auction. NextWave wasn't about to give up its winning ticket without a legal fight.

Another small problem—NextWave was forced to file for Chapter 11 bankruptcy protection when it ran completely out of cash while fighting to retain its spectrum rights in court. At that point, in 2001, in a move of dubious legality, the FCC seized the spectrum rights from NextWave and sold them off to the highest bidders, raising (at least on paper) $15 billion. NextWave went to court and succeeded in getting an injunction against the FCC. NextWave argued this was a taking, according to the Fourth Amendment to the U.S. Constitution, and the Court agreed.

As we write this, it appears that only an act of Congress can put together a deal that both the FCC and NextWave will agree to. Such a deal is on the table—Next Wave gets $10 billion, of which half goes to the U.S. Treasury as back taxes—while the FCC once again sells the spectrum rights for $15 billion in a repeat of its previous resale. Both sides come out winners, if Congress ever passes the legislation necessary to make this bargain legal. However, Congress has yet to pass such an act; meanwhile, the large telecomm companies have been released from their obligations to pay $15 billion for the spectrum, and may not want to bid that high again. So, the proposed deal may be history.

In the meantime, if you're wondering why your cell phone isn't working optimally, maybe it's because a big chunk of spectrum is unemployed. And maybe the next time the FCC runs an auction, it will make sure winning bidders can pay for their winning bids.

◼ 13.6 SEQUENTIAL BARGAINING WITH PERFECT INFORMATION

We have been modeling bargaining games in normal form, where each party to the bargain makes an offer and there is a deal or there isn't. This simple model of bargaining takes us a long way. Sometimes, however, we need to go to the extensive form to explain certain real-world phenomena. Of special interest is the behavior known as holding out for a better deal. A **holdout** is someone who refuses to reach an agreement until better terms are offered. This section shows that in **sequential bargaining** with complete information, holding out does not take place along the subgame perfect equilibrium path. In the next section, where information is incomplete, holding out may indeed take place along that path—if it is the only way to make private information credible.

Bargaining in extensive form is modeled as a sequence of offers and counteroffers, sequential bargaining. Suppose there is a sum of money M on the table. Let $a_i(t)$ represent the amount that player 1 asks for at time t. Player 1 is the first to move at time $t = 0$. Player 1 asks for an amount $a_1(0)$ of the money, with the rest of the money, $M - a_1(0)$, going to player 2 if player 2 accepts at once. If player 2 rejects player 1's proposal, then after one period of time has elapsed, player 2 gets to make a counterproposal, $a_2(1)$. It is then player 1's turn to accept or reject. The game can go on indefinitely, with player 1 making proposals during even-numbered periods and player 2 making proposals during odd-numbered periods. The first offer and counteroffer in sequential bargaining are shown schematically in Figure 13.10.

Players do not have an incentive to stall in their bargaining. Time is money, as the saying goes, and there is a considerable opportunity cost attached to having the money M tied up on the table. This opportunity cost is the interest forgone because a split of the money has not been agreed on—a cost we measured with the discount factor R in our study of infinitely repeated games in chapter 8. In particular, suppose that for each player, $1 paid

FIGURE 13.10 **SEQUENTIAL BARGAINING, FIRST TWO PERIODS**

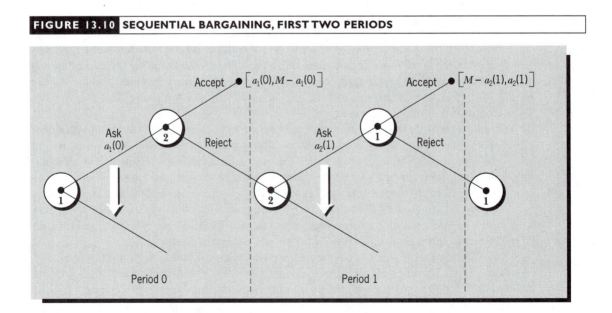

today is worth the same as R dollars paid one period hence, with $0 < R < 1$. Thus, since the amount of money M on the table is constant, its value to the players drops exponentially as the negotiations drag on. In particular, the value of the money after T periods have passed is only MR^T. If the two players never agree, then the money on the table eventually becomes worthless. This is the meaning of disagreement in sequential bargaining.

There is a reason for modeling bargaining in extensive form as a game that could go on forever. If there is a finite time limit, then we tend to get very extreme solutions to the game. For instance, suppose that the time limit is 0—that is, player 2 must take or leave the offer made by player 1 and the game ends. This is ultimatum bargaining, as described in the appendix to chapter 7. At subgame perfect equilibrium, player 1 gets all or almost all the money. If the game can last another period, allowing player 2 to make a counterproposal, then player 1 can no longer get away with almost all the money.

Since the amount of money on the table is shrinking , player 1 would like to make an offer enticing enough that player 2 accepts immediately. Suppose that player 1 has asked for $a_1(0)$, and so is offering player 2 the remainder, $M - a_1(0)$. When should player 2 accept? The guide to our thinking is the following principle, which captures subgame perfection in the case of bargaining that can go on forever:

Bargaining Consistency. You should never ask for something later that you have rejected before. You should never reject something now that you plan to ask for later.

If you are consistent in bargaining, at least you won't look stupid. You would look really stupid if you were to reject an offer of \$1 million early on in the negotiations, and then later on asked for \$1 million or even less. Bargaining consistency says, a bird in the hand now is better than a bird in the hand later—the time cost breaks the tie.

We now construct a subgame perfect equilibrium outcome for sequential bargaining, using bargaining consistency. Suppose that player 1 asks $a_1(0)$ initially, thus leaving $M - a_1(0)$ for player 2. If player 2 rejects this amount, then player 2 should ask for at least as much when it is his turn to propose. That means player 2 should plan to ask at least $a_2(1)$, satisfying

$$a_2(1) = M - a_1(0)$$

Next, notice the subgame that begins with player 2 making an offer at time $t = 1$ with amount M on the table looks exactly like the subgame that begins with player 1 making an offer at time $t = 0$ with amount M on the table, with the roles of the players reversed. Suppose player 1 makes an acceptable ask $a_1(0)$ right now. Then player 2's ask one period hence is also acceptable, provided that

$$Ra_1(0) = a_2(1)$$

where the discount factor R appears to adjust for the time difference between the two subgames.

Putting these two equations together and solving, we get

$$a_1(0)^* = M/(1 + R)$$
$$a_2(1)^* = RM/(1 + R)$$

A subgame perfect equilibrium outcome is for player 1 to ask for $a_1(0)^*$ and for player 2 to agree immediately. This wastes no time, and allocates the money M efficiently. Notice that the player moving first, player 1, has a first-mover advantage, since for $R < 1$,

$$M > RM$$

while the denominators of the two payoff terms are the same. Holding out doesn't pay here. Since the terms are never going to get better, it is best to accept them now. This solution, first noted by Stahl in 1971, was rediscovered by Rubinstein a dozen years later.[6] This solution is now called the **Stahl-Rubinstein bargaining solution** in their honor.

Figure 13.11 shows the Stahl-Rubinstein solution for $M = \$100$ and $R = 0.5$. At an R this low, there is a big first-mover advantage. The player who moves first gets two-thirds of the money on the table, as opposed to the player who moves second, who gets one-third. As the discount factor approaches 1—thereby reducing the time cost of holding out—the first mover advantage shrinks. In the limit as R approaches 1, the Stahl-Rubinstein solution converges to an even division of the money on the table, just the same division as any bargaining solution satisfying efficiency and symmetry would do.

13.7 SEQUENTIAL BARGAINING WITH IMPERFECT INFORMATION

The Stahl-Rubinstein solution depends crucially on both players knowing exactly how much money there is on the table at the outset.[7] Holding out does not pay if both sides

---

FIGURE 13.11 SEQUENTIAL BARGAINING: COALITION FUNCTION FORM, $R = 0.5$

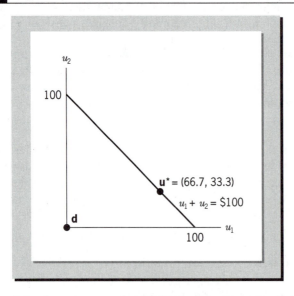

---

[6] The relevant sources are Ingolf Stahl, *Bargaining Theory* (Stockholm: Stockholm School of Economics, 1972) and Ariel Rubinstein, "Perfect Equilibrium in a Bargaining Model," *Econometrica* 50 (1982): 97–109. Rubinstein also proved that this was the unique subgame perfect equilibrium when money is infinitely divisible.

[7] For readers interested in going more deeply into this topic, I heartily recommend the survey by John Kennan and Robert Wilson, "Bargaining with Private Information," *Journal of Economic Literature* 31 (1993): 45–104.

know exactly how much money is at stake. If information is imperfect and one of the players does not know how much money is at stake, then holding out might pay. In such a situation, the rejection of a proposal and the subsequent counterproposal by an informed player can signal the other side what the true amount of the money on the table is.

Here is an example of **sequential bargaining with imperfect information.** Player 1 is a novelist, who is about to offer a novel to a motion-picture company as the basis for a movie. The novelist makes the first move. However, the novelist has only a vague idea of what the novel is worth as a movie property. This vague idea takes the form of a probability distribution. The probability is 90 percent that this novel is an okay movie property, in which case it is worth $100,000; the probability is 10 percent that this is a blockbuster property, in which case it is worth $1,000,000. This is a fairly optimistic assumption. Sylvia Nasar has written a lot of good books, but only one *A Beautiful Mind*. Player 2, the movie company, actually knows what the novel is worth—but for obvious reasons is not telling.[8]

What we have is a screening game, with the uninformed player moving first. Suppose everyone involved is risk neutral. The parties have agreed in advance that they will split any money on the table evenly, once an agreement has been reached.[9]

Given the even-split provision, the best thing the novelist can do at the outset is ask for $500,000—half the value of the novel if it is a blockbuster. If the novel is a blockbuster movie property, then the movie company knows this, and should accept at once. The same reasoning that underlies perfectly informed sequential bargaining applies to the movie company in this situation. If the novel is an okay movie property, then the movie company knows this and rejects the novelist's proposal. Now the movie company waits before coming back with a counterproposal. This is the holdout phase. The movie company has to wait to make its information—that the novel is merely an okay movie property—credible. If the movie company rejects the $500,000 proposal and immediately turns around and says we'll give you $50,000 instead, the novelist should reject the offer, because it could just as well be a $450,000 lie. However, if the movie company holds out long enough, then its counteroffer does become credible. In fact, the movie company has to hold out long enough for the profit from a $450,000 lie to completely vanish. If the movie company lies and rejects a sure gain of $500,000, it is looking at $(\$950,000)R^T$ during the holdout phase. This $950,000 is the movie company's $500,000 gain from getting hold of a blockbuster plus the $450,000 lie. The movie company's possible lie has lost all its value when

$$\$500,000 = (\$950,000)R^T$$

Rearranging, we get

$$(500,000)/(950,000) = .526 = R^T$$

Taking the logarithm of both sides, we have

$$\log(.526) = T \log(R)$$

where $\log(.)$ represents the logarithm of the term inside the parentheses.

Solving for T, we get

$$T = \log(.526)/\log(R)$$

---

[8] Yes, this is a heroic assumption, given how many bad movies get made every year. The point of the example still goes through if the movie company has merely a better signal of underlying value than does the novelist.
[9] For instance, by using a symmetrical and efficient shortcut such as the Nash bargaining solution.

The lower the discount factor, the shorter the time the movie company has to wait before getting back to the novelist with the $50,000 counteroffer. For instance, if the discount factor is exactly $R = .526$, and discounting is in annual terms, then the holdout phase lasts exactly 1 year. If the discount factor is .90 instead, then the holdout phase lasts much longer, about 5 years. This is one of the reasons that Hollywood negotiations can be so protracted. If you as a writer think you have any chance at all of having a hot property, it may take years for someone to convince you otherwise.

We now turn to a real-world instance of protracted negotiations under incomplete information. Note the sequence of proposal and counterproposal in these events.

■ 13.8 UNITED STATES–JAPAN TRADE NEGOTIATIONS

The United States and Japan are the two largest national economies in the world, and trade between them results in large gains to both sides. Exports sold by a nation make its economy bigger, whereas imports make its economy smaller, as measured by GDP. When trade is balanced, and exports equal imports, then the gains from trade are fairly evenly divided between two countries.

Under current arrangements, Japan gets a larger share of the gains from trade than does the United States. This disparity in gains shows up in the $50 billion trade surplus that Japan enjoys annually with the United States. At this level, Japan accounts for more of the U.S. trade deficit than any other country. The gains from trade would be shared a lot more equally if this trade deficit were closer to zero.

In a perfectly competitive world, trade deficits of this magnitude would not persist. Prices—here, exchange rates—would adjust until the deficit disappeared. The yen has risen from 225 yen = $1 to about 120 yen = $1 in the past 20 years, but the trade deficit has persisted. Thus, the primary explanation for the trade deficit is imperfections in competition. The Clinton administration began bargaining for trade concessions from Japan as soon as Clinton took office. Then-President Clinton and then-Prime Minister Miyazawa met on April 18, 1993, to announce a new framework for United States–Japan trade.[10] At a news conference following a day of meetings, the president said he was deeply concerned about the inadequate access for American firms, products, and investors in Japan. For his part, Prime Minister Miyazawa said that improvements could be realized neither with managed trade nor under the threat of unilateralism. The sense of these meetings was that it would take months or even years of bargaining before the trade-deficit issue could be fully resolved. The two leaders did agree to set up an agenda for talks on the new framework at the G-7 summit in July 1993.

A week later in Tokyo, Secretary of the Treasury Ron Brown said, "It is a little disingenuous for the Japanese to complain about managed trade. I mean, after all, they have been some of the most successful and obvious managers of trade over many years."[11] The secretary's remarks provoked a sharp response from the Japanese. One high-ranking Japanese official spoke of Japanese retaliation, for instance, by reducing its investments in the United States. Secretary Brown countered by saying that he had been quoted out of context. In any

---

[10] Bob Davis, "U.S., Japan Endorse Trade Framework, But Outlook Is for Continued Haggling," *Wall Street Journal*, 19 April 1993.

[11] Jacob M. Schlesinger and Quentin Hardy, "War of Words between U.S. and Japan over Trade, Exchange Rates Heats Up," *Wall Street Journal*, 26 April 1993.

event, Secretary Brown was clearly urging Japan to agree to measurable results in a number of trade areas. "Our goal is not better rules, it is demonstrably open markets," he said. The administration's position was that Japanese restrictions on imports from the United States were primarily responsible for the trade imbalance—a position captured in the metaphor of an unlevel playing field. The United States' push for a level playing field was an effort to share the gains from trade more evenly.

The official Japanese response to Secretary Brown's remarks and other initiatives by the Clinton administration was sure and swift. On May 11, 1993, Japan issued a report accusing the United States of unfair trade practices and calling the United States the worst offender among the large economies.[12] According to the Japanese report, the United States broke the General Agreement on Tariffs and Trade (GATT; the predecessor to today's World Trade Organization—WTO) rules in 9 of 12 major sectors. Furthermore, the Japanese government announced in late May that the new framework must include an agreement on underlying principles. One of these underlying principles was bilateralism: if either side invoked unilateral measures, the other will reserve the right to suspend those talks.[13]

Just prior to the G-7 meetings in Tokyo, Japan made a major concession on the issue of measurable results. Japan said that it would be willing to consider illustrative examples of numbers in certain product areas—numbers that would not be binding, but would serve as dimensions along which to measure agreement.

After the G-7 summit, Clinton and Miyazawa agreed on a framework for trade. In this agreement, called the framework agreement, each side made two major commitments. Japan agreed to open its markets to more imports, making the rules and regulations more transparent to foreign companies. Japan also agreed to reduce its trade surplus—a surplus that reached $120 billion in 1992—with the rest of the world, not just with the United States. For its part, the United States agreed to reduce its government deficit considerably and to raise the competitiveness of its manufacturers. The framework agreement was finalized and signed at a summit meeting between the two leaders in Washington, D.C., on February 11, 1994. The threat of a trade war between the United States and Japan had been averted.

■ 13.9 BARGAINING IN THE LABORATORY

A wide variety of experiments on bargaining behavior have been run in the laboratory.[14] A veteran of this activity is Alvin E. Roth at Harvard University. This section reports on some of what Roth and his coauthors have found.[15]

The basic setup for a bargaining experiment is as follows. There are two players, recruited from the student population as subjects. Each subject is told that both a large prize and a small prize are available. If the subject does not win the large prize, the small prize is automatically awarded. The large prize is awarded by a lottery at the end of the

---

[12] Jacob M. Schlesinger, "Japan Accuses U.S. of Unfair Trade Policies," *Wall Street Journal,* 12 May 1993.

[13] Jacob M. Schlesinger, "Japanese Say They'll Impose Conditions in Trade Talks Contrary to U.S. Views," *Wall Street Journal,* 28 May 1993.

[14] Material in this section was drawn from Alvin E. Roth, "Bargaining Phenomena and Bargaining Theory," in *Laboratory Experiments in Economics,* ed. Alvin E. Roth (Cambridge, UK: Cambridge University Press, 1987), 14–41.

[15] For a good survey of the activity in this field, the interested reader should consult Alvin E. Roth, "Bargaining Experiments," in *Handbook of Experimental Economics,* ed. John H. Kogel and Alvin E. Roth (New York: North Holland, 1994).

experiment. The large prize goes to the player holding the winning number. At the start of bargaining there are 100 lottery tickets on the table, numbered 1 to 100. The more lottery tickets a subject obtains by bargaining, the greater that subject's chance of winning the large prize. The winning number is drawn by chance from the uniform distribution, so that each number is equally good. The lottery tickets on the table represent money on the table. Subjects bargain over how many of the tickets each will get. In the event of disagreement, there is no lottery for the large prize, and each subject gets his or her small prize.

Figure 13.12a shows the ticket possibilities with this setup. If player 1 gets all the tickets, player 1 is sure to win the large prize; if player 2 gets all the tickets, player 2 will win the large prize. In the event of disagreement, neither player gets any tickets. We can convert tickets into utilities by the following transformation:

$$u_i = t_i A_i + (1 - t_i)a_i$$

where t_i is the number of tickets player i holds, A_i is player i's grand prize, and a_i is player i's small prize. In the simplest experiments, the large prize $A_i = \$1$ for both players and the small prize $a_i = \$0$ for both players. The utility possibilities that result are shown in Figure 13.12b. This figure represents one particular set of rules for dividing a dollar between two players. When human subjects played the game in Figure 13.12b, every single pair (11 in all) picked the 50–50 ticket distribution, just as predicted by the Nash and Kalai-Smorodinsky bargaining solutions.

Now suppose that player 2 is allowed to receive at most 60 tickets. According to the independence of irrelevant alternatives, this restriction should not matter. Figure 13.13 shows the ticket possibilities and the utility possibilities that result. Many pairs of subjects played this game, and the results were somewhat different from the results of the other

FIGURE 13.12 BARGAINING IN THE LABORATORY, M = 1: (a) TICKET POSSIBILITIES; (b) UTILITY POSSIBILITIES

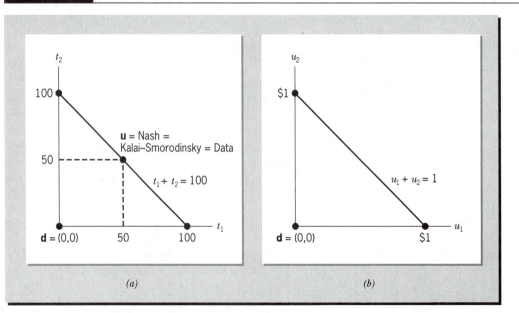

(a)   (b)

FIGURE 13.13 | BARGAINING IN THE LABORATORY, INDEPENDENCE OF IRRELEVANT ALTERNATIVES: (a) TICKET POSSIBILITIES; (b) UTILITY POSSIBILITIES

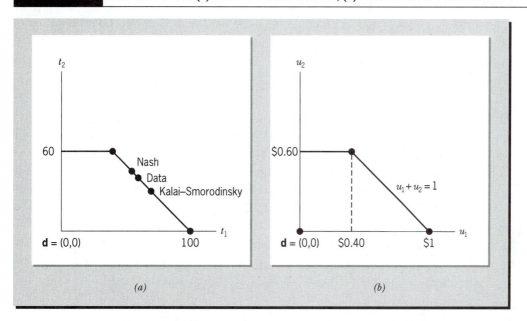

version. On average over all pairs, player 2 got 1.9 fewer tickets than player 1, whereas the Nash bargaining solution says that there should be no difference. The large standard deviation of the ticket difference, 12.2, suggests that it is not statistically significant.

The Kalai-Smorodinsky solution says that the restriction should make a difference, and in player 1's favor. However, according to the Kalai-Smorodinsky solution, the tickets should be split in the ratio 5:3, so that player 1 gets 25 more tickets, rather than just 2 more. The upper bound on player 2's tickets injected a great deal of noise into the data, and subjects had a difficult time dealing with the bargaining problem they faced. The observed data are not terribly supportive of either bargaining solution in this treatment.

At this point, the experimenters varied the sizes of the large prizes (the small prizes were still worth $0 to each player). The large prize was worth $1.25 to player 1, but $3.75 to player 2. There were no limits on how many tickets player 2 could get. The utility possibilities that result from this setup are shown in Figure 13.14 (b). According to the Nash bargaining solution, the players split the money in the ratio 1:3, with player 1 getting $0.625 and player 2, $1.875. This result follows from linear invariance. The Nash bargain over the money implies a 50–50 ticket split. Since the Kalai-Smorodinsky bargaining solution satisfies linear invariance, it agrees with the Nash bargaining solution in this case. When this game was played in the laboratory, something remarkable happened. Instead of splitting the tickets evenly, player 1 got on average 34.6 more tickets (the standard deviation of this difference was 19.3) than player 2, an observed ratio of more than 2:1, shown in Figure 13.14 (a). The standard deviation of this difference was again quite high, 19.3. This average ticket difference is certainly not what either bargaining theory would predict. What happened was that ticket agreements tended to cluster between the 50–50 ticket split predicted by the bargaining solutions and the 75–25 split that led players to get the same expected

FIGURE 13.14 BARGAINING IN THE LABORATORY, LINEAR INVARIANCE: (a) TICKET POSSIBILITIES; (b) UTILITY POSSIBILITIES

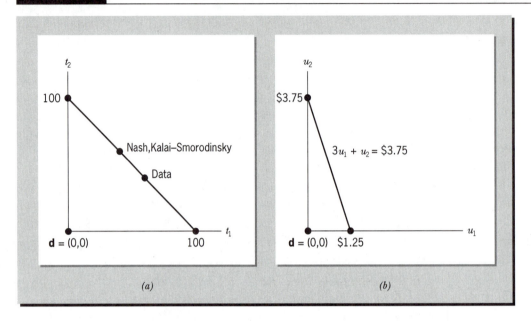

payoff. The average of these two types of agreements led to the observation in between them, namely, a ticket difference between 0 and 50.

As a final treatment, the sizes of the prizes were kept the same as in this last setup, but player 2 could ask for at most 60 tickets. The joint treatment of linear invariance and independence of irrelevant alternatives is shown in Figure 13.15. The Nash bargaining solution continues to predict that the tickets will be split evenly. The Kalai-Smorodinsky solution says that utility will be split in the ratio 5:9, which implies a ticket split of 61 for player 1 and 39 for player 2, both shown in Figure 13.15 (a). When 11 pairs reached agreements in this bargaining game, the average ticket difference was 21.6 tickets in favor of player 1.[16] This outcome, shown in Figure 13.15 (b), is remarkably close to the Kalai-Smorodinsky prediction of 22 more tickets to player 1, and quite different from the Nash prediction of no ticket difference.

The conclusions from this series of experiments are mixed; each bargaining solution gets some support, but also some disconfirmation. Data from the real world—and laboratories are part of the real world—are never as clean and clear-cut as game theory would like. In addition to the mixture of results reported here, some other things happen in bargaining experiments that are even more puzzling. First, we have been speaking only about agreements. In roughly 20 percent of all pairs in bargaining experiments, no agreement is reached. Disagreement should never happen according to the efficiency condition, but, unfortunately, it does. It would seem that one or both players are holding out for a better deal when time runs out. (There are time limits on all bargaining sessions, typically on the order of 6 minutes.) Second, and apparently related, there is a pronounced deadline effect. More agreements are reached in the last 30 seconds of bargaining than in the rest of the

[16] With a standard deviation of 22.5.

FIGURE 13.15   BARGAINING IN THE LABORATORY, BOTH TREATMENTS: (a) TICKET POSSIBILITIES; (b) UTILITY POSSIBILITIES

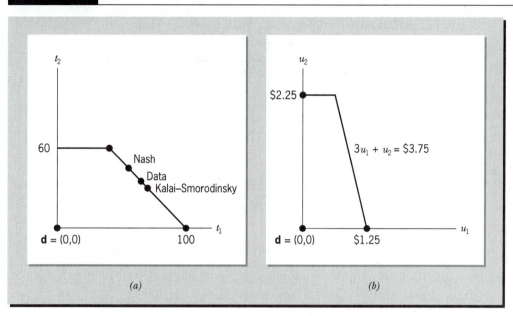

(a)   *(b)*

time combined, with a peak number of agreements in the last 5 seconds. You can expect future bargaining experiments to address these issues of efficiency and timing.

SUMMARY

1. In a bargaining game, two players stand to gain if they can come to an agreement. The coalition form of a game is useful for describing and solving bargaining games.

2. A bargaining game is described by its disagreement point and its utility possibilities set. The disagreement point tells what happens if negotiations break down. The utility possibilities set tells how much the bargainers could get from various agreements.

3. The principle of bargaining symmetry says that the solution of a symmetrical bargaining game is symmetrical. The principle of efficient bargaining says that the solution of a bargaining game is efficient. Together, these two principles select a unique solution to symmetrical bargaining games.

4. Even when bargainers have all necessary information, four asymmetries can affect the outcome of a bargaining game: the medium of payment, attitudes toward risk, outside options, and legal limits on asks. The concept of linear invariance says that the medium of payment really shouldn't matter to the outcome of bargaining.

5. The Nash bargaining solution is the only bargaining solution that satisfies symmetry, efficiency, linear invariance, and independence of irrelevant alternatives. This bargaining solution embodies the notion of risk dominance in bargaining games.

6. The Kalai-Smorodinsky bargaining solution is the only bargaining solution that satisfies symmetry, efficiency, linear invariance, and monotonicity. It gives more appealing solutions to bankruptcy games than does the Nash bargaining solution.

7. Bargaining games in the corporate sector are often played for billion-dollar stakes. The outcomes of such games are a complicated mixture of bargaining solution principles.

8. In sequential bargaining with perfect information, the player who goes first has an advantage. The Stahl-Rubinstein bargaining solution solves such games.

9. In sequential bargaining with imperfect information, the informed player has an informational advantage. However, the informed player may have to hold out in such a game in order to make its private information credible to the other side.

10. In bargaining between nations, business goes on as usual, which reduces the time cost of bargaining and the pressure to reach an agreement. Thanks to the trade agreement between the United States and Japan in 1994, after years of conflict over trade issues, these countries were able to avert a trade war.

◼ KEY TERMS

bargaining games
disagreement point
utility possibilities
efficient division
coalition-function form
Nash bargaining solution
bargaining symmetry
bargaining efficiency

linear invariance
bankruptcy game
independence of irrelevant
   alternatives
monotonicity
Kalai-Smorodinsky
   bargaining solution
holdout

sequential bargaining
Stahl-Rubinstein bargaining
   solution
sequential bargaining with
   imperfect information

◼ PROBLEMS

1. Two risk-neutral bargainers have $500 on the table. If they disagree, player 1 gets nothing, whereas player 2 has an outside option worth $100. Find the Nash bargaining solution.

2. Same data as in problem 1. Find the Kalai-Smorodinsky bargaining solution. Compare this solution to the Nash bargaining solution in problem 1. Do they agree or disagree?

3. In problem 1, player 1 can only ask for up to $40 on the table. Find the Nash bargaining solution, and compare to the answer in problem 1.

4. Same data as in problem 3. Find the Kalai-Smorodinsky bargaining solution. Compare this solution to the Nash bargaining solution in problem 3, and to your answer in problem 2.

5. Players 1 and 2 are claimants in a bankruptcy game. Player 1 has a claim worth $1 million; player 2 has a claim worth $5 million. Both are risk neutral. Work out the Nash and Kalai-Smorodinsky bargaining solutions when the assets at stake are $1 million, $3 million, and $5 million. How do the two solutions compare?

6. You are called to testify in a bankruptcy case as an expert witness for a small claimant. You will be asked in court why the Nash bargaining solution should be used in this case. Prepare your testimony—you will be well paid.

7. There is $1 trillion on the table in United States–Japan trade. Trade talks are sequential, there is perfect information, and the annual discount factor is .9. All trade is suspended for the duration of the talks. The United States gets to make the first offer. What should it offer Japan? What should Japan do with this offer?

8. Show that when the discount factor $R = 1$, the formula for the Stahl-Rubinstein bargaining solution divides the money on the table equally.

9. In the novelist–movie company negotiations, suppose that an okay novel is worth $400,000 as a movie property and the discount factor is .80. Describe the solution to the bargaining. How long does the movie company hold out? Would it be right to say that the novelist is making the movie company hold out?

10. Besides having trade disagreements with Japan, the United States also has trade disagreements with the European Union (EU), most notably involving steel, bananas, and the tax treatment of profits earned overseas. You represent the United States at upcoming trade talks with the EU. Describe your negotiating stance—what you would hope to get out of the talks, what you would be willing to do in case of disagreement, what sort of counterproposals you would bring. What role does a deadline play in negotiations?

■ APPENDIX. RISK AVERSION AND BARGAINING SOLUTIONS

Attitude toward risk has a visible effect on the shape of a bargaining game—it makes it curved. It also has an effect on the payoffs—the more risk-averse a player is, the less that player gets at a Nash or a Kalai-Smorodinsky bargaining solution. This makes sense intuitively. If you are risk averse, then you are averse to disagreement, or even the risk of disagreement. That aversion will make you willing to give up more in the bargaining, to reach an agreement.

We now illustrate this effect of risk aversion on bargaining, for the Nash bargaining solution. Suppose that player 1 is risk neutral but that player 2 is risk averse, with

$$u_2 = (m_2)^{0.5}$$

or

$$u_2^2 = m_2$$

where m_2 is payoff in money. Start with cash payouts:

$$M = m_1 + m_2$$

Converting cash to utility by substituting into the efficient division line, we get a curve:

$$u_1 + u_2^2 = M$$

This curve is shown in Figure 13.16 for $M = 100$. You can see that the Nash bargaining solution occurs at the highest indifference curve for the product of the two utilities:

$$u_1^* = 66.7, u_2 = 5.77$$

At these utilities, the cash of 100 is paid out in a ratio of 2:1. The risk-neutral player 1 gets paid 66.7, while the risk-averse player 2 gets paid 33.3 (that's the square of 5.77). Since risk-neutral players would split the 100 equally, risk aversion has made all the difference to the outcome.

We can also compute the Kalai-Smorodinsky bargaining solution for the risk-averse case. From Figure 13.16, we have $\mathbf{U} = (100, 10)$. The line between disagreement and $\mathbf{U}$ satisfies

$$u_2 = (0.1)u_1$$

FIGURE 13.16 **BARGAINING GAME, RISK ATTITUDE ASYMMETRY**

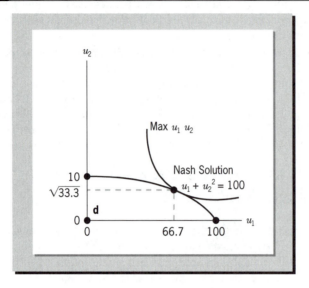

Substituting this line into the efficiency curve, we have

$$10u_2 + u_2^2 = 100$$

Solving this quadratic equation for player 2's utility, we get

$$u_2^* = 6.18$$

Substituting into the line between disagreement and **U**, we get

$$u_1^* = 61.8$$

At the Kalai-Smorodinsky bargaining solution, the risk-neutral player again gets more than the risk-averse player. The risk-neutral player gets 61.8 out of 100, while the risk-averse player gets what's left, 38.2.

The moral of all this is, if you are risk averse, it is best to keep that to yourself. If someone you are bargaining with knows you are risk averse, that information will cost you money in terms of the overall bargain reached.

CHAPTER 14

n-Person Bargaining and the Core

The bargaining games studied in the last chapter had exactly two sides, the two players. This is fairly restrictive. In many real-world cases, there are more than two sides in a bargaining game. For instance, there may be hundreds of creditors involved in a bankruptcy game. In the G-8 talks among the United States, its allies, and Russia, eight sides are represented. This chapter looks at bargaining when more than two sides are involved.

First, the basic model of a bargaining game is extended to accommodate three or more players. Each of the players in an n-person bargaining game has a *veto;* that is, any player can kill any proposed agreement by refusing to agree. A function, called the coalition function, is introduced to represent such a game. The Nash bargaining solution and the Kalai-Smorodinsky bargaining solution for n-player bargaining games are studied next. These two solution concepts are applied to n-player bankruptcy games, and the differences are highlighted. The second largest bankruptcy in U.S. history, Enron, is described. This ongoing case involves 54 pages of creditors in a bankruptcy game where tens of billions of dollars of corporate value have vanished.

If some or all of the players lack a veto, then bargaining becomes much more complicated. In particular, coalitions with fewer than all players may still be able to reach valuable agreements on the side. The bargaining game solution concept that captures this notion is the *core.* A bargain is in the core if no coalition can create a better deal for itself relying only on its own strategies. The core may be empty. A sufficient condition for the core to exist in a 3-person game is given. The core is very useful in studying issues of defense economics, especially alliance formation and burden sharing within an alliance. These ideas are illustrated with a study that finally came to fruition at Dayton, Ohio, in 1995: it is a study of peace plans for the war in Bosnia.

14.1 n-PERSON BARGAINING GAMES

In the bargaining and arbitration games of the last two chapters, there were exactly two sides, two players. This chapter studies what happens if there are more than two sides, more than two players. The set of players is $N = [1, 2,..., n]$, which contains n players in all. Just as in 2-person bargaining, in **n-person bargaining** there is a sum of money, M, at stake and each player i can ask for part of the money, x_i. Let $\mathbf{x} = (x_1, x_2, \ldots, x_n)$ be a vector of asks, and suppose for now that all players are risk neutral. If the sum of all the asks does not exceed the money on the table, then each player gets what he or she asked for; otherwise, no one gets anything. The payoff function for a typical player i, $u_i(\mathbf{x})$, is

$$u_i(\boldsymbol{x}) = x_i \text{ if } \Sigma \, x_i \leq M$$
$$0 \text{ if } \Sigma \, x_i > M$$

This is just the Nash demand game with n players, instead of 2.

The efficient division line for the n-person bargaining game is

$$\Sigma \, x_i = M$$

Any vector of asks that exhausts the money on the table is efficient. Substituting the utility functions into the efficient division line gives us the efficient payoff line:

$$\Sigma \, u_i = M$$

A payoff is efficient if it exhausts all the money on the table.

Nash equilibria for the n-person bargaining game in normal form have precisely the same nature as those for the 2-person bargaining game. First, there are efficient Nash equilibria of the form

$$\Sigma \, x_i{}^* = M$$

which also satisfy the boundary condition $x_i{}^* \geq 0$. In a bargaining game, it is a strategic mistake to ask for less than zero—you might very well get exactly what you asked for. Such a strategy is weakly dominated by asking for zero. There are also inefficient equilibria, where everyone gets zero. To construct an inefficient equilibrium, you need only two players, each of whom asks for all the money. Then, no matter what the other $n - 2$ players ask for, there is no agreement and everyone gets the payoff 0. Even if one of the greedy players were to reduce his or her demand all the way to zero, it would not raise the payoff to that player. These two classes of equilibria meet at the vectors $\mathbf{x} = (M, 0, \ldots, 0)$, $\mathbf{x} = (0, M, \ldots, 0)$, and so on, where the equilibrium is efficient but one greedy player gets all the money on the table.

This n-person bargaining game, like the 2-person bargaining game with all risk-neutral players, is symmetrical. In particular, it has a symmetric, efficient Nash equilibrium, where each player gets an equal share of the money M:

$$u_i{}^* = M/n$$

In a symmetrical bargaining game, an efficient agreement is reached and every player comes out the same.

There is a special interpretation of this result when $M = 1$, which deserves our attention. Interpret $M = 1$ as the amount of political power to be shared among the n players. Next, suppose that every player has **veto power,** that is, the ability to derail any proposal by simply voting against it. Then the bargaining game solution represents *power sharing*—each player in the power game has $1/n$ of the political power available. An example of such a polity is the European Union (EU). On very serious matters, like the Treaty of Maastricht or questions of enlargement, each of the 15 member countries has a veto. This is a 15-player bargaining game, where each of the players is a member country. Denmark alone could stop the Treaty of Maastricht simply by voting no—which it did, the first time it voted, in May of 1993. (The second time, Denmark voted yes, barely.) In this game,

Denmark, with 8 million inhabitants, has the same power as Germany, with over 80 million. Polities where every player has a veto are heavily weighted toward the status quo—you have to build the biggest possible tent to get *everyone* in it.

The bargaining game solution just given is a special case of both the Nash and Kalai-Smorodinsky bargaining solutions for *n*-person games. We review the *n*-person generalizations of these two bargaining solutions in the next section.

◼ 14.2 Solutions for *n*-Person Bargaining Games in Coalition Function Form

Let's begin with the bargaining game where *n* risk-neutral players are bargaining over *M* dollars. In the event of disagreement, the outcome of the game is the disagreement point

$$\mathbf{d} = (d_1, d_2,\ldots, d_n)$$

Since the players are risk neutral, the efficiency line is

$$\Sigma\, u_i = M$$

The efficiency line and the disagreement point constitute the representation of the game in coalition function form.

The Nash bargaining solution for two players generalizes to *n* players in an obvious way. Define the **Nash product** as the product of utility gains over disagreement:

$$\text{Nash product} = \Pi\,(u_i - d_i)$$

Nash bargaining solution $\mathbf{u}^\star$ is the outcome that maximizes the Nash product over all available bargains. Since the Nash product is increasing in each of its arguments, the maximum occurs on the efficiency line.

We can gain insight into the *n*-person Nash bargaining solution by looking at the case of three bargainers, which can be studied graphically. Suppose that $M = 1$ and $\mathbf{d}$ the vector of zeroes. Figure 14.1 shows the payoff tetrahedron representing this bargaining game. This tetrahedron has vertices at the disagreement point $\mathbf{d} = (0,0,0)$, as well as at the best agreements for each of the parties, $(1,0,0)$, $(0,1,0)$, and $(0,0,1)$, respectively. This coalition function form is shown in Figure 14.1a. Since the Nash bargaining solution is efficient, it suffices to restrict attention to the efficiency line, here the equilateral triangle atop the coalition function form, which is enlarged in Figure 14.1b. The vectors on the boundary of this triangle have at least one component equal to zero, so that the Nash product on the boundary is zero. In the interior of the triangle, the Nash product is positive. Given that the disagreement point is the zero vector, the maximum Nash product occurs at the median of the triangle, the vector $(1/3, 1/3, 1/3)$, with the Nash product $(1/3)^3 = 1/27$. You can show numerically that every other point on the triangle leads to a lower Nash product. For instance, the vector $(1/4, 1/4, 1/2)$ has the Nash product $= (1/4)(1/4)(1/2) = 1/32 < 1/27$.

This result is the same as that for this bargaining game in normal form, and it checks with the result for 2 players in chapter 12. The Nash bargaining solution of the bargaining game in coalition form splits the gains equally, and it embodies the notion of risk dominance.

The Nash bargaining condition for *n* players satisfies bargaining efficiency, bargaining symmetry, linear invariance, and independence of irrelevant alternatives, just as it does for two players. We have just seen how it satisfies bargaining efficiency and symmetry. The following

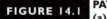

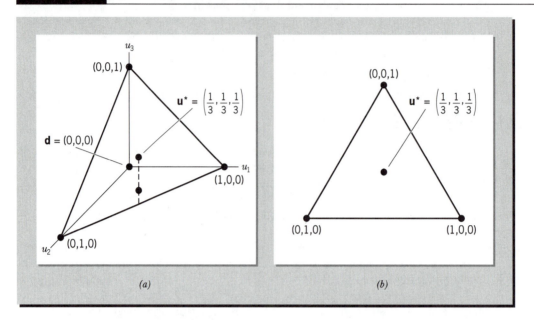

(a)   *(b)*

two examples illustrate how it satisfies linear invariance. First, suppose that M is a million dollars, $M = \$1$ million. The players split this amount equally. If there are 10 players, each gets \$1 million/10 = \$100,000. Now suppose that M is 1.1 million euros, $M = €1.1$ million, an equivalent amount of money. The players split this amount equally, each getting €1.1 million euros/10 = €110,000 = \$100,000. This is linear invariance. We would get the same outcome if some players were paid in euros and others were paid in dollars. As a second example of linear invariance, this time with respect to the disagreement point, suppose that $M = \$1$ million and disagreement means \$0 to every player except player 1, who gets \$100,000. We subtract this \$100,000 from the money on the table, since it really isn't money on the table. Player 1 does not walk away from this bargaining game with nothing. That leaves \$900,000 for the players to split evenly. If there are still 10 players, that leaves \$900,000/10 = \$90,000 for each player. Player 1 gets the \$90,000 gain plus the outside option of \$100,000, for a total of \$190,000. Notice that the resulting sum of \$190,000 + 9(\$90,000) = \$1 million exhausts the money on the table. This is precisely the answer you get if you maximize

$$\max \Pi \, (u_i - d_i) \text{for all } i$$

The Nash bargaining solution for n players also satisfies independence of irrelevant alternatives. The easiest way to see this is by an example. Figure 14.2 shows the same efficient payoff triangle as in Figure 14.1b, with the added restriction that in any agreement player 1's utility u_1 must be at least 0.25. Note that this added restriction does not hold in case of disagreement, so the disagreement point remains the vector of zeroes. This restriction cuts off a large chunk of the triangle, including the vertices (0,0,1) and (0,1,0). However, since it doesn't disturb the previous Nash bargaining solution at the median,

$\mathbf{u^\star} = (1/3, 1/3, 1/3)$, that $\mathbf{u^\star}$ is still the solution. The Nash bargaining solution considers this lower bound of player 1's payoff in case of agreement irrelevant—although player 1 might consider it very relevant. The next section shows how such restrictions can arise in the context of *n*-player bankruptcy games.

We can just as easily extend the Kalai-Smorodinsky bargaining solution to *n* players. Suppose that the disagreement vector is **d**, each player *i* is risk neutral, and each player *i* has the right to ask for all the money on the table, $x_i = M_i = M$. Here M_i represents the largest payoff that player *i* could conceivably get from a bargain. Now draw the line from the disagreement point **d** to the **vector of maximal asks, U,** where

$$\mathbf{U} = (U_1, U_2, \ldots, U_n)$$

The Kalai-Smorodinsky solution occurs where this line crosses the efficiency line.

The Kalai-Smorodinsky solution is easy to find. Let's take the case of three players. When the disagreement point **d** is (0,0,0), the amount on the table is *M* dollars, and each player has the right to ask for all the money, then the line between disagreement and maximal asks crosses the efficient payoff plane at the point $(M/3, M/3, M/3)$. This result occurs because the line between (0,0,0) and (M,M,M) can be written parametrically as (s,s,s), where *s* is between 0 and *M*. The point (s,s,s) crosses the efficient payoff plane when $s + s + s = M$, or $s = M/3$. We have just found the Kalai-Smorodinsky bargaining solution.

The Kalai-Smorodinsky bargaining solution satisfies bargaining symmetry and bargaining efficiency, as this result illustrates. The Kalai-Smorodinsky bargaining solution also satisfies linear invariance. Suppose that player 3 is paid in euros and the other players are paid an equivalent amount in dollars. Now convert disagreement and maximum ask for player 3 into euros:

$$d_3 = 0, M_3 = 1.1\,M$$

FIGURE 14.2 INDEPENDENCE OF IRRELEVANT ALTERNATIVES

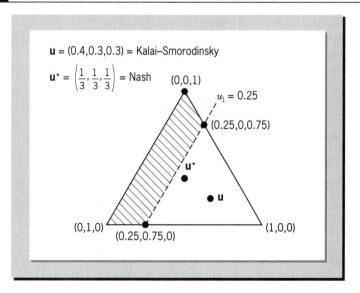

$\mathbf{u} = (0.4, 0.3, 0.3) = $ Kalai–Smorodinsky

$\mathbf{u^\star} = \left(\dfrac{1}{3}, \dfrac{1}{3}, \dfrac{1}{3}\right) = $ Nash

The line between $(0,0,0)$ and $(M, M, 1.1M)$ is written parametrically as $(s, s, 1.1s)$, where s is between 0 and M. The point $(s, s, 1.1s)$ crosses the efficient payoff plane:

$$u_1 + u_2 + u_3/1.1 = M$$

at the point $u_1 = u_2 = u_3 = M/3$, just as before.

The Kalai-Smorodinsky bargaining solution also satisfies monotonicity. If the efficient payoff plane moves out in a player's direction, that player cannot lose as a result. At worst, the payoff will remain the same because the shift did not affect where the line between disagreement and the maximal ask vector hit the efficient payoff plane. In every other case, the payoff will go up.

However, the Kalai-Smorodinsky bargaining solution continues to violate independence of irrelevant alternatives—just as the Nash bargaining solution continues to violate monotonicity. Consider the game in Figure 14.2 from the standpoint of the Kalai-Smorodinsky bargaining solution. Players 2 and 3 can ask at most 0.75, since player 1 is guaranteed at least 0.25. Player 1 can still ask for all the money on the table. The vector of maximal asks is $(1, 0.75, 0.75)$. Disagreement is $(0,0,0)$. We can write the line between these two points parametrically as $(s, 0.75s, 0.75s)$, where s is between 0 and 1. This line crosses the efficiency line at

$$s + 0.75s + 0.75s = 1$$

or $s = .4$. The Kalai-Smorodinsky bargaining solution is $(0.4, 0.3, 0.3)$. This solution considers the lower bound on player 1's payoff to be quite relevant to the outcome. The Kalai-Smorodinsky bargaining solution violates independence of irrelevant alternatives—the even split is still available, but it is no longer the solution.

To get a Nash bargaining solution violation of monotonicity, start with the payoff plane $\Sigma u_i = 1$, whose Nash solution is $(1/3, 1/3, 1/3)$. Now take the vector $\mathbf{u} = (1/2, 1/2, 1/4)$ and add it to the feasible set. The Nash product of $(1/2, 1/2, 1/4)$ is $1/16$, which is greater than the Nash product of $(1/3, 1/3, 1/3) = 1/27$, the old solution. Thus, we now have a Nash solution of $(1/2, 1/2, 1/4)$. This solution violates monotonicity. We have added utility possibilities, including more for player 3, but player 3's payoff has gone down.

The differences between these two bargaining solutions are quite pronounced when dealing with n-person bankruptcy games.

■ 14.3 n-PERSON BANKRUPTCY GAMES

This section focuses on n-person bankruptcy games, for two reasons. First, bankruptcy occurs all the time in a modern capitalist economy, and most bankruptcies involve many creditors. Second, bankruptcy games highlight the differences between the two major solution concepts for bargaining games.

Consider a set of n creditors, with claims on the bankrupt firm that can be ranked as follows:

$$C_1 < C_2 < \ldots < C_n$$

Claimant 1 has the smallest claim on the bankrupt firm; claimant n has the largest. The bankrupt firm has assets, A, which fall short of total claims:

$$A < \Sigma \, Ci$$

If the claimants can reach an agreement, they can divvy up all or part of the assets of the bankrupt firm. Otherwise, each claimant walks away from the proceedings empty-handed. Thus the disagreement point

$$\mathbf{d} = (0, 0, \ldots, 0).$$

As in the case of two players, the Nash bargaining solution creates a seniority system among the *n* creditors—even though all of them have equal seniority. Indeed, if one of the creditors, say, creditor 1, were truly senior to the rest, then that creditor would be paid off in full before any of the other creditors got so much as a penny out of the assets. In such a case, the coalition form of the game would consist of all the junior claimants, with the money on the table equal to what is left after the senior claim is paid off. The endogenous seniority system created by the Nash bargaining solution directly generalizes the solution when there are two claimants.

We will work out the Nash bargaining solution to the bankruptcy game with three claimants in detail, leaving the more general cases as problems. As with two claimants, the solution is sensitive to how many assets *A* are at stake. There are three cases to consider, one case per claimant.

- *Case 1.* There are very few assets relative to even the smallest creditor, $A < 3C_1$. The Nash bargaining solution treats all claimants equally. Each is paid the same, $A/3$.
- *Case 2.* *A* exceeds this threshold, $3C_1 < A$, but not by too much: $A < C_1 + 2C_2$. The Nash bargaining solution treats the smallest claimant as senior and pays that claimant off in full. The remaining two claimants are paid equally from what is left. The solution is $\mathbf{u}^\star = [C_1, (A - C_1)/2, (A - C)/2]$. This case is shown in Figure 14.3a.
- *Case 3.* $C_1 + 2C_2 < A$. Once *A* exceeds this threshold, the Nash bargaining solution treats the two smallest claimants as senior and pays them off in full. The largest claimant gets what is left after the other claimants are paid off. The solution is $\mathbf{u}^\star = (C_1, C_2, A - C_1 - C_2)$. This case is shown in Figure 14.3b.

The Nash solution easily generalizes to *n* claimants, using the following algorithm. See if you can pay all the claimants equally (case 1). If you cannot, because you are paying one or more of them too much, then pay off the smallest claimants in full. Divide the remainder of the proceeds equally among the remaining claimants. If no one is being paid more than the claim, stop. If at least one claimant is being paid more than the claim, pay that claimant off in full and divide the remainder among the remaining claimants. Complete this process until all assets have been exhausted.

This process of creating senior claims where none really exist is quite elegant, but it might strike the large claimants as rather arbitrary. After all, it means they are getting stuck with large losses whereas the small claimants get all their money back. Such is not the case with the Kalai-Smorodinsky solution. Every claimant is treated as equally senior in this solution. Nevertheless, we have to treat $n + 1$ cases—one more case than the number of players—because, if a player's claim is larger than the assets available, the most that player can ask for is all the assets. Let us consider the solution for $n = 3$ in detail.

Case 1: $A < C_1$. In this case, the vector of maximal asks is (A,A,A). The line between the disagreement point and (A,A,A) is given by (s,s,s), where *s* is between 0 and *A*. This line crosses the efficient payoff line when $s + s + s = A$, or $s = A/3$.

The solution in this case is to pay all the claimants equally—since there is almost nothing left anyway.

| FIGURE 14.3 | **BANKRUPTCY, NASH BARGAINING SOLUTION, $n = 3$: (a) CLAIMANT 1 IS SENIOR; (b) CLAIMANTS 1 AND 2 ARE SENIOR** |

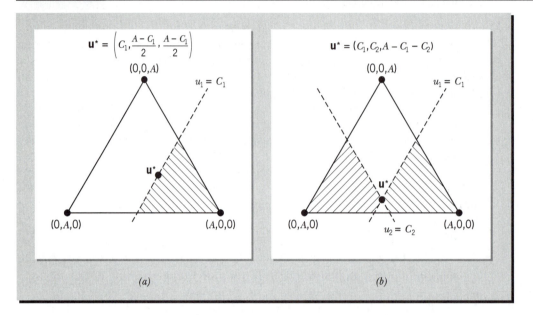

$$\mathbf{u}^\star = \left(C_1, \frac{A - C_1}{2}, \frac{A - C_1}{2}\right)$$

$$\mathbf{u}^\star = (C_1, C_2, A - C_1 - C_2)$$

(a)   *(b)*

Case 2: $C_1 < A < C_2$. In this case, claimant 1 is constrained to claim only what he or she is owed, and the other claimants are constrained by the available assets. The vector of maximal asks is (C_1, A, A). The line between the disagreement point and (C_1, A, A) is parameterized by $[(C_1/A)s, s, s)]$, where s is between 0 and A. This line crosses the efficient payoff line when

$$(C_1/A) s + s + s = A$$

Solving, we get $s = A^2/(C_1 + 2A)$.

The resulting solution is

$$\mathbf{u}^\star = [(C_1 A)/(C_1 + 2A), A^2/(C_1 + 2A), A^2/(C_1 + 2A)]$$

The smallest claimant gets rationed according to the claim.

Case 3: $C_2 < A < C_3$. In this case, both claimant 1 and claimant 2 are constrained to claim only what is owed them, and the remaining claimant is constrained by the available assets. The vector of maximal asks is (C_1, C_2, A). The line between the disagreement point and the vector of maximal asks is parameterized by $[(C_1/A)s, (C_2/A)s, s]$. This line crosses the efficient payoff line when

$$(C_1/A)s + (C_2/A)s + s = A$$

Solving, we get $s = A^2/(C_1 + C_2 + A)$. The resulting solution is

$$\mathbf{u}^\star = [(C_1 A)/(C_1 + C_2 + A), (C_1 A)/(C_1 + C_2 + A), A_2/(C_1 + C_2 + A)]$$

The smallest two claimants get rationed according to their claims.

Case 4: $C_3 < A$. In this case, all claimants are constrained to claim only what is owed them. The vector of maximal asks is simply the vector of claims (C_1, C_2, C_3). The line between the disagreement point and the vector of maximal asks is parameterized by $[(C_1/A)s, (C_2/A)s, (C_3/A)s]$, where s is between 0 and A. This line crosses the efficient payoff line when

$$(C_1/A)s + (C_2/A)s + (C_3/A)s = A$$

Solving, we get $s = A^2/(C_1 + C_2 + C_3)$. The resulting solution is

$$\mathbf{u}^\star = [(C_1A)/(C_1 + C_2 + C_3), (C_2A)/(C_1 + C_2 + C_3), (C_3A)/(C_1 + C_2 + C_3)]$$

All three claimants get rationed according to their claim. This particular formula is often used by courts to apportion claims of equal seniority.

The Kalai-Smorodinsky solution to the bankruptcy game readily generalizes to n claimants. The only thing you need to keep track of is the relationship of assets to the sizes of the various claims. Once assets exceed even the largest claim, then the proportional rationing formula, where each claimant i gets a share of the assets proportional to the share of total claims (C_i/C_i), yields the Kalai-Smorodinsky solution. We now turn to the largest bankruptcy case in U. S. history—at least when it was filed in December 2001—unfolding right before our very eyes, and involving thousands of players.

■ 14.4 ENRON: THE BIGGER THEY ARE, THE HARDER THEY FALL

On January 1, 2001, **Enron** was the seventh largest corporation in the United States in terms of market capitalization, with a stock trading at $90/share and a market capitalization in excess of $100 billion.[1] On December 2, 2001, Enron declared bankruptcy, with assets of $50 billion, liabilities in excess of $100 billion, a stock price below $1, and a market capitalization of less than $1 billion—the biggest bankruptcy in U.S. history at that time. The $100 billion question is, what happened? Where did the money go? And what happens to the 54 pages of creditors listed in the bankruptcy filing?

A dozen congressional committees and a legion of lawsuits will try to find answers to these questions and determine where the money went. It is quite clear at this time that Enron had been using "aggressive accounting," in the words of its auditor, Arthur Andersen, for several years. Indeed, Andersen met in February 2001, to decide whether to drop Enron as a client. Enron was paying Andersen $50 million for its services as auditor and as consultant—making this Andersen's biggest client—but if Enron got in serious trouble, so would Andersen.

---

[1] Material for this study was drawn from the following sources: Jathon Sapsford, "Enron Debacle Puts J. P. Morgan in the Spotlight," *Wall Street Journal*, 11 January 2002; Jathon Sapsford and Mitchell Pacelle, "Citigroup's Enron Financing Stirs Controversy," *Wall Street Journal*, 17 January 2002; Reed Abelson and Jonathan D. Glater, "Auditors under Fire after Enron's Failure," *San Francisco Chronicle*, 15 January 2002; David S. Hilzenrath and Peter Behr, "Secret Letter Warned Enron of Problems Last Summer," *San Francisco Chronicle*, 15 January 2002; and the Enron Web site at www.enron.com; and www.siliconinvestor.com.

And there was plenty for Andersen to worry about. The first sign publicly of trouble was the sudden resignation of CEO Jeffrey Skilling on August 15, 2001. Although this resignation made the front page of the *Wall Street Journal,* no one suggested that the company was in serious trouble, and the stock price held its own. Inside the company, however, the picture was very different. Vice President Sherron Wilkins, an attorney, warned both Enron President Ken Lay and the auditors at Andersen that she feared the entire company could "implode in a wave of accounting scandals." Ms. Wilkins was a prophet ahead of her time—by about 3 months.

In October of 2001, Enron announced it was correcting 4 years' worth of financial statements in an SEC filing, and that it had lost $684 million in the previous quarter—a staggering amount. This was the beginning of the implosion forecast by Wilkins. At the same time, Chief Financial Officer Andrew Fastow suddenly resigned. Fastow was in charge of billions of dollars of debt kept off the books of Enron via **special-purpose entities (SPEs)**, entities with colorful names like "Raptor," which helped inflate Enron's earnings at the same time that they made Enron's liabilities appear small. The debt held in SPEs helped send the company into bankruptcy once it was acknowledged. Enron stock, which had still been holding on at $40/share, quickly dipped into the teens, and then plunged further once the SPEs started to be made public.

Enron's entire world was crumbling as December 2001 approached. Not for nothing had this corporation donated millions of dollars to the campaigns of both Republicans and Democrats (90 percent to the former), including being the single largest to President George W. Bush in the past decade. Enron officials called on the administration for a bailout—but various cabinet secretaries resisted these calls. None of this was released to the public. It was determined inside the administration that Enron was going down, but that the impact on the entire economy would be slight; hence, unlike the airlines, no bailout.

By the end of November, Enron debt had been downgraded to junk status, and its biggest lenders on Wall Street were scrambling to cover their positions before they lost every cent. J. P. Morgan has the biggest exposure to Enron, with some $2.6 billion owed it. Notice that this number is still far less than Enron's total assets. If Enron's assets are indeed half of its liabilities, then Morgan can expect to see half of what it is owed gone forever. Citigroup is also on the hook for about $1 billion—but is in much better shape than Morgan. In late October, Enron asked Citigroup for $1 billion in an emergency loan. Citigroup obliged—but only on two conditions. First, Enron had to repay an existing $250 million loan to Citigroup immediately out of the $1 billion, and the entire $1 billion loan had to be secured. Thus, Citigroup stands to see a lot more than half of its $1 billion back.

As if all this wasn't colorful enough, when word reached Andersen that the SEC was subpoenaing documents related to the bankruptcy filing, Andersen went on a shredding party, destroying tens of thousands of documents relating to its audit. That's got a name—obstruction of justice—and it led to Andersen's being convicted in Federal District Court in Houston for obstruction of justice. Thus was destroyed the brand name of Andersen, once considered the finest accounting firm in the world.

This story isn't over by a long shot—high-ranking former Enron officials have begun to be indicted—but Enron itself might be done for. When the management of a publicly held corporation watches $100 billion in market capitalization evaporate, someone is to blame.

■ 14.5 THE COALITION FUNCTION WHEN INTERMEDIATE COALITIONS HAVE POWER

One hallmark of bargaining games, whether they have two players or *n* players, is that any player can stop any deal. Every player has a veto. The minute that some or all players lack a veto, then groups of players, called coalitions, may be able to walk away from the bargaining table with money, even in the absence of an agreement. A **coalition** is any group of players. An **intermediate coalition** in an *n*-person game has from two to *n* – 1 players. A coalition with a single player is called a **singleton.** The coalition consisting of all *n* players is called the **grand coalition.** This section studies games where intermediate coalitions can negotiate their own side agreements if they choose.

First we need a bit of set notation. Coalitions are sets of players. Let *S* represent a coalition in an *n*-player game. The grand coalition in this game is $N = \{1, 2, \ldots, n\}$. A singleton is denoted $S = \{1\}$ if player 1 is alone, $\{2\}$ if player 2 is alone, and so on. $S = \{1,2\}$ is an intermediate coalition, consisting of players 1 and 2. As a real-world example, NATO is a coalition consisting of 19 countries. Let N = NATO. Within NATO, there are various groupings. For instance, the set S = {Belgium, Netherlands, Luxembourg} represents the coalition of the low countries; set S = {United States, Canada}, the NATO countries in North America; the set S = {Poland, Hungary, Czech Republic}, the set of newest members. For any given S, the set $N - S$ represents the members of N that do not belong to S. For S = {United States, Canada}, the set $N - S$ is the set of 17 NATO countries that are in Europe, not North America.

In the rest of the chapter, it is assumed that all players are risk neutral. The *coalition function* then shows how much money the members of a given coalition can guarantee themselves if they walk away from the bargaining table. The coalition function, written $v(S)$, associates to every coalition S the guaranteed value of its outside option.

The coalition function of a bargaining game with *M* dollars on the table and disagreement point **d** (here the zero vector) is easy to write down. First, the only coalition that can walk away from the table with any guaranteed money is the grand coalition, so we have

$$v(N) = M$$

If any other coalition walks away from the table, it does so empty-handed:

$$v(S) = 0, \text{ for } S \text{ not equal to } N$$

What $v(N) = M$ means is that the members of N can divide up the M dollars on the table any way they choose:

$$M = v(N) = \Sigma \, u_i, \text{ where } i \text{ is in } N$$

Thus, $v(N)$ is shorthand for the efficiency line. Similarly, $v(S) = 0$ means that the members of N can divide up \$0 on the table any way they choose:

$$0 = v(S) = \Sigma \, u_i, \text{ where } i \text{ is in } S$$

Thus, $v(S)$ is shorthand for the disagreement point as it applies to each coalition S not equal to the grand coalition.

Now suppose that the disagreement point **d** is not the zero vector, but some other vector. In this event, intermediate coalitions can walk away from the table with their disagreement values. If player 1 walks away from the table, he or she gets $v(\{1\}) = d_1$. If players 1 and 2 walk away from the table together, they get $v(\{1,2\}) = d_1 + d_2$. In general, a coalition S walking away from the table will get

$$v(S) = \Sigma\, d_i, \text{ where } i \text{ is in } S$$

We can convert a bargaining game with a nonzero disagreement point into a bargaining game with a zero disagreement point via the following trick. Transform every player's utility in the following way:

$$u_i' = u_i - d_i$$

Simply subtract every player's disagreement value from that player's utility. In the new utility coordinates,

$$v(S) = \Sigma\, u_i' = \Sigma\, (u_i - d_i) = 0, \text{ where } i \text{ is in } S$$

while for the grand coalition N,

$$v(N) = u_i' = M - \Sigma\, d_i, \text{ where } i \text{ is in } N$$

The players take their disagreement values from the money on the table and bargain over what is left. So, in any bargaining game, intermediate coalitions still play no role.[2]

In the game **Majority Rule,** intermediate coalitions play a manifest role. There are three players, $N = \{1,2,3\}$. For the coalition function, we have the following:

$$v(N) = 1$$

meaning that the grand coalition can achieve 100 percent political power (this is one way of expressing the notion of popular sovereignty, if N is equal to the people, or Rousseau's notion of the general will);

$$v(\{i\}) = 0$$

meaning that any singleton is powerless; and

$$v(S) = 1, \text{ if } S \text{ has two members}$$

meaning that any majority can rule. In a 3-player polity a coalition with two members is a majority, and under majority rule a majority can take 100 percent of the power. Majority Rule can be played with any number of players n. In the general case, its coalition function is

$$v(S) = 0, \text{ if } S \text{ is not a majority, but is a minority or exactly } 1/2 \text{ of } N$$
$$v(S) = 1, \text{ if } S \text{ is a majority}$$

Of course, what is used to measure size is important. Under the principle of one person, one vote, each player counts the same. Under the principle of one share, one vote, each share of voting stock counts the same.

A second example of a game in which intermediate coalitions matter is drawn straight from the market. Suppose that players 1, 2, and 3 are firms in the same industry. Any firm going it alone earns a normal rate of return ($u_i = 0$). If firms 1 and 2 merge, they earn an above-normal rate of return:

$$v(\{1,2\}) > 0$$

---

[2] This conclusion remains true if players have attitudes toward risk different from risk neutrality.

Similar opportunities await any pair of firms in the industry. Finally, if all three firms in the industry merge, they form a monopoly and earn a way-above-normal rate of return:

$$v(\{1,2,3\}) > 0$$

Mergers among competitors create intermediate coalitions with considerable profit potential—which is why antitrust authorities are keen to prevent them.

We can adapt the triangle diagram for bargaining games to this game, as in Figure 14.4. The corners of the triangle represent maximum utility for each of the three firms in the game. The line $v(\{1,2\}) = 0.15$ shows the various ways in which firms 1 and 2 can divide their above-normal profits should they form a joint venture. Similarly, $v(\{1,3\}) = 0.10$ and $v(\{2,3\}) = 0.05$ show the same thing for those coalitions. Once the number of firms exceeds three, it is hard to depict the coalition function—but we can still study such games using systems of inequalities.

Once intermediate coalitions have value, solving a game becomes much more difficult. There are so many more aspects to take into consideration. How will this or that coalition react to a proposal? Can some coalition upset an agreement? Which coalitions are likely to form, and which are unlikely to form? We will now turn to a solution concept that addresses these questions.

14.6 THE CORE OF A GAME IN COALITION-FUNCTION FORM

A bargain has to have something to offer to everybody at the table. Suppose that some individual or group S is contemplating walking away from the bargaining table. If the players walk away from the table and make their own side agreement, it is worth $v(S)$ to them. If

---

FIGURE 14.4 **JOINT VENTURE, COALITION-FUNCTION FORM**

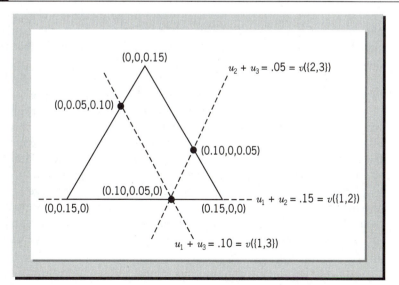

the proposal on the table is worth at least that much to them, then they don't gain by walking out. Such a proposal should appeal to them—it definitely has something to offer them. A proposal is in the **core** of a game in coalition-function form when it has something to offer every possible coalition.

Let $\mathbf{u} = (u_1, u_2, \ldots, u_n)$ be a proposal on the table. In order to have something to offer every coalition, this proposal must satisfy $2^n - 1$ inequalities of the following sort:

$v(S) \leq \Sigma u_i$, where i is in S

There are $2^n - 1$ inequalities, because that is how many different coalitions can be formed from a group of n members. One of these inequalities is actually an equality:

$v(N) = \Sigma u_i$, where i is in N

This is the efficiency condition. With at most M dollars on the table, everybody involved can get no more than M dollars if they all walk away from the table.

This system of inequalities may or may not have a solution. There is an existence problem for the core, just as there is an existence problem for Nash equilibrium. We will see that large classes of games in coalition function form, including market games, matching games, and bankruptcy games, have solutions in the core. The game Joint Ventures has a unique solution in the core. There are $2^3 - 1 = 8 - 1 = 7$ inequalities that have to be satisfied:

$$v(\{1\}) = 0 \leq u_1$$
$$v(\{2\}) = 0 \leq u_2$$
$$v(\{3\}) = 0 \leq u_3$$
$$v(\{1,2\}) = 0.15 \leq u_1 + u_2$$
$$v(\{1,3\}) = 0.10 \leq u_1 + u_2$$
$$v(\{2,3\}) = 0.05 \leq u_2 + u_3$$
$$v(\{1,2,3\}) = 0.15 = u_1 + u_2 + u_3$$

Solving a large system of linear inequalities usually involves a machine. Fortunately, in this case we can see the solution graphically. Figure 14.5 reproduces Figure 14.4 with some new information. First, note that if a vector $\mathbf{u}$ lies in the triangle, it satisfies both the requirement that the individual payoffs be nonnegative and the requirement that the individual payoffs sum to .15. This leaves three inequalities to solve for. Take the inequality for the joint venture of firms 1 and 2, $v(\{1,2\}) = 0.15 \leq u_1 + u_2$. All the points on the base of the triangle have $u_1 + u_2 = 0.15$. Since firms 1 and 2 should not settle for less, this inequality eliminates all points in the triangle except along the base (Figure 14.5a). This elimination is reflected by the crosshatching. The other two inequalities, involving the joint venture between firms 1 and 3 and the joint venture between firms 2 and 3, cross at the point of the triangle $\mathbf{u} = (0.10, 0.05, 0)$ in Figure 14.5b. Since this point is on the base of the triangle, it satisfies firms 1 and 2. Thus it satisfies all the inequalities. The proposal $\mathbf{u} = (0.10, 0.05, 0)$ is in the core of the game Joint Ventures (Figure 14.5c).

This proposal is the only one in the core. Since firms 1 and 2 together have to get a rate of return of .15, the situation between them is constant sum. Suppose that firm 1 got more than a 10 percent return—say, an 11 percent return. Firm 2 is getting only 4 percent. Then firm 2 could propose a joint venture with firm 3, offering firm 3 a 0.5 percent return and itself

FIGURE 14.5	JOINT VENTURES, CORE: (a) COALITION ({1,2}); (b) COALITIONS ({1,3}) AND ({2,3}); (c) CORE

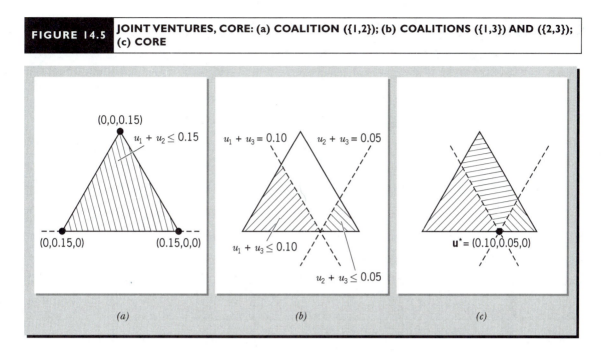

(a)   *(b)*   *(c)*

a 4.5 percent return. At this point, firms 2 and 3 could walk away from the table and be better off. So firm 1 can't get more than 10 percent. Similar reasoning shows that firm 1 can't get less than 10 percent either, since then it could walk away from the table with firm 3.

Majority Rule is an example of a game whose core is empty. Any proposal in the core of Majority Rule would have to satisfy the following inequalities:

$$v(\{1\}) = 0 \le u_1$$
$$v(\{2\}) = 0 \le u_2$$
$$v(\{3\}) = 0 \le u_3$$
$$v(\{1,2\}) = 1 = u_1 + u_2$$
$$v(\{1,3\}) = 1 = u_1 + u_3$$
$$v(\{2,3\}) = 1 = u_2 + u_3$$
$$v(\{1,2,3\}) = 1 = u_1 + u_2 + u_3$$

These inequalities have no solution, as illustrated by Figure 14.6. Each of the inequalities for the 2-player coalitions requires that the payoff lie on one side of the triangle. However, there is no point on the triangle that lies simultaneously on all three sides. Hence, Majority Rule has an empty core.

Games that lack cores can be quite turbulent. In Majority Rule, any proposal to share power can be upset by another proposal. If player 1 offers to share power equally with player 2, player 3 can upset this relationship by offering player 2 a larger share of the power, and so on. Some real-world polities using majority rule, such as Italy, exhibit just such instability. The instability can be avoided, or at least lessened, if certain coalitions cannot

---

FIGURE 14.6 | **MAJORITY RULE, EMPTY CORE: (a) v({2,3}); (b) v({1,3}); (c) v({2,3})**

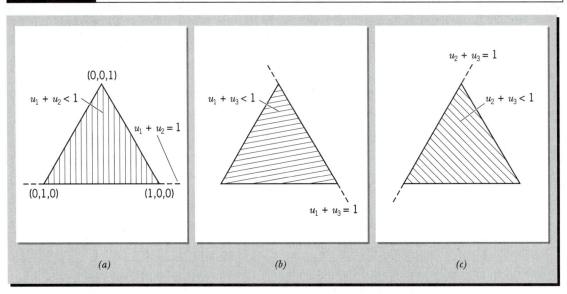

(a)   *(b)*   *(c)*

---

form for ideological reasons. For instance, suppose that player 1 represents the Left; player 2, the Center; and player 3, the Right of the political spectrum. Further, suppose (which is the case in a country like Italy) that players at the opposite ends of the spectrum refuse to have anything to do with one another. Then the only coalitions that will share power in practice are {Left, Center} or {Center, Right}. The player at the Center will anchor every possible government, thereby providing stability.

There is an easy sufficient condition for a core in a 3-person game. Suppose that the disagreement point is zero and that the amount on the table is M dollars. Suppose each player can guarantee a payoff of at least zero. Then add the three inequalities for the intermediate coalitions, to get

$$v(\{1,2\}) + v(\{1,3\}) + v(\{2,3\}) \leq 2(u_1 + u_2 + u_3)$$

At the same time, the sum of all utilities must equal M. Substituting, we get

$$v(\{1,2\}) + v(\{1,3\}) + v(\{2,3\}) \leq 2M$$

Basically, what this condition says is that if the intermediate coalitions do not have claims too large against the money on the table, then there is an outcome in the core.[3] Notice that this checks for Majority Rule; substituting, we get

$$1 + 1 + 1 = 3 > 2(1) = 2$$

so Majority Rule has an empty core.

---

[3] There is an elegant generalization of this condition for a nonempty core when there are n players. For details, see Herbert Scarf, *The Computation of Economic Equilibria* (New Haven, Conn.: Yale University Press, 1973).

14.7 SHARING DEFENSE BURDENS

Chapter 15 studies the cores of market games and matching games. This section presents a game that arises in a nonmarket setting, in particular, among the members of an international alliance. The game, called **Mutual Defense,** involves alliance formation against an external threat. Suppose that players 1, 2, and 3 are three countries situated as in Figure 14.7. Each country is 1 unit square, arrayed in a line with the others, and is surrounded by external threats against which each wishes to defend. The cost of defending a country against a surrounding external threat is proportional to the perimeter of the area being defended. According to NATO doctrine, for instance, it takes one armored division to defend a front 20 miles long against hostile attack.

In Mutual Defense, a coalition is an alliance, and the coalition function $v(S)$ represents the cost of defending that alliance. If an alliance walks away from the bargaining table, it will have to defend itself. Suppose that it costs 1 unit to defend one side of a country. Then $v(\{1\}) = -4$, the cost of defending country 1 when it is by itself, and so on. The coalition function for the entire game is

$$v(\{1\}) = -4 \leq u_1$$
$$v(\{2\}) = -4 \leq u_2$$
$$v(\{3\}) = -4 \leq u_3$$
$$v(\{1,2\}) = -6 \leq u_1 + u_2$$
$$v(\{1,3\}) = -8 \leq u_1 + u_3$$
$$v(\{2,3\}) = -6 \leq u_2 + u_3$$
$$v(\{1,2,3\}) = -8 = u_1 + u_2 + u_3$$

The alliances $\{1,2\}$, $\{2,3\}$, and $\{1,2,3\}$ all involve cost savings because they all involve adjacent states. When countries 1 and 2 form an alliance, neither of them has to defend

FIGURE 14.7   MUTUAL DEFENSE, PHYSICAL SITUATION

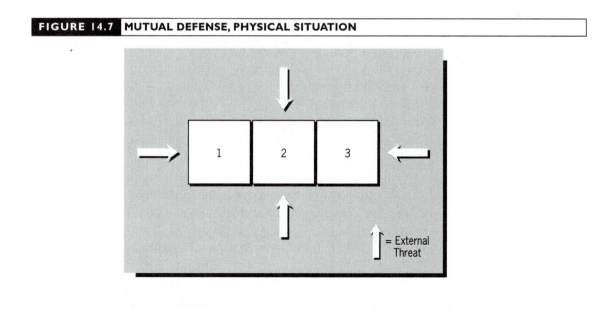

against their common boundary. The United States–Canada alliance has saved an enormous amount in defense costs for both countries. For graphic purposes, it is convenient to transform the payoffs so that the disagreement point is zero. This can be accomplished by the transformation $u_i = u_i + 4$. The coalition function that results is

$$v(\{1\}) = 0 \le u_1$$
$$v(\{2\}) = 0 \le u_2$$
$$v(\{3\}) = 0 \le u_3$$
$$v(\{1,2\}) = 2 \le u_1 + u_2$$
$$v(\{1,3\}) = 0 \le u_1 + u_3$$
$$v(\{2,3\}) = 2 \le u_2 + u_3$$
$$v(\{1,2,3\}) = 4 = u_1 + u_2 + u_3$$

The transformed coalition function values represent the cost savings available to the countries in a given alliance. For instance, if all three countries form an alliance, then they save 4 units of defense.

Mutual Defense always has proposals in the core, and usually many such proposals. Figure 14.8 shows the core of this version of Mutual Defense. Countries 1 and 2 can walk away from any proposal, such as (0,0,4), that does not offer them 2 units of cost savings. Countries 2 and 3 can likewise walk away from any proposal, such as (4,0,0), that does not offer them 2 units of cost savings. The remaining rhombus of proposals is the core. This is a lot of proposals—an entire convex set. Thus, the average of any two proposals in the core is itself a proposal in the core. In particular, the center of gravity of this rhombus, $\mathbf{u} =$ (1,2,1), would strike many people as very appealing. It gives country 2 a bigger share of the cost savings, and without country 2 in the alliance, there aren't any costs to save.

Like any model of real life, Mutual Defense leaves out many of the complexities surrounding negotiations among members of an alliance or a projected alliance. Nevertheless, it gives us some insight into the war in Bosnia, the bloodiest fought in Europe since World War II.

FIGURE 14.8 | **MUTUAL DEFENSE: TRANSFORMED PAYOFFS, CORE**

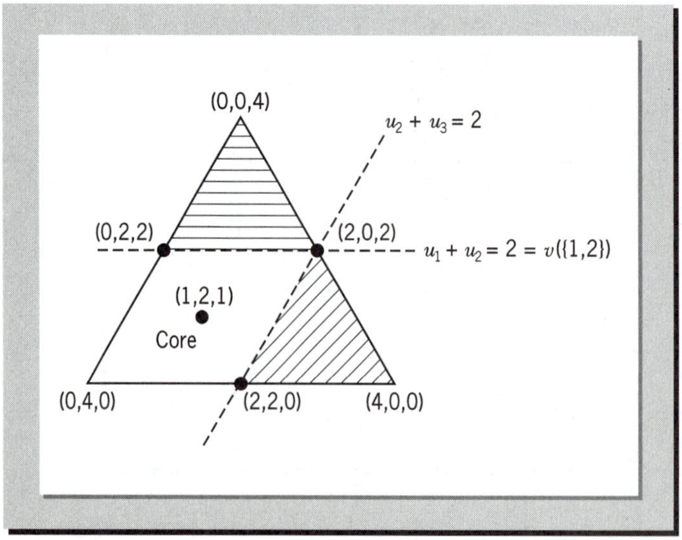

◼ 14.8 BOSNIAN PEACE PLANS

The area comprising present-day Bosnia has been a fault line through Europe for two millennia.[4] During the time of the Roman Empire, the language line separating the Latin-speaking empire to the west and the Greek-speaking empire to the east ran through there. After Slavic-speaking peoples entered the area in the seventh century, the Latin/Greek separation was replaced by a common Slavic tongue. The current inhabitants of Bosnia speak very similar languages, Serbian and Croatian. Indeed, until recently, these were considered to be a common language, Serbo-Croatian. However, Croatian is written in the Latin alphabet and Croats are predominantly Roman Catholic; Serbian is written in the Cyrillic alphabet and Serbs are predominantly Orthodox. When the Turks invaded Europe in the fifteenth century, their conquests included Byzantium in 1453, Serbia in 1489, and Bosnia soon thereafter.

For the next four centuries, Bosnia was part of the Ottoman Empire. During this period, a large part of the population converted to Islam. As part of the rollback of the Turks from Europe, at the Congress of Berlin (1878) Serbia regained its independence and Bosnia was attached to the Austro-Hungarian Empire. It was in the capital of Bosnia, Sarajevo, that a Serbian nationalist assassinated the heir to the throne of Austria-Hungary, precipitating World War I. Bosnia became part of the southern Slavic confederation, Yugoslavia, after the war. That confederation began to crumble in 1991, with the secession of Slovenia and Croatia. This is a lot of history in a rather small place.

On the verge of its declaration of independence in 1992, Bosnia was a mosaic of three religions. Muslims were in the areas surrounding Sarajevo, which itself was ethnically mixed, as well as in the Bihac region. Croatians were centered around Mostar. Serbs were scattered in pockets around the rest of the country. Bosnia declared independence in the summer of 1992, and hostilities immediately broke out. Sarajevo became the military headquarters of the Muslims; Mostar, of the Croats; Pale, of the Serbs. The Bosnian Serbs, with military assistance from the Former Republic of Yugoslavia (FR Yugoslavia), made enormous gains in the initial fighting. By the end of 1992, Serbs controlled 45 percent of the territory of Bosnia; Muslims, 35 percent; Croats, 20 percent. At the beginning of peace talks in 1993, Serbs controlled 64 percent of the territory; Croats, 25 percent, Muslims, 11 percent. The ferocity of the fighting rivaled that of World War II. More than 130,000 people had died, and another 2 million had been displaced, by the time serious negotiations began to end the war in Bosnia.

In an effort to stop the fighting, representatives of the United States (Vance) and the United Kingdom (Owen) proposed a **Bosnian peace plan** under the aegis of the United Nations (see Figure 14.9). The Vance-Owen plan proposed a Bosnian confederation along ethnic lines, retaining the percentage of territory held by the combatants before the war. This plan was accepted by the Croats (who broke even, so to speak) and by the Muslims (who thereby avoided serious losses of territory). The Bosnian Serbs, facing the prospect of giving up enormous territorial gains, initially rejected the plan.

Negotiations dragged on, while a battlefield stalemate persisted. A breakthrough—at terrible cost—took place on both the military and diplomatic fronts in the spring of 1995. The UN had designated several cities along the front lines between the Muslim-Croat and Bosnian-Serb forces as safe havens, among them Srebrenica. Each safe haven was protected

---

[4] This material was informed in part by the trenchant analysis of John J. Mearsheimer and Robert A. Pope, "The Answer," *New Republic,* June 14, 1993, pp. 22–28.

FIGURE 14.9 **VANCE-OWEN PEACE PLAN**

SOURCE: From *Wall Street Journal,* 17 May 1993, p. 12.

by a token UN military force. Bosnian Serb forces, violating the safe haven status, attacked Srebrenica. The UN peacekeepers stood by while Bosnian Serbs committed the largest single atrocity in Europe since World War II, killing some 5,000 people, mostly men and boys. This war crime, in full view of the entire world, cost the Bosnian Serbs greatly. NATO immediately intervened in the war, and the subsequent NATO bombardment of Bosnian Serb and FR Yugoslavia positions brought the Bosnian Serbs to the negotiating table in a hurry. Suddenly, the prospect of breaking even in terms of territory did not seem so unacceptable.

At Dayton, Ohio, in 1996, an accord very much along the lines of Vance-Owen was reached among the warring parties. This settlement, shown in Figure 4.10, divides the former Yugoslav republic of Bosnia and Herzegovina into two parts: the Federation of Bosnia and Herzegovina, and the Serb Republic ("Republika Srpska"). The Federation of Bosnia and Herzegovina controls an area roughly the size of the prewar Croat and Muslim areas; the Serb Republic, an area roughly the size of the prewar Serbian area.

FIGURE 14.10 **DAYTON SETTLEMENT**

SOURCE: Government Printing Office

The Bosnian War has been brought to a peaceful conclusion, with NATO peace-keepers on hand ever since 1996 to keep the peace. But the memory of the atrocities and war crimes lives on. Some of the war criminals would eventually be brought to justice before the War Crimes Tribunal in the Hague, Netherlands. The tribunal is still in session at this writing.

◼ SUMMARY

1. In *n*-person bargaining there is a sum of money M at stake, and each player i can ask for part of the money. Every player has to agree to a proposal before it is a deal. Any player can veto a deal. In the event of a veto, each player gets the disagreement payoff.

2. There are two kinds of equilibria, efficient and inefficient, for *n*-person bargaining games in normal form. The solution of such games is efficient. If the game is also symmetrical, then so is the solution.

3. There is a special interpretation for the bargaining game with 1 unit of value on the table. This unit can be interpreted as political power; the object of negotiations is then to share that power. When every player has a veto, power is shared equally.

4. The Nash and Kalai-Smorodinsky bargaining solutions generalize to *n* players. Even with *n* players, they retain their distinctive properties.

5. In the *n*-person bankruptcy game, the Nash bargaining solution creates senior rights, with the smallest creditor the most senior. In contrast, the Kalai-Smorodinsky bargaining solution treats all creditors proportionally if no creditor's claim exceeds the available assets.

6. Enron, once the seventh largest firm in the U.S. economy, became the largest bankruptcy in U.S. history in December of 2001—all in the space of a single year. Several Wall Street firms stand to be among the biggest losers as the bankruptcy case plays out, but the legal list of creditors is 54 pages long.

7. An intermediate coalition in an *n*-person game has from 2 to $n - 1$ players. A coalition with a single player is called a singleton. A coalition consisting of all *n* players is called a grand coalition.

8. When intermediate coalitions have value, bargaining is much more complicated. The coalition function expresses the value of intermediate coalitions.

9. A proposal is in the core when no coalition can do better by walking away from the bargaining table than by accepting the agreement. Being in the core means satisfying a set of linear inequalities. Not all games have nonempty cores.

10. The game Mutual Defense has a large core. This game is a model of savings in defense costs available to alliance partners.

◼ KEY TERMS

n-person bargaining	Enron	core
veto power	coalition	Mutual Defense
Nash product	intermediate coalition	Bosnian peace plan
vector of maximal asks	singleton	
special-purpose entities (SPEs)	grand coalition	
	Majority Rule	

◼ PROBLEMS

1. There are three bargainers and $100 on the table. All bargainers are risk neutral. Find the set of efficient payoffs. Then find the Nash bargaining solution.

2. Find the Kalai-Smorodinsky bargaining solution for problem 1. Then compare the solution you get to the solution in problem 1.

3. Suppose that there are three players in a bargaining game. Give an example of a Nash bargaining solution that violates monotonicity and of a Kalai-Smorodinsky bargaining solution that violates independence of irrelevant alternatives.

4. In a bankruptcy game, claimant 1 can claim $1 million; claimant 2, $2 million; claimant 3, $3 million; claimant 4, $4 million. All claimants are risk neutral. There is $5 million in assets available. Find the Nash and the Kalai-Smorodinsky bargaining solutions, and compare them.

5. Solve problem 4 if only $2.5 million in assets is available.

6. Give three examples of signals in the saga of Enron that could have indicated to stockholders to unload their stock before it was too late. If you had $100,000 (1250 shares) in Enron stock on January 1, 2001, how much would this be worth today? What if you had loaned Enron $100,000 on January 1, 2001?

7. In the game Joint Ventures, we claimed that firm 1 will walk away from the table if offered a return of less than 10 percent. Prove this in detail.

8. Suppose that in Mutual Defense, the intermediate coalitions are not allowed to form and so have coalition value 0. Find the Nash and Kalai-Smorodinsky bargaining solutions, and show that they are in the core.

9. Find the coalition function for the 4-country version of Mutual Defense in Figure 14.11. Each country is 1 unit square. Then find a proposal in the core.

10. Write down a coalition function for the three warring parties in the recent war in Bosnia (see section 14.8), under the assumption that each warring party can hold on to one-half of its prewar territory in the event that no agreement to end the war is reached. Show that the resulting game has a nonempty core. Is the ultimate settlement (see Figure 14.10) in the core?

FIGURE 14.11 | **MUTUAL DEFENSE, FOUR COUNTRIES**

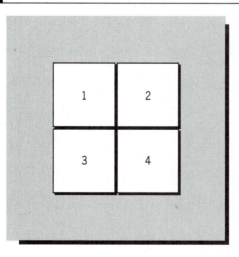

PART FIVE

Games, Marketing, and Politics

Two-Sided Markets and Matching Games

The market games in chapter 6 were in normal form, with strategies either chosen by buyers and sellers alike, or just by the sellers, with the buyers modeled as passive players represented by revealed market demand. In the auctions in chapter 12 bids were chosen by the buyers, and the seller was a passive player willing to take any winning bid above the reserve price. A **one-sided market game** occurs when one side of the market or the other has all the strategies. Chapters 13 and 14 looked at economic deals struck through bargaining. These situations were two-sided or many-sided: every party to a deal influenced the outcome.

This chapter studies **two-sided market games** in coalition-function form, where all players are risk neutral. It provides an algorithm for computing market equilibria of two-sided games, based on market fundamentals, and then uses those market fundamentals to construct the coalition function for a two-sided market game. The coalition function for such games, suitably normalized, measures **gains from trade,** which is the motive for all market transactions. A famous and important result, the core equivalence theorem, is proved. Core equivalence says that every market equilibrium is in the core of the market game and that every bargain in the core of the market game is a market equilibrium. This is a major strategic reason for the observed stability of market outcomes—they have something to offer to everyone who trades. Core equivalence is then considered in light of various imperfections of information. The RJR Nabisco takeover is studied to see what light the core sheds on it; the outcome lies in the core of the market game for this company.

A game can be two-sided even if no money is at stake. Matching processes, such as those that match dates for the prom or pledges to fraternities and sororities, are a case in point. These two-sided matching games have a lot in common with two-sided market games. They also satisfy a version of core equivalence. Sorority rush—which some of you may have gone through—is an interesting real-life matching game, matching recruits to sororities on college campuses.

■ 15.1 TWO-SIDED MARKETS: THE FUNDAMENTALS

This section models markets in which each buyer is interested in buying 1 unit of an indivisible commodity, and each seller is interested in selling 1 unit of that same commodity.

The markets for houses and cars conform to this pattern pretty closely. For a given commodity in question, there is a set $N(\text{buy})$ of buyers, and a set $N(\text{sell})$ of sellers. We will denote the buyers with odd numbers, $N(\text{buy}) = \{1, 3, \ldots, 2n - 1\}$ and the sellers with even numbers, $N(\text{sell}) = \{2, 4, \ldots, 2n\}$. As we shall see in a moment, we lose no generality by assuming that the number of buyers and the number of sellers are the same, n. Let's turn first to the demand side of the market.

Each buyer i has a utility function, u_i, of the form

$u_i(M_i, p) = M_i + b_i - P$ if the item is bought

M_i if the item is not bought

The parameter b_i represents the marginal utility of the item to buyer i. It is also the highest price that buyer i can pay for the item without losing utility overall. The expression $(b_i - P)$ measures buyer i's gain from trade at the price P. Use of the same notation used in chapter 12 for bidding behavior is deliberate. In a complete information framework, there is no reason not to bid what an item is worth to you, since everyone knows what it is worth to you anyway. Later we will distinguish between bids (which are publicly observable) and private information (which is not). Since utility is assumed linear in money M_i, the buyers are risk neutral. This assumption will also be relaxed later. It will prove useful to have the buyers ranked by bid, with high bid first:

$$b_1 \geq b_z \geq \ldots \geq b_{2n-1} \geq 0$$

Most of the time, these inequalities are strict. One exception is a *dummy* buyer i, for whom the item is worthless: $b_i = 0$. We can include as many dummies as we need on the demand side of the market to make the two sides of the market have the same number of traders. Figure 15.1 shows the demand function that results when there are three buyers, with $b_1 = \$15$, $b_2 = \$10$, and $b_3 = \$5$. At a price above $15, there is no willing buyer. At a price below

---

FIGURE 15.1 | TWO-SIDED MARKET, DEMAND SIDE, $n = 3$

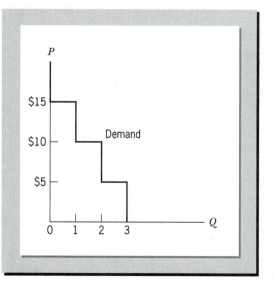

$5, there are three willing buyers. Notice that demand in a market like this must obey the law of demand.

We can model the supply side of the market in a similar fashion. Each seller j has a utility function, u_j, of the form

$u_j(M_j, p) = M_j + P - a_j$ if the item is sold

M_j if the item is not sold

The parameter a_j represents the marginal cost of the item to seller j. It is also the lowest price that seller j can receive for the item without losing utility. The expression $(P - a_j)$ measures seller j's gain from trade at the price P. Again, use of the same notation as that in chapters 13 and 14 for bargaining behavior is deliberate. In a complete information framework, there is no reason not to ask what an item costs you to sell, since everyone knows this already anyway. Later we will distinguish between asks (which are publicly observable) and private information (which is not). Since utility is assumed to be linear in money M_j, the sellers, like the buyers, are risk neutral. It will prove useful in a minute to have the sellers ranked by ask, with low ask first:

$$0 \le a_2 \le a_4 \le \ldots \le a_n$$

Most of the time, these inequalities are strict. One exception is a *dummy* seller u, for whom the item is infinitely costly. We can include as many dummies as we need on the supply side of the market to make the two sides of the market have the same number of agents. Figure 15.2 shows the supply schedule that results when there are three sellers, with $a_2 = 8, $a_4 = 12, and $a_6 = 16. At a price above $16, there are three willing sellers. At a price below $8, there are no willing sellers. Notice that supply in a market like this must obey the law of supply.

A market is in equilibrium at a price P^* when demand equals supply. Figure 15.3 shows the equilibrium that results when the demand of Figure 15.1 meets the supply of Figure 15.2. There is 1 unit transacted. The lowest-cost seller, seller 2, sells this unit to the highest

---

FIGURE 15.2 | **TWO-SIDED MARKET, SUPPLY SIDE, $n = 3$**

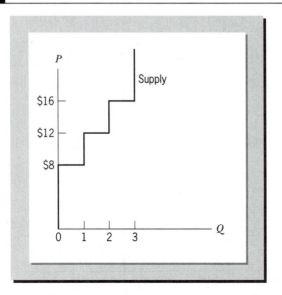

bidder, buyer 1, at a price P^*, between \$10 and \$12. If the price were lower than \$10, demand would exceed supply, $2 > 1$. The excess demand would drive the price up, a strategic process that will be made precise in the next section. If the price were higher than \$12, supply would exceed demand, $2 > 1$. The excess supply would drive the price down, a strategic process that will be made precise in the next section as well. Notice that although the equilibrium quantity is unique, there is an entire interval, [\$10, \$12], of equilibrium prices. The lowest price in this interval maximizes gain for the buyers; the highest price in this interval maximizes gain for the sellers.

Austrian economist Eugen von Boehm-Bawerk has developed a simple algorithm for finding an equilibrium in a two-sided market.[1] His method, called the **method of marginal pairs**, mimics the way an auctioneer would work in an auction with many units being auctioned all at once. Start with the first pair of traders, buyer 1 and seller 2. If $b_1 > a_2$, then have these two traders trade and go on to the next pair. If $b_1 < a_2$, stop. There are no gains from trade available in this market if the lowest-cost seller cannot make money by selling to the highest bidder. The next two traders are buyer 3 and seller 4. If $b_3 > a_4$, then have these two traders trade and go on to the next pair. If $b_3 < a_4$, stop. All gains from trade have been exhausted. Continue the algorithm until reaching the nth pair of traders, or stop, whichever comes first. The last pair of traders before stopping is called the *marginal pair*. The equilibrium price lies between the individual bid and ask of the marginal pair. Often, an equilibrium price can lie anywhere in this entire interval. In this example, however, the equilibrium prices lie in an even narrower band, given by the individual bid and ask of the pair next in line after the marginal pair.

In the market of Figure 15.3, the method of marginal pairs starts with buyer 1 and seller 2. Since

$$b_1 = \$15 > \$8 = a_2$$

FIGURE 15.3 **TWO-SIDED MARKET, EQUILIBRIUM, $n = 3$**

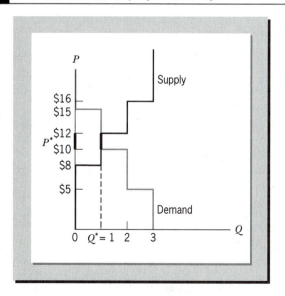

[1] Eugen von Boehm-Bawerk, *Positive Theory of Capital* (New York: G. E. Stechert, 1923; originally published in German in 1891).

these two trade, and we go to the pair consisting of buyer 3 and seller 4. Since

$$b_3 = \$10 < \$12 = a_4$$

we stop at this point. One unit is sold at equilibrium. The marginal pair is {1,2}, and the equilibrium price is between \$10 and \$12. The next section shows that one reason the method of marginal pairs works is that it mimics, or reproduces, the reasoning that underlies the core of the market game.

15.2 THE COALITION FUNCTION OF A TWO-SIDED MARKET GAME

This section derives the coalition function $v(S)$ of a market game, where S is a set of buyers and sellers trading only among themselves. We begin with singleton coalitions. Take buyer i. This buyer can't create a gain from trade all alone, and so $v(\{i\}) = M_i$, the amount of money buyer i starts with. The same is true for seller j: $v(\{j\}) = M_j$. Only coalitions with two or more traders can effect gains from trade. Even then, however, two conditions must be met. First, both buyers and sellers must be present in the coalition. A coalition composed of all buyers or all sellers has nothing to trade among its members. If the coalition S consists of all buyers, then

$$v(S) = \Sigma\, M_i, \ i \text{ in } S, \ i \text{ in } N(\text{buy})$$

Similarly, if the coalition S consists of all sellers, then

$$v(S) = \Sigma\, M_j, \ j \text{ in } S, \ j \text{ in } N(\text{sell})$$

Second, at least one pair in the coalition must gain from trade; that is, there must be one pair $\{i,j\}$ such that $b_i > a_j$. A coalition builds up value by matching up such pairs and having them trade. Suppose that $\{i,j\}$ is just such a pair. Then $v(\{i,j\})$ is realized when buyer 1 buys from seller 2:

$$v(\{i,j\}) = u_i(M_i, P) + u_j(M_j, P) = M_i + b_i - P + M_j + P - a_j$$
$$= M_i + M_j + b_i - a_j$$

Notice that the coalition value of $\{i,j\}$ exceeds the no-trade outcome, $M_i + M_j$, only when trade is mutually beneficial between buyer i and seller j. This formula holds for any buyer-seller pair that enjoys gains from trade.

Now is a good time to introduce an extremely useful normalization. You have probably noticed that the amount of money each player starts the game with—for buyer i, M_i, and seller j, M_j—shows up in every formula. The problem does not change at all—it is merely a linear transformation of the data—if we subtract this term from every coalition where player i appears. In the new coordinate system, we have

$v(\{I\}) = v(\{j\}) = 0$

$v(\{S\}) = 0$ if S is a subset of $N(\text{buy})$ or $N(\text{sell})$

$v(\{i,j\}) = b_i - a_j$ if $b_i > a_j$

0 otherwise

In this new coordinate system, $v(S)$ represents the gains to trade accruing to coalition S if its members should happen to trade among themselves in an optimal fashion.

Now consider a coalition with three members, two buyers (players 1 and 3), and one seller (player 2). If both {1,2} and {2,3} enjoy gains from trade, then from what we have just seen

$$v(\{1,3\}) = 0$$
$$v(\{1,2\}) = b_1 - a_2$$
$$v(\{3,2\}) = b_3 - a_2$$

From this foundation, we can find $v(\{1,2,3\})$. Seller 2 can sell to only one buyer, either buyer 1 or buyer 3. Buyer 1 values the item as least as much as does buyer 3. Therefore, we have

$$v(\{1,3\}) = b_1 - a_2 \geq b_3 - a_2 = v(\{2,3\})$$

The best the coalition {1,2,3} can do is to have buyer 1 buy from seller 2:

$$v(\{1,2,3\}) = v(\{1,3\}) = b_1 - a_2$$

Notice that we could have gotten the same answer by applying the method of marginal pairs within the coalition {1,2,3}: identify the pair with highest gains from trade and match them; then go on to the next pair; and so on until all gains from trade have been exhausted. The resulting outcome will maximize gains from trade for the coalition S.

We can now write down the coalition function for the 6-player, two-sided market game, with $N(\text{buy}) = \{1,3,5\}$, $N(\text{sell}) = \{2,4,6\}$, bid vector $\mathbf{b} = (\$15, \$10, \$5)$, and ask vector $\mathbf{a} = (\$8, \$12, \$16)$. All 2-player coalition values are zero except for the following:

$$v(\{1,2\}) = 15 - 8 = 7$$
$$v(\{1,4\}) = 15 - 12 = 3$$
$$v(\{3,2\}) = 10 - 8 = 2$$

We can build up the value of larger coalitions based on the 2-player coalition values, since all gains from trade are realized in bilateral exchange. For instance, for three players we get

$$7 = v(\{1,2,3\}) = v(\{1,2,4\}) = v(\{1,2,5\}) = v(\{1,2,6\})$$
$$3 = v(\{1,4,3\}) = v(\{1,4,5\}) = v(\{1,4,6\})$$
$$2 = v(\{2,3,5\}) = v(\{2,3,4\}) = v(\{2,3,6\})$$

The other 3-player coalitions have zero value. If a 4-player coalition contains {1,2}, it has value 7; if it contains {1,4} but not {1,2}, it has value 3; if it contains {3,2} but not {1,4} and not {1,2}, it has value 2; otherwise, it has value zero. Each 5-player coalition must have a positive value:

$$v(\{1,2,3,4,5\}) = 7 \ (1 \text{ and } 2 \text{ trade})$$
$$v(\{1,2,3,4,6\}) = 7 \ (1 \text{ and } 2 \text{ trade})$$
$$v(\{1,2,3,5,6\}) = 7 \ (1 \text{ and } 2 \text{ trade})$$
$$v(\{1,2,4,5,6\}) = 7 \ (1 \text{ and } 2 \text{ trade})$$
$$v(\{1,3,4,5,6\}) = 3 \ (1 \text{ and } 4 \text{ trade})$$
$$v(\{2,3,4,5,6\}) = 2 \ (2 \text{ and } 3 \text{ trade})$$

Finally, for the grand coalition N consisting of all buyers and all sellers, we have

$$v(N) = 7 \ (1 \text{ and } 2 \text{ trade})$$

The grand coalition cannot do any better than the coalition consisting of buyer 1 and seller 2.

Even for as few as six players, the coalition function is complicated. It has to specify $2^6 - 1 = 63$ different values. As we have just seen, in a two-sided market game, depending on how many pairs can create value, the specification of the coalition function is somewhat less complicated. For instance, when only three pairs can create value, as in the example given, then the coalition function has a lot of zero values.

15.3 THE CORE OF A TWO-SIDED MARKET GAME

We are now in position to find the core of the two-sided market game. We can save a lot of time with the following observation. A player i in a game is a *dummy* if every time that player joins a coalition S, zero value is added to the coalition's value $v(S)$:

$$v(S \text{ and } i) - v(S) = 0 \text{ for every coalition } S$$

This usage corresponds to that for markets. A buyer who doesn't want to bid more than zero for something is a dummy buyer; and a seller who wants to ask infinitely many dollars for something is a dummy seller. Such a buyer or seller is not going to bring any gains from trade when he or she joins a coalition.

In the market game whose coalition function we derived earlier, buyer 5 and seller 6 are dummies. Buyer 5 is a dummy because this buyer's bid of $5 is below the ask of any seller—buyer 5 can't create gains from trade with anybody else in the market. Similarly, seller 6 is a dummy because this seller's ask of $16 is above the bid of any buyer—seller 6 can't create gains from trade with anybody else in the market, either. A coalition can't count on any help from any of its dummy members when it is pondering whether to walk away from the negotiating table or walk out of the market. The core of a two-sided market game reflects this situation in the dummy principle:

Dummy principle. If player i is a dummy player, or player j a dummy seller, in a market game, then $u_i = u_j = 0$ in any outcome in the core of the game.

According to the dummy principle, we will find the core when we have solved the following system of inequalities:

$$u_1 + u_2 \geq 7 = v(\{1,2\})$$
$$u_3 + u_2 \geq 2 = v(\{2,3\})$$
$$u_1 + u_4 \geq 3 = v(\{1,4\})$$
$$u_1 + u_2 + u_3 \geq 7 = v(\{1,2,3\})$$
$$u_1 + u_2 + u_4 \geq 7 = v(\{1,2,4\})$$
$$u_1 + u_3 + u_4 \geq 3 = v(\{1,4,3\})$$
$$u_2 + u_3 + u_4 \geq 2 = v(\{2,3,4\})$$

along with the efficiency condition that all utilities add to 7:

$$7 = v(N)$$

We have already set $u_5 = u_6 = 0$, since buyer 5 and seller 6 are dummies. Figure 15.4 shows solutions to this set of inequalities.

One solution has

$$u_1 = 5, u_2 = 2, u_3 = u_4 = 0$$

Another solution has

$$u_1 = 3, u_2 = 4, u_3 = u_4 = 0$$

It is easy to see that these two vectors are in the core. Take the first of them. Substituting into the system of inequalities, we get

For players 1 and 2: $5 + 2 = 7 = v(\{1,2\})$
For players 2 and 3: $3 + 0 > 2 = v(\{2,3\})$
For players 1 and 4: $5 + 0 > 2 = v(\{1,4\})$
For players 1, 2, and 3: $5 + 2 + 0 = 7 = v(\{1,2,3\})$
For players 1, 2, and 4: $5 + 2 + 0 = 7 = v(\{1,2,4\})$
For player 1, 3, and 4: $5 + 0 + 0 > 2 = v(\{1,3,4\})$
For players 2, 3, and 4: $2 + 0 + 0 = 2 = v(\{2,3,4\})$
And finally, for the grand coalition, $5 + 2 + 0 + 0 + 0 + 0 = 7 = v(N)$

You can check that the other solution is in the core. You can also show that any point on the line between these two solutions is in the core; for instance, the point $u_1 = 4$, $u_2 = 3$, $u_3 = u_4 = 0$. Moreover, the outcome in Figure 15.4 must be all the outcomes in the core, since traders 1 and 2 have to get all the gains from trade in the grand coalition, $v(\{1,2\}) = v(N)$.

Let's now squeeze some intuition out of what we have just seen. The core says that buyer 1 and seller 2 get all the gains from trade, but there are limits on what each can get. Buyer 1 has to get at least a $3 gain, but can get no more than a $5 gain. Here is why. Suppose that buyer 1 was getting only a $2 gain. This means that buyer 2 would be paying a price of $13. At a price of $13, buyer 1 would not have to buy only from seller 2. Buyer 1

FIGURE 15.4 CORE OF THE MARKET GAME, $n = 3$

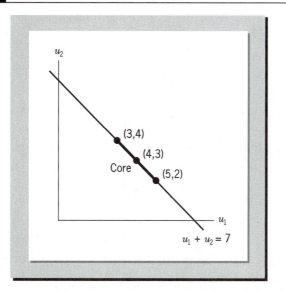

could switch to seller 4, who would also be willing to sell at a price of $13. Indeed, seller 4 would be interested in selling at any price above the reservation price of $12. This potential excess supply on the part of the next most costly seller puts an upper bound on the price seller 2 can get, and therefore a lower bound on the gain buyer 1 can get, in the two-sided market game.

Next, consider what happens if buyer 1 gets more than a $5 gain—say, $6. In this case buyer 1 would be paying a price of only $9. At a price of $9, seller 2 would not have only buyer 1 to sell to. Seller 2 could switch to buyer 3, who would also be willing to buy at a price of $9. Indeed, buyer 3 would be interested in buying at any price below the reservation price of $10. This potential excess demand on the part of the next highest bidder puts a lower bound on the price buyer 1 can pay, and therefore an upper bound on the gain seller 2 can get, in the two-sided market game.

Now compare the gains from trade corresponding to the market equilibrium in Figure 15.5 with the core of the market game in Figure 15.4. Market equilibria gains from trade are parameterized by the equilibrium price P^*:

$$u_1 = 15 - P^* \text{ (buyer's gain)}$$
$$u_2 = P^* - 8 \text{ (seller's gain)}$$

where P^* is between 10 and 12. Take the market equilibrium $P^* = 10$. This is the lowest possible equilibrium price, which is best for the buyer. This price corresponds to $u_1 = 5$, $u_2 = 2$, which is at one end of the core. Take the other extreme market equilibrium price, $P^* = 12$. This is the highest possible equilibrium price, which is best for the seller. This price corresponds to $u_1 = 3$, $u_2 = 4$, which is at the other end of the core. All the market equilibrium prices in between these two extremes line up, one to one, with points in the core. For instance, the price $P^* = 11$ corresponds to the core outcome $u_1 = 4$, $u_2 = 3$.

The phenomenon whereby market equilibria correspond to outcomes in the core, and vice versa, is known as the **core equivalence theorem.** You can show that for any two-sided

---

FIGURE 15.5 **GAINS FROM TRADE, MARKET EQUILIBRIUM**

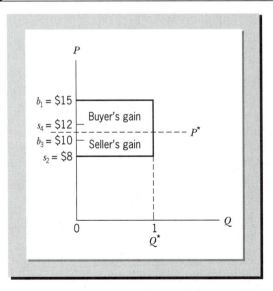

market game with a finite number of players, the market equilibria and the core outcomes are equivalent.[2] When goods are perfectly divisible, the situation becomes much more complicated. For instance, the existence of a market equilibrium or of outcomes in the core is no longer guaranteed, but requires more structure. In such situations, if there are infinitely many players, none of whom is risk seeking, then core equivalence holds.

Core equivalence explains why market outcomes hold up so well to criticism. If any group could do better by not being in the market, it is free to get out of the market and do its own thing. However, if the market is in equilibrium, then there is no such group. All participants in the market are doing at least as well as they would on their own. The market has something to offer everyone who is active at a market equilibrium.

15.4 LIMITATIONS ON CORE EQUIVALENCE

In settings where markets are likely to fail, core equivalence is likely to fail also. The link between competitive markets, where price is set by supply demand, and the core of an associated game may be tenuous indeed, or it may even disappear. There are two obvious places to look for market failure. One involves the formation of conspiracies on the buyers' or sellers' side to fix the price in their favor. Another, which may exploit imperfect information, involves shaving asks and bids to move the price in one's favor. We will consider these phenomena in turn.

First let's look at attempts to monopolize the market. Suppose that all the sellers in a market merge to form a single player, a **merger** that we will call player 2. This single entity, which still has the same costs of production of its individual members, henceforth will act as the only seller in the market. The impact of this merger will be to extend the core beyond the set of market equilibria and in a direction favorable to the monopoly.

Here's how monopoly works in a two-sided market game. Take the bid and ask data from the market game of the previous section, only now seller 2 can sell as many as 3 units. There are still independent buyers, 1, 3, and 5. Using the coalition function we have already derived, we have

$$v(\{1,2\}) = 7$$
$$v(\{3,2\}) = 2$$
$$v(\{1,3,2\}) = 7 = v(N)$$

and all other coalitions have value zero. We have already set $u_5 = 0$, since buyer 5 continues to be a dummy player. An outcome in the core must satisfy the following set of inequalities:

$$u_1 + u_2 \geq 7 = v(\{1,2\})$$
$$u_3 + u_2 \geq 2 = v(\{3,2\})$$
$$u_1 + u_2 + u_3 = 7$$

The solution to these inequalities is shown in Figure 15.6. The core consists of the line segment between (5,2,0) and (0,7,0) on the bottom edge of the gains from trade triangle. In particular, the monopoly player can get as much as $u_2 = 7$ at a core outcome. Prior to the merger, the maximum gain to the sellers in the core was only 5. All the points from

---

[2] The easiest proofs require linear programming, which is beyond the mathematical scope of this book. For a particularly insightful treatment, see Lloyd S. Shapley and Martin Shubik, "The Assignment Game I: The Core," *International Journal of Game Theory* 1 (1972): 111–130.

(5,2,0) to (0,7,0) have been added to the core, thanks to monopolization. The core is now larger than the set of perfectly competitive market equilibria, and all the new points in the core are better for sellers who have monopolized the market.

What the monopoly has done is repeal the effect of excess supply on market price. In order to achieve a gain of 7, the sellers have to get a price of $15 for 1 unit sold. At this price, there would ordinarily be 2 units for sale, not 1. The monopoly prevents the second unit from being sold. Moreover, from the total gain of 7 units, the monopoly can distribute *side payments* to its participating members:

$$7 = u_2 + u_4 + u_6$$

The monopoly can parcel out the gains to make everybody in the merger better off, for instance by paying $5.50 to (pre-merger) seller 2, $1 to seller 4, and $0.50 to seller 6. Compare this to the best possible pre-merger core outcome, where the payoffs were $5, $0, and $0. Pre-merger seller 2 could justify the side payment to seller 4 as a reward for not spoiling the fun by offering a unit for sale at the price of $15, and the side payment to seller 6 as a reward for keeping quiet about the whole business. What we have just described is a conspiracy to fix prices. Since such conspiracies are a felony in the United States, it behooves the participants to keep things quiet. However, firms may still try to get away with mergers whose sole objective is to raise prices to monopoly levels, a phenomenon that the antitrust authorities (the Department of Justice Antitrust Division; the Federal Trade Commission) monitor closely.

Sellers aren't the only ones who can monopolize a market. Buyers can, too—witness the $280 million fine levied on the owners of Major League Professional Baseball for fixing the prices of free agents below market levels in the late 1980s. You can show that when buyers form a monopoly ("monopsony"), the core expands in a direction favorable to them (see end-of-chapter problem 4).

FIGURE 15.6 MONOPOLIZED MARKET (THE CORE DOES NOT EQUAL PERFECTLY COMPETITIVE EQUILIBRIUM

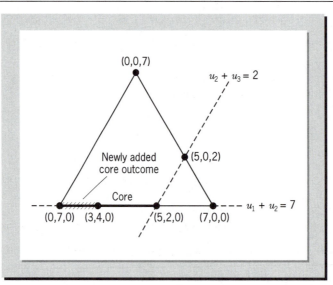

We have just seen core equivalence fail when one side or the other of the market is monopolized. In this case, the set of outcomes in the core expands, and the set of market equilibria stays the same. Another route by which core equivalence may fail is when bids or asks are made strategically. To adapt our notation to this possibility, let z_i be the underlying value of the item for buyer i; z_j, the cost of producing the item for seller j. These underlying values are known to all players. This crucial assumption means that the coalition function and the inequalities defining the core do not change. Buyer i *bids honestly* when $b_i = z_i$; seller j *asks honestly* when $a_j = z_j$. The market demand and supply schedules, such as in Figures 15.1 and 15.2, presuppose that all buyers bid honestly and all sellers ask honestly. Unfortunately, the market participants usually have an incentive to act otherwise.

Suppose that the market is run by an English auction, where the auctioneer raises the price until demand equals supply. The auction will stop at the lowest competitive equilibrium price. Suppose that k knits have been sold, so that the marginal pair at equilibrium consisted of buyer $2k - 1$ and seller $2k$. Then this auction rule sets

$$P^* = a_{2k}$$

From a strategic standpoint, seller $2k$ would like to raise his or her ask. By doing so, seller $2k$ increases the gain he or she gets from trade. This seller can afford to raise the ask until it is just below the cost of the next seller in the cost ranking:

$$a_{2k} = z_{2(k+1)} - e$$

where e is the minimum monetary unit. The reasoning here is just like the reasoning for the equilibrium behavior in a complete information first-price auction; the only difference is that now there are many units on the auction block instead of just one.

Let's apply this conclusion to the market data of Figure 15.3 (see Figure 15.7). If sellers are bidding strategically, then seller 1 asks $11.99, not $8. The supply schedule that is

---

FIGURE 15.7 **STRATEGIC ASKS IN THE MARKET (THE CORE DOES NOT EQUAL PERFECTLY COMPETITIVE EQUILIBRIUM**

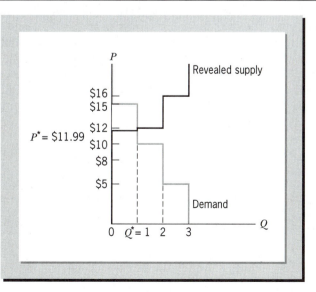

revealed to the market is not the true supply schedule, but a supply schedule shifted upward in the vicinity of the market equilibrium quantity. The sellers who aren't active do not have an incentive to misrepresent their costs, but the marginal seller (here, seller 1) certainly does. The outcome corresponding to $P = \$10$, which is still in the core, is no longer a market equilibrium outcome.

You can show that strategic bidding can also occur in an auction among buyers. Suppose that the market is run by a descending auction, in which the auctioneer lowers the price until demand equals supply. The auction will stop at the highest competitive equilibrium price. Suppose that k units have been sold, so that the marginal pair at equilibrium consisted of buyer $2k - 1$ and seller $2k$. Then this auction rule sets

$$P^* = b_{2k-1}$$

From a strategic standpoint, buyer $2k - 1$ would like to lower the bid. By doing so, this buyer raises the gains from trade. Buyer $2k - 1$ can afford to lower the bid until it is just above the underlying value of the next buyer in the value ranking:

$$b_{2k-1} = z_{2k} + e$$

where e is the minimum monetary unit. The reasoning here is again just like that for the equilibrium behavior in a complete information first-price auction. Now the outcome corresponding to $P = \$12$, which is still in the core, is no longer a market outcome. The details are left for an end-of-chapter problem.

Recall from chapter 12 that there is an institution to combat the problem of **dishonest asks** and **dishonest bids** when there is one item on the auction block: the second-price auction. We can adapt this institution to the present situation, where there are k units being transacted at equilibrium. In a $k + 1$ price auction among buyers, all bids greater than the $k + 1$ highest bid win and pay a price equal to the $k + 1$ highest bid. In a $k + 1$ price auction among sellers, all asks less than the $k + 1$ highest ask win and receive a price equal to the $k + 1$ highest ask. If $k = 4$, there are four items being transacted at equilibrium, and these would be fifth-price auctions. A $k + 1$ auction among buyers gives each buyer an incentive to bid honestly. Indeed, this is a weakly dominant strategy, just as it was in second-price auctions, and for exactly the same reasons. Your bid, if it wins, does not affect the price you pay; but if you underbid, you may lose an auction you should otherwise win. A $k + 1$ auction among sellers gives each seller an incentive to ask honestly. Unfortunately, there is no way to provide incentives to ask and bid honestly to both sides of the market at the same time. Thus there is a second major limitation to core equivalence, resulting from strategic bidding behavior. Such behavior played a major role in the bidding for RJR Nabisco during the takeover episode of 1989.

◧ 15.5 BARBARIANS AT THE GATE: THE CORE

In 1989, the largest corporate takeover up to that time occurred. RJR Nabisco was on the block, and several groups were actively trying to buy it.[3] You may have seen the movie, with the same name as the book. In any event, here is how this takeover looks as a two-sided market game.

---

[3] Material for this analysis was derived from Bryan Burrough and John Helyar, *Barbarians at the Gate: The Fall of RJR Nabisco* (New York: Harper & Row, 1990).

RJR Nabisco shares were trading at $55, before all the excitement started. Two outsiders, Kohlberg Kravis Roberts (KKR) and First Boston (FB), were especially keen to acquire the company. So was a group headed by RJR Nabisco's CEO, Ross Johnson—this group was trying to conduct a leveraged buyout. They would borrow billions of dollars (that's leverage) and buy out all the shares, taking the company private.

We take up the story at the point in the bidding where the stock price had reached $100/share. We will call the three buyers:

> Player 1—the leveraged buyout group, led by CEO Ross Johnson
> Player 3—KKR
> Player 5—FB

The single seller is the board of directors of RJR Nabisco (player 2). The board was inclined to accept $100/share as a purchase price, as this represented a whopping $45/share premium over the stock price at the start of the takeover event. The board's oft-stated goal throughout the proceedings was to maximize shareholder value, which here meant maximum gains from trade for the seller.

Figure 15.8 shows the market demand and supply schedules for the RJR Nabisco leveraged buyout (LBO). Since the company has to be bought lock, stock, and barrel, there is 1 indivisible unit of company for sale. The board has already shown its willingness to accept $100/share, hence the supply schedule with the company for sale at any price above that. Based on inside information (buyer 1), due diligence (buyer 3), and sheer guts (buyer 5), there are three willing buyers at any price up to $106/share, and two willing buyers at any price up to $109/share.[4] The market equilibrium—where demand equals supply—occurs at a unique price, $109/share, with either buyer 1 or buyer 3 getting the company.

FIGURE 15.8 DEMAND AND SUPPLY FOR THE RJR NABISCO LBO

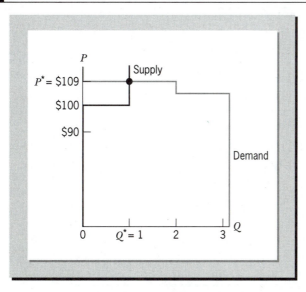

---

[4] The management group actually bid $112/share at the end. After reading the fine print and evaluating the heavy load of junk bonds in this bid, the board of directors ruled that it was equivalent to the KKR bid of $109/share.

As we have seen, the winning bidder has an incentive not to bid that high and would much prefer to get the company for a lower price. Thus, when the first bidding deadline occurred (end of October 1988), none of the bids was that close to underlying value. The management group had bid $100/share and KKR, $94/share. First Boston had come closest to its underlying valuation, at $101/share.

At that point the seller did something quite unusual. The board asked each of the buyers for a new bid. The implication of this move was clear: the seller suspected the buyers of holding out and expected the new bids to be higher than the old ones. Indeed, the new bids were higher: the management group went up $1/share, KKR went up $12/share, and First Boston went up $5/share. This strategy worked so well the first time that the board tried it once more. This time, the board asked each bidder for a final bid. The final bids reached market equilibrium levels, with First Boston no longer an active bidder.

The inequalities that describe the core of this game are as follows:

$$u_1 + u_2 = 9 = v(\{1,2\})$$
$$u_3 + u_2 = 9 = v(\{3,2\})$$
$$u_5 + u_2 = 6 = v(\{5,2\})$$

together with the efficiency condition

$$9 = v(N)$$

The gains from trade are the $9/share available to split between the seller and either buyer 1 or buyer 3, or the $6/share between the seller and buyer 5. Even though buyer 5 is not a strategic dummy, this buyer still gets shut out at any core outcome: $u_5 = 0$. Figure 15.9 shows the core of this two-sided market game. The core is the single outcome (0,9,0)—the seller gets all the gains from trade. This is equivalent to the market equilibrium price—a

---

FIGURE 15.9 CORE OF BARBARIANS AT THE GATE

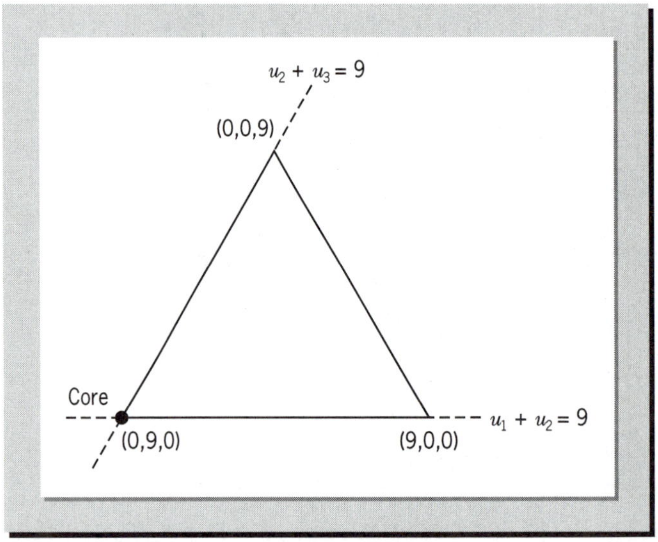

share price of \$109. This is core equivalence with a vengeance—but it took a really clever move on the part of the seller to get the price this high.

15.6 TWO-SIDED MATCHING GAMES

In every market there are two sides, the buyers and the sellers, and gains from trade at stake. In nonmarket situations there may still be two sides, but something different from money at stake. Consider what happens prior to a high school **prom.** There are two sides, boys and girls. Individuals from the two sides get matched somehow, and form dates to the prom. Each person who goes to the prom would like to be matched with his or her preferred date. Although it may not look like it, this, too, is a game—a **two-sided matching game.** And even though there is no money at stake, it has strategic properties very reminiscent of those of two-sided markets. This stands to reason because markets also perform a matching function, namely, matching buyers to sellers. In particular, the core will prove to be just as important to a two-sided matching game as to a two-sided market game.

To fix notation, let the odd numbers represent one side of the matching game, $N(I) = \{1, 3, \ldots, 2n-1\}$ and let the even numbers represent the other side of the matching game, $N(II) = \{2, 4, \ldots, 2n\}$. The grand coalition N is simply the union of these two sides, $N(I)$ and $N(II)$. A player i on side I of the market has a ranking of the players on the other side in terms of preference as a date. A player also has the option (NO) of not going to the prom at all. Suppose that $n = 3$. Then player i could have preferences of this sort:

> i: 4,6,NO,2

Player i's preferred date is player 4, followed by player 6. Player i would rather not go to the prom than go with player 2.

Similarly, a player j on side II of the market has a ranking of the players on the other side in terms of preference as a date. This player also has the option of not going to the prom at all. Player j might have preferences of the sort:

> j: 1,3,5,NO

Player j's preferred date is player 1, followed by player 3, followed by player 5. The absolute worst for this player is not to go to the prom at all.

To motivate the idea of equilibrium for the prom, we will study a small prom with $n = 3$. The preferences are as follows. On side I, we have

> 1: 2,4,6,NO
> 3: 2,6,NO,4
> 5: 2,NO,4,6

All the players on this side rate player 2 first. This is obviously a very popular player. On side II we have

> 2: 1,5,NO,3
> 4: 5,3,1,NO
> 6: 3,1,NO,5

There is no clear favorite on side II for a date to the prom.

The definition of an **equilibrium matching** is a bit abstract[5]; it contains two parts. First, suppose that players *i* and *j* are matched up. Then it must not be the case that either or both of them can find a more preferred date, either among those already matched or among those not yet matched. If either one of them could still get a better date, then that player has an incentive to break the date they currently have—a clear sign of disequilibrium. Absent that possibility, then both have the best date they are going to get. Second, suppose that player *i* or player *j* is not yet matched. Then the unmatched player prefers not going to the prom to going with any of the dates still available. If an acceptable person were still available, player *i* or player *j* could ask that person to the prom—another clear sign of disequilibrium.

Although there is no simple graphic for describing an equilibrium matching, there is a simple algorithm for arriving at one. A variant of this algorithm is enshrined in the custom expressed as "the boy asks the girl to the prom." We will call this the **boy-asks-girl algorithm,** and it goes like this. Each of the boys asks his favorite date to the prom. Each of the girls says yes to the best offer she gets, or says no to all of them if she ranks not going to the prom higher. All boys who get accepted stand pat. The boys who have not yet heard yes next ask out the girl they rank highest who is still available. The girls compare offers they have just received to dates they already have, breaking any date in favor of a better one. This process continues until all the dating possibilities are exhausted.

Let's apply the boy-asks-girl algorithm to the 6-player prom data given. We interpret side I as the boys; side II, as the girls. At the first step, each boy invites his favorite date, player 2, to the prom. Player 2 accepts her favorite among these, player 1. She says no to the other two boys. So after the first step, we have a match [1,2]. Boys 3 and 5 are left at step two. Boy 3 asks girl 6, and boy 5 says no to the whole process. If boy 5 can't go with girl 2, he's not going at all. Girl 6 ranks boy 3 first, and is thrilled to say yes. We have a second match, [3,6]. Since boy 5 has hit NO in his rankings, this completes the algorithm.

Now let's check that the matching [1,2], [3,6], and 4 and 5 stay home is an equilibrium. Since players 1, 2, and 6 get their first choice, they have to be in equilibrium. Likewise player 5, who prefers not going to the prom to going with anyone other than player 2. Player 3 gets his second choice, but player 3's first choice is getting her first choice, so there is nothing player 3 can do about it. Player 4 would like to go to the prom, but all her choices are either taken or unwilling to go with her.

The boy-asks-girl algorithm always leads to an equilibrium matching. You can turn the process completely around in the form of a girl-asks-boy algorithm. This algorithm, too, will always lead to an equilibrium matching, although usually not the same matching as when boys ask girls (see end-of-chapter problem 8). Indeed, you can show that if there is more than one stable matching, then the boy-asks-girl algorithm leads to the stable matching that does best for the boys, while the girl-asks-boy algorithm leads to the stable matching best for the girls. Who does the asking out does make a difference.

We now turn to the coalition form of a matching game and show that an equilibrium matching is equivalent to being a core outcome.

---

[5] The term *stable matching* is often used as well. See Alvin E. Roth and Marilda A. Oliveira Sotomayor, *Two-sided Matching: A Study in Game-Theoretic Modeling and Analysis* (Cambridge, UK: Cambridge University Press, 1990), for an admirable treatment of this entire subject.

◼ 15.7 Matching Games in Coalition-Function Form

The first task in constructing a coalition function is to find a way to represent preferences. It will suffice for our purposes to use an **ordinal utility**. Suppose there are n possible dates to the prom, plus the option NO. Then attach $n + 1$ utility points to the highest-ranked option, n utility points to the next-highest-ranked option, and so on down to 1 utility point to the lowest-ranked option. This process yields an ordinal scale that expresses preferences numerically.

Armed with a numerical utility, we can now find the coalition function. First, take a singleton i. The only thing that a player in a matching game acting alone can guarantee is the outcome NO. It takes two players, one from each side of the game, before gains from going to the prom together can be realized. This gives the coalition-function value

$$v(\{i\}) \geq u_i(\text{NO})$$

The only dates you should consider are those that are better than staying home from the prom. Now consider a doubleton $\{i, j\}$, one from each side of the market. Here, one of two things can happen. First, each member of this pair may prefer going to the prom with the other member to staying home. In this case, their coalition value is the vector of utilities they achieve by going to the prom together:

$$v(\{i,j\}) \geq (u_i(j), u_j(i))$$

Second, at least one member of this pair may prefer staying home to going to the prom with the other member. In that case, the best this pair can do is stay home:

$$v(\{i,j\}) \geq [u_i(\text{NO}), u_j(\text{NO})]$$

Clearly, such a coalition will never form.

The remarkable thing about two-sided matching games is that all the information in the coalition function is contained in the values for singletons and doubletons. There are two reasons for this phenomenon. First, there isn't any money on the table to divide: you either go to the prom with someone or you don't. Second, to go to the prom, all you need is one other person. If you were in a coalition with a lot of other people, you would still break down into pairs for prom night. This should become clearer when we write down the coalition function for the prom we just studied.

First, we check out the singletons. On the boys' side, $N(\text{I})$, we have

$v(\{1\}) \geq 1$ since boy 1 ranks NO fourth

$v(\{3\}) \geq 2$ since boy 3 ranks NO third

$v(\{5\}) \geq 3$ since boy 5 ranks NO second

On the girls' side, $N(\text{II})$, we have

$v(\{2\}) \geq 2$ since girl 2 ranks NO third

$v(\{4\}) \geq 1$ since girl 4 ranks NO fourth

$v(\{6\}) \geq 2$ since girl 6 ranks NO third

Next, we check out the pairs. There are nine possible pairs with one member from each of the two sides of the game. Of these, five lead to possible dates:

$v(\{1,2\}) \geq (4,4)$ These are each other's top choice.

$v(\{1,4\}) \geq (3,2)$ These are each other's second and third choice, respectively

$v(\{1,6\}) \geq (2,3)$ These are each other's third and second choice, respectively

$v(\{3,6\}) \geq (3,4)$ These are each other's second and first choice, respectively

$v(\{5,2\}) \geq (4,3)$ These are each other's first and second choice, respectively

With the other four possible pairs, $\{3,2\}$, $\{3,4\}$, $\{5,4\}$, and $\{5,6\}$, one or the other member of the pair would rather stay home. As far as the core is concerned, we only have to satisfy the demands of the five pairs who could conceivably date.

Now consider a coalition with three members, say, $\{1,2,4\}$. This coalition can do one of two things: send $\{1,2\}$ to the prom or send $\{1,4\}$ to the prom. The former achieves $v(\{1,2\})$; the latter, $v(\{1,4\})$. So $v(\{1,2,4\})$ is simply $v(\{1,2\})$ or $v(\{1,4\})$, the set union of these two payoff vectors. Larger coalitions break up into couples as far as their coalition value is concerned.

A vector $\mathbf{u} = (u_1, \ldots, u_6)$ is in the core of the matching game if it satisfies the preceding 10 inequalities. That's a lot of inequalities to satisfy. Let's show that the equilibrium matching we found earlier—$\{1,2\}$, $\{3,6\}$, and 4 and 5 stay home—is in the core. This matching generates the utility vector

$$\mathbf{u} = (4, 4, 3, 1, 3, 4)$$

Notice first that $\mathbf{u}$ payoff dominates the vector of stay-at-home utilities, $(1, 2, 2, 1, 3, 2)$. Everyone except players 4 and 5 gets a better utility from the stable matching than from staying at home. Players 4 and 5 break even by staying home.

Next, let's look at pairs. Pair $\{1,2\}$ can guarantee utilities $(4,4)$ by going out together, and this is exactly what they get. Similarly, pair $\{3,6\}$ can guarantee the utilities $(3,4)$ by going out together, and this is exactly what they get. The last pair left, $\{4,5\}$ can guarantee the utilities $(1,3)$ by staying home, and this is exactly what they get. You can check that none of the other seven possible pairs can do better, either. Since no coalition by itself can do better than what the vector $\mathbf{u}$ gives them, the vector $\mathbf{u}$ is in the core.

This is true in general: an equilibrium matching is in the **core of the matching game.** Even more remarkable, the converse is true. If an alternative is in the core of the matching game, then it is an equilibrium matching. Since the prom has a unique equilibrium matching, there is a unique solution to this set of inequalities. Just as in a two-sided market game, in a two-sided matching game the set of equilibria is equivalent to the core.

We can squeeze some intuition out of this result by observing the following. The way a coalition gets its coalition value is by making a date. The coalition $\{1,2\}$ can walk away from any matching that gives them payoffs less than what they can get by making a date, namely the payoffs $(4,4)$. Equilibrium means that no individual or pair can gain by walking away from a proposed matching. At the same time, equilibrium is the test that outcomes in the core must pass as well.

This chapter closes with a look at a matching game played across the nation—sorority rush on U.S. college campuses.

◼ 15.8 SORORITY RUSH

Each year brings a familiar sight on campuses—female students all dressed up and lined up in front of a sorority they hope to join.[6] This ritual is part of the **sorority rush.** Rush is the

[6] Some material for this study came from Susan Mongell and Alvin E. Roth, "Sorority Rush as a Two-sided Matching Mechanism," *American Economic Review* 81(1991): 441–464.

recruitment process of the sorority system as a whole. It is supervised by the Panhellenic Council (Panhel), a nationwide organization with local chapters, one per campus. The point of rush is to match sororities with recruits, known as **rushees,** taking into account the preferences of both.

Rush begins with a series of parties. The first parties are called open houses. These parties allow the rushees to inform themselves, and so form preferences, about the various sororities. The parties also allow the sororities to inform themselves about the rushees. Later parties are called preference parties. A rushee may attend at most three preference parties. Panhel urges sororities to invite to preference parties only rushees in whom they are interested.

When the parties are over, the matching process begins in earnest. Each rushee fills out a preference card. On this card, she is supposed to list in order, from the top on down, all the sororities she is interested in joining. If a rushee does not list a sorority on her preference card, she cannot be matched. If a rushee lists only one sorority, she is said to have suicided. If that sorority doesn't want her, she cannot be matched, and she must wait a year before the next rush to try to get in to a sorority. Panhel explicitly urges rushees not to **suicide.** While rushees are filling out preference cards, the sororities are filling out something analogous, called *bid lists*. On its bid list, each sorority lists all the rushees it is willing to accept. Each sorority has a quota to fill—this is the number of names it can put on its bid list.[7]

Panhel has its own matching algorithm, called the preferential-bidding-system (PBS) algorithm, which it has used since 1928. The PBS algorithm works as follows. The rushees' preference cards are put in alphabetical order. The first choice on each preference card is called out. If that choice is on the bid list of the sorority named, this is a match. That person is removed from the pile, and the sorority's quota is reduced by one. If that choice is not on the bid list of the sorority named, and this person has not suicided, she is put into the hold pile. If this person has suicided, her card is discarded.[8] When all the first choices have been processed, then all the cards still in the pile are read for the second choices. This process continues until no further matches are possible, either because all the sororities are full, or because no sorority wants any of the rushees left in the pile.

The matching process surrounding sorority rush is a lot like the matching process surrounding the prom. The only real difference is that each sorority can recruit more than one rushee, whereas each rushee can be matched to only one sorority. The PBS algorithm does not have all the properties of the boy-asks-girl or girl-asks-boy algorithms for the prom. In particular, it may lead to matches that are not equilibria, and therefore not in the core. In practice, however, most rushees appear to get their top choices, and so have no incentive to walk away from the matching.

Two economists, Susan Mongell and Alvin E. Roth, have studied sorority rush at four campuses in the northeastern United States for several years.[9] The data from 1987 are typical. On one campus, 56 of 68 rushees got their first choice, and 59 of 68 were matched overall. On another campus, 93 of 125 rushees got their first choice, and 105 of 125 were matched overall. On a third campus, 91 of 119 rushees got their first choice, and 105 of 119

---

[7] The exact procedures vary across campuses. At one large Midwestern university, rushees are allowed to put on their preference cards only the names of sororities to whose preference parties they have been invited. At this same university, the Panhel algorithm is worked from the other side, with sorority bid lists read first, and the algorithm is run on a computer.

[8] Panhel officials may, if they wish, contact the rushee and ask if she wants to reconsider before they discard her card.

[9] Panhel is very reluctant to divulge information about rush. The researchers were able to use data from these four universities only on condition of anonymity.

were matched overall. Averaging over all three campuses, 77 percent of rushees got their first choice, and 86 percent got matched. It is interesting to note that 184 of the 312 rushees suicided, even though they were told not to. Of these 184, 149 (or 81 percent) got their first and only choice. A rushee had a slightly better chance of getting her first choice if she suicided than if she didn't. With suicide rates this high, the possibility that the PBS will lead to an outcome outside the core is remote.

This isn't the only place in the economy where matching takes place. Students applying to college, graduates applying to medical school, and people with Ph.D.s applying for jobs—they are all going through matching processes too.

■ SUMMARY

1. A market is one-sided if only one side of the market has strategies. A market is two-sided if both sides have strategies.

2. Two-sided markets in which each buyer buys at most 1 unit of an indivisible good, and each seller sells at most 1 unit of that good, always obey the law of supply and the law of demand.

3. Equilibria of a two-sided market can be found using the method of marginal pairs. There are usually many equilibria in a two-sided market; there is always at least one.

4. The coalition function of a two-sided market game measures gains from trade. When all buyers and sellers are risk neutral, the coalition-function value is a dollar number.

5. The core of a two-sided market game is a proposal from which no coalition can profitably walk away. Every market equilibrium is in the core of a two-sided market. The converse is also true, a result known as the core equivalence theorem.

6. The fact that market equilibria are in the core of a market game accounts for their considerable stability.

7. The core equivalence theorem breaks down when competition is imperfect or when agents on one side of the market bid strategically.

8. A two-sided matching game differs from a two-sided market game in that no money is at stake on the table. Otherwise, the two kinds of games are quite similar. In particular, they both exhibit core equivalence.

9. Two-sided matching games are analyzed using ordinal preferences. The coalition-function value for a doubleton in such a game is a single vector.

10. Sorority rush on campus is a two-sided matching game. In practice, most rushees get their first choice of sororities.

■ KEY TERMS

one-sided market games	merger	boy-asks-girl algorithm
two-sided market games	dishonest asks	ordinal utility
gains from trade	dishonest bids	core of the matching game
method of marginal pairs	prom	sorority rush
dummy principle	two-sided matching game	rushees
core equivalence theorem	equilibrium matching	suicide

■ PROBLEMS

1. Suppose that buyers have bids $b_1 = \$100$ and $b_3 = \$50$, and that sellers have asks $a_2 = \$25$ and $a_4 = \$40$. Plot the market demand and supply schedules. Find the market equilibria. Find an outcome in the core of the market game.

2. Two new traders, one buyer and one seller, have entered the market in problem 1. The buyer has bid $b_5 = \$40$; the seller has ask $a_6 = \$50$. Find the market equilibria. Find two outcomes in the core of this market game. What, if anything, has changed?

3. Compare the core in problem 1 to the symmetric, efficient Nash equilibrium outcome you would get according to the market rules in chapter 6, with a bid/ask increment of $5. What does this tell you about the relationship between symmetric efficient Nash equilibria and the core?

4. The sellers in problem 2 merge to monopolize the market. Find an outcome in the core that is not a perfectly competitive equilibrium.

5. Suppose that in a two-sided market, there are three buyers and three sellers on each side. Two units are transacted at equilibrium. Define a third-price auction for buyers. Show that in this third-price auction, honest bidding is a weakly dominant strategy for the buyers.

6. Suppose that in a market with two buyers and one seller, a second-price auction is used to sell the item. However, if the second price is lower than what the seller is asking, the seller's ask becomes the sale price. Give a numerical example in which the seller has an incentive to overstate the costs of production.

7. Suppose that in Barbarians at the Gate, First Boston had an underlying value for RJR Nabisco of $115/share. What would the outcome of the game have been? Derive the core while you are at it. Is the outcome you predicted in the core?

8. Consider a prom-matching algorithm that is just like boy-asks-girl, except that the girls ask the boys. Work out the details of this algorithm, and then apply it to the prom problem in section 15.6. Do you get a different answer from the one derived using the boy-asks-girl algorithm? Can you explain why or why not?

9. In the prom problem of section 15.6, suppose that player 5 has the rankings:

    5: 2,4,6,NO

    Nothing else has changed. Derive the coalition function. Find all outcomes in the core.

10. There are 2 sororities and 10 rushees participating in rush. Rushees are identified by the odd numbers 1 through 19. Sorority Alpha Alpha Alpha finds rushees 1 through 9 acceptable and so notes on its bid sheet. Sorority Zeta Zeta Zeta finds all rushees whose numbers are prime (i.e., 1, 2, 3, 5, 7, 11, 13, 17, 19) acceptable and so notes on its bid sheet. Each sorority has a quota of 10. Rushees numbered 10 and below prefer Alpha Alpha Alpha to Zeta Zeta Zeta; rushees numbered 11 and above prefer just the opposite. Every rushee wants to get into a sorority. Work out the result of the PBS algorithm, on the assumption that every rushee suicides (the sororities go in Greek alphabetical order). Is the outcome you get a matching equilibrium? Why or why not?

C H A P T E R   1 6

Voting Games

Voting is a major part of business and economic life. As Thoreau wrote in his essay *On Civil Disobedience,* "All voting is a sort of gaming, like checkers or backgammon, with a slight moral tinge to it, a playing with right and wrong, with moral questions; and betting naturally accompanies it." Proxy fights, votes to oust a CEO, and an industry lobbying for votes on Capitol Hill are just a few of the many actual economics examples. This chapter looks at some of the strategic aspects of voting games.

The first section sets up voting games in extensive form, where candidates move first and voters move second. Subgame perfection is used to solve the voting game. When voters are distributed symmetrically on a discrete issue spectrum, then each candidate has a dominant strategy to move to the center. This result is generalized as the median voter theorem.

The chapter then turns to 3-candidate elections and voting rules proposed for them. Plurality rule, which is most often used in the United States, is examined first. Three-candidate elections make possible strategic voting, where voters vote in a way that differs from their true preferences in order to get a better outcome. The only way to avoid strategic voting is by dictatorial elections. These complications show up in a major way in the three-way presidential elections that have occurred, albeit infrequently, in U.S. history—most recently, in the year 2000 election. Three-way elections pose special difficulties for voters who want to maximize their utility, rather than simply send a message to the politicians. The Borda voting rule is used in elections such as those for Most Valuable Player (MVP) or for the weekly coaches' rankings in college football. Strategic voting is rampant in such elections.

Finally, voting games in coalition-function form are reviewed. Such games are especially suited to the study of party formation and coalition governments. An index of voting power is developed for voting games in coalition-function form. This index is used extensively to explore the power implications of expanding the United Nations Security Council to include Brazil, a large developing country that is lobbying hard for a permanent seat.

■ 16.1 TWO-CANDIDATE VOTING GAMES WITH A DISCRETE ISSUE SPECTRUM

This section studies voting games with two candidates, named 1 and 2. Each candidate adopts a position along an **issue spectrum.** Figure 16.1 shows two kinds of issue spectra, discrete and continuous. In a discrete spectrum (Figure 16.1a), each candidate can pick a position on the Left (L), in the Center (C), or on the Right (R). In a continuous spectrum (Figure 16.1b), each candidate can pick a position anywhere between the far left (0) and the far right (1). The basic difference between discrete and continuous spectra lies in their ability to distinguish among various political positions. For simplicity, the issue spectrum is couched in terms of the political spectrum, from Left to Right. Other interpretations are also possible. For instance, the candidates can be vying for CEO of a corporation, and the points on the spectrum can represent various corporate strategies, from conservative (risk averse) to liberal (risk seeking), which lie on the risk-return frontier. A more conservative strategy accepts less risk and gets less expected return. A third interpretation could be in terms of a proxy fight, involving various strategies for managing a corporation, again aligned on a spectrum.

In the voting game, the candidates move first. Simultaneously, each candidate i chooses a position s_i on the spectrum. The voters move second. Each voter rates candidates based on how close they are to what the voter wants most. Suppose that each voter j has a favorite position on the spectrum, v_j. We call this favorite position the voter's **ideal point,** since in an ideal world (for that voter) the point v_j is precisely what would happen. Then voter j's utility, u_j, from a candidate taking position s_i is measured in terms of distance from the voter's favorite position:

$$u_j = -d(v_j, s_i)$$

The minus sign reflects the fact that the further away a candidate is from the voter's preferred position, the lower the voter's utility from that candidate. A voter maximizes utility by voting for the candidate closest to the favored position. In the event that two candidates are equally distant from the position, the voter plays a mixed strategy, tossing a coin and voting for each with probability .5.

FIGURE 16.1 | **ISSUE SPECTRA: (a) DISCRETE SPECTRUM; (b) CONTINUOUS SPECTRUM**

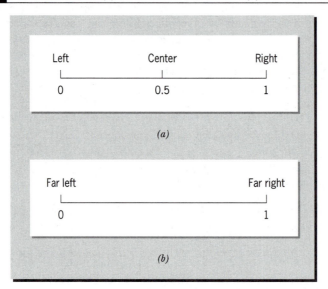

Candidates' utility is measured by how many votes they receive. Suppose there are 4 million voters, distributed on the discrete issue spectrum as follows:

- On the Left—1 million
- In the Center—2 million
- On the Right—1 million

As we will see later, the optimal strategies for the candidates depend on how the voters are distributed. In this case, the voters are distributed *symmetrically* on the issue spectrum. Since the candidates move before the voters do, they do not necessarily know how the voters will vote. However, an appeal to subgame perfection will remove any doubt. For instance, suppose that candidate 1 chooses Left and candidate 2 chooses Center. Then candidate 1 will get all the votes on the Left (1 million), since candidate 1 is closest to these voters, at distance 0. Candidate 2 will get all the rest of the 3 million votes. This candidate is right on top of the Center with its 2 million votes, and a lot closer to the Right, with its 1 million votes, than candidate 1 is. Using subgame perfection in this way generates the 3 x 3 normal form matrix game between the two candidates in the first stage of the voting game (see Figure 16.2). The result is recorded in the cell (L,C). Note that whenever both candidates occupy the same position, they split the total votes.

As is clear from Figure 16.2, the voting game has a unique subgame perfect equilibrium. Each candidate adopts a position at the Center. Indeed, this is a strictly dominant strategy for each candidate. The voters then respond by voting for each candidate in equal numbers. The candidates split the total votes, with 2 million each.

FIGURE 16.2 | **VOTING GAME: DISCRETE ISSUE SPECTRUM, SYMMETRICAL DISTRIBUTION (VOTE TOTALS IN MILLIONS)**

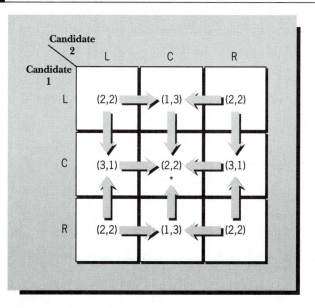

This result, when both candidates in a 2-candidate election move to the middle of the political spectrum, is called the **median voter theorem**.[1] If the average, or median, voter is in the middle of the political spectrum, that is also where the candidates want to be. This theorem explains the persistent tendency for candidates for national office in the United States to establish positions in the middle. Woe unto candidates who get stuck on the far left or far right—they will pay a big price in lost votes on election day. We will establish this result in a fairly general form in the next section.

Before doing so, however, it is useful to solve a voting game where the candidates do not seek out the Center. Suppose that the distribution of voters is heavily stacked toward the Right:

- On the Left—1 million voters
- In the Center—0.5 million voters
- On the Right—2.5 million voters

The median voter isn't in the middle anymore, but on the Right. Proceeding as before, and using subgame perfection, we get the first-round matrix game in Figure 16.3. Taking a position on the Left is dominated twice, by taking a position in the Center or on the Right. The unique equilibrium has both candidates taking positions on the Right, again splitting the total vote. Both candidates being in the Center is not a subgame perfect equilibrium. A candidate can move to the Right and pick up an extra 500,000 votes. The political calculation is straightforward. At the Center, the candidate was getting the Left and the Center for 1.5 million votes. By moving to the Right, the candidate gives up half the Left (0.5 million votes) and half the Center (0.25 million votes), but gets half the Right (1.25 million). The

| FIGURE 16.3 | VOTING GAME: DISCRETE ISSUE SPECTRUM, ASYMMETRICAL DISTRIBUTION (VOTE TOTALS IN MILLIONS) |

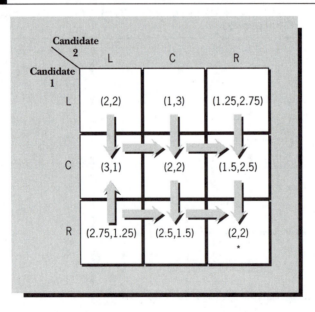

[1] This result is sometimes called Black's theorem, in honor of the British mathematician Duncan Black, who first proved it. See Duncan Black, *The Theory of Committees and Elections* (Cambridge, UK: Cambridge University Press, 1958).

total is a half-million more votes. In a voting equilibrium, the median voter gets exactly what he or she wants, whether that is a centrist outcome or an extremist outcome.

16.2 TWO-CANDIDATE VOTING GAMES WITH A CONTINUOUS ISSUE SPECTRUM

This section studies voting games on a continuous spectrum and extends the results of the previous section. This extension is a famous result in political science. The median voter theorem, introduced in the previous section, can be formally stated as follows:

Median Voter Theorem. Suppose that there are two candidates and voters are arrayed in a continuous distribution on the issue spectrum [0,1]. Let s^* be the median of the voter distribution. Then the candidate position vector (s^*, s^*) solves the voting game.

We will establish this result when voters are distributed uniformly on the issue spectrum [0,1] (see Figure 16.4). For voters to be distributed in a continuous fashion, there must be infinitely many of them. This is one way to model mass elections involving millions of voters.

As before, candidates move first. Each candidate i picks a point s_i on the issue spectrum. At the end of the candidate stage, the voters are faced with a vector $s = (s_1, s_2)$ of candidate positions. Each voter ranks candidates according to how close the candidate's position is to his or her own position. A voter j whose ideal position is located at point v_j would maximize utility as follows:

$$u_j(s) = -d(v_j, s_1) \text{ if } d(v_j, s_1) < d(v_j, s_2)$$
$$= -d(v_j, s_2) \text{ if } d(v_j, s_2) < d(v_j, s_1)$$

FIGURE 16.4 **CONTINUOUS ISSUE SPECTRUM, UNIFORMLY DISTRIBUTED VOTERS**

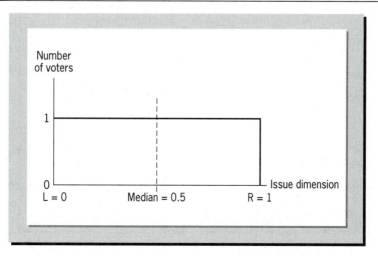

where $d(.)$ is the distance function. For instance, suppose that $\mathbf{s} = (0.4, 0.8)$ and $v_j = 0.5$. Then the distance from voter j to candidate 1 is 0.1, and the distance from voter j to candidate 2 is 0.3. Since candidate 1 is closer, voter j votes for this candidate.

Using subgame perfection in this way, we can establish vote totals for the two candidates at the voting stage, based on the vector of positions they have taken, $\mathbf{s}$. These vote totals establish a utility function in the first stage for the candidates. Solving this first-stage game will lead to a solution for the entire voting game. The biggest challenge is establishing the vote totals. We make our task a lot simpler by noticing that for the candidates, the voting game is symmetrical. Both candidates have the same strategy set, $[0,1]$. If both candidates pick the same strategy, they split the vote. Finally, if candidates trade places, they trade vote totals, as illustrated by Figure 16.5. In Figure 16.5a, the candidate position vector $\mathbf{s} = (0.4, 0.8)$. Candidate 1 gets all the votes to the left of the position 0.6, which amounts to 60 percent of all votes. Candidate 2 gets all the votes to the right of position 0.6, which amounts to 40 percent of all votes. In Figure 16.5b, the can-

FIGURE 16.5 | **CONTINUOUS ISSUE SPECTRUM: CANDIDATES TRADE PLACES**

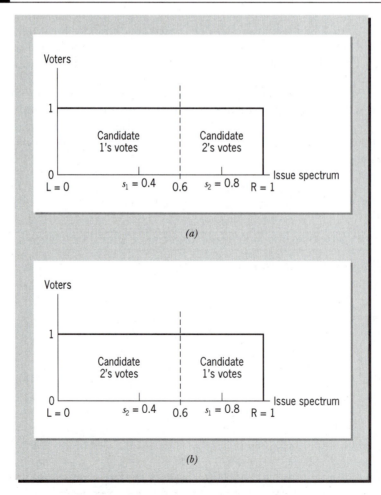

didates trade places, with the position vector $\mathbf{s} = (0.8, 0.4)$. Now candidate 1 gets 40 percent of the votes, and candidate 2 gets 60 percent of the votes. Trading places means trading vote totals. In terms of candidate utilities, we have

$$u_1(s_1, s_2) = u_2(s_1, s_2)$$

We have just verified all that we need for symmetry.

We are now ready to write down a general utility function for the two candidates in the first stage of the game. By symmetry, it is enough to write down the utility function for candidate 1, $u_1(\mathbf{s})$. There are three cases to consider, depending on the relationship between the two candidates' strategies:

Case 1: $s_1 < s_2$. This is the case illustrated in Figure 16.5a. Candidate 1 gets all the voters from 0 up to the boundary value $(s_1 + s_2)/2$. Since the distribution of voters is uniform, we get

$$u_1(\mathbf{s}) = (s_1 + s_2)/2$$

Notice that candidate 1's utility is increasing in the candidate's own strategy in this case.

Case 2: $s_1 = s_2$. In this case, the candidates split the vote

$$u_1(\mathbf{s}) = 0.5$$

Case 3: $s_1 > s_2$. This is the case illustrated in Figure 16.5b. Candidate 1 gets all the voters from the boundary value $(s_1 + s_2)/2$ up to 1. Since the distribution of voters is uniform, we get

$$u_1(\mathbf{s}) = 1 - (s_1 + s_2)/2$$

Notice that candidate 1's utility is decreasing in the candidate's own strategy in this case.

This exhausts the possible relationships between the two candidates' positions and therefore completes the derivation of candidate 1's utility function. Since the total vote percentage is 100% = 1, the game is one sum, so candidate 2's utility function is

$$u_2(\mathbf{s}) = 1 - u_1(\mathbf{s})$$

The indifference lines for candidate 1's utility function are shown in Figure 16.6. Notice that there is a big discontinuity in candidate 1's utility in the vicinity of the line $s_1 = s_2$. For instance, at $\mathbf{s} = (0.24, 0.26)$, $u_1 = 0.25$, whereas at $\mathbf{s} = (0.26, 0.24)$, $u_1 = 0.75$. In between, at $\mathbf{s} = (0.25, 0.25)$, $u_1 = 0.5$.

Let's find a subgame perfect equilibrium. By symmetry, we know that there must be a symmetric equilibrium on the line where $s_1 = s_2$ and where $u_1 = u_2 = 0.5$. Since the game is constant sum, the solution theorem from chapter 3 applies. Candidate 2 can guarantee that candidate 1's utility is never greater than 0.5 by setting $s_2 = 0.5$. As you can see from Figure 16.6, this choice of s_2 puts u_1 in the interval [0.25, 0.5]. Since u_1 has to equal 0.5 at equilibrium, this means that $s_2^* = .5$ supports the equilibrium. Then by symmetry, we have as the equilibrium $\mathbf{s}^* = (0.5, 0.5)$. The solution of the game has each candidate staking out a position in the middle of the issue spectrum, precisely where the median voter is. This establishes the median voter theorem for the uniform **distribution of voters' ideal points.**

The median voter theorem holds for any symmetrical distribution of voters' favorite points, not just for the uniform distribution. The median for any symmetrical distribution on [0,1] is at $s^* = 0.5$. Although the indifference curves for u_1 will look different, the argument just given still holds, and the median voter will be where candidates locate. If the distribution of voters' favorite points is symmetrical, then the median need not be in the middle, but candidates will still locate at the median voter. Finally, if the distribution of voters' favorite

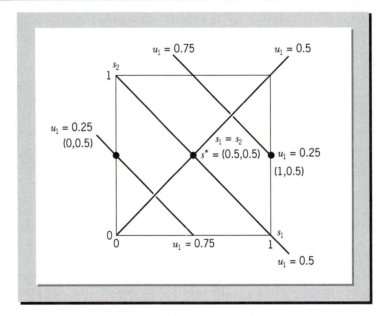

points contains gaps, there may be two median voters. In this case, there may be a candidate at each of two medians (see end-of-chapter problems 2 through 4 for details).

16.3 MULTICANDIDATE VOTING GAMES

The voting games considered so far have had exactly two candidates. It turns out to be an important restriction. Once there are three or more candidates, the strategic considerations increase enormously. In particular, voter preferences may be quite a bit more complicated, and voters may do well to vote strategically, rather than according to their preferences. The very notion of majority rule becomes somewhat ambiguous when there are three or more candidates. This section takes up these issues. To keep the complexity manageable, we will assume throughout that *candidates have already adopted positions.* One explanation for this situation is that they are bound by party platforms or by other credible commitment devices. This assumption puts all the complexity on the side of the voters.

Consider an election with three candidates, represented by the vector of candidate positions $\mathbf{s} = (s_1, s_2, s_3)$. In the United States an election with three candidates is conducted by **plurality rule.** Each voter receives a ballot with all three candidates' names on it and a box beside each name. The voter may mark one candidate's box. The candidate with the most marks wins. Since the winning candidate will have more marks than any other candidate, this candidate will have a plurality.

To see how plurality rule works, suppose that there are three types of voters. Voters rank the candidates, from top to bottom, as follows:

- Voter type 1: $s_1 > s_2 > s_3$
- Voter type 2: $s_2 > s_3 > s_1$

■ Voter type 3: $s_3 > s_1 > s_2$

Furthermore, there are 20 voters of type 1, and 15 voters each of types 2 and 3. Voters vote *honestly* when they fill out the ballot exactly in accordance with their ranking of candidates. In this case, honest voting leads to the election of candidate 1. The type 1 voters vote for candidate 1; the type 2 voters, for candidate 2; the type 3 voters, for candidate 3. The vote totals are candidate 1, 20; candidate 2, 15; and candidate 3, 15. Candidate 1 wins.

Several problems with plurality voting are readily apparent from this example. First, a minority candidate can be and often is elected. Candidate 1 wins with 20/50 = 40% of the votes in this election. Second, the winning candidate may actually have a majority opposed to his or her election. For instance, in this election, all type 2 and 3 voters rank candidate 3 above winning candidate 1. In this example 30/50 = 60% of the voters favor candidate 3, a loser, over candidate 1, the winner. This is a majority in opposition. Third, any time there is a majority in opposition, there is a strong incentive to vote *strategically*. **Strategic voting** is any voting not in accordance with the voter's true preferences. When it succeeds, strategic voting leads to an outcome that the voter prefers to the outcome that results from voting honestly. Suppose that type 2 and 3 voters all vote for candidate 3. This is honest voting for type 3, but strategic voting for type 2. Candidate 3 is elected, by a 60 percent to 40 percent margin, over candidate 1. The election of candidate 3 is preferred by the type 2 voters to the election of candidate 1. Strategic voting by the type 2 voters has succeeded.

Given all the problems inherent in plurality voting, there have been many attempts to find a better way of conducting elections with three or more candidates. A short list of commonly accepted desiderata for an election would include at least efficiency, decisiveness, truthfulness, and neutrality:

■ **Efficiency.** The winner of the election is efficient. This means there is no candidate that every voter ranks higher than the winner. The need for this condition is pretty self-evident. Every voter would clamor for electoral reform if a three-way election chose a candidate that every voter ranked last.

■ **Decisiveness.** The electoral process leads to a unique winner each time. The whole point of an election is to reach a decision, which is not accomplished by a tied election. Tie-breaking mechanisms are therefore needed. In the United States, these mechanisms include the extraordinary vote of the vice president when the Senate is tied (then Vice President Al Gore broke two 50–50 ties in 1993), recounts of ballots, and as a last resort, runoff elections.

■ **Truthfulness.** No voter ever has an incentive to vote strategically. In a truthful election, every voter would get his or her best possible outcome by voting honestly.

■ **Neutrality.** The winner does not depend on the names of the candidates or on the way in which the names are arrayed on the ballot. There are many ways to steal an election that is not neutral. The presidential election held in South Vietnam in 1971 was definitely not neutral. The number 9 is very important in Vietnamese culture, and the incumbent President Thieu made sure that he was listed as candidate number 9 on the ballot.

Unfortunately, if there are at least three voters and three candidates, there is only one voting rule that satisfies efficiency, decisiveness, truthfulness, and neutrality. This voting rule has a very familiar name: *dictatorship*. In a dictatorship, only one voter's preferences matter—those of the dictator. This is one-man, or one-woman, rule. It is easy to check that dictatorship satisfies the four desiderata. First, a dictator is efficient. A dictator picks what he or she wants most. There can be no alternative that everyone, including the dictator, likes better. Second, a dictator is decisive. As long as the dictator has a unique favorite, the dictator picks that favorite and the election is over. A dictator who has multiple favorites can decide among them by tossing a coin or by some even more whimsical procedure. Third, a dictator is truthful. Since the dictator gets what he or she wants anyway, lying on the ballot isn't necessary. The same holds true for the other voters, since in a dictatorship the outcome is whatever the dictator wants, regardless of how the other ballots are filled out. Fourth, a dictator is neutral. It doesn't matter what the ballot looks like or how the candidates are named—the dictator's first choice always wins. Despite these appealing features, however, dictatorship is inconsistent with democratic principles. The immense concentration of power in the hands of a Hitler or a Stalin can lead to disastrous consequences for human rights and world peace.[2]

The reason dictatorship shows up here is a fundamental result in economics called **Arrow's impossibility theorem,** after the Nobel Prize–winning economist Kenneth J. Arrow, who discovered it.[3] Arrow's theorem shows that under conditions similar to those given, the only possible social welfare function is dictatorship. You can show, although the proof is involved, that the four desiderata imply the existence of an Arrow social welfare function, and hence imply dictatorship.[4]

An appealing voting scheme that comes close to satisfying the four desiderata without being dictatorial was derived by the Marquis de Condorcet. Condorcet was one of the major figures of the Enlightenment and the French Revolution. His contributions to economic science include the invention of national income accounting and the voting proposal that bears his name.[5] Condorcet proposed that the winner in a 3-candidate election should have a majority against every other candidate in two-way comparisons. When such a winner exists, then every voter has a weakly dominant strategy to vote honestly. Here's an example in which Condorcet's proposal works fine. There are three types, with the rankings

Voter type 1: $s_1 > s_2 > s_3$

Voter type 2: $s_2 > s_3 > s_1$

Voter type 3: $s_3 > s_2 > s_1$

Suppose that there is one voter of each type. Candidate 2 has a 2-to-1 majority over candidate 1 and a 2-to-1 majority over candidate 3. Therefore, candidate 2 is the winner. Note that plurality voting would lead to a three-way tie instead of a clear-cut winner.

---

[2] The list of dictators or near dictators who were good guys is very short. One nominee would be George Washington, who, as commander in chief of the Continental army, was in a position to become King of America. Instead, he gave up his army command and later ran for president.

[3] See K. J. Arrow, *Social Choice and Individual Values,* 2nd ed. (New York: Wiley, 1963). Arrow won the Nobel Prize in part for this work.

[4] See Alan Gibbard, "Manipulation of Voting Schemes: A General Result," *Econometrica* 41 (1973): 587–601. Also see Mark Satterthwaite, "Strategy-Proofness and Arrow's Conditions: Existence and Correspondence Theorems for Voting Procedures and Social Welfare Functions," *Journal of Economic Theory* 10 (1975): 187–217. One way to prove this theorem is to show that the conditions imply the existence of a social welfare function satisfying Arrow's conditions, which then runs afoul of the Arrow impossibility theorem.

[5] Condorcet was a fervent believer in human progress, which he thought unstoppable. The economist Malthus wrote his gloomy *Essay on Population* in direct opposition to Condorcet's position. In a final irony, Condorcet was one of the 30,000 victims sentenced to death at the guillotine during the French Revolution.

Moreover, strategic voting would lead to a worse outcome for any voter that tried it. For instance, suppose that voter type 1, in an attempt to manipulate the outcome, voted for candidate 3 instead of candidate 2 in the contest between candidates 3 and 2. Then candidate 3 would win a majority against both candidate 2 and candidate 1 and would be elected. This outcome, however, would be the worst possible for voter 1, who would be getting the bottom candidate instead of the middle candidate.

Condorcet's proposal satisfies neutrality, efficiency, and truthfulness. If we model the previous election as a game in coalition-function form, then the election of candidate 2 is the unique outcome in the core of the voting game. Unfortunately, however, Condorcet's voting scheme is not decisive. Suppose that we replace the earlier rankings for voter type 3 with the following rankings:

Voter type 3: $s_3 > s_1 > s_2$

Candidate 2 has a 2-to-1 advantage over candidate 3, candidate 3 has a 2-to-1 advantage over candidate 1, and candidate 1 has a 2-to-1 advantage over candidate 2. No candidate has a majority against every other; hence no decision is reached. What is worse, Condorcet's voting scheme is forced to be decisive. By picking a minority outcome in this case, an opportunity for strategic voting is created.

Suppose that, for the sake of decisiveness, a minority decision is forced and that decision elects candidate 2. This creates a golden opportunity for voter type 3 to vote strategically. If voter type 3 switches sides on the contest between candidates 1 and 3, in effect revealing the rankings

$$s_1 > s_3 > s_2$$

then candidate 1 has a majority against both candidates 2 and 3. The voting scheme has just become untruthful.

In a way, the fact that we are caught on the horns of a dilemma between dictatorship and untruthfulness is not so surprising. It is yet another indication that strategy matters. Thoreau may not have approved of the way things are in this respect, but this is the price we must pay if we want a democracy. Given all the problems that arise with multicandidate elections, it should come as no surprise that these have proved very troublesome in U.S. presidential politics, as we shall now see.

◾ 16.4 MULTICANDIDATE PRESIDENTIAL ELECTIONS, 1824–2000

The members of the Constitutional Convention were familiar with the problems surrounding plurality voting, and so created an institution, the electoral college, to limit its role. This system has nevertheless worked remarkably like plurality voting in 2-candidate races. In all but two such races, the candidate with the most popular votes was also the candidate with the most electoral votes, and so was elected president. The exceptions were Rutherford Hayes versus Samuel Tilden in 1876 and Benjamin Harrison versus Grover Cleveland in 1888, both of which were extremely close in the popular vote.

With **multicandidate elections,** however, the results have been much more volatile and have left great scope for strategic voting, as might be expected. In the first multicandidate race,[6] in 1824, four candidates received votes in the electoral college. Andrew Jackson received a plurality of both the popular and the electoral college votes, but not a majority of the latter. Thus the election went to the House of Representatives. Meanwhile, the second-place candidate, John Quincy Adams, was busy assembling a winning coalition. He promised (and delivered) the office of secretary of state to Henry Clay of Tennessee in exchange for Clay's support in the House vote. This move gave the Adams bloc the votes to win in the House. Jackson and his supporters screamed they had been robbed by a crooked bargain, conveniently forgetting that they could have made the same deal with fellow southerner Clay, and perhaps at a lower price.

The next multicandidate race was in 1860. The incumbent Democrats were favored to win the election, until they split into Northern and Southern factions, led by Stephen Douglas and John Breckenridge, respectively. This split in their ranks opened the door for Abraham Lincoln's Republicans, who ran only in the North and were therefore in no danger of splitting along North-South lines. Lincoln won the ensuing election, with less than 40 percent of the popular vote but with a majority of the electoral vote. This was an outcome that neither northern nor southern Democrats wanted. Had the Democrats been able to preserve their party, or at least to vote strategically, they might have been able to preserve the Union without a Civil War. But it would have been a very different Union from that of today.

Lincoln's repeat victory in 1864, and the Union victory in the Civil War, led to a Republican dynasty that lasted half a century.[7] Republican presidential dominance did not cease until 1912, thanks to a split in the Republican ranks between incumbent president Howard Taft and former president Theodore Roosevelt. The Republican split allowed a Democrat, Woodrow Wilson, to capture the White House with only a minority of the votes—once again, an outcome that strategic voting could have prevented. Wilson's victory ushered in a period of Democratic dominance that lasted 40 years.[8]

One of the most intriguing multicandidate races of all time occurred in 1968. This race pitted Republican Richard Nixon against Democrat Hubert Humphrey in a battle of vice presidents; and it pitted them both against Alabama governor George Wallace, a southern Democrat. In hindsight, it appears that Wallace played the role of the spoiler (see chapter 5), making certain that Humphrey, a political enemy of the southern Democrats since 1948, was denied the White House. Nixon won handily in the electoral college, even though he had only 43 percent of the popular vote. The Democratic split handed the White House to the Republicans, and they held on to it for all but one election (Carter, 1976) until 1992.

Multicandidate races occurred in both 1992 and 2000. The 1992 race pitted incumbent Republican President George Bush against Democratic challenger Bill Clinton and third-party candidate Ross Perot. Perot dropped out of the race suddenly in midsummer, when he was leading in the polls. He reentered the race in September, in a move widely regarded as playing the spoiler. Perot split the political right and thus helped hand the election to the left-of-center Democratic governor of Arkansas, Bill Clinton. Democrat Clinton, in a now

[6] *Multicandidate race* refers to a race in which at least three candidates receive 10 percent or more of the popular vote. Every presidential election includes a wide assortment of crank, protest, or otherwise minor candidates, whose presence has no effect on the outcome or the strategies employed. There were over 4000 officially registered candidates for president in 1992. All races since the constitutional reform of 1804 are considered here. Prior to 1804, there was no distinction between candidates for president and candidates for vice president. The candidate with the most electoral votes was named president; the candidate with the next most electoral votes was named vice president.

[7] Cleveland's victories in 1884 and 1892 were the only Democratic victories between 1860 and 1912.

[8] Between 1912 and 1952, the only Republican victories were those of Harding in 1920, Coolidge in 1924, and Hoover in 1928.

familiar pattern, won the election with 43 percent of the popular vote and a large majority of the electoral vote.

The 2000 race pitted Vice President Al Gore against Republican challenger George W. Bush (son of former President George H. Bush) and third-party candidate Ralph Nader. This was the closest race since 1876. The election came down to the recount of a few thousand votes in Florida (again, just as in 1876). Since Nader drew most of his support from Gore voters, and since Nader received tens of thousands of votes in Florida, it is clear that Nader played the role of spoiler, throwing the election to Bush.

In every case of multicandidate elections since 1824—1860, 1912, 1968, 1992, and 2000—the losers had an opportunity to vote strategically, an opportunity that, once lost, meant they faced a very bad outcome. Even a modified form of plurality voting, as in the form of the electoral college, exhibits all the drawbacks that game theory leads us to expect from plurality voting.

■ 16.5 POSITIONAL VOTING RULES

In the period of Enlightenment before the French Revolution, another Frenchman, the Count de Borda, proposed an improvement on plurality voting. His system is based on attaching point values to various positions in the rankings, with the final ranking based on total point values. Such systems are now called **positional voting rules.** The **Borda voting rule** belongs to this class and is used today in contexts such as voting for the Most Valuable Player and the Cy Young Award in professional baseball and the coaches' rankings of top football teams in college football.

Borda's original example considered a 3-candidate election. He proposed a 3-line ballot. On the first line, the voter would put the highest-ranked candidate, and this candidate would be awarded 3 points. On the second line, the voter would put the second-highest-ranked candidate, and this candidate would be awarded 2 points. On the bottom line, the voter would put the lowest-ranked candidate, and this candidate would be awarded 1 point. All the points would be added for each candidate. The final ranking of the candidates would be according to their total point counts.

To see how Borda's voting rule works in practice, consider again the 3-candidate election with the following three voter types:

- Voter type 1: $s_1 > s_2 > s_3$
- Voter type 2: $s_2 > s_3 > s_1$
- Voter type 3: $s_3 > s_2 > s_1$

There are 20 type 1 voters, and 15 voters each of the other two types. Suppose that all voters vote sincerely. Then candidate 1 gets 20 first-place rankings worth 60 points, 15 second-place rankings worth 30 points, and 15 third-place rankings worth 15 points, for a total of 105 points. Candidate 2 gets 15 first-place rankings worth 45 points, 20 second-place rankings worth 40 points, and 15 third-place rankings worth 15 points, for a total of 100 points. Candidate 3 gets 15 first-place rankings worth 45 points, 15 second-place rankings worth 30 points, and 20 third-place rankings worth 20 points, for a total of 95 points. The outcome is

1. Candidate 1: 105 points
2. Candidate 2: 100 points
3. Candidate 3: 95 points

In this case the winner is the same under both Borda and plurality voting. However, just like plurality voting, Borda voting is very susceptible to strategic voting.

Type 2 and 3 voters have every incentive to try to get candidate 3, currently in last place, elected instead of candidate 1. Moreover, they have the votes to do this. What they have to do is fill out their ballots as follows:

- Voter type 2: $s_3 > s_2 > s_1$
- Voter type 3: $s_3 > s_2 > s_1$

Candidate 1 now gets 20 first-place votes and 30 third-place votes for a total vote of 90, substantially less than before. Candidate 3 now gets 30 first-place votes worth 90 points, and 20 third-place votes worth 20 points, for 110 points, much more than before. Candidate 2 gets 50 second-place rankings, worth 100 points, the same as before, for a total of 105. The outcome of this fine piece of strategic voting is

1. Candidate 3: 110 points
2. Candidate 2: 100 points
3. Candidate 1: 90 points

The former winner is now ranked last. The key to this result was having all voter types 2 and 3 rank candidate 1 last.

This example is by no means unusual. Strategic voting can and does happen all the time in the voting used to rank the top teams in college football. Each voter (either the college coaches or media voters) fills out a ballot with 25 places. The top place on the ballot gets 25 points, and so on down to the 25th team, which gets 1 point. All teams not ranked (roughly 100 teams are eligible for the Division I rankings) get 0 points. The rankings derived from this voting, as well as other variables, determine who will play in the Bowl Championship Series (BCS)—the teams ranked 1 and 2 according to the BCS numbers at the end of the regular season. Depending on which team a voter wants to see in the BCS game, that voter can manipulate his or her ballot. Clearly, the result of such behavior can be very far from the goal of the NCAA—to name the best college football team in the country the national champion.[9]

16.6 VOTING GAMES IN COALITION-FUNCTION FORM

In a voting game, the more the voters are organized as a bloc, the more likely they are to get what they want. This is the reason for the existence of political parties, coalition governments, international alliances, and cliques within a board of directors. The easiest way to study the phenomenon of voting coalitions is with games in coalition-function form.

Let N be the set of voters, $N = \{1, 2, \ldots, n\}$. A coalition S, which is a subset of N, can either be *winning* or *not winning*. A **winning coalition** can take control of the political process to achieve its ends. Any coalition that is not winning cannot take control of the political process to achieve its ends. For the coalition function, we have

$v(S) = 1$ if S is a winning coalition

$v(S) = 0$ if S is not a winning coalition

---

[9] The same phenomenon appears in MVP or Cy Young voting in baseball, when top contenders are left off sportswriters' ballots.

In this representation, the coalition value 1 means 100 percent control of the political process. We have encountered an example of such a coalition function before, in our study of *n*-player bargaining games in chapter 14. The coalition function corresponding to a bargaining game is

$v(S) = 1$ if $S = N$

$v(S) = 0$ otherwise

In a bargaining game, the only coalition that controls things is the grand coalition. Any other coalition that walks away from the table is powerless to affect outcomes.

Any game in coalition-function form that is limited to the values 0 or 1 is called a **simple game.** Some restrictions on simple games are necessary to avoid contradiction. For instance, two winning coalitions cannot coexist, since only one coalition at a time can be in charge. This contradiction would occur if there were disjoint coalitions S and T, both with $v(S) = v(T) = 1$. This situation is avoided by the exclusivity condition:

Exclusivity. If S is winning, then $N - S$ is not winning. In equation form, $v(S) = 1$ implies $v(N - S) = 0$.

Exclusivity says that if a coalition S is winning, then the countercoalition, $N - S$, consisting of all players in N not in S, is not winning.

Another contradiction would occur if a coalition S was winning, but a larger coalition T that included S was not. This contradiction is avoided by the monotonicity condition:

Monotonicity. If S is winning, and T includes S, then T is winning. In equation form, if $v(S) = 1$ and T includes S, then $v(T) = 1$.

A final regularity condition is that at least one coalition, the grand coalition, is winning. This condition is called nonnullity:

Nonnullity. The grand coalition N is winning, $v(N) = 1$.

In the case of bargaining games, only the grand coalition is winning. All the voting games worth our attention satisfy exclusivity, monotonicity, and nonnullity.

Here are two examples of how winning coalitions are generated in real life. First, consider the process by which a bill becomes law in the United States. The set of players in the voting game by which a bill becomes law consists of the president, the Senate, and the House of Representatives. There are two recipes for a winning coalition. A bill becomes law if it gets a majority (218 votes of 435 seats) in the House of Representatives, a majority in the Senate (51 votes of 100 seats), and the signature of the president.[10] This kind of winning coalition—the win is the bill being passed into law—needs the president, at least 218 representatives, and at least 51 senators—270 people in all, in just the right places. A bill can also become law if Congress overrides the president's veto—his refusal to sign the bill. An override requires a two-thirds majority in both the Senate and the House. This kind of winning coalition—the kind without the president—needs at least 290 representatives (exactly double the remaining 145) and at least 67 senators (more than double the remaining 33). The U.S. Constitution makes it difficult, but not impossible, to form winning coalitions. The voting game that results satisfies exclusivity, monotonicity, and nonnullity, as you can show in an end-of-chapter problem.

Corporate voting is another example of how winning coalitions are formed. Here the set N of voters consists of all stockholders with voting stock in a corporation. Let i be a stockholder and $w(i)$ be the number of his or her shares. The total shares in the corporation are $\Sigma\, w(i)$. Each share is worth one vote. A winning coalition has to have a majority of the shares in the corporation:

$$v(S) = 1 \text{ if } \Sigma\, w(i), i \text{ in } S > 1/2\, \Sigma\, w(i), i \text{ in } N$$

Needless to say, a winning coalition can be very small as long as it includes some big owners. Proxy fights and other struggles for corporate control center on getting 51 percent of outstanding shares because this is the magic number for a winning coalition.

16.7 MEASURING POWER

Now that we have a representation of political structure in a voting game, let's solve such games. As we saw in chapter 15, the core will not be of much help, since it is empty in the game Majority Rule—and, as it turns out, in most other simple games. Thus we need a different concept for solving simple games. The concept presented here, the **Shapley value,**[11] is based on the idea that power consists in the ability of a player to turn a coalition that is not winning into a coalition that is winning.

Recall the definition of player i's **marginal product** to the coalition S, $MP(i,S)$:

$$MP(i,S) = v(S \text{ and } i) - v(S)$$

In a simple game, a player's marginal product can take only two values, 0 or 1. For instance, suppose that coalition S is winning before player i joins. By monotonicity, {S *and* i} is still winning, so player i's marginal product is

$$MP(i,S) = 1 - 1 = 0$$

Next, suppose that coalition S is losing before player i joins and is still losing after player i joins. We have

$$MP(i,S) = 0 - 0 = 0$$

---

[10] As we have seen, if the vice president can be trusted to vote with the president, then 50 senators and the vice president suffice to win in the Senate.

[11] The index of voting power was first introduced in Lloyd Shapley and Martin Shubik, "A Method for Evaluating the Distribution of Power in a Committee System," *American Political Science Review* 48 (1954): 787–792. This index is a special case of a more general concept, the Shapley value. See Lloyd S. Shapley, "A Value for *n*-Person Games," in *Contributions to the Theory of Games,* vol. 2, ed. Harold W. Kuhn and A. W. Tucker (Princeton, N.J.: Princeton University Press, 1953), 307–317.

In both these cases, player i's marginal product to the coalition is 0. This player adds nothing. There is exactly one way for a player's marginal product to be positive—when coalition S is not winning before player i joins and is winning afterward. We have

$$MP(i,S) = 1 - 0 = 1$$

In this case, player i is **pivotal** to the coalition's winning.

The Shapley value says that a player's political power is the likelihood of that player being pivotal. If a player will never, under any circumstances, be pivotal, then that player is powerless. No one would ever need such a player's vote. As before, such a player is called a **dummy.** On the other hand, if a player is always, under all possible circumstances, pivotal, then that player is all-powerful. Such a player—there can be at most one, by exclusivity— is called a **dictator.** These are the two extremes between which most players are found.

To compute the likelihood that a player will be pivotal, we need a mechanism for generating probabilities. Of the many stories for such a mechanism, we will adopt that of the *veil of ignorance.*[12] Imagine that players have not yet been assigned their identities in the game. It is as if they are waiting backstage to play various parts in a play; but the curtain (or veil) hasn't risen yet, and they don't know which part they will play. All they know is that each of them has the same probability of playing a given role. Imagine further that the parts are going to be assigned at random. What the Shapley value does is identify a player's role with that player's position in a random ordering of all players. When each random ordering is equally likely, then each player is equally likely to be in first place, second place, and so on, through last place. For instance, if there are 2 players, then there are $2! = (2)(1) = 2$ random orderings:

  1, 2 (player 1 is first)

  2, 1 (player 2 is first)

Each of these random orderings occurs with probability 1/2 when the veil of ignorance is lifted.

The Shapley value of player i, written Shap(i), is the expected value of that player's marginal product in a random ordering of all the players:

Shap(i) = $EV\, MP(i,S)$

  = (probability of being pivotal)(1) + (probability of not being pivotal)(0)

  = probability of being pivotal

A player's marginal product is equal to 0 or 1, so the expected value of this marginal product is positive only when a player is pivotal. When a player is pivotal, his or her marginal product is 1. The probability at which a player is pivotal is precisely that player's Shapley value.[13]

This is all rather abstract. Let's look at some sample calculations. Take 3-player Majority Rule. Figure 16.7 spells out the required computations. Since there are three players, there are $3! = 6$ possible random orderings of players: 123, 132, 213, 231, 312, 321. Each

---

[12] This notion comes from the Nobel Prize–winning game theorist John C. Harsanyi, "Cardinal Welfare, Individualistic Ethics, and Interpersonal Comparisons of Utility," *Journal of Political Economy* 63 (1955): 309–321. Although Harsanyi uses the veil of ignorance to argue for utilitarianism, John Rawls's theory of justice uses the veil of ignorance to argue just the opposite.

[13] There are other ways to measure power in addition to this one. One such alternative is the power index of John F. Banzhaf III, "Weighted Voting Doesn't Work: A Mathematical Analysis," *Rutgers Law Review* 19 (1965): 317–343.

of these random orderings is equally likely, hence probability 1/6. In the first row, the random ordering is 123. Player 1's marginal product in this random ordering is 0, since neither the coalition with 0 members nor the coalition {1} is winning. Player 2's marginal product in this random ordering is 1, since the coalition {1} is not winning but the coalition {1,2} is winning. Player 2 has been pivotal in creating a winning coalition. Player 3's marginal product in this random ordering is 0, since coalition {1,2} is winning and so is coalition {1,2,3}. This reasoning underlies the marginal product calculations in the figure. Finally, since each random ordering is equally likely, each of a player's marginal products is multiplied by 1/6, yielding the bottom-line Shapley value. For instance, for player 1,

$$\text{Shap}(1) = 1/6(0 + 0 + 1 + 0 + 1 + 0) = 2/6$$

Figure 16.7 shows that in one-person, one-vote Majority Rule, each player has the same power, 1/3.

When all the players have the same impact on the vote, as in a bargaining game or in one-person, one-vote Majority Rule, the Shapley value says that power is equally divided. When the players have differential impact, the Shapley value picks that up, too. Here is an extreme case. There are three players. Any coalition that includes player 1 is winning; and only coalitions that include player 1 are winning. Figure 16.8 contains the relevant calculation for the Shapley value. As you can see, player 1 is always pivotal and gets a Shapley value of 1. Player 1 is a dictator. Players 2 and 3 are never pivotal. These players, with Shapley value equal to zero each, are powerless.

Sometimes a player can be a dummy in a voting game, even though the player apparently has influence. Suppose in the example just given that player 1 has 51 percent of the voting stock in a corporation; player 2 has 25 percent; and player 3 has 24 percent. Player 1 alone can win any vote. Players 2 and 3, despite all their stock, cannot win a vote without player 1. Such a situation is exactly what happens in a 51–49 percent takeover, where corporate ownership of 51 percent in the hands of one player is much less than 100 percent, but still amounts to complete control, with a Shapley value of 100 percent.

FIGURE 16.7 MAJORITY RULE: SHAPLEY VALUE, $n = 3$

Majority Rule, Shapley Value, $n = 3$

Random Ordering	MP (1,S)	MP (2,S)	MP (3,S)
123	0	1	0
132	0	0	1
213	1	0	0
231	0	0	1
312	1	0	0
321	0	1	0
	2/6	2/6	2/6
Shap (i)	i = 1	i = 2	i = 3

| FIGURE 16.8 | DICTATORSHIP: SHAPLEY VALUE, $n = 3$ |

Dictatorship, Shapley Value, n = 3

Random Ordering	$MP\,(1,S)$	$MP\,(2,S)$	$MP\,(3,S)$
123	1	0	0
132	1	0	0
213	1	0	0
231	1	0	0
312	1	0	0
321	1	0	0
	6/6	0/6	0/6
Shap (i)	$i = 1$	$i = 2$	$i = 3$

Player i has a *veto that cannot be overridden* if no coalition can win unless player i is a member. Such a player is called a **veto player.** The president of the United States is not a veto player, since his or her veto can be overridden. However, there are numerous examples of veto powers that cannot be overridden. For instance, if the commissioner of baseball vetoes a player deal, the teams involved must annul it. If an arbitrator rules in a certain way, the parties involved cannot appeal the decision. If one of the permanent members of the United Nations Security Council vetoes a Security Council resolution, the resolution is dead. We will next study the power structure of the Security Council in considerable detail, and especially the implications of adding Brazil to the Council.

16.8 EXPANDING THE UNITED NATIONS SECURITY COUNCIL

The United Nations was founded by the victorious powers of World War II in 1945.[14] Their purpose was to ensure world security in the aftermath of the world's greatest conflagration and to prevent further world war. To this end, the United Nations included a Security Council, to deal with matters of world security, and in particular to sanction the use of force by the members of the United Nations in disputes threatening world peace and order. The five great powers that won World War II—the USA, USSR, France, the United Kingdom, and China—had permanent seats on the **United Nations Security Council.** Seven (later 10) other seats were held on a rotating basis by other United Nations member states.

The Security Council uses three-fifths majority rule for its decisions. Under its current configuration, this means a winning coalition needs 9 of the 15 members. However, each of the five permanent members has a veto over any proposal. This veto cannot be overridden: its exercise kills a proposal. In 1950, the USSR could have vetoed the proposal to send

[14] This material was drawn from "Putin Backs Brazil's Bid for UN Security Council," *Wall Street Journal*, 15 January 2002.

United Nations forces to defend South Korea against attack by North Korea, a Soviet ally. For reasons still unexplained, the Soviet ambassador to the United Nations was not present at the Security Council deliberations and did not veto the United Nations initiative in South Korea. Thus, not only does a winning coalition need to have nine members, but it also needs to have every country with a veto. Currently, the five members with a veto are the United States, Russia (inheriting the USSR's veto), France, the United Kingdom, and the People's Republic of China (inheriting the Republic of China's veto).

Recently, Russia has endorsed enlarging the Security Council with the addition of Brazil. This proposal has been vigorously opposed by some current Security Council members. The Shapley value will help explain their opposition.

To compute the Shapley value for a political system with 15 players, like the current Security Council, requires the examination of $15! = (15 \times 14 \times \ldots \times 1)$ random orderings, more than 1.3 trillion in all. This entire book could not contain the calculation. Obviously, we are going to need some cunning to pull this off. The best way in science is to start with a simple model and work your way up. That's what we've done before in this book, and that's exactly what we will do here. Let's start with a model security council, like the current one, only divided by 5—one country, 1, with veto power, and two countries, 2 and 3, without veto power. Figure 16.9 contains the relevant computation. With three countries, we only have to worry about $3! = 6$ random orderings.

There are several useful things to note about this computation. First, the only time a country without a veto is pivotal is when it is in second place preceded in the random ordering by the country with a veto. So, in the random ordering 123, country 2 is pivotal; in the random ordering 132, country 3 is pivotal. It is easy to see why this is so. If the country with a veto is not already present in the random ordering, then adding a nonveto country cannot make the coalition a winning one. If all the countries with vetoes are already present in the random ordering, then adding a nonveto country is pivotal only when the coalition is one country short of a majority. This reasoning explains why the nonveto country has to be in second place to be pivotal. Second, each nonveto country has the same

FIGURE 16.9 **SECURITY COUNCIL: SHAPLEY VALUE, $n = 3$**

Security Council, Shapley Value, $n = 3$

Random Ordering	MP (1,S)	MP (2,S)	MP (3,S)
123	0	1	0
132	0	0	1
213	1	0	0
231	1	0	0
312	1	0	0
321	1	0	0
	4/6	1/6	1/6
Shap (i)	$i = 1$	$i = 2$	$i = 3$

Shapley value, 1/6. This makes sense, since each is a perfect substitute for the other; that is, every time country 2 is pivotal, so is country 3, and vice versa. Finally, note that each country is in second place in a random ordering 1/3 of the time.

Based on these three observations, we will use the following shortcut to obtain the Shapley value for this mini security council. We need to compute the probability that a given nonveto country is pivotal. Once that is done, everything else will follow. To compute the probability that country 2 is pivotal, argue as follows. Country 2 will be in second place in a random ordering 1/3 of the time. We need to compute the probability that country 1 is ahead of country 2 in this ordering. To do so, we need to know how many different combinations could precede 2 in the random ordering and how many of these combinations contain country 1. This is a problem in combinatorics, for which the combinations function $C(n,m)$—choose m items of n available—is essential. The value of $C(n,m)$ is given by

$$C(n,m) = n!/[m!(n-m)!]$$

There are two countries available for first place in the random ordering, one with a veto and the other without. Clearly, the probability of choosing the one with the veto power from these two is 1/2. Here is how to get this probability, using the combinations function. Start with

$C(1,1)$ = the number of ways of choosing one country with a veto from the set containing one country with a veto

$C(1,0)$ = the number of ways of choosing 0 countries without a veto from the set containing one country without a veto

$C(2,1)$ = the number of ways of choosing 1 country from the set containing two countries

Then the probability of choosing one country with a veto from the set containing two countries is

$$[C(1,1)][C(1,0)]/C(2,1) = (1)(1)/(2) = 1/2$$

the same as before. This more complicated method is the one used for bigger security councils.

Next, the probability is 1/3 that country 2 is in second place. Multiplying these two probabilities, we get

$$\text{Shap}(2) = (1/3)(1/2) = 1/6$$

as before. Now apply symmetry to get

$$\text{Shap}(2) = \text{Shap}(3) = 1/6$$

Finally, to account for all the power, we have

$$\text{Shap}(1) = 1 - \text{Shap}(2) - \text{Shap}(3) = 1 - 1/6 - 1/6 = 4/6$$

These answers check with our previous ones, and we didn't have to go through all the random orderings to get them.

Now we are ready to tackle the Security Council as it currently stands. A nonveto country has to be in ninth place in a random ordering to be pivotal. The probability of this is 1/15. Moreover, all five veto countries have to be in the random ordering already in order for this nonveto country to be pivotal. The probability of a nonveto country being preceded by all five veto countries and three nonveto countries is given by

$$[C(5,5)][C(9,3)]/C(14,8) = 1/33$$

Multiplying these two probabilities leads to the Shapley value for a nonveto country,

$$\text{Shap(nonveto country)} = (1/15)(1/33) = 1/495$$

or about 0.2 percent, a very small number. A nonveto country as things now stand has minimal power in the Security Council. Even the 10 nonveto countries taken together have only about 2 percent of the power. This leaves 98 percent of the power to be divided evenly among the five countries with veto power. Each of these has 98%/5 = 19.6% of the available power.

If Brazil joins the Security Council, and it has a permanent veto, then the Security Council grows to size 16. To see the implications of this situation, we need to perform some more Shapley value calculations. Intuitively, it seems this would have a big impact on the power of every current veto player. As we shall see, not only do the veto countries become substantially less powerful, but there is also a marked negative impact on the power of non-veto countries.

Consider a Security Council with 6 veto countries and 10 nonveto countries. Under three-fifths majority rule, it would take 11 countries, including all 6 veto countries, to form a winning coalition. A nonveto country would have to be in eleventh place in a random ordering to be pivotal. The probability of being in eleventh place in a random ordering of 16 players is 1/16. Moreover, all 6 veto countries would have to be present already in the random ordering in order for this nonveto country to be pivotal. The probability of this event is given by

$$[(C(6,6)][C(9,3)]/C(15,9) = 12/715$$

Multiplying these two probabilities, we get

$$\text{Shap(nonveto country)} = (1/16)(12/715) = 12/11440$$

or about 0.1 percent. Each nonveto country loses about one-half of its power, which wasn't that big to begin with.

All nonveto countries taken together have 1 percent of the power. This leaves 99 percent of the power to be divided among the 6 veto countries. Each of them would get 99%/6 = 16.5% of the available power. For a current veto power, this represents a drop from a Shapley value of 19.6 percent to 16.5 percent—a bitter pill to swallow. Under this scenario, both Third World countries and current veto-power members are losers.

To change the Security Council requires a two-thirds approval among the 189 member states. Hence, 126 member states must approve. Next, these member states must get the approval of their national legislatures. Finally, every veto-power state must refrain from vetoing the proposal. This is a tough set of requirements to meet. It will be a long time before Brazil or any other country is in any position to take a seat with a permanent veto on the United Nations Security Council.

■ SUMMARY

1. Voting is a major part of economic life. Proxy fights, votes to oust a CEO, and lobbying to affect economic policy are all examples.

2. The median voter theorem gives conditions under which, in a 2-candidate election, the candidates will appeal to the voter in the middle of the distribution of voters' favorite points. When the distribution of voters' favorite points is symmetrical, the candidates position themselves in the middle of the political spectrum.

3. When there are more than three candidates, the median voter theorem no longer holds. Many voting rules try to extend majority rule to this case, including plurality rule and Condorcet's rule.

4. Plurality rule has several defects, among them that it may elect a minority candidate. This result has happened several times in U.S. elections for president, most recently in 2000.

5. Strategic voting occurs when a voter fills out the ballot other than in accord with personal preferences and thereby gets a better outcome. A voting rule is truthful if no voter ever has an incentive to vote strategically. Plurality voting is not truthful.

6. In a multicandidate election, if a voting rule is efficient, decisive, truthful, and neutral, then it must be dictatorial. Conversely, dictatorship is efficient, decisive, truthful, and neutral—but not very appealing, given its massive concentration of power.

7. Positional voting rules are used in many sports elections, for instance, for the coaches' poll ranking college football teams. Strategic voting can be rampant in such voting rules.

8. The coalition function for a voting game focuses on whether a coalition is winning or not. A winning coalition can take control of the voting process to achieve its ends.

9. A voter is pivotal when adding that voter to a coalition turns it into a winning coalition. The Shapley value of a player in a voting game is the probability that the player is pivotal. The Shapley value provides a measure of voting power.

10. The Russian proposal to add Brazil to the UN Security Council as a permanent member with veto power would decrease the Shapley value of existing Security Council members by about 10 percent each.

■ KEY WORDS

issue spectrum	truthfulness	Shapley value
ideal point	neutrality	marginal product
median voter theorem	Arrow's impossibility	pivotal
distribution of voters'	theorem	dummy
ideal points	multicandidate elections	dictator
plurality rule	positional voting rules	veto player
strategic voting	Borda voting rule	United Nations Security
efficiency	winning coalition	Council
decisiveness	simple game	

■ PROBLEMS

1. In a discrete issue spectrum, there are 2.5 million voters on the Left, 1 million voters in the Center, and 0.5 million voters on the Right. Draw the normal form of the 2-candidate election and find the solution.

2. Suppose that the distribution of voters' favorite points is triangular and symmetrical, as shown in Figure 16.10. Prove the median voter theorem in this case. A diagram of candidate utility, like the one in Figure 16.6, may help.

FIGURE 16.10 **TRIANGULAR DISTRIBUTION OF VOTERS' IDEAL POINTS**

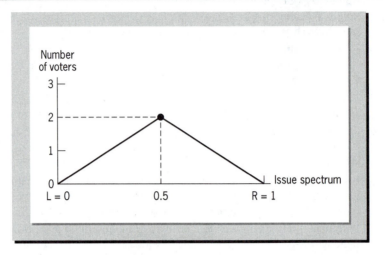

3. Suppose that the distribution of voters' favorite points is asymmetrical, as shown in Figure 16.11. Find the median voter. Prove the median voter theorem in this case.

4. In a discrete issue spectrum, half the voters are on the Left, and half are on the Right. Find an equilibrium where the candidates stake out different positions. Does this kind of situation deserve to be called polarized?

5. Define the core of a voting game. (*Hint:* Compare this to the core of a matching game.) Show that the Condorcet winner in section 16.3 is in the core of the voting game.

6. Suppose that there are three candidates for MVP and that Borda's rule is being used. Show that a coalition with more than 4/7 of all the voters can guarantee any outcome it wants.

7. Which of the following conditions does Borda's rule satisfy: efficiency, decisiveness, truthfulness, or neutrality? Which does it fail?

8. Show that the provisions of the U.S. Constitution for making a bill law satisfy nonnullity, monotonicity, and exclusivity. What would happen if the Constitution did not satisfy these provisions?

9. Consider the following mini security council. There are four members, one of which has a veto. Compute the Shapley value. Describe the power when a veto country is added.

10. It is hard to explain why Russia is pushing to get Brazil on the United Nations Security Council in view of the effect this change would have on its own power. Try to explain this. Could it be part of a larger bargain?

FIGURE 16.11 **ASYMMETRICAL DISTRIBUTION OF VOTERS' IDEAL POINTS**

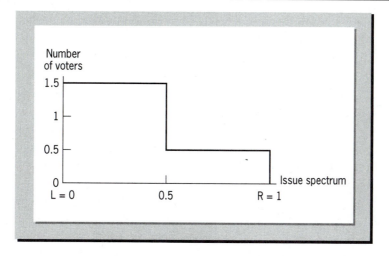

Games List

The following games are explored in this book:

Always the Low Price
Asymmetrical Hawk versus Dove
Asymmetrical Market Niche
Bankruptcy
Barbarians at the Gate
Battle of the Networks
Blackjack
Buyer versus Seller
Caveat Emptor
Centipede
Chess
Chicken
Cigarette Television Advertising
Competitive Advantage
Conscription in the Civil War
Coordination
Depositor versus S & L
Divide a Dollar
Escape and Evasion
Frogs Call for Mates
Gambler versus Casino
Hawk versus Dove
Lemons
Let's Make a Deal
Liar's Poker
Mutually Assured Destruction (MAD)
Majority Rule
Market Niche
Market Niches (repeated Market Niche)
Matching Pennies

Money-Back Guarantee

Mutual Defense

Nash Demand

Pick the Largest Number

Poker

Pot of Gold

Principal versus Agent

Prisoner's Dilemma

Roulette (American and European)

Screening

Small Business

Solitaire

Sorority Rush

Stag Hunt

Subsidized Small Business

Take-It-Or-Leave-It

Telex versus IBM

Ten

This Offer is Good for a Limited Time Only

Tic-Tac-Toe

Tragedy of the Commons

Ultimatum

Video System Coordination

To locate these games, check the Index.

Index